ALSO BY JEFFRY D. WERT

*A Brotherhood of Valor: The Common
Soldiers of the Stonewall Brigade, C.S.A., and
the Iron Brigade, U.S.A.*

*Custer: The Controversial Life of
George Armstrong Custer*

*General James Longstreet: The Confederacy's Most
Controversial Soldier—A Biography*

*Mosby's Rangers: The True Adventures of the
Most Famous Command of the Civil War*

*From Winchester to Cedar Creek:
The Shenandoah Campaign of 1864*

GETTYSBURG

D A Y   T H R E E

JEFFRY D. WERT

A Touchstone Book
Published by Simon & Schuster
New York   London   Toronto   Sydney   Singapore

TOUCHSTONE
Rockefeller Center
1230 Avenue of the Americas
New York, NY 10020

Copyright © 2001 by Jeffry D. Wert
All rights reserved,
including the right of reproduction
in whole or in part in any form.
First Touchstone Edition 2002

TOUCHSTONE and colophon are registered trademarks
of Simon & Schuster, Inc.

For information about special discounts for bulk purchases,
please contact Simon & Schuster Special Sales at
1-800-456-6798 or business@simonandschuster.com

Designed by Leslie Phillips
Manufactured in the United States of America

10   9   8   7   6   5   4   3   2   1

The Library of Congress has cataloged
the Simon & Schuster edition as follows:
Wert, Jeffry D.
    Gettysburg, day three / Jeffrey D. Wert.
        p.   cm.
    Includes bibliographical references (p.) and index.
    1. Gettysburg (Pa.), Battle of, 1863.   I. Title.
E475.53 .W5   2001
973.7'349—dc21   2001031071
ISBN 0-684-85914-9
        0-684-85915-7 (Pbk)

All photographs are from the United States Army Military History Institute (USAMHI), Carlisle
Barracks, Pennsylvania.

To the memory of my father
MERLE W. WERT

and my father-in-law
RALPH E. LONG

whom we miss

CONTENTS

PREFACE AND ACKNOWLEDGMENTS

M y fascination with the Battle of Gettysburg began when I was barely a teenager, an eighth-grader in a central-Pennsylvania high school. On a class trip, we visited the battlefield, stood on Little Round Top and looked upon storied fields, climbed the tower on Culp's Hill, gazed up at Robert E. Lee and Traveller on the Virginia monument, pointed toward the clump of trees like the wounded soldier on the North Carolina monument, and knelt behind the stone wall on Cemetery Ridge, trying to imagine how it must have felt to watch and to wait as Confederate infantry, coming on in serried ranks behind red flags, crossed the fields toward where we were. It was good to know that fellow Pennsylvanians stood behind the wall on July 3, 1863.

That fascination, rekindled with many subsequent visits, has never waned. I look at war differently now. It is not the wondrous dreams of a fourteen-year-old boy. Gettysburg was once a terrible place where good men gave "the last full measure of devotion" to two opposing causes. On Gettysburg's fields the country's past and future collided. On July 4, when the Confederate army began its retreat away from Gettysburg, and when another Confederate army surrendered at Vicksburg, Mississippi, America's future course was redirected.

For a number of years, I have wanted to return to Gettysburg as a historian. I have revisited it, in part, in my previous books on James Longstreet, George Custer, and the men of the Stonewall and Iron Brigades. For me, this book is the closing of a long journey begun four decades earlier, when I visited for the first time.

July 3 at Gettysburg remains a day in which drama seems to fill each hour. The fighting began at daylight on Culp's Hill and ended near where a setting sun touched the western face of Little Round Top. My book covers the entire twenty-four hours of July 3 at Gettysburg. It recounts not only "Pickett's Charge," but the seven hours of combat on Culp's Hill, the deadly work of skirmishers throughout the morning, and the four cavalry engagements, including the clash at Fairfield, Pennsylvania.

Like the entire battle and campaign, the final day of fighting at Gettysburg is replete with enduring controversies. My book will undoubtedly renew some of the arguments. Some readers will question its conclusions. In making my judgments I have tried to rely on as much primary-source material as I could locate, favoring contemporary accounts in letters and diaries over postwar memoirs and reminiscences whenever possible. I have allowed the participants to speak for themselves, for their words possess an immediacy and poignancy few historians can match. I have let their spelling and grammar stand, except in rare instances when I made changes for clarity. The story of July 3 belongs to them, and I have tried to let them tell it.

All of history walks in the shadows. Accounts of participants conflict, omit critical information, or are cursed with memory's fallibility. My book offers, I believe, the most detailed recounting of the day yet published. It is a study both of the armies' high commands and of the common soldiers in the ranks. It seems appropriate that the officers and enlisted men of both armies share the pages, for one army lost on this day and one army won.

On July 3, 1863, the nation began its final, long march on a road that would make it whole again. Approximately seventeen thousand men were either killed, wounded, or captured on the final day at Gettysburg. It is their story, as well as the survivors', that drew me to this day. Most of them were ordinary Americans, men who had been farmers, clerks, dockworkers, laborers, artisans, and schoolboys before a country's descent into civil war summoned them behind the banners of a cause. And it was those banners that brought them to Gettysburg.

☼   ☼   ☼

THIS BOOK HAS BEEN A COLLECTIVE ENDEAVOR, possible only through the efforts of numerous individuals. To them, I extend my sincere appreciation and gratitude. Their knowledge, assistance, and insight have made this a better book, but all errors are solely the responsibility of the author.

First of all, I wish to thank the archivists and librarians at the institutions cited in the bibliography for their understanding, expertise, and patience with my requests for material.

Other individuals deserve my particular recognition:

Dr. Richard Sommers and David Keogh, archivists, and Michael Winey, photograph curator, United States Army Military History Institute; John Coski, historian, The Museum of the Confederacy; William Brown, archivist, North Carolina Department of Archives and History; John Heiser, historian and librarian, Gettysburg National Military Park; Ralph G. Poriss of Williamsburg, Virginia; and J. Marshall Neathery of Rolesville, North Carolina.

Bonny Moellenbrock, a former student of mine, for conducting research for me at the University of North Carolina and Duke University.

Daniel and Alice Hoffman, owners of the Rummel farm, for a delightful visit and tour of their historic land.

Charles Romig, a friend and colleague, for reading portions of the manuscript.

Wayne Motts, a Civil War historian and authority on Lewis Armistead, and a friend, for sharing his ideas about July 3 with me.

Dr. Carol Reardon, professor of history at the Pennsylvania State University, author of an acclaimed book on Pickett's Charge, and a friend, for reading portions of the manuscript and providing critical comments.

Eric J. Wittenberg, a historian of Civil War cavalry operations, and a friend, for reading my chapter on the cavalry on July 3 and correcting errors.

Richard Rollins, a student and historian of July 3 at Gettysburg, for reading the entire manuscript, correcting errors, and offering numerous insights.

Frank Acosta, a retired Air Force officer, longtime student of Gettysburg, and a friend, for reading the entire manuscript, correcting errors, and providing a different perspective on leadership.

Daniel Laney, a Civil War historian and preservationist, president of the Austin Civil War Round Table, and a dear family friend, for reading the entire manuscript, editing passages, and challenging my conclusions, particularly about the Confederate high command.

Dr. Charles C. Fennell, Jr., a Gettysburg licensed battlefield guide and an authority on Culp's Hill, for reading my chapters on that combat and offering perceptive insights.

Nicholas Picerno, Sr., an avid Civil War collector and longtime family friend, for sharing items from his collection.

Robert Gottlieb, my agent, for his advice and efforts on my behalf.

Bob Bender, my editor, for his steadfast support, counsel, and friendship; and Johanna Li, associate editor, for her patience and constant willingness to answer my questions.

Our children, Jason and Natalie Wert, our daughter-in-law, Kathy Neese Wert, our granddaughter, Rachel Wert, and our grandson, Gabriel Wert, for their love and support.

My wife, Gloria, who has been with me from my beginnings as a historian, has shared the work, has typed all of the pages, and, most of all, has understood and given her love.

I write this on what would have been my father's, Merle W. Wert's, seventy-sixth birthday. He passed away last year, as did Gloria's father, Ralph E. Long. They were the two most important men in my life. They taught me that decency, kindness, and honesty distinguish good men. We miss them and honor them by dedicating this book to them, two good men.

Jeffry D. Wert
Centre Hall, Pennsylvania
December 3, 2000

To a Crossroad

T HE PAST CAME AS AN INTRUDER to a "shabby little farm house" near Gettysburg, Pennsylvania, on the night of July 2, 1863. It was there as the senior officers of the Union Army of the Potomac gathered. For two days, their units had been engaged in a fearful struggle, with staggering casualties, in the fields and woodlots that surrounded this south-central-Pennsylvania village. Rarely, if ever, had the army's rank and file fought so well as they had on this Thursday, but would their past, a history of defeats and humiliation at the hands of the Confederate Army of Northern Virginia, haunt them one more time? It was an intruder that could herald a nation's fate.[1]

Each officer who attended the meeting at the farmhouse had been present for all or much of that history. Each had witnessed the sacrifices, the forlorn assaults, the bitter retreats, and the succession of army commanders. This time, however, it was different. The army now defended Northern soil in a free state where colonial leaders had adopted the Declaration of Independence and where the country's founders had crafted the Constitution. As one of these officers had written just three days earlier: "We run a fearful risk, because upon this small army everything depends. If we are badly defeated the Capital is gone and all our principal cities and our national honor."[2]

The army's ranking generals had been summoned to army headquarters—the small, nondescript home of a widow, Mrs. Lydia Leister—by the commander, Major General George G. Meade. Only five days earlier, Meade had been one of them, a corps commander, until the administration in Washington accepted the resignation of Major General Joseph Hooker on June 27, and appointed Meade to the post. The change in commanders received the endorsement of the officers and men, but few American soldiers given command of an army had faced a more difficult burden, both of the present and of the past, than Meade.[3]

The campaign's pace had accelerated rapidly after June 27, conspiring against the cautious general. On July 1, advance elements of the army collided with the vanguard of General Robert E. Lee's forces north and west of Gettysburg. By late afternoon, two Federal corps had been routed, and one of its popular commanders, Major General John F. Reynolds, had been killed. The Northerners fled through the town to the south and regrouped. During the night and the morning of July 2, most units in both armies reached the area, with Meade's troops occupying a series of hills and a ridge. It was good ground to defend, and against it came the Southerners on the afternoon and evening of July 2. The combat had barely ceased when Meade ordered his corps commanders to headquarters.

Meade called the council—"consultations," as he described it later—wanting, in his words, "to obtain from them the exact condition of affairs in their separate commands, and to consult and advise with them as to what, if anything, should be done on the morrow." He knew that the casualties had been frightful—in fact, more than eighteen thousand Federals had been killed, wounded, or captured during the two days—but he also had learned from enemy prisoners that all of Lee's divisions, except that of Major General George E. Pickett, had been bloodied.[4]

Before his senior officers arrived at headquarters, Meade had decided to maintain the position at Gettysburg. He was uncertain whether the army would assume the offensive or remain on the defensive. "The most difficult part of my work," he admitted to his wife later, "is acting without correct information on which to predicate action." For that information on this night, Meade turned to his corps commanders.[5]

The meeting began sometime after nine o'clock in the bedroom of the Leister house. It was a small room, measuring perhaps ten feet by twelve feet, containing a bed, a few chairs, and a table with a solitary candle held upright by its own wax. It was an unlikely setting for such a council.[6]

A dozen officers, including Meade, crowded into the room. A few lounged on the bed, some stood, others used the chairs, and one of them sat in a corner and slept. All but three of them were West Pointers, professional soldiers, who had learned their trade from the bottom of the officers' ranks. Like Meade, they had most likely not changed clothes for days, and their faces bore the marks of exhaustion. Cigar smoke hung from the ceiling.[7]

The discussion began informally, with each general commenting on the two days of fighting and "the moral condition of the troops." The casualties were evident, and three of the seven corps—the First, Third, and Eleventh—had suffered grievous losses. They believed that the army still counted about fifty-eight thousand enlisted men in the ranks, but rations had been so depleted that the troops would have to subsist for a few days on half-rations. Only one of the officers, John Newton, argued that "Gettysburg was no place in which to fight a battle." Meade spoke seldom, merely asking an occasional question.[8]

Later in the meeting, Daniel Butterfield, the army's chief of staff, suggested that questions should be written down and each member voice his opinion on them. Meade nodded approval, and Butterfield sat at the table and prepared three questions: Should the army hold its present position or retreat to a line closer to its base of supplies? Should they attack or await an assault? If they decided to wait, how long?[9]

John Gibbon, the junior officer present, answered first, followed by the others according to seniority—Alpheus S. Williams, David Birney, George Sykes, John Newton, Oliver O. Howard, Winfield Scott Hancock, John Sedgwick, and Henry W. Slocum. No one bothered to wake Gouverneur K. Warren, Meade's engineer officer, from his sleep. Although a number of them offered refinements to their answers, the consensus was clear and unanimous—the army would stay, and remain on the defensive, for at least another day. Butterfield recorded each general's opinion and handed the paper to Meade, who remarked, "Such, then, is the decision."[10]

As the generals left the meeting, Meade approached Gibbon, whose Second Corps division manned the center of the Union line, marked by a small clump of trees, on the ridge west of army headquarters. "If Lee attacks tomorrow," Meade told Gibbon, "it will be *in your front*." When Gibbon asked why Meade thought so, the army commander replied, "Because he had made attacks on both our flanks and failed and if he concludes to try it again, it will be on our centre." Gibbon responded that he hoped the Confederate commander would try such an assault, adding, "We would defeat him."[11]

It was nearly midnight when the council adjourned. Within a few minutes, it would be Friday, July 3, 1863. Before this new day would end, the Federals would confront their past once again, while their old nemeses would confront a disturbing future.[12]

○ ○ ○

THE INITIAL MOVEMENTS of the campaign that would bring both armies to a crossroad in south-central Pennsylvania had begun a month earlier, on June 3. Their genesis lay with one man, General Robert E. Lee. Since his accession to command of the Army of Northern Virginia on June 1, 1862, Lee had fashioned a succession of victories that reshaped the war's course in Virginia. Only one setback, a strategic defeat at Antietam or Sharpsburg, Maryland, on September 17, 1862, marred Lee's first year in command. Most recently, on May 1–5, 1863, Lee and the army had won a brilliant tactical victory at Chancellorsville, Virginia. In the battle's aftermath, Lee saw opportunity and moved to seize it.[13]

While the opposing armies returned to their pre-Chancellorsville positions along the Rappahannock River, near Fredericksburg, midway between Washington and Richmond, Lee journeyed to the latter city to confer with President Jefferson Davis and the Cabinet. Lee stayed in the Confederate capital from May 14 until May 18, sequestered in meetings with the civilian authorities. The army commander proposed a second offensive movement into Northern territory, arguing that the incursion would garner a harvest of supplies for the army, spare the Old Dominion further ravages for weeks, and disrupt the enemy's operations for the summer.[14]

Lee's plan sparked hours of debate among the participants. Confederate fortunes in Virginia appeared to be at a zenith, but in the West, along the Mississippi River, another Southern army was being driven into a siege at Vicksburg, Mississippi. If the river city fell, the Mississippi would be under Union control. Secretary of War James Seddon and Postmaster General John Reagan favored sending a detachment of units from Lee's army west. In the end, however, the Cabinet voted five to one for Lee's northward movement, and Davis approved. Afterward, Seddon noted that Lee's views "naturally had great effect in the decisions of the Executive."[15]

On returning to Fredericksburg, Lee began preparations at once for the campaign. Not only had the victory at Chancellorsville cost the army thousands of troops, it had resulted in the death of Thomas J. ("Stonewall") Jackson, mortally wounded by Confederate troops while scouting at night in the woods between the two battle lines. To one of his sons, Lee confessed upon learning of Jackson's death: "It is a terrible loss. I do not know how to replace him." [16]

Since the previous autumn, the army had functioned with two infantry corps—the First Corps, under James Longstreet, and the Second, under Jackson. Lee, however, had been contemplating a reorganization for months, and with Jackson gone, he believed the time had come to restructure the units. "I have for the past year," he explained to Davis, "felt that the corps of this army were too large for one commander. Nothing prevented my proposing to you to reduce their size and increase their number but my inability to recommend commanders." [17]

Lee proposed the creation of a third corps, with Richard S. Ewell taking command of Jackson's old corps, the famed "foot cavalry," and Ambrose Powell Hill receiving the new Third Corps. Although Ewell had been away from the army since losing a leg at Second Manassas in August 1862, Lee described him as "an honest, brave soldier, who has always done his duty well." Hill, in Lee's judgment, had been the army's finest division commander, "the best soldier of his grade." [18]

The administration approved the reorganization, and it was announced to the rank and file in a special order on May 30. The addition of a new corps necessitated further changes at the divisional and brigade levels. Lee moved one division from the First Corps into the Third, and created two new divisions by transferring units to Hill's command. Deserving officers received promotions. Lee also completed the restructuring of the artillery units, begun before Chancellorsville, by assigning five battalions to each corps. Finally, on "a beautiful bright" day, June 3, elements of the army marched up the Rappahannock River, beginning Lee's second offensive operation beyond the Potomac River. [19]

During the next several days, additional infantry and artillery units followed, joining the vanguard and the cavalry brigades of Major General James Ewell Brown ("Jeb") Stuart concentrated near Culpeper Court House. Onlookers undoubtedly watched the passing columns, and they saw lean men in ragged uniforms of various hues of gray and brown. Many were barefoot; nearly all wore slouch hats, in an array of shapes and colors. It was a fearsome weapon on the roads of central Virginia. Except for unanswered questions about the new commanders, Lee commanded, in the judgment of an artillery officer, "the best and largest army . . . that he ever had in hand." [20]

"An overwhelming confidence possessed us all," claimed one of Lee's staff officers. "If General Lee can carry out what I believe are his designs," a Virginian asserted at this time, "he will achieve the greatest victory of the war. At all events this army cannot be routed, and will hold its own against any force which will be brought against it." Already rumors about the army's destination filled the ranks, moving one infantryman to predict, "We will have a good Deal of hard fighting" before they returned to Virginia.[21]

An Alabamian boasted in a letter home, "No army ever commenced a campaign under more brilliant prospects, or with firmer hopes of success than ours." Much of this confidence, even cocksureness, resulted from contempt for their opponent, whose camps lay beyond the Rappahannock, a barrier as much psychological as geographical. While the victors of Chancellorsville had prepared for a new campaign, the losers, the rank and file of the Army of the Potomac, sought answers for another defeat.[22]

The spring campaign had begun with optimism for the Federals but ended with despair and recrimination. The army blamed its commander, Major General Joseph Hooker, whose bold pronouncements about victory before the battle now rang hollow. To many of the officers and men, it had been a simple matter—Lee had "out-generaled" Hooker, in the word of one of them. Chancellorsville, concluded an officer, revealed that the "Rebellion" could not "be crushed here, unless we may *annihilate* the great army in front of us."[23]

Chancellorsville still festered within the Union ranks when "the great army in front of us" marched away from Fredericksburg. The Federals detected the movement, and Hooker sent his cavalry upriver to attack Jeb Stuart's mounted brigades and to gather information about the reported Southern concentration in Culpeper County. On June 9, the blue-jacketed horsemen crossed the Rappahannock, surprised Stuart's troopers, and ignited a daylong engagement at Brandy Station on the Orange & Alexandria Railroad. Before the fighting ended with a Union withdrawal, the opponents assailed each other in mounted attacks and counterattacks. At times, the Northerners nearly swept the Rebels off of Fleetwood Hill, the dominant terrain feature, only to be hammered back by gray-clad reserves. The Yankees failed to destroy their enemy or to confirm the presence of Confederate infantry and artillery in the area, but they had fought Stuart's proud cavalrymen to a standstill.[24]

The next day, the Confederate advance resumed, with Ewell's Second Corps leading the march toward the Blue Ridge Mountains and the Shenan-

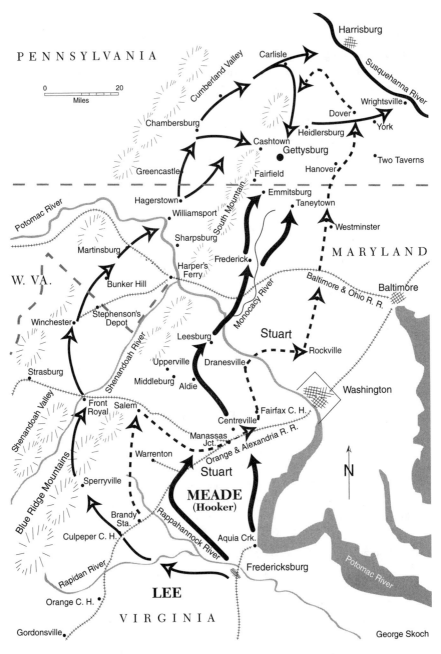

PENNSYLVANIA

Harrisburg

Susquehanna River

Cumberland Valley

Carlisle

0   20
Miles

Chambersburg

Dover

Wrightsville

York

Cashtown

Heidlersburg

Gettysburg

Greencastle

Fairfield

Hanover

Two Taverns

Potomac River

Hagerstown

Williamsport

South Mountain

Emmitsburg

Taneytown

Martinsburg

Sharpsburg

Frederick

Westminster

MARYLAND

W. VA.

Bunker Hill

Harper's Ferry

Monocacy River

Baltimore & Ohio R. R.

Baltimore

Winchester

Stephenson's Depot

Leesburg

Stuart

Rockville

Strasburg

Shenandoah River

Upperville

Dranesville

Washington

Middleburg

Aldie

Shenandoah Valley

Front Royal

Salem

Fairfax C. H.

Centreville

Warrenton

Manassas Jct.

Orange & Alexandria R. R.

Stuart

Blue Ridge Mountains

Sperryville

MEADE
(Hooker)

N

Brandy Sta.

Rappahannock River

Culpeper C. H.

Aquia Crk.

Potomac River

Rapidan River

Fredericksburg

LEE

Orange C. H.

VIRGINIA

Gordonsville

George Skoch

TROOP MOVEMENTS, GETTYSBURG CAMPAIGN,
JUNE 3–JULY 1, 1863.

doah Valley beyond. Jackson's old foot cavalry raced across the mountains and then turned north, down the valley. It was a familiar land to them, the killing grounds of 1862 and homes to hundreds of them before civil war had divided their country. By June 13, the Second Corps had reached Winchester, where Major General Robert Milroy's Union force blocked the roads to the Potomac River. Ewell's veterans overwhelmed the Federals the next day, however, routing Milroy's command and seizing cannon, supplies, wagons, and nearly four thousand prisoners. On June 17, one of Ewell's divisions crossed the Potomac into Maryland.[25]

While the cutting edge of the Confederate army entered Union territory, Longstreet's corps passed through the gaps of the Blue Ridge, and Hill's divisions approached the mountains. Stuart's horsemen patrolled the gaps, screening the movement as Lee's army, from its head to its tail, stretched across the Old Dominion for more than a hundred miles.[26]

Meanwhile, Hooker's army marched on roads heading north through the Piedmont region. The Union commander had reacted slowly, even reluctantly, to Lee's movement, arguing with authorities in Washington for an advance on Richmond. When President Abraham Lincoln rejected the proposal, Hooker abandoned his lines at Fredericksburg, directing his columns in pursuit of the Southerners toward another uncertain rendezvous.[27]

On June 17, Union cavalrymen re-established contact with the Confederates east of the Blue Ridge gaps. During the next four days, the Federals clashed with Stuart's troopers at Aldie, Middleburg, and Upperville, but were unable to penetrate the Rebel screen and locate Lee's infantry and artillery. Within days, Longstreet's and Hill's corps resumed their march toward the Potomac fords as Ewell's men entered Pennsylvania, moving along a number of roads toward the state capital at Harrisburg and points south on the Susquehanna River.[28]

To Ewell's veterans, the Keystone State appeared as a Biblical land of milk and honey. Their letters home during this time consist of a chorus about the lushness of the soil, the neatness of the farms, and the size of the farmers' bank barns. One soldier asserted, in typical fashion, "The country is the most beautiful I ever beheld, and the wheat and corn crops are magnificent." Another Rebel described it as "the prettiest country I ever saw in my life, they have the finest land in the world."[29]

"It is a great place to feed an army," observed one Confederate. Although Lee had issued an order against foraging, his troops, like locusts in gray and butternut, reaped a bounty. They feasted on milk, butter, molasses, honey, apple butter, chickens, sugar, coffee, cheese, and whiskey. The men had been suffering from "sore mouth" until Pennsylvania's larders were opened to them. "Every thing to eat that hart could wish," boasted one scavenger, adding that "every thing was cheap all it cost us was to go after it."[30]

The cupboards brimmed with such riches that even Longstreet's and Hill's men shared in the bounty when they entered the state. An officer in the 53rd Virginia informed his wife, "I have eaten many nice meals in Yankee land." To a fellow Virginian in the same division, the Confederates' plundering was about more than just securing food. "We are doing all the injury we can," he wrote, "to pay back for what they have done in our country." The cavalry units with the infantry corps seized hundreds of head of horses and cattle. When regiments passed through towns, the men raided merchants' stores for other goods.[31]

Although the Southerners praised the region's natural wealth and beauty, they sneered at the inhabitants, many of whom were of German descent, the so-called Pennsylvania "Dutch." Almost to a man, the Rebels described the civilians as "ignorant" and the women as "ugly." A Mississippian scribbled in his journal, "Apparently this is the place they get the comic pictures they put in the almanac." A Texan believed that "they thought we were all hungry Methodist preachers," and a South Carolinian noted that "the whole country is frightened almost to death." A Virginian put his feelings bluntly: "I could rather fight them a hundred years than to be Subjugated by Such a worthless race."[32]

The morale of the Confederates soared as they fanned out across the state, filling their knapsacks and stomachs. "Never did soldiers appear more buoyant and cheerful than Lee's army," a Louisiana lieutenant told his father in a letter. A Virginia officer stated, "Our army is in fine spirits and willing to be led everywhere and anywhere." They knew that their pleasant sojourn on Northern soil would have to end when the enemy located them, but, as one soldier put it for many of his comrades, "we will clear the Yankees out this summer and whip them."[33]

The opportunity to "whip them" was approaching with a swiftness few, if any, in the Confederate army anticipated. By June 27, Lee had established his headquarters in Chambersburg—a town, wrote a Southerner, that "had the appearance of a deserted village on a wet Sunday"—with Longstreet's and Hill's divisions either encamped nearby or en route. Farther east, across South Mountain, Ewell's units marched through the Cumberland Valley, like rivulets before an oncoming flood, occupying Carlisle, passing through Gettysburg to York and beyond, and edging closer to Harrisburg. Unfortunately for Lee, the whereabouts of the Federal army remained a mystery. He had been awaiting reports from Jeb Stuart and the cavalry, but none had come.[34]

While in Virginia, Lee had given Stuart permission to move north with three brigades and "pass around" the Union army. Lee expected the cavalry commander to advance on the Confederate right flank, gathering supplies and information and establishing contact with Ewell in Pennsylvania. The instructions, dated June 22 and 23, were vague and discretionary, however. With the options of either crossing the Blue Ridge and marching down the Shenandoah Valley or keeping east of the mountains, riding between the enemy and Washington, Stuart chose the latter route. At 1:00 A.M. on June 25, Stuart led his three best brigades east and out of the campaign for the next week.[35]

"An army without cavalry in a strange and hostile country," Major Walter H. Taylor of Lee's staff wrote afterward, "is as a man deprived of his eyesight and beset by enemies; he may be ever so brave and strong, but he cannot intelligently administer a single effective blow." Although Lee had with him two of Stuart's brigades, he had not used them for reconnaissance, perhaps expecting word from Stuart at any time. Crippled by a lack of information, Lee became anxious and cautious.[36]

Not until ten o'clock on the night of June 28 did Lee receive the first reliable report about the Union army, when a "dirt-stained, travel-worn, and very much broken down" spy named Henry Harrison reached army headquarters. At the campaign's outset, Longstreet had employed Harrison to travel to Washington and to secure any information he could obtain, providing the operative with gold coins for expenses. When Harrison inquired where he could find the general, Longstreet answered: "With the army. I shall be sure to be with it."[37]

Harrison's words surprised Lee's senior officer—the enemy had crossed the Potomac into Maryland and was marching toward Pennsylvania. Longstreet sent the spy with a staff officer at once to Lee, who accepted the information only after the aide assured the general of Longstreet's confidence in Harrison. With his units scattered across southern Pennsylvania, separated at points of more than sixty miles, Lee reacted that night to the news.[38]

The Confederate commander recalled Ewell's corps and a cavalry brigade to Chambersburg, but countermanded the order the next morning, redirecting them to either Gettysburg or Cashtown, across South Mountain from

Longstreet's and Hill's troops. On June 30, Hill's corps led the march from Chambersburg east, with two divisions bivouacking for the night near Cashtown, roughly eight miles west of Gettysburg. To the north and east, two of Ewell's three divisions approached the latter town, where ten roads converged. Lee and Longstreet shared a campsite west of South Mountain. Most likely on this day, Lee learned that George Meade now commanded the Union army. When informed of the news, Lee allegedly remarked, "General Meade will commit no blunder in my front, and if I make one, he will make haste to take advantage of it."[39]

Joseph Hooker's tenure as commander of the Army of the Potomac had lasted exactly five months. Since Chancellorsville, he no longer had the confidence of the army or of the administration in Washington. At the end, his removal resulted from a dispute with the War Department over the Union garrison at Harper's Ferry, Virginia. Hooker wanted the place, located at the northern end of the Shenandoah Valley, abandoned, and the troops attached to his army. In the capital, Secretary of War Edwin Stanton and General-in-Chief Henry W. Halleck refused to order an abandonment. When Hooker tendered his resignation, Lincoln accepted it with no remorse, and on June 27, appointed Meade to command. "As we say in the army," wrote an officer, " 'Hooker is not worth a tinkers damn.' He is removed."[40]

Meade learned of the change in commanders at three o'clock in the morning on June 28, when an officer from Halleck's staff woke him in his tent, pitched near Frederick, Maryland. The news was, according to one of Meade's aides, "a complete surprise to General Meade." Most of the speculation in the army as to a possible successor to Hooker had centered upon the commander of the First Corps, John F. Reynolds, a highly popular officer. Reynolds, however, had rejected an offer to command the army after Chancellorsville because the administration would not grant him a "free rein" with the army. To Lincoln, Stanton, and Halleck, Meade was the best available candidate, and the president issued the order, giving the general the option of either accepting the command or resigning his commission. A professional soldier all his adult life, Meade had no recourse and went to army headquarters to meet with Hooker.[41]

With such a crisis at hand, the administration understood the immense responsibility it had placed upon Meade. It granted him authority over all forces "within the sphere of . . . [his] operations," including the garrison at Harper's Ferry and the militia units in Pennsylvania, along with the power to remove any subordinate officer and to appoint a replacement. Halleck, however, dispatched a letter to Meade explaining to the commander that the army's primary role was to "maneuver and fight in such manner as to cover the capital and also Baltimore, as far as circumstances will admit. Should General Lee move upon either of these places, it is expected that you will either anticipate him or arrive with him so as to give battle."[42]

Like Lee, Meade confronted the uncertainties of his enemy's whereabouts. Since the Rebels had entered the Keystone State, wild rumors of their locations and plans had inundated Washington. Enjoined to cover both the national capital and Baltimore and to find the Confederates, Meade decided to advance the army's seven corps and cavalry units along a broad front that secured both cities. Consequently, on June 28, he concentrated the corps around Frederick, twenty-five miles south of the Pennsylvania border. He ordered a march north for the next morning, planning to have the units on a twenty-mile line from Emmitsburg on the west to Westminister on the east by nightfall.[43]

It was an exhausted beast, however, that Meade commanded. A one-day march turned into two days. Throughout June 29, the columns were plagued by delays, jammed roads, miscarried orders, and bone-weary troops. On June 30, the Federals made better progress. By nightfall, elements of Reynolds's First Corps had crossed the Mason-Dixon Line with all but one of the other corps in supporting distance. During the day, Meade received reports that indicated that the Confederates were advancing toward Gettysburg, where Brigadier General John Buford's Union cavalry division had been sent. A battle appeared imminent, but nothing could be certain for either Meade's army of ninety-three thousand effectives or Lee's seventy thousand as they bedded down for the night. It was as if a siren's call—the road network at Gettysburg—drew them both to a terrible rendezvous.[44]

The rendezvous came on the morning of Wednesday, July 1. It began as a routine encounter between Buford's horse soldiers and Confederate infantrymen of Major General Henry Heth's Third Corps division, but it escalated throughout the day into a fierce struggle as units from both armies marched toward the reckoning. Events and the decisions of subordinates conspired against Lee and Meade, neither of whom sought a major engagement on this day. By 10:00 A.M., however, it had passed beyond their control with the arrival of Reynolds's Union First Corps on the field. Gettysburg stood at the edge of American history.[45]

Reynolds's infantry replaced Buford's troopers, who had fought a three-hour delaying action against Heth's men, as an assault by two Confederate

brigades began to roll forward. Although Reynolds was killed at the very outset of the action, the Northerners repulsed the attackers. Behind the First
Corps came Major General Oliver O. Howard's Eleventh Corps, which
passed through town into the fields to the north. A lull ensued as Hill brought
forward Major General William D. Pender's division, and as Ewell's two Second Corps divisions, under Major Generals Robert E. Rodes and Jubal A.
Early, approached on the Carlisle and Harrisburg roads. In a matter of hours,
more than twenty-eight thousand Confederates and twenty-two thousand
Federals had converged on Gettysburg.[46]

At midafternoon, with Lee on the field, the Confederates went forward
against the Federal lines on McPherson's Ridge, Oak Ridge, Seminary Ridge,
and in the lowlands north of town. (For clarity, the modern names of the battlefield will be used throughout.) The Federals fought tenaciously at points,
but the Rebel lines overlapped both their flanks. The collapse came about
four o'clock and rapidly degenerated into a rout through Gettysburg's streets.
The pursuing Southerners bagged more than four thousand prisoners. Total
casualties in both armies exceeded fourteen thousand.[47]

The Northerners rallied south of town on Cemetery Hill, where previously
Howard had posted some regiments and artillery batteries. Lee, meanwhile,
followed his victorious troops to Seminary Ridge, surveyed the ground beyond the village, and ordered Ewell to advance, "if practicable," against the
heights. But when Lee could not assure Ewell of support, and a reconnaissance revealed the presence of enemy troops, the corps commander hesitated. Whether an attack could have been organized and undertaken in a
timely fashion and would have succeeded remains one of Gettysburg's enduring questions.[48]

The Rebel victors, a Confederate staff officer argued subsequently, "never
seemed to me as invincible as on July 1, 1863." Once more, they had swept
their opponents from a field of battle. Their "profound contempt" for the
enemy seemed to be justified again. Few Southerners in the ranks speculated
about the location of the other five Union infantry corps or looked closely at
the ground south of town now occupied by the Yankees. These matters, however, troubled their commander.[49]

Lee had found himself on this day in a battle he had not wanted. "It had not
been intended to fight a general battle at such a distance from our base," he
explained in his report, "unless attacked by the enemy." But that had
changed, and his splendid army had won another clear victory. Despite the
continuing lack of information about his opponent's remaining units, Lee was

reluctant to relinquish the initiative to Meade. "A battle thus became, in a measure, unavoidable," Lee further argued. "Encouraged by the successful issue of the engagement of the first day, and in view of the valuable results that would ensue from the defeat of the army of General Meade, it was thought advisable to renew the attack" on July 2. Lee would have with him on the morrow eight of nine infantry divisions and most of his artillery battalions.[50]

While Lee had watched his legions rout the enemy, George Meade had spent July 1 redirecting his units toward Gettysburg from army headquarters at Taneytown, Maryland. He had prepared a contingency plan for his army to hold a line along Pipe Creek in Maryland, but that changed with the news of the fighting at Gettysburg. When Meade learned of Reynolds's fall, he sent Major General Winfield Scott Hancock to Gettysburg to assume command. "If you think," he wrote to Hancock, "the ground and position there is a better one to fight a battle under existing circumstances, you will so advise the general, and he will order all the troops up."[51]

Hancock arrived at Gettysburg as the Federals were being chased through the streets of the town. Assuming command, he organized the defense of Cemetery Hill and nearby Culp's Hill. Meade, meanwhile, had not waited to hear from his subordinate but prodded his other corps commanders to hurry their marches. At 5:30 P.M., the Twelfth Corps reached the field. The Second, Third, and Fifth corps were en route and would arrive during the night or early on the 2nd. Only the Sixth Corps, the army's largest command, would not reach the field until late on Thursday afternoon, after a march of thirty-four miles in eighteen hours from Manchester, Maryland.[52]

Meade followed the army to Gettysburg during the early-morning hours of July 2, arriving before dawn. Halting on Cemetery Hill, he was soon joined by Howard, Henry Slocum, Daniel Sickles, and a coterie of officers. He inquired about the army's position. When told it was good ground, he responded that he was pleased to hear it, for "it was too late to leave it." In fact, the army had never defended better ground.[53]

The Union position which Meade examined before daylight possessed natural strengths and a convex character that would expedite the movements of troops from one section of the line to another. One Union general termed it "our defensive triangular army formation." In time, however, it would be described simply as a fishhook. Cemetery Hill, rising sixty to eighty feet above its base, formed the hinge of the line. To the east, several hundred yards away, stood Culp's Hill, 140 feet high and the anchor of the Union right flank, the barb of the fishhook. To the south, Cemetery Ridge extended for nearly a mile and a half, its elevation diminishing into a lowland before abutting against the base of Little Round Top. A quarter-mile to the southwest, Big Round Top, heavily wooded and with a steep ascent, rose roughly 135 feet above the smaller hill. With its western face cleared of timber, Little Round Top was the dominant terrain feature on the left flank of the Union line.[54]

The Confederate line framed the fishhook-shaped Federal position. It began east of the town, opposite Culp's Hill, and passed through the streets of Gettysburg to Seminary Ridge before turning south along the crest of the ridge. Five miles in length, the Southern line possessed a major drawback—its distance and concave character would hamper the expeditious movement of units from one point to another along its length.[55]

Cultivated fields and pasture, patterned by various types of fences, covered the mile of ground between Seminary Ridge and Cemetery Ridge. Emmitsburg Road, angling from the southwest to the northeast, passed between the ridges, its roadbed defined by stout post-and-rail fences. The area mirrored the fertile fields, lush with ripening crops, elsewhere in the state that had elicited the admiration and praise of the Southerners. Here families such as the Codoris, Blisses, Spanglers, McMillans, Weikerts, Trostles, Klingles, Roses, and Sherfys had worked the soil's richness until war's fury came to them.[56]

The storm broke across the fields and woodlots at four o'clock on the afternoon of July 2, when a pair of Confederate divisions, under Major Generals John B. Hood and Lafayette McLaws, advanced against the Union left flank. Since midmorning, Lee had settled upon an offensive operation against the Federal position, but delays ensued. Now, hours later, fourteen thousand of his best troops from Longstreet's First Corps moved to the attack. "Then was fairly commenced," Longstreet declared afterward, "what I do not hesitate to pronounce the best three hours' fighting ever done by any troops on any battle-field."[57]

Hood's and McLaws's veterans and their Federal opponents, troops from three different corps, savaged each other in places that would be seared into America's collective memory—the Peach Orchard, the Wheatfield, Devil's Den, and the Slaughter Pen. Artillery fire ripped into ranks; musketry flashed continuously, creating killing walls of flame. "I could hear bones crash like glass in a hail storm," wrote a Confederate; a comrade admitted a week later in a letter, "It seemed to me that my life was not worth a straw."[58]

Meade and his subordinates shifted units from other sections of the line to meet the onslaught. Furious counterattacks blunted the Southern thrusts, only to be ravaged. Six times the triangular-shaped Wheatfield changed hands. On Little Round Top, the Rebels clawed their way nearly to the crest. A Texan who survived the combat likened it to "a devil's carnival."[59]

As Longstreet's assault stalled at last, additional Confederate brigades attacked the long spine of Cemetery Ridge. A brigade of Georgians drove to the crest but, like their comrades in other units, were repulsed by Union reserves. At last, the Confederate offensive faltered through a combination of Union mettle and bungling Confederate command.[60]

On the Confederate left, meanwhile, Ewell's Second Corps did not advance against Culp's Hill and Cemetery Hill until after seven o'clock. On Culp's Hill, the Rebels made a lodgment in the Federal works, since Meade had stripped the height of its defenders, except for a solitary brigade that fought a valiant action against superior numbers. On Cemetery Hill, two Southern brigades charged up its northeast slope. Here, the fighting was vicious and hand-to-hand until the Yankees pounded them back. Spasms of musketry and cannon fire continued even as Meade met with his corps commanders at the Leister house. Approximately 16,500 men had been either killed, wounded, or captured on this second day of battle.[61]

The Southerners had come close, stretching the Union line until it nearly snapped. But at critical moments, the attacks foundered. "The whole affair was disjointed," grumbled Walter Taylor of Lee's staff. "There was an utter absence of accord in the movements of the several commands, and no decisive result attended the operations of the second day."[62]

Despite the outcome, Lee thought that opportunity for victory still beckoned. "The result of the day's operations," he stated in his report, "induced the belief that, with proper concert of attack, and with the increased support that the positions gained on the right would enable the artillery to render the assaulting columns, we should ultimately succeed, and it was accordingly determined to continue the attack. The general plan was unchanged."[63]

To a common soldier, a Floridian who had crossed the fields in front of Cemetery Ridge and had met the Yankees, the day revealed a different truth. "The fighting was most desperate," he told his father in a letter on July 8, "the enemy fighting much harder on their own soil & having the best position."[64]

1

Night on the Battlefield

L IEUTENANT GEORGE G. BENEDICT had never heard the sound before in his life. Like his comrades in the Second Vermont Brigade, the staff officer had been a soldier less than a year, most of that time spent on garrison duty at Washington, D.C. Attached to the Army of the Potomac as it marched north toward Pennsylvania, the Vermonters faced the terribleness of combat for the first time on July 2. Now, with night's darkness across the battlefield, Benedict heard the sound that rolled over the crest of Cemetery Ridge, where he rested with his fellow soldiers, and likened it to "a low, steady, indescribable moan."[1]

It came from hundreds of voices, pleading cries for help or for "water, give me water." These were the voices of war's wreckage, of dying and wounded men who lay amid the blackness. Everywhere death and maiming had walked on July 2, leaving furrows of victims in the Peach Orchard and the Wheatfield, on Little Round Top, and along Emmitsburg Road. To Benedict and the others who had been spared, the wounded men's "mingled imprecations, prayers & groans . . . were literally heart rending."[2]

Only the living received attention during the night of July 2–3. Aided by a moon just past full, ambulance crews, assisted by soldiers searching for

31

friends, roamed the fields and woodlots, gathering up the wounded. Hour after hour, the ambulances passed to the rear and returned for more cargo. Their movement was marked, according to a New Yorker, by "the line of *red lights*" from their lanterns. Men on picket duty from both armies allowed stretcher-bearers from either side to pass through their lines. "It was the saddest night on picket duty," wrote an officer, "that I ever passed."[3]

A Union staff officer found among the fallen Confederate Brigadier General William Barksdale. A former congressman and a fiery advocate of states' rights, Barksdale had led his brigade of Mississippians in an attack that swept across the fields north of the Peach Orchard. He fell wounded, and when his men were driven back, he was left behind. He had been shot in the back, and two bullets had broken his left leg.[4]

A stretcher crew carried the general to the Jacob Hummelbaugh house, where surgeons from the Second Corps had established a hospital. Dr. A. T. Hamilton of the 148th Pennsylvania attended to Barksdale, whom the surgeon described as "large, corpulent, refined in appearance, bald." Several times Barksdale asked if his wounds were mortal, and Hamilton told him that he would not survive them. Later on July 3, Barksdale died for the cause he had so vigorously espoused.[5]

The suffering men ended the night's journey as Barksdale had, at either a house or a barn converted into a makeshift hospital. The stream of ambulances was endless. The chief ambulance officer for the Union Fifth Corps reported that, from 4:00 P.M. on the 2nd to 4:00 A.M. on July 3, eighty-one ambulances brought in thirteen hundred wounded men to his corps's hospitals. The army commander had issued an order forbidding baggage wagons and ambulances to accompany the army to the battlefield. But doctors and generals ignored the directive, which George Meade admitted later had not included hospital wagons. "I do not know," confessed a member of the medical corps, "what could have been done with the wounded" if the order had been obeyed.[6]

The surgeons and their assistants worked all night on the flood of patients. A Georgia doctor scribbled in his diary, "I did not sleep a moment last night." But the hospitals were wretched places, "miserable death Holes" to a Confederate officer. A New York soldier exclaimed that words could not describe "the frightful picture of a field hospital." An ambulance-corps sergeant confided to his diary that "the suffering is awful," for the wounds "are mostly severe." A Pennsylvanian who visited a Union Third Corps hospital in a barn at dawn on the 3rd, said that it reminded him of a Philadelphia slaughterhouse.[7]

During the night, George Benedict was sent to the rear to obtain ammunition for the Vermonters. Since no one knew the location of the ordnance train, Benedict stopped at a dozen or more barns—"the great Pennsylvania barns, looking more like large factory buildings than our New England barns," as he described them. At the door of one of them, Benedict found a common sight, "a ghastly pile of amputated arms and legs."[8]

Sometime, perhaps even before midnight, the army's bands were instructed to place themselves between the troops on the line and the hospitals. "They played by detachments all night," recalled a New York captain, "to drown out the cries of the wounded and those who were being operated upon." At one point, a number of bands joined together and played "When This Cruel War Is Over." "While we sympathized with the sentiment," the captain added, "we execrated the doleful and monotonous music."[9]

✿   ✿   ✿

FOR THE SURVIVORS of the combat on July 2, lying in the Union line from Cemetery Hill to Big Round Top, little else mattered than food and sleep. With cooking fires prohibited, the troops chewed on hardtack, a square, quarter-inch-thick cracker made of unleavened flour. In a number of regiments and batteries, the rations had been exhausted, and the officers and men had nothing to eat. An officer in Battery I, 1st United States Artillery, recalled that the unit's quartermaster sergeant disobeyed orders, went to the rear, and returned with forage for the horses and three days' rations for the gun crews.[10]

Sleep came easily, exhaustion overtaking the men despite the pleas of the wounded and the music from the bands. Many of them used their knapsacks as pillows, and all bedded down with their weapons beside them. Captain Silas Adams of the 19th Maine looked at the starlit night, brightened by the moonlight, and wondered if the one he loved at home was gazing at the same stars. When "I saw what I thought was a roguish twinkle in one of them," he wrote later, "I was satisfied that I was right, and I was happy and went to sleep."[11]

In the fields along Emmitsburg Road, west of Cemetery Ridge, detachments from several regiments manned picket posts. It was a long night for these soldiers as they lay amid the dead and the wounded. Required to stay awake, many of the Yankees passed the hours conversing with their Rebel counterparts, who in some places were less than seventy yards away. When relief parties moved forward to occupy the picket lines, a brief exchange of gunfire ensued. Many of the opponents had piled fence rails for protection, and few casualties resulted from the outbursts. It was a warm night, even an uncomfortable one, with the temperature in the seventies.[12]

Farther south, on Little Round Top, members of the Fifth Corps were directed to occupy Big Round Top. The first regiment to be assigned the task was the 20th Maine, under the command of Colonel Joshua Lawrence Chamberlain. During the fighting for possession of Little Round Top, Chamberlain and the Mainers had held the end of the Federal line and repulsed the assaults of two Alabama regiments. Their valiant defense would subsequently earn Chamberlain the Medal of Honor.[13]

The 20th Maine began the ascent of the steep, wooded height sometime after 9:00 P.M. The 83rd Pennsylvania, a companion regiment in the brigade, followed three or four hours later. By dawn, the 5th and 12th Pennsylvania Reserves had joined the pair of regiments on the hill, and secured at last the Federal left flank on Big Round Top. The movement of the units had not gone unnoticed and drew the fire of Texas skirmishers at the base of the hill.[14]

The rattle of musketry from the foot of Big Round Top indicated that elements of the Confederate army, like Federal units, were active in the hours before dawn. The 1st Texas of Brigadier General Jerome B. Robertson's brigade had been ordered to move from the Devil's Den area to the base of Big Round Top. Before the Texans complied, however, a detail of officers and men crawled to the crest of Houck's Ridge, above Devil's Den, to retrieve three ten-pounder Parrott rifles of the 4th New York Battery, which the Confederates had seized earlier in the day. Speaking in whispers, the Texans cleared a path by removing stones, wrapped blankets around the wheels, and dragged the guns down the western slope without alerting the enemy on Little Round Top.[15]

The 1st Texas filed through the woods to the southeast about 2:00 A.M. on July 3. The regiment secured its position at the base of the hill probably in time to detect the movement of the two Pennsylvania Reserve regiments toward the crest. The Texans triggered a round or two up the wooded hillside. Not long afterward, Confederate batteries to the west shelled the area.[16]

No troops appeared to be more active on the southern portion of the battlefield during the night than Southern artillerists. One gunner complained in his diary that he "spent the whole of last night getting ammunition" for his 2nd Company, Richmond howitzers. The artillerymen fed their horses, killed crippled animals, refilled ammunition chests, tended to their wounded, buried their own while leaving the Federal dead untouched, and obtained rations for the next day. A few batteries shifted their positions, and others were brought up from the rear.[17]

Overseeing these labors was Colonel Edward Porter Alexander. At twenty-eight years old, the Georgian was one of the finest artillery commanders in the army, a West Pointer who was exceptionally bright and exceedingly capable. Although only a battalion commander, Alexander had been given tactical control of the First Corps's batteries by James Longstreet on July 2. He rewarded Longstreet's trust by directing the fire in support of the assaults by Lafayette McLaws's and John Hood's divisions.[18]

After nightfall, Alexander attended to the myriad details in preparation for the next day and then rode to Longstreet's headquarters near Pitzer's Woods. There he learned from the lieutenant general that Lee had issued orders for a resumption of the offensive at daylight on July 3. "My impression," Alexander recounted later, "is the exact point for it was not designated, but I was told it would be to the left of the Peach Orchard." Longstreet informed Alexander that George E. Pickett's division would arrive on the field and join in the attack. Longstreet also directed the artillery officer to move the Washington Artillery forward and put its four companies in line by dawn.[19]

Alexander rode back to the Peach Orchard, fashioned a bed from two fence rails, using his saddle as a pillow, and slept for two hours. Dead men and horses shared the ground with him among the fruit trees. Before 3:00 A.M., he rose, resaddled his mount, and proceeded north along the row of silent cannon, waiting for the arrival of the additional batteries.[20]

Major Benjamin F. Eshleman's four batteries of the Washington Artillery and Captain W. W. Parker's Virginia Battery soon appeared. Alexander placed eighteen of the twenty cannon in a line that began about one hundred yards north of the Peach Orchard. Two howitzers of the Washington Artillery were placed in reserve. While the Confederate gunners wheeled their guns into position, Captain Charles W. Squires and Sergeant John Payne of the 1st Company, Washington Artillery, nearly rode into a Union picket line. Only a warning voiced by a fellow Southerner saved them from a prison camp.[21]

Alexander completed his preparations by four o'clock or shortly thereafter. Dawn would be breaking from the east in less than forty-five minutes. With his gunners, Alexander could only wait. For all of them, it would be a day unlike any in their experience.[22]

✿   ✿   ✿

THE STRUGGLE FOR CULP'S HILL, at the opposite end of the Union position, frittered away at last about 10:00 P.M. on July 2. Richard Ewell had been ordered "to make a diversion" when James Longstreet's two divisions moved against the Federal left flank and convert it "into a real attack if an opportunity offered." The assault had begun at 7:00 P.M., after an artillery cannonade. At that hour, three brigades of Major General Edward Johnson's division waded Rock Creek and ascended the wooded, rugged slope of Culp's Hill. Fortunately for the Southerners, only a single Union brigade waited behind breastworks on the hillside.[23]

The two infantry divisions of Major General Henry Slocum's Twelfth Corps, numbering about ninety-two hundred officers and men, had occupied Culp's Hill since the morning of July 2, erecting fieldworks of logs, rocks, and dirt from its summit, down the southern slope, to the edge of a large meadow. When the crisis mounted on the Union left and center during the late afternoon and evening, however, Meade sent instructions to Slocum to send troops to Cemetery Ridge. Slocum complied, but through either a misunderstanding or garbled orders, five of the corps's six brigades abandoned their positions on the Union right and marched away. Brigadier General Alpheus S. Williams's three brigades departed at 6:30 P.M., followed thirty minutes later by Brigadier General John W. Geary's two brigades. Left behind were 1,350 New Yorkers of Brigadier General George S. Greene's brigade. Only minutes after Geary's troops departed, Johnson's Confederates appeared through the trees, moving toward the New Yorkers.[24]

Culp's Hill actually consisted of two hills, an upper and a lower, which were divided by a saddle, running east to west, about four hundred yards south of the summit. Greene's troops manned the works from the crest to the saddle, where the rifle pits formed an angle and extended south and east toward the meadow. It was too long a line for too few men to defend.[25]

Against the New Yorkers came nearly forty-eight hundred Confederates. From behind the breastworks, Greene's men fought with a valor and desperation that rivaled the defense of Little Round Top by Joshua Chamberlain and the 20th Maine. For three hours the opponents hammered each other in the enveloping darkness. A Virginian stated that he and his comrades located the Yankees by "flashes of the guns." At the southern end of the Confederate line, Brigadier General George H. Steuart's troops seized the abandoned works on the lower hill and forced Greene's right regiment, the 137th New York, back up the slope beyond the angle in the works. Only the tenacity of these New Yorkers and the arrival of reinforcements from other corps prevented Steuart's men from penetrating deeper into the Federal position. When the combat ended, Steuart's brigade lay only five hundred yards from Baltimore Pike, Meade's primary supply line and, if necessary, his escape route.[26]

The provost guard of the Twelfth Corps, 250 members of the 10th Maine Battalion under Captain John Q. Adams, had been posted to the rear of Culp's Hill, along Baltimore Pike. When the fighting on the hill stopped, Adams sent a detail of men east to reconnoiter the lower hill. They returned about thirty minutes later and reported that the enemy held the works in that area. Adams hurried the information to army headquarters at the Leister house, where Meade and his generals were conferring.[27]

About the same time Adams sent his message, Brigadier General Thomas L. Kane's brigade of Geary's division came up Baltimore Pike, returning to Culp's Hill. When Geary had been instructed to follow Williams's division, he had started a half-hour later and mistakenly turned his column onto Baltimore Pike, leading it away from the battlefield. He halted his march on the road at a bridge over Rock Creek, and deployed Colonel Charles Candy's and Kane's brigades. About nine o'clock, Kane began his countermarch, under orders from either Slocum or Geary.[28]

Kane's three regiments of Pennsylvanians turned off Baltimore Pike and angled northeast through woods toward the works on the lower hill, which they had constructed and manned before being withdrawn. Although the moon shone brightly, the trees' canopy darkened the area. The 29th Pennsylvania led the brigade, approaching a stone wall that ran roughly parallel to and southwest of the Union rifle pits. Someone shouted for a cheer. The Yankees hurrahed, and a blast of musketry from behind the wall ripped into the column, killing four and wounding ten. The 29th turned about and scrambled back to the pike.[29]

The regiment's commander, Colonel William Rickards, Jr., believed that Greene's troops had mistakenly fired the volley. He spurred his horse into the woods, halted, and identified himself. Another volley flashed from behind the wall, hurrying the colonel rearward.[30]

Kane then resumed the march on the pike with 111th Pennsylvania in the lead, trailed by the 109th and 29th Pennsylvania. At the farmhouse of Henry Spangler, the troops left the road and followed a farm lane that led to the saddle between the upper and lower hills. The 111th continued on about one hundred yards to the angle in the works. Evidently, the Federals remained unconvinced that enemy troops held a portion of the works on the lower hill.

Colonel George A. Cobham, Jr., who shared command of the brigade with Kane, directed the 111th's acting commander, Lieutenant Colonel Thomas M. Walker, to deploy the regiment in its former position.[31]

Walker managed to place two companies in the works before another volley, fired at a distance of thirty paces, chased the Pennsylvanians. Walker wheeled his regiment to face the unseen riflemen. Minutes later, Cobham repeated his order to hold the entrenchments. The lieutenant colonel protested against it, and Cobham relented.[32]

Walker extended his left flank up the hillside until it connected with Greene's New Yorkers. The 109th and 29th arrived and went into line next to the 111th. Kane's troops faced southeast, covering the saddle and the end of the stone wall. There was no doubt that the Confederates were in their front, but Kane wanted more information about the enemy's location. He sent a reconnaissance party from the 29th, under Captain Charles E. Johnson, down the hillside. All the effort accomplished for the Rebels was the capture of Johnson and five men. With that, the Pennsylvanians lay down and slept.[33]

Charles Candy's brigade of six Ohio and Pennsylvania regiments also returned by Spangler's farm lane, arriving about 1:30 A.M. The colonel halted his units in a hollow behind Greene's and Kane's lines, reorganized them, and, at Geary's direction, formed a double line along the lane. Candy's front stretched from Kane's right flank to an orchard north of the Spangler house. Sergeant Aaron Bennyhoff of the 28th Pennsylvania sneaked forward to a large spring on the land of Abraham Spangler (Spangler's Spring) and then returned to his regiment, declaring that "Johnnies were thicker than bees" around the spring. Like Kane's men, the Ohioans and Pennsylvanians slept on their arms.[34]

Farther south, meanwhile, the two brigades of Williams's division stumbled into the same dark nightmare that had engulfed Geary's men. Brigadier General Thomas H. Ruger held temporary command of the division—Williams was attending the council at the Leister house—and acted with caution. He told both of his brigade commanders—Colonels Archibald H. McDougall and Silas Colgrove—to send skirmishers ahead to learn whether the enemy held the works. If these were vacant, they were to bring up the brigades and man them without delay.[35]

McDougall proceeded, with his regiments in a double line. Halting them on a rise, he ordered one company each from the 123rd New York and 5th Connecticut forward as skirmishers. They had advanced only a short distance when a blast of musketry exploded in the darkness. The Southerners' fire drove the blue-clad skirmishers rearward into their regimental ranks. The 123rd New York had begun to retire when the 145th New York, lying behind them, mistook their comrades for Confederates and triggered a wild volley before running away. McDougall's rear units halted the rush, and the brigade withdrew behind the rise, to bivouac for the night. Many of the men had to lie down in a muddy cornfield.[36]

On McDougall's right, Colgrove's four regiments fared better. They moved ahead—"we crept quietly along . . . not a word spoken," in the description of Major Charles F. Morse of the 2nd Massachusetts—toward their former position in McAllister's Woods, south of the meadow. A company of the 2nd Massachusetts led the march as skirmishers, passing through the woods into the meadow, where they captured a solitary Confederate. They brought the captive back to the brigade and reported that no other enemy troops occupied the woods. The regiments proceeded into the meadow and halted.[37]

Lieutenant Colonel Charles R. Mudge of the 2nd Massachusetts ordered Morse to cross the lowland with a company and to determine whether the Rebels were in the woods on the lower hill. Morse led Company F across the meadow into the trees, where they stumbled upon a Confederate captain and twenty-two men. Mudge reported the capture of the enemy party to Colgrove and perhaps to Ruger. Colgrove thought the Southerners were stragglers and instructed Mudge to send in another company of skirmishers, supported by the regiment. The 107th New York was ordered to move forward on the left of the Bay Staters.[38]

This time the Yankees found what they were seeking. When Captain John A. Fox of Company K demanded the surrender of the Southerners whom his men had located, the Confederates replied with gunfire. The outburst wounded three of Fox's men, and the others bolted for the meadow. Convinced, Colgrove withdrew the troops into McAllister's Woods and posted pickets. It was, as Morse related in a letter to his mother, "enough skylarking for one night."[39]

Alpheus S. Williams had rejoined his command by this time, only to receive "the astounding intelligence" that the enemy had taken the works on the lower hill. He met with several officers and reportedly told a group of them, "We will hold the position we now have until morning. Then, from these hills back of us, we will shell hell out of them."[40]

By morning, there would be more Confederates to "shell hell out of" on Culp's Hill. To bolster the attack that Lee had ordered for daylight on July 3, Ewell pulled Brigadier General James A. Walker's Stonewall Brigade from guarding the corps's left flank and ordered three brigades from his other two divisions to report to Johnson. Walker's Virginians rejoined their comrades in Johnson's division well before sunrise, while two of the brigades—Brigadier General Junius Daniel's North Carolinians and Colonel Edward A. O'Neal's Alabamians—marched throughout the night, arriving about thirty minutes before daylight. When the sun rose, Johnson had six brigades and another one approaching for the difficult and assuredly bloody work ahead.[41]

Before he rested that night, one of Walker's men, Sergeant David Hunter of the 2nd Virginia, wrote a letter to his mother. "We are in all probability on eve of a terrible battle," the Stonewall Brigade member wrote. "The two contending armies lie close together and at any moment may commense the work of death. Great results hang upon the issue of the battle. If we are victorious peace may follow if not we may look for a long and fierce war. We trust in the wisdom of our Gens, and the goodness of our Father in Heaven who doeth all things well."[42]

Perhaps a mile away in a direct line from where Hunter wrote his letter, on Cemetery Ridge, Captain Silas Adams of the 19th Maine thought of home. He was the one who had wondered if his love in Maine was looking upon the same stars as he gazed at in the moonlit sky. He later remembered, however, that on this night, "I felt sad, and dreaded the next day." He spoke for more men than he probably knew.[43]

2

Lee and Meade

G ENERAL ROBERT E. LEE woke well before dawn on the morning of July 3, 1863. Whatever rest or sleep he had managed to get had been brief. His headquarters tent lay in a field south of Chambersburg Pike, across the roadbed from the stone house of a widow, Mary Thompson. Undoubtedly, he talked with his staff officers and probably ate breakfast before asking for Traveller, his favorite horse. Lee then mounted and nudged Traveller south. The moon still brightened the fields behind Seminary Ridge as the long strides of the six-year-old iron-gray horse brought Lee toward the army's right flank.[1]

Lee was fifty-six years old on this morning, and a professional soldier all of his adult life. A son of Revolutionary War hero Henry ("Light-Horse Harry") Lee, the Confederate commander had ranked second in his class at West Point, served on the staff of General Winfield Scott during the Mexican War, held the superintendency at West Point, and led the detachment that captured abolitionist John Brown at Harper's Ferry in October 1859. When his native Virginia seceded in April 1861, Lee resigned his commission in the Regular Army and accepted command of the state's forces as the Old Dominion prepared for war. Commissioned a general in the Confederate army, he commanded forces in western Virginia and supervised the construction of coastal defenses in South Carolina and Georgia before being appointed military adviser to President Jefferson Davis. On June 1, 1862, Lee assumed command of the Army of Northern Virginia when General Joseph E. Johnston was wounded at the Battle of Seven Pines or Fair Oaks.[2]

Lee's accession to command of the army was the turning point of the war in the East for the Confederacy. In a year, under Lee's generalship, the army won battlefield victories that bolstered Southern morale and opened the road north into Pennsylvania, where another Confederate success might bring the nation independence. Whether he knew it or not, Lee had come to embody Southern nationalism. As long as he and his army remained in the field, an independent Confederate States of America appeared to be an obtainable goal. Lee had outgeneraled a string of Federal opponents—George McClellan, John Pope, Ambrose Burnside, and Joseph Hooker. With a string of victories culminating at Chancellorsville, he had become the South's pre-eminent general.[3]

Lee's achievements resulted from his abilities as a soldier and from his aggressiveness as a strategist and tactician. "No one," wrote Porter Alexander, "could meet Lee and fail to be impressed with his dignity of character, his intellectual power, and his calm self-reliance." He possessed an exceptional intelligence of both discernment and depth. Where others saw dim outlines, Lee could seemingly visualize, as if magnified, strategy across a broad landscape and tactics across the terrain of a battlefield. He had an aptitude for the art of warfare, excelling with deductive reasoning in the interpretation of often confusing and contradictory information. He also understood the administrative details that underpinned the workings of an army. He labored tirelessly at organizational, commissary, and supply problems. Lee forged the weapon that he commanded, and it bore his imprint.[4]

Within days of Lee's appointment to army command, Porter Alexander spoke with a member of President Davis's staff, Captain Joseph C. Ives. Alexander wondered if Lee would be audacious enough as a commander. To Alexander, that attribute was an *"absolute requisite"* if the Confederacy, with its inferior resources and manpower, were to have *"any chance"* at all." "Alexander," Ives responded, "if there is one man in either army, Federal or Confederate, who is head & shoulders, far above every other one in either army in audacity that man is Gen. Lee, and you will very soon have lived to see it. Lee is audacity personified. His name is audacity, and you need not be afraid of not seeing all of it that you will want to see."[5]

As Ives had predicted, Alexander and the army witnessed Lee's audacity in the Seven Days, Second Manassas, Antietam, and Chancellorsville campaigns. A Texan in the army compared his commander's temperament to that of "a game cock." "The mere presence of an enemy aroused his pugnacity," thought the soldier, "and was a challenge he found it hard to decline." James Longstreet described this trait in Lee as "headlong combativeness." Like the Texan, Longstreet declared that, once Lee encountered the enemy on a battlefield, "his impatience to strike" was evident. Alexander called it Lee's "combative instinct."[6]

Lee's audacity or aggressiveness, however, reflected more than a personal characteristic. It was his reasoned assessment of how the Confederacy could achieve victory over a numerically superior opponent with unlimited resources. In Lee's judgment, the South had a limited opportunity before the industrial and human might of the North doomed the Confederacy to defeat. He understood that ultimate victory and independence could be attained not militarily but politically. Behind the Union host lay the will of Northerners to withstand the sacrifices, casualties, and defeats. If that will endured, the Confederacy faced certain defeat.[7]

Within the broad framework of the Confederacy's offensive-defensive strategy, Lee saw the offensive as the only course that could possibly achieve the nation's independence. To adopt a passive, defensive posture meant a slow death. The fires in Northern steel mills, the harvests reaped by farmers, the belching smokestacks of factories, and the pool of volunteers or conscripts doomed the South if it awaited the inevitable onslaught. Time was the silent, insidious enemy of the Confederacy.[8]

Lee chose the offensive, with its attendant risks, not because of an innate aggressiveness, but from a calculated and stark assessment of his country's chances for victory. The offensive allowed Lee to dictate operations and to acquire and to retain the strategic initiative. Risks meant desperate measures, but they also offered opportunities. Lee believed that his army had to inflict a series of battlefield defeats upon its opponent within a narrow, and diminishing, framework of time. He guided his army to a fork in the road and led it down the route no other general dared to take.[9]

To achieve tactical victories and to hold the initiative in the Virginia theater of operations, Lee used maneuver, particularly the turning movement. At Second Manassas, it was a broad turning movement; at Chancellorsville, a flank attack. Although he had not attained it, he conducted operations in each campaign to inflict a crippling, if not fatal, blow upon the enemy. Once he seized the tactical momentum upon the battlefield, he pressed it. Lee's correspondence bristles with words such as "destroy," "ruin," "crush," and "wipe out" when discussing the most desirable fate for Union forces. At Chancellorsville, his outnumbered army achieved a stunning tactical victory but to Lee it was not the decisive, overpowering victory he had sought. After a year of unmatched battlefield success, such a victory still eluded him.[10]

For a second time, then, in Chancellorsville's aftermath, Lee, retaining the strategic—in modern terms, operational—initiative in the theater, turned his army northward. His reasons for the offensive beyond the Potomac River he had explained to Davis and the Cabinet in mid-May. On June 8, in a letter to Secretary of War James A. Seddon, Lee provided arguably his primary motivation, an encapsulation of his strategic and tactical views. "As far as I can judge," he wrote to Seddon, "there is nothing to be gained by this army remaining quietly on the defensive, which it must do unless it can be reenforced. I am aware that there is difficulty and hazard in taking the aggressive with so large an army in its front, intrenched behind a river, where it cannot be advantageously attacked. Unless it can be drawn out in a position to be assailed, it will take its own time to prepare and strengthen itself to renew its advance upon Richmond, and force this army back within the entrenchments of that city. This may be the result in any event; still, I think it is worth a trial to prevent such a catastrophe."[11]

Lee followed his letter to Seddon with another to Jefferson Davis, written on June 10. In it, the general expanded upon the consequences of inactivity, "conceding to our enemies the superiority claimed by them in numbers, resources and all the means and appliances for carrying on the war." Lee argued, "We have no right to look for exemptions from the military consequences of a vigorous use of these advantages." In turn, the resources of the Confederacy "are constantly diminishing, and the disproportion in this respect between us and our enemies, if they continue in their efforts to subjugate us, is steadily augmenting."[12]

To Lee, the Federals were unassailable behind their works beyond the Rappahannock River; on open terrain, they were vulnerable to the killing blow Lee had sought for months. Such a victory on Northern soil offered incalculable possibilities, military and political. The Confederates must, Lee added in his letter to Davis, encourage "the rising peace party of the North." "Should the belief that peace will bring back the Union become general," Lee wrote, "the war would no longer be supported, and that, after all, is what we are interested in bringing about." It was, then, toward Pennsylvania that Lee turned, seeking a showdown engagement that could result in a political solution to the conflict.[13]

Once in Pennsylvania, Lee hoped by maneuver to force the Union army to attack him. Senior officers in the army, notably James Longstreet, and members of Lee's staff stated in postwar accounts that, once the enemy had been met, the Confederates would fight a defensive battle. Longstreet termed it "the ruling idea of the campaign." "Under no circumstances," he declared to Lafayette McLaws in a postwar letter, "were we to give battle, but exhaust our skill in trying to force the enemy to do so in a position of our own choosing." Major Walter H. Taylor of Lee's staff echoed Longstreet's assertion. Lee's design was, according to Taylor, to select "a favorable time and place in which to receive the attack which his adversary would be compelled to make on him, to take the reasonable chances of defeating him in a pitched battle."[14]

Lee said as much in his report: "It had not been intended to fight a general battle at such a distance from our base, unless attacked by the enemy." But the absence of Stuart and of information about the Union army crippled Lee's operations. "The movements of the army preceding the battle of Gettysburg had been much embarrassed by the absence of the cavalry," wrote Lee. The news brought by the spy Henry Harrison forced Lee's hand, and he ordered the concentration of the army east of South Mountain at or near Cashtown or Gettysburg.[15]

Nevertheless, on July 1, Lee found himself and his army in an engagement he did not want at that time. Circumstances or fate or human error, as occurs so often in war, had intervened and altered plans. Lee could only react to what he had witnessed and what lay before him. "A battle thus became, in a measure, unavoidable," Lee explained. "Encouraged by the successful issue of the engagement of the first day, and in view of the valuable results that would ensue from the defeat of the army of General Meade, it was thought advisable to renew the attack" on July 2.[16]

Lee made the decision to assume the offensive on the next day even as the Federals fled through the streets of Gettysburg late on the afternoon of July 1. He tried to press the pursuit, directing Ewell to take Culp's Hill "if practicable." When Longstreet joined Lee on Seminary Ridge about 5:00 P.M., and proposed a broad turning movement beyond the Union flank into Maryland, Lee rejected the idea. Instead, Lee pointed to the Union position south of town and stated firmly to his corps commander, "If the enemy is there tomorrow, we must attack him." Lee, wrote Longstreet afterward, "seemed under a subdued excitement, which occasionally took possession of him when 'the hunt was up,' and threatened his superb equipoise. The sharp battle fought by Hill and Ewell on that day had given him a taste of victory."[17]

The day's outcome provided Lee and the army with momentum and the tactical initiative, two critical factors on any battlefield. To the Confederate commander, these advantages had to be exploited as had happened at Second Manassas and at Chancellorsville, the army's finest victories. He believed, as a historian has argued, that once a battle was joined "it was imperative to finish the fighting on the same field." And as Lee watched the rout of two enemy corps on July 1, he saw before him, in the words of one of his officers, "this great prize [the defeat of the Union army], which he believed within his grasp."[18]

The fighting on July 1 confirmed another belief of Lee's, that the combat prowess of the men in his army's ranks remained unparalleled. In May, before the campaign began, he told John Hood: "I agree with you in believing that our Army would be invincible if it could be properly organized and officered. There never were such men in an Army before. They will go anywhere and do anything if properly led."[19]

On July 2, then, Lee once again asked his vaunted infantry to assail an enemy position. They fought magnificently, but Lee's command system faltered at crucial moments, perhaps denying him the crushing victory he thought essential for Southern independence. As Walter Taylor noted, "The whole affair was disjointed." In his method of command, at least to this point in the war, Lee had left the tactical direction of the troops to subordinates. He watched the action from Seminary Ridge, seemed nervous to eyewitnesses, but did not intervene when the unfolding events arguably required more direction over them from him.[20]

Lee's assault plan required active and timely actions by subordinate officers. In the center of the Confederate line, however, Hill failed to exercise close supervision over his units. Consequently, only three of his Third Corps brigades assailed Cemetery Ridge and were repulsed when additional units from the corps did not move forward either in an attack or as support. On the Confederate left, Ewell seemed unprepared to join in the offensive despite having hours to ready his infantry and artillery. Longstreet's attacks had been bloodied and stopped by the time Ewell ordered forward infantry against Cemetery and Culp's hills. Ewell's actions lacked foresight and initiative. In the end, the valor of Lee's troops could not overcome the advantages of the Union position and the breakdown of command within the army.[21]

On the night of July 2, Lee ordered Longstreet and Ewell to renew their attacks against the ends of the Union line at daylight on July 3. How much Lee knew of the tactical situation each general faced remains unclear. He would, however, have the entire army on the field, for Jeb Stuart and his three brigades of cavalry were en route that afternoon, and George E. Pickett's infantry division had bivouacked a few miles west of Seminary Ridge. Lee instructed Stuart to operate beyond Ewell's left flank and expected Pickett's three brigades to join Longstreet by daylight for the assault. If, as Lee said later, "one determined and united blow [could] have been delivered by our whole line," the "great prize" was attainable.[22]

In a conversation after the war, Lee discussed Gettysburg with one of his former officers. "Everything was risky in our war," the listener recorded Lee saying. "He knew oftentimes that he was playing a very bold game, but it was the only *possible* one." His "very bold game" had brought him into Pennsylvania, and he was determined to see it to the end. Lieutenant Colonel G. Moxley Sorrel, Longstreet's chief of staff, put it simply: "Lee could not retreat without another effort," on July 3.[23]

So Lee rode Traveller through the predawn darkness of this Friday morning with his army committed to bloody work ahead. He was willing, if not compelled, to take the gamble. His generalship in previous campaigns had shown to him the benefits of pressing the tactical initiative by assailing his opponents. If he could achieve a concerted attack, his army might deliver a decisive blow against the Federals, who still appeared vulnerable after two days of fighting. On July 3, the road to Confederate independence crossed Culp's Hill and Cemetery Ridge.[24]

To the officers and men who saw him pass on this morning, he would have been a striking man. A British officer with the army thought him to be, "almost without exception, the handsomest man of his age I ever saw." Lee stood nearly six feet tall, broad-shouldered, with an erect bearing and prematurely gray hair and beard. He wore a plain long gray coat, blue trousers, a black felt hat, and Wellington-styled boots. "He is," noted the Englishman, "a perfect gentlemen in every respect."[25]

At Gettysburg, however, Lee still suffered from the effects of a serious illness that had struck him in the spring. It appeared to be the onset of cardiovascular difficulties, probably angina pectoris, or it might have been a severe case of pneumonia. Colonel Charles Marshall of Lee's staff claimed after the war that it was pneumonia, saying that Lee complained "very much" of pain in his chest. Its effects continued to plague him into the fall, but no conclusive evidence exists that Lee had a relapse or was afflicted otherwise during the three-day battle.[26]

The night had not yet given way to the morning sun when Lee halted at the headquarters of James Longstreet. His orders had been issued hours ago, and he would watch the beginning of the assault on this portion of the line with his senior subordinate. But as they had on the previous two days, events would disrupt Lee's plans.

✸   ✸   ✸

MAJOR GENERAL GEORGE GORDON MEADE slept little, if at all, during the night of July 2–3. While members of his staff lay on the floor of the Leister house and snatched a few hours of sleep, he probably worked through the early-morning hours after the conclusion of the meeting with his corps commanders about midnight. Since his appointment to command of the army on June 27, Meade had labored ceaselessly, day and night, with almost no rest. His burdens were enormous. "I feel fully the responsibility resting upon me," he wired Major General Henry W. Halleck on the afternoon of July 2, "but will endeavor to act with caution."[27]

Meade was forty-seven years old, born in Cádiz, Spain, the son of a prominent Philadelphia merchant. An 1835 graduate of West Point, Meade had been in the Regular Army, except for a brief stint as a civilian engineer, for nearly three decades. Meade served throughout the antebellum years in the Corps of Topographical Engineers, constructing lighthouses and breakwaters along the Atlantic coast. He earned a brevet as first lieutenant during the Mexican War and was a captain when the Civil War began. At the urging of Pennsylvania Governor Andrew Gregg Curtin, the Lincoln administration commissioned Meade a brigadier general on August 31, 1861.[28]

Assigned to command of a brigade in the Pennsylvania Reserve division, Meade led it through the Peninsula Campaign in the spring of 1862, and at Second Bull Run in August, suffering two wounds in combat. At Antietam, on September 17, he commanded the division, and after the battle was given temporary command of the First Corps. Three months later, at Fredericksburg, his division breached the Confederate line only to be repulsed by enemy reserves. It was the one Union success on a terrible field of battle. On December 23, 1862, Meade was appointed commander of the Fifth Corps. He led the corps at Chancellorsville and was at its head when the administration promoted him to command of the army.[29]

Meade's promotion received almost universal approbation within the army. "Everyone seems satisfied," wrote one of his staff officers on July 1, "and a great many are rejoicing over it." Meade's son, George, who served on his father's staff, wrote the same day to his mother: "I never saw such universal satisfaction, everyone is delighted. Reynolds, Slocum, & Sedgewick have all given in and behaved very well, as far as I know." Young Meade added that he and his father were "astonished" at the appointment. "I think Papa's first thought in seeing Col Hardee, of Halleck's staff, was his own removal and not Hooker's."[30]

The army's reaction to the news came, in part, because of the officers' and men's desire to rid themselves of Joseph Hooker. Brigadier General Alpheus S. Williams spoke for many when he stated, "I had no confidence in Hooker after Chancellorsville," describing the commander's performance in that campaign as "imbecility and weakness." Many in the ranks, however, had hoped that George B. McClellan would succeed Hooker. In fact, while Meade examined the army's position early on the morning of July 2, regiments stood and cheered as a rumor scurried through the ranks that McClellan had arrived on the battlefield. Despite his lack of success, McClellan—or "Little Mac," as the men called him—had an enduring hold on the army's rank and file.[31]

Meade was an unknown quantity to the common soldiers outside of the Fifth Corps. He seemed not to be a popular corps commander, because of his strict discipline and his demands on the men. A Pennsylvania captain in the corps claimed that he was "universally despised." But to fellow generals and members of his staff, Meade was, in the words of one of them, "a thorough soldier, and a mighty clear-headed man." When John Gibbon learned of Meade's appointment, he declared to his wife, "I now feel my confidence restored & believe we shall whip these fellows." Gibbon added that morale had improved and that "we shall at least have an honest administration of affairs at Hdqts. Which was far from the case before."[32]

Numerous officers who knew or would come to know Meade remarked about his honesty, straightforwardness, personal bravery, and moral courage. He had avoided the political intrigues that had afflicted the army's officer corps, a fact that Lincoln and Secretary of War Edwin Stanton found appealing. Whatever ambition stewed within the man, he concealed. A thorough, painstaking man, he demanded the best from himself and from those under his command. "He will pitch into himself in a moment," a staff officer stated, "if he thinks he has done wrong; and woe to those, no matter who they are, who do not do right!"[33]

When angered by incompetence or misdeeds, Meade would explode "like a firework," according to an aide. His temper was notorious to those who served with him. A corporal thought that Meade "might have been taken for a Presbyterian clergyman, unless one approached him when he was mad." To many other soldiers, he was "a damned old goggle-eyed snapping turtle." When his temper flared, staff officers waited in "semi-terrified states" for the fury to spend itself. His fearful demeanor boiled constantly just beneath the surface.[34]

Like Lee, Meade looked older than his years. Lieutenant Frank A. Haskell of Gibbon's staff described Meade as "a tall, spare man, with full beard, which with his hair, originally brown, is quite thickly sprinkled with gray—has a Romanish face, very large nose, and a white large forehead, prominent and wide over his eyes, which are full and large, and quick in their movements." A captain in the 20th Massachusetts wrote that Meade reminded him of "a good sort of a family doctor."[35]

Rather ungainly and nearsighted, he cared little about his uniform or personal appearance and wore spectacles. An aide observed that, "as for clothes, General Meade was nowhere," while Haskell thought that "it would be rather difficult to make him look well-dressed." Because of his eyeglasses, troops had nicknamed him either "Old Four Eye" or "Old Goggle Eyes."[36]

It was this blunt-speaking, forthright, exacting career engineering officer, then, who had been given command of the army on June 27. By temperament, training, and experience, Meade was a careful man who shunned risks. The responsibility handed to him by the authorities in Washington demanded that he act with caution. He knew, as did others, that his appointment came at a critical time, or, as an artillery officer remarked, "it is a very dangerous experiment on the eve of battle." He reacted by working tirelessly.[37]

From the time Meade assumed command of the army, he based his plans on the need to protect Washington and Baltimore and to find Lee's army. Meade explained his thinking afterward: "My object being at all hazards to compel him [the enemy] to loose his hold on the Susquehanna and meet me in battle at some point. It was my firm determination, never for an instant deviated from, to give battle wherever and as soon as I could possibly find the enemy." Once a battle was joined, he continued, his operations would be governed by circumstances on the field, "with a view to secure advantages on my side in the battle, and not allow them to be secured by him."[38]

Throughout June 29 and 30, Meade had advanced his corps toward Pennsylvania on a broad front, covering the cities and hunting for the Confederates. Except for the Sixth Corps, he had the army's units well deployed by nightfall on the second day. When the clash came at Gettysburg on July 1, Meade acted decisively in redirecting that corps toward the battlefield. Like Lee's, Meade's hand had been forced by the encounter. His army had found the enemy—"my main objective point," as he had told Halleck—and Meade followed it to Gettysburg.[39]

After Meade had arrived on the field and finished a reconnaissance of the army's position early on July 2, he considered an attack against the enemy's left flank. Subordinates advised against it for a number of reasons, and Meade canceled it. For the rest of the morning, he examined his lines, posted units, and awaited developments. Although he preferred to fight a defensive battle, Meade continued not to rule out an offensive strike of his own. When the Confederate assault came, late in the afternoon, Meade and his subordinates shifted units to plug gaps in the lines, repulsing the enemy thrusts. They had exploited the army's interior lines in a masterful fashion. Meade had, as Lee had predicted, made few mistakes, and his army had fought valiantly.[40]

That night, at the council in the Leister house, Meade and his corps commanders decided to stand at Gettysburg for another day and await perhaps another offensive from Lee. He and his army had been fortunate—the terrain and the nature of the combat had favored them. If Lee chose to renew the attacks, Meade would be prepared.[41]

Before that might occur, however, Meade had agreed during the night to initiate an attack. He had learned that Confederate troops had seized a portion of the Federal works on Culp's Hill, and he wanted them retaken. It would be Meade, not Lee, who would strike first on July 3. When daylight touched Culp's Hill, the "devil's carnival" at Gettysburg would resume.

3

"The Whole Hillside Seemed Enveloped in a Blaze"

THE SOLDIERS IN HIS BRIGADE called him affectionately "Old Pop" or "Old Man Greene." At sixty-two years of age, George S. Greene was old enough to be their grandfather and was the oldest Union general on the field at Gettysburg. An 1823 graduate of West Point, he had spent most of his adult life as a civilian engineer, enduring the tragedy of losing his wife and three children in a span of seven months. Appointed a colonel of the 60th New York in January 1862, Greene then received a commission as brigadier general three months later. He led a division at Antietam, but a subsequent illness forced him to request a leave of absence. When he returned to the army, Brigadier General John W. Geary had the division, and Greene resumed command of a brigade of New York regiments.[1]

Greene was a short, stocky man with gray hair and beard. Like George Meade, he wore a plain uniform, looking much like one of his old foremen on a railroad project. He was a plain-speaking, no-nonsense general, as tough as dried leather. His men might have grumbled about his firm methods, but they respected "Old Pop." When he and his New Yorkers filed onto Culp's Hill on the morning of July 2, the Federal army had the right man at the right place.[2]

As Greene's regiments and the other two brigades in the division occupied the hill, Geary met with the brigade commanders. The officers discussed building fieldworks along the eastern slope, but Geary opposed the idea, arguing that works "unfitted men for fighting without them." Greene replied that saving men's lives was more important to him than "any theories as to breastworks." If he had time, his men would build them along their front. Geary acquiesced, and the troops began the work.[3]

The soldiers griped as they felled oak, chestnut, walnut, and hickory trees, gathered fence rails, and dug a trench, piling the dirt on the logs and rails. To them, "it was the old trade of building works never to be used." When completed, the entrenchments stood nearly three feet high, with a "head log" on top and a six-inch gap to fire through.[4]

The line of works extended from the crest of Culp's Hill south to the saddle between the upper and lower hills, where they angled southeast through the woods, ending near the meadow by Spangler's Spring. At the angle or elbow in the line, members of the 137th New York dug a traverse trench that extended to the west as flank protection for units on the upper hill. "Troops stationed in these trenches," recalled a soldier, "were entirely protected from infantry fire from our front except their faces." A staff officer declared that the fieldworks blended into the terrain and "could not be distinguished fifty yards to front."[5]

By noon on July 2, Greene reported, "we had a good cover for the men." To the Federals' front, "a heavy growth of timber, free from undergrowth," in Greene's description, extended roughly three hundred yards east to waist-deep Rock Creek. Large boulders and rock ledges scarred the slope among the trees. If the Confederates were to attack the Union position, the ascent toward the upper hill was "very steep," whereas a "gentle slope" rose from the stream to the lower hill. The terrain's natural strength, augmented by the breastworks, made Culp's Hill a formidable position, or, as a Rebel who faced it exclaimed, it was "as strong as *eny Gnl ort* to want for it was a very steep place indee."[6]

When the Southerners came at last in the enveloping twilight of July 2, only "Old Man Greene" and his New Yorkers manned the works from the crest to the angle in the works. As three Confederate brigades ascended the slope, the woods resounded with musketry. Behind their handiwork, the New Yorkers "did as hard fighting as I ever saw men do," remarked a Federal soldier. Although the Confederates occupied the empty works on the lower hill and drove the 137th New York, on Greene's right, up the hill from the angle in the works, the Yankees held the upper hill. Greene's insistence that his men construct fieldworks paid rich dividends. "Our 3rd Brigade, under Gen. Greene," asserted Lieutenant Colonel Eugene Powell of the 66th Ohio, "is entitled to everlasting honor for the stubborn, heroic fight they made to hold these works against overwhelming force."[7]

The combat ended finally, "by degrees and by common consent," in the words of a New Yorker, about ten o'clock. As recounted earlier, the New Yorkers' comrades in the Twelfth Corps returned to Culp's Hill and the surrounding area during the nighttime hours, stumbling into collisions with the Confederates and sparking outbursts of gunfire. The Southerners retained their hold on the works south of the angle, and each side waited for daylight.[8]

When Brigadier General Alpheus S. Williams, acting commander of the Twelfth Corps, returned from the council at the Leister house, and learned of the situation on Culp's Hill, he rode to report the information to his superior, Major General Henry W. Slocum. Known as "Old Pap" in the corps, Williams was a former attorney, judge, and newspaper owner from Detroit, Michigan, who had risen from instructing recruits to divisional command in eight months. His troops had suffered grievously but fought well at Chancellorsville. A natural leader, he had demonstrated his capability as a division commander.[9]

Williams met with Slocum most likely at the latter's headquarters at Powers Hill, along Baltimore Pike. Slocum was thirty-five years old, an Academy graduate who had been in command of the Twelfth Corps since October 1862. He was a short man with undoubted ability and intelligence and with a combative disposition. He dressed well, if not elegantly, in striking contrast to other generals, such as Greene. George Meade so trusted Slocum's generalship that he had made him a wing commander as the army moved toward Gettysburg. Unfortunately, Slocum believed that he retained the authority once the battle began, complicating command arrangements in the corps between him and Williams.[10]

Earlier, at the council, Slocum responded to the questions with a terse, "Stay and fight it out." So, when Williams explained the situation on Culp's Hill, Slocum replied, "Well! Drive them out at daylight." Later, Williams wrote that Slocum's response was "an order that I then thought was more easily made than executed." Slocum, however, relayed the information to army headquarters, where Meade approved the decision.[11]

Williams had about nine thousand officers and men for the work ahead, sprawled across the woods and fields from the crest of Culp's Hill on the north to McAllister's Woods on the south, a distance of nearly twelve hundred yards. Though Greene's New Yorkers still held the works on the upper hill, the corps's other five brigades lay where they had halted during the night, either because of encounters with the Rebels or by orders from commanders. Williams would fashion the attack from these dispositions.[12]

"The plan was simply to open upon the ridge they occupied with several batteries of artillery at daylight," Williams explained later, "and after a cannonading of fifteen minutes to attack them from the left (Greene's position) while the 1st Division held a threatening position on the right and felt them cautiously by skirmishers." Geary's Second Division, or so-called White Star Division because of its distinctive corps badge, would have to bear the burden of the attack on both the upper and lower hills, because the Confederate position on the Federals' right was "quite impregnable for assault."[13]

Geary's division consisted of Greene's New Yorkers and the brigades of Brigadier General Thomas Kane and Colonel Charles Candy. Kane's three Pennsylvania regiments had led the return march to Culp's Hill. After their brush with Confederates in the lower works, they had deployed on Greene's right, facing southeast, covering the saddle between the two hills and the end of the stone wall that paralleled the lower works and ran to Rock Creek. To Kane's right, Candy's six regiments of Ohioans and Pennsylvanians had stopped along Henry Spangler's farm lane and fronted to the southeast. Before them lay a seven-acre field, edged on the northeast by the stone wall and encircled by trees. In time, it would become known as Pardee Field for Lieutenant Colonel Ario Pardee, Jr., of the 147th Pennsylvania in Candy's brigade. Geary had perhaps thirty-seven hundred officers and men in his division.[14]

South and west of Geary's troops, Williams's division, commanded by Brigadier General Thomas H. Ruger, occupied the area between Baltimore Pike and Rock Creek. Colonel Silas Colgrove's five regiments held McAllister's Woods after exchanging gunfire with Confederates on the lower hill. Colgrove had deployed his regiments to face north, toward the meadow between his position and the Southerners', and toward Rock Creek to the east. Two hundred yards southwest of McAllister's Woods, near the D. Lightner farmhouse, Colonel Archibald L. McDougall's brigade lay in reserve. To McDougall's left, Brigadier General Henry H. Lockwood's three regiments supported two artillery batteries posted along Baltimore Pike. Approximately fifty-two hundred troops stood in the ranks of the 1st Division.[15]

According to the plan, Williams would open the effort to retake the works with artillery. For that duty, he had the four batteries of the corps and one from the Artillery Reserve of the army. Fourteen cannon were posted on

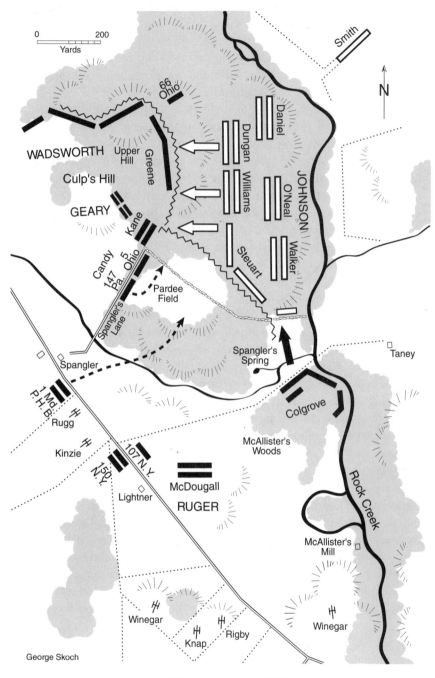

0   200
Yards

Smith

66
Ohio

WADSWORTH

Upper
Hill

Culp's Hill

Greene

GEARY

Kane

Candy

147
Pa.

5
Ohio

Spangler's Lane

Spangler

1 Md.
P. H. B.

Rugg

Kinzie

107 N.Y.

150
N.Y.

Lightner

Pardee
Field

McDougall

RUGER

Dungan

Williams

Daniel

O'Neal

JOHNSON

Walker

Steuart

Spangler's
Spring

Colgrove

McAllister's
Woods

Taney

Rock Creek

McAllister's
Mill

Winegar

Knap

Rigby

Winegar

N

George Skoch

CULP'S HILL, 4:30 A.M.–7:00 A.M.

Powers Hill—six ten-pound Parrotts of Knap's Independent Pennsylvania Battery E, under Lieutenant Charles A. Atwell; six three-inch Ordnance rifles of Battery A, 1st Maryland, under Captain James H. Rigby; and two ten-pound Parrotts from a section of Battery M, 1st New York, under Lieutenant Charles E. Winegar. The other section of Winegar's battery unlimbered on McAllister's Hill, located two hundred yards east of Powers Hill. From Powers Hill, the artillerists had a clear field of fire to the wooded slopes of lower Culp's Hill.[16]

At 1:00 A.M. on July 3, the other two batteries had been placed on a rise west of Baltimore Pike, about three hundred yards southwest of Henry Spangler's farm. Lieutenant Sylvanus T. Rugg's Battery F, 4th United States Artillery deployed on the left of Lieutenant David H. Kinzie's Battery K, 5th United States Artillery. Between them, Rugg and Kinzie had ten bronze, smoothbore Napoleons. The Regulars covered the meadow south of the lower hill, and at the range of about eight hundred yards could use canister against any Confederate force that entered the open ground.[17]

Williams instructed the artillery officers to open fire at 4:30 A.M. and continue for fifteen minutes, until Geary's troops advanced. When Williams had finished discussions with subordinates about the orders, he lay down on a flat rock beneath an apple tree and rested for thirty minutes.[18]

❖   ❖   ❖

FOR THE VIRGINIANS, Louisianans, North Carolinians, and Marylanders in the woods along the base and on the eastern slope of Culp's Hill, the night of July 2–3 surely passed with an unwanted swiftness. After the fighting had ended, between ten and eleven o'clock on July 2, the return of Federal units to the area brought shouts of identification in the darkness and outbursts of gunfire. While many Confederates managed to sleep for a few hours, others gathered ammunition from their dead and wounded comrades. A few Rebels even crawled into the works near the angle and collected abandoned enemy rifles from the 137th New York, whose members had been forced up the slope during the action on July 2.[19]

On the Confederate right, opposite the steepest portion of Culp's Hill, which a Southern officer in his report called "Red Hill," the Virginia brigade of Brigadier General John M. Jones had retired to the foot of the hill along Rock Creek. Jones had suffered a thigh wound during the attack, and Lieutenant Colonel Robert H. Dungan of the 48th Virginia now led the five regiments. On the Virginians' left, Colonel Jesse M. Williams's Louisianans held the center of the line. During the assaults, the Louisianans had clawed up the slope to within forty yards of the Union works before withdrawing. They now lay one hundred paces from the enemy, still close enough that they spoke in whispers and heard the Yankees astir on the hill. One of Williams's officers claimed later that, "to mask our weakness," they decided to open fire at daylight.[20]

Farther south, Brigadier General George H. Steuart's mixed brigade of Virginians, North Carolinians, and Marylanders clung to the breastworks below the saddle between the upper and lower hills, and to sections of the stone wall. Directly in front of the Rebels lay Kane's and Candy's Union brigades, while on their left, beyond the meadow on McAllister's Hill, were Colgrove's troops. From their position, the Southerners could hear wagons roll on Baltimore Pike, five hundred yards to the west. Some of Steuart's men speculated that perhaps the enemy was retreating. Steuart believed that "we had gained an admirable position" and must have reported that judgment to division commander Major General Edward Johnson.[21]

Like his corps commander, Lieutenant General Richard S. Ewell, Johnson had received his new command in the May reorganization of the army. Known in the army as "Allegheny," Johnson was a West Pointer who had suffered a severe wound to an ankle during the Battle of McDowell in May 1862. He had returned to duty a year later, when he assumed command of the division. He walked with a noticeable limp, using a staff that was "about as long as a rail and almost as thick as the club of Giant Despair" to assist him. Less charitable soldiers called him "Old Clubby."[22]

"A heavy, thick-set man," according to an officer, Johnson had a personality and manners as rough as the bark of a hickory tree. He was ill-tempered, cursed at the troops, and when he came upon skulkers from the ranks, he hit them with his walking club. One of his men called him simply a "brute." But he was an obstinate fighter who would hammer at the enemy just as he swung his club at soldiers who shirked their duty.[23]

In his report, Johnson stated that his assault on July 2 "was as successful as could have been expected, considering the superiority of the enemy's force and position," which he described as "formidable." It would seem, however, that he informed corps headquarters after the fighting had ended that his troops—probably referring to Steuart's men—had gained an advantage that could be exploited in the morning. How Johnson planned to accomplish this remains uncertain other than for his division to resume the frontal attacks that had been repulsed by a single Union brigade and a few additional regiments. Undoubtedly, he learned of the return of at least some of the Twelfth Corps units. Against a determined opponent on that ground, it was, as a historian has asserted, "an impossible assignment." [24]

In the end, the decision rested at army and corps headquarters. Before midnight, Ewell had received an order from Robert E. Lee "to renew my attack at daylight," as the corps commander reported it. When Lee issued the directive, he could not have known of the tactical situation on Ewell's front. His order, however, caused an argument at Second Corps headquarters, located in a barn near the intersection of Carlisle Street and Heidlersburg Road. When Ewell proposed to comply with another attack on Culp's Hill, some officers voiced their opposition to the idea. Ewell allegedly responded "that he knew it could be done, and that the assault should be renewed." [25]

"Johnson's position was the only one affording hopes of doing this to advantage," Ewell explained later. He had no other choice. Two Confederate brigades from Major General Jubal A. Early's division, shielded by a deepening twilight on July 2, had charged up the eastern slope of Cemetery Hill and into Union batteries before being repulsed by Federal reserves. To attempt that attack in daylight without considerable reinforcements would result in a slaughter. With no alternative, and apparently buttressed by a favorable report from Johnson, Ewell sent the order to the division commander.[26]

Since the assault at Culp's Hill would be his primary effort on July 3, Ewell strengthened the attack force by drawing two brigades from Major General Robert E. Rodes's division and one brigade from Early's division. Rodes sent the brigades of Brigadier General Junius Daniel and Colonel Edward A. O'Neal, while Early complied with the three regiments of Brigadier General William Smith's brigade. Johnson, meanwhile, recalled Brigadier General James A. Walker's Stonewall Brigade, which had been guarding the corps's left flank on Hanover Road on July 2. Ewell also ordered Lieutenant Colonel William Nelson and his artillery battalion to report to Johnson and to support the infantry attack. Nelson, however, could not find favorable ground for his batteries, and he posted them in the rear of the Confederate line behind some hills and would not be engaged.[27]

Walker's famous command of five Virginia regiments arrived first on Culp's Hill, forming in the rear of Steuart's brigade on the lower hill, east of the saddle. Daniel and O'Neal began their march about 1:30 A.M. from west of the town, and reported to Johnson about four o'clock. Johnson placed O'Neal's Alabamians and Daniel's North Carolinians as support for the center of the line. Smith's troops would not reach the area until nearly seven o'clock. When all the units were at hand, Johnson had slightly more than nine thousand officers and men to oppose an equal number of Federals.[28]

Ewell had committed thirty-three regiments from seven brigades to the assault. Except for July 1, when he had attacked with two divisions, Ewell had not used this many troops for an action at Gettysburg as he had for this morning at Culp's Hill. Before a wound cost him a leg in August 1862, he had been one of the army's finest division commanders. His performance during the army's movement toward and into Pennsylvania had been outstanding, fulfilling Lee's confidence in him as a corps commander. But once on the field at Gettysburg, his generalship seemed to be characterized by indecisiveness and a lack of firm direction to his subordinates. Now, as daylight approached, the forty-six-year-old Virginian had assigned more than half the troops left in his corps to an offensive against a Federal position that he had not personally examined. Ominously, he seemed to have little appreciation of the difficulties his soldiers confronted.[29]

On Culp's Hill, meanwhile, Daniel's and O'Neal's men, after crossing Rock Creek, were filing up the slope and forming into lines. Numbers of Johnson's troops were still asleep. One of them, Lieutenant John H. Stone of the 1st Maryland Battalion, had jotted in his diary under July 2, "The worst was to come."[30]

◦   ◦   ◦

ALPHEUS WILLIAMS ROSE from his brief rest on a flat rock about four o'clock on the morning of July 3. He had issued the orders to his subordinates, and now all he could do was wait until 4:30 A.M., when the artillery would begin firing. The five batteries were under the capable direction of Lieutenant Edward D. Muhlenberg, the corps's chief of artillery. Muhlenberg had the twenty-six-gun crews ready, and at the designated time, the cannon erupted with a wave of shells toward the Confederate position.[31]

Instructed to fire for fifteen minutes, Muhlenberg's artillerists concentrated on the lower hill, where the Southerners held the trenches. "We poured shot and shell into them," stated a Federal gunner. The shells exploded among the trees, raining jagged pieces of metal and severed branches and limbs upon the Rebels. Mercifully for the Southerners, the fire ended a quarter-hour later. This would prove to be only a respite, however: the battery crews resumed their work at 5:30 A.M., continuing to discharge their cannon at intervals until ten o'clock. Without opposition from enemy batteries, "the artillery was of essential service," in Muhlenberg's judgment.[32]

When the Union gunners ceased the cannonading, their infantry comrades prepared to advance as Williams had directed. Before they could move, however, "defiant yells" rolled up the eastern slope of Culp's Hill, emitted by oncoming Confederates. Then, as if someone had yanked open the doors to hell, sheets of flame, from thousands of rifled muskets, flashed in the darkened woods. In what seemed to be an instant, "the fire was awful," wrote a Confederate, "and the whole hillside seemed enveloped in a blaze."[33]

The Confederate attack came from the right and center—Dungan's Virginians and Williams's Louisianans, supported by O'Neal's Alabamians—toward George Greene's New Yorkers on the upper hill. The New York line ran from the crest down the slope four hundred yards to where the works, a New Yorker wrote, "turn an elbow east." The 137th New York held the right flank, with the 149th on its left, then the 60th, 78th, and 102nd New York. Colonel Henry A. Barnum of the 149th New York declared that the enemy "furiously attacked us. His charges were most impetuous and his fire terrific."[34]

Down the slope, the Southerners used trees and rocks as protection, trying to inch their way up the hillside. Like their opponents, the Rebels described the gunfire as "incessant," as "one continuous roar," and as "murderous." A member of the 12th Alabama wrote in a letter that O'Neal's brigade advanced at five o'clock, and "we were into it hot and heavy. I thought I had been in hot places before—I thought I had heard Minnie balls; but that day capped the climax."[35]

Colonel David Zable of the 14th Louisiana recalled that the smoke was so heavy that the enemy line could only be distinguished by the flashes from the rifles. "The roar of musketry was so intense," Zable declared, "that it was useless to attempt to give command unless shouted into the men's ears." He believed that if the Yankees had fired with more "deliberation" they "would have annihilated the Brigade."[36]

Southern gains were measured in feet, secured at a dear price. On the Confederate right, Dungan's Virginians "were compelled to climb up the very steepest kind of cliffs to get to them," grumbled one man in the 21st Virginia. Robert Slaughter of the 44th Virginia fell mortally wounded. In the attack on July 2, his brother, William, had been cut down with a fatal wound. During the night, Robert had to listen to his brother plead for water but could not come to his assistance. The cries ceased at last, and the Slaughter family lost two sons on Culp's Hill.[37]

Dungan's attack foundered from the outset, caught in a scissors of musketry from the front and from the right. It would appear from the few extant Southern accounts that only a portion of the brigade managed to climb up the slope to a midway point about 150 yards from the Federal entrenchments. The commander of the 50th Virginia reported, for instance, that his men remained along Rock Creek and spent the morning "without any important operations on our part." Robert Slaughter perhaps died near a rock ledge reached by the 44th Virginia. The Virginians struggled against the steepness of the hill and a deadly enfilading fire upon its right flank.[38]

Before daylight, Union division commander John Geary had ordered Colonel Charles Candy, whose brigade lay along the Spangler farm lane, to send a regiment to the crest of the hill beyond the Union works and have it form a line perpendicular to Greene's, down the hillside. Candy selected the 66th Ohio, under Lieutenant Colonel Eugene Powell. The Ohioans followed a ravine to the crest, where Powell apparently met George Greene. It was still dark, and Powell did not know who Greene was. When he repeated his orders to the New Yorker, Greene barked: "My God young man. The enemy are right out there. I am expecting an attack any moment. If you go out there with your Regiment they will simply swallow you."[39]

Greene gave Powell a guide, and the two men crossed the works, seeking a good position for the regiment. Powell wrote later that Greene "expected that we would be annihilated and I thought so myself." Returning to his regiment, Powell ordered the men forward past Greene's left flank and down the slope. It was now daylight, and Dungan's Virginians were advancing. Some of the Confederates saw the Ohioans and fired. The blast mortally wounded Major Joshua G. Palmer, who was standing just below the crest and hurrying the Ohioans across the works. The Northerners fanned out as skirmishers, "every man sheltering and caring for himself as much as possible," according to Powell.[40]

Powell admitted later, "I did not know exactly what I was to do or where I was to go except to get under fire with the enemy which was not difficult of doing on that morning." His men, however, sheltered behind rocks, trees, and stumps, raked the Southern flank with a murderous fire. Private William Sayre wrote his family two days later, "You had better think we give them what they needed this time if they never got it before. Well I could not say that I killed one myself, but I can say that I shot enough at them. . . . I done my best to kill to."[41]

The 66th Ohio clung to its perch beyond the Union works throughout the morning. Their fire and that of Greene's troops stopped Dungan's advance, forcing the Virginians down the hillside. From along Rock Creek, the Virginians skirmished with the Ohioans and New Yorkers but made no further attempt to ascend the slope.[42]

Geary, meanwhile, bolstered his left on the upper hill by pulling additional regiments from Candy's brigade and placing them in a hollow to the rear of Greene's line. A native Pennsylvanian, Mexican War veteran, first mayor of San Francisco, and former governor of Kansas Territory, Geary towered physically over a battlefield, standing six feet six inches tall and weighing more than two hundred pounds. He had been wounded twice, captured once, and paroled during the previous year. Though he possessed a fearsome temper, he had earned his men's respect.[43]

One of Geary's soldiers saw him on this morning and later penned a description. The division commander was "dressed in an old blouse with few of the outward appearances of a general. He bore evidence of the wear and tear. His hair was uncombed, his face was brown and rusty, his garments were shockingly soiled, and he might have been taken for a 'tramp' who had suddenly appeared upon the field, ready to lead where any would dare to follow."[44]

Geary and Alpheus Williams understood that the critical sector of the Twelfth Corps's line was on the upper hill, where Greene's New Yorkers manned the works. Accordingly, Geary strengthened the line, first with the 66th Ohio and then with the 7th and 29th Ohio and the 28th Pennsylvania. When the order came, the three regiments, numbering nearly nine hundred officers and men, hurried up the western slope and halted in a hollow about fifty yards behind Greene's troops.[45]

To their front, the musketry continued unabated, sounding as if some giant bellowed in defiance. The New Yorkers crouched behind the works, aiming and firing their Springfield and Enfield rifles through the gap beneath the head logs. Nevertheless, the Confederates hit Yankees, inflicting head and shoulder wounds. At first, the New Yorkers carried their dead to the rear, but as the number mounted, the survivors ignored the bodies, caring only for their wounded comrades. Captain George K. Collins recalled that an unidentified soldier stood on a bank behind the 149th New York, loading and shooting his rifle. Suddenly, Collins heard a sound "like a blow given upon fresh meat." The soldier stood motionless, dropped his gun, and then "began to tip forward and fell like a falling tree. He was a lifeless corpse," from a bullet in the head.[46]

A member of the 149th New York claimed in a letter, written on July 9, that the leg wound he had sustained resulted from fire in the rear of their line. "It is not the Rebs that done it," Perry Norton wrote his father, "it was are [sic] own men—they took us to be Rebs and they fired tremendous volleys in on our own men and I tell you that there was many a man fell by our own mens shots." Whether Norton's allegation was accurate remains uncertain.[47]

About six o'clock, the Federals began a rotation of regiments on the upper hill. The 7th Ohio of Candy's brigade went into the works first, relieving the 60th New York in the center of Greene's line. The Ohioans emerged from the hollow, cheering and double-quicking across the ground to the trenches, where the New Yorkers scrambled out and passed through the files of the incoming regiment. The exchange of regiments exposed the Federals to enemy fire, which the Rebels "were not slow to improve." Minutes later, the 29th Ohio ran forward to replace the 137th New York on Greene's right.[48]

While the fresh troops engaged the enemy, the New Yorkers cleaned their weapons, acquired more ammunition, and rested. Corporal James S. Hyde of the 137th New York asserted later, "They would all rather be in the trenches than in the hollow." The rotation of regiments continued throughout the morning, with the Northerners cheering when they went back in. "The men were always comparatively fresh," reported Greene, "and their arms in good order." In time, the 28th Pennsylvania of Candy's brigade, the regiments of Henry Lockwood's brigade, and the 14th Brooklyn and 147th New York from the First Corps joined the struggle on the upper hill.[49]

The rotation of regiments allowed the Federals to maintain a continuous fire of musketry. A soldier in the 7th Ohio described his regiment's work: "the command, 'Front rank—Ready—Aim Low—Fire!' was given and executed, and immediately the rear rank the same." The unrelenting gunfire, according to another Ohioan, took nearly "*all* the bark from the trees." Lieutenant Harry Dean of the 7th Ohio observed that it was the first time the regiment had fought behind fieldworks, and "all agree it is a pretty good way to fight."[50]

Although not as sustained, the Confederate gunfire was described by the Federals as "terrific" and "fearfully destructive." "If a man exposed himself," avowed an Ohioan, "he was sure to get shot." Many of his comrades placed their caps on ramrods and raised them above the works, drawing immediate responses from the Southerners. From where acting corps commander Williams stood, the woods "were ablaze with continuous volleys." The Confederates had to deal with fouled rifles from the many discharges and a dwindling supply of ammunition. It was an uneven struggle for the gray-coated soldiers from the outset, and their situation never improved.[51]

o   o   o

IN THE SADDLE BETWEEN upper and lower Culp's Hill, where the Union breastworks turned "an elbow east," the combat was as unremitting and fearful as the fighting on the higher elevation. Here, Edward Johnson and Richard Ewell had hoped to exploit the advantage gained on the night of July 2, when George H. Steuart's brigade had occupied the abandoned trenches. Instead, Steuart's troops, supported by James A. Walker's Stonewall Brigade, met a wall of musketry.[52]

The gunfire came from some of George Greene's New Yorkers, three Pennsylvania regiments in the brigade of Thomas L. Kane, and the 147th Pennsylvania and 5th Ohio in Charles Candy's brigade. Kane's officers and men, numbering about 625, covered the saddle, the angle in the works, and the northern end of the stone wall that paralleled the Federal entrenchments. From behind a rock ledge above the saddle, Kane's fellow Pennsylvanians raked Steuart's right flank and Walker's Virginians farther down in the woods. "A constant fire of musketry was kept up," reported one of Kane's officers.[53]

Kane's men had led the return march of the Twelfth Corps to Culp's Hill on the night of July 2, and had discovered, at the loss of several men, that the Rebels held the works that the Pennsylvanians had built. The Federals then receded into the darkness, halting above the saddle. Before daylight on July 3, Kane had realigned his front. The 111th Pennsylvania connected its left flank with Greene's right. The 109th Pennsylvania formed beside the 111th, its line extending west to Candy's units. Behind the pair of regiments, Kane placed the 29th Pennsylvania in reserve. As the engagement progressed, the three Pennsylvania regiments rotated from the front line to the rear, as their comrades were doing on upper Culp's Hill.[54]

For Thomas Kane, this fighting marked another day in more than a decade of being at war because of his principles. During the 1850s, he had embraced abolitionism, resigned as a federal commissioner in protest of the Fugitive Slave Act, and was jailed for contempt of court on an order from his father, the presiding judge. Unbowed when released by the United States Supreme Court, he aided runaway slaves. When the Civil War began, he had recruited fellow townsmen and backwoodsmen from Kane, a town he had founded and named in northwestern Pennsylvania, into the famed "Pennsylvania Bucktails." In time, he proved to be an excellent officer, earned promotion to brigadier general, suffered two wounds, and endured a brief imprisonment in the Confederacy.[55]

After the Chancellorsville campaign in May 1863, Kane developed pneumonia, and was at home on leave when he learned of the Confederate movement into his native state. Although not recovered, he hurried south, first to Washington and then to Baltimore, trying to overtake the army. Sharing a carriage with an army surgeon, Kane arrived at Gettysburg early on the morning of July 2. He reassumed command of the brigade on that day, but his lingering illness forced him to share it with Colonel George A. Cobham, Jr., of the 111th Pennsylvania.[56]

Kane was, in the estimation of one of his men, "the bravest little man that ever lived," an "old-time warrior." His superior officer, Alpheus Williams, said that the brigadier possessed "pluck and will." He had leaned into numerous winds in his lifetime and had come to Gettysburg looking for a fight. On this morning on Culp's Hill, the physically diminutive soldier and his men faced a furious gale.[57]

The accounts of the combat on lower Culp's Hill echo those of the fighting on the higher elevation. A soldier in the 111th Pennsylvania claimed that he and his comrades discharged sixty rounds in less than an hour, "as fast as we could." A veteran in the 10th Virginia, in Steuart's brigade, described the struggle in his diary as "the heardest contested battle of the war"; a Marylander stated that a man was almost certain to be shot if he exposed any part of his body. "So terific was the strife," declared another Southerner, "that scarcely a leaf or limb was left on the surrounding trees."[58]

On Steuart's right, nearest the saddle, the 3rd North Carolina and 1st Maryland Battalion suffered the worst, caught between Greene's New Yorkers and Kane's and Candy's troops. Major William M. Pausley of the 3rd North Carolina asserted that the regiment was "exposed to a very heavy fire." When the commander of the Marylanders, Major William W. Goldsborough, checked on his right-flank company, he found it and the 3rd North Carolina "nearly annihilated." Behind these two units, members of the Stonewall Brigade suffered nearly as badly. Like the Marylander, a Virginian wrote home, "I think it was the hardest battle we ever had."[59]

The fury increased for the Confederates on the lower hill when the Union batteries on Powers and McAllister's Hills and along Baltimore Pike resumed their shellfire at 5:30 A.M. "At times," Lieutenant John H. Stone of the 1st Maryland scribbled in his diary, "one could feel the earth tremble, so fearful was the cannonading." According to an officer, Steuart and members of his staff sheltered themselves behind an "immense rock." "It was a very trying place," in the terse estimation of one Confederate.[60]

Like the Southerners, Kane's Pennsylvanians contended with overheated and fouled weapons. Many of the rifles became "so clogged as to be useless," but, unlike their opponents, the Yankees were relieved on the line and had time to clean the guns. Sergeant Castor G. Malin of the 111th Pennsylvania conducted a personal duel with a Confederate. When he saw smoke come from an opening between rocks, he fired at the target. Each time he triggered a round, however, another puff reappeared. He shot six times, grumbling about his poor marksmanship. When the fighting had ended and the enemy had withdrawn later in the day, Malin walked to the site and found five dead Rebels, proving, perhaps, that his marksmanship was not as bad as he had thought.[61]

On Malin's and his comrades' right, meanwhile, Charles Candy's two remaining regiments—the other four had been sent by Geary as support for Greene—had been engaged since daylight. Candy's troops had spent the night along Spangler's farm lane, many of them "prostrate" from the exertions on July 2. Sometime the next morning, probably when the Union cannon opened its initial fire, Candy moved his front line forward to a "thin skirt of trees" along the northwestern edge of a seven-acre field—Pardee Field. Across the open ground, the stone wall, which roughly paralleled the captured Union works, ran from the saddle diagonally along the field's eastern side. If the Federals could seize and hold the stone wall, they could enfilade the flank of any Confederate force that advanced through the saddle toward the upper hill.[62]

Geary ordered Lieutenant Colonel Ario Pardee, Jr., and the 147th Pennsylvania to drive Steuart's gray-coated skirmishers from the wall and hold it. Minutes earlier, the 1st Maryland Potomac Home Brigade (1st Maryland PHB), a regiment in Brigadier General Henry H. Lockwood's brigade, had tried to take the wall but been repulsed. The Marylanders were regrouping for a second attack when Pardee led his men across the field that would eventually bear his name. Supported on their left by gunfire from the 5th Ohio, the Pennsylvanians seized the wall, scattering the enemy skirmishers. Back on the ridge, among the narrow stand of trees, the 147th's pet dog scampered into a hole beneath the rocks and stayed there.[63]

Candy's six hundred Ohioans and Pennsylvanians rendered valuable service. On the ridge beside Kane's men, the 5th Ohio directed their fire toward the works held by Steuart's Confederates, while the 147th Pennsylvania, from behind the stone wall, scorched the ground through the saddle. The Pennsylvanians' gunfire added to the casualties and miseries of the 3rd North Carolina and 1st Maryland Battalion of Steuart's brigade, and Walker's Virginians. Later during the action, Company F of the 5th Ohio joined Pardee's troops at the wall.[64]

At some time on this morning, Lieutenant William L. Tourison of the 147th Pennsylvania was killed at the wall. When the fighting ceased, the lieutenant's father and company commander, Captain A. S. Tourison, had four soldiers wrap his son's body in a blanket and carry it to the rear. As the party proceeded, Captain Tourison, who had served in the 28th Pennsylvania, met a member of his former unit. When the soldier said that he was glad to see the captain, Tourison could only reply, "My poor boy is dead."[65]

After the 1st Maryland PHB of Lockwood's command had been repulsed and had watched Pardee's successful attack, the regiment rejoined its comrades near Baltimore Pike. The brigade consisted of the 1st Maryland PHB, the 1st Maryland Eastern Shore regiment, and the 150th New York. The eighteen hundred members of the brigade had been on garrison duty at Baltimore until June 25, when the War Department attached it to the Twelfth Corps. Dressed in new uniforms and carrying "bright burnished arms," the officers and men of the brigade were readily distinguishable among the faded uniforms of the veteran units in the army. Neither Lockwood, a West Pointer, nor most of his men had been in combat before they arrived at Gettysburg.[66]

Assigned to Alpheus Williams's division as a provisional brigade, the novice soldiers had not long to wait to join the brotherhood of combat veterans. They had led the corps's units toward Cemetery Ridge on July 2, and were rushed into the cauldron aboil in the fields west of the ridge. They retook three captured Union cannon before being recalled. Upon their return to the Culp's Hill area, they halted along the pike. From there, the 1st Maryland PHB had advanced to charge the stone wall.[67]

Lockwood received his orders directly from Williams. When Williams had been given acting command of the corps, Lockwood became the senior officer in the division, outranking Brigadier General Thomas H. Ruger. Neither Williams nor Henry Slocum wanted an untested Lockwood in command of the division, so Williams designated Lockwood's troops as an "unattached brigade pending the existing operations." In turn, Ruger commanded the other two brigades, and Lockwood reported to Williams.[68]

Between six and seven o'clock, Williams directed Lockwood to march his three regiments to upper Culp's Hill as support for Geary's division. The brigade followed Spangler's farm lane before ascending the hill's western face and halting in the ravine behind the Union line. When Lockwood's troops were en route to Gettysburg, one of them declared that he was "ready for anything that comes along in the shape of a Rebel." If he had not seen enough Rebel shapes on the afternoon of July 2, he would see more than his fill before this morning ended.[69]

When the 1st Maryland PHB tried unsuccessfully to seize the stone wall, the regiment received support on its right from the 20th Connecticut of Colonel Archibald L. McDougall's brigade. McDougall's six regiments had halted upon their return during the night near the D. Lightner house, east of Baltimore Pike. Many of the men slept in a muddy cornfield at the base of a ridge. Before daylight, McDougall, who had been in the army less than a year, received orders to advance against the works on the lower hill held by the enemy. McDougall chose the 20th Connecticut to lead the brigade.[70]

Lieutenant Colonel William B. Wooster deployed his men as "a heavy force of skirmishers," with orders to move ahead slowly and cautiously. At five o'clock, the 20th Connecticut stepped out, ascending the ridge and halting on its crest at the edge of a treeline. Before them lay Pardee Field, the stone wall, and the captured trenches. Steuart's Confederate skirmishers welcomed the Yankees, who responded with a volley. "The awful work of retaking their old position began," wrote a Northerner.[71]

The 20th Connecticut became engaged evidently about the time the 1st Maryland PHB suffered its repulse, and before the charge of the 147th Pennsylvania. Wooster pushed his line forward beyond the trees and halted. The musketry escalated between the opponents. After a while, Wooster withdrew the regiment into the shelter of the trees and rocks. From there, the Connecticut men fought, in Wooster's words, "as best we could."[72]

McDougall, meanwhile, brought forward his other five regiments as support. The 123rd New York and the 46th Pennsylvania halted behind Wooster's troops on the crest, while the 5th Connecticut moved up on the right of the 20th Connecticut, extending its line south toward Colonel Silas Colgrove's brigade in McAllister's Woods. The 3rd Maryland and 145th New York remained farther to the rear in reserve.[73]

When the Union batteries along Baltimore Pike and on Powers Hill resumed firing at 5:30 A.M., some of the rounds fell far short of the Confederate
position and into the ranks of McDougall's units. One shell exploded prematurely above the 20th Connecticut, its shards mangling both arms of Private
George W. Warner. Carried to the rear, Warner did not learn until he was
being treated at a hospital that he had lost both limbs—not just the right arm,
as he had thought when wounded.[74]

Additional shells burst within the ranks of the 123rd and 145th New York
and 46th Pennsylvania. Wooster and McDougall sent aides to the artillery
crews, complaining about the fire. Colonel James L. Selfridge of the 46th
Pennsylvania was so furious he warned McDougall that, if the artillerists continued to either aim low or short-cut the fuses, he would personally go to the
rear and shoot them. The gunners corrected the problems, and their infantry
comrades were spared further losses.[75]

McDougall's troops settled in once the dangerous artillery rounds ceased.
On the ridge's crest, Wooster's 20th Connecticut maintained a constant fire
toward lower Culp's Hill as the other regiments lay in reserve. For Wooster's
men, the fighting became routine, without an apparent end.[76]

◦   ◦   ◦

LIEUTENANT COLONEL CHARLES R. MUDGE of the 2nd Massachusetts listened with disbelief to the order for an attack. His veteran soldiers had bled
and died in Miller's Cornfield at Antietam on September 17, 1862, but for
them to cross the meadow that lay between their position in McAllister's
Woods and the Confederate-held works on lower Culp's Hill meant almost
certain death. Turning to his field and staff officers, Mudge declared that the
directive was "murder but it was the order."[77]

The order had originated with Henry Slocum, who instructed acting division commander Thomas Ruger to retake the trenches on lower Culp's Hill
occupied by the enemy on July 2. A West Pointer and career army officer,
Ruger reacted cautiously, asking Slocum if he could determine Confederate
strength in the works before undertaking a charge. Slocum approved, and
Ruger dispatched a staff officer, Lieutenant William M. Snow, with instructions for Colgrove. Before he departed, Snow repeated the oral order that
Ruger had given him.[78]

Snow found Colgrove on wooded McAllister's Hill about 5:30 A.M. (In his report, Ruger badly mistimed the order at 10:00 A.M.) At the time, Colgrove's troops were skirmishing with the Southerners on the lower hill and from across Rock Creek around the stone farmhouse of Zephaniah Taney. The opponents had been exchanging gunfire for an hour when Snow arrived. The staff officer told Colgrove that the colonel should advance skirmishers, and if the Rebels were "not found in too great force, to advance two regiments and dislodge them from the breastworks."[79]

In his report, Colgrove stated that Snow said that Ruger wanted the colonel "to advance your line immediately." Colgrove then wrote that "it was impossible to send forward skirmishers" or to attack with more than two regiments. As he saw it, his only chance to comply with the order was "by storming" the enemy position.[80]

A former lawyer and state legislator, Colgrove had served as colonel of the 27th Indiana since its organization in the autumn of 1861. He had demanded much from his Hoosier volunteers, and they came to respect and to admire his courage in battle and his concern for their welfare. He led them through the 1862 campaigns and at Chancellorsville in May 1863. He was an able regimental commander who would be a key figure in a tragic drama on this morning.[81]

Colgrove chose his own regiment and the 2nd Massachusetts for the attack. He ordered Mudge and the 2nd Massachusetts to charge the works on the lower hill directly in their front, and Lieutenant Colonel John R. Fesler and the 27th Indiana to oblique to the right and carry the enemy position behind a rock ledge. Ahead of them, beyond the one-hundred-yard-wide meadow, were roughly a thousand Confederates—the left wing of Steuart's brigade in the trenches, and the 2nd Virginia of the Stonewall Brigade behind the stone wall that ran from the saddle of Culp's Hill to Rock Creek. The two Union regiments had about 650 officers and men in the ranks.[82]

Charles Mudge was twenty-four years old, a Harvard graduate, class of 1860, who had assumed command of the regiment when its colonel had been wounded at Chancellorsville. He had already voiced his opinion on the order when he stood in front of his fellow Bay Staters and shouted to them, "Rise up, over the breastworks, forward, double-quick." His men cheered, crossed the works, and emerged into the meadow. To their right and slightly behind them came the Hoosiers of the 27th Indiana.[83]

"They had scarcely gained the open ground," Colgrove reported, "when they were met with one of the most terrible fires I have ever witnessed." The

Confederates reloaded and triggered another volley, and cut gaps in the ranks of both regiments. The "boggy" ground of the meadow slowed the Federals' rush, subjecting them longer to the "galling fire."[84]

The Confederates exacted a fearful price. Mudge was slain. Near him in the 2nd Massachusetts, Color Sergeant Levitt C. Durgin was killed before the regiment reached the midpoint of the meadow. Corporal Rupert J. Sadler picked up the flag and died. Corporal James Hobbes then seized it, only to be severely wounded. The men were "dropping on every side," in the words of Major Charles F. Morse. But the Massachusetts veterans crossed the meadow and fought from behind rocks and trees. They opened fire, Morse wrote, "at the shortest range I have ever seen two lines engaged at."[85]

"From behind every tree and rock above the rebel fire poured in," recalled a Massachusetts man. A Private Cody of Company I had taken the flag when Hobbes fell wounded, carrying it across the meadow. As his comrades battled with the enemy, Cody jumped on a boulder, waving it in the faces of the Confederates until he was killed. Another soldier picked it up and soon went down with a wound. For ten minutes the Yankees stood and fought, until the Southerners pushed out from the works and threatened their right flank. Major Morse, now in command, looked to his right for assistance from the 27th Indiana. The Hoosiers, however, had been stopped in the meadow, their ranks thinning before a frontal and enfilading fire.[86]

Advancing on the right of the 2nd Massachusetts, the Indianans rushed through the middle of the meadow. From behind the stone wall, the 2nd Virginia scorched the Hoosiers' front, while Rebel sharpshooters, east of Rock Creek, lashed their flank. The first Southern volley leveled nearly the entire color guard of the 27th. When Fesler's men reached the center of the meadow, a "scathing, fatal volley" seemed to knock down entire companies. The Federals pressed forward several paces, with a handful of bolder soldiers continuing forward and shouting for the others to follow. More Confederate volleys ripped through the ranks in the open field. By now, additional Southern troops had joined the action, their gunfire increasing the scythe of musketry from the lower hill.[87]

The newly arrived Confederates belonged to the brigade of Brigadier General William ("Extra Billy") Smith of Jubal Early's division. Soon after the fighting had begun on Culp's Hill, Edward Johnson had sent Major Henry Kyd Douglas of his staff to locate Smith's Virginians and to hurry them to the front. When Douglas found the command, he volunteered to lead the three regiments to the lower hill. The van of Smith's column, the 49th and 52nd Virginia, arrived on the left of the 2nd Virginia as the two Union regiments were crossing the field.[88]

Kyd Douglas, who had served on the staff of Stonewall Jackson until the general's death, rode at the head of Smith's troops. A burst of rifle fire from the Federals struck the column, one bullet hitting Douglas in the left shoulder. The young staff officer remained mounted until weakened by loss of blood. He was carried to an ambulance and taken to a hospital. When the Confederate army retreated after the battle, Douglas was left to the care of Union surgeons. He eventually recovered and was imprisoned.[89]

Shortly after Douglas was hit, the Union attackers retreated. Morse would write that Colgrove ordered the withdrawal. The Indianans recrossed the meadow "rapidly," according to one of them, whereas a Bay Stater asserted that his regiment retired "slowly and sullenly." Two weeks later, Morse declared to his mother in a letter, "I never saw men behave so splendidly." He knew of only one man who had shirked his duty. "It was awful and yet grand," he wrote, "to see men expose their lives and lose them, as they did."[90]

Perhaps there had been a grandeur to it, but the awfulness of it could be seen in the meadow and among the rocks and trees near Spangler's Spring. Morse admitted that "it was a sad thing calling the rolls" after the charge had ended. The 2nd Massachusetts reported losses of twenty-two killed or mortally wounded, including Mudge and two other officers, and 112 wounded, a casualty rate of more than 40 percent. The 27th Indiana counted eighteen killed or mortally wounded and ninety-three wounded, a loss of one-third of the regiment. Colgrove concluded in his report, "It seemed that the two regiments were devoted to destruction."[91]

A Federal affirmed later that "the order to advance was a palpable blunder." Primary responsibility for it, however, remains unassigned. Ruger's decision to have an oral order delivered by a staff officer contributed undoubtedly to either a misstatement by Snow or a misunderstanding by Colgrove. Years afterward, in a letter, Ruger stated that "it was impossible to ascertain" whether Snow or Colgrove "was responsible for the mistake." In his report, Alpheus Williams concluded that Colgrove either "misapprehended the orders sent him or they were incorrectly communicated" to him.[92]

For his part, Lieutenant Snow remained steadfast that he had repeated the order to Colgrove as Ruger had given it to him. "I could never quite understand," Snow wrote in a postwar letter, "why General Colgrove should have advanced two regiments under the order delivered by me, when he, being on the spot, must have known that it was 'murder,' as poor Mudge exclaimed."

The staff officer thought that Colgrove should have apprised Ruger of the situation, because the latter "could only have had a general idea" about the tactical conditions. The order should have granted Colgrove discretion, Snow concluded.[93]

Snow had served in the 3rd Wisconsin before his staff appointment. A fellow officer in the regiment commented later in a letter that he "always considered" Snow to be "one of the most reliable men of a very reliable regiment."[94]

As noted previously, Colgrove stated in his report that Snow said, "The general directs that you advance your line immediately." But a careful reading of the report, dated August 8, 1863, appears to support the staff officer's version of the order. Colgrove argued that he could advance neither skirmishers nor more than two regiments, both elements of the order as reported by Ruger. It would seem that Colgrove concluded, as he said, "The only possible chance I had to advance was to carry his [the enemy's] position by storming it." Apparently, he interpreted Ruger's instructions as an order for an assault. Primary responsibility for the "palpable blunder" rested most likely with Colgrove.[95]

The tragedy in the meadow by Spangler's Spring ended as Confederates on Culp's Hill prepared for another assault up the hillside. Three hours of killing and maiming had brought no resolution. Hell had come with the daylight. It would stay a while longer.

4

"None but Demons Can Delight in War"

CULP'S HILL TOOK THE MEASURE of men on the morning of July 3, 1863. Amid the awful combat, some men wanted for courage, most of them stood. "There is a great deal of the hum-drum in heroism," a New Yorker observed later. "The man who made the good soldier was not the swaggering swash-buckler, not the street brawler, but the respectable plain man who at home had always done his duty, faithfully, whatever it might be." [1]

For thousands of plain men on Culp's Hill, it had been a fearful measurement, an unrelenting ordeal that had begun with the morning's light. The killing and the maiming seemed to have no end—accompanied by a deafening roar, as if some creature were in its death throes. The carnage mounted, taking more ordinary men whose sense of duty held them there. "Some places in the trenches," wrote a member of the 137th New York, "the ground was saturated with Human blood." Below the works, on the slope, "the hillside was slippery from human blood." Heroism wore a common uniform. [2]

About eight o'clock—more than an hour after the repulse of the 2nd Massachusetts and 27th Indiana in the meadow—the combat intensified when the Confederates undertook a second attack against the entrenchments on the upper hill. Edward Johnson had ordered that the effort be undertaken by

James A. Walker's Stonewall Brigade on the left, Jesse M. Williams's Louisianians in the center, and Edward A. O'Neal's Alabamians on the right. As with the initial assault, the Southerners pushed up the slope in a frontal charge.[3]

Smoke hung everywhere on the hillside as the Confederates advanced. When Lieutenant Colonel Charles B. Randall of the 149th New York of George S. Greene's brigade saw the Rebels at last, he shouted to his men: "There they come boys. Give them hell boys, give it to them right and left." Randall's New Yorkers triggered a volley, and the entire Union line behind the works flamed. To their right, the troops above the saddle and the 147th Pennsylvania from behind the stone wall directed their fire toward the oncoming Confederates, the Virginians of the Stonewall Brigade. From above the saddle, Thomas Kane said that the enemy "appeared to us only as closed in mass."[4]

The Federal musketry raked the front and left flank of the Stonewall Brigade. Walker had only four of his regiments, because the 2nd Virginia had been sent across Rock Creek to the Taney farm and deployed as sharpshooters against Silas Colgrove's Union brigade in McAllister's Wood. The 33rd Virginia was on the left of Walker's line, and it suffered the most punishment. From behind the stone wall, Ario Pardee's Pennsylvanians lay perpendicular to the Virginians' line and could fire through the low ground of the saddle into the Rebels' flank.[5]

It was during this attack, arguably, that Captain George R. Bedinger of the 33rd Virginia was killed. A student at the University of Virginia when the war began, he enlisted in the regiment, and by Gettysburg he commanded Company E. Bedinger was a popular officer, "whose presence imparted an electric touch to those around him," according to a fellow Virginian. He called his men "Greeks," and beside them he died on Culp's Hill. He fell "perhaps farther in advance of the line of battle than any other officer or man." He would have been twenty-three years old a week later.[6]

The Virginians withdrew before this combined fire, retiring nearly to the base of the hill. They needed rest, ammunition, and time to clean their rifles. On their right, the Louisianans pulled themselves up the slope into a "galling fire." Like the Virginians, they soon retreated, leaving behind more wounded and dead comrades. Culp's Hill was becoming a Confederate burial ground.[7]

To the Louisianans' right, O'Neal's Alabamians "moved forward in fine style," in their colonel's words. Within minutes, they were hit, with "a terrific fire of grape and small-arms." The Alabamians pushed ahead, however, reaching a small knoll or rise on the hillside. Here they stayed for the next

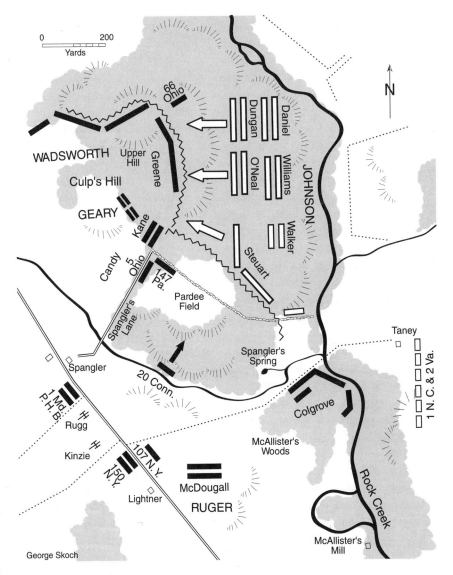

0
200
Yards

66 Ohio

Dungan
Daniel

WADSWORTH
Upper Hill
Greene

O'Neal
Williams

JOHNSON

Culp's Hill

GEARY
Kane

Walker

Candy
5 Ohio
147 Pa.
Steuart

Pardee Field

Spangler's Lane
Spangler's Spring

Taney

1 N. C. & 2 Va.

20 Conn.

Spangler

1 Md. P.H.B.
Rugg

Kinzie
107 N.Y.
150 N.Y.
Lightner
McDougall
RUGER

Colgrove

McAllister's Woods

Rock Creek

N

McAllister's Mill

George Skoch

CULP'S HILL, 8:00 A.M.–10:00 A.M.

three hours, "exposed to a murderous fire." "Many gallant men were lost," admitted O'Neal.[8]

With the repulse of this second Confederate assault, the fighting on Culp's Hill resumed its previous pattern—an unremitting slugfest, marked by unbroken rolls of musketry. The gunfire was so continuous, so fearful, that it moved one Pennsylvanian to write his parents three days later, "It seems as though to look at the field that nothing could have lived." He was not alone in his judgment.[9]

On upper Culp's Hill, the Federals rotated regiments from the works to the hollow in the rear, as they had done during the initial hours of combat. A member of Greene's brigade described the process in his diary. "Just back of the breast work was a hollow where the reinforcements stayed," the New Yorker wrote. "A regiment would use up their ammunition in about two hours, when another would relieve them and they fall back to the hollow where the balls would whistle over their heads." While the men were in the rear, they cleaned their rifles and replenished their cartridge boxes. "In this way," he added, "we could have stood as long as the rebs chose to show themselves below."[10]

As one regiment emerged from the hollow, its members cheered and double-quicked across the exposed ground to relieve another unit in the works. "Back and forth, back and forth, staggering through the heat and smoke of battle, red-eyed, gasping," was how one Federal described the exchange of units. Greene thought that at no time were there more than thirteen hundred troops in the trenches on the upper hill.[11]

Once in the works, the men received a simple command—load and fire until relieved. "We keep a constant fire," jotted a sergeant in his diary. The soldiers worked their rifles until either the barrels overheated, they expended their ammunition, or they were replaced by other troops. One New Yorker, viewing the intensity of the gunfire, believed that "the woodlands looked like a cyclone of hail had swept over them." Another Northern soldier confessed in a letter to his sister, however, "In the smoke of a battle field all that we see or know is confined to our own regiment."[12]

The men's faces became black from the smoke. Their lips cracked and bled from the saltpeter in the cartridges, whose paper ends they had to bite before pouring the gunpowder and bullet into the barrel. A captain recalled that the troops in his regiment "resembled more the inhabitants of the bottomless pit than quiet peaceful citizens of the United States of America." A spirit animated them. "I know that my feelings was to conquer or die on free soil," avowed a New Yorker to his parents.[13]

One of the regiments that rotated in and out of the works on the upper hill was the 150th New York of Henry Lockwood's brigade. Like their Maryland comrades in the command, the New Yorkers had never been in combat before the afternoon of July 2. Now they were brought forward from the hollow into a cauldron that few of them could have imagined before this morning. They wrote about the experience shortly afterward and remembered it for years.[14]

Known as the "Dutchess County Regiment," the 150th New York entered the works about 6:00 A.M., relieving the 78th and 102nd New York of Greene's brigade. "My men rallied to the front in double-quick time, cheering loudly," reported Colonel John H. Ketcham, "and they fought earnestly and bravely." One member of the regiment believed that only ten or fifteen men stayed in the hollow, while "the remainder went into it about as cool as they would go to dinner." He marveled in a letter to his father about their conduct, noting that they were "raw troops."[15]

"The enemy," Ketcham stated, "kept up a continuous, direct, and terrible firing of musketry during the whole time engaged." Many men fell with wounds, but the works sheltered most of them from death. Charles Howgate of Company A was believed to be the first one killed, when a bullet tore away part of his head. One Confederate minié ball killed seventeen-year-old Johnny Wing and Levi Rust, one of the regiment's oldest soldiers. Wing was standing behind Rust as the bullet passed through the latter. For their part, one of the Dutchess County men claimed, "we did terrible execution."[16]

The breastworks saved the lives of countless Union soldiers, but few, regardless of rank, were spared from either wounds or death if they exposed themselves for a long time. Lieutenant Charles Randall of the 149th New York was struck in the left arm and chest by a bullet. He was acting commander of the regiment, because Colonel Henry A. Barnum had become ill on July 2 from the effects of a wound he had suffered a year before at Malvern Hill. Before daylight on July 3, Randall had given each officer a drink of whiskey from a bottle, telling them that "it was probably the last drink they would take together." Randall would survive the wound only to be killed on July 20, 1864, near Atlanta, Georgia.[17]

The members of Randall's regiment stuck their flag on the works. Confederate gunfire shattered the staff twice, but Color Sergeant William C. Lilly repaired it, splicing together the pieces, and returned it to the works. A Rebel sergeant ran forward at one point in the action to seize the banner. He made it to within two feet of the line before being struck by five bullets and killed. When the fighting ended, the New Yorkers counted eighty-one holes in the flag.[18]

At times, the Federals could not find safety even in the hollow. When the 28th Pennsylvania of Charles Candy's brigade returned from the front line, its men came under fire from a Confederate sharpshooter in a tree. Adjutant Samuel Goodman borrowed a rifle from a sergeant. When the enemy marksman fired again, Goodman triggered a round. The Southerner toppled from the tree, striking the ground with his head wedged in the crevice of a rock. The next day, some of the Pennsylvanians tried to remove his body but could not pull it from the rock.[19]

The volume of musketry defies belief. A soldier in the 111th Pennsylvania of Thomas Kane's brigade described a typical expenditure of ammunition in a letter to his sister. He wrote that he and his comrades fired sixty rounds "as fast as we could," were relieved, and then returned to the works, firing another sixty to eighty rounds. The colonel of the 150th New York estimated that his men discharged an average of 150 rounds. In his report, John W. Geary claimed that his division expended 277,000 cartridges. "The only wonder is," a New Yorker declared, "that there is a live rebel left."[20]

The wonderment of the New Yorker must have been shared by many in the Confederate ranks who were subjected to this relentless and merciless gunfire. A North Carolina officer described the fighting as "desperate." An enlisted man penned in his diary a more graphic depiction of the effects of Union musketry and cannon fire: "Had every lump of ice in a hail-storm been a bullet, the woods in our rear could not have been more effectually peeled & riddled & swept with lead & iron."[21]

An Alabamian put it tersely in a letter: "All day long it was one continuous roar." Some of the Confederates, overcome with exhaustion, dozed off until awakened by bullets that struck the ground, rocks, or trees close to them. One soldier was reported to be killed while asleep. A staff officer of George Steuart, Lieutenant Randolph McKim, and a three-man detail braved the gunfire, carrying blankets full of ammunition from the rear to the works on the lower hill. A bullet grazed McKim's shoulder as he crossed the exposed ground, and he fell asleep briefly when he reached the line.[22]

Private John Futch of the 3rd North Carolina, like his comrades, probably sought as much shelter as he could. His regiment had suffered the most punishment in Steuart's brigade, holding the right of the line near the saddle between the hills. Part of the time, Futch worried about his brother, Charles, who lay dying in the rear from a head wound. Charles would succumb to the injury that afternoon. Several days later, John comforted himself with the loss by writing to his wife that, although Charles "suffered greatly" before he died, "I believe he is happy and no doubt is better off than eny of us."[23]

The Confederates fought as tenaciously as their opponents, despite the Federal's advantages of terrain, breastworks, and the rotation of units into and out of the line. Henry Slocum admitted later, "The task of regaining our line proved to be more difficult than I had anticipated." Probably by seven o'clock or shortly afterward, Slocum had asked George Meade for additional troops. Meade had approved the Twelfth Corps's effort to retake the works and followed developments by reports once the fighting began. When he received Slocum's request, Meade directed Major General John Sedgwick to send some units from the Sixth Corps and alerted Oliver O. Howard to be prepared to shift Eleventh Corps troops from Cemetery Hill to Culp's Hill.[24]

Sedgwick complied with Meade's instructions by ordering two brigades to Culp's Hill. Brigadier General Alexander Shaler's five regiments of New Yorkers and Pennsylvanians marched first from the corps's reserve position along the southern portion of Cemetery Ridge, trailed by Brigadier General Thomas H. Neill's command of Mainers, New Yorkers, and Pennsylvanians. Shaler's nearly eighteen hundred troops reached the Henry Spangler house about 8:45 A.M., followed the farm lane toward the fighting, and then turned north into the ravine behind the Union position. Before long, Shaler was ordered to relieve a regiment on the firing line with one of his units. He selected the 122nd New York. A member of the brigade described the action at that time as "very hottempered."[25]

The officers and men of the 122nd New York formed ranks in the ravine and then crawled on their hands and knees to the rim of the hollow. Ahead of them was the 111th Pennsylvania of Thomas Kane's brigade, manning the traverse trench above the saddle, which had been dug by the 137th New York on July 2. At a signal, the Sixth Corps troops stood, scrambled over the edge of the ravine, and, in the words of Corporal Sanford Truesdell, ran "as fast as our legs could carry us." "O! How the balls whistled," wrote Truesdell, adding that "it seemed impossible" for any of them to reach the works.[26]

The Pennsylvanians raced to the rear, while the New Yorkers opened fire at Steuart's Confederates on the lower hill. "We poured it into them with a vengeance," declared Truesdell, firing "almost as fast as you could count."

The members of the 122nd New York soon discovered that the 149th New York of Greene's brigade held the trenches to their left. Both regiments consisted of men from Onondaga County. When the New Yorkers in both regiments learned that their neighbors from home were beside them, they cheered.[27]

When Neill's Sixth Corps troops arrived, Slocum ordered them to cross Rock Creek, to secure the Union right flank, and to dislodge Confederate skirmishers from the Zephaniah Taney farm. Since the repulse of the 2nd Massachusetts and 27th Indiana, Silas Colgrove's Federals in McAllister's Woods had been dueling with the 2nd Virginia and four companies of the 1st North Carolina beyond the stream. Although the Northerners had the shelter of trees, rocks, and fieldworks, many of them were struck when they exposed themselves. Colgrove's regimental commanders rotated companies in and out of the skirmish lines. When the Rebels shot a litter bearer who was picking up wounded men in the meadow, an angry Colgrove asked for an artillery battery to shell Taney's stone house, where some of the Southerners were located. The left section of Battery M, 1st New York, shifted across Baltimore Pike until it had a clear field of fire. The gunners hurled percussion shells into the house, silencing the sharpshooters.[28]

Neill's fourteen-hundred-man brigade passed behind Colgrove's troops, forded Rock Creek south of McAllister's Woods (most likely beyond a pond used for McAllister's Mill), and then turned north, moving toward Wolf Hill, located several hundred yards east of Culp's Hill. Rebel skirmishers, probably from the 2nd Virginia, engaged the Federals, killing Captain William H. Gilfillan of the 43rd New York. Earlier, Edward Johnson had shifted "Extra Billy" Smith's three Confederate regiments east of the creek to protect his left flank and rear, but evidently they were not involved in the action. Neill's advance stalled, and his men occupied the hill.[29]

In a 10:05 A.M. dispatch, Slocum assured Meade that he did not need additional reinforcements. Minutes later, a Confederate battle line appeared, stretching for more than six hundred yards from the woods of the lower hill into Pardee Field. The troops belonged to George Steuart's brigade and formed one-third of an attack force ordered forward in a final push to take Culp's Hill. On Steuart's right, Junius Daniel's North Carolinians were aligning ranks for an assault against the lower section of the works on the upper hill, while, farther north, James Walker's Stonewall Brigade prepared to advance up the steepest part of the hillside.[30]

Second Corps commander Richard Ewell apparently ordered this attack, forwarding the directive through Edward Johnson to the brigade commanders. According to Lieutenant Randolph McKim of Steuart's staff, both his commander and Daniel "strongly disapproved of making the assault." Daniel stated in his report, "The hill in front of this position was, in my opinion, so strong that it could not have been carried by any force." Furthermore, Steuart's troops had been under fire for nearly six hours, clinging to the works on lower Culp's Hill and in the swale between the two heights.[31]

George Steuart was a career army officer, an 1848 graduate of West Point. A native Marylander, Steuart had resigned from the army after Fort Sumter and offered his services to the Confederacy. Known throughout the Confederate army as "Maryland" Steuart to distinguish him from Virginian Jeb Stuart, he had fought under Stonewall Jackson in the 1862 Shenandoah Valley Campaign, suffering a wound that kept him on leave for nearly a year. He was given command of his brigade upon his return in May 1863. When the Second Corps had crossed the Potomac River on its march into Pennsylvania, Steuart dismounted on the northern bank, knelt down, and kissed the ground of his home state. Onlooking troops of the 1st Maryland Battalion cheered for "My Maryland."[32]

Before he undertook the attack, Steuart sent forward the 10th Virginia as skirmishers to dislodge Ario Pardee's 147th Pennsylvania from the stone wall. The Virginians stepped out and swept the Pennsylvanians across Pardee Field into the woods beyond. They then redeployed to the south, toward Spangler's Spring and the meadow. Behind them, their comrades in the brigade were pivoting their line until it was nearly perpendicular to the works they had held and facing northwest.[33]

Steuart's line consisted of, from left to right, six companies of the 1st North Carolina, 23rd Virginia, 37th Virginia, 1st Maryland Battalion, and 3rd North Carolina. When Major William W. Goldsborough, commanding the Marylanders, received the order to charge, he also protested against it, describing it to a fellow officer as "nothing less than murder." "I moved slowly down the line to my position with feelings I had never before experienced on the battle field," wrote Goldsborough. "I felt that I had but a few minutes to live. I gazed into the faces of men and officers and saw the same feelings depicted there." One of his men confessed to his diary, "We knew at that time we were marching to almost certain death."[34]

The Confederates advanced at the command of "Attention! Forward, double quick! March!" As soon as Steuart's three units on the left cleared the trees and swung into Pardee Field, they met a storm of musketry from the

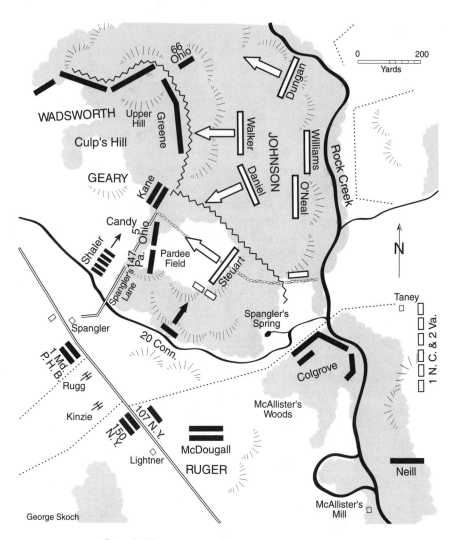

66
Ohio

WADSWORTH
Upper
Hill
Culp's Hill
Greene
GEARY
Kane
Candy
Shaler
Spangler's Lane
147 Pa.
5 Ohio
Pardee
Field
Spangler
20 Conn.
1 Md.
P.H.B.
Rugg
Kinzie
107 N.Y.
150 N.Y.
Lightner
McDougall
RUGER

Dungan
Walker
Daniel
JOHNSON
Williams
O'Neal
Rock Creek
Steuart
Spangler's
Spring

Taney
1 N.C. & 2 Va.

Colgrove
McAllister's
Woods
Neill
McAllister's
Mill

N

0   200
Yards

George Skoch

CULP'S HILL, FINAL CONFEDERATE ASSAULT,
10:00 A.M.–11:00 A.M.

front and from the left. Union batteries on Powers Hill and along Baltimore Pike unleashed charges into the Confederate flank. From above the saddle and along the ridge, Kane's Pennsylvanians, supported by other Federal regiments, and the 147th Pennsylvania raked the Rebels with musketry. Farther south, the 20th Connecticut of Archibald McDougall's brigade engaged the 10th Virginia. The Northerners fired deliberately, with "well-aimed precision." The Rebels came on, wrote a Pennsylvanian, "with the usual yell in closed column in mass." [35]

The 1st North Carolina, 23rd Virginia, and 37th Virginia stopped in the field about seventy paces from the enemy line, unable to go farther against the fury that seared their front and flank. "It was the most fearful fire I ever encountered," affirmed Randolph McKim, "and my heart was sickened with the sight of so many gallant men sacrificed." The line began to waver and then broke. "The greatest confusion ensued," McKim continued, "regiments were reduced to companies and everything mixed up. It came very near being a rout." Another Confederate said simply, "The men were being mowed down." [36]

On the right of the brigade, the 1st Maryland Battalion and 3rd North Carolina encountered the same deadly musketry. "What a fire greeted us," remembered a Marylander. The officers shouted to the men, "Steady"— "Steady." As Goldsborough had predicted, however, "flesh and blood could not withstand that circle of fire." Goldsborough fell with a severe wound, and a captain took command of the battalion. A captain in the 3rd North Carolina asserted later, "That last charge on the third day was a cruel thing for the Third." [37]

Directly in front of the 1st Maryland Battalion, standing on a rise above Kane's Pennsylvanians, were five companies of the 1st Maryland Eastern Shore regiment of Henry Lockwood's brigade. Both of the Maryland units had been recruited from the same section of the state, and the members had relatives and friends in the other unit. Sergeant Robert W. Ross held the flag of the Federal regiment during the action; his cousin, P. M. Moore, was the color sergeant of the Confederate battalion. Moore went down with four wounds and would be captured by former friends. [38]

Colonel James Wallace of the 1st Maryland ES wrote afterward that their fellow Marylanders in Steuart's brigade "were cut to pieces." Randolph McKim, who had his wrist bruised when a bullet struck a brass button on his gauntlets, was near the gray-coated Marylanders' line. A friend of his, Private James Iglehart, had been shot through both thighs and yelled at the staff officer, "McKim, McKim, for God's sake, help me." The lieutenant carried Igle-hart to the shelter of a rock, where he laid his friend down to die. McKim be-lieved afterward that the enemy must have taken pity on him and withheld its fire.[39]

"The end came soon," said McKim. The Marylanders and North Carolini-ans retreated, joining their other comrades in the works on the lower hill. Steuart declared in his report that to continue the assault was "futile," if "not total annihilation." Steuart allegedly had tears on his cheeks when he saw the thinned ranks and exclaimed: "My poor boys! My poor boys!" A soldier in the 37th Virginia stated that his regiment had been "almost wiped out," adding that "the dead lay one on top the other." "Our column," concluded McKim, "had been dashed back like a wave breaking spray against a rock."[40]

One of the wounded Confederate Marylanders left behind lay in view of many of the Federals. He had been mortally wounded in the abdomen and seemed to know his fate. He loaded his rifle "very deliberately," placed the muzzle beneath his chin, and, using the ramrod, pushed the trigger. He died instantly.[41]

When the Confederates later abandoned their positions on Culp's Hill, Kane's Pennsylvanians and the blue-clad Marylanders would walk across the ground where Steuart's men had charged. The Marylanders searched for their wounded friends and acquaintances from the 1st Maryland Battalion and "had them carefully & tenderly cared for." That redoubtable soldier Thomas Kane had a few of his men bury a dog. During the attack, the three-legged animal had run into the Union line before scampering back into the ranks of the Confederates. He stopped by a fallen soldier and was licking his hand until killed. "Regarding him as the only christian being on either side," Kane wrote, "I ordered him to be honorably buried."[42]

On Steuart's right, meanwhile, Daniel's and Walker's brigades had ad-vanced against the trenches on upper Culp's Hill. Daniel's line had the 43rd North Carolina on the left, then the 32nd, 45th, and 53rd North Carolina. The North Carolinians went forward, according to Daniel, "in a most gallant manner." The 43rd North Carolina spearheaded the charge, seizing the southern end of the Union works near the elbow in the line. Although Colonel Thomas S. Kenan suffered a wound, his regiment clung to the trenches under both artillery and rifle fire. When Steuart's troops withdrew, the 43rd North Carolinians had to retreat.[43]

Their comrades in the other three regiments pushed up the slope, reaching points within fifty paces of the Union works. The 45th North Carolina found shelter in a depression, and from there raked the Federals. An officer in the regiment claimed that "we killed more than in all our fighting before and after" during the morning. When the 43rd North Carolina withdrew, Daniel ordered back the other three regiments. "My troops were much exposed," the brigadier stated in his report, and he abandoned the effort.[44]

With the repulse of Daniel's brigade, the struggle for Culp's Hill was ending, or had already ceased, on the hillside's sheerest ground. The Virginians of the Stonewall Brigade had withdrawn after their failed assault at 8:00 A.M. to the base of the hill, where they rested and refilled cartridge boxes. This was where Johnson found them an hour or so later, when he ordered them to make the attack with Daniel's and Steuart's troops. James Walker re-formed the ranks, with the 33rd Virginia on the left, then the 27th, 4th, and 5th Virginia on the right. The veterans moved ahead, following the assault path taken nearly six hours earlier by Dungan's Virginians.[45]

Walker's troops ascended the slope into the same frontal and enfilading gunfire that Dungan's men had encountered. Troops from Greene's and Candy's brigades triggered volleys down the hillside, while the 66th Ohio, still perched beyond the works and aligned perpendicular to them, opened a slicing fire into the right flank and along the front of the Virginians. Colonel J.H.S. Funk of the 5th Virginia called it "a murderous and enfilading fire." His men recoiled from the maelstrom and turned back.[46]

To the 5th Virginia's left, the men in the other three regiments pushed ahead until they could go no farther. On the right center of the line, the 4th Virginia reached a rock ledge and huddled under it. From above, the bullets came in waves, pinning down the Virginians, who could neither advance nor retreat. One of the soldiers raised a white cloth above the ledge. When Corporal John T. McKee saw it, he asked his captain if he could shoot the man. The officer refused, suggesting that McKee hurl rocks at him. The corporal did, and the cloth came down. Other men braved the gunfire and broke for the rear.[47]

As they scrambled down the slope, Major Benjamin W. Leigh, Johnson's chief of staff, mounted and with a drawn sword, tried to stop them. He was a conspicuous target on horseback, and the Federals cut him down. Later, when the Northerners found his body, an officer noticed five bullet holes in it. He described Leigh as having a "fine intellectual appearance, and well dressed." A burial detail carried Leigh up the hill, and at Greene's order to honor a brave man, interred him in a grave with their own dead comrades. Before he was buried, a member of the 29th Ohio removed his shirt studs.[48]

At last, Walker stopped the senseless bloodletting by recalling the regiments. "The fire became so destructive," he explained in his report, "that I suffered the brigade to fall back to a more secure position, as it was a useless sacrifice of life to keep them longer under so galling a fire." The valiant but ill-considered Confederate efforts to take Culp's Hill had ended.[49]

At the rock ledge below the Union works, however, scores of men from the 4th Virginia remained trapped by the "galling" musketry. One of the Virginians raised a white cloth again, and the Federals ceased firing. The Confederates emerged from behind the ledge, walking toward the crest. The 7th Ohio collected seventy-eight officers and men of the 4th Virginia, while other Union defenders gathered up handfuls from other units. A Northern soldier secured the flag of the 4th Virginia. On the lower hill, additional Rebels surrendered. Like the Virginians, "they were in a tight fix," in the words of a Federal corporal, and gave up the fight. John Geary claimed in his report that his division took five hundred prisoners and two more flags from unidentified regiments. "The day was," observed Geary, "a most disastrous one to Ewell's corps."[50]

When the Northerners realized that their opponents had abandoned the struggle and withdrawn, "great cheers on our side" arose, according to a New York sergeant in Greene's brigade. After nearly seven hours of unremitting combat, from 4:30 A.M. to minutes past 11:00 A.M., they had won a decided victory. A soldier in the 147th Pennsylvania had it right when he jotted in his diary, "We made them quit."[51]

◊   ◊   ◊

PRIVATE WILLIAM SAYRE of the 66th Ohio walked into the woods in front of his regiment's position near the crest of Culp's Hill after the Confederates had disappeared through the trees. "The Rebs lay thicker than I ever saw them before," he informed his family in a letter. About one hundred yards from the Ohioans' line, Sayre counted twenty-five enemy dead in a grassy area he estimated to be no more than five yards wide. Corporal Sanford Truesdell of the 122nd New York had fought on the terrible battlefield at Antietam on September 17, 1862, and believed that the dead on Culp's Hill were as thickly piled up as they had been at the earlier battle.[52]

Like Sayre and Truesdell, many other Northerners walked among the Confederate dead, searching for "relicks," retrieving the wounded, or digging graves after the fighting had ceased. Nothing seemed to have been spared, neither man nor nature. An Ohioan described the hillside as "the deadened woods." Limbs of trees, cut off by artillery fire, seemed to lie everywhere. "On some trees there was not a piece of bark left as large as your hand," remembered Corporal James S. Hyde of the 137th New York. "The white spots [from bullets] were also very thick on the rocks."[53]

It was the carnage, however, that both fascinated and appalled them, and which moved them to write in letters and diaries. "Dead rebbs lay almost as thick as leves on the ground and in all shapes mangled in all kinds of sights," an Indiana soldier told his sister. "There is acres of Ground there that is covered with dead rebbs graves." A member of the 107th New York wrote in a letter on July 5: "I never saw a more horrid sight in my life. Rebels lay in piles all over the field dead." A fellow New Yorker exclaimed a day later, "I cannot describe what I saw it was too horrid—truly thought as I passed over the field none but Demons can delight in war."[54]

Major Philo B. Buckingham of Alpheus Williams's staff penned a graphic description of the Southern dead. Some of the slain Confederates, Buckingham wrote, were "sitting up against trees or rocks stark dead with their eyes wide open staring at you as if they were still alive—others with their heads blown off with shell or round shot[,] others shot through the head with musket balls. Some struck by a shell in the breast or abdomen and blown almost to pieces, others with their hands up as if to fend of[f] the bullets we fired upon them, others laying against a stump or stone with a testament in their hand or a likeness of a friend, as if wounded and had lived for some time. O it was an awful sight, Terrible! Terrible!"[55]

By July 4 and 5, the sights were more gruesome. Because of the heat the corpses had turned black and their heads had "swelled up to twice their natural size." Numerous Yankees remarked that most of the enemy dead lay within yards of the Union breastworks. The burial details gathered the awful harvest and interred it in mass graves. One soldier recalled that on one tree someone had nailed a paper with the words "Here lie 45 Rebels." Similar signs, with various numbers, dotted other trees. A member of the 150th New York voiced a sentiment undoubtedly shared by many others, veterans and novices: "I never was on a battlefield before and the Lord preserve me from such a sight again."[56]

A Gettysburg civilian, J. Howard Wert, toured the battlefield soon after the fighting had ended and before the fallen had been buried. He visited most of the scenes of the three-day battle. In the Culp's Hill area, Wert found the slain, both Union and Confederate, in heaps. "It was scarcely possible to walk anywhere without treading on them," he avowed. In front of the Federal breastworks, "the Confederate dead were piled against the works almost as high as the rampart itself." Wert concluded that the corpses at Culp's Hill lay in greater numbers "no where else, on the Gettysburg battle-field, on the same limited area."[57]

The casualty lists testified to the fierceness and length of the combat, the frontal assaults, the valor of the opponents, and the advantages of terrain enjoyed by the Federals. Accurate figures for losses on July 3 are nearly impossible to calculate. In their post-battle tabulations, commanders combined the numbers for all three days at Gettysburg. It would seem, however, that the seven Confederate brigades at Culp's Hill on this day incurred more than three hundred killed or mortally wounded, perhaps fifteen hundred wounded, and at least another six hundred captured or missing, for an estimated total of twenty-four hundred. Casualties thus exceeded 25 percent of the force.[58]

Ironically, the only member of the 2nd Virginia of the Stonewall Brigade killed at Gettysburg was Private John Wesley Culp of Company B. A former resident of Gettysburg, the twenty-four-year-old Culp had moved to Virginia to pursue work as a carriage maker before the war. Having enlisted in the regiment in 1861, Culp returned to Gettysburg with the Confederate army. The evidence conflicts as to whether he was slain on July 2, on the Christian Benner farm, east of Rock Creek, or on July 3, possibly on land owned by his father's first cousin, Henry Culp. Wherever the young man died, his remains lie in an unmarked grave.[59]

Union casualties totaled less than the Confederate losses, since the Yankees fought either behind works or from the shelter of higher ground. The Northerners sustained casualties of nearly two hundred killed or mortally wounded, approximately seven hundred wounded, and about fifty captured or missing, for a total of approximately 950, or a rate of slightly more than 10 percent. Roughly eighteen thousand officers and men—Federal and Confederate—struggled for possession of Culp's Hill on July 3, and of that number, about thirty-four hundred became casualties.[60]

The ferocity and tenacity of the Confederates had amazed their opponents. Some Federals thought the Rebels were madmen to make successive charges against the Union position. A Pennsylvanian was convinced that the Southerners "were certainly made drunk or bribed in some way or they would never have run up so close to our works." Alpheus Williams wrote subsequently, "The wonder is that the rebels persisted in an attempt that the first half hour must have told them it was useless." Williams added, "The advantage of ground and position on Geary's front was all on our side."[61]

Numerous Confederates shared Williams's assessment of the engagement. A North Carolinian asserted, "The enemy occupied an elevated position and fortified it well which saved them from their usual fate." A surgeon in the 37th Virginia informed a cousin, "Our men fought desperately and overcame many almost incredible difficulties, but did not succeed in dislodging the Yanks from their last stronghold." Lieutenant James E. Green of the 53rd North Carolina confided to his diary, "It was almost impossible to rout them from sutch a Position as they held." Like many others, a Virginian believed that "it was the hardest battle we ever had."[62]

Staff officer Randolph McKim recorded his disappointment in his diary: "I went into the last battle feeling that victory *must* be ours—that such an army could not be foiled, and that God would certainly declare Himself on our side." It was not to be—at least not on Culp's Hill, against an able foe on high ground behind breastworks.[63]

Private Ted Barclay of the 4th Virginia knew whom to blame for the defeat and the sacrifice of so many of his comrades. "The whole division suffered proportionately through the folly of our hard fighting Johnson," Barclay groused to his sister in a letter of July 8. "He has none of the qualities of a general but expects to do everything by fighting. Three or four times did he throw our gallant band against powerful breastworks and Yankees without number each time mowing them down."[64]

Had he read the Virginia private's words, "Allegheny" Johnson would have agreed, in part, with the soldier's observation. "The enemy," Johnson stated in his report, "were too securely intrenched and in too great numbers to be dislodged by the force at my command." Why, then, had he persisted in assailing the Union lines after the initial failure? Orders and duty required that he try to seize the hill, and the eight o'clock attack came at his direction. Ewell, however, apparently ordered the final assault two hours later. Whether Johnson protested against it or whether he had voiced concerns earlier to Ewell about the unlikelihood of success remains unknown. He and Ewell demanded too much of good men whose courage and determination could not achieve the impossible. And these good men paid the toll to hell with their lives and blood.[65]

By noon, nearly all of the Confederates had withdrawn to the marshy lowland along Rock Creek. Skirmishers deployed to the front, but the fighting was finished. Ewell stated that Johnson had retired to the stream because of "repeated reports"—which would prove to be unfounded—of the approach of Union infantry against his left flank and rear. In fact, Johnson had been defeated and wisely withdrew. He could do nothing more except sacrifice additional men. Later, the skirmishers at the Taney farm rejoined their units, and Smith's brigade recrossed to the western side of the creek. The Southerners would remain in position until after dark, when they marched to beyond the town and bivouacked.[66]

Behind them on Culp's Hill, the Federals reoccupied the works on the lower hill. A member of the 123rd New York claimed that a number of Confederates were still in the area, and when his regiment arrived, "they were on a wild run through the woods beyond." Other regiments extended the Twelfth Corps's southern flank beyond McAllister's Woods. At 12:20 P.M., Slocum wrote Meade, "I think I have gained a decided advantage," and said he could spare one or two brigades if needed elsewhere. Culp's Hill, and with it the army's right flank, had been secured.[67]

The defenders of Culp's Hill had won a decisive and crucial victory. A Confederate seizure of the height would have rendered untenable the Union position on Cemetery Hill and would have endangered control of Baltimore Pike, the army's main supply line and retreat route. Credit for the successful defense belonged to various commanders—notably, Alpheus Williams, John Geary, George Greene, Thomas Kane, and Charles Candy—to regimental field and company officers, and to the soldiers in the ranks. Slocum declared in his report, "The conduct of the entire command during this campaign was such as entitles it to the gratitude of the country, and justifies me in the indulgence of a deep and heartfelt pride in my connection with it."[68]

Williams and Geary understood that the key to Culp's Hill lay on the upper summit, to which they funneled regiments. The rotation of units from the entrenchments to the hollow allowed them to maintain a constant fire on the Southerners and to give their men time to rest and to secure ammunition. The defense of the ground above the saddle fell primarily to Kane's and Candy's troops. They fought with a stubbornness that secured the flank of the units on the upper hill.

No Union officer, however, deserved more credit for the retention of Culp's Hill than "Old Pop" Greene. His foresight in demanding the construction of fieldworks undoubtedly saved many lives and secured the position. One of his privates put it simply: "We had brest works and they did not."

Slocum cited the brigadier and his New Yorkers in particular: "General Greene handled his command with great skill," and "his men fought with gallantry never surpassed by any troops under my command."[69]

Ultimately, the issue was settled by the men in the fieldworks, along the edge of a ridge, behind the stone wall near Pardee Field, in the meadow beside McAllister's Woods, and with the Union batteries along Baltimore Pike. John Geary asserted that on this morning he had witnessed many deeds "of bravery and that higher grade of true courage—self-denial under trying difficulties and hardships—throughout the entire command." On no other battlefield of the war would the rank and file who wore a star as a corps insignia achieve more than at Culp's Hill.[70]

Alpheus Williams underscored the importance of the Union achievement on Culp's Hill. Had the Confederates seized the height and Baltimore Pike to its rear, Williams observed, "it requires no great stretch of fancy to imagine the direful consequence. It is not too much to say, therefore, that had the 12th Corps failed on the morning of July 3rd there would have been no victory at Gettysburg."[71]

Once quiet had returned to Culp's Hill, Corporal Horatio Dana Chapman of the 20th Connecticut walked with his comrades among the fallen Confederates on the hillside. He came upon one dead Louisianan, who had a letter in his breast pocket. Chapman pulled it out and began to read. It was from the soldier's wife. She hoped the war would end soon and he could come home. Then, as Chapman recorded it in his diary, "she says our little boys gets into my lap and says now Mama I will give you a kiss for Papa. But oh how I wish you could come home and kiss me for yourself." Chapman thought about her words and the husband and father who would never return and concluded, "But such is war and we are getting use to it."[72]

5

"No Fifteen Thousand Men"

🕊🕊
🕊

T HE STRUGGLE FOR CULP'S HILL had barely begun on July 3 when
Robert E. Lee reined up Traveller at the field headquarters of his senior
subordinate officer and commander of the army's First Corps, Lieutenant
General James Longstreet. The two generals had not spoken to each other
since the afternoon of July 2, but Lee had issued orders to Longstreet to
renew the offensive at daylight on this morning in a coordinated assault with
Richard S. Ewell's strike against Culp's Hill. Although the Confederate army
had failed to execute such a timely attack on the previous day, Lee held to the
belief that victory "would have been gained could one determined and united
blow have been delivered by our whole line." [1]

Longstreet and his staff were at work when Lee arrived. Like Lee,
Longstreet was a career army officer, West Pointer, and Mexican War veteran. When the Civil War began, Longstreet resigned from the Regular
Army, commanded a Confederate brigade at First Manassas or Bull Run, and
by the spring of 1862 was one of the army's promising major generals. At the
conclusion of the Seven Days Campaign, Lee had described Longstreet as
"the staff in my right hand," and on the battlefield of Sharpsburg or Antietam,
Lee greeted him with the words, "Here's my old *war-horse*!" An admiring

staff officer described the Georgian's performance at Sharpsburg as "magnificent."[2]

Longstreet was a physically striking man, standing about six feet two inches tall and weighing about two hundred pounds. He worked long hours, never seeming to tire. While on the march to Pennsylvania, after spending an entire day and much of the night with his troops, Longstreet told a staff officer, who had said that the general must be exhausted, "No, I have never felt fatigue in my life." Taciturn, possessed of self-confidence, he surrounded himself with the army's best staff. The British army officer who accompanied the Confederates north, Lieutenant Colonel James Arthur Lyon Fremantle, noted in his diary, "By the soldiers he [Longstreet] is invariably spoken of as 'the best fighter in the whole army.' "[3]

The Englishman had observed closely the relationship between Lee and Longstreet, describing it as "quite touching—they are almost always together." After the war, Longstreet stated, "The relations existing between us were affectionate, confidential, and ever tender, from first to last. There was never a harsh word between us." Their meetings and letters were "almost always of severe thought and study." As the army marched toward Pennsylvania, the two men discussed matters almost daily.[4]

Longstreet had endorsed Lee's decision to undertake a strategic offensive beyond the Potomac River. He understood also that the Confederates, as he put it, had "to impair the *morale* of the Federal army and shake Northern confidence in the Federal leaders." A military victory on Northern soil offered the opportunity for political results. In this, he and Lee agreed.[5]

Longstreet believed, however, that by the spring of 1863 the Confederacy had reached its limits. To him, the manpower disparities between the opponents doomed the South to defeat if the bloodletting was not stanched. "One mistake of the Confederacy was pitting force against force," he argued in a postwar article. "The only hope we had was to outgeneral the Federals. We were all hopeful and the army was in good condition, but the war had advanced far enough for us to see that a mere victory without decided fruits was a luxury we could not afford. . . . The time had come when it was imperative that the skill of generals and the strategy and tactics of war should take the place of muscle against muscle."[6]

In Longstreet's judgment, casualties could only be reduced if the army used the tactical defensive when a battle was joined. A careful, methodical, even conservative officer, Longstreet favored defending ground instead of attacking the enemy. He alleged after the war that Lee had agreed to wage a defensive battle when the army encountered the Federals in Pennsylvania. When queried about this later, Lee responded, "The idea was absurd. He had never made any such promise, and had never thought of doing any such thing." Lee should be taken at his word, for he and Longstreet knew that circumstances on a battlefield dictated decisions. Nonetheless, Longstreet and other officers in the army expected, if not believed, that the army would wage a defensive fight.[7]

Longstreet joined Lee on the battlefield late on the afternoon of July 1. He found the army commander on Seminary Ridge, most likely near the Lutheran Theological Seminary. Longstreet arrived after the fields north and west of the town had been swept clean of Federals. As he recounted it, Lee "was engaged at the moment," so the First Corps commander examined the terrain south of Gettysburg, where their opponents had rallied. He did not like what he saw—it had the appearance of a naturally strong position. "It was entirely different with me [compared with Lee]," Longstreet wrote later. "When the enemy was in sight I was content to wait for the most favorable moment to strike—to estimate the chances, and even decline battle if I thought them against me."[8]

When Lee had finished, Longstreet approached him and said: "We could not call the enemy to position better suited to our plans. All that we have to do is file around his left and secure good ground between him and his capital." Lee did not like the proposal of a broad flank movement—it could not be readily executed without cavalry to screen it and to locate the remaining Union corps. Lee reacted to the idea by jabbing a fist toward the Union line and exclaiming, "If the enemy is there tomorrow, we must attack him." Longstreet rebutted, "If he is there, it will be because he is anxious that we should attack him—a good reason, in my judgment for not doing so."[9]

Longstreet admitted subsequently that he "was not a little surprised" at Lee's "impatience" and decision to attack the enemy. But Lee had witnessed, despite his desire not to fight a general engagement on this day, the rout of two Union corps. The prospect of a victory that could achieve Confederate independence seemed within reach. During his thirteen months in command, Lee had never abandoned a field once a battle had been joined. That night Longstreet told his staff that the Federal position was "very formidable" and that it would require the "whole army" to take the ground, and "then at a great sacrifice."[10]

Early on the morning of July 2, Longstreet rejoined Lee on Seminary Ridge. It was before daylight, and Lee had not settled upon a specific plan for the day except for a determination to attack the enemy. The two men talked, Lee indicating that he wanted to resume the offensive with the First Corps divisions of John Hood and Lafayette McLaws. Longstreet objected to it and reiterated his proposal for a turning movement beyond the Northerners' left flank. Again, Lee rejected the idea.[11]

Lee's response silenced Longstreet, but his opposition to an attack affected his role in the operations. Moxley Sorrel, Longstreet's chief of staff, observed that his commander "failed to conceal some anger. There was apparent apathy in his movements." In time, his performance on this day would generate a heated—and continuing—controversy. Duty required him to comply with the thoroughness and vigor that had marked his leadership on previous battlefields. Once the divisions of Hood and McLaws charged, the officers' and men's bravery and skill nearly secured a victory. As noted earlier, Longstreet said it was "the best three hours' fighting ever done by any troops on any battle-field." When the day's combat had ended, Longstreet remarked to another visitor with the army, "We have not been so successful as we wished." Later that night, he received Lee's orders for another assault the next morning.[12]

While members of his staff slept on blankets in a meadow behind the lines, Longstreet sent a detail of scouts to determine whether the Union position, now anchored on Big Round Top, could be turned. Whether Longstreet interpreted Lee's instructions as granting him the authority to alter the direction of the assault remains unclear. His scheme appears to indicate further his objections to the battle's course and bears the characteristics of a hastily conceived idea to avoid another attack on the Union position, which had cost his two divisions more than four thousand casualties.[13]

Lee's plan had been predicated upon limited knowledge of the tactical situation along Longstreet's front when the fighting had ended and what seems to have been a lack of appreciation of the strength of the ground and the location of Meade's units. Lee seems to have overestimated the advantage of the ground near the Peach Orchard seized by Longstreet's troops. It could, and did, serve as a platform for artillery, but the modest ridge did not command the surrounding terrain. Lee should have, and most likely had, assumed that the Federals would strengthen their position on this section of the field. Nevertheless, as if still blinded, Lee had ordered another assault.[14]

The Confederate commander was unswerving in his determination to deliver a "united blow." "Our only hope was to make our attacks simultaneous," Porter Alexander concluded. Alexander believed, however, that the five-mile length of the Confederate line at Gettysburg rendered such a coordinated strike an "impossibility." Too many factors could intrude and result in failure. Lee had seen this occur on July 2, but he was convinced that the army could succeed in overcoming "the difficulties by which we were surrounded." His unbending commitment to offensive strikes was, in Alexander's judgment, an "example of the forcing game."[15]

Consequently, when Lee halted at Longstreet's headquarters early on July 3, he expected to see final preparations for an attack being completed and George E. Pickett's three brigades of Virginians ready to join in the effort. He saw neither. Longstreet met him with the news that he had issued orders for a movement around the flank of the Union army. More critical to Lee's plans, Pickett's division was nowhere to be seen. The army commander must have been stunned.[16]

Pickett and his troops had been left at Chambersburg on July 1, with orders to guard a wagon train until Brigadier General John Imboden's cavalry brigade arrived. About one o'clock the next morning, Pickett received instructions to march to Gettysburg at once. Within an hour or so, the Virginians were under way. A civilian in town awoke as he heard them marching by his house. "They were quite jubilant in their passage thru town," he wrote in his diary, "pulling my bell at the door and hooting at me."[17]

The division approached Gettysburg that afternoon and halted about three to four miles west of town. Pickett and a few aides rode ahead to the sounds of battle. Major Walter Harrison reported the command's arrival to Lee, who told the staff officer, "Tell General Pickett I shall not want him this evening, to let his men rest, and I will send him word when I want them." Pickett located Longstreet. They were old friends and watched the action together for some time. Before Pickett departed, Longstreet told him to bivouac the men and stay there "until they were wanted."[18]

No one, either from Lee's or Longstreet's headquarters, sent orders to Pickett to have his division on the battlefield by daylight. Responsibility for this oversight or failure of duty rests with Longstreet. Evidently, Lee's instructions for the attack on July 3, which included Pickett's division, were delivered orally to Longstreet. As noted previously, Longstreet had told Alexander that Pickett would be on the field on that morning. Either through a misunderstanding or by mistake, however, he or his staff failed to forward the orders to Pickett.[19]

Pickett's men stirred from their bivouac sites between two and three o'clock on the morning of July 3. They cooked breakfast, had roll call, and then prepared for the march. The column started at daylight, the time Lee had wanted the Virginians on the battlefield. It would be a few hours before they came into view.[20]

The failure to order up Pickett's division by daylight wrecked Lee's plan for simultaneous attacks on both flanks of the Union line. Lee rejected Longstreet's proposal for a flank movement as soon as his subordinate explained it. In one of his postwar accounts, Longstreet wrote that Lee, pointing toward Cemetery Ridge, replied, "The enemy is there, and I am going to strike him." The sound of cannon fire and musketry continued to roll south from Culp's Hill. Although he did not know at the time that the enemy had initiated the fight for the hill, Lee must have concluded that Ewell had obeyed orders. A concerted attack by the Confederates could not be salvaged now by delaying Ewell's assault.[21]

"General Longstreet's dispositions were not completed as early as was expected," Lee offered as an explanation for the breakdown of his plan. He did not mention in his report the failure of Pickett's division to be brought forward in time. The result was that Lee needed to fashion another effort. Determined to "strike" the enemy, Lee proposed to Longstreet that they proceed with the original operation, attacking with Hood's and McLaws's divisions, supported by Pickett's, when the latter's troops reached the field and deployed.[22]

Longstreet raised objections at once. If Hood and McLaws advanced from their positions west of Little and Big Round Top, argued Longstreet, they would expose their right flanks to an enemy counterattack. Both units had suffered serious casualties the day before and were worn out. The Federals, moreover, had had all night to strengthen their lines and to reinforce the position. Longstreet's scheme to move around the Union flank indicates that he had had these concerns the night before when he had received Lee's orders for a daylight attack. Why had he not ridden to army headquarters and expressed his doubts in person to Lee? Instead, he fashioned an alternative plan that he must have suspected Lee would reject. Now, confronted with Lee's determination to assault the enemy, Longstreet once more voiced opposition to an offensive operation.[23]

It would have been better for both of them and for the army, however, had Longstreet objected the previous night. His reasons for not using Hood's and McLaws's units were sound, and, in his defense, he owed it to Lee as the army's senior subordinate officer to express his views. Lee listened and concurred with Longstreet's judgment. In his report, Lee said that Longstreet "now deemed it necessary to defend his flank and rear with the divisions of Hood and McLaws."[24]

This exchange between the two generals occurred either at Longstreet's headquarters or after they had ridden forward, accompanied by their staffs, to the fields north of the Peach Orchard and west of Emmitsburg Road. Lee had wanted a better look at the enemy position, and perhaps it was after he had viewed it that he accepted Longstreet's argument. But when the two generals arrived to inspect their lines, their presence drew rifle fire from Union pickets. The officers dismounted and continued their examination of the Federal line. At some point, A. P. Hill, commander of the Third Corps, and one of his division commanders, Henry Heth, joined the group. Further discussions ensued.[25]

At last, Lee focused his attention on the crest of Cemetery Ridge, south of Cemetery Hill. A grove and a small clump of trees broke the horizon on this section of the ridge. Union infantry and artillery batteries were visible, but it appeared that the enemy had not constructed substantial fieldworks along the ridge. Low stone walls offered protection to some of the Northerners, but the ridge's open ground exposed the Federal gun crews and infantrymen to Confederate artillery fire.[26]

Lee might have witnessed personally or probably had heard about the charge of Brigadier General Ambrose R. Wright's brigade across the fields early on the evening of July 2. Wright's brigade of about fourteen hundred Georgians had swept forward, pushing back two Union regiments and overrunning three abandoned cannon. Two of Wright's three regiments then hit a gap in the Union line and reached the crest of the ridge just south of the copse of trees. But Union reserves repulsed the Georgians, who retreated to Seminary Ridge. Wright believed that he could have held his position had he been supported. "The trouble is not in going there," the brigadier later told Porter Alexander. "The trouble is to stay there after you get there, for the whole Yankee army is there in a bunch."[27]

Wright's Georgians had benefited from the disarray in the Union lines as regiments and brigades had been rushed into the fight against Hood's and McLaws's troops. If the Federals were prepared and waiting with units in place, the difficulty would be not only staying there but "getting there." But the advance of Confederates across the fields between Seminary and Cemetery ridges on July 2 had revealed that the terrain had no hidden features that could wreck formations. Furthermore, the ground undulated with swales or depressions that could provide brief shelter and concealment to an attack force during the advance.[28]

Numerous fences, however, crisscrossed the fields, and a pair of stout post-and-rail fences framed Emmitsburg Road. All of these structures could be obstacles to the troops, particularly the ones along the roadbed. When the Southerners reached the road, they would be within effective musketry range of Union infantry and well within canister range of cannon. The Confederate high command evidently surmised that the fences would not seriously impede or disorganize an assault force.[29]

As Lee viewed the Union line on Cemetery Ridge—"Apparently it never occurred to him that the position could not be taken," a historian has contended—he knew that a successful attack hinged upon two critical factors. First, the infantry commands had to cross the distance between the ridges with minimal losses while maintaining unit cohesiveness. Second, he had to assign enough troops to the assault force and supporting units to ensure that once a breach was made in the Federal position it could be held and exploited. If the infantrymen advanced at "common time," or seventy yards per minute, they would need about twenty minutes to cover the fourteen hundred yards. Throughout much of that time, various enemy batteries could rake their ranks with solid shots and shells. Lee's artillery would have to silence or seriously cripple the Federal batteries on the ridge and on Cemetery Hill. This could only be achieved with a sustained cannonade prior to the attack.[30]

When the guns fell silent, the Confederate infantry would advance. Although this was not explicitly stated, Lee decided upon a bayonet charge or the use of shock tactics. A bayonet charge consisted of a rapid forward movement, with the troops holding their fire until close to the opposing line. Once a breakthrough was attained, the attackers would create a gap by changing fronts and advancing down the enemy lines. Behind them would come the supporting troops, to exploit the gains and to rout their opponents. Those tactics entailed "a higher risk in order to achieve a more decisive result." For the men in the attacking ranks, such tactics demanded discipline and a willingness to withstand punishment before they could respond with their own gunfire. "Thus commanders who asked their men to use shock tactics," argued a historian of Civil War combat, "were asking for an unnatural response to fear. It took exceptional leadership, or exceptionally high-quality soldiers, to make the system work." The tactic was difficult to achieve unless "one's own troops were entirely reliable or the enemy's were markedly inferior."[31]

Lee was a career soldier, one of the finest generals in American history. He certainly weighed the difficulties and knew the risks. In the opinion of Gettysburg historian Edwin B. Coddington, "For basic simplicity and audacity of concept his plan evokes admiration." The preparations would require time; the details could be addressed. When he had decided upon it, Lee turned to Longstreet and outlined the basics of the attack. Longstreet would command the assault force, Lee said, which would consist of Pickett's division and units from Hill's Third Corps. As many batteries as could be brought to bear on the Union position would be assigned to the cannonade.[32]

Longstreet could not believe it. The attack force would, he thought, amount to about fifteen thousand troops. Then, as Longstreet recounted it later, he felt "that it was my duty to express my convictions." He said to Lee: "General, I have been a soldier all my life. I have been with soldiers engaged in fights by couples, by squads, companies, regiments, divisions, and armies, and should know, as well as any one, what soldiers can do. It is my opinion that no fifteen thousand men ever arrayed for battle can take that position." He pointed toward Cemetery Ridge as if to emphasize his words.[33]

Lee listened, but Longstreet could see his impatience. The professional and personal relationship between the two men allowed for such an exchange. "I should not have been so urgent," Longstreet admitted, "had I not foreseen the hopelessness of the proposed assault. I felt that I must say a word against the sacrifice of my men; and then I felt that my record was such that General Lee would or could not misconstrue my motives."[34]

It was left at that, with Lee turning to the matter of which troops from Hill's corps should be assigned to the effort. After some deliberation, which surely included Hill and probably Heth, Lee selected Heth's division of four brigades and two brigades from Major General William Dorsey Pender's division. All of the units had been engaged heavily on July 1, but had been spared from the next day's fighting. As support for the right flank of the main attack force, Lee drew the brigades of Brigadier General Cadmus Wilcox and Colonel David Lang from Major General Richard Anderson's division. Both of the commands had participated in the attack on July 2, but they were close at hand, lying in the fields west of Emmitsburg Road and north of the Peach Orchard.[35]

It appears that Lee selected Hill's units because they had not been engaged on July 2 and they were posted nearby. It also appears that neither Hill nor Heth had accurate figures on the commands' losses. Heth had sustained a wound on July 1, when a piece of a shell struck his head. Before the battle, he had acquired a new hat too large for him and had used wadded newspaper to make it fit. The newspaper lining likely saved his life. Unable to continue in command, Heth had relinquished it to his senior brigadier, J. Johnston Pettigrew. Additionally, Dorsey Pender had been wounded on the second day, disrupting command in his division. Brigadier General James H. Lane had succeeded Pender. Thus, the extent of damage incurred by the brigades seems to have gone unreported.[36]

Although members of Lee's staff insisted after the war that Hood's and McLaws's divisions were assigned roles in the operation, the evidence, including Lee's report, suggests otherwise. McLaws claimed that neither could he see the infantry brigades as they formed for the assault nor "was I informed, officially or otherwise, that an advance of troops was to be made." Porter Alexander, who would direct the artillery of the First Corps, remarked that, if either of the two divisions had been used in the attack, "it would have been simply impossible to hold the firing line, upon which our guns were placed." Both commands could have been withdrawn only under enemy observation. The Federals then would have advanced, in Alexander's view, "a cloud of skirmishers" against his batteries.[37]

Either at this time or later, Lee placed Anderson's three remaining brigades under Longstreet's direct authority. The units—those of Brigadier Generals William Mahone, Carnot Posey, and Ambrose Wright—stretched along Seminary Ridge from near the David McMillan farm to a point almost opposite the copse of trees on Cemetery Ridge. These Virginians, Mississippians, and Georgians would act as supports, prepared to follow the main attack force. Lee's decision left Third Corps commander Hill with only two brigades from Pender's division—Colonel Abner Perrin's South Carolinians and Brigadier General Edward L. Thomas's Georgians—under his immediate command.[38]

Approximately five hundred yards in front of Seminary Ridge, on Long Lane, a narrow roadbed that began at High Street in Gettysburg and ran southwesterly three-fourths of a mile through fields, Major General Robert E. Rodes of Ewell's Second Corps had troops from his division deployed beside the brigades of Perrin and Thomas. Rodes's orders would be the same as they had been on July 2, "to co-operate with the attacking force as soon as any opportunity of doing so with good effect was offered." With Junius Daniel's and Edward O'Neal's brigades engaged on Culp's Hill, Rodes counted eighteen hundred men in line. The division commander remained under Ewell's authority and would have to decide for himself when "any opportunity" offered.[39]

In all, Lee committed seventeen brigades, completely or in part, to the offensive operation. Nine brigades—three from Pickett and six from Heth and Pender—constituted the main strike force, with Wilcox's and Lang's brigades in flank support. The remaining units would act as a reserve and, if ordered forward, would advance as a second wave. Command responsibility for the fourteen infantry brigades rested with Longstreet.[40]

As Coddington noted, the plan combined simplicity and audacity. The historian added, however, "It could work only if an almost infinite number of pieces in its pattern fell into the right places at the right time." In fact, the plan had serious flaws from its conception. The main elements—the cannonade and the bayonet charge—required an execution and coordination that had not been evident in the army on the field. Lee's method of command, granting wide latitude to subordinates, would be tested.[41]

The initial and critical component, a cannonade by massed batteries, fell upon the army's weakest arm. The artillery was directed to cripple or to break Union resistance on Cemetery Ridge, and to follow Confederate infantry during the advance and assault. Lee's artillery, however, was plagued with ordnance inferior to that of the Federals, inadequate and faulty ammunition, and no centralized leadership that would orchestrate cohesive operation of the batteries and battalions.[42]

Each battery assigned to the operation had at least two different cannon in the unit. The Confederates needed more three-inch Ordnance rifles and tenpound Parrotts, guns that had greater range and more accuracy at a distance than the more numerous twelve-pound bronze Napoleons. Their exterior line, however, gave them the advantage of bringing a converging fire upon the targets. It would have to be carefully plotted and coordinated to be effective. In turn, although the Confederate gunners faced an opponent with better and more weapons, their dispersed batteries would hamper the effectiveness of Union counterfire.[43]

The curse of Lee's artillery was the quantity and quality of its ammunition. Many of the batteries had been engaged on either July 1 or 2, or on both days, depleting their artillery chests. Each gun had begun the campaign with an average of two hundred rounds of shell, shrapnel, solid shot, and canister. By the morning of July 3, according to Porter Alexander, "Our reserve wagons, I knew, must be now very nearly empty of all but canister." Alexander observed, "We had no artillery ammunition to waste," which meant that his gunners and those from the other battalions did not possess the ammunition to make the cannonade "a long business."[44]

The shortage of long-range ammunition was exacerbated by its quality. Both the gunpowder and the fuses for the shells were notoriously poor. Nearly all of the Confederate batteries used the Bormann Time Fuse on the shells. A small circular device edged with a ring of soft lead filled with fine powder, the fuse was screwed into the base of a projectile. A gunner cut the circle at a mark according to the range of a target. If it worked as designed, the fuse would detonate the shell over an enemy battery or troops. Alexander estimated, however, that only 20 percent of Bormann fuses functioned properly during the war. Most failed to detonate or seemed to be misaimed, flying over the targets.[45]

Past experience with the premature explosions of shells had shown that Confederate infantry opposed, even threatened to fire upon, their own gunners when the latter discharged cannon over the soldiers' heads. "Our Confederate artillery," stated Alexander, "could only sparingly & in great emergency, be allowed" to follow infantry in close support, as Lee planned. Both arms needed their "own fighting front free" during an attack. Infantry and artillery, concluded Alexander, "do not mix well in a fighting charge."[46]

The final consideration vis-à-vis the artillery concerned leadership. Brigadier General William N. Pendleton served as the army's chief of artillery. A fussy individual who resembled Lee in facial appearance, Pendleton had abandoned the military, after graduation from West Point, for teaching and the ministry. He had risen from a battery commander to a brigadiership and his present post in less than a year. By Gettysburg, however, his inadequacies as artillery chief had become evident. Lee had bypassed his fellow Virginian for tactical control of batteries on a battlefield. But only Pendleton retained the authority over the entire field, to oversee and to coordinate the battalions from the different corps, during the preparations and cannonade. If the batteries were to exploit the advantage of an exterior line, it would have to be done under Pendleton's direction.[47]

The army commander knew of the deficiencies that had hampered the performance of his artillery in previous engagements. Lee would overcome the problems with a bombardment unparalleled in the annals of the army. He hoped that the storm of fire that would rain down upon the enemy on the relatively open ridge would inflict so much havoc upon the Federals as to shield his oncoming infantry from crippling counterfire. For his artillery officers and gun crews, it would be a formidable undertaking.[48]

In the wake of this hurricane of shell and solid shot would come the infantry. Pickett's three brigades of Virginians had not been bloodied during the campaign. Counting slightly more than fifty-eight hundred officers and men in the ranks, they would be rested when they arrived on the battlefield. On their left would be the six brigades from Hill's Third Corps, each of which had suffered serious, if not grievous, casualties on July 1.[49]

Accurate or reasonably precise numbers of officers and men left in the ranks of Hill's half-dozen brigades on the morning of July 3 are difficult, if not impossible, to calculate. Lee's officers did not list casualties for each day of the battle but combined them for the battle. On May 14, 1863, Lee had issued an order to unit commanders not to count slightly wounded men as casualties. Consequently, soldiers who had suffered such wounds on July 1 but were unable to return to duty by July 3 lowered the casualty figures for the battle yet increased the number not present on the final day.[50]

Heth's division, commanded by Pettigrew, seems to have had about five thousand officers and men in the four brigades, and the two units from Pender's division added roughly twenty-five hundred troops. With Pickett's fifty-eight hundred men, Longstreet would have nearly 13,500 veterans for the main assault force. Wilcox's and Lang's brigades, assigned to the role of flank support, counted probably twelve hundred in the ranks. If Anderson's remaining three brigades are included, the total number designated for the assault amounted to about 18,500 officers and men.[51]

Questions remained, however, about the combat-readiness of Hill's troops, particularly the six brigades that would advance with Pickett. The regiments in the commands had lost an inordinate number of field and company officers on July 1. One of Pettigrew's staff officers, Louis G. Young, asserted that on the third day his brigade suffered from "the disadvantage of impaired organization, caused by its heavy losses, especially of officers." Captain George M. Whiting of the 47th North Carolina, in another brigade, said that his unit's efficiency "was doubtless much impaired by the loss of many of our best and bravest officers" on July 1. A North Carolina private stated it bluntly: "We had been very roughly handled on the 1st day and were in bad shape" on the third day.[52]

In the past, Lee had asked much of the army's rank and file. With him, they had ascended the long, terrible slope into a wall of Union cannon at Malvern

Hill; had stood in thinned ranks with their backs to a river on the war's blood-iest day, at Sharpsburg; and had given him a surprising victory in the woods around Chancellorsville. He shared with them a belief in their matchless combat prowess. When he had summoned them forth, they had answered on all fields, despite the odds and the conditions. What he would ask of some of them now exceeded any previous request. Before long, they would learn of the task ahead of them, would look across the fields at the dark figures of the enemy and the unmistakable shapes of cannon on the ridge, and would once again answer the call.

Lee had examined the same ground, noted the batteries and infantrymen on the ridge, conferred with subordinates, and decided upon a plan. He had ordered a different attack to take place at daybreak, but when it had to be scrapped, he fashioned a new one. He had been unbending, however, in his desire to strike the enemy. Did he believe that on this day, on this field, the fate of the Confederacy hung? Did he order another attack because he simply wanted to attack? A recent biographer of Lee has written, "He confronted the moment of truth at Gettysburg and never flinched."[53]

By Lee's side on these early-daylight hours of July 3 stood James Long-street. He had looked at the same fields, the same ridge, the same enemy that Lee had seen and that their men would view. But the corps commander saw a different truth. He had expressed his views forthrightly to Lee; he had tried to be unequivocal in his opposition to Lee's planned assault. In his report, he wrote, "The distance to be passed over under the fire of the enemy's, and in plain view, seemed too great to insure great results." Nevertheless, Lee had assigned command of it to him, and now, as he said, "nothing was left but to proceed."[54]

6

"We Were on the Eve of Something Desperate"

REVEILLE SOUNDED IN THE CAMPS of George E. Pickett's division about three o'clock on the morning of July 3. The Virginians stirred from their camps near Marsh Creek, roughly three miles west of Gettysburg, ate breakfast, and prepared for the march. They had known since the previous night "that our services would be required in the morning." Morale was high. One of them said, "I rarely ever saw troops more inspirited." The outcome of the battle, they believed, "was yet undecided."[1]

At some point during the early morning, Pickett had evidently received orders to bring forward his troops. About daylight or before, the Virginians filed into column on the pike and marched east a short distance, before turning south into a farmer's lane. They followed it for a half-mile and then swung east on another narrow road that paralleled the pike. The column crossed Fairfield Road and Willoughby Run, passing the Emmanuel Pitzer farm before halting in the fields west of Seminary Ridge. Spangler's Woods lay directly in front of the troops. It was probably between seven and eight o'clock.[2]

The Virginians could only speculate about what would be required of them. But they were veterans and understood the signs. They had been issued an extra twenty rounds of ammunition, and while they waited in the fields, officers conducted an inspection of their weapons. The war had been kind to them during the past nine months. They had been spared from the worst of Fredericksburg's combat and had been stationed in southeastern Virginia during the Chancellorsville Campaign. Two of the division's five brigades had been retained by Richmond authorities in Virginia because of concern about the capital's defenses while the army operated in Pennsylvania. Whatever work lay ahead, it would be shouldered by the men in these three brigades.[3]

As they stood in the fields, offering their rifles for inspection and waiting for orders, they shared the bond of the Old Dominion. These Virginians hailed from more than forty counties in the state, from the counties along the Potomac River, through the Tidewater and the Piedmont, to the lowlands along the Atlantic coast. A number of companies had their roots in antebellum militia units, with the lineage of the 1st Virginia dating from George Washington's presidency. Brothers stood beside brothers; cousins shared canteens with cousins. In the 8th Virginia, for instance, two sets of four brothers—the Presgraves and the Berkeleys—served together. Theirs was the only division in the Confederate army at Gettysburg consisting entirely of men from the same state.[4]

At their head rode, in the words of Longstreet's chief of staff, "a singular figure indeed." George Pickett was an unforgettable man at first sight. He wore his hair in long, flowing ringlets to his shoulders, perfumed them and his beard, and "was very foppish in his dress." An aide thought him to be "a very dashing officer," but James Fremantle, the British officer, described him as "rather a desperate-looking character." He was regarded among fellow officers as a "good fellow" who enjoyed liquor. Questions percolated in the army, however, about Pickett's "self-control and self-discipline."[5]

Pickett was thirty-eight years old, a member of Virginia's slaveholding gentry. He had entered West Point in 1842, a classmate of Stonewall Jackson and George B. McClellan, and graduated four years later, ranking last in the class. He served in Mexico, lost his first wife in childbirth, and fathered a son to an Indian woman while stationed in Washington Territory. Like scores of fellow Southerners, he resigned his commission in 1861, accepting a colonelcy in the Confederate army. A brigadiership and brigade command followed. He suffered a wound at Gaines's Mill in June 1862. Upon his return to command, Pickett was promoted to major general in October with command of a First Corps division.[6]

By the summer of 1863, Pickett was passionately in love with LaSalle Corbell, a young woman more than fifteen years his junior. Sallie, as she was called, rekindled his youthful ardor, and he wrote letters to her as often as he could. Unfortunately for history, before publication she either embellished his letters or personally wrote a number of them.[7]

Within the army, Pickett's mentor and perhaps closest friend was James Longstreet. Both of them had served in the 8th United States Infantry in Mexico. When Longstreet fell with a wound in the attack on Chapultepec while carrying the regimental flag, he handed it to Pickett, who bore it over the wall. According to Moxley Sorrel, Longstreet "was exceedingly fond" of Pickett. Sorrel noted that during combat "I could always see how he looked after Pickett, and made us give him things very fully; indeed, sometimes stay with him to make sure he did not get astray." Longstreet had been instrumental in Pickett's appointment to divisional command.[8]

After the Virginians reached the battlefield, Pickett reported to his commander and old friend. Longstreet went with Pickett to the crest of Seminary Ridge, explained Lee's plan to him, and indicated the direction of the advance. Pickett "seemed to appreciate the severity of the contest upon which he was about to enter," wrote Longstreet, "but was quite hopeful of success." Longstreet then instructed his subordinate to "form his line under the best cover he could get from the enemy batteries, and so that the center of the assaulting column would arrive at the salient of the enemy's position." Longstreet added that he should form his line with two brigades in front and the third as support. The friends then separated. Longstreet stated afterward, "My heart was heavy when I left Pickett."[9]

Pickett rejoined his troops and issued the necessary orders. Officers shouted the commands, and the men re-formed ranks. Brigadier General James L. Kemper's brigade had led the morning's march to the field and now stepped off into Spangler's Woods. Kemper had been a prominent attorney and politician before the war, serving as speaker of the House of Delegates. A Mexican War veteran, he was commissioned colonel of the 7th Virginia and led it at First Manassas. A brigadier since June 1862, Kemper was known in the division for his capability as an officer, his personal charm, and his fiery temper. His brigade had originally belonged to Longstreet.[10]

Behind Kemper came the officers and men of Brigadier General Richard B. Garnett's brigade. Colonel Eppa Hunton of the 8th Virginia had been in temporary command of the brigade off and on for two weeks, since Garnett was kicked on the ankle by a horse during the march into Pennsylvania and became unable to mount a horse. On this morning, however, Garnett felt well enough to ride. He relieved Hunton as his regiments formed in line west of Spangler's Woods.[11]

"Old Dick" Garnett, as he was known to fellow officers, could not sit out this day's fight. A West Pointer, he had commanded the renowned Stonewall Brigade from the fall of 1861 until the spring of 1862. At the Battle of Kernstown, on March 23, 1862, with his men nearly out of ammunition and being pressed by superior numbers, Garnett had ordered a withdrawal without direct instructions from his commander, Stonewall Jackson. Garnett's action, however, unraveled the Confederate line, resulting in a defeat for Jackson's troops.[12]

Jackson had regarded Garnett as a lax disciplinarian—an unforgivable failing in an officer, by Jackson's stern standards. He disliked the brigadier personally, believing apparently that Garnett owed his appointment to command of Jackson's former brigade to his aristocratic family's influence. A week after Kernstown, Jackson relieved Garnett and ordered his arrest. Lieutenant Sandie Pendleton, Jackson's acting chief of staff, delivered the order to Garnett. "I am exceedingly sorry for it," Pendleton informed his mother, "and was utterly amazed by it." Garnett had not "behaved in any but the most gallant manner," the staff officer explained, "but he was guilty of a breach of orders and partly to his mismanagement it is owing that we did not gain a victory." Officers in the Stonewall Brigade protested against Jackson's action, and for weeks the men in the ranks greeted Jackson with silence when he passed by them.[13]

Garnett traveled to Richmond, where he asked for a court of inquiry into the matter. The War Department suspended his arrest, and on August 6, the court convened. Only Jackson and Pendleton had testified when Jackson ordered an advance of his troops against a Union force, suspending the inquiry. The court never reconvened. In October, with Pickett's promotion to divisional command, Garnett was assigned to that officer's former brigade. A staff officer who knew Garnett wrote that the brigadier "felt keenly the aspersions Genl Jackson cast upon him," and he was "determined to show how unfounded they were by his conduct in the field."[14]

Jackson was among the very few who disliked Garnett. "No one was more universally beloved," claimed a staff officer. Major Walter Harrison described him as kind, courteous, warmhearted, and magnanimous. Pickett called him "a fine fellow, a brave splendid soldier." On July 3, as he resumed command of his brigade, the men noticed that he wore a new uniform. If his personal redemption were at hand, he would be dressed as a warrior.[15]

The division's third brigade belonged to another member of a family of proud military and Virginia heritage, Brigadier General Lewis A. Armistead. His father, Walter Keith Armistead, had been a brevet brigadier general in the Regular Army, and his uncle, Major George Armistead, had commanded Fort McHenry during the British attack on the installation in 1814. Major Armistead had commissioned a garrison flag to be made of exceptional size to be flown over the fort. It was his colors that moved Francis Scott Key to write "The Star-Spangled Banner."[16]

Lewis Armistead continued the family's tradition, entering West Point in 1834. On January 16, 1836, in an altercation in the mess hall, Armistead cracked a plate over the head of Cadet Jubal Early, now one of the Confederate army's division commanders. Dismissed from the academy, Armistead re-entered the army as a second lieutenant in 1839 and fought in Mexico, earning two brevet ranks for gallantry. After the war, he served at various posts on the frontier, losing his wife to cholera in 1855.[17]

In May 1861, Armistead resigned his commission to join the Confederacy while stationed at Camp Fitzgerald, near Los Angeles. His dearest friend in the army was Winfield Scott Hancock, whose Second Corps troops held the Union line on Cemetery Ridge, at the clump of trees. Before Armistead and other Southerners departed for the East, Hancock's wife, Almira, held a farewell party. It was an evening of music and difficult separations. At its end, Armistead, with tears on his face, went to Hancock and said, "Good-by; you can never know what this has cost me." He then handed to Almira a satchel with some personal souvenirs and asked her to send them to his family if he should die during the war. One of the items, a small prayer book, was for her. On its flyleaf, Armistead had written his name and the words, "Trust in God and fear nothing."[18]

Armistead reached Richmond in September. He briefly commanded companies of Texas volunteers before being appointed colonel of the 57th Virginia. Promoted to brigadier general on April 1, 1862, he led his command at Seven Pines and during the Seven Days Campaign. His officers and men soon learned that he possessed the stiff hide of an old Regular Army man and demanded discipline in camp, on a march, and in battle. "Obedience to duty he regarded as the first qualification of a soldier," wrote a subordinate. On this morning at Gettysburg, few brigadiers in the army were better prepared, from personal character and military experience, to lead men across the fields than Armistead. As his men formed ranks, he probably did not know that an old friend, Winfield Hancock, walked with his men on the distant ridge.[19]

Kemper's veterans cleared Spangler's Woods first and turned southeast. Nearby, burial details worked at their grisly duty. "In many instances," wrote Captain John Dooley of the 1st Virginia, "they have only the ghastly and mangled remnants of their gallant friends to deposit in these hastily dug pits. I pass very close to a headless body; the boy's head being torn off by a shell is lying around in bloody fragments on the ground." The Virginians moved behind the crest of a rise or low ridge that angled from the northwest to the southeast, from opposite the northeast corner of the woods to beyond the Henry Spangler farmhouse and outbuildings. The swale at the foot of the ridge would offer the troops some shelter from Union cannon on Cemetery Ridge. When Kemper's men had passed beyond the Spangler farmstead, the brigadier deployed them into a battle line. Skirmishers were posted fifty yards to the front, and the troops were directed to lie down.[20]

Garnett's regiments followed Kemper's and extended the divisional front northwest from the Spangler place. Like Kemper, Garnett instructed his men to lie down. Behind Garnett, Armistead halted near the eastern edge of Spangler's Woods. When his regiments shifted into a line, the two left units remained among the trees, while the other three deployed in the fields. Part of Armistead's line overlapped Garnett's, which lay about one hundred yards in its front. Armistead's troops also lay down. To the division's rear, surgeons began to establish field hospitals.[21]

"As the day progressed," recalled Lieutenant John H. Lewis of the 9th Virginia, "it became a certainty that we were on the eve of something desperate, and finally each regiment was informed what it had to do and what was expected of it." A sergeant in Lewis's regiment wrote in his diary after they had received the instructions that they were "to Charge that Hill and take those cannon." Lieutenant Colonel Rawley W. Martin of the 53rd Virginia remarked that the men's morale "could not have been better," though he noted he heard "none of the usual jokes, common on eve of battle."[22]

Many of the officers and men walked to the crest of the rise to view the enemy position. Walter Harrison described it as "frightful to look at." A surgeon compared it to "Gibraltar," and a chaplain told some soldiers upon his return "that it would require a very bloody battle to win the day." Private Samuel F. Pawlett of the 18th Virginia wanted to see it for himself. "My heart almost failed me," he remembered as he looked across the fields to Cemetery Ridge. He turned to a comrade and declared: "This is going to be a heller! Prepare for the worst!"[23]

Rawley Martin believed that each man "felt the gravity of the situation" and "realized that he had the most stupendous work of his life before him." Eppa Hunton wrote: "All appreciated the danger and felt it was probably the last charge for most of them. All seemed willing to die to achieve a victory there, which it was believed would be the crowning victory and the end of the war." A staff officer, James Crocker, recalled that "the sense of the importance of the issue, and the responsibility of fully doing duty equal to the grand occasion, impressed on us a deep solemnity and a seriousness of thought." They "fully intended to take" the enemy's position.[24]

⚬   ⚬   ⚬

BRIGADIER GENERAL J. JOHNSTON PETTIGREW received instructions to report to James Longstreet about midmorning on July 3. Pettigrew had been in command of Henry Heth's division since the afternoon of July 1, when Heth suffered his head wound. A native North Carolinian, Pettigrew was renowned in the army for his intellect and personal charm. While attending the University of North Carolina, he had earned the highest grades of any student in the school's history. During the 1850s, Pettigrew had enjoyed an eclectic career and interests as an astronomer, lawyer, author, state legislator, and militia officer. He had traveled widely in Europe, learning a number of languages.[25]

A slender, darkly handsome man, with black eyes and a mustache, Pettigrew had been a brigadier general since the spring of 1862. At the Battle of Seven Pines he was dangerously wounded and left for dead on the field. Captured by the Federals and later exchanged, he returned to duty that autumn. In the army's reorganization in May 1863, his brigade and another one were transferred from North Carolina to Virginia, and assigned to the newly created Third Corps. Pettigrew had a reputation for icy composure in combat. His troops, said a staff officer, "were devoted to him and felt the most implicit confidence in him."[26]

When Pettigrew reported to Longstreet, the latter officer outlined Lee's plan. Once the cannonade had ceased, Longstreet said, Pettigrew's division would advance to the attack, "keeping dressed to the right, and moving in line with Major-General Pickett's division." Captain Louis G. Young of Pettigrew's staff claimed later that Longstreet assigned Pettigrew's troops initially as support for Pickett, but the order was "countermanded almost as soon as given." Instead, Young wrote, they would move forward on the "same line with Pickett." There might have been some brief misunderstanding, but Lee had designated the Third Corps units as part of the main assault force.[27]

Pettigrew's troops had been held in reserve in the fields west of Seminary Ridge, south of Fairfield Road, on July 2, after the battering they had taken the previous day. They had bivouacked there for the night, and were enjoying a restful morning when Pettigrew rejoined them after his conference with Longstreet. He probably summoned his brigade commanders, explained the situation, and issued the requisite orders for the troops to move forward to the crest of Seminary Ridge. According to one of his subordinates, Pettigrew said in part, "They [the enemy] will of course return the fire with all the guns they have; we must shelter the men as best we can, and make them lie down."[28]

The four brigades began the movement forward about ten o'clock. A Union signal station on a mountain south of Emmitsburg, Maryland, detected the advance and relayed the information to George Meade's headquarters. Pettigrew brought the division into line behind the crest of Seminary Ridge, with the brigades aligned along a single front. From this position, they were about two hundred yards to the rear and to the left of Pickett's front ranks.[29]

Colonel Birkett D. Fry's brigade of Alabamians and Tennesseans manned the division's right. The unit's commander, Brigadier General James J. Archer, had been captured on July 1, and Fry had succeeded. A native Virginian, Fry had attended the Virginia Military Institute and West Point but had not graduated from either school. He had fought in Mexico and was described as "a man with a gunpowder reputation." When he had fallen seriously wounded with his left arm shattered by a bullet at the head of the 13th Alabama at Sharpsburg, he refused an amputation. A surgeon told him that if the arm were not removed his odds of surviving the wound were one in three hundred. "Then I'll take it," replied Fry, who kept his limb and survived.[30]

To the left of Fry's troops were the North Carolinians of Pettigrew's brigade, now under Colonel James K. Marshall of the 52nd North Carolina. A grandson of Supreme Court Chief Justice John Marshall, the colonel was an 1860 graduate of the Virginia Military Institute. He had been teaching and studying law in North Carolina when the war began. In the reorganization of Confederate forces in the spring of 1862, the rank and file of his regiment elected him colonel. A staff officer called him a "man of brilliant promise." Like Fry, however, Marshall had not led a brigade in combat before this day.[31]

The next brigade in line—North Carolinians and Mississippians—belonged to the nephew of President Jefferson Davis, Brigadier General Joseph R. Davis. An attorney and state senator before the war, Davis had held a colonelcy in a Mississippi regiment before joining his uncle's staff in Richmond. When President Davis recommended his kinsman for a brigadiership, the Confederate Senate rejected the commission, accusing the chief executive of nepotism. Davis prevailed, however, with the promise of patronage to the recalcitrant senators. The new brigadier received his command in January 1863. An acquaintance described Davis as "a very pleasant and unpretending gentleman." His lackluster performance on July 1 demonstrated his inexperience and lack of military training.[32]

The division's smallest brigade, three regiments and a battalion of Virginians, held the left flank of the line. Its commander, Colonel John M. Brockenbrough, was a VMI graduate who had been in command of the unit for ten months. At best, his leadership could be described as mediocre. Soon after the Virginians went into line on Seminary Ridge, Brockenbrough assigned Colonel Robert M. Mayo to command of the brigade's two left-front regiments—Mayo's own 47th Virginia and the 55th Virginia. Brockenbrough retained direct authority over the 40th Virginia and the 22nd Virginia Battalion. Why Brockenbrough decided upon this arrangement was never explained.[33]

After the brigades reached their positions behind the crest of the ridge, the troops lay down. Some of them sought shelter behind trees and stumps; others dug holes on the western slope. "We were assessed to the scope of our situation," wrote a North Carolinian. Like their comrades with Pickett, Pettigrew's officers and men viewed the ground between Seminary and Cemetery ridges. Although a narrow strip of woods screened their front, most of the men lay in open fields under a midday sun. Lieutenant W. B. Taylor of the 11th North Carolina informed his mother that "the men were fainting all along" the line from the heat.[34]

Pettigrew could ill afford further losses before the assault. The thinned ranks revealed the casualties the command had sustained on July 1. Most critical was the loss of field officers in the regiments. Captains now led regiments; lieutenants commanded companies. Longstreet admitted long after the war that it was "a grievous error" to have included Pettigrew's troops in the main assault force.[35]

In the planning for the attack, however, Lee and Longstreet had decided to augment Pettigrew's portion of the line by adding two brigades from William D. Pender's division as support. Consequently, during the late morning,

Brigadier General James H. Lane, who had succeeded Pender when the latter was wounded on July 2, was ordered by Hill to report with two brigades to Longstreet. Lane complied, meeting with the First Corps commander. Longstreet told the brigadier to place the two brigades behind Pettigrew's troops and to follow as support during the advance.[36]

Hill had directed Lane to take the two brigades from the division's second line, his own and Brigadier General Alfred M. Scales's. Scales had been wounded in the fighting on July 1, and his regiments had suffered serious losses, including fifty-five officers killed or wounded. A private claimed that the regiments "were in bad shape." Colonel William L. J. Lowrance of the 34th North Carolina now commanded the brigade. A colonel for less than five months, Lowrance had never before led a brigade in combat.[37]

The two brigades, ten regiments of North Carolinians, filed into position about 150 yards behind Pettigrew's ranks at noon or shortly afterward. In his report, Lane wrote that Longstreet had ordered him to form in the right rear of Pettigrew's line. Lowrance led the march and deployed behind Fry, while Lane brought his men into line behind Marshall. "Heth's [Pettigrew's] division was much larger than Lowrance's brigade and my own, which were its only support," Lane noted, "and there was consequently no second line in rear of its left."[38]

Lane had been a brigade commander since the autumn of 1862. When the brigade's previous commander fell at Sharpsburg, the officers and men petitioned for Lane's appointment. They called him "Little Jim," and he had led them capably at Fredericksburg and Chancellorsville. On this day, however, Lee decided he needed an officer with more experience to lead the units. As Lane finished the deployment of the North Carolinians, Major General Isaac R. Trimble rode up with orders from Lee to supersede Lane in command of the two brigades.[39]

This was the kind of assignment Trimble coveted. At sixty-one years of age, he was one of the oldest generals on the field, but few younger men were more combative than this native Virginian. A graduate of West Point, Trimble had left the army in 1832, and prospered as a railroad engineer and superintendent. When the war began, he embraced the struggle, securing a brigadiership in August 1861. During the 1862 Shenandoah Valley Campaign, Trimble's aggressiveness and temperament on a battlefield impressed Stonewall Jackson, who recommended him for promotion. Trimble once proclaimed to Jackson, "Before this war is over, I intend to be a major general or a corpse."[40]

On August 28, 1862, Trimble suffered a serious leg wound at Brawner's Farm. While convalescing, he was promoted and assigned to command of a division in Jackson's corps. When he had a relapse in his recovery, Edward Johnson received the division, and Richmond relegated Trimble to the Shenandoah Valley.[41]

Here Trimble was serving when Lee's army passed through en route to Pennsylvania. Refusing to miss active operations, Trimble attached himself to the army as a voluntary aide to his old comrade Richard S. Ewell. He arrived at Gettysburg with Ewell on the afternoon of July 1 and, according to his post-war account, urged the corps commander to seize Culp's Hill. When Ewell refused, Trimble threw down his sword and stomped away, swearing that he would never serve under Ewell again. It was this warrior of fiery disposition whom Lee selected to lead Lane's and Lowrance's brigades.[42]

After Trimble replaced Lane, the major general briefly addressed the rank and file. Blessed with a voice that could resound across a battlefield, Trimble introduced himself to the North Carolinians. He told them that he wanted none of them to fire his weapon until the enemy line had been broken on the ridge. Then, he promised them, he would be with them to the "farthest point."[43]

Whether the North Carolinians cheered the old fighter's words, Trimble did not recount. Like many of Pettigrew's men, they were sweltering under the "intense" heat in the open fields. They also had been informed by their officers of the work ahead of them. "It was understood all during the day," wrote a private, "that every man on that part of the line was to be sent against that ridge and *carry it.*" Until the order came to advance, however, they could only wait and endure the punishment from the sun.[44]

The final component of troops assigned to Longstreet's direction, the five brigades of Major General Richard Anderson's division, had been in position throughout most of the morning. The commands of Brigadier Generals William Mahone, Carnot Posey, and Ambrose Wright lay where they had bivouacked during the night, on Seminary Ridge, south of Pettigrew's line and behind Pickett's ranks. Anderson's other two brigades, of Brigadier General Cadmus Wilcox and Colonel David Lang, had spent the night in the fields near the Henry Spangler farm. When Lee and Longstreet discussed the details of the plan, Lee placed Anderson's five brigades under Longstreet's direct authority.[45]

Anderson's orders were "to hold his division ready to take advantage of any success which might be gained by the assaulting column or to support it, if necessary." In compliance, he moved Wilcox and Lang forward "to eligible positions" from which they could render immediate support to Pickett's right flank. Before Pickett's men deployed behind the rise, Wilcox and Lane advanced about two hundred yards closer to Emmitsburg Road, in front of the Confederate artillery batteries. Lang's Floridians were on the left, posted in a depression north of the Spangler farm lane. Wilcox's Alabamians extended the line south from the lane. Lang directed his men to dig a ditch for protection from Federal artillery fire.[46]

Before long, an aide from Anderson delivered an order to Lang. As Lang remembered it, Anderson stated that once the cannonade had begun it "would be so hazardous to communicate with me, that he would send no further orders to me, direct," but would communicate with Wilcox. Lang "was to observe closely what Wilcox did, and conform my movements to his."[47]

Anderson's instructions troubled Lang, and he went to speak with Wilcox. Lang asked the brigadier what he should do if ordered to advance once the main attack had been repulsed, "as we both felt confident it would be." Wilcox replied, as Lang recalled, "in substance, that he would not again lead his men into such a deathtrap" as he had done on July 2. Lang pressed the matter, inquiring what Wilcox would do if the orders were "imperative," without discretion. He would protest it, responded Wilcox. With that, Lang returned to his command. The fate of his men would be in the hands of Wilcox.[48]

Back on Seminary Ridge, meanwhile, Pettigrew had sent Birkett Fry, whose brigade held the right of the division's line, to discuss with Pickett "the *dress* in the advance" of the two commands. Fry found Pickett in "excellent spirits," and the two Mexican War veterans reminisced briefly about their service in the conflict. Richard Garnett joined them. Together, they agreed that Fry's regiments would be the brigade of direction. Garnett's troops would dress on Fry's line or adjust their attack route to that of the Tennesseans and Alabamians.[49]

During the return to his brigade, Fry perhaps recalled a conversation he had had with Hill on the afternoon of July 2. Both of them were standing on Seminary Ridge, viewing the Federal position on Cemetery Ridge. When Hill asked Fry what he thought of it, Fry answered that it appeared to be "an exceedingly strong one." Fry then sought Hill's opinion. The corps commander shut his eyeglass "emphatically" and said that it was "entirely too strong to attack in front."[50]

        ❧   ❧   ❧

WHILE THE INFANTRYMEN of George Pickett, Johnston Pettigrew, and Isaac Trimble filed into their assigned positions, their artillery comrades labored throughout the morning in preparation for a cannonade unprecedented in the army's experience. Robert E. Lee had predicated his assault plan on the belief that a bombardment of massed batteries upon Union cannon on Cemetery Ridge would "silence those of the enemy." Lee would use guns from each of the three corps with orders "to open simultaneously." It would be a difficult undertaking, requiring a clear understanding of orders, supervision, and coordination.[51]

A number of Confederate artillery crews had been active before daylight on the southern portion of the battlefield, in the fields along Emmitsburg Road north of the Peach Orchard. Under the direction of Porter Alexander, the batteries either had redeployed or moved forward from the rear into line. Alexander was readying his cannon for an anticipated attack at daylight. As the eastern sky brightened, Alexander discovered that he had pushed some of his guns too far forward, vulnerable to enfilade fire from Union batteries. "It scared me awfully," he wrote; he withdrew them to safer positions.[52]

Alexander had finished the work by daylight. William N. Pendleton, the army's chief of artillery, soon joined him. The two officers rode along the line of cannon, with Pendleton approving the colonel's dispositions. Pendleton mentioned that Colonel R. Lindsay Walker, commander of the Third Corps artillery, had available nine twelve-pound howitzers, which he could not use because of their limited range. Would Alexander want them? asked Pendleton. "I jumped at the idea," stated Alexander. He could advance them as support for the infantry, whom he expected to attack the Federals at any time.[53]

In his postwar accounts, Alexander wrote that he personally led Major Charles Richardson, who commanded the nine guns from Lieutenant Colonel John H. Garnett's battalion, and the howitzers to a hollow behind some woods. The difficulty with Alexander's versions of events is that Richardson had nine rifled pieces, not howitzers, a fact that Alexander should have readily seen. Perhaps Alexander was confused when he penned his memoirs years later or he might not have seen the long-range guns, believing that they were howitzers. If not, he misused them during the cannonade.[54]

Upon Alexander's return to his batteries, Lee joined him. The commanding general informed the artillerist of a change in plans. Lee did not provide many specifics, except to tell Alexander that his artillery would participate in a cannonade. Later, however, Lee, Longstreet, and their staffs returned. In the discussions, Alexander received "more exact ideas of where Pickett was to direct his march." Someone pointed to "a clump of trees" as the target. Lee left the details of Alexander's role to Longstreet and Pendleton.[55]

Alexander wrote after the war, "Longstreet was as good & kind & considerate to me as if he were my father." Longstreet had recognized Alexander's talent for a long time. When Longstreet had an opening for an artillery battalion commander in the fall of 1862, he asked for Alexander, who had been serving as the army's chief of ordnance. Although his decision on July 2 to give the twenty-eight-year-old Georgian tactical control of the corps's batteries rankled his artillery chief, Colonel James B. Walton, it indicated Longstreet's trust in Alexander's judgment and skill.[56]

The instructions Alexander received from Longstreet were "quite specific." "Moreover," he wrote later, "they were identical with the usual practice, both of our army and the Federals, in attacking each other in position, from the beginning of the war to the end of it." As he explained, he was directed "to give the enemy the most effective cannonade possible. It was not meant simply to make a noise, but to try & cripple him—to tear him limbless, as it were, if possible." Once the infantry advanced, Alexander was to follow with his guns and give fire support.[57]

Alexander wrote extensively about Gettysburg after the war. No member of the army proved to be a finer and fairer chronicler of its operations than he. Trained as an engineer, he thought analytically, examining the campaigns with precision and incisiveness. In particular, he analyzed the army's conduct on July 3. He cited the quality and quantity of the artillery ammunition, stating that once he learned of the cannonade he knew that "I had not the ammunition to make it a long business. It must be done inside of an hour if ever."[58]

Nothing, however, troubled Alexander more than the target for the assault. "God knows who selected the spot at which Pickett was to direct his charge," he confided to a former staff officer in a letter. "While it was perhaps as good as any on our front it was an awful spot." In his published writings, Alexander described it as "almost as badly chosen as it was possible to be." He asserted elsewhere, "The point selected and the method of the attack would certainly have been chosen for us by the enemy had they had the choice."[59]

In Alexander's judgment, the obvious target had lain in front of the Confederates for two days—Cemetery Hill. The bend in the Union line was a salient that could be enfiladed by Confederate artillery. "That was the one solitary advantage of our bad position," he declared. Any military engineer, he wrote, would have selected Cemetery Hill as *"the only hopeful point of attack upon the enemy's entire line."* Batteries from Hill's and Ewell's corps *"should have been put to that work from [as] close up as possible."* He admitted, however, "that advantage was *entirely ignored.*" Blame for that failure he assigned to Lee, Pendleton, and the lack of trained staff officers.[60]

Alexander concluded that once Lee had chosen Cemetery Ridge the "peculiarities of the topography . . . here left no reasonable method of making our attack at the point selected but the one adopted." On this morning, remembered Alexander, "the fact is that like all the rest of the army I believed that it would come out right, because Gen Lee had planned it."[61]

When Alexander received his instructions, he went to work. He thought that it was about eight o'clock or shortly before—Pickett's troops were halting in the fields west of Spangler's Woods—when he began to reposition batteries and issue orders. Each of the three Confederate infantry corps had five artillery battalions attached to it—one assigned to each of the three divisions, and two placed in a corps reserve. Alexander's First Corps artillery consisted of eighty-four cannon in twenty-two batteries. In the three infantry corps, the figures were 248 cannon in sixty-two batteries.[62]

The change in plans and new target necessitated a shift in the alignment that Alexander had fashioned before daylight. Alexander's line of cannon began in the Peach Orchard, south of Wheatfield Road, and extended across Emmitsburg Road into the fields east of the Henry Spangler farmhouse. Major Mathis Henry's battalion of four batteries anchored the right of the artillery line. Two of the batteries—Captain Alexander C. Latham's Branch Artillery and Captain Hugh R. Garden's Palmetto Light Artillery, totaling nine cannon—were shifted into the Peach Orchard south of Wheatfield Road and placed to oppose Union cannon on Little Round Top. Another of Henry's batteries, Captain William Bachman's German Light Artillery, with four pieces, remained farther south along Emmitsburg Road, to join in the fire on Little Round Top. Captain James Reilly's Rowan Artillery was positioned beyond Bachman to provide support for the army's infantry on the right flank.[63]

Six cannon from three batteries of Colonel Henry C. Cabell's battalion, under Captain Basil C. Manly of the 1st North Carolina Artillery, extended Alexander's line north from Wheatfield Road. Manly unlimbered the guns near the John and Mary Wentz house in the northern portion of Joseph Sherfy's Peach Orchard. Manly had four three-inch Ordnance rifles and two ten-pound Parrotts.[64]

Beside Manly's gun crews, running north along Emmitsburg Road, were four batteries from Alexander's own battalion, under the command of his good friend and fellow West Pointer Major Frank Huger. The row of sixteen cannon followed the roadbed from the Sherfy farm buildings to the David Klingle house. Huger's line consisted of, from south to north, Captain Tyler C. Jordan's Bedford Artillery, Captain George V. Moody's Madison Light Artillery, Captain William W. Parker's Richmond Battery, and Captain Osmond B. Taylor's Bath Battery. Huger had a mix of cannon—seven three-inch Ordnance rifles, four twenty-four-pound howitzers, four twelve-pound Napoleons, and one ten-pound Parrott.[65]

Before daylight, Alexander had brought forward Major Benjamin Eshleman's Washington Artillery battalion. One of its members recalled that as they passed the Sherfy farmstead they could hear the cries of the wounded inside the barn. The battalion's four companies, as they were designated, went into position west of Emmitsburg Road. The 1st and 3rd Companies, under Captain Merritt B. Miller, unlimbered on a rise near the intersection of the road and Spangler's farm lane. After sunrise, Captain Joseph Norcom's Fourth Company and Captain John B. Richardson's Second Company refused or bent the line to the left and rear, en echelon upon Miller's guns. At either Alexander's or Cabell's direction, five cannon from the latter's battalion deployed between Norcom and Richardson.[66]

Before the companies shifted their line, Richardson saw an abandoned Union three-inch Ordnance rifle, with its team of horses dead, outside of the Federal skirmish line. Privates William Forest and Jim Brown, two drivers, volunteered to retrieve it. Riding a pair of horses, the privates unhitched the dead team, attached the cannon to their animals, and hurried back under fire from the Yankees. The limber held fifty rounds of ammunition, and Richardson placed the captured piece in line. Eshleman and Cabell now had fourteen cannon readied, with two twelve-pound howitzers in reserve.[67]

Between nine and ten o'clock, Major James Dearing's battalion rumbled across the fields and swung into line on the left of the Washington Artillery. The battalion was attached to George Pickett's division and had accompanied the infantrymen from Chambersburg on July 2. Dearing had ridden ahead of his gun crews and assisted Alexander during the fighting on July 2. Dearing, whom Alexander described as "a fine, handsome fellow," had resigned from West Point in April 1861, when his native Virginia seceded. At twenty-three years old, this dark-complexioned man was an excellent officer. When he re-

ceived orders to report to Alexander on this morning, he led his four batteries
from their bivouac site on the Samuel Pitzer farm. They came into position as
if on review.[68]

Federal artillerists watched this display of precision and greeted it with
some fire. As one of Dearing's gun crews wheeled into line, an artillery round
struck the buttock of a lead horse. "I never saw so much blood fly," wrote
Alexander, "or so much grass painted red before." It was the battalion's only
casualty during the deployment.[69]

When Dearing completed the alignment, his cannon lay north of the Spangler farm lane, fronting on a northwest-to-southeast line. Captain Robert M.
Stribling's Fauquier Artillery was posted on the right, followed by Captain
Miles C. Macon's Fayette Artillery, Captain William H. Caskie's Hampden Artillery, and Captain Joseph G. Blount's Lynchburg Artillery. The four Virginia
batteries had fourteen twelve-pound Napoleons, three ten-pound Parrotts,
and a three-inch Ordnance rifle.[70]

The final two batteries put in line belonged to Alexander's or Huger's battalion. Lieutenant S. Capers Gilbert's Brooks Artillery of four twelve-pound
howitzers unlimbered to the left and rear, en echelon, of Dearing's row of
guns. On Gilbert's left, Lieutenant James Woolfolk's Ashland Artillery, consisting of two twelve-pound Napoleons and a pair of twenty-pound Parrotts,
moved into position. Alexander thought that he had finished the deployment
by ten o'clock. He had, with the captured Union gun, seventy-six cannon in
line, with nine in reserve.[71]

Mounted on his horse Dixie, Alexander had supervised the placement of
the batteries. The cannon "had all been carefully located and made ready."
He had been pleased with the limited reaction from enemy batteries. The
Federals were "most remarkably amiable all that morning, in allowing our
batteries to move about in easy range, & often in columns & masses wh[ich]
presented the prettiest possible targets, & annoying us so little." He had estimated the range at generally twelve hundred yards and assigned to each battery a specific target, primarily an enemy battery. He instructed the gunners
to fire slowly and deliberately. They could neither test ranges beforehand nor
fire rapidly, wasting their limited supply of long-range ammunition. Alexander waited another hour or more to inform Longstreet that he had completed
the preparations.[72]

While Alexander constructed his line of bronze and iron, his fellow artillery
commanders in the Second and Third corps oversaw their preparations.
Since most of the batteries in the two corps had been posted since July 2, the

deployment for the cannonade required minimal movement. Colonel R. Lindsay Walker's Third Corps battalions had participated in the action on July 2 from Seminary Ridge and would extend Alexander's left north along the crest. Walker described his position as "very favorable ground" for artillery. He counted eighty-three cannon available. He would use, however, only fifty-five pieces in the cannonade, placing Lieutenant Colonel John H. Garnett's battalion and a Georgia battery in reserve and keeping six short-range twelve-pound howitzers out of the bombardment.[73]

Major William T. Poague's battalion connected with Alexander's line on the rise east of Spangler's Woods. Poague, who had learned the artillerist trade under Stonewall Jackson, had four batteries in place—the Albemarle Artillery, Charlotte Artillery, Madison Light Artillery, and Warrenton Artillery—totaling sixteen cannon. Of that number, however, six were the twelve-pound howitzers, which remained silent.[74]

To Poague's left and rear, on the crest of Seminary Ridge, Walker's main line of batteries began, extending north past the David McMillan house and across Fairfield Road nearly to the Lutheran Seminary. Major John Lane's Companies A and C of the Sumter Battalion held the right end of the line. Next to Lane's Georgians were the five batteries of Major William J. Pegram's battalion—the Crenshaw Battery, Fredericksburg Artillery, Letcher Artillery, Pee Dee Artillery, and Purcell Artillery. Lane's Georgians and Pegram's Virginians and South Carolinians manned a total of thirty cannon, including four three-inch Navy rifles.[75]

The Danville Artillery, Hardaway Artillery, 2nd Rockbridge Artillery, and Virginia Battery, Richmond Artillery, of Major David G. McIntosh's battalion, completed Walker's line of Third Corps artillery. McIntosh's thirteen cannon were aligned behind a stone wall to Fairfield Road. Two of his pieces from the Hardaway Artillery, a pair of long-range British-made Whitworth cannon, were moved to Oak Ridge, north of Chambersburg Pike and the railroad cut. The Whitworths had been ordered there by A. P. Hill to enfilade Union guns on Cemetery Hill.[76]

Colonel J. Thompson Brown's Second Corps artillery units continued the Confederate line beyond Fairfield Road. Four batteries of Captain Willis J. Dance's 1st Virginia Artillery Battalion—the 2nd and 3rd Richmond Howitzers, Powhatan Artillery, and Salem Flying Artillery—covered the ridge from the road to near the Lutheran Seminary. The gun crews manned ten three-inch Ordnance rifles and four ten-pound Parrotts and would concentrate their fire upon Cemetery Hill.[77]

Posted near the two Whitworths, on both sides of the railroad cut, were ten cannon of Lieutenant Colonel Thomas H. Carter's Second Corps battalion. Because of the range, Carter employed six three-inch rifles and four ten-pound Parrotts in the Jeff Davis Artillery, King William Artillery, and Orange Artillery. The Morris Artillery consisted of four twelve-pound Napoleons and were held in reserve.[78]

The remaining Second Corps batteries ringed the town to the north and east. Of these crews, only nine guns from three batteries—Lee Artillery, Georgia Battery, and 1st Rockbridge Artillery—would be assigned to the cannonade. These artillerists stood to their guns on Benner's Hill, a broad-crested height that lay astride Hanover Road, east of Gettysburg. Brown's gunners had fought from there on July 2, drawing a firestorm from Union cannon. Cemetery Hill lay fifteen hundred yards to the southwest of Benner's Hill. Of the twenty Second Corps batteries, all or part of thirteen batteries would not be engaged.[79]

The Confederates had committed 164 cannon to what Alexander termed the "grand assault." Of that total, sixty-five were either Napoleons or twelve-pound howitzers, smoothbore weapons more suited for defensive action than a long-range cannonade. An equal number of three-inch Ordnance rifles and ten-pound Parrotts remained in reserve and did not take a part in the action. Alexander's line held a majority of the Napoleons and had the shortest range to the Federal batteries.[80]

If the Confederates were to succeed and to wreak havoc upon the Federals on Cemetery Ridge, as Lee planned, the artillery officers and men would have to create a fearful and coordinated blanket of fire upon the target. With the limitations of their ammunition and ordnance and the shallowness of the enemy position, there was "little room for error." The operation demanded strong leadership that brought numerous batteries from three corps together into a combined bombardment. The requirements were, however, beyond the abilities of the army's chief of artillery, William Pendleton.[81]

Known in the army as "Granny" and "Old Mother Pendleton," the former minister was, in Alexander's estimation, "too old & had been too long out of army life to be thoroughly up to all the opportunities of his position." Another battalion commander stated that Pendleton was "lacking in force" and "regarded in the army as a sort of joke." One of Longstreet's staff officers contended that Pendleton served as little more than an "*ordnance* officer."[82]

Pendleton stated in his report that "proper directions" were given to the artillery commanders. It would appear, however, that Pendleton failed to tell Lindsay Walker that Poague's Third Corps battalion was expected to advance with the infantry. When the cannonade commenced, he would be more concerned about the location of the ordnance trains than the execution of his artillerists and the effectiveness of their fire.[83]

Unfortunately for the Confederates, only Pendleton possessed the authority to achieve a cohesiveness among his commands. He neither saw the possibilities of enfilading Cemetery Hill nor added more batteries to the cannonade. In turn, the corps artillery commanders acted independently, without a firm understanding of the crucial importance of their roles. Only Alexander, who reported directly to Longstreet, had received detailed instructions. Pendleton's failings would have a critical impact upon the effectiveness of the Confederate artillery.[84]

Pendleton's performance was symptomatic of the Confederate high command's shortcomings during the morning's preparation. Lee, Longstreet, Hill, and their staffs were a constant presence along the lines, seen by numerous officers and men. Longstreet stated that once the troops had been arrayed he and Lee rode twice along the ranks "to see that everything was arranged according to his wishes. He [Lee] was told that we had been more particular in giving the orders than ever before." Longstreet had met with Pickett, Pettigrew, and Trimble, "carefully designated" the point of attack, and told the officers to confer with their subordinates. Longstreet wanted the men in the ranks informed about "the work that was before them, so that they should nerve themselves for the attack, and fully understand it."[85]

If they "had been more particular in giving orders than ever before," questions haunt Confederate history. The Southerners were about to undertake a terrible mission, against a formidable opponent, across open killing fields, with the battle's outcome and, perhaps, much more at stake. Lee had brought his army north, seeking an engagement that might bring resolution to the war. When Lee had pointed toward Cemetery Ridge, it had been a resounding summons. But on this morning, the ghosts of the army's past gathered along Seminary Ridge.

The Army of Northern Virginia had operated under Lee with a loosely organized command structure. His personal staff amounted to a handful of officers. He once described his method of command: "I do everything in my power to make my plans as perfect as possible, and to bring the troops upon the field of battle; the rest must be done by my generals and their troops,

trusting to Providence for the victory." For most of the past year, Lee had relied upon Stonewall Jackson and James Longstreet to execute his plans. But
Jackson was dead, and Longstreet opposed the assault.[86]

Although Lee accompanied Longstreet at least twice during their inspec-
tions of the troops, he seems to have continued his passive role. It has been
argued that Lee "intended" Trimble's two brigades to form en echelon on
Pettigrew's left flank—instead of behind his right front, as directed by
Longstreet. If that were Lee's intent, he did not correct the alignment. In
fact, he, Longstreet, and Hill appeared to be unconcerned about the lack of
direct support for Pettigrew's left front, manned by the division's weakest
brigade, Brockenbrough's, and by one of its most inexperienced, Davis's.
"The arrangement of all the troops," contended Alexander in a private letter,
"*must* have been apparent to Gen Lee when he was going about the lines between 11 & 12, & his not interfering with it stamps it with his approval."[87]

According to an officer in the ranks of Lowrance's brigade, Lee halted in
front of the unit and noticed a number of men with bandaged heads. Turning
to Trimble, Lee remarked, "Many of these poor boys should go to the rear,
they are not fit for duty." He then added, "I miss in this brigade the faces of
many dear friends." Before he nudged Traveller to leave, he said to Trimble
that "the attack must succeed."[88]

The incident and Lee's words might be apocryphal, but Lee undoubtedly
rode along Pettigrew's and Trimble's lines. He had nearby troops from the divisions of Richard Anderson, Robert Rodes, and Dorsey Pender who had suffered minimal casualties during the first two days. Pettigrew's and Trimble's
units would have served better as support troops than as components of the
main attack force. It must be assumed that the actual condition of the six
brigades was unknown to Lee and not readily evident from what he saw as he
passed by their ranks.[89]

Pettigrew's and Trimble's troops belonged to the Third Corps, whose commander's role on this day defies historical scrutiny. In 1862, Powell Hill had
been one of the army's finest warriors at the head of his renowned "Light Division." But on July 1 at Gettysburg, he had allowed the action between
Henry Heth's infantrymen and their Union opponents to escalate beyond
Lee's strictures against bringing on a general engagement. After that day, for
reasons unknown, Hill became a shadow, lurking in the background but not
exercising active leadership of his corps. The breakdown in the unfolding
Confederate attacks on July 2 occurred along Hill's sector. He spent portions
of the afternoon by Lee's side but did not intervene personally in the tactical

direction of his units, even after Dorsey Pender had to relinquish command of his division because of a wound.[90]

Whatever information or counsel Hill provided to Lee and Longstreet on the morning of July 3 remains unknown. Hill possessed a combative personality and an inordinate sensitivity. He had clashed with both Jackson and Longstreet while he had served under them in 1862. His and Longstreet's relationship probably remained less than cordial. Whether Hill withheld some measure of cooperation because of the past cannot be ascertained. Longstreet might have chosen to ignore Hill. Lee's plan to put Hill in direct command over only two brigades indicates the commanding general's possible dissatisfaction with his subordinate's performance on this field of battle. When Lee needed critical information about troops in the Third Corps, Hill either did not know or perhaps remained silent.[91]

Porter Alexander attributed some of these failings to the inadequacy of the staffs. "None of our Armies *ever* had enough staff to keep our Generals perfectly informed and in touch with all parts of the Army," he declared. "Hence it was so common to have hitches and things go wrong and recriminations afterward. If ever a field got big and complicated hell got to pay somewhere." But on this morning, the field was not "big and complicated" where the artillery and infantry formed. Furthermore, the generals and their staffs had several hours to oversee the preparations, to make corrections, and to ensure that orders were understood and implemented.[92]

Direct authority over and responsibility for the assault, in the end, belonged to James Longstreet. "Old Pete," as his troops called him, had voiced his opposition to the assault. Nevertheless, Lee had entrusted it to him. Longstreet believed, or at least argued later, that Lee "should have put an officer in charge who had more confidence in his plan." But Lee had no one else who possessed Longstreet's experience and skills. Despite his judgment about the wisdom of Lee's decision, duty required of Longstreet that he fulfill Lee's plans to the best of his abilities.[93]

Longstreet attended to numerous details. He met with the three division commanders, discussed with Alexander the artillerist's role in the cannonade, designated areas for the infantry, and inspected the lines at least twice. He was never informed by Pickett, however, that Fry's brigade, not Garnett's, would be the unit of direction in the charge. Furthermore, no evidence exists that he met personally with Richard Anderson to clarify any questions about support troops. Neither he nor Lee inquired about the supply of artillery ammunition, assuming that the batteries had an ample number of rounds for the cannonade and then to follow the infantry. Longstreet gave most of his attention to Pickett's troops and Alexander's gun crews. He seems to have been too parochial in his concern for the First Corps while neglecting his wider responsibility for the other elements of the force.[94]

What is undisputed is that, as the morning lengthened, Longstreet's mood darkened. Walter Harrison of Pickett's staff observed that Longstreet "seemed to be in anything but a pleasant humor at the prospect 'over the hill.' " The general confessed later, "Never was I so depressed as upon that day. I felt that my men were to be sacrificed, and that I should have to order them to make a hopeless charge."[95]

About 11:00 A.M., Porter Alexander reported to Longstreet. Not all of the infantry units were in place, Longstreet said, and he would give the signal for the artillery to open. He wanted two cannon fired in rapid succession on Alexander's line. Longstreet directed Alexander to find a location where he could observe the effect of the cannonade. Alexander should have one of Pickett's couriers with him and, as the colonel recalled it, "exercise my judgment in selecting the moment for Pickett's advance to begin." Longstreet then lay down for a nap.[96]

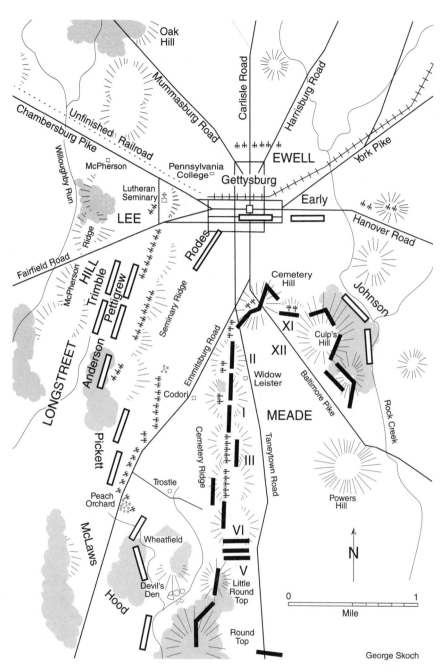

UNION AND CONFEDERATE DEPLOYMENTS
PRIOR TO CANNONADE.

7

"They Are Determined to Do or Die"

⚑⚑
⚑

L IEUTENANT FRANK HASKELL watched his comrades in Brigadier General John Gibbon's division of the Union Second Corps stir on Cemetery Ridge on the morning of July 3. They were "roused early," shortly after daylight. "Then ensued the hum of an army, not in ranks, chatting in low tones, and running about and jostling among each other, rolling and packing their blankets and tents," wrote Haskell. "They looked like an army of rag-gatherers." They gathered in knots to share cups of coffee and to chew on hardtack. Behind them, to the northeast, the smoke and sound of cannon fire and musketry billowed up from Culp's Hill.[1]

These "rag-gatherers" were veterans, some of the Union army's finest combat soldiers. They wore faded, dirty blue uniforms. Their equipment consisted of a knapsack, capped by a rolled gray blanket, a haversack or "satchel," a belt with a cartridge box, cap box, and bayonet attached, and a rifled musket which shone "like silver." "It is curious," thought a staff officer, "how everything has, by sheer hard service and necessity, been brought down to the lowest point of weight and complication." Messmates took turns carrying their coffeepot and frying pan, items "more precious to them than gold."[2]

From where they stood on the ridge's crest, near a small copse of trees, they had a panoramic view of the fields that stretched to Seminary Ridge, of Little and Big Round Top, of Cemetery and Culp's hills, and of Baltimore Pike and Taneytown Road. It was good ground to defend, and they knew it. On July 2, they had repulsed Confederate attacks against it. A captain in the division described it to his father a few days later: "The advantages of our position were that the comdg. General could look over almost the whole line, a rare thing in this country, & that moving on the chord of the circle while the enemy moved on the arc, we could reinforce any part of the line from any other part much quicker than they could."[3]

The advantages noted by the captain had underpinned the decision of George Meade and his corps commanders to stand and to fight on the ground for another day. Meade's prediction to Gibbon that Lee would test the Union center on July 3 would have to await developments. Before Gibbon's men and troops in other units on Cemetery Ridge awoke, the commanding general was at work. He had approved earlier the effort to retake the captured works on Culp's Hill by the Twelfth Corps and now needed to attend to matters along the army's center and left flank.[4]

At 4:30 A.M., as Henry Slocum's artillery opened up on the Confederates on Culp's Hill, Meade conferred with Brigadier General Henry J. Hunt, the army's chief of artillery. Meade directed Hunt to examine the Union line from Cemetery Hill to Little Round Top, rectifying, if necessary, the position of batteries, and bringing forward additional pieces. He then ordered his cavalry commander, Major General Alfred Pleasonton, to guard the army's right flank and rear along Hanover Road, east of the town. He knew, as one of his staff officers had put it, the magnitude of the battle's outcome. "I do hope this time," the aide had written two days before, "the Army of the Potomac may meet with success. We cannot always be so unfortunate as we have been thus far."[5]

Meade left army headquarters at the Lydia Leister house a short time later on a personal inspection of the lines. On this morning, he rode one of his spare mounts. His favorite horse, Old Baldy, which Meade had bought early in the war and named, had been wounded on the afternoon of July 2. A bullet had struck the animal in the stomach, barely missing Meade's leg before it penetrated his saddle into the animal. At first, Meade despaired of his horse's recovery, but he reported to his wife afterward that "the old fellow has such a wonderful tenacity of life" and seemed to be healing.[6]

During this initial tour, Meade stopped near Culp's Hill for a report on the fighting, probably visited Cemetery Hill, and then proceeded south along Cemetery Ridge. Major General Winfield Scott Hancock, commander of the

Second Corps, accompanied Meade on the ride toward Little Round Top. Whether Meade examined the line beyond Hancock's position is uncertain. Two of Hancock's divisions covered the ground from Ziegler's Grove to a point a few hundred yards south of the copse of trees. From the end of his line to Big Round Top, units from five of the army's corps were posted as a result of the combat on July 2. It would take time to rectify the lines in this area.[7]

Perhaps, before Meade began his ride, he received a message from Major General John Newton, acting commander of the First Corps. When John Reynolds was slain on July 1, his senior division commander, Major General Abner Doubleday, had assumed command. But Meade had little confidence in Doubleday's abilities and supplanted him with Newton, a division commander in the Sixth Corps and junior in rank to Doubleday, early on July 2. An aide to Doubleday described Meade's action as "a gross outrage."[8]

A West Point classmate of James Longstreet with more than two decades of service in the army, Newton was a tall, muscular man with blue eyes and "a thick head" of brown hair. An artillery officer in the army thought him to be "a gentlemanly man, and quite affable." Frank Haskell noted that he walked "very erect" and had "somewhat of that smart sort of swagger, that people are apt to suppose characterizes soldiers." During the council at Meade's headquarters on the night of July 2, only Newton had argued that Gettysburg "was no place in which to fight a battle."[9]

Newton had been awakened on July 3 by the cannon fire from along Baltimore Pike. His headquarters lay behind Doubleday's division on Cemetery Ridge. The corps's other two divisions were posted in the Cemetery Hill–Culp's Hill area. Brigadier General John C. Robinson's two brigades acted as support for the Eleventh Corps infantry and artillery units on Cemetery Hill, while Brigadier General James S. Wadsworth's command, including the famous Iron Brigade, held the northwest slope of Culp's Hill, on the left of the Twelfth Corps. Unable to direct these latter two divisions personally, Newton concerned himself with the area around Doubleday's troops.[10]

Like Meade, Newton decided to survey the line, riding south to Little Round Top. Beyond Doubleday's left, he found the ground to be "almost denuded of troops." He sent a courier to Meade with a message about his discovery. Meade suggested that he ask Major General John Sedgwick, Sixth Corps commander, for units to fill the gap. When Newton rode to find Sedgwick, he came upon Brigadier General John C. Caldwell's division of the Second Corps. Caldwell's four brigades had been ravaged in the fight for the

Wheatfield the previous day, losing two brigade commanders and nearly thirteen hundred officers and men. Caldwell agreed to shift forward, in his words, "what was left of the division" in line with Doubleday's ranks. Caldwell's men then advanced to the crest of a slight rise and erected some modest fieldworks. Eventually, the Sixth Corps brigades of Brigadier General A.T.A. Torbert and Colonel Henry L. Eustis extended the line to the George Weikert house.[11]

Behind Newton's refashioned line, the battered remnants of the Third Corps had spent the night of July 2–3. When Major General Daniel E. Sickles had decided to occupy the ground at the Peach Orchard on July 2, he had led his two divisions into a furious cauldron. Longstreet's Confederates crushed the salient and wrecked the Third Corps's lines. Sickles's misjudgment cost the general a leg and hundreds of his troops. The officers and men had little left to give.[12]

Major General David B. Birney had succeeded the wounded Sickles. The son of James G. Birney, a renowned antebellum abolitionist who twice ran for the presidency in the Liberty Party, Birney was practicing law in Philadelphia when the war began. He had served under Philip Kearny, one of the army's best combat officers, and succeeded Kearny in September 1862, upon the latter's death in an engagement at Chantilly, Virginia. Physically, Birney was a small man, noted for his "cold covert manner." One of his men stated that the general "reminds me of a graven image and could act as a bust for his own tomb, being utterly destitute of color." When his troops had passed through Frederick, Maryland, en route to Gettysburg, Birney had his orderlies draw sabers "to clear the way" for a band, the general, and his staff. "Such feats are not common in the army," groused an officer, "and do not take."[13]

Few in the army, however, questioned Birney's personal courage and capabilities as a general. While his men prepared their breakfasts and refilled their cartridge boxes, Newton asked Birney to provide support for the front line if needed. Birney agreed. As the morning lengthened, his two divisions formed a reserve line from behind Doubleday's position to the lower ground at the southern end of Cemetery Ridge. Birney probably had upward of five thousand officers and men left in the ranks.[14]

The members of the Union Fifth Corps, who had secured Little Round Top and had stopped the Confederate thrusts on July 2, remained in the positions they had held when the fighting had ended. During the night, four regiments had occupied Big Round Top while other units built fieldworks of stones on the lower peak. Several regiments lay behind a stone wall across Wheatfield Road in the valley between Houck's Ridge and Little Round Top. Additional units filled the line between Little Round Top's northern base and the Weikert house. If the Southerners decided to renew the struggle in this area, it would be far more difficult for them than it had been on the previous day.[15]

One of Meade's best commanders, Major General George Sykes, led the Fifth Corps. Sykes was forty-one years old but seemed older, a career soldier and West Pointer who appeared on the surface to be constantly angry about something. Haskell thought he possessed "the general air of one who is weary, and a little ill natured." According to a captain in the corps, Sykes was "a thorough soldier, brave and accomplished, in whom the men have the greatest confidence, fear, and respect." But the old Regular Army man, the officer added, could not disguise his "contempt and hatred of the volunteers." He spoke rarely to the troops, who still regarded him as "one of the great men of the army." John Gibbon called him "a very fine soldier." Duty governed this small, thin man's character. The ground now belonged to his volunteers and Regulars, and Sykes would see that they kept it.[16]

Unlike Sykes, Major General John Sedgwick was universally liked by the citizen soldiers of his Sixth Corps. A large, heavyset man, kindhearted and generous, with "a cheery soul," Sedgwick had "no enemy" in the army. One soldier in the corps wrote his mother a week after the battle: "I wish you could see Gen. Sedgwick. You would take him to be a farmer or wagon master. He does not wear any mark by which anyone would know him but wears a straw hat, dark blue blouse & pants, and a checked cotton shirt. . . . He rides a powerful bay horse which seems to be proud of its rider."[17]

The men in the ranks called this Academy graduate and career soldier "Uncle John," but never within earshot of the general. Sedgwick was a cautious, steady, and imperturbable officer. Haskell thought that, like Meade, "he looks, and is honest and modest." Sedgwick commanded the army's largest infantry corps, more than thirteen thousand troops. It had not arrived at Gettysburg until the afternoon of July 2. Placed in support behind lower Cemetery Ridge and Little Round Top, the rank and file bivouacked in the area. Although exhausted from their forced march to the field, the officers and men had suffered few casualties and provided Meade with a large reserve of manpower.[18]

At 8:00 A.M. on July 3, Sedgwick received instructions from Meade to have his units ready to march, if needed, along the line. Before long, army headquarters ordered him to send two brigades to Culp's Hill. When Newton requested support, Sedgwick complied with another pair of brigades, ordering them to Cemetery Ridge. Meanwhile, he had bolstered the army's left rear, east of Big Round Top, by dispatching Brigadier General David A. Russell's brigade and two batteries to that area, where they joined Colonel Lewis A. Grant's Vermonters astride Taneytown Road. These detachments left Sedgwick with two brigades, which he placed behind the Fifth Corps, north of the base of Little Round Top. He remarked later that he had "not a man or gun under his command except a few orderlies" and thought that "he might as well go home." [19]

From the time Newton found a portion of the line "almost denuded of troops" until late morning, Meade and his subordinates cobbled together a continuous line, with reserves in place, from an amalgam of commands. Approximately twenty-three thousand troops manned this portion of the field. Meade might have served himself and the army better if he had created two wings, with Hancock in command of all the units from Ziegler's Grove south to the George Weikert house, including Doubleday's First Corps division and Birney's Third Corps, and with Sedgwick in charge of the units south of the Weikert house, on both Round Tops, to the Taneytown Road. Instead, Meade had divisions detached from their corps and brigades, separated from their divisions, under the apparent authority of other commanders. Newton, however, reported that by noon he thought the line was "very secure." [20]

At 8:30 A.M., Meade wired Major General Darius Couch, commander of the Department of the Susquehanna, headquartered in Harrisburg, Pennsylvania. "The result of my operations may be the withdrawal of the rebel army," Meade stated. "The sound of my guns for these three days, it is taken for granted, is all the additional notice you need to come on. Should the enemy withdraw, by prompt co-operation we might destroy him. Should he overpower me, your return and defense of Harrisburg and the Susquehanna is not at all endangered." [21]

Fifteen minutes later, Meade penned a letter to his "Dearest Love," his wife, Margaret. In an earlier letter he had asked her to "pray earnestly, pray for the success of my country." Now he was brief. "All well & going on well with the army," he assured her. "We had a great fight yesterday, the enemy attacking & we completely repulsing them—both armies shattered—today at it again with what result remains to be seen. Army in fine spirits & they are determined to do or die. George [their staff officer son] & myself well." [22]

○　○　○

BRIGADIER GENERAL HENRY JACKSON HUNT, chief of artillery of the Army of the Potomac, looked at war with an unblinking eye. He had reduced it to a basic element—massed cannon spewing forth hot iron into human flesh. In its fearful starkness, it was a philosophy of man-made fury against the bodies and souls of men. Henry Hunt could create hell on a battlefield unlike any other warrior at Gettysburg.

Artillery had been his life's work since his graduation from West Point in 1839. The son and grandson of army officers, Hunt had distinguished himself in Mexico, earning brevets as captain and major for gallantry in battle. In 1856, the War Department selected him and two other officers to revise the army's manual on light-artillery tactics. Adopted by the department four years later, their report became the instructional guide for artillerists in the opposing armies throughout the conflict. By the time the Civil War began, Hunt had devoted more than three decades, including his combat experience in Mexico, to the study of artillery in battle.[23]

Hunt believed that the use of artillery on a battlefield should be governed by three basic principles. Batteries can be maneuvered or shifted with rapidity, enabling commanders to fill gaps in lines or to follow in close support for infantry assaults. The mobility of cannon allowed artillerists to mass batteries, to forge a wall of concentrated fire upon enemy guns and troops. Finally, the array of cannon should be aligned to create a convergence of fury or a crossfire, a swirling gale of solid shot and jagged pieces of iron. Northern factories wrought for him the tools, and he wielded them unlike any other artillerist in the East.[24]

Friend and foe alike had witnessed Hunt's handiwork on some of the war's bloodiest fields in 1862. At Malvern Hill, on July 1 of that year, Union gun crews, aligned in an unbroken row, erased the ranks of Confederate attackers. At Antietam, on September 17, Hunt's batteries created a maelstrom of destruction—"artillery hell," as it was termed. And on the awful field at Fredericksburg for the Union army, on December 13, Hunt's dark line of iron and bronze across the Rappahannock River prevented the Southerners from exploiting their victory.[25]

The debacle at Fredericksburg and the subsequent, ignominious "Mud March" brought Major General Joseph Hooker into command of the Union army. Hooker and Hunt clashed almost at once over the creation of a corps of artillery, fueled by a personal antipathy between the two generals. Hunt had been an outspoken supporter of George B. McClellan, was strong-willed, and backed down to few men. "He showed so much ill feeling," Hooker declared afterward, "that I was unwilling to place my artillery in his charge." The army commander relegated Hunt to administrative duties, restricting him to limited authority over batteries in battle, and only upon Hooker's direct orders.[26]

At Chancellorsville, Hooker paid a price for his decision. The dispersed authority over the batteries negated the army's superiority in artillery. On the afternoon of May 3, Hooker quietly returned tactical control of the gun crews to Hunt. By then, Confederate batteries covered the plateau of Hazel Grove, dominating the field and dooming the Federals. After the defeat, Hooker restored Hunt to field command and granted him authority to unify control over the army's finest branch.[27]

An organizational genius, Hunt created fourteen artillery brigades, with four or five batteries in each. He assigned one brigade to each of the seven infantry corps and two brigades of nine batteries to the Horse Artillery in the cavalry corps. The remaining five brigades formed the army's Artillery Reserve, a separate and self-sufficient command. He appointed officers who were loyal to him and whom he trusted. When the Union army—"a ponderous machine," in the words of a staff officer—headed north in pursuit of the Confederates in June, Hunt commanded 370 cannon in sixty-two batteries.[28]

Meade's accession to command surely pleased, if not elated, Hunt. Both men possessed strong personalities, but they shared similar views on the use of artillery. Hunt accompanied Meade to Gettysburg early on July 2, riding with the army commander as he inspected the Union position before daylight. Meade directed Hunt "to see to the position of the artillery and make such arrangements respecting it as were necessary." Hunt wrote afterward, "These orders recognized, in fact necessarily vested in me all the powers of a commander-in-chief of the artillery in their plentitude."[29]

Hunt seemed to be everywhere along the Union line during July 2. He issued orders, posted batteries, and witnessed the loss of a number of guns, their crews overrun by the Confederate attackers. When the fighting ceased, he had ammunition chests refilled and batteries reorganized because of the day's casualties. During the action, Meade had expressed to him a concern about the army's supply of artillery rounds. Unknown to Meade and to his two predecessors in command, Hunt had since the fall of 1862 been stockpiling supplies, foodstuffs, and ammunition in a wagon train that did not exist officially in army documents. Hunt had requested supplies for the artillery in duplicate, or even in triplicate, to secure the necessary items. Only he and

Quartermaster General Rufus Ingalls among the army's ranking officers knew about the train. At Gettysburg, it consisted of nearly sixty wagons, with twenty extra rounds of ammunition for each cannon.[30]

The artillery chief rose early on July 3, and watched as Union gunners along Baltimore Pike initiated the combat on Culp's Hill. From there, he inspected the batteries from Cemetery Hill to Little Round Top. Most of the gun crews remained where they had been when the fighting had ceased on July 2. The army's Artillery Reserve, from which Hunt had drawn units during the day, stood parked near the army's center, in fields east of Taneytown Road. If the Southerners were to come again on this Friday, Hunt wanted his officers and men prepared. Before the morning ended, his own and his subordinates' efforts would result in a formidable line of batteries directed toward the fields of wheat, corn, and pasture between Cemetery Ridge and Seminary Ridge.[31]

Cemetery Hill bristled with more than fifty cannon. East of Baltimore Pike, covering the approaches from the north and northeast, Colonel Charles S. Wainwright, artillery commander of the First Corps, had seven batteries, with thirty-four guns. Across the road, placed among the gravestones in Evergreen Cemetery—"one of the prettiest burial places I ever saw," thought an Ohioan—were thirty-eight cannon, under Major Thomas W. Osborn, commander of the Eleventh Corps artillery. Two of Osborn's batteries—1st New Hampshire Light Artillery and 5th New York Independent Battery—supported Wainwright's units, aligned toward the northeast.[32]

Osborn's remaining twenty-nine cannon were, in his description, "in position as in park." Each gun stood fourteen feet from the one beside it. Facing to the west and northwest toward Seminary Ridge, the line consisted of, from north to south: a section of Captain Michael Wiedrich's Battery I, 1st New York; Captain Hubert Dilger's Battery I, 1st Ohio; Lieutenant Eugene Bancroft's Battery C, 4th United States; Lieutenant Philip Mason's Battery H, 1st United States; Captain Wallace Hill's 1st West Virginia Light Artillery; and Lieutenant George Norton's Battery H, 1st Ohio. These units had seventeen twelve-pound Napoleons, eight three-inch Ordnance rifles, and four ten-pound Parrotts.[33]

South of Cemetery Hill, along the ridge from Ziegler's Grove to a few hundred yards beyond the clump of trees, lay five batteries of the Second Corps, posted among the infantrymen of Alexander Hays and John Gibbon. Confederate artillerist Porter Alexander admitted later that Cemetery Ridge offered the Federals "good cover behind it & endless fire positions for batteries."

Captain John G. Hazard commanded the corps artillery. Hazard counted twenty-seven pieces in the batteries.[34]

Lieutenant George A. Woodruff's Battery I, 1st United States, with a half-dozen Napoleons, held the right of Hazard's position in a field west of Ziegler's Grove. On July 2, Rebel sharpshooters had shot about one-third of Woodruff's men, and he had to borrow soldiers from a nearby infantry brigade to fill his ranks. Woodruff also had one cannon disabled when an enemy solid shot struck a wheel, bending the spindle of an axle. Taken to the rear, the gun's spindle was repaired, a new wheel mounted, and the cannon returned to the battery on the morning of July 3.[35]

Adjacent to and west of Ziegler's Grove of oak and hickory trees were the house and barn of Abraham Bryan or Brien, an illiterate free black. When the Confederates passed through the area days before the battle, Bryan and his family had fled. A low stone wall ran south from the southeast corner of the barn 775 feet until it turned west. From this angle, the wall continued nearly 250 feet to the west before resuming its southerly direction for another several hundred feet. A hundred yards south of the first angle in the wall stood the copse of trees.[36]

Captain William A. Arnold's Battery A, 1st Rhode Island, with six three-inch Ordnance rifles, was placed behind the wall from the Bryan barn to the initial angle. Arnold's line began near the angle and ran north, covering roughly one-third of the distance to the barn. Like Woodruff, Arnold had to use infantrymen to serve some of the guns because of losses on the previous day.[37]

Hazard had two batteries stationed south of the section of the wall between the angles and behind the westernmost extension of the wall. Lieutenant Alonzo H. Cushing's six three-inch Ordnance rifles in Battery A, 4th United States, filled the space north of the copse of trees. On Cushing's left and south of the small woodlot was Lieutenant T. Frederick Brown's Battery B, 1st Rhode Island, now under the command of Lieutenant Walter Perrin. Brown's crews had been overrun by Ambrose Wright's Georgians on July 2, suffering heavy casualties in men and horses—including Brown, who was severely wounded in the neck. Perrin had five Napoleons left in his line. Both batteries' cannon lay beneath the ridge's crest, on its western slope.[38]

One hundred fifty yards south of the Rhode Islanders were four ten-pound Parrotts of Battery B, 1st New York. On July 2, one section of the 14th New York Independent Battery had been consolidated with Battery B. Later in the day, Captain James M. Rorty replaced Lieutenant Albert S. Sheldon as commander. Originally assigned to the 14th New York, Rorty had been serving as chief artillery-ordnance officer of the Second Corps. He had impressed Hancock with his competence. When the section of Rorty's former command reported to Sheldon, Hancock intervened, ordering Hazard to reassign Rorty to the section and to command of the consolidated batteries.[39]

Beyond Rorty's left flank and to its rear, posted in reserve, was Captain Andrew Cowan's 1st New York Independent Battery of six three-inch Ordnance rifles. A Sixth Corps battery, Cowan's guns had been ordered into position by Colonel Charles H. Tompkins at the request of John Newton, commander of the First Corps. Cowan's men parked their cannon in the rear of Abner Doubleday's division.[40]

Farther south on the crest of Cemetery Ridge (where the present-day Pennsylvania Monument towers over the field), a formidable line of cannon began and extended six hundred yards to the George Weikert farm. At daylight on July 3, Lieutenant Colonel Freeman McGilvery, commander of the 1st Volunteer Brigade of the Artillery Reserve, had only a dozen guns posted on this section of the battlefield. He requested additional batteries, and throughout the morning, units wheeled into place. Once completed, McGilvery's line angled from the northeast to the southwest.[41]

Captain James Thompson's Batteries C and F, Pennsylvania Independent Artillery, held the right end of McGilvery's position. On Thompson's left came Captain Charles A. Phillips's Battery F, Fifth Massachusetts, then Captain Patrick Hart's 15th New York Independent Battery and Captain John W. Sterling's 2nd Connecticut Light Artillery, whose members had never before been engaged in a pitched battle. Next to Sterling was a section of Captain William D. Rank's 3rd Pennsylvania Heavy Artillery of the Horse Artillery, followed by Captain James H. Cooper's Battery B, 1st Pennsylvania; Lieutenant Edwin B. Dow's Battery F, 6th Maine; and Captain Nelson Ames's Battery G, 1st New York. It was a line patched together with units from three brigades of the Artillery Reserve, from the First Corps, and from the Horse Artillery.[42]

McGilvery ordered the gun crews to build a slight fieldwork for the thirty-seven cannon. Before noon, he added the six three-inch Ordnance rifles of Captain Jabez J. Daniels's 9th Michigan Battery of Horse Artillery, placing them to the front and right of Thompson's Pennsylvania gunners. From their position, McGilvery's artillerists could sweep Plum Run Valley from the Joseph Sherfy home to the Nicholas Codori farm, located along Emmitsburg Road west of the copse of trees. A small knoll, paralleling Cemetery Ridge and separating a ravine at the western foot of the ridge from Plum Run Valley, extended almost the entire length of McGilvery's line and masked much of it from view by the Confederates. It appears that this array of Union cannon was unknown to Lee's gunners.[43]

Two Fifth Corps batteries completed the Union line of cannon. Six Napoleons of the 1st Ohio Light Artillery, under Captain Frank C. Gibbs, rested on a northwest spur of Little Round Top. With the twelve-pounders' limited range, Gibbs's crews were deployed to stop any Confederate attack against the hill. Above the Ohioans, below the crest, lay Battery D, 5th United States, commanded by Lieutenant Benjamin Rittenhouse, a native Pennsylvanian. Rittenhouse had assumed command on the afternoon of July 2, when Lieutenant Charles E. Hazlett was killed. The Regulars' six ten-pound Parrotts could reach the fields beyond the Sherfy farm, raking the flank of any Southern force that advanced against Cemetery Ridge.[44]

Between 10:00 and 11:00 A.M., as the combat on Culp's Hill neared its end, Henry Hunt conducted an inspection of his batteries from Cemetery Hill to Little Round Top. When he first rode onto the crest of Cemetery Ridge, he stopped and looked west toward Seminary Ridge. He watched with admiration—batteries coming into line, horses' flanks to the front, dust as if it were a blanket on the drivers, the glint of the sun on polished bronze and iron. He called it "a magnificent display" as Porter Alexander's Confederate artillerymen deployed in the fields from the Peach Orchard to Henry Spangler's farm.[45]

Hunt knew at once that the enemy was preparing for either an anticipated Union advance, a withdrawal of its infantry for a movement, or, as he said, "the most probable case," a prelude to an assault on the Federal center. He spurred his horse, Bill, riding to each artillery chief and battery commander. Be prepared for a heavy cannonade, he told them, but wait fifteen or twenty minutes before replying, and then concentrate fire on individual Rebel batteries until they are silenced. "Under all circumstances to fire deliberately," he added, "and to husband their ammunition as much as possible." He compared it to *"target practice,"* and instructed them to save at least half of their rounds for the Confederate infantry. An old artilleryman could ask for nothing better than massed lines of charging infantry in open fields, with each step reducing the range, bringing them closer into a killing furnace of heated iron.[46]

A painstaking, cautious officer like the army commander, Hunt saw to details. He ordered that as many batteries as possible from the Artillery Reserve be readied. By noon, he would have eighty-one pieces from eighteen batteries posted in reserve. If the Confederates came, Hunt had, either on line or at hand, from Cemetery Hill to Little Round Top, 213 cannon to respond to a cannonade and to an infantry charge. Given an opportunity, it would be a fine day for Federal artillerymen. The industrial might of their society and Henry Hunt would see to it.[47]

*   *   *

SERGEANT BENJAMIN HIRST of the 14th Connecticut had written a letter to his wife from Uniontown, Maryland, on June 30, during a pause in a march. In it he said: "To day we expect to be in old Pennsylvania and I feel ready to go. I should give up on the Road Side, but I want to be counted in if there is a Big Battle in the old Keystone State."[48]

A fellow member of Hirst's regiment, Corporal Thomas W. Gardner, also wanted to be present if a battle occurred. Gardner saw the prospects for an engagement on Northern soil in a broad context. "I feel as if our country is worth fighting for, our government worth maintaining," he declared to his sister in a letter dated a week before Hirst's. "No one can ever convince me that slavery is right. I believe it has been the principle cause of all our troubles. I want to see it uprooted, root and branch. I believe the Rebels crossing into Maryland and Penn. will prove a good thing. I believe it will shorten the days of the rebellion. It will wake up the North."[49]

Less than two days after Hirst wrote home, he and Gardner would "be counted in" at Gettysburg. With their comrades in the Union Second Corps, the pair of Connecticut men marched through the night of July 1–2, arriving on the battlefield an hour or so after daylight. Later, the officers and men of the corps found themselves on Cemetery Ridge, the center of their line, near a copse of trees. Toward evening, the fighting came to them from across the fields to the west. They repulsed the Confederate attacks and then welcomed nightfall. One of the defenders avowed in his diary that they "were determined not to be drove."[50]

When dawn came on July 3, the 14th Connecticut and most of the Second Corps were still on Cemetery Ridge. At first, many of them grumbled about having neither rations nor coffee, and little tobacco left to fill their pipes. Private John W. Haley of the 17th Maine wrote: "We turned out early. Hunger had such a grip on us that it dragged us forth." As the morning hours passed, however, they saw what Henry Hunt had looked upon and admired. If the growing line of Confederate cannon portended another enemy assault, it appeared the Rebels would be coming directly at the men in the Second Corps. Only those who had used its shade had probably noticed the small clump of trees on the ridge's crest.[51]

Staff officer Frank Haskell asserted in a letter two weeks after the battle: "The Army of the Potomac was no band of school girls. They were not the men likely to be crushed or utterly discouraged by any mere circumstances in which they might find themselves placed." And within the army, the rank and file of the Second Corps believed that they were the least "likely to be crushed or utterly discouraged." They had been caught in a savage crossfire in the West Woods at Antietam and had charged up the long, awful slope before a stone wall until their blood reddened the ground at Fredericksburg. To them, any man who wore a trefoil, the corps insignia, on his cap belonged to the army's finest corps. Their commander wanted them, thought Sergeant Hirst, "to show that we can outmarch as well as outfight anything in the army."[52]

That demanding general was Winfield Scott Hancock, who had been appointed to command of the Second Corps on May 22. Since then, he had worked tirelessly to make them even better soldiers. "No commander ever more carefully prepared in camp for success in the field," wrote an officer in the corps. Hancock possessed "unflinching resolution" and "almost magical influence over men." Haskell believed that, if Hancock rode onto a battlefield in citizen's attire, unknown to troops, and issued orders, that "he would be likely to be obeyed at once, for he had the appearance of a man born to command." When George Meade needed an officer whom he could trust on the field at Gettysburg on July 1, he had sent Hancock.[53]

At thirty-nine years old and standing six feet two inches tall, Hancock was a physically imposing man. Officers and men regarded him as "the best looking officer in the army." Regardless of the weather or circumstances, he invariably wore a clean white shirt beneath his uniform coat. One staff officer observed that his servant "must have a hard time of it washing those shirts." He was well groomed, clean-shaven except for a mustache and goatee, had blue eyes and a ruddy complexion. A native Pennsylvanian and Academy graduate, Hancock passed through a campsite or rode behind a battle line with regal magnificence.[54]

One of his staff officers compared him to "a kind of meteor on the battlefield." Hancock was a superb tactician, with an eye for terrain and an instinctive feel for combat. He possessed a fearsome temper, which often exploded during a battle into a string of oaths. A fellow general declared, "Hancock always swore at everybody, above all on the battlefield." In calmer moments, when a day's fighting had subsided, he managed to send a telegram to his wife, Almira, usually telling her simply, "I am all right, so far."[55]

Colonel Wheelock G. Veazey of the 16th Vermont, whose brigade lay next to Hancock's troops on the morning of July 3, observed later, in speaking of Hancock and the Second Corps on this day, that "leader and men were never better suited to each other." Hancock had in line on Cemetery Ridge's crest the divisions of Alexander Hays and John Gibbon, with John Caldwell's bloodied brigades in reserve farther south on the ridge, to the left of Abner Doubleday's First Corps veterans. Between them, Hays and Gibbon had perhaps fifty-three hundred officers and men, covering a front of roughly two thousand feet.[56]

The Second Corps line began in the Ziegler's Grove area, near the Bryan farm, with troops from Hays's division. Like Hancock, Hays was a West Pointer and native Pennsylvanian. When the Confederates entered Pennsylvania, Hays and his brigade were pulled from the defenses of Washington and assigned to the Third Division of the Second Corps. On June 28, because of seniority, Hays assumed command of the division upon the transfer of its commander, Major General William H. French. Two days later, Hays informed his wife: "We have a promise of a fight. My command will do its duty."[57]

Hays came to the division with a reputation as a fighting man. Badly wounded at Second Bull Run, with a shattered leg, he "seemed happiest when in the thickest of the fight," claimed an officer in his brigade. Another officer declared that Hays possessed an "extraordinary vivacity in battle." He compared strategy to "a humbug. Next thing to cowardice." Red-haired, rough-mannered, with a temper similar to Hancock's, he was "idolized" by his troops, in the estimation of Captain Winfield Scott of the 126th New York, and "we would have followed him to the death." Colonel Clinton D. Mac-Dougall of the 111th New York described Hays as "a great friend of the volunteer soldier and deservedly popular." But Brigadier General Alexander S. Webb of Gibbon's division confided to his wife a month after the battle that Hays "is a real specimen of a weak ignorant political appointment. He is nothing but a personally brave man. No head no education & vulgar beyond measure."[58]

Webb had a number of facts wrong about Hays, except for the man's personal courage and rough language. He was the kind of man and soldier Hancock wanted on this day on Cemetery Ridge. Hays had with him on the ridge only two of his three brigades. When the Southerners charged up the northeastern slope of Cemetery Hill in the twilight of July 2, Hays had rushed Colonel Samuel S. Carroll's brigade to the fighting. Carroll's troops assisted in the repulse of the Rebels, and Oliver O. Howard, commander of the Eleventh Corps, insisted that they remain on the hill. One of Carroll's regiments, the 8th Ohio, had been on skirmish duty along Emmitsburg Road and had not gone with the brigade. Hays kept the Ohioans on the line, and they were there on the morning of July 3, with three companies in the fields west of the road.[59]

Three regiments of Colonel Thomas A. Smyth's brigade—the 12th New Jersey, 1st Delaware, and 14th Connecticut—held the stone wall, which a soldier described as a "remnant of a fallen stone wall," that ran from the Bryan barn to the angle, where the wall turned west down the slope of the ridge. The men in the regiments had piled rails on top of the wall, raising its height to nearly three feet. The 108th New York of the brigade was posted to the right and rear as support for Lieutenant George Woodruff's Battery I, 1st United States. Smyth's final unit, the 10th New York Battalion, rested behind the crest to the left and rear of the 14th Connecticut.[60]

Hays's former brigade of New Yorkers lay among the trees of Ziegler's Grove to the rear of Smyth's ranks. The unit consisted of four companies of the 39th New York, a cosmopolitan command of various immigrant groups known as the "Garibaldi Guards," and the 111th, 125th, and 126th New York. The 111th and 126th had been a part of the Harper's Ferry garrison that had surrendered to Stonewall Jackson during the Antietam Campaign in September 1862. During the action, the 126th New York had been accused of "a shameful panic." The New Yorkers denied the allegation, but they and their comrades in the 111th were branded the "Harper's Ferry Cowards." On July 2, when ordered into the fight, the New Yorkers charged William Barksdale's Mississippians, shouting, "Remember Harper's Ferry!" They drove back the Southerners and earned some redemption.[61]

Colonel George L. Willard had assumed command of the brigade when Hays took the division. During the action against the Mississippians, Willard was killed instantly by a cannonball that blew away part of his head. Colonel Eliakim Sherrill of the 126th New York succeeded Willard and ordered a withdrawal. Hancock rode up, learned of the colonel's decision, and had him arrested. On the morning of July 3, Hays and Colonel MacDougall of the 111th New York asked Hancock to reconsider. The corps commander relented, and Sherrill resumed command of the brigade.[62]

The 111th, 125th, and the four companies of the 39th New York were aligned directly behind Smyth's three regiments along the stone wall. The 126th New York supported Woodruff's battery, on the right of the 108th New York. Hays had roughly twenty-three hundred officers and men, either on the ridge or on skirmish duty to the front. The men in the division called themselves the "Blue Birds" because of the blue trefoils they wore, signifying the Third Division. Hays boasted to his wife later, "My division is the fighting kind I love."[63]

John Gibbon's Second Division continued the corps's line south along the ridge. Gibbon was one of Hancock's favorite subordinates. Born in Philadelphia, he had grown up in North Carolina and had three brothers in the Confederate army. When the war began, Gibbon, an 1847 graduate of West Point, commanded a battery in Utah Territory and marched it across the plains, arriving in the East in July 1861. He then served as a chief of artillery until promoted to brigadier general and assigned to command a brigade of Western regiments in the spring of 1862.[64]

A private in Gibbon's new command remarked about the general, "You'll just feel that you hadn't better call him Johnnie." At first, the Wisconsin and Indiana volunteers hated Gibbon's discipline and constant drills. Regular Army to his last fiber, Gibbon was determined to make these citizen soldiers as good as any Regular unit. He had them issued the Regular Army's long frock coats and high-crowned Hardee hats. In time, the men adopted the hats as their brigade's distinctive badge. When the tests came at Brawner's Farm, Second Bull Run, South Mountain, and Antietam, the Westerners forged a record for valor and prowess in combat unmatched by any other unit in the army. "Those damned black hats," as the Confederates called them, became known as the Iron Brigade. When Gibbon was promoted to divisional command, he told his wife that he had prepared his farewell address to the brigade "*almost* with tears in my eyes."[65]

During the army's march north in pursuit of Lee's troops, Gibbon had visited the field at Brawner's Farm, near Groveton, Virginia, where he had led the Westerners into battle for the first time. He wrote to his wife afterward, stating that he "could without difficulty trace the direction of my line by the broken cartridges and the bodies of the men, which appear to have been simply covered over with earth right where they fell." He then concluded, "It will not be very long however before most of the trace of these battles is obliterated, and I only wish traces on the country could be wiped away as easily and as soon." [66]

A staff officer who would come to know Gibbon wrote, "A tower of strength he is, cool as a steel knife, always, and unmoved by anything and everything." Frank Haskell, his aide, described Gibbon as "compactly made, neither spare nor corpulent, with ruddy complexion." Except for a mustache, the brigadier was clean-shaven and, like Hancock, "always looks well dressed." Haskell said that he had an "air of calm firmness in his manner." Whenever they could, Gibbon and Hancock shared a campsite together. While en route to Gettysburg, Gibbon confided to his wife that Hancock "really does depend a good deal upon me." [67]

On the morning of July 3, Gibbon's three brigades covered the corps's front between Hays's line and the troops of the First Corps, farther south on the ridge. Brigadier General Alexander Webb's so-called Philadelphia Brigade held the stone wall in front of the copse of trees, with its right unit connecting with the left flank of the 14th Connecticut of Hays's division. Webb was twenty-eight years old, a West Pointer from a distinguished New York family. He had been serving as chief of staff of Meade's Fifth Corps until June 25, when Gibbon selected him to replace Brigadier General Joshua T. ("Paddy") Owen, the Philadelphia Brigade commander, whom Gibbon had placed under arrest for an alleged violation of orders. Five days later, Gibbon boasted to his wife, "Webb has taken hold of his Brig, with a will, comes down on them with a heavy hand and will no doubt soon make a great improvement." [68]

The Philadelphia Brigade was predominantly composed of immigrants or Americans of Irish descent. Rumors had circulated through the Second Corps that the Irishmen "never were known to stand fire." A captain in another command said that one of the brigade's regiments, the 72nd Pennsylvania, had done all of its fighting from the rear. Gibbon seems to have seized the opportunity to shelve Owen and place an officer whom he trusted at the head of the brigade. Webb was, in the words of a staff officer, "a thorough soldier, wide-awake, quick and attentive to detail." [69]

Most of Webb's troops had fought well on July 2, repulsing Ambrose Wright's Georgians and retaking a captured cannon. Later, Webb sent eight companies of the 106th Pennsylvania—two companies of the regiment were on picket duty—to Cemetery Hill, and the 71st Pennsylvania to Culp's Hill. The latter unit briefly supported George S. Greene's brigade against the Confederate assaults until its commander, Colonel Richard Penn Smith, withdrew it, claiming that "he would not have his men murdered." Smith's soldiers were, in the words of a captain, "much mortified at the conduct of the Colonel." While the 106th Pennsylvania stayed on Cemetery Hill, Smith's regiment rejoined the brigade on Cemetery Ridge.[70]

Webb had with him fewer than one thousand officers and men on the morning of July 3. The 72nd Pennsylvania, a former Zouave unit whose members had discarded the distinctive uniforms months before, was deployed behind the clump of trees. Webb ordered it to be ready to advance to the front if necessary. Half of the 71st Pennsylvania lay next to the 14th Connecticut behind the upper stone wall. The regiment's left wing was down the slope, its ranks extending from the outer angle of the wall to the companies of the 69th Pennsylvania. The 69th manned the wall in front of the copse between the batteries of Cushing and Perrin. Later, two companies of the 106th Pennsylvania returned from Cemetery Hill and were put in reserve beside the 72nd Pennsylvania.[71]

Throughout the morning, members of the 69th and 71st Pennsylvania stockpiled abandoned rifles. They tore open ball and buckshot cartridges made in England, removed the ball, and loaded each weapon with a dozen buckshot. Eventually, they had amassed "a large pile of guns." A pasture lay in front of them, extending to Emmitsburg Road and to an orchard and buildings of the Nicholas Codori farm. A small grassy knoll broke the pasture's slope about one hundred yards beyond the wall.[72]

Next to the 69th Pennsylvania's left company, separated by a small gap in the stone wall, was the 59th New York of Colonel Norman J. Hall's brigade. Two years younger than Webb and a fellow Academy graduate, Hall had been in command of the brigade since the fall of 1862. Although his conduct seemed to merit it, he had not received a promotion to brigadier general. Like Webb, he had his regiments posted in two lines on the morning of July 3.[73]

Before the battle, the 59th New York, numbering only 120 men, had been reorganized into a battalion of four companies, and now formed the right of Hall's line. Next to it was the 7th Michigan, and then the 20th Massachusetts. The latter unit was known as the "Harvard Regiment" because of the many officers who were alumni of the college. On the afternoon of July 2, the regiment had lost its commander, Colonel Paul J. Revere, mortally wounded by an artillery shell. The stone wall ended before it reached the Massachusetts men. During the night, they had dug "a little rut" about a foot deep and piled the dirt in front of them. Hall's remaining two regiments—the 42nd New

York, known as the "Tammany Regiment," and the 19th Massachusetts—were deployed to the rear along the ridge's crest.[74]

The final brigade in Gibbon's line was four regiments under Brigadier General William Harrow. A native of Kentucky, Harrow had been an attorney before the war, riding the circuit with Abraham Lincoln in Illinois and Indiana. By the spring of 1862, he held the colonelcy of the 14th Indiana and was commended for his conduct at the First Battle of Kernstown in the Shenandoah Valley. Serious health problems plagued him during the next year, but he rejoined the army in April 1863 with a brigadiership. As the army marched toward Pennsylvania, Harrow's health worsened again. He refused to relinquish command of the brigade, but questions arose about his ability to lead his men in battle. One officer grumbled that Harrow "toadies the men & calls them boys." At forty years of age, he was the division's oldest brigade commander and its ranking subordinate.[75]

Harrow's line consisted of the 82nd New York, 19th Maine, 1st Minnesota, and 15th Massachusetts. Each of these veteran regiments had been engaged on July 2, but none had been so bloodied as the 1st Minnesota. Hancock had ordered it forward to slow a Confederate brigade until he could gather more units. The Minnesotans charged and were slaughtered, losing more than two-thirds of their comrades. Reinforcements arrived and repulsed the Confederates.[76]

Harrow's "boys" dug a shallow trench during the morning of July 3. Using their bayonets and plates, they piled the dirt and topped it with stones, rails, sticks, brush, knapsacks, and blankets. One soldier did not think much of the effort, describing it as "the molehill line which passed for a barricade."[77]

Although Gibbon might have had some concerns about the grit of Webb's Philadelphia Brigade and Harrow's leadership, he could not have asked, for the most part, for better officers and men. Numbering about three thousand, they were lean, suntanned veterans who thought of themselves as "tough as a knot." Casualties on July 2 had thinned the ranks and placed subordinates at the head of some regiments, but those left in the ranks still remembered that cold, terrible day at Fredericksburg in December 1862.[78]

First Corps troops from Major General Abner Doubleday's division extended the Union line south along the ridge. On Harrow's left were the 80th New York and 151st Pennsylvania of Brigadier General Thomas A. Rowley's brigade. They had been sent as reinforcements from Cemetery Hill on the afternoon of July 2, and were halted on the ridge, remaining there during the night. Colonel Theodore B. Gates of the 80th New York commanded the pair of regiments. The New Yorkers and Pennsylvanians had torn down "an old rail fence" and built a modest fieldwork.[79]

The division's largest brigade, three regiments of nine-month Vermont troops, completed Doubleday's front. The Vermonters had been serving in the capital's defenses until attached to the army. In their new uniforms, they contrasted sharply with the veteran outfits. It did not take long for their new comrades to nickname them the "Paper Collar Brigade." As they trudged through Maryland, many of the Vermonters either straggled or simply quit the ranks. "They count their time by days," their commander, Brigadier General George J. Stannard, noted in his diary. "Consequently, they do not have any heart in the work."[80]

By the afternoon of July 2, their ranks had been reduced by the loss of the 12th and 15th Vermont to guard duty with wagons. Stannard had left the 13th, 14th, and 16th Vermont, none of whom had been in combat. Stannard, the former colonel of the 9th Vermont, had taken command of the brigade in April after its first commander, Brigadier General Edwin Stoughton, had been captured in his bed at Fairfax Court House, Virginia, by Confederate guerrilla officer John S. Mosby. A private wrote of Stannard, "You would take him for a private, if he had not any shoulder straps on."[81]

The Vermonters' baptism came on the evening of July 2. Hours before, Corporal Francis Long of the 16th Vermont had written to his wife, "We are well prepared to meet the rascals and I hope that none of them will escape." Five companies of the 13th Vermont counterattacked, retaking a Union battery and capturing about eighty Rebels and two of their cannon. It had been an auspicious beginning for the nine-month men.[82]

On the morning of July 3, Stannard placed the 13th and 14th Vermont Regiments on the line, some companies of the 16th Vermont on skirmish duty, and the others in reserve. Behind the Vermonters, Colonel Roy Stone's three regiments of Pennsylvanians formed the division's rear support. Doubleday's command numbered about three thousand officers and men, either on the line or in close reserve. Like their comrades in Gibbon's and Hays's divisions, they could readily watch the row of Confederate cannon lengthen in the fields to the west. Something was afoot with the "rascals."[83]

◦   ◦   ◦

MINUTES AFTER NOON ON July 3, John Gibbon went to army headquarters to invite George Meade to a midday meal. Meade looked, thought Gibbon, "worn and haggard." At first, the army commander objected, arguing that he had to be at headquarters to receive reports from subordinates. Gibbon was persuasive, and Meade consented.[84]

Meade, Gibbon, Hancock, and some aides gathered in a hollow behind Cemetery Ridge. Servants had prepared a chicken stew—using "an old and tough rooster"—with potatoes and coffee. The officers sat on stools or the ground, resting their plates on the top of an empty hardtack box or a camp chest. John Newton and Alfred Pleasonton, accompanied by staff officers, joined them. When they had finished, the generals smoked cigars and speculated whether Lee would attack them again.[85]

About 12:30 P.M., Meade returned to the Leister house. In case the Confederates renewed the offensive, he had prepared well for the possibility. The fighting on Culp's Hill had ended with that critical position secure. Throughout the morning, the signal station on Little Round Top had kept him informed of Confederate movements along Seminary Ridge. He knew that Henry Hunt had readied his batteries, with more than two hundred cannon deployed or in reserve. Meade had issued orders to the infantry corps. Whether he knew the numbers or not, he had positioned and alerted roughly thirteen thousand troops to support their comrades on Cemetery Hill and Cemetery Ridge. He had even directed that members of his headquarters guard who could be spared should be added. If the Confederates charged the center of the Union line on the ridge, Meade had more than twenty-two thousand officers and men either on the front line or in close reserve.[86]

Two days earlier, on July 1, while Meade awaited developments from Gettysburg at his headquarters in Taneytown, Maryland, his son, George, wrote a letter to his mother. "This is a very important point in the History of this war," he stated, "as the next fight will decide something." Now, as he and his father waited, that decision approached. It had been building all morning in the fields west of Cemetery Ridge. While the generals had prepared, men were dying, not only on Culp's Hill but there, amid the grass, wheat, and corn.[87]

8

"Bloodthirsty Business"

☙☙
☙

THE WORLD OF A SOLDIER on a battlefield was a confining one. Orders placed him at a specific location; duty governed his work. Although his experiences were unique to himself, they shared a commonality with others nearby or at his side. For hundreds of officers and men in both armies assigned to skirmish lines, the morning of July 3 passed within another reality on the battlefield. It would not equal the fearful combat on Culp's Hill, but it possessed a deadliness of its own.

Skirmish duty had a symmetry to it, as if it were a choreographed dance. Division and brigade commanders delegated usually three or four companies from regiments to advance a few hundred yards to the front. Once the details moved forward, the companies divided, with one or more placed on the line while the others formed a reserve. As the hours passed, the companies rotated from the line to the reserve. The exchange of troops invariably ignited more gunfire from opponents. The entire business frayed men's nerves and cost men's lives.[1]

Officers and men on the line used any shelter or protection they could find—depressions in the ground, fence rails, stones, and knapsacks. Some of the soldiers worked together in small groups, firing volleys at times. Most of them, however, fought as isolated individuals. All of them lay on the ground—"hugged" was the word they used—and either fired from the prone position or from a knee. Drill manuals specified seventeen movements to load and to fire a rifled musket, but veterans had learned to shorten the routine. Nevertheless, reloading meant that a soldier must expose himself. Exposure along a skirmish line meant an almost certain wound and possible death. Every time skirmishers fired their weapons, the white smoke marked their positions.[2]

Captain Benjamin W. Thompson of the 111th New York served on the skirmish line west of Cemetery Ridge on this morning. "Line fighting is barbarous, but skirmishing is savage—nay, devilish," as he described it. "To juke and hide and skulk for men and deliberately aim at and murder them one by one is far too bloodthirsty business for Christian men." Captain Silas Adams of the 19th Maine, who was posted several fields south of Thompson, said later that he and his men "had a severe and terrible day out there . . . putting it very mildly."[3]

The duel began with the morning's sun—"Enemy feel of us at diglight," in the words of a 1st Minnesota soldier. Companies from the divisions of Alexander Hays, John Gibbon, and Abner Doubleday opposed units from the Confederate divisions of Richard Anderson, William D. Pender, and Robert Rodes. Ohioans, New Yorkers, Pennsylvanians, Mainers, Minnesotans, and Connecticut and Massachusetts men fought Mississippians, Georgians, Floridians, North Carolinians, and Alabamians. With the morning's light, "we were soon popping away as lively as crickets," declared a member of the 14th Connecticut.[4]

Descriptions of the fighting varied. Some participants termed it as "spasmodic," "a hectoring fire," and "a lively popping all along the line." Captain Winfield Scott of the 126th New York claimed, "Without exception, I think it was the hottest skirmish I was ever in." Conversely, a Mississippian noted in his diary that because of the heat the men "shoot lazily." The fiercest exchanges seemed to have occurred along Hays's and Gibbon's front. A Union officer in this area was ordered "to hold on as long as he could."[5]

At times, groups of skirmishers rushed their opponents' picket line, driving it back and grabbing a few prisoners. Colonel Abner Perrin reported that the Yankees charged his pickets in "a perfect torrent," forcing the 14th South Carolina to counterattack. Much of the aggressiveness came from the Federals. Most often, it was warfare reduced to the basic—two enemies seeking to kill or to maim the other. As a Union captain put it, "Both sides were doing each other all the harm they could."[6]

Casualties mounted. When a relief party from the 14th Connecticut replaced their comrades on the line, the men found Corporal Samuel Huxham dead, shot through the head while aiming his rifle. Nearby, the 126th New York had three captains slain. Captain Orin Herendeen, a Quaker, bled to death when the femoral artery in his thigh was severed. Captain Isaac Shimer was killed instantly when a bullet passed through his open mouth and the back of his head. The third officer, Captain Charles M. Wheeler, fell as he led his men in a charge on Rebel pickets. Soldiers called a gunshot wound "a buttonhole," and numbers of men had buttonholes before the morning ended.[7]

Skirmishers of the 108th New York depleted their ammunition. A lieutenant with them ordered Corporal William H. Raymond, acting ordnance sergeant, to take a detail and to secure more cartridges. When no soldier volunteered to go with Raymond, the corporal hurried alone to the rear and grabbed a box of ammunition with one thousand rounds. Raymond raced back to the picket line and, moving along it, distributed the cartridges. He was an inviting target for the Confederates, who directed their fire at him. The corporal completed his mission unscathed but with seven bullet holes in his coat. He would receive a Medal of Honor for his action.[8]

Sergeant Benjamin Hirst, who had wanted "to be counted in" if there were a battle, fought with his comrades in the 14th Connecticut on the skirmish line. When his rifle became fouled with a bullet lodged in the barrel, Hirst placed the weapon's butt against a fence rail, removed a shoestring, tied it to the trigger, and pulled. The rifle fired but did not explode. The sergeant cleaned the barrel, reloaded, and continued "to be counted in."[9]

To the right of the 14th Connecticut—closer to the town, near the Emanuel Trostle house—about one hundred men of the 111th New York spent the morning engaged with the Confederates from regiments in Long Lane. When a relief party from the 39th New York arrived, its commander, Major Hugo Hildebrand, demanded that the men of the 111th move immediately. Captain Sebastian D. Holmes of the 111th objected, apparently with some heated words. A furious Hildebrand threatened to shoot the captain and reached for his revolver. Holmes drew his first and pointed it at the major, who suddenly turned his horse and rode to the rear.[10]

A Second Corps soldier recounted in a letter to his parents that in front of his division's pickets "nearly the whole line [of enemy skirmishers] threw down their arms and ran into our lines, the rebel batteries shelling them as they ran." The deserters told the Federals that "it was the hardest fight they had ever been in, and they were whipped this time sure." The Confederates claimed that their generals had lied to them, telling the troops "they would have nothing but militia to fight, who would fire one round and run, but instead of that they found the Army of the Potomac."[11]

The struggle between the pickets for narrow swaths of ground was accompanied on occasions by the bellow of cannon. Nearly all of the artillery fire came from Confederate batteries in Hill's Third Corps, usually lasting about ten minutes at a time. A Union gunner stated, "We could see them all the forenoon getting their batteries in position but wasnt allowed to open on them." Federal skirmishers, however, fired on the Rebel gun crews, drawing a few rounds from the artillerists in response. The Southern rounds exploded a few limbers and caissons, injuring or killing artillerymen and nearby infantry soldiers. One unfortunate victim was Private Myron Clark of the 14th Vermont. On July 1, Clark had fallen out of the ranks during the march to Gettysburg. He rejoined the regiment the next day, then died on July 3, when a solid shot smashed into him.[12]

The round that killed Clark could have come from Captain William W. Parker's Richmond Battery, one of the more active Confederate units. While Parker's men were engaged, Pat McNeil, a driver with the battery, relieved one of the gunners. McNeil had deserted in the winter of 1863 and was captured and court-martialed. Several days before the battle, Confederate authorities had granted a general pardon for noncapital offenses, which included McNeil. As he worked with a crew, McNeil saw a wounded Union soldier who lay in front of the cannon. He crawled to the man and dragged him back to the battery. When McNeil stood, a Federal artillery shot struck him, ripping off both of his legs. McNeil exclaimed, "Oh, my wife and children!" Unconscious, he was carried to a field hospital, where he soon died.[13]

Some of the nastiest fighting occurred between Union infantry and artillery on Cemetery Hill and Confederate sharpshooters huddled behind barricades in streets and alleys and sequestered in buildings in Gettysburg. The Southerners, mainly members of a battalion of the 5th Alabama, occupied the second stories and garrets of houses, church steeples, and outbuildings. They fired from windows, usually from behind piles of mattresses and furniture, or through holes they had cut in walls. The houses and businesses manned by the Alabamians extended north from the intersection of Baltimore Pike and Emmitsburg Road to a hill where High Street crossed Baltimore Pike. This section of the town became a dangerous area for both soldiers and civilians.[14]

Major Eugene Blackford, who commanded the battalion of Alabamians, wrote, "My orders were to fire incessantly, without regard to ammunition."

He instructed his men to focus on Union batteries on Cemetery Hill, which Blackford noted appeared as an inverted "V" from town. The Alabamians opened fire at the sound of a bugle. From Cemetery Hill, Union infantrymen replied.[15]

The gray-coated sharpshooters kept up a sustained, harassing fire throughout the morning. After a while, the Alabamians complained of sore shoulders from the constant kicks of their rifles. They rapidly depleted their ammunition, and Blackford sent a detail of men through the streets with "a small baker's cart" to collect discarded cartridges. The major also put the buglers to work at baking bread and raiding grocery stores for meat, cheese, and coffee. Blackford even grabbed a rifle and, by his count, fired eighty-four shots at the enemy.[16]

On the height, Union generals and privates alike cursed the Rebels. One Federal recalled that a group of Southerners behind a barricade in a street drew the Northerners' fire by placing their hats on sticks and holding them above the makeshift protection. When the Yankees fired, the Confederates stood and returned it. As more men were hit and the frustrations grew among the Federals, batteries opened on a church and houses. Ten volunteers from the 45th New York advanced and silenced a nest of Rebels at the edge of town.[17]

When Oliver O. Howard, commander of the Eleventh Corps, wanted a party of Southerners in a small brick building on Washington Street eliminated, five soldiers from the 55th Ohio stepped forward. Readying themselves, they waited for a signal. When it came, however, only Private Benjamin Pease rushed ahead to the front of the house. Pease pounded on the door with his rifle butt, shouting for the Rebels to surrender. Five Confederates walked through the door, met by a solitary Yankee with a leveled weapon. Pease's act earned him a Medal of Honor.[18]

At places in the southern end of the town, the opponents dueled from nearby buildings. A number of Federals occupied Snider's Wagon Hotel at the intersection of Baltimore Pike and Emmitsburg Road. From windows and holes punched through the roof, the Northerners engaged some Rebels in John Rupp's tannery, less than one hundred paces up the pike. Neither side incurred many casualties, although the numerous nearby buildings that still stand today bear the marks of the intense gunfire. Blackford claimed that the Yankees could not inflict "any great harm" on the Alabamians because of the protection afforded by the structures.[19]

Civilians residing in this section of Gettysburg either had abandoned their homes or sheltered themselves inside the buildings. Some attended to chores despite the fighting around them. About 150 yards south of the Wagon Hotel, where the pike began its ascent of Cemetery Hill, stood a double brick house. In the northern half of the residence lived Mrs. Georgia Anna Wade McClellan, who had given birth to a son on June 26. With her husband away in the army, she had her mother and twenty-year-old sister, Mary Virginia Wade, to help her with the infant. On July 3, as Mary Virginia—nicknamed Ginnie (not Jennie, as frequently reported)—kneaded dough for biscuits, she was killed by a stray Confederate sharpshooter's bullet that had passed through the door and struck her. Mary Virginia Wade was the only Gettysburg civilian to be slain during the battle.[20]

Death had come through a door to the young woman, suddenly, accidentally, devoid of meaning. The skirmishing and sharpshooting were indeed work unfit "for Christian men." The "bloodthirsty business" went on, however, through the morning, to a climax marked by smoke and flames.[21]

⁂   ⁂   ⁂

THE STONE-AND-BRICK BARN of William Bliss loomed above the surrounding landscape as if it had been built for a medieval lord. Seventy-five feet in length and thirty-three feet in width, the structure rose forty or more feet above the ground. Vertical slits decorated the front and rear of the upper story, while its northern and southern ends held double rows of windows. The barn's bank or bridge of ground to the upper story abutted against the stable's western wall. Five doors opened into the stable along its eastern wall. A Federal, who could see it plainly from Cemetery Ridge, described it as "an expensively and elaborately built structure, as barns go." The Northerner also called it "almost a citadel in itself," a "paradise for sharp-shooters with long range rifles."[22]

Since the morning of July 2, the Bliss farm had been contested ground. Skirmishers from both armies fought for possession of the barn, the family home—a weatherboarded log-and-frame house located nearly two hundred feet north of the barn—and an extensive ten-acre orchard west of the buildings. At 10:00 A.M. on July 2, the Confederates seized the two structures and opened fire on Cemetery Ridge, situated seven hundred yards to the east. Whichever side held the barn and the "damned white house," as the Yankees termed the Bliss home, controlled the nearby fields between Cemetery and Seminary ridges.[23]

The Southerners clung to the "citadel" and house until late in the afternoon, when four companies of the 12th New Jersey charged and scattered the Rebels. The Bliss family had evacuated the farm the day before, leaving its possessions in the house and barn. When the New Jerseymen took the place, some of them grabbed jars of preserves, stuffing them into their knapsacks. The Federals' stay was brief, however, as Brigadier General Carnot Posey's Mississippi brigade advanced across the fields toward Cemetery Ridge, chasing the New Jerseymen. When Posey's attack faltered and receded, the brigadier ordered Colonel William H. Taylor and the 12th Mississippi to hold the Bliss barn overnight.[24]

At daylight on July 3, Taylor's Mississippians resumed their sharpshooting toward Cemetery Ridge and Union skirmishers along Emmitsburg Road. After three hours of this fire from the barn, Alexander Hays selected five companies of the 12th New Jersey, under Captain Richard Thompson, to re- take the structure. Thompson led them across the road and into the fields beyond, where they halted and formed a column by companies.[25]

In front of the New Jersey veterans, a 350-yard-wide flat knoll rose, concealing them from the Confederates and blocking their view of the farm. A spur of Cemetery Ridge, the knoll ran from Ziegler's Grove southwest for a half-mile. Emmitsburg Road had been cut through its spine, and at its western base Stevens Run flowed north from the Bliss farm into town. The 8th Ohio had been fighting on it throughout the morning, sparring with the Mississippians and Confederate troops in the Long Lane, which turned west about three hundred yards north of the Bliss farm.[26]

When Thompson had readied his troops, they moved to the attack. As the Yankees passed over the knoll's broad crest, the Mississippians and skirmishers from Brigadier General Edward L. Thomas's Georgia brigade in front of Long Lane unleashed bursts of gunfire into the Federals. The Rebels' initial blast knocked down a lieutenant and mortally wounded three soldiers. Thompson's men kept going, now at a double-quick toward the barn. Fanning out, they burst through the stable doors and began climbing up ladders into the main floor. The Mississippians bolted out the rear doors and into the orchard, where they rallied and returned the fire. The Federals bagged a major and four enlisted men, thrusting their bayonets into straw piles to try to get others.[27]

Thompson's men dueled with their opponents, who began inching closer to the barn. On Seminary Ridge, Confederate batteries hurled solid shots against the walls, creating a cloud of lime dust in the barn. Sergeant Frank M.

Riley climbed up on a crossbeam to a window and fired at the Rebels as his comrades passed rifles up to him. The Mississippians and Georgians kept closing in. Without orders to hold the barn, Thompson ordered a withdrawal. On the knoll, the 8th Ohio pressed ahead and covered the New Jerseymen's retreat. More of the Federals fell as they raced over the knoll and to shelter on the opposite slope. When Thompson re-formed the companies, he had lost a pair of officers and more than twenty men. Behind them, the Mississippians reoccupied the barn and entered the house.[28]

Now the Confederates seemed to direct their shots at Captain William A. Arnold's Battery A, 1st Rhode Island, posted north of the copse of trees behind the inner stone wall. Arnold soon complained to Colonel Thomas A. Smyth, whose brigade manned the wall in front of the cannon, asking Smyth if he could not burn the barn. Alexander Hays had decided, meanwhile, to try to retake and to hold the buildings one more time. Hays gave the order to Smyth, who assigned the work to Major Theodore G. Ellis and the 14th Connecticut. With two companies on the skirmish line, Ellis divided his eight companies into two detachments. Captain Samuel A. Moore took half the command, sixty men in all, and started for the barn.[29]

Like Thompson's 12th New Jersey detail earlier, Moore's troops crossed Emmitsburg Road and halted in the fields. This time there would be no formation; the order was, "Each man reach barn as best he could." The men scattered and ran toward the barn. When they reached the knoll, the Confederates from the Bliss barn and house and from along Long Lane raked them. One Connecticut soldier said it was like "dodging ten thousand shafts of lightning." One bullet struck Jeff Brainard, a nineteen-year-old illiterate farm boy who was known as "the life of his company, full of rollicking fun." At first, his comrades thought it was another of his antics, until he screamed, "My God! My God, I'm hit!—Oh, how it hurts me!" His friends carried him back to the ridge, where he died with a chaplain at his side.[30]

Once again, the Mississippians scampered from the barn into the orchard. Moore's Federals regained the stable and upper floor, returning the fire from the orchard and the house. From Cemetery Ridge, Smyth and Ellis could see that Moore's detachment was outnumbered and could be trapped in the building. Smyth ordered Ellis to seize the house with his four remaining companies. They started down the slope.[31]

When they crossed the knoll, Ellis's detachment encountered a more scathing fire than Moore's men had. From Long Lane, Thomas's Georgians triggered a volley that enfiladed the Federals. Numbers of them went down, but the others kept going. On reaching the house, the Connecticut men opened fire through the windows on the Rebels inside. One Mississippian fought from the doorway until Sergeant Samuel Scanton killed him "as he would have shot a squirrel on his fathers farm." Most of the Confederates escaped as Ellis's men poured into the house.[32]

Within minutes, the struggle intensified. Thirty Confederate cannon on Seminary Ridge opened with solid shot and case shot on the barn and house. From his line of guns, Porter Alexander watched the Third Corps artillerists work their pieces and grumbled about the waste of vital ammunition before the cannonade. "I would not let one of my guns fire a shot," he wrote later.[33]

Inside the house, the Federals discovered quickly that the weatherboarding could stop neither artillery rounds nor minié balls. Ellis ordered it evacuated. Some of his men ran outside and sheltered themselves behind a woodpile, while most of them darted for the barn through a gauntlet of fire. The Confederate gunners then poured shells into the brick upper story, their explosions raining shards of metal upon the occupants. From the orchard, the Mississippians targeted the windows. One of their shots hit Corporal Thomas W. Gardner, who had been firing from a window, and "plowed a permanent furrow along the top of his head."[34]

On Cemetery Ridge, Alexander Hays had had enough. Granted discretionary orders by Winfield Hancock to burn the buildings, Hays turned to Colonel Clinton D. MacDougall of the 111th New York and asked him for a volunteer to carry the order to the barn. MacDougall shouted the request to his men, and Sergeant Charles A. Hitchcock stepped forward. Hays told the sergeant what he wanted done. When he had gathered some matches and paper, Hitchcock headed for the barn at a double-quick, running a jagged route across the fields.[35]

No sooner had Hitchcock departed than Hays decided, as a precaution, to send a mounted courier with the order. Captain James P. Postles of Smyth's staff volunteered to deliver it. Postles rode his horse at a walk across Emmitsburg Road and then spurred it into a "gentle lope." The Rebels saw him coming and aimed at horse and rider. "It was a constant wonder and surprise to me," he remembered, "that none of the bullets, which I heard whistling and so close to me, had hit me. . . . It immediately flashed upon me that my only chance of safety was in keeping my horse in motion." Both he and his mount made it through unscathed. When he reined up before the barn, he shouted, "Colonel Smyth orders you to burn the house and barn and retire." Behind him came Hitchcock, who repeated the order to Ellis.[36]

Ellis instructed the men to gather the hay and straw into piles and sent a detail to the house. While some of them obeyed the orders, others removed their dead and wounded comrades from the buildings. In the house, the Federals stacked furniture and bedding together. When ready, a few men lit the piles and joined their comrades in the barnyard. Ellis waited until the smoke and flames would provide them some concealment before he led them back to Cemetery Ridge. As they watched the fire embrace both buildings, chickens flew from the barn and were grabbed by the soldiers. At the least, they would have a noonday meal for their efforts. Finally, Ellis ordered them away. They did not halt until they reached Emmitsburg Road.[37]

When the flames caved in the roof of the barn, Union skirmishers in the fields and their comrades on Cemetery Ridge cheered. The fires would smolder for a long time. The "citadel" and the "damned white house" had come down. With them, William Bliss and his family lost their home and livelihood. In time, they would relocate to New York, and file a claim with the government for $3,256.08 in damages. Bliss sold the land to Nicholas Codori for one thousand dollars, but the family never received any money from the government. For his ride, James Postles would receive a Medal of Honor.[38]

✧   ✧   ✧

THE SMOKE FROM THE BLISS BARN and house hung in the air as if it were a funeral pyre. But the fires had brought a silence to the battlefield. The early morning's clouds—"a thick morning," in the words of one Union artillerist—had dissipated into a sky of bright sunshine and cumulus clouds. A breeze from the southwest provided little comfort from the increasing heat and humidity. By noon, the temperature had probably passed eighty degrees, and an "intolerable" sun beat down upon men in both armies—the Confederates lying in the fields waiting for the order to charge, and the Federals resting behind stone walls and small mounds of dirt and rails on Cemetery Ridge. As if by mutual consent, the armies paused, taking a midday respite from the slaughter of their fellow men.[39]

It was the stillness that they would remember. "The silence and sultriness of a July noon are supreme," thought Frank Haskell. The quietness enveloped the field. A Union artilleryman claimed that he heard honeybees at work on Cemetery Hill. A Confederate artillery officer on Seminary Ridge believed that the silence and atmosphere "produced a feeling of nervous expectancy, which sometimes is felt when an electrical storm is pending."[40]

Men attended to matters during this welcome interlude. The 8th Ohio withdrew all its skirmishers to Emmitsburg Road, where the soldiers rested in a ditch by the roadbed, cooked coffee, and replenished their cartridge boxes. Nearby, knots of soldiers walked to the Nicholas Codori farm and filled canteens from its well. On the ridge, details from the three nine-month Vermont regiments gathered more fence rails for their modest fieldworks. Colonel Francis V. Randall of the 13th Vermont instructed a private to take his two horses and his drummer-boy son to the rear. Randall expected "a hot fight." [41]

Private Patrick Taylor and two friends in the 1st Minnesota had finished a sad duty, the burying of Taylor's brother, who had been killed on July 2. Not far away, on the Lewis A. Bushman farm, Lieutenant William H. Crennell of the 140th New York had overseen the interment of his commander, Colonel Patrick O'Rorke, and Brigadier General Stephen H. Weed. Both of the officers had been slain on Little Round Top. In his diary, Crennell wrote that it was "a very perplexing job on account of the lack of material etc for the coffins." [42]

In the Union Third Corps, Private Michael Duddy of the 114th Pennsylvania sat gagged and bucked with bayonets tied behind his knees and in his mouth. Earlier in the morning, a barrel of whiskey had been given to the regiment. Duddy became drunk and threatened to kill Captain Henry M. Eddy. A sergeant intervened, throwing Duddy to the ground. Comrades bound up the private until he had sobered. Elsewhere in the corps, a young woman distributed loaves of bread that she had baked. The corps's commander, Major General Daniel Sickles, was en route to a hospital after his leg had been amputated. [43]

Henry Hunt had seldom rested since he had arrived at Gettysburg, and continued to work during the lull. He shifted forward Captain Andrew Cowan's 1st New York Independent Battery to below the crest of Cemetery Ridge. To the left and rear of Cowan, Captain Jabez J. Daniels's 9th Michigan Battery unlimbered in low ground north and slightly west of Lieutenant Colonel Freeman McGilvery's line of cannon. Near Ziegler's Grove, a section of the 9th Massachusetts Light Artillery was posted about seventy-five yards north of the Bryan barn, and two Napoleons of Batteries F and K, 3rd United States Artillery, moved into place in the Bryan orchard, facing southwest toward the Codori farm and the outer angle of the stone wall. [44]

Nearly fifty miles to the northwest, residents of Mercersburg, Pennsylvania, were eating their midday meals. Earlier in the morning, they had come together in the Methodist church for "the first united prayer-meeting" in the village. It had been "called forth by the peculiar condition of the country." On the battlefield at Gettysburg, meanwhile, a Union soldier recorded in his diary, "I think it will bee a day long to bee Remembered in Gathersburgh." At noon, a North Carolina civilian, who had joined the army in search of a friend, wrote in a letter, "The enemy fight harder than usual." [45]

❂ ❂ ❂

CONFEDERATE ARTILLERIST PORTER ALEXANDER read the contents of the note from Longstreet. "If the artillery fire does not have the effect to drive off the enemy or greatly demoralize him so as to make our effort pretty certain," stated the lieutenant general, "I would prefer that you should not advise Gen Pickett to make the charge. I shall rely a great deal upon your good judgment to determine the matter, and shall expect you to let Gen Pickett know when the moment offers." [46]

The words hit Alexander, as he put it, with a "sudden shock." Longstreet had placed the responsibility for whether the assault should go forward or not on the young officer, and Alexander understood that at once. "I was by no means ready to go for that place on my own judgment," he declared afterward. Securing a piece of paper, Alexander replied: "I will only be able to judge the effect of our fire on the enemy by his return fire as his infantry is but little exposed to view & the smoke will obscure the whole field. If as I infer from your note there is any alternative to this attack it should be carefully considered before opening our fire, for it will take all the arty ammunition we have left to test this one thoroughly & if the result is unfavorable we will have none left for another effort & even if this is entirely successful it can only be so at a very bloody cost." [47]

Robert E. Lee had proposed this charge. Longstreet had opposed it, believing that it could not succeed and would result in a needless sacrifice of valuable lives. Then, when Lee had assigned him command of the operation, Longstreet had not wanted it. He knew, however, when he wrote the note to Alexander at about 11:30 A.M., that there was no turning back. Instead, he tried, seemingly, to shift his responsibility to a trusted subordinate. As he read Alexander's response, Longstreet must have understood how close he had come to abdicating his duty. He hurriedly penned another note, which Alexander received at 12:15 P.M.: "The intention is to advance the Inf. If the Arty. Has the desired effect of driving the enemy off or having other effect such as to warrant us in making the attack. When that moment arrives advise Gen P. and of course advance such artillery as you can use in aiding the attack."[48]

Although ambiguous, Longstreet's second message sought the artillery colonel's opinion as to the most opportune time for the infantry's advance. Brigadier General Ambrose R. Wright was with Alexander when both notes arrived. Wright's Georgians had reached Cemetery Ridge on the afternoon of July 2, and Alexander discussed the contents of each note with the brigadier. The problem, Wright affirmed, was not to get there but "to *hold it* as the whole Federal Army was massed so close to it, & our supports necessarily so far off & scattered." Alexander replied that he had heard that Lee had planned to use every available brigade in the assault. This seemed to allay Wright's concern about support troops.[49]

Alexander decided to talk with Pickett to "see how he felt about the charge, without telling him my object." When Alexander found Pickett, the general "was entirely sanguine of success in the charge and was only congratulating himself on the opportunity." With that, Alexander returned to his post, convinced, as he stated it, that only "one supreme effort" by the artillery might result in success, and that "*if the artillery opened Pickett must charge.*" He scribbled quickly a second note to Longstreet: "General: When our artillery fire is doing its best I shall advise General Pickett to advance."[50]

When Longstreet read Alexander's brief response, he had an order prepared for his chief of artillery, Colonel James B. Walton. "Let the batteries open," Longstreet directed. "Order great care and precision in firing. If the batteries at the Peach Orchard cannot be used against the point we intend attacking let them open on the enemy on Rocky Hill [Little Round Top]." Longstreet gave the order to a courier and then walked into Spangler's Woods, where he lay down in hopes of "some new thought that might aid the assaulting column."[51]

The courier reined up behind the guns of the Washington Artillery in a field west of Emmitsburg Road, opposite the David Klingle house. Walton read the contents and instructed Major Benjamin F. Eshleman, commander of the battalion, to have the two signal guns fired. The gunners of Captain Merritt B. Miller's 3rd Company stood by a pair of Napoleons. It was 1:00 P.M., or a few minutes after. As one of Longstreet's staff officers had predicted only three hours before, "This will be a great day in history."[52]

9

"The Air Seethed with Old Iron"

T HE LOUISIANA GUNNERS of the Washington Artillery pulled the lanyards on the Napoleons. The sharp, distinct explosions from one cannon and then the other ended the stillness. Buglers with the Confederate batteries sounded "Commence Firing." Scores of gunners yanked on more lanyards, and a roar of hellfire engulfed the battlefield. A watching Alabamian thought he was seeing the Judgment Day. "When the heavens are rolled together as a scroll in the last days," he marveled, "I doubt whether it will present a more awe inspiring spectacle."[1]

The Confederate artillerymen reloaded the cannon and fired again—working "slowly and deliberately," as ordered. But the discharges were "incessant." Smoke rolled back with each shot, smothering the ground and creating a curtain of white. "The very air seemed as if about to take fire," wrote Lieutenant Colonel Hilary Hebert of the 8th Alabama. From where Hebert watched, fifty yards behind the row of pieces, "the artillerists seemed like weird specters of the damned in the place of departed spirits plying the hellish work of destruction."[2]

Other onlooking Confederates shared the awe of the Alabamian. "Nothing you've ever heard or read of can give you an idea of the terrific fire Lee

opened on their heights," exclaimed a Georgian. A North Carolinian declared, "It was awfully grand and excelled anything I had ever conceived
of. . . . The very earth shook and the tremendous roar was deafing." Another
Alabamian wrote, "I thought that I had heard cannonading before, but not
so." A recruit in the 14th North Carolina asserted, "The men that have been
in service from the beginning, say they never heard anything like this."[3]

Union soldiers on Cemetery Hill and Cemetery Ridge, the targets of the
cannonade, also thought of Biblical images to describe the fury. "It seemed as
if all the Demons in Hell were let loose," avowed Sergeant Benjamin Hirst of
the 14th Connecticut, "and were Howling through the Air." A soldier in the
1st Minnesota wrote that the massed Confederate cannon looked like "banks
of white vapor, from beneath which tongues of fire were incessantly darting."
The shells came "howling, shrieking, striking, exploding, tearing." He admitted that "we had been badly scared many times before this but never quite as
badly as then. We commended our soul to God, shut our teeth *hard* and lay
flat on the ground, expecting every minute to be blown to atoms."[4]

The Minnesotans were not alone in their supplications to the divine or in
their fearfulness. "The Command was given to keep well down which was re-
ligiously obeyed," recalled a Maine soldier. A 69th Pennsylvania man, lying in
front of the copse of trees, declared, "After the cannonading began, we were
all hugging the earth and we would have liked to go into it if we could." To the
Pennsylvanian's right, a member of the 12th New Jersey believed that the
cannonade "was awful and sublime," but then added, "We fairly rooted and
felt most grateful and thankful that we were alive to root." Another Yankee
sheltered himself behind the root of "a small bushy tree" and was glad for the
modest protection.[5]

"The air seethed with old iron," wrote Private John W. Haley of the 17th
Maine. "We hardly knew what it meant." The 13th Vermont's Sergeant
George H. Scott said, "We hardly dared rise on our elbows." One of Scott's
comrades told his wife the exploding shells churned up so much dirt that they
believed they would be buried under it. Captain Josiah C. Fuller of the 32nd
Massachusetts described the sounds of solid shots and shells as "wizz, bang,
bun, chug." When shells burst above their heads, the detonations were like
the discharge of a cannon next to their ears. For days afterward, men complained of deafness. Alexander Webb, whose brigade lay at the seeming vortex of the onslaught, confessed to his father, "I have been through many
battles, in all sorts of places, under all fires but never have I heard such cannonading as they opened on our lines." It was, Webb added, "terrible."[6]

Up and down the Union line the infantrymen endured the maelstrom, helpless to respond to the ceaseless bombardment. For the troops of Alexander Hays's division in Ziegler's Grove, severed limbs from the oak and hickory trees added to the danger. It was "perfectly awful, murderous," according to a 108th New York man. One Federal soldier noted that the birds in the grove began to fly wildly in the air, "all out of their wits with fright." Numbers of men in the New York regiment "were so shook up" they began to waver. Lieutenant David Shields of Hays's staff rode to them, shouting encouragement and telling them to stay at their posts. Some of them broke for the rear. "It was an appalling sight," complained Shields.[7]

Officers in the 108th drew swords, threatening to use them on any man who left the ranks. Brigade commander Colonel Thomas Smyth went to the regiment to restore order and was struck in the face with a piece of a shell. When Hays learned of it, he sent Lieutenant Theron E. Parsons, one of Smyth's aides, to inform Lieutenant Colonel Francis E. Pierce of the 108th that he now commanded the brigade. As Parsons approached his horse, a shell killed the animal. "I went across the field towards the colonel," Parsons wrote later in his diary, "but no more expected to reach him than to fly."[8]

On the right of the 108th New York, lying in support of George Woodruff's battery, the 126th New York suffered a fearful punishment. Seeing that the men could not withstand much more, Colonel Clinton MacDougall decided to move them into the grove behind the crest. Few of the soldiers wanted to stand up and march through the torrent of cannon fire. "We attempted to form our men, but it was impossible," stated a captain. "We drove them before us up the hill more like cattle than soldiers." Hays and aides assisted MacDougall and his officers in pushing the troops over the crest.[9]

Hays passed along the ranks constantly, exposing himself to the rain of fire and trying to steel the troops while they endured the pounding. "I must say," wrote a New Yorker the next day, "I think he is the bravest division general I ever saw in the saddle. Most of the time he was riding up and down the lines in front of us, exhorting the 'boys' to stand fast and fight like men." Hays told them to clean and to load all discarded rifles. He believed that the cannonade was a prelude to an infantry assault.[10]

Shortly after the Confederate fire began, Hays ordered the 111th New York out of Ziegler's Grove and into line near the stone wall. The New Yorkers hurried forward through "this infernal shelling" and deployed behind the Bryan barn, with their left companies overlapping the right of the 12th New Jersey at the wall. Most of the New Yorkers lay on the ground; a few took shelter behind the barn. These latter men stayed there until a shell blew through the wooden wall, decapitating one soldier and severing both legs of another.[11]

David Shields was with Hays throughout most of the bombardment. Hays had known Shields when he commanded the 63rd Pennsylvania. When the general needed staff officers, he selected Shields as one of them. Months after the battle, Hays recommended the lieutenant's promotion to Governor Andrew Gregg Curtin, stating, "Although he is quite a young man I know no equal to him for cool courage, except Charlie Campbell [former colonel of the 57th Pennsylvania], and he does not know the difference between minnie balls and Brandorths pills."[12]

When Hays sent Shields to army headquarters during the cannonade, the staff officer encountered Lieutenant Colonel Levi Crandall, commander of the 125th New York, behind the crest of Cemetery Ridge. Crandall was sitting on the ground holding the reins of his horse and claiming that he was ill. On his return ride, Shields stopped a second time and urged Crandall to rejoin his regiment, arguing that it was safer on the ridge. Crandall refused. "He was a coward in action," declared Shields.[13]

As the storm of iron continued, Hays became increasingly concerned about the stability of Alexander Webb's brigade on his left and in front of the copse of trees. He sent Shields, telling the lieutenant, "Dave, go over to Webb and see how he is standing it." When Shields had delivered Hays's message, Webb replied that "he was doing all that could be expected." Could Webb's men hold the line if the Rebel infantry attacked? Shields asked. Webb said that they could and would.[14]

Probably few officers and men in his brigade or in Gibbon's division shared Webb's confidence. They must have thought that the entire Confederate artillery corps had targeted them specifically. Colonel Richard Penn Smith of the 71st Pennsylvania exclaimed later: "My God it was terrible. . . . The field was a grave. Such a sight you never saw." Frank Haskell described the flash of shell bursts as "a bright gleam of lightning radiating from a point." He saw the knapsack of one of Webb's men ripped from his back, leaving the soldier unharmed. Another soldier cowered with his nose on the ground in terror behind a stone "the size of a common water-bucket." Webb was struck three or four times with pieces of stone. "I knew then," he told his wife, "we were to have a fierce attack."[15]

"All we had to do while undergoing the shelling was to chew tobacco, watch caissons explode, and wonder if the next shot would hit you," remembered a soldier in William Harrow's brigade, posted south of Webb's regiments on the ridge. "On the whole it was not a happy time." A member of the 1st Minnesota in the same brigade concluded, after he had seen a solid shot plow into the ground where a soldier had been lying moments before, "I had just as leave and be a thousand miles from here as not." The Rebels, he thought, "could not kill me any younger & that they cant do it but once."[16]

Like Alexander Hays, Gibbon moved among his units on horseback and on foot. At the cannonade's outset, Gibbon's "faithful old orderly," John Sheehan, was killed by a piece of a shell as he went to the rear for the general's horse. An old artilleryman, Gibbon noted that a shell from a twelve-pound Napoleon could be seen in its final flight as "it curved gracefully." Rifled cannon shells were, however, "invisible" and "came tumbling along through the air in their crooked flight and soul shuddering noise which gave you the impression they were liable to strike any where and every where."[17]

Gibbon told Frank Haskell once: "I am not a member of any church, but I have always had a strong religious feeling; and so in all these battles I have always believed that I was in the hands of God; and that I should be unharmed or not, according to his will. For this reason, I think it is, I am always ready to go where duty calls, no matter how great the danger."[18]

The division commander walked the entire length of his line, even crossing the stone wall held by Webb's Pennsylvanians and going into the field beyond. He stopped frequently, with arms folded, and watched the explosions of shells near his men. One of his troops wrote that as he and his comrades looked at Gibbon the general was "seeming to say, Boys, this is the way to face danger. We all noticed it and many said, See There, see Gen. Gibbons."[19]

Within the ranks of Abner Doubleday's First Corps division on Gibbon's left, the nine-month volunteers of the Vermont Brigade held up well under the pummeling. One of the Vermonters stated that veterans told them later that the artillery fire at Malvern Hill and Antietam was "but a salute" as compared to this cannonade. When it began, George Stannard shifted the 13th and 14th Vermont forward about fifteen rods to shelter the men behind "some rocky points." The Vermonters hurriedly gathered loose rocks and rails and piled them on the ground. Nineteen-year-old Private Silas Mozier stood up, tossed aside his rifle and gear, and ran away. Men in his regiment shouted, "Shoot the damn coward," but apparently none did.[20]

Behind the Vermonters, a shell cut off the top of a soldier's head in the 143th Pennsylvania. When another man inquired if it had killed him, "the boys roared with laughter," recounted Sergeant Simon Hubler, "and called him a d——d fool for asking such a foolish question." Other shells wounded

Doubleday and Brigadier General Thomas A. Rowley. Doubleday was struck in the neck and knocked from his mount.[21]

During the initial minutes of the cannonade, however, no Union troops endured worse punishment than the artillerists and infantrymen on Cemetery Hill. As Porter Alexander had argued, the Federal position on the height was vulnerable to enfilading fire. When the Confederate batteries opened, the pair of Whitworth rifles and the rifled pieces located north of Chambersburg Road and the cannon on Benner's Hill targeted the salient in the Union line. From the Southerners' first shot, according to Major Thomas W. Osborn, commander of the Eleventh Corps artillery, the Rebels had the range and elevation "exactly." "They commanded my guns to absolute perfection," declared Osborn. The havoc, he said, "was fearful."[22]

The shells and solid shots struck caissons filled with ammunition, slaughtered teams of horses, shattered and overturned tombstones in the cemetery, and disabled cannon. "The cannonade was truly frightful," said Major General Carl Schurz, who walked among his troops in his Eleventh Corps division, smoking a cigar and joking with them. He stated that only he himself and the battery crews were on their feet. One shell smashed into a fence in front of the 45th New York, killing "a large number of men, sending hats, limbs & bodies flying through the air." Another shell nearly killed or wounded Oliver O. Howard, the corps commander, as he stood near the gate of Evergreen Cemetery. One round passed through six horses who were standing broadside to each other.[23]

The two Whitworth cannon fired an elongated "steel bolt" that had a distinctive "sharp whistle" as it passed through the air. When the Federals saw one of the rounds plow into the ground, they joked that the enemy was firing "railroad bars." When an infantry brigade received orders to change its position, a captain reported that as they marched it seemed "as though every portion of the atmosphere contained a deadly missle." Colonel Charles S. Wainwright, the First Corps artillery commander, noted in his diary afterward that he had never known of Confederate batteries "to be so lavish of ammunition."[24]

Despite the destruction wrought on Cemetery Hill, Wainwright and Osborn claimed that many of the Confederate rounds passed over their heads or the shells failed to detonate. Wainwright estimated that nine out of ten shots sailed past, but this seems to be inflated. Most accounts of Union troops on the skirmish line west of Cemetery Hill and Cemetery Ridge note that many of the men slept during the cannonade, except for two companies of the 14th

Connecticut. Where these units lay, they would have been subjected to over-shots from Confederate guns on Benner's Hill. One of the Connecticut soldiers described their plight as "a terrible situation to be in, midway between the two armies. How we did hug the ground, expecting every moment to be our last! No matter who was hit, you dare not move hand or foot; to do so was almost sure death."[25]

But many Confederate rounds fired from Seminary Ridge and the fields east of it did fly over Cemetery Ridge. Either the Southern gun crews miscalculated the range or, most likely, many of the fuses on the shells failed. Consequently, the area behind Cemetery Ridge, in the fields along Taneytown Road and Baltimore Pike, received a pounding. As soon as the Confederates opened fire, "the plain behind the ridge," an officer asserted, "was almost immediately swept of all camp followers and the unordered attendants of an army." Teamsters lashed their horses, driving headquarters and ammunition wagons farther to the rear. Stragglers or "loose men," remarked a soldier, disappeared immediately.[26]

Surgeons and assistants, tending to the wounded in houses and barns that served as field hospitals along the two roads, evacuated patients as fast as they could. One doctor stated that there was a "general stampede" from one barn. At another site, a string of nearly thirty ambulances filled rapidly, and within minutes the clover field where the vehicles had been parked looked "as if it had been plowed" by the artillery rounds. A team of Union surgeons fled from one house, deserting the wounded soldiers who lay in the yard. Lieutenant Zilba B. Graham of the 16th Michigan found them there. Most of the men were Confederates, and they pleaded with Graham to get them drinks of water. The owner of the house had removed the crank from his well, growling that he would not have it pumped dry. Graham found him, "a mean Dutchman," in the cellar with his family. The man refused Graham's request for the crank until the lieutenant threatened to shoot him.[27]

When solid shots struck large rocks and split them, recalled a soldier, it sounded as if they had been "exploded by gunpowder." A Sixth Corps private in the rear related to a friend that he was seated on the ground when a shard of a shell removed a piece of pork from his hand just as he was about to eat it. An orderly in the corps was sent with a message by Brigadier General Gouverneur K. Warren from Little Round Top to army headquarters. The courier rode at "a breakneck pace." As he passed by some troops, they yelled at him, "You better stop orderly, you will never get through." He reached headquarters, but at such speed he nearly killed his horse.[28]

The scene that the messenger from Warren encountered at the Lydia Leister house was one of bedlam. Located a few hundred feet east of the copse of trees, army headquarters had been hammered by overshots. An aide wrote that the place "seemed to be the point of all others where the rebels fire converged." Major James C. Biddle told his wife, "It was horrible, they burst all around us & were going over our heads every second." One round tore off the front steps of the house, another leveled the porch posts, a third passed through the attic, and a fourth howled inside through the open door. The solid shots and shells killed sixteen horses who were tied to the fences.[29]

George Meade was inside the house when the cannonade began. When he walked outside and saw his staff members scrambling for cover, he laughed at them. Turning to a group of them, he remarked: "That now reminds me of a feller at the Battle of Buena Vista, who having got behind a wagon, during a severe cannonade, was there found by General [Zachary] Taylor. 'Wall, Gin'ral,' said he, looking rather sheepish, 'this ain't much protection, but it *kinder feels as it was.*'" Seconds later, a spherical case round exploded, wounding Lieutenant Colonel Joseph Dickinson of the staff.[30]

Aides pleaded with Meade to evacuate the building. At first, he refused, arguing that he needed to be there to receive reports from the generals. When someone suggested that he could leave a signal officer behind who could communicate with another man on Powers Hill, Meade acquiesced. Mounting Blackey, one of his spare horses, Meade crossed Taneytown Road and halted in a field. He had with him several staff members and orderlies, while at least a dozen officers huddled in the cellar of the Leister house, beneath the "fiery inferno" above them. When more rounds struck near Meade's party, the general continued on to Powers Hill, site of Henry Slocum's Twelfth Corps headquarters.[31]

Meade stayed briefly on Powers Hill. When a signalman reported that he was not getting a response from army headquarters, Meade started back toward the Leister house. The army commander had with him only a handful of orderlies, most of his staff having become scattered during the change in headquarters. Upon his return to the house, Meade learned that the signal officer had fled soon after the general had departed. Meade then rode toward Cemetery Hill to get a view of the action, which was now at a crescendo. The Union line on the hill and along Cemetery Ridge was wreathed in smoke: Federal gunners were working their cannon at last.[32]

Henry Hunt's artillery crews had stood at their posts, the cannon loaded and primed, waiting under "a mighty hurricane" of Confederate fire. The artillery chief's orders had been clear—withhold fire for fifteen minutes and then reply "deliberately and slowly as at target practice." So they faced the fury and paid the price. A watching surgeon described the carnage: "The horses rolled in heaps everywhere tangled in their harness with their dying struggles—wheels knocked off, guns capsized and artillerists going to the rear or lying on the ground bleeding in every direction."[33]

With each passing minute, the maelstrom worsened. Enough Confederate rounds were hitting their targets, spewing shards of metal down on the gun crews and the infantry ranks. At last, before Hunt's prescribed time limit had expired, the five Second Corps batteries on Cemetery Ridge exploded with a roar. It had been one thing to withstand the wrath of the enemy; it was another matter to cross a furious Winfield Scott Hancock.[34]

The Union Second Corps commander had been relaxing in a hollow behind the ridge after John Gibbon's midday meal when the Confederate artillery opened. Mounting quickly, he spurred his horse up the slope onto the ridge. Hancock had been on some of the conflict's bloodiest fields, had heard cannon belch forth sheets of iron, but this was, as he reported, "the heaviest artillery fire I have ever known." "The air was filled with projectiles," he added, "there being scarcely an instant but that several were seen bursting at once. No irregularity of ground afforded much protection." He knew from experience that infantry would not take such punishment for long unless the artillery replied to the enemy guns.[35]

Hancock wasted little time demanding to know why the batteries were silent. When told of Hunt's orders, the general must have unleashed a string of oaths, probably cursing Hunt and his interference with Hancock's artillery. Saying he would take responsibility, he ordered the batteries to reply at once. Captain John G. Hazard, the corps artillery chief, stated in his report that he withheld his fire until the Confederate onslaught had become "too terrible." He never mentioned Hancock's pre-emptive order.[36]

The artillerymen of George Woodruff, William Arnold, Alonzo Cushing, Walter Perrin, and James Rorty answered the Southern fire. A wall of sulfurous smoke rolled up from Ziegler's Grove to south of the copse of trees, flames flashing as each gun discharged. The crews worked the pieces with "no flurry and no fuss." Veterans, they followed the prescribed routine—"Number one, fire! Number two, fire!" Nevertheless, the smoke became so thick that it obscured targets and the effects of their rounds. "It was pretty much guesswork," admitted an officer. Frank Haskell sat on the ground behind Cushing's guns and, watching the discharges, likened "these great guns" to "great infuriate demons, not of the earth."[37]

Before long, the Union batteries on Cemetery Hill entered the duel. Thomas Osborn had shifted cannon to counter the Confederate fire from Benner's Hill. When his crews opened, they hammered the open height. On July 2, Southern gunners had been subjected to what one of them termed "a hell inferno." Now, on July 3, it became a similar place. The Confederate crews began to fire "wildly," said Osborn, and soon ceased firing altogether. This ended the terrible crossfire that had scoured the Federal infantry and artillery on Cemetery Hill.[38]

Osborn's other batteries joined Hazard's Second Corps guns against the Confederate cannon arrayed on Seminary Ridge and in the fields east of it. The Union gunners concentrated on their Southern counterparts, punishing the gray-jacketed crews. "The very air seems to quiver," exclaimed a Rebel. A Third Corps artillerist on Seminary Ridge said in a letter on July 7, "I never heard guns roar as they did in my life, and you know we 'heard guns' at Seven Pines, Sharpsburg, Chancellorsville, &c. Our position was one of the hottest we were ever in—shell, and solid shot were hurled as thick as hail over our battalion." The storm they had visited upon Cemetery Ridge was being returned.[39]

Hancock, meanwhile, had passed slowly along his lines, trying to inspire his troops. When he reached Lieutenant Colonel Freeman McGilvery's line of batteries along the southern portion of Cemetery Ridge, he halted in front of Captain Patrick Hart's 15th New York Independent Battery. Hancock wanted to know, "not in a very mild manner," why the captain had not begun firing. Hart repeated his orders from Hunt and McGilvery, which directed the battery commanders to wait at least fifteen minutes before replying to the Confederate batteries. Hancock demanded that Hart open fire, declaring that these batteries were part of his line and under his authority. Hart asked for a written order. He would open fire, but only "under protest."[40]

At this point, McGilvery rode up. Hancock turned to him and fumed, "Why in hell do you not fire with these Batteries." McGilvery said he had instructions to reserve his fire as long as possible. Hancock cursed, using "very profane language," telling McGilvery that unless he opened on the Confederates "his troops would not stand it much longer." Hancock then headed back to the center of his line. Hart's gunners and Captain Charles A. Phillips's Battery F, 5th Massachusetts, fired several rounds before McGilvery stopped them. McGilvery's cannon had not been subjected to the Confederate barrage, and his crews would wait for the Rebel infantry that he and Hunt had anticipated would be coming in the cannonade's wake.[41]

Following the battle, Hancock complained to Meade about the artillery officers' refusal to obey his orders. When Meade confronted Hunt about the matter, the two generals exchanged, as Hunt put it, "some warm words between us." For his part, Hunt believed afterward that Hancock's interference with the batteries "seriously imperilled the battle." In fact, Hunt seemed to become obsessed with the dispute in the postwar years. Hancock emerged from the battle as one of its heroes, whereas the performance of Hunt and the artillery appeared to be given secondary status after the battle. Hunt resented this deeply and gathered information from other officers to support his argument.[42]

Hancock was right in his concern about the steadiness of the infantry without counterbattery fire from its own guns. Although Meade had returned Hancock to corps command, the subordinate acted as if he still retained authority over all units along Cemetery Ridge. When he told Hart that his guns were in his line, Hancock must have believed that he commanded this sector of the field. Conversely, Hunt had been given field command of all artillery units. In his mind, his authority over artillery superseded that of a corps commander. Hunt was also convinced that his crews had to conserve long-range ammunition for the Confederate infantry. This was a clash between two confident, strong-willed men, both of whom knew their business.[43]

The Union response to the Confederates rested primarily, then, with Osborn's cannon on Cemetery Hill and with Hazard's guns from Ziegler's Grove to beyond the copse of trees. Thirty minutes into the cannonade, the discharges of the guns had blended into a "mighty thunder"—in the words of soldier, "the like of which we thought we never heard before." And with this deafening noise, the carnage mounted in the ranks of both opponents. Wounded and dying men screamed in agony. A Southern artilleryman described the scenes as "more appaling & heart rending the like I never saw. The like I never want to see again."[44]

Among Hazard's five Union batteries the destruction was staggering. In Walter Perrin's Battery B, 1st Rhode Island, deployed just south of the copse of trees, a round hit the muzzle of a piece, exploded, and killed William Jones and Alfred Gardner. A piece of the shell cut off the top of Jones's head, and another mangled Gardner's shoulder, nearly severing his arm. Before he died, Gardner asked his comrades to send his Bible to his wife and write her that he had died a happy man. Perrin asked for troops from the 19th Massachusetts to help work the cannon because of the casualties.[45]

Similarly, on Perrin's right, Alonzo Cushing secured infantrymen from the 71st Pennsylvania to man his six cannon. The Confederate fire came at them with such intensity that a wheatfield beyond Emmitsburg Road seemed to wave as if hit by "gusts of wind." Some of Cushing's gunners could not endure it and broke toward the rear. Cushing drew his revolver and threatened that if any man fled he would "blow his brains out." One round passed through a horse and exploded inside another. Wrecked limbers and the debris of exploded caissons lay scattered across the ground.[46]

The losses among officers and men were even worse in Battery B, 1st New York, aligned south of Perrin's Rhode Islanders. Captain James M. Rorty, whom Hancock had assigned to command of the battery on July 2, was killed, and Lieutenant Albert S. Sheldon fell severely wounded. Nearly two dozen artillerists also went down. A rumor circulated in the army afterward that Hazard had been angry with the battery for withdrawing without orders on July 2, and "purposely put them in a most exposed position" on this day.[47]

Tragically, when the New Yorkers opened fire, a shell exploded as it left the muzzle. A fragment of it struck Lieutenant John Ropes of the 20th Massachusetts. Ropes, who had been sitting under a tree and reading a volume of Charles Dickens, blurted out, "I am killed," and died.[48]

Across the fields to the west, the Confederates manned their cannon; in the estimation of one officer, "Never were guns served more splendidly, and never did men behave more heroically." It was courage of the finest, but at a cost. Within ten minutes of the Federal response, Captain Hugh Garden's Palmetto Light Artillery lost every man and horse in one section of guns. The South Carolina officer said it was a "carnival of hell." In two companies of the Washington Artillery, the Union fire silenced three cannon because of losses among the crews. In Captain Alexander Latham's North Carolina Battery, five gunners were killed and "quite a number" wounded. The brains and parts of the head of a horse splattered over one of Latham's men, who believed that he had been mortally wounded until he learned the cause of the gore and blood. Major James Dearing, carrying a flag, rode behind his battalion, encouraging his crews.[49]

The bloodshed "was enough to try the stoutest heart," admitted a Southern battery member. A watching infantryman wrote that it "presented a sad spectacle of war's destructive work." The artillerymen obeyed orders and maintained a steady, deliberate fire. Nevertheless, the constant discharges began to drain the ammunition chests of long-range charges. The thick smoke made it nearly impossible to assess the damage they had inflicted on the enemy. But duty and orders required them to keep to the work until the infantry advanced.[50]

o   o   o

THE THOUSANDS OF CONFEDERATE infantrymen in the commands of George Pickett, Johnston Pettigrew, and Isaac Trimble knew that the whirlwind was inevitable. Their officers had warned them about it, ordering them to lie down. When the Union batteries replied to the cannonade, the storm blew over the Southern gun crews and their comrades in the infantry regiments. A Virginian in Pickett's division asserted that when the Federals opened fire "it seemed that death was in every foot of space, and safety was only in flight, but none of the men did that."[51]

It was among Pickett's three brigades that the whirlwind raged the fiercest. Lying in the swale directly behind Porter Alexander's and William Poague's batteries, the Virginians had no natural protection from the shell bursts above them. Some of the men lay behind small piles of stones that they had collected earlier. Captain John Dooley of the 1st Virginia in James Kemper's brigade remembered that "orders were to lie as closely as possible to the ground, and *I like a good soldier* never got closer to the earth than on the present occasion."[52]

The 7th Virginia's Sergeant David E. Johnston confessed that "it was really a praying time" after he saw one shell decapitate two men. Nearby, in the 3rd Virginia, a shell killed two soldiers, splattering their blood and brains on Colonel Joseph Mayo. The 3rd Virginia also had its color-bearer mortally wounded; Lieutenant John C. Arthur was killed, and his brother, Lieutenant Patrick H. Arthur, was wounded. The shelling created "fearful havoc" in the regiment, according to Mayo. "When the line rose to charge," thought one of Mayo's soldiers, "it appeared that as many were left dead and wounded as got up."[53]

Another of Kemper's Virginians wrote, "I know I felt almost paralyzed, and would have dug a hole in the ground to escape if it had been possible." A round killed two brothers in the 11th Virginia, privates Thomas and William

Jennings. Chaplain John Granberry of the 11th Virginia walked along the ranks of the regiment during the cannonade, kneeling and praying with each wounded man. "I never knew a more divine specimen of a man," stated one officer.[54]

On Kemper's left, Richard Garnett's Virginians, lying behind James Dearing's battalion, also sustained losses. "The enemy succeeded in getting quite an accurate range," contended Major Edmund Berkeley of the 8th Virginia. In Berkeley's regiment, a shell killed privates Benjamin Jackson and Albert Morris, "devoted friends" who were lying next to each other on a blanket. Lieutenant Colonel John T. Ellis of the 19th Virginia was mortally wounded when a solid shot, bounding down the hillside, smashed into his face as he raised his head to see why someone shouted, "Look out." Carried to the rear, Ellis lingered only a few hours before dying. Casualties in the brigade probably exceeded fifty men killed and wounded.[55]

To the rear of Garnett, Lewis Armistead walked among his men trying to calm them. The solid shots and shells sounded like "the whistling blast of winds" to one of his men. Armistead told them to "lie still boys, there is no safe place here." One shell exploded above Company H of the 14th Virginia, killing a captain and several men. Another round wounded the 53rd Virginia's Colonel William R. Aylett, who relinquished command of the regiment to Lieutenant Colonel Rawley W. Martin and went to the rear. At one point, Armistead reminded his troops that, "unless the artillery succeeded in dislodging the enemy" from the hill and ridge, they would have to charge the Federals.[56]

On Seminary Ridge, behind the batteries of the Third Corps, Johnston Pettigrew's troops hugged the ground like their comrades in Pickett's division. "The air seemed to be in a state of vibration," wrote a Mississippi officer, "and produced a very strange feeling in one's head." The ranks were "almost entirely unprotected." Birkett Fry and James Marshall lost dozens of officers and men. Fry called the bombardment "that deadly storm of hissing and exploding shells." The colonel suffered a painful wound in his right shoulder but stayed with his command.[57]

One of the first soldiers hit in the division was Private Jeremiah Gage of the 11th Mississippi. A fragment of a shell ripped Gage's upper left arm and tore open his abdomen. When a surgeon told him that the wound was fatal, Gage asked for a pencil, paper, and a knapsack for a desk. Despite the agony, he wrote to his mother: "This is the last you may ever hear from me. I have time to tell you that I died like a man. Bear my loss the best you can. Remember that I am true to my country and my greatest regret at dying is that she is not free and that you and my sisters are robbed of my worth whatever that may be. I hope this will reach you and you must not regret that my body can not be obtained. It is a mere matter of form anyhow. This is for my sisters too as I can not write more. Send my dying release to Miss Mary . . . you know who."[58]

When Gage had finished, his comrades of Company A, the University Greys, gathered around him. Like many in the company, Gage was a graduate of the University of Mississippi. He asked them to join him in a toast to the Confederacy and to victory. Gage died four hours later. By then, each of his friends who shared in the toast had been either killed or wounded.[59]

Federal projectiles crashed among the trees or spewed dirt into the air among the ranks of the Confederate infantry in the Long Lane and on Seminary Ridge, directly behind Pickett's troops. Officers passed along the ranks, encouraging the men to be "steady." Soldiers in William Mahone's brigade counted twenty-three pieces of shells that struck their "little breastwork." Carnot Posey's Mississippians had to shoot frightened and wounded artillery horses that had bolted to the rear. One of the men told his wife afterward, "I never was scard as bad in my life." Another man described the fury to his wife a few days later: "If the crash of worlds and all things combustible had been coming in collision with each other, it could not have surpassed it seemingly. To me it was like the 'Magazine of Vengeance' blown up."[60]

When the Union fire seemed to be at its most furious, Longstreet rode past the ranks of Pickett's brigades. A Virginia captain who watched Longstreet stated afterward, "He was as quiet as an old farmer riding over his plantation on a Sunday morning." Some of the troops shouted at him to go to the rear. James Kemper also saw the corps commander and contended, "His bearing was to me the grandest moral spectacle of the war. I expected to see him fall every instant."[61]

As Longstreet approached, Kemper walked forward and said, "General, this is a terrible place." Was his command suffering? Longstreet inquired. When Kemper replied that it was, Longstreet asked if he could not move them to a safer position. "No," offered the brigadier, "we are exactly behind the line of this crest—the very safest place about here."

"I am greatly distressed at this—greatly distressed at this," Longstreet responded, "but let us hold our ground a while longer; we are hurting the enemy badly, and we'll charge him presently."[62]

✿   ✿   ✿

A RELATIVE QUIET, broken by sporadic cannon fire, returned to the battle-field at 2:00 P.M. or several minutes before. Most of the Union batteries had ceased firing earlier, because of the complete expenditure of long-range ammunition or by orders. Confederate batteries stopped as the Southern infantry prepared to advance. Eyewitnesses in both armies timed the duration of the cannonade from forty-five minutes to two hours or more, but the most reliable evidence places it at about an hour. The Confederates could not have sustained a two-hour bombardment, given their limited supply of solid shots and shells. By the time the infantry troops moved forward, many, if not most, of the gun crews had expended all or nearly all of these rounds. Porter Alexander's timed notes to George Pickett provide the best documentary evidence of the duration of the cannonade and the beginning of the charge.[63]

While it lasted, the Confederates poured thousands of rounds into the Union positions on Cemetery Hill and Cemetery Ridge. A Northern artillery officer asserted later, "Viewed as a display of fireworks, the rebel practice was entirely successful, but as a military demonstration it was the biggest humbug of the season." In fact, the gray-jacketed gun crews had inflicted serious losses upon a number of Federal batteries. The Rebels had disabled a dozen cannon and destroyed "a great many" caissons and limbers. Casualties among the Union crews exceeded one hundred.[64]

Captain John Hazard's Second Corps batteries incurred the most damage. Alonzo Cushing's Battery A, 4th United States, had only two serviceable cannon left of its six. On its left, Walter S. Perrin's Battery B, 1st Rhode Island, was virtually destroyed and was ordered to the rear by Henry Hunt during the cannonade. Battery B, 1st New York, posted south of Perrin, had two of its four ten-pound Parrotts still available. All of the Second Corps batteries, including George Woodruff's Battery I, 1st United States, and William Arnold's Battery A, 1st Rhode Island, had drained their ammunition chests of long-range rounds. When the Confederate infantry advanced, these batteries would have to withhold their fire until the lines came within case-shot and canister range.[65]

James Thompson's Batteries C and F, Pennsylvania Independent Artillery, had held the right end of Freeman McGilvery's line of cannon along southern Cemetery Ridge. This was the only unit in this section clearly visible to the Confederates, and it was pummeled with artillery rounds. Hunt ordered it withdrawn, telling Thompson to report to the Artillery Reserve and to have a replacement battery sent forward. Two other Union cannon had burst during the action, killing and maiming members of their crews.[66]

In all, thirty-four of the 111 Union cannon in place from Cemetery Hill to Little Round Top at the beginning of the cannonade had been either disabled or withdrawn at its conclusion. Most of the remaining seventy-seven guns were on Cemetery Hill or on McGilvery's line, with sufficient long-range ammunition.[67]

Although the Confederates had achieved limited success, they had failed to silence enough enemy pieces to clear the way for their infantry. The valiant efforts of the Southerners could not overcome crippling handicaps—the quantity and quality of their ammunition; the undulating terrain between the lines, which distorted the distance and elevation of the targets, contributing to the overshooting; the lack of overall leadership from Lee, Longstreet, and Pendleton, which might have clarified orders and coordinated the fire from the dispersed batteries; the limited use of Second Corps batteries; and the failure of the Southerners to locate most of McGilvery's line. Sergeant Frederick Fuger of Cushing's battery concluded perceptively, "As a demonstration, or rather as a spectacle, it was superb, but as a military operation, it was not effective, because its destructiveness was not such as to impair the power of our Infantry to resist and repulse the great charge for which it was designed to pave the way, nor did it cripple our own artillery."[68]

The final factor contributing to the failure of the cannonade was the response of Union batteries. Once the Yankees opened fire, they wreaked their own havoc upon the Rebels. The rapid smothering of Confederate guns on Benner's Hill demonstrated the might of Federal firepower. As the Union discharges increased, the effectiveness of Confederate fire was reduced. This array of Union cannon foretold a terrible reckoning for the waiting Confederate infantry. In the end, Lee had expected too much from his artillery. The miscalculation would cost him and the army dearly.[69]

Even as the Confederate guns went silent, more Union batteries were moving forward to replace those withdrawn. When the cannonade began, Henry Hunt was with Benjamin Rittenhouse's artillerists on Little Round Top. After reminding Rittenhouse to withhold his fire for at least fifteen minutes, Hunt rode to the Artillery Reserve and directed that all the batteries "be ready to move at moment's notice." From there, Hunt proceeded to army headquarters, where he learned that Meade had left earlier. He then hurried to McGilvery's line, checked ammunition supplies, and continued north along the ridge, watching the effects of the enemy rounds, before finally ascending Cemetery Hill.[70]

Hunt dismounted and walked into Evergreen Cemetery, where he met

Thomas Osborn, the artillery commander on the hill. Hunt learned from Osborn that Meade had been there, expressing concern about the ammunition and whether the Eleventh Corps artillery could maintain its position on the crest. When Osborn told him, "I will stay here, General, and so will my men," Meade rode away. Soon Oliver Howard and Carl Schurz joined the two artillery officers. The four men talked, concluding that Lee planned to assault the Union line with infantry. They decided that if Osborn ceased firing it might mislead the enemy into thinking the guns had been driven off the height. Hunt issued the order, and Osborn instructed each battery to stop and to have the men lie down.[71]

Hunt remounted and raced south along the ridge, silencing the remaining batteries. At this time, he sent Perrin's Rhode Islanders and Thompson's Pennsylvanians to the rear. Hunt halted along McGilvery's line and was with that officer when the Confederates halted fire. To Hunt's surprise, however, the Union Second Corps batteries had resumed firing. Hancock had learned of Hunt's cease-fire order and was irate. When the corps commander told John Hazard to reopen fire, Hazard objected but complied. The resumption lasted only a few minutes.[72]

Hunt knew that it would not be long before Confederate infantry followed. He issued instructions to bring up additional batteries and then spurred his horse toward the center of the line. Earlier, he had bolstered Hazard's guns with two sections of four cannon—one from the 9th Massachusetts Battery and another from Batteries F and K, 3rd United States—placing them near the Bryan farm buildings. Now Lieutenant Augustin Parson's Battery A, 1st New Jersey, and Captain Robert Fitzhugh's Battery K, 1st New York, with the 11th New York Independent Battery attached to it, arrived. Hunt posted both of them among McGilvery's guns. He kept Lieutenant Gulian Weir's Battery C, 5th United States, in reserve north of the Jacob Hummelbaugh farm. Finally, two more batteries from the Artillery Reserve were en route, and five batteries from the Sixth Corps were moving toward Cemetery Hill.[73]

On Cemetery Hill, meanwhile, Osborn had been shifting batteries and bringing forward additional crews. When he had finished, he had forty-one cannon deployed, aimed at the fields between the two ridges and south down Emmitsburg Road. The gunners had sufficient long-range ammunition and stood to their pieces.[74]

More than a half-mile south of Cemetery Hill, Hunt waited with the gunners of Captain Andrew Cowan's 1st New York Independent Battery. For hours he had sensed this time would come, and he had done all that he could to prepare his artillery command for it. He had performed masterfully. Perhaps he saw them first, or heard a shout that the Confederate infantry were coming. He would undoubtedly have agreed with the words of a Union infantryman: "There is one thing that our government does that suits me to a dot. That is, we fight mostly with artillery. The rebels fight mostly with infantry." [75]

      °   °   °

PORTER ALEXANDER HAD WATCHED the effects of the Confederate artillery fire through field glasses from behind a tree. It was difficult, because the "smoke soon hid almost everything," and the "shot and shell flew in flocks." His responsibility was to determine at what time the Southern infantry would advance. "I had intended fully to start Pickett on his travels after the Arty had been at it about ten minutes," he stated afterward, "for he had a long way to go & ammunition burns up very fast in an affair like that." But when the Federals replied, their fire was "so perfectly terrific that I did not believe any Infantry could traverse half the necessary distance under it & . . . at the end of ten minutes I could not bring myself to do it." [76]

He waited another fifteen or so minutes—as he said, "in great anxiety." During this time, an aide returned with the surprising news that Major Charles Richardson and his nine cannon had disappeared from the hollow where Alexander had placed them with orders "to wait there until I sent for him." These were the guns that Alexander had designated to follow the infantry. He learned later that William Pendleton had removed three or four of them without informing him. Then, during the artillery exchanges over the Bliss farm action, Richardson had come under fire and withdrawn the other pieces. "God knows where he went to but it was where he could not be found." Although Alexander felt "bitterly" about the episode, he admitted that Richardson's nine cannon "would not have made any difference in the result of the battle." [77]

At 1:25 P.M., knowing he had to act despite the volume of Union fire, Alexander wrote a note to George Pickett: "If you are to advance at all you must come at once or we will not be able to support you as we ought, but the enemy's fire has not slackened materially and there are still 18 guns firing from the cemetery." He gave it to a courier and sent a copy of the message to Johnston Pettigrew. [78]

Alexander resumed his study of the Union line, looking for any evidence that the enemy fire had abated or that batteries had been silenced. Shortly, he thought that the cannon on Cemetery Hill were limbering up and withdrawing. He probably mistook the decision by Meade, Hunt, and others to cease firing for a retirement of the batteries. He also noticed that elsewhere along the ridge the Union discharges had lessened. "Then I began to believe that we stood a good chance for the day," Alexander commented. At 1:40 P.M., Alexander scribbled a hurried, second note to Pickett: "The 18 guns have been driven off. For God's sake come on quick or we cannot support you ammunition nearly out." A courier raced with the note to Pickett, followed minutes later by another courier sent by Alexander to relay the message orally.[79]

When Pickett received Alexander's first note, he was with his staff near his troops. He read it and then mounted his horse. "Boys," he said to his aides, "let us give them a trial." He ordered them to go to the brigade commanders and have them form ranks. With that, Pickett rode to meet with Longstreet.[80]

10

"Like Feathers
Before the Wind"

❧ ❧
❧

G EORGE PICKETT HANDED Porter Alexander's 1:25 P.M. note to his old friend and commander, James Longstreet. The attack could not be stayed. Longstreet accepted the words—"with dejection, it seemed," to a staff officer. "General, shall I advance?" asked Pickett. Longstreet hesitated and then nodded his head. "Sir, I shall lead my division forward," Pickett said as he saluted. Longstreet watched him ride toward his division, thinking that Pickett "seemed rather like a holiday soldier." "That day at Gettysburg," Longstreet wrote later, "was one of the saddest of my life." [1]

Longstreet waited a few minutes and then spurred Hero, his favorite mount, toward the line of cannon. He rode alone and halted when he came to Alexander. The young artillery officer described the situation quickly to Longstreet, explaining that he could not give the infantry effective support because the batteries had nearly expended all their ammunition. "Go and halt Pickett right where he is," Longstreet declared, "and replenish your ammunition."

"General, we can't do that," replied Alexander. "We nearly emptied the trains last night. Even if we had it, it would take an hour or two, and meanwhile the enemy would recover from the pressure he is now under. Our only chance is to follow up now—to strike while the iron is hot."

Longstreet looked at the Union position through his field glasses and then said, with slight pauses, as if he had to force the words from his soul: "I don't want to make this attack—I believe it will fail—I do not see how it can succeed—I would not make it even now, but that General Lee has ordered and expects it."

Alexander said nothing in response, though he admitted later, "I felt that a word of concurrence from me would have stopped the charge then & there. But I had done my duty & was not willing to take any responsibility wh[ich] did not belong to me." In a few minutes it did not matter, for the Confederate infantry passed Longstreet and Alexander, and "the thing was done." Leaving Longstreet alone, Alexander galloped his horse along his cannon to select guns with ammunition to follow the foot soldiers. In his report, Longstreet stated, "The order for this attack, which I could not favor under better auspices, would have been revoked had I felt that I had that privilege."[2]

o   o   o

"ATTENTION, BATTALION," or similar commands echoed along a line of more than a mile and a half in length. Officers and men rose to their feet, discarded their knapsacks and blankets, piling them in heaps by companies, and fixed bayonets to their Springfield and Enfield rifles. They had endured an unrelenting sun and the wrathful fire of Union cannon. Their time had come.[3]

They had been "thoroughly posted as to what they were up against" and had resolved themselves to it. Many of them thought, as an officer said, "that it was almost sure death." A Virginian confessed later: "I never expected to get out alive when I went up in line of battle & saw where we had to go across that Valley. . . . No better men went into battle than our division was & more dangerous place was hard to find to put them in."[4]

Despite their shared foreboding about the "bloody work" ahead of them, they stood in the ranks because of things more than themselves—duty, cause, and comrades. These were precious commodities to them, worth more than a man's or many men's lives. "They knew," as Adjutant James Crocker of the 9th Virginia explained it, "that victory meant so much more to them than to the enemy. It meant to us uninvaded and peaceful homes under our own nationality. With us it was only to be left alone. With this end in view, all felt that victory was to be won at any cost. All were willing to die, if only their country could thereby triumph."[5]

So thousands of Virginians, North Carolinians, Alabamians, Tennesseans, and Mississippians rose to their feet at the command and formed ranks. On the far right of the Confederate line, James Kemper brought his five Virginia regiments into line—from left to right, the 3rd, 7th, 1st, 11th, and 24th. He gathered his three staff officers and gave them "brief instructions" as "to the character of the movement, the points to be watched and particulars reported." The brigadier remarked afterward that the enemy line, particularly where the stone walls angled in front of the copse of trees, appeared to him as "a *cul-de-sac* of death."[6]

Many of Kemper's troops had not risen from where they lay. Captain J. Risque Hutter of the 11th Virginia claimed that there were "many men" unable to go forward with their comrades because of heat exhaustion and sunstroke. He appealed to those in his regiment in the name of Virginia. And there were those, he said, in all the regiments, "in whom there is not sufficient courage to enable them to rise."[7]

On Kemper's left, Richard Garnett received his orders to advance with "apparent cheerfulness." Mounted on a "magnificent bay" named Red Eye, Garnett issued commands, and his Virginians shifted into ranks. The 56th Virginia formed the left on the line, then the 28th, 19th, 18th, and 8th Virginia. Pickett had passed by as the officers and men came into line and halted beside Garnett, telling the brigadier "to get across the field as soon as you can, for I believe you are going to catch hell." Earlier, Cadmus Wilcox, whose troops had attacked the Union position on July 2, had spoken to Garnett and claimed that Cemetery Ridge was "twice as strong as" the Federal line at Gaines's Mill on June 27, 1862. In one of the regiments, a chaplain knelt with soldiers and led them in a prayer.[8]

Minutes before the brigade aligned its ranks, Major Nathaniel C. Wilson of the 28th Virginia took out his diary and wrote: "July 3rd. In line of battle, expecting to move forward every minute. With our trust in God, we fear not an earthly enemy. God be with us." Nearby, the 18th Virginia's Lieutenant Colonel Henry A. Carrington sought out Dr. J.S.D. Cullen, a First Corps surgeon, and said, "If I am wounded look out for me."[9]

Behind Garnett's regiments, the Virginians of Lewis Armistead's brigade listened as their commander shouted in his booming voice: "Men, remember what you are fighting for. Remember your homes and your friends, your

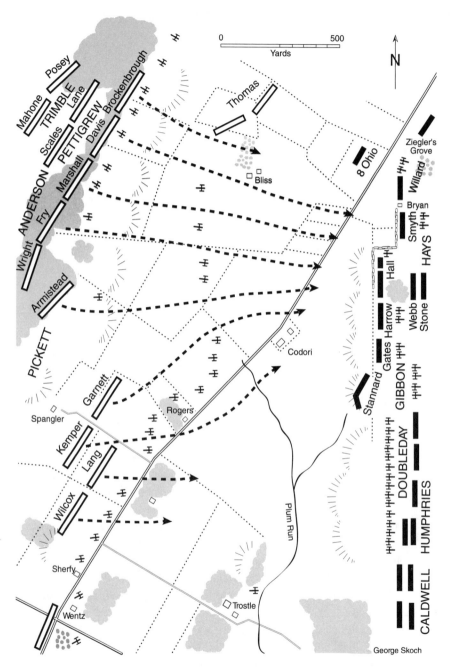

CONFEDERATE ADVANCE ON CEMETERY RIDGE,
AFTERNOON OF JULY 3.

wives, mothers, sisters and your sweethearts." Prayers had already been said, surgeons alerted to be prepared. From left to right, the line consisted of the 38th Virginia, 57th Virginia, 53rd Virginia, 9th Virginia, and 14th Virginia. As the men rose to form ranks, a rabbit scampered through the line. When a soldier saw it, he shouted, "Run old heah; if I were an old heah I would run too."[10]

When the officers and men had aligned themselves into a single line of two ranks, Armistead walked to the color sergeant of the 53rd Virginia, the regiment of direction for the brigade, and said, "Sergeant, are you going to put those colors on the enemy's works today?"

"I will try Sir," Sergeant Leander Blackburn replied, "and if mortal man can do it, it shall be done."

Armistead then turned away and walked twenty paces in front of his men. Removing his hat, he stuck it on his uplifted sword. Minutes earlier, he had told Garnett, "The issue is with the Almighty, and we must leave it in his hands."[11]

On the western slope of Seminary Ridge, meanwhile, Johnston Pettigrew and Isaac Trimble had brought their men to their feet and aligned the ranks. Most likely, when Pettigrew received the message from Porter Alexander, he relayed the contents to Trimble, whose line lay about 150 yards down the slope. Neither general conferred with Longstreet, who might have sent staff officers to them with orders to move forward. The uncertainty about these matters was characteristic of the loose Confederate command system and the lack of documentary evidence that surrounds critical aspects of the assault.[12]

Unlike Pickett's troops, Pettigrew's men formed double lines, with two ranks in each line, five companies of a regiment followed by five companies. Birkett Fry's brigade held the right flank, its line, from left to right, consisting of the 5th Alabama Battalion, 7th Tennessee, 14th Tennessee, 13th Alabama, and 1st Tennessee. Fry recalled that since they had been subjected to "that deadly storm of hissing and exploding shells, it seemed a relief to go forward to the desperate assault. At the command the men sprang up with cheerful alacrity."[13]

James Marshall's and Joseph Davis's brigades extended the front north along the ridge. The 52nd North Carolina of Marshall's command connected with the left flank of Fry's 5th Alabama Battalion. To the left of the 52nd came the 47th North Carolina, 26th North Carolina, and 11th North Carolina. Beyond them, the 55th North Carolina began Davis's double lines, followed by the 42nd Mississippi, 2nd Mississippi, and 11th Mississippi. A Mississippian noted in his diary that many of his comrades had "ashen" faces when the order came to form ranks.[14]

John M. Brockenbrough's three regiments and a battalion of Virginia troops completed Pettigrew's deployment. Earlier, Brockenbrough had assigned Colonel Robert M. Mayo of the 47th Virginia to command of his regiment and the 55th Virginia. Brockenbrough retained control of the 22nd Virginia Battalion and 40th Virginia, which formed the right half of the brigade front with the battalion beside Davis's 11th Mississippi. The 47th Virginia stood next to the 40th Virginia; the 55th Virginia held the left end of the division's line.[15]

As Brockenbrough's troops prepared to advance, the officers of the 47th and 55th Virginia could not locate Mayo. Colonel William S. Christian of the 55th and Lieutenant Colonel John W. Lyell of the 47th conferred, uncertain what to do in Mayo's absence. Consequently, when the right wing of the brigade stepped off with the division, their two units stayed behind the crest for a number of minutes. Brockenbrough's understrength command of eight hundred officers and men went forward at the outset with only half of its units.[16]

One hundred fifty yards to the rear of Pettigrew's division, Trimble finalized the formation of his two brigades. William L. J. Lowrance's five regiments were behind Birkett Fry's units, deployed from right to left: 16th North Carolina, 22nd North Carolina, 34th North Carolina, 13th North Carolina, and 38th North Carolina. On Lowrance's left, James Lane had, from right to left, five more North Carolina regiments: 7th, 37th, 28th, 18th, and 33rd. Lane's ranks were in rear of James Marshall's brigade and part of Joseph Davis's. Trimble's front evidently was arrayed in double lines similar to Pettigrew's deployment.[17]

It had taken probably thirty minutes from the time Porter Alexander sent the first note to Pickett and Pettigrew until the final preparations had been completed. Skirmishers dotted the front of each regiment about one hundred yards to the front. Field officers in each regiment had taken their posts in the rear, with file closers two paces behind the ranks to keep men in the line. The color guards, with flags unfurled, stood ready to the left and in front of the right-center companies. It was humid, with the temperature in the mid-eighties, and according to one soldier, "The heat can be seen quivering along the line." About two o'clock, "Forward" echoed along the lines of slightly more than thirteen thousand officers and men.[18]

The tread of so many feet resounded from the ground as the Confederate infantry moved ahead at quick time. A gentle breeze from the south-southwest had cleared the smoke from the field, and they marched under a bright-blue sky. A band behind Pickett's division began playing as their comrades started. Pickett rode behind Garnett's and Kemper's men, encouraging them with "Remember Old Virginia." Pettigrew's ranks cleared the skirt of trees on Seminary Ridge's crest while Pickett's troops ascended the slope of the rise on which Alexander's and William Poague's guns were aligned. Men wounded during the cannonade and still on the field shouted to their comrades: "Goodbye, boys! Goodbye!" [19]

On they went, these Southern infantrymen. Union staff officer Frank Haskell noted that the Federals had a low opinion of the Confederate artillery, but not the foot soldiers of Robert E. Lee. "This army of the rebel Infantry, however, is good—to deny this is useless," he contended. They "fight well, even desperately." Another Northerner, who would see them closely the next year, declared of them, "A more sinewy, tawny, formidable-looking set of men could not be." He thought that "their great characteristic is their stoical manliness." [20]

Their Confederate comrades in other, nearby units watched in awe and admiration as the attackers proceeded. A Georgian exclaimed, "I am sure that I have never seen troops start better than this storming party did." A North Carolina captain in Long Lane who had a clear view of Pettigrew's troops wrote in a letter weeks later: "As far as the eye can reach on the right long rows of infantry clear the woods and enter the field and move down towards the line occupied by us to the right of us. It was a grand sight, never did men move in better lines—never did a flag wave over a braver set of men." Not far from the captain was a Georgia lieutenant who declared afterward, "We were surprised to see this charge ordered we did not expect to see any of the men return from the assault." Another onlooker wrote his mother that the Yankees "had the finest position I ever saw and I knew it would require the most desperate fighting to drive them from it." [21]

They marched as if on a review—"slowly, steadily out in perfect order." Pickett's instructions to Garnett and Kemper were "to keep closed to left" toward Birkett Fry's brigade, the unit of direction. Accordingly, Kemper's five regiments on the right of the line marched initially by the left flank the entire length of a regiment. Kemper claimed later that the only order he received that day was to advance. He was undoubtedly mistaken or had forgotten, since he complied at the outset with Pickett's directions. He had even placed one of his staff officers, Captain Thomas G. Pollock, at the right end of his line to oversee the movement.[22]

Garnett's and Kemper's Virginians passed through the row of cannon on the rise as Pettigrew's men closed the distance between the commands. On the far left of Pettigrew's line, the members of the 47th and 55th Virginia, having started late because of Mayo's absence, were running to overtake their comrades. A post-and-rail fence ran east from the northwest corner of Spangler's Woods, past the smoldering Bliss buildings, to Emmitsburg Road, intersecting with it about three hundred yards north of the Nicholas Codori farm. Fry's brigade followed the fence on its northern side, while Garnett, obliquing left, would move along its southern side when it closed the gap between the two units.[23]

When the Confederates started out, Cemetery Ridge lay three-fourths of a mile ahead. At quick time, or roughly eighty-two yards per minute, they could cover the distance in less than twenty minutes. Depressions in the undulating ground would offer momentary protection and places to re-form ranks. But the fences that divided farm properties would hamper the rate of march. Their courage and morale would be tested during the advance once the Union artillery opened fire. They knew the fury of iron would come and braced themselves for it. Within a handful of minutes, it came.[24]

°   °   °

ON CEMETERY HILL AND CEMETERY RIDGE, the Federals, probably to a man, paused and looked to the west. Coming across the fields, in the words of a 1st Minnesota soldier, was "a rising tide of armed men rolling towards us in steel crested billows." They saw Pettigrew's ranks clear the fringe of trees on Seminary Ridge first, and then Pickett's Virginians top the rise as if they had risen from the ground. "Their appearance was truly a relief from that terrible fire of their artillery," stated a Union private.[25]

It was "a splendid sight," remarked a Connecticut soldier, and an unforgettable one. "I never saw troops march out with more military precision," asserted a New Yorker. "Their lines were unbroken and they looked in the distance like statues. On they came, steady, firm, moving like so many automatons." A New Englander remembered "their beautiful battle flags flying open to the breeze." Captain Winfield Scott of the 126th New York compared the lines to "a stream or river of silver." A 12th New Jersey captain thought it was "the grandest sight I ever witnessed," adding, "The lines looked to be as straight as a line could be, and at an equal distance apart."[26]

Sergeant Benjamin Hirst of the 14th Connecticut said, "It was a Glorious Sight to see, Rebels though they were." The Southerners marched as "though upon Parade, and were confident of carrying all before them." Captain William Davis of the 69th Pennsylvania declared in his report, "Onward they came, and it would seem as if no power could hold them in check."[27]

When Lieutenant Tully McCrea, an artillery officer, saw the Confederates, he believed that "our chances for Kingdom Come, or Libby Prison were very good." Captain Henry L. Abbott of the 20th Massachusetts thought otherwise. "The moment I saw them," Abbott claimed, "I knew we should give them Fredericksburg. So did every body." A soldier in Abbott's regiment wrote to his father a few days later, "Our men realized that they were fighting on their own ground. . . . They were now to fight for their own homes and their own friends." A Pennsylvanian recalled that his comrades' faces "were not as pale as I have seen them."[28]

As they watched, the blue-clad infantrymen and artillerists busied themselves. The foot soldiers piled more stones on the walls, checked the rails on the fieldworks, and dumped cartridges on the ground beside them or on top of the walls. Company officers and sergeants paced behind the troops, admonishing them not to fire until the Rebels reached Emmitsburg Road. Some of the color-bearers waved their flags defiantly at the enemy. Frank Haskell noted that the men slid percussion-cap boxes to the front of their bodies and officers unholstered their pistols, stating that "such preparations, little more, was needed."[29]

Alexander Hays sent officers to round up stragglers and brought forward the 125th New York and the four companies of the 39th New York of Eliakim Sherrill's brigade from the Bryan orchard to behind Thomas Smyth's three regiments at the stone wall south of the Bryan barn. A private in the 125th New York confided in his diary, "Here we waited in almost breathless suspense for the enemy who was moving on toward us like a vast avalanche." North of the Bryan house and barn, the 108th and 126th New York marched out of Ziegler's Grove and aligned on the other units in the division. In the 108th New York, Lieutenant Colonel Francis E. Pierce walked up to his former classmate at the University of Rochester, Captain Winfield Scott. Locking arms with his friend, Pierce said: "Well, Scott, we have sat beside each other in the classroom many a day; but this is a new experience. This isn't much like digging out Greek roots."[30]

Hays rode along his entire line, reminding the men to withhold their fire until the Confederates reached Emmitsburg Road. Then, Hays bellowed, they should "give them hell!" With some troops, he joked that they would now "see some fun." He stopped in front of one unit and led the troops in the manual of arms. One of Hays's officers believed that once the Federals opened on the Rebels it would be "impossible that one of them could reach the breastwork."[31]

Like Hays, John Gibbon passed along his ranks trying to reassure the men. When the cannonade had ended, Gibbon was standing behind the crest of Cemetery Ridge. A staff officer came to him and said that the Rebel infantry was advancing. Gibbon mounted Fanny, a gray horse, and crossed the crest. To the west, he wrote, "the line moved steadily to the front in a way to excite the admiration of every one, and was followed by a second and third, extending all along our front as far as the eye could reach." He sent Frank Haskell to army headquarters to report the attack to George Meade and to ask the commanding general for "all the help he could send us." Gibbon then rode forward among the troops.[32]

In "an unimpassioned voice," Gibbon spoke to his veterans. "Do not hurry, men," the general said, "and fire too fast,—let them come up close before you fire, and then aim low, and steadily." One soldier remembered Gibbon declaring, "We must hold this line *to the last man!*" He ordered William Arnold's Battery A, 1st Rhode Island, closer to the wall where Hays's troops and the right wing of the 71st Pennsylvania lay north of the inner angle.[33]

In front of the copse of trees, Alexander Webb knew that his Philadelphia Brigade needed help. He had ordered Captain Charles H. Banes, a staff officer, to find a battery that could replace Walter Perrin's cannon, which had been withdrawn by Henry Hunt from its position south of the clump of trees. Webb then walked over to Alonzo Cushing and told the battery commander, "This is going to be a hot place." Cushing suggested that he could roll his two serviceable guns to the outer wall. Webb agreed, and Cushing's Regulars shouldered the pieces down the slope, placing them between the 69th Pennsylvania and the left wing of the 71st Pennsylvania. The gunners loaded the pair of cannon with canister and stacked additional rounds on the ground near them.[34]

Colonel Dennis O'Kane of the 69th Pennsylvania ordered his men, who must have thought that the entire Confederate force was heading directly toward them, that they should not fire on the Southerners until they "could distinguish the whites of their eyes." He reminded the troops that they were defending their home state. If any man flinched, added O'Kane, "the man nearest him would kill him on the spot." Webb told them that if they fought as well as they had on July 2 he would be satisfied.[35]

Staff officer Banes or another aide, meanwhile, had halted at Andrew Cowan's 1st New York Independent Battery. The officer, whom Cowan did not identify, said to the artillery captain, "Report to General Webb at the right." The battery had ceased firing only minutes before, after discharging forty-five rounds during the cannonade. Having been posted under the orders of First Corps commander John Newton, Cowan hesitated to comply with the request of an unknown staff officer. When he looked toward the copse of trees, however, he saw an officer who was waving his hat in Cowan's direction. Although the captain could not recognize him, it was Webb. Cowan decided to risk disobeying his previous orders and shouted to his crews, "Limber to the right, forward!"[36]

The New Yorkers cheered, limbered the six three-inch Ordnance rifles, and lashed the teams into a gallop. The battery arrived within minutes, wheeling by the left flank into position. The lead crew had passed beyond the small woodlot and unlimbered north of it, while the other five pieces came into position where Perrin's Rhode Island gunners had been, south of the copse of trees. Webb met Cowan and pointed toward the oncoming enemy lines. Cowan ordered his crews to load the cannon with shells. His men had stripped down to their shirts.[37]

By the time Cowan's crews were redeploying, the other Union batteries that Henry Hunt had ordered forward either had arrived and unlimbered or were coming into position. Hunt's prior preparations and swift reaction to the cannonade would add at least seventy-five cannon to the Union line. As the Confederates advanced, more than 120 guns were in place, with dozens more en route. The smoke had dissipated, and the Federal artillerists had a clear field of fire. As one of them exclaimed later, "Never was there such a splendid target for Light Artillery."[38]

❊   ❊   ❊

THE LINES OF CONFEDERATE INFANTRY had covered barely two hundred yards—the brigades of Richard Garnett and James Kemper had passed through the row of Confederate artillery on the rise, and Johnston Pettigrew's division had cleared the trees on Seminary Ridge, descending the slope. Officers shouted to the men, "Steady boys." Now they were a "splendid target," marching in full view across open ground. On Cemetery Hill, Cemetery Ridge, and Little Round Top, Union gunners unleashed their fire. Solid shots, shells, and spherical case shots came howling and shrieking toward the gray-coated ranks.[39]

A watching Northern newspaperman reported that the initial discharges "seemed to smite the column of attack as if it had been struck by some unseen power, some great physical body, causing the column to waver, reel, and for a moment halt." "Deep gaps" appeared, but in a matter of seconds they closed. The lines kept moving. "Some unseen mighty power . . . impelled them forward," he recalled thinking. Major Thomas Osborn, Eleventh Corps artillery commander, contended, "From the very first minute our guns created sad havoc in that line."[40]

The Federal battery crews who used solid shots resorted to a "rolling" fire, in which the cannonballs bounded or ricocheted along the ground. The effect was fearful on closed ranks, for a shot could level several men. In turn, bursting percussion shells and case shots rained down from above, spewing fragments of iron across the length and width of the lines. A Mississippian called it "a perfect tempest" of fire.[41]

Some of the most devastating Union fire came from Freeman McGilvery's line of batteries on southern Cemetery Ridge, and from Lieutenant Benjamin Rittenhouse's Battery D, 5th United States Artillery, on Little Round Top. These crews, with thirty-four cannon, could fire obliquely into the Confederate lines, enfilading the length of the Southern ranks. "We had a raking fire through all three of these lines," reported McGilvery. "The execution of the fire must have been terrible, as it was over a level plain, and the effect was plain to be seen." An onlooking North Carolina captain thought that the enemy batteries hit the charging lines "with as much precision as if in 100 yards." A Virginian claimed that the discharges ignited the grass in the fields.[42]

Within the Confederate ranks, it was a boiling cauldron of hellfire. On the right of the line, Kemper's Virginians received the worst of the punishment from McGilvery's and Rittenhouse's cannon. A soldier in the 7th Virginia would remember that as they passed through the ranks of Cadmus Wilcox's brigade the Alabamians expressed their pity for the Virginians: "Boys that's a hot place, we were there yesterday." Captain John Dooley of the 1st Virginia stated that when the Federal artillery opened "now truly does the work of death begin. The line becomes unsteady because at every step a gap must be

closed and thus from left to right much ground is often lost." Company officers implored the troops to "Close up! Close up!" Numbers of men fell out,
running for cover in depressions in the ground.[43]

Captain Richard Irby of the 18th Virginia avowed that the troops exhibited
"admirable conduct" in closing the gaps made by the solid shots and shells.
The 7th Virginia lost seven color-bearers before the regiment reached Emmitsburg Road. Corporal Jesse B. Young carried the flag beyond the road
until he fell. In the 11th Virginia, Adjutant Hilary V. Harris seized its flag after
three bearers had been cut down. The 1st Virginia's Private Willie Mitchell, a
sixteen-year-old former student at the University of Paris, took the colors
from a fallen comrade, suffered a wound, but kept advancing in front of the
regiment until killed.[44]

Colonel Lewis B. Williams, commander of the 1st Virginia, had been
granted permission to ride a horse because of illness. As he followed the line
on his mount, a shell struck him on the shoulder and passed down his back,
severing his spinal cord. When he toppled off his saddle, he fell onto his
drawn sword. A graduate of the Virginia Military Institute, Williams suffered
intense agony until his death four or five days later.[45]

Porter Alexander, riding forward with some cannon, came upon one of
Kemper's Virginians sitting against rails in a fence, his mouth and chin torn
away by a solid shot. "This poor fellow looked up at me," recalled Alexander,
"& I even noted powder smut from the ball showing on the white skin of the
cheek."[46]

Throughout the destructive onslaught, Kemper's men maintained reasonable order as they kept dressing to the left, narrowing the gap between them
and Garnett's troops. They marched "alternately by the front & by the left
flank" as blasts of Union fire from the right blew across the ranks. Kemper
claimed afterward, "I never saw the behavior of men in battle equal to that
shown by my command in this advance."[47]

The Union enfilading fire from lower Cemetery Ridge and Little Round
Top that scoured Kemper's ranks also raked Garnett's line. A lieutenant in the
56th Virginia described it as "fearfully destructive." One shell nearly swept
away the lieutenant's entire company. The regiment's commander, Colonel
William D. Stuart, fell mortally wounded from a piece of a shell early in the
advance, and died on July 29 at his home in Staunton, Virginia. The 56th Virginia's entire color guard was also struck down by the fire.[48]

In the 28th Virginia, on the right of Stuart's troops, Major Nathaniel Wilson

sank to the ground when struck with another shell fragment. Carried to a field
hospital behind Seminary Ridge, Wilson said to a chaplain, "Tell my mother I
died a true soldier, and I hope a true Christian."[49]

About one hundred paces behind Garnett's veterans came Lewis Armistead's Virginians. When they reached the crest of the rise where the cannon
stood, "it seemed to me," wrote a soldier in the 53rd Virginia, "that the whole
of Cemetery Ridge was a blaze of fire and the blaze continued." Within minutes, the solid shots, shells, and case shots "poured in" like "hail." Another
Virginian declared in a letter, "Now and then a man's hand or arm or leg
would fly like feathers before the wind."[50]

The casualties mounted with each step. The 53rd Virginia's commander,
Colonel William R. Aylett, was carried to the rear with a severe wound. In one
company, a bursting shell killed a captain and "a great many others." When a
shell exploded above Company K, it leveled every member as if it had been a
scythe in the hands of a giant.[51]

Sergeant Drewery B. Easley marched behind the ranks of the 14th Virginia
with orders to watch closely the "playouts who would run once the fighting
started" and to "take them into the fight or kill them." He paid particular attention to a former classmate who, Easley said, "had done more talking and
less fighting than anyone in the company." The line had gone only a short distance when this soldier lay down on the ground. Easley went to him, asking
the man to show him a wound. The soldier jumped up and ran toward the
rear, chased by another sergeant.[52]

Few men, however, shirked their duty. "Our line was steady and unbroken," Major Joseph R. Cabell of the 38th Virginia reported, "except the gaps
made by the enemy's fire, which were speedily closed and all necessary ma-
neuvers were performed with the same promptitude and precision as when
on Battalion drill." Lieutenant Colonel James J. Phillips agreed with Cabell,
stating that the men of the 9th Virginia filled "the awful gaps" and dressed the
lines "until there were none to order and almost none to obey."[53]

Beyond Garnett's and Armistead's left, Pettigrew's four brigades pushed on
in the face of the "destructive fire" which "told sadly upon our ranks." Like
the Virginians, these Southerners sealed the gaps in the ranks made by the
Union artillery rounds and, according to Joseph Davis, "displayed great coolness." Twice during the advance they were ordered to slow the pace and to
dress the line. "It required more courage to dress the line under fire," asserted a captain, "than to continue the charge" into what he described as "that

galling fire." Another captain, in James Marshall's brigade, said that the artillery rounds caused "the decimation of our ranks."[54]

When Pettigrew's troops passed the smoking ruins of the Bliss house and barn, they halted in the swale along Stevens Run. They had covered more than half the distance to Emmitsburg Road and now probably came abreast of Garnett's Virginians, who also most likely halted. The Confederates re-formed ranks and redressed the lines. At this point, the 47th and 55th Virginia overtook the other two units of Brockenbrough's brigade, the 40th Virginia and 22nd Virginia Battalion. But as Colonel Robert M. Mayo of the 47th Virginia reported, the two regiments "arrived on the field just in time to meet a flanking party of the Enemy."[55]

The Union "flanking party" consisted of about 160 members of the 8th Ohio, who had been on picket duty since the afternoon of July 2. During the cannonade, the Ohioans had taken shelter in the ditch along Emmitsburg Road. When it ended, the regiment hurried across the road into the fields beyond, halting at a rail fence, where they had engaged Rebel skirmishers from Long Lane earlier in the morning. They were on the western slope of the ridge, north of the Bliss farm site. As the Confederates halted in the swale, the Ohioans rose and opened fire upon the left flank of the Southerners' line, Brockenbrough's brigade.[56]

Brockenbrough's Virginians had just passed through a scene about which one of them declared, "Hell could never be so bad," when a volley from the 8th Ohio ripped into their flank. The gunfire was sudden and unexpected, triggering a rout by hundreds of Virginians. The casualties were minimal, but an apparent panic seized the men. One Confederate alleged that two privates in the 22nd Virginia Battalion bolted toward the Federals and deserted. To the rear, Major J. McLeod Turner of the 7th North Carolina, in James Lane's oncoming brigade, ordered his men to "charge bayonets," to force the Virginians to run around his line. Although an unknown number of Brockenbrough's men stood and returned the musketry, the brigade had dissolved as a fighting force.[57]

Colonel William S. Christian of the 55th Virginia and Colonel Mayo of the 47th Virginia claimed that their regiments, as a whole, stayed on the field until the charge had been repulsed. Christian wrote years later, "We stood there to be shot at, and that was about all that we did." In his report, Mayo stated, "We succeeded . . . in holding the enemy in check until everything on our right had given way. Our Brigade was the last to leave the field . . . after the flags of every other Brigade had disappeared." Evidently, the remnant of the brigade advanced to the crest of the ridge beyond the swale, but probably went not much farther beyond that point. It could have been there when the other troops retreated after the repulse. Whatever the Virginians did and wherever they stood, it mattered little after their dissolution along Stevens Run.[58]

Pettigrew's remaining three brigades and Garnett's and Kemper's Virginians had continued on to the ridge past the swale. During the advance, the troops had to pass through or scale a number of fences, which disordered ranks and slowed the pace. Additional fences hampered their progress as they approached Emmitsburg Road. Now, however, they were well within canister range—less than four hundred yards—of some of the Union batteries. The gunners switched to these charges, which consisted usually of from three to four dozen one-inch slugs packed in sawdust in a tin cylinder. When the Federals discharged these rounds, it was as if gigantic shotguns were being wielded by titans.[59]

The swirling gale of iron and lead slugs blew into the Confederate ranks. But still the Southerners came. Yankees on the ridge marveled at their discipline and valor. A Pennsylvania captain wrote soon afterward, "They continued to move on unflinchingly, and it was a grand sight to see them, their splendid behavior calling forth bursts of admiration from us all." One of Hays's men told his wife that the Rebels "marched on like brave men to accomplish their purpose." A Union artilleryman stated, "They suffered terribly getting to us but they marched up as tigers keeping perfect line." One of Gibbon's soldiers believed that "no one looked at their uniforms or no uniforms, hats or caps, or bare heads. Everybody looked at the beautiful way in which they arrayed themselves in order of attack."[60]

As the Confederates neared Emmitsburg Road, Federal skirmishers who had been firing at the Southerners withdrew up the slope of Cemetery Ridge. Some of the companies retired in order, turning around and triggering a volley as they pulled back. One Yankee on the ridge contended that the skirmishers in front of his regiment fled "like so many frightened sheep." Two men of the 14th Connecticut, William H. Hall and James Inglis, stopped during their retreat to find their comrade Augustus Guild wounded but alive. They picked him up and carried him to safety.[61]

On Cemetery Ridge, the Union infantrymen steadied themselves—the Confederates were closing on Emmitsburg Road. Sergeant Benjamin Hirst of the 14th Connecticut recalled for his wife the moments just before the

Rebels reached the roadbed. He looked along his regiment's ranks at his comrades: "One is looking at the Far off Home he will never see again. Another is looking at his Little ones, and he mechanically empties his Cartridge Box before him determined to part with Life as Dearly as possible. Other ones you can see are communing with Him before whom so many of us will have to shortly appear."[62]

11

Into the "Vortex of Death"

❧ ❧
❧

H AMMERS CLINKED. RIFLES CAME to shoulders. Men braced themselves and touched triggers. A flash of musketry flamed from the Union
line on Cemetery Ridge. It was not a simultaneous, singular explosion, but a
series of flames as individual regiments unleashed volleys. The command—
"Fire! Fire! Fire!"—reverberated up and down the ranks until the discharges
blended into a deafening roar. The time had come for the Federal infantrymen.[1]

The volleys caught the Confederates as they climbed "the hither fence" on
the western side of Emmitsburg Road. Stoutly built, with five rails of chestnut
wood, the pair of post-and-rail fences framed the roadbed from beyond the
Joseph Sherfy farm to its intersection with Baltimore Pike. This barrier
seemed not to have figured in the planning of the assault. Now the fences became, in the words of a Confederate officer, "a very great obstruction." Unable to level sections between the posts, the Southerners had no choice but to
scale the fence and expose themselves to enemy fire.[2]

When the initial Union musketry hit the Southerners on the fence, the
front rank, according to a Yankee, "dropped from the fence as if swept by a gigantic sickle swung by some powerful force of nature." A Tennessean with

Birkett Fry recalled: "We reached the first slab or plank fence and the men clambered over with the speed of a stampeded retreat. The time that it took to climb to the top of the fence seemed to me an age. It was not a leaping over; it was rather a tumbling to the ground." He thought the bullets "rattled [against the rails] with the distinctness of large raindrops pattering on a roof."[3]

A Virginian in Richard Garnett's brigade declared, "It seemed as if we should all be killed." Another Virginian wrote that the "men were falling all around us, and cannon and muskets were raining death upon us." Regimental lines and organization became disrupted as the Southerners strove to cross both fences while the "withering fire" continued relentlessly. Scores, if not hundreds, of men stayed in the two-foot-deep roadbed, refusing to climb over the second fence. Colonel John A. Fite estimated that of the roughly two hundred men in the 7th Tennessee only fifty went beyond the road. Those not shot, Fite stated, "fell down" and stayed.[4]

Lieutenant John H. Moore of the 7th Tennessee wrote: "Our line was greatly weakened by a great part of the charging column I mean the front line . . . remaining in the Emmitsburg Road. I think not more than two thirds crossed it. I know when I reached the top of the second fence there seemed to remain a line of battle in the road." He believed that "the immediate cause" of their eventual repulse was the fences and the roadbed. Nothing could impel these men who huddled in the road to face the fire any longer. The Confederates' passage across the road had been "a dreadfully bloody one."[5]

Once the Confederates had scrambled over the second fence, they leaned into the musketry and the waves of canister. The Union fire sliced through the disjointed Southern ranks, staggering the Rebels. The range was barely two hundred yards, a killing zone of fearful carnage. A soldier in the 12th New Jersey boasted to his wife in a letter three days later, "We opened on them and they fell like grain before the reaper." Major Theodore G. Ellis of the 14th Connecticut described the effect of the Union fire as "a clean cut through both the rebel lines."[6]

The disruption in Confederate ranks caused by the fences worsened as they advanced up the slope. A Union artillery officer thought that "it was a mass of men without organization." Although Johnston Pettigrew's three brigades appeared to have retained relative order in their ranks, Garnett's Virginians seemed to have crowded together as their front narrowed. On Garnett's right, James Kemper's brigade was pressing against his flank, adding to the merging of regiments and ranks.[7]

Kemper's veterans crossed Emmitsburg Road along the section from the Nicholas Codori farm to the Peter Rogers house. Because the road ran diagonally, from the southwest to the northeast, across the Virginians' attack path, the brigade's right regiments, the 11th and 24th Virginia, reached it first. The two regiments crossed the roadbed around the Rogers house, whereas the other units—the 1st, 7th, and 3rd Virginia—crossed it at or near the Codori buildings. Once they were across the road, the Virginians descended into the low ground along Plum Run, passing behind the knoll in front of Freeman McGilvery's line of Union batteries. For several minutes at least, they were spared from the fire of these cannon.[8]

As Kemper's Virginians marched through the shallow valley, however, they moved by the left flank, opening the right end of the line to the Federal infantry. George Stannard's Vermont volunteers stood and blasted Kemper's flank. "When they got in about the right spot," wrote a New Englander, "we rose up and gave them" a volley. "It was a terribly costly move for the enemy," stated an officer. One of Kemper's captains, writing about his regiment, admitted that it "was a mass or ball, all mixed together." The Federals could hardly miss. Another Vermonter contended that the effect of their fire "was better than I had anticipated. It decimated their ranks and threw them into utter confusion."[9]

The Virginians continued north as if blown in that direction by the Union musketry. At the Codori farm, the brigade veered to the east, its left-flank regiments coming in behind Garnett's right flank. They were now well in range of Norman Hall's and William Harrow's blue-coated regiments south of the copse of trees, and exposed again to McGilvery's batteries. When Harrow's men fired their initial volley at Kemper's troops, "their front line went down like grass before the scythe," a 1st Minnesota soldier contended. Another Federal maintained that the enemy's first line "seemed to disappear." Some of the Yankees began shouting, "Fredericksburg," invoking the memory of that most terrible of days, December 13, 1862, when they had charged a stone wall held by the Confederates. A thick blanket of smoke covered the ridge and rolled down the slope. "We could see nothing clearly."[10]

Behind Garnett's and Kemper's ranks rode George Pickett and his staff. The division commander had followed the two brigades during the advance. When his Virginians reached Emmitsburg Road, Pickett sent Lieutenant Robert A. Bright to the rear, instructing the aide to tell General Longstreet that they "would take the Hill, but could not hold it, without reinforcements."

As Bright spurred across the fields, Pickett moved ahead, probably crossing the road south of the Codori farm.[11]

Porter Alexander, meanwhile, had pushed forward perhaps a dozen cannon as support for the infantry. When the infantry had passed through his batteries, Alexander hurried along his line, ordering forward every artillery piece that had at least fifteen rounds of ammunition. "It was the duty of artillery," he wrote later.[12]

The Confederate crews went ahead a few hundred yards and soon drew a response from a number of Union batteries. One of the Confederate gunners described this action as an entry into "the very mouth of hell." Within ten minutes, the Federals had killed or wounded every man and horse in one two-gun Confederate section. Volunteers from other guns rushed forward and retrieved the cannon in what a captain called a "carnival of hell." Elsewhere, the Union artillerists disabled a piece and cut down every member of the crew except one man. But a handful of Southern crews withstood the punishment and directed their fire against Union infantry.[13]

It was on the western slope and crest of Cemetery Ridge, however, that the afternoon's drama and tragedy were unfolding. There had been fearful minutes in awful places in the war before this day, but nothing seemed to compare to this struggle. As it had hours earlier on Culp's Hill, valor wore the uniforms of both sides. And, once again, good men slaughtered each other.

◦   ◦   ◦

THE CONFEDERATES EMITTED, in the words of John Gibbon, "a kind of savage roar" as they ascended the slope from Emmitsburg Road. Other Federals thought the sound was the familiar "demonic yells" of the Rebels. Whether primordial or fiendish, the screams came from men impelling themselves forward into a maelstrom of staggering proportions and intensity.[14]

The combat raged ferociously between Gibbon's Second Corps veterans and Garnett's and Kemper's Virginians. "The incessant rattle of musketry sounded like the grinding of some huge mill," wrote a Union captain. The smoke was so thick that it blinded troops on both sides. A Federal soldier declared, however, that he and his comrades had "no trouble" making their shots count. A number of Northern regiments aimed at the legs of the attackers, the only parts of their enemies' bodies that they could see. A captain in the 20th Massachusetts wrote that the New Englanders "bowled them over like nine pins."[15]

"Every man fired as rapidly as he could handle cartridges and adjust caps," claimed Sergeant James A. Wright of the 1st Minnesota. Along the stone wall in front of the copse of trees, Alexander Webb's Pennsylvanians used the rifles that they had readied and stockpiled before the assault, creating a devastating and ceaseless fire. The Federals fought without commands as the din of musketry and cannon fire drowned out the words of their officers. "I never saw such slaughter," Private Cyril Tyler stated in a letter to his father on July 7. "Never saw men mowed so by canister as they was there."[16]

The butchery consumed not hours but minutes. Although the Rebels "staggered realed and yelled like demons," they kept coming. A Union sergeant likened their push forward to "the oceans surge upon the solid rock." A New York lieutenant marveled at the courage of the enemy, writing that "their determination was to effect a storm or dye in the attempt." A member of the 69th Pennsylvania put it simply: "The slaughter was terrible."[17]

Kemper, Garnett, and their officers urged the men ahead. Kemper's five regiments had passed on both sides of the Codori farm buildings. South of the buildings, part of the 1st Virginia, 11th Virginia, and 24th Virginia followed a broad swale toward the Union line. North of the house and barn, the left wing of the 1st Virginia and the 3rd and 7th Virginia marched through the Codori orchard in the rear of Garnett's line. The regimental ranks had become, for the most part, a jumble of men, with Kemper's and Garnett's troops intermingled with each other as they closed on the Union position.[18]

Captain James T. James of the 11th Virginia stated years later, "I am even now almost persuaded that I was saved in that charge by some kind of a miracle or other." Too many men, however, were not so fortunate. In James's regiment, captains David G. Houston and Andrew Houston, brothers from Rockbridge County, went down. Andrew was wounded and captured; David died of his wounds the next day. Another company commander, Captain J. Risque Hutter, was struck in the back by a bullet that exited through his chest. "I am a dead man," Hutter exclaimed to a fellow officer. As he stood up, a shell burst over his head, stunning him and others. Eventually, the Yankees found him and took him prisoner.[19]

A minié ball smashed into the face of Colonel Waller Tazewell Patton of the 7th Virginia, breaking his jaw and ripping apart his tongue. Patton had had a premonition of his death on this day. Captured afterward by the Federals, he would die as a prisoner on July 21. Three color-bearers of the 1st Virginia were shot down in succession. Sergeant William Lawson grabbed the flag and carried it toward the stone wall, then had his arm nearly torn off by

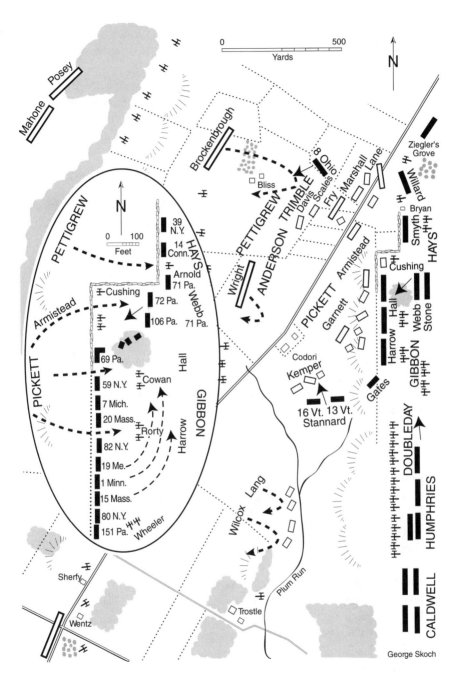

0   500

Yards

N

Mahone

Posey

Brockenbrough

Bliss

8 Ohio.

Ziegler's Grove

Willard

Bryan

Smyth

PETTIGREW

N

0   100

Feet

39 N.Y.

14 Conn.

Arnold

71 Pa.

Cushing

72 Pa.

106 Pa.

69 Pa.

59 N.Y.

7 Mich.

20 Mass.

82 N.Y.

19 Me.

1 Minn.

15 Mass.

80 N.Y.

151 Pa.

HAYS

Webb

71 Pa.

Hall

Cowan

Rorty

Harrow

Wheeler

GIBBON

PETTIGREW

ANDERSON

TRIMBLE

Wright

Davis

Scales

Fry

Marshall

Lane

Cushing

Webb

Stone

Hall

Harrow

Armistead

Garnett

Kemper

Codori

Gates

GIBBON

PICKETT

Armistead

PICKETT

Armistead

16 Vt. 13 Vt.

Stannard

DOUBLEDAY

HUMPHRIES

Wilcox

Lang

Plum Run

Sherfy

Wentz

Trostle

CALDWELL

George Skoch

CLIMAX AND REPULSE OF CONFEDERATE ASSAULT ON
CEMETERY RIDGE, AFTERNOON OF JULY 3.

the gunfire. A private seized it and was wounded; his body and those of others concealed it beneath them.[20]

Captain Thomas G. Pollock of Kemper's staff had been assigned to the right flank of the brigade during the advance. One of the mounted officers, Pollock stayed with the troops as they ascended the slope. As they neared the Union line, a volley knocked the staff officer from his horse, killing him "instantly." Kemper wrote afterward to a family member that Pollock was his "cherished friend and confidential counsellor at all times." They had often discussed religion together.[21]

Kemper's Virginians still pressed on into what the general had called a "vortex of death." An officer in the brigade reported that the men "moved forward steadily and earnestly and stood the shock of battle with fortitude." As they neared the Federal ranks, they were now triggering their own volleys. Although "nearly exhausted," they "rushed" the enemy when they were within a hundred yards of the Yankees, cheering again as they closed on the wall and fieldworks.[22]

Beside and among Kemper's Virginians came Garnett's men. The casualties in this brigade, from its crossing of the road to this point, had been equally staggering. A lieutenant in the brigade penned a dramatic description of the charge up the slope: "Grape and canister scour the ground. Down! Down! Go the boys. The remainder press forward." They also loaded and fired as they advanced "rapidly forward."[23]

Garnett's right regiment, the 8th Virginia, split into halves as it passed on both sides of the Codori house. The regiment had lost its commander, Colonel Eppa Hunton, before it reached Emmitsburg Road. Hunton, who suffered from a fistula and had been granted permission to ride a horse in the charge, was struck in the right leg, below the knee, by a bullet probably fired by a Union skirmisher. The minié ball missed his leg bone and hit his mount, mortally wounding the animal. Hunton's orderly led the colonel and dying horse to the rear.[24]

Lieutenant Colonel Norbonne Berkeley assumed command of the 8th Virginia and led it across the road and beyond the Codori house. Within minutes, two of his brothers, Major Edmund Berkeley and Captain William N. Berkeley, fell wounded. As he urged his men up the slope, Norbonne Berkeley went down with a bullet in the foot. Norbonne, William, and a fourth brother from this landowning family from Loudoun and Prince William Counties, Charles F. Berkeley, would be captured, eventually imprisoned together on Johnson's Island, Ohio.[25]

The four Presgrave brothers in the regiment fared even worse. Each of them were tall men. Pickett and Hunton had joked about "our twenty-four feet of Presgraves." Privates George and William Presgrave were captured; Lieutenant John Presgrave suffered a severe leg wound that necessitated an amputation. He died on July 8, cared for by Corporal James Presgrave, who was reported as missing. When John died, James buried his brother and proceeded home. After the war, he would return to Gettysburg, disinter his brother's remains, and bury them in a cemetery in Middleburg, Virginia.[26]

The entire color-guard and four flag-bearers in the 8th Virginia were either killed or wounded. A fifth bearer then tore off the flag and hid it in his coat. In the 18th Virginia, after two flag-bearers went down, Lieutenant Colonel Henry A. Carrington grabbed the banner, waving it in front of the regiment as they charged toward the wall. A VMI graduate and an opponent of secession, Carrington held the flag until Union fire knocked him down with a wound. Before the assault, it had been Carrington who had asked Dr. J.S.D. Cullen to "look out for me" if he were wounded. Cullen would be unable to fulfill the request.[27]

Shortly after the 28th Virginia marched north of the Codori house and cleared the family orchard, Captain Michael P. Spessard knelt beside a fallen soldier, his son Private Hezekiah Spessard. The young man had been in the regiment less than five months. Now his life was draining away from a mortal wound. His father gave him a drink of water from a canteen and then rejoined his company.[28]

Like Henry Carrington, the 28th Virginia's Colonel Robert E. Allen took the regimental flag when his color-guard was shot down. Allen carried it to the stone wall, where he was hit by enemy fire. Handing the colors to a lieutenant, Allen sat down, asked another man about the flag, placed his hat on his head, and died.[29]

Men from Garnett's 56th, 28th, 19th, and 18th Virginia and from Kemper's 3rd and 7th Virginia surged toward the stone wall held by Webb's Pennsylvanians and Alonzo Cushing's pair of cannon. Garnett trailed them on horseback, shouting, "Faster men, faster, we're almost there." Cushing's gunners rammed in more loads of double canister when the Confederates were less than seventy yards away. The Southerners could see the muzzles of the guns. "I remember distinctly," wrote a Union artillerist, "that they pulled their caps down over their eyes and bowed their heads as men do in a hail storm. They knew what was coming."[30]

The artillerymen waited until they could see the Virginians' entire bodies and then pulled the lanyards. Dozens of Rebels went down in a gale of canister. "I felt distinctly the flame of the explosion," recalled a lieutenant of the 56th Virginia. But the others screamed "a savage yell" and kept closing on the wall. "I did not think there was rebbels enough in the Southern Confederacy to run over that line of Arty," asserted Corporal Thomas Moon of Cushing's battery, "though they kept a cumming until they did run over us." [31]

Other groups of Virginians had halted behind the bushy knoll about one hundred yards from the stone wall and raked the Federals with musketry. Beyond the wall, Webb's Pennsylvanians were reeling from the Rebel fire. The 69th Pennsylvania refused to break and clung to the wall. On its right, however, the left wing of the 71st Pennsylvania abandoned the wall as the Southerners closed, running up the slope. On the 69th Pennsylvania's left, the 59th New York buckled and then cracked. Earlier, Webb had ordered forward the 72nd Pennsylvania and two companies of the 106th Pennsylvania from behind the crest. Now, as their comrades raced past them, these Federals stood on the western slope below the crest, refusing to counterattack. [32]

Alonzo Cushing was already dead when the Virginians reached the wall. As the twenty-two-year-old West Pointer directed the fire of his gunners, he was hit in the shoulder with one bullet and in the testicles with another. Refusing to go to the rear, Cushing stood with his men until a third bullet struck him in the mouth, killing him instantly. He reeled and collapsed into the arms of Sergeant Frederick Fuger. Lieutenant Joseph A. Milne shouted to the gunners that he now commanded the battery. Almost immediately, he crumpled to the ground with a mortal wound. Fuger succeeded him. In his report, Captain John Hazard wrote that Cushing "especially distinguished himself for his extreme gallantry and bravery, his courage and ability, and his love for his profession." [33]

At the wall, meanwhile, the Virginians poured musketry over it and up the slope, getting some retribution. Along the section of the wall held by the 69th Pennsylvania, the opponents stood paces apart. The green Irish flag and blue state flag of the Pennsylvanians were only yards from the red flags of the Virginians. "Everybody was loading and firing as fast as they could," declared a Federal. Pennsylvania Sergeant Henry W. Murray had both eyes shot out. As Corporal John Buckley led the blinded soldier to the rear, Murray pleaded with his friend to shoot him. [34]

"It was a *fearful scene*," stated a Union sergeant who watched the struggle from the rear. A Virginia major described the fighting at the wall as "of the most desperate character." Near the crest, the members of the 72nd and

106th Pennsylvania staggered as Rebel volleys sliced through their ranks, killing and wounding nearly a fourth of them. At these close ranges, neither side could miss.[35]

About twenty-five paces from the wall, behind the Virginians, Richard Garnett lay dead on the ground. Garnett had been waving his black hat and urging his men forward when a Union volley killed him, a bullet striking the general in the head. "I felt sure," wrote a Confederate staff officer, "that Genl Garnett's death on a battle field was but a question of time." The aide knew that the brigadier was "determined to show how unfounded" were Stonewall Jackson's charges about his conduct at Kernstown. It had taken Garnett nearly sixteen months, but he had his redemption.[36]

As Garnett fell beside scores of his fellow Virginians on the bloody slope, the Confederate surge stalled at the wall for a handful of minutes. While the combat continued, Lieutenant George Finley of the 56th Virginia looked to the north, where Pettigrew's troops were ascending the slope against Hays's Federals. To Finley, it appeared as if "there was but a fragment" of the Confederate force left in the ranks.[37]

¤   ¤   ¤

BIRKETT FRY, THE MAN with a "gunpowder reputation," had looked into hell at a number of places. He had glimpsed it in Mexico and had had a fuller view at Seven Pines and Sharpsburg. But now, as Fry faced Cemetery Ridge with the officers and men of Johnston Pettigrew's division, it might have seemed to him that the doors were wide open and Lucifer himself was beckoning them inside. And, like Richard Garnett's and James Kemper's Virginians, the Tennesseans, Alabamians, North Carolinians, and Mississippians stepped through the portal.[38]

Along a front of roughly 250 yards, Pettigrew's three brigades cleared the second fence along Emmitsburg Road and ascended the slope. Ahead of them, behind the stone wall from the Bryan barn to the inner angle, were the "Blue Birds" of Alexander Hays's Second Corps division. The Yankees had loosed their initial volley as the Southerners climbed over the fences. The blast had swept through the Rebel ranks, according to Hays, "like a tornado," but it had not stopped them, and they were coming up the ridge.[39]

In a flash of time, "the fire now became general," reported Colonel Clinton MacDougall of the 111th New York. "As the effect of each volley could be seen, the cheers and the confusion were wild." Screeching their yell, the

Rebels replied with volleys. A dense smoke covered the slope, in which the flames from the muzzles appeared as long, lurid sparks.[40]

On Pettigrew's right, Fry's four regiments and a battalion of Tennesseans and Alabamians moved ahead directly against part of the 71st Pennsylvania, 14th Connecticut, and 1st Delaware. Birkett Fry, however, had made it only a few paces beyond the roadbed when a bullet smashed into his leg, breaking his thigh bone. He would remember that while he lay on the ground he shouted to his men, "Go on—it will not last five minutes longer!" Although he could see little of the action, he "was so confident of victory."[41]

The fallen colonel's brigade braved the "incessant" musketry, triggering their own volleys as they advanced. The Confederates followed a narrow spine of ground that ran east to west and separated them from Garnett's Virginians on their right. They pushed ahead over the remnants of a stone wall and "a low rail fence" that extended north of the outer angle, where Garnett's veterans were silencing Cushing's guns. Later, Fry's troops argued that they had overrun the Federals' first line, mistaking these "rough stones" for the enemy's initial defenses.[42]

The Yankees behind the wall hammered the Tennesseans and Alabamians. Two companies of the 14th Connecticut were armed with Sharps breech-loading rifles. The Connecticut men worked in pairs, one firing and the other loading the breechloaders. The Federals discharged the rifles so rapidly that they had to pause momentarily and pour water from canteens down the barrels to prevent overheating. The intensity of the gunfire, delivered at a range of less than ninety yards, defied belief.[43]

Supporting the Union infantrymen was Lieutenant Gulian V. Weir's Battery C, 5th United States Artillery. Ordered to the crest by one of Hunt's aides, Weir's crews had arrived at a gallop, following a farm lane that ran up the ridge's eastern slope. Minutes earlier, William Arnold had withdrawn his six cannon of Battery A, 1st Rhode Island, after his crews had fired their last rounds of canister. Someone pointed Weir toward the gap created by Arnold's departure, and his Regulars unlimbered their six Napoleons. Ramming in loads of double canister, the gunners unleashed the rounds toward Pettigrew's Southerners. With each discharge, a gunner wrote, "the flashes of our pieces would scorch and set fire to the clothing" of the Union dead and wounded who lay in front of the cannon.[44]

The Confederates leaned ahead into the fire. Entire regimental color-guards and a succession of bearers disappeared, only to have another soldier grab the colors and wave on his comrades. By the time the Rebels crossed the remains of the wall and fence on the slope, "our lines all along," stated Lieutenant Colonel Samuel G. Shepard of the 7th Tennessee, "as far as I could see, had become very much weakened." As more Union volleys ripped into the Confederates, Shepard added, "there was but little left" of the line.[45]

Major Theodore G. Ellis of the 14th Connecticut described the carnage in the Southern ranks as Colonel Shepard had. The enemy was, reported Ellis, "being rapidly mowed down by our terribly destructive fire." Echoing Shepard's words, Ellis asserted that the Rebel line "seemed to melt away." Sergeant Benjamin Hirst, in Ellis's regiment, claimed the Southerners "got within 30 rods of us, then such a Volley of rifles we gave them you cannot imagine. Soon the first line was Shattered to pieces."[46]

Fry's troops clung to the ground at the remnant of the wall for five to ten minutes. Every flag in the brigade had fallen under the Union fusillades. Captain Archibald D. Norris saved the 7th Tennessee's banner by tearing it from the staff. When Private Thomas Holloway of the 7th Tennessee heard a man suggest that they surrender, he raised up from the ground and barked, "Let's never surrender." Before he could lower his head, a bullet shattered his skull, killing him instantly.[47]

Behind the stone wall, eighteen-year-old Connecticut Corporal William Goodell exclaimed to all that could hear him, "I would rather be killed than beaten to-day." Minutes later, the young man died, struck by a Confederate minié ball as he loaded his rifle.[48]

"It was the strongest position I have ever seen," Lieutenant James M. Simpson of the 13th Alabama affirmed in a letter to his mother five days later, "and I wondered at our Genls making any attempt to storm them. I saw that they could not be taken before the charge." So, with the other survivors in the brigade, Simpson fought on, unable to advance any farther as more Tennesseans and Alabamians gave their blood and lives on a slope where only courage walked.[49]

Beside Fry's shattered ranks, James Marshall's four North Carolina regiments climbed the slope into a slaughter pit as fearful as the one that had consumed the Tennesseans and Alabamians. Marshall's men pushed forward against the center of Hays's line, drawing fire from the 1st Delaware, 12th New Jersey, 111th New York, 125th New York, and four companies of the 39th New York. To the Confederates' left, in front of Ziegler's Grove, five cannon from Lieutenant George Woodruff's Battery I, 1st United States Artillery, scorched the slope with enfilading fire. For the understrength Confederate brigade, it was a hopeless effort.[50]

The participants recorded the grim truth. "We let them come up within easy range and then opened fire," noted Captain Richard Thompson of the 12th New Jersey. "They came up to our line, but only to die." The New Jerseymen, armed with smoothbore muskets, blasted the North Carolinians with loads of buckshot and ball, a particularly lethal combination at close range. "It looked like murder," thought a surgeon in the regiment. Another New Jersey captain scribbled in his diary that the Rebels "fell like wheat before the garner." An officer on Winfield Scott Hancock's staff, writing about Woodruff's artillerymen, stated, "The effect of the fire of the battery I have never seen surpassed."[51]

The Federals along the stone wall unloosed various shouts:

"Give Them Hell."

"Now we've got you."

"Sock it to the Blasted Rebels."

"Fredericksburg on the other leg."

"Hurrah, Hurrah."

"Give them hell again."[52]

A North Carolina lieutenant described the carnage to his mother: "The fighting was perfectly fearful, and the slaughter tremendous. Our men fought with the accustomed valor and determination of Southern soldiers but in vain." Their bravery and the price of it defied reason.[53]

The Federals' gunfire simply erased the North Carolinians' ranks. Their brigade commander, James Marshall, died within fifty yards of the stone wall, struck in the head by two bullets. Minutes before, the colonel had told an aide, "We do not know which of us will be the next to fall." Not far from Marshall, Captain N. C. Hughes, a staff officer and "a favorite in the brigade," lay on the ground with a mortal wound. In the 52nd North Carolina, Marshall's own regiment, Lieutenant Colonel Marcus A. Parks fell wounded, and Major John Q. Richardson went down "very near" the Union line, his life ebbing away on the slope.[54]

Although the Union volleys were "beyond description," according to a Confederate officer, the North Carolinians drove up the slope to within feet of the stone wall. No soldiers displayed more courage than the color guards and bearers. The 11th North Carolina lost all eight members of its guard, with Captain Francis W. Bird saving the flag from capture. A flag-bearer in the 47th North Carolina took the banner to within ten feet of the Federals; Private Thomas Cozort carried the colors of the 26th North Carolina to near the wall and died. Captain S. W. Brewer gathered up the standard and was cut down. Another soldier then seized it and took it to the wall, where a Federal shouted to him, "Come over to this side of the Lord!" A Yankee shot him; Private Daniel Thomas picked up the flag and placed it on the wall.[55]

Captain Albert S. Haynes, who was shot twice, recalled afterward that in his Company I of the 11th North Carolina "we were all cut down—no one but wounded left in my company, save two." A captain in the 52nd North Carolina who had been wounded about fifty feet from the wall wrote, "The ground between the enemy's works and where I lay was thickly strewn with killed and wounded." Some of the wounded crawled to the wall and sheltered themselves beside it. "It was a second Fredericksburg affair," complained a staff officer the next day, "only the wrong way."[56]

The North Carolinians had nothing left to give, and few of them left to give it. But they stood and exchanged gunfire with the Federals for a few more minutes, which must have seemed like an eternity to those still in the ranks. They clung to the slope until they received a "murderous fire upon our left flank." Joseph Davis's brigade had been there, but, like Marshall's North Carolinians, Davis's line had disappeared in the cauldron of musketry and artillery fire that had engulfed them near the Bryan barn.[57]

Davis's Mississippians and North Carolinians charged up the ridge into what their brigadier described as "a most galling fire of musketry and artillery." A staff officer called it simply "murderous." The 111th New York and the right companies of the 12th New Jersey lashed the front of the Confederate ranks, while the 108th and 126th New York and Woodruff's artillerists raked the Rebels' left flank with an oblique fire.[58]

The Union fusillades felled scores of officers and men. Five of the brigade's seven field officers remaining after the fighting on July 1 were struck down, including the 42nd Mississippi's Colonel Hugh Reid Miller, mortally wounded, and the 2nd Mississippi's Lieutenant Colonel David W. Humphries, killed. "No one seemed to be in command," claimed a Mississippian after the officers fell. As they ascended the slope, according to another soldier, the "lines became so shortened and thin as they neared the wall as to be nearly or wholly undiscernible and indistinguishable in the smoke, even nearby, and much more so at a distance."[59]

On the brigade's right, the 11th Mississippi lost both of its field officers and all of its captains. Thirteen of its members clustered around the regimental flag. With a yell, they "rushed through the 'hell of fire' of all arms to near the wall, continuing the battle there at close quarters for a short time." When they reached the Bryan barn, Lieutenant A. J. Baker ordered them to charge.

Corporal William O'Brien, the third color-bearer, was wounded. Private Joseph Smith grabbed the colors and went down. Private William P. Marion then picked them up and was killed; the staff was cut in two pieces by the fire.[60]

Rushing to the fallen banner and severed staff, Private Joseph Marble placed it on the wall. A Federal soldier flattened the Mississippian. Near the barn, Captain George W. Bird and Captain W. T. Magruder died. Lieutenant Baker, who had ordered the final surge, was slain a few feet north of the barn. A Mississippian swore later that there seemed to be Yankees ten deep at the wall. Everyone who remained unscathed in the regiment huddled around the barn, under the command of a lieutenant.[61]

The other regiments in the brigade also pushed toward the Bryan structure. A member of the 55th North Carolina thought that its ranks looked like "a mere skirmish line" by the time they reached the barn. A handful or more of the North Carolinians drove on almost to the wall. These Southerners later claimed that Captain E. Fletcher Satterfield, Lieutenant T. D. Falls, and Sergeant J. A. Whitley went farther than any other men. All of them died in their attempt.[62]

Not far away, Sergeant Luke Byrn of the 2nd Mississippi lay on the ground bleeding from a wound. On July 1, the regiment had its flag captured, and on this day, Byrn carried a new one. He had taken it to within yards of the Union line before being shot. Now, as he lay with it, he gathered the folds and tried to conceal it. He was determined that the enemy not seize a second flag of the 2nd Mississippi.[63]

Davis stated later that the Confederates' effort to take the Union line was "hopeless." Like the other two brigades in Pettigrew's division on the slope, his had been decimated, with only remnants of companies and regiments left unscathed. Pettigrew's command teetered on the edge of dissolution. A push by the Yankees would ensure a collapse, making that, in the estimation of one of Pettigrew's aides, an "impossibility" to prevent.[64]

о   о   о

WINFIELD SCOTT HANCOCK, commander of the Union Second Corps, reined up his horse beside George Stannard's Vermont brigade as the Confederate infantry reached the wall in front of the copse of trees and approached the inner stone wall manned by Alexander Hays's troops. Accompanied by Sergeant Thomas M. Wells with the corps's headquarters flag, Hancock had ridden the entire length of his line from Ziegler's Grove south to the Vermonters' position. En route, he had ordered the 19th Massachusetts and 42nd New York toward the clump of trees and had learned that John Gibbon had been taken from the field with a wound. Now, as he halted, one of Stannard's Vermont regiments was wheeling to the right, advancing into a field toward the right flank of George Pickett's troops.[65]

Lieutenant George G. Benedict of Stannard's staff, who observed Hancock when the general joined them, later wrote, "I thought him the most splendid looking man I ever saw on horseback, and magnificent in the flush and excitement of battle." Hancock and Stannard conversed; the corps commander apparently approved Stannard's maneuver. Hancock then turned his white-faced bay horse around to the north. On his left the 13th Vermont, trailed by the 16th Vermont, was rushing toward the Confederates.[66]

The mount had proceeded only a short distance when the major general suddenly reeled in the saddle and grunted "an exclamation." Benedict and two other officers rushed to Hancock's assistance, lowering the corps commander to the ground. A bullet had struck the pommel of his saddle, driving a piece of a bent ten-penny nail into his thigh. Stannard came to the fallen general, who pointed to where he had been hit. Blood was "pouring profusely" from the wound as they cut open his pants. Hancock said: "Don't let me bleed to death. Get something around it quick."[67]

Benedict tied a handkerchief around the leg, noticing that the blood was neither dark nor spurting. "This is not arterial blood, General," Benedict assured him, "you will not bleed to death." Hancock thanked the staff officer, believing him to be a surgeon. Minutes later, Major William G. Mitchell of Hancock's staff arrived, found his wounded commander, and rode for a doctor.[68]

Hancock refused to leave the field until the outcome of the Confederate assault had been decided. Lying on the ground and looking over, as he remembered it, "the remains of a very low, disintegrated stone wall," he watched the Vermonters shift into a line perpendicular to the Rebel ranks in front of Gibbon's troops. His wait would not be long.[69]

❖   ❖   ❖

AT THE OPPOSITE END of Hancock's line, on Cemetery Ridge, Alexander Hays was sealing the opposite flank of the Confederate force. Hays had appeared to his men to be everywhere as the Southern infantry charged up the slope. A New Yorker wrote in a letter on July 4, that neither "shell, shot, nor the bullets of the Rebel sharpshooters seemed to intimidate him in the least; in fact, he paid not the least attention to them." Hays rode among his men, exhorting them, "Hurrah! Boys, we're giving them hell!" The soldier concluded that Hays "is the bravest division general I ever saw in the saddle." [70]

Hays had two horses shot from under him, and one of his staff officers had the shoulder of his coat blown off by a shell. Nearly three-fourths of his twenty orderlies had been either killed or wounded. Colonel Eliakim Sherrill, who had been restored to command by Hancock at Hays's insistence during the morning, was dead, slain by a bullet. Colonel Clinton MacDougall had been wounded but refused to relinquish his command. Yet, despite the intensity of the combat, the division had not suffered serious casualties. On the slope in front of them, however, it was a different scene. "The angel of death alone can produce such a field as was presented," Hays wrote. [71]

Finally, as the Confederate onslaught crested before the wall and around the Bryan barn, Hays rushed the 108th and 126th New York and a detachment of the 1st Massachusetts Sharpshooters from Ziegler's Grove to the Bryan farm lane, which ran from the house to Emmitsburg Road. George Woodruff sent a two-gun section from his battery, under Lieutenant John Egan, to the left, where Hays posted it at the head of the lane, directing its fire obliquely across the slope. When the New Yorkers and Massachusetts men reached the lane, Pettigrew's Southerners were caught, as Pickett's Virginians would be by the Vermonters, in a closing vise of Union manpower. Lucifer prepared to collect his toll. [72]

12

"Come On, Come On,
Come to Death"

BRIGADIER GENERAL LEWIS A. ARMISTEAD, WITH sword upraised, walked about twenty paces in front of his brigade of Virginians as they approached Emmitsburg Road. Union batteries had torn gaps in the ranks during the advance across the fields, but Armistead's veterans had kept going, filling the breaks in the line. Officers encouraged them with "Steady, boys," and "Forward." Ahead of them, on Cemetery Ridge, they could see "nothing but smoke and flame."[1]

When they reached the fences along the road, Union musketry pelted them, shells bursting over their heads. Like their comrades before them, Armistead's Virginians were helpless as they scaled the five-rail fences or crowded through openings. "The bullets continued to bury themselves into the bodies of the victims and the sturdy chestnut rails," wrote one of them. The roadbed was a charnel house of dead and wounded men—those who had fallen minutes earlier, and now these Virginians. Scores, if not hundreds, of frightened troops still cowered on the ground, refusing to go forward and too scared to flee.[2]

Lieutenant J. Irving Sale of the 53rd Virginia would remember that a shell exploded above his Company H, killing a dozen men, including one man who was cut in two. Sale tried to crawl between the rails, but his head became stuck. "I recall the horror of the thought that I might be killed and left hanging there dead," the lieutenant wrote. He managed to free himself and climbed over the fences. "It was awful the way men dropped."[3]

After they cleared the fences and cluttered roadbed, "we moved steadily forward," a captain wrote later in his diary. Passing through and around the Codori orchard and buildings, Armistead's men ascended the slope, which was littered with hundreds of fallen Virginians from Richard Garnett's and James Kemper's commands. A member of the 53rd Virginia thought that these two brigades "had disappeared almost entirely now." From the crest, "a murderous fire" slammed into Armistead's ranks.[4]

One of the Virginians who went down just beyond the road was Color Sergeant Leander Blackburn. Before the advance had begun, Blackburn vowed to Armistead that, "if God is willing," he would place the regimental flag on the Union works. The sergeant carried it across the road until a shell fragment struck him, inflicting a mortal wound. Corporal John Scott grabbed the colors and bore them forward. Blackburn died days later in a Union field hospital.[5]

About 150 yards from the stone wall, Armistead's men triggered their initial volley and then pushed ahead. A sergeant major in one of the regiments shouted above the thunderous clamor: "Home, home, boys! Remember home is over beyond those hills." By now, the well-maintained ranks of the advance had become a mass of mingled regiments, which were denoted only by the star-crossed red flags. Then, as if impelled by an unseen force, the Virginians surged toward the wall, where the survivors of Garnett's and Kemper's shattered units still fought. As one of Armistead's men described it, "We landed right in to the 'Bloody Angle.' "[6]

Armistead's Virginians jammed against the wall, sharing the shelter with Garnett's and Kemper's troops. One field officer in the 38th Virginia estimated that his regiment on the left of the brigade had already lost two-thirds of its officers and men. The 38th Virginia's Colonel Edward C. Edwards died instantly with a bullet in the head. Lieutenant Colonel Powhatan B. Whittle succeeded Edwards, only to be hit in the leg and shoulder by two bullets.[7]

In the 9th Virginia, Lieutenant Colonel William J. Richardson suffered a wound and Major John C. Owens was mortally wounded. "A large woolen shawl" draped over the shoulder of Lieutenant Colonel James J. Phillips spared him from serious harm or death when a case shot buried into it, only bruising his chest.[8]

Colonel James Gregory Hodges led the 14th Virginia to the wall and died. Nearby, Lieutenant Colonel William White collapsed to the ground with a severe wound, and Major Robert H. Poore was killed. Private George Neathery of Company G also went down, shot in the left shoulder. "I tried to raise my rifle to shoot," the private recalled, "but I could not. Then, someone hollered for me to 'go back'—that I had been wounded. My shoulder began to burn like fire. I couldn't raise my left arm."[9]

Corporal John Scott, who had taken the flag of the 53rd Virginia after Sergeant Blackburn had fallen, tried to carry it to the wall, as Blackburn had hoped to do. Within a few yards of the wall, however, Scott sank to the ground with a wound. Private Robert Tyler Jones, grandson of former President John Tyler, seized the colors and took them to the Union line, where a minié ball grazed his head. Undaunted, Jones jumped on the wall, and waved the flag until another Yankee bullet toppled him. The colors fell inside the wall.[10]

At last, after only a handful of minutes, with the Federal fire blazing in their faces, perhaps two to three hundred of Armistead's troops and some of Garnett's and Kemper's "rushed over the wall." The Rebels poured over from the angle in the wall to the front of the 69th Pennsylvania. Armistead crossed the works, exclaiming to all that could hear him, "Now give 'em the cold steel, boys."[11]

Lieutenant Colonel Rawley W. Martin of the 53rd Virginia likened the Confederate thrust across the wall to "a lance-head of steel." In fact, it was more like a torrent of Rebels spilling over the rocks of a burst dam. The left wing of the 71st Pennsylvania and troops from the 59th New York and 7th Michigan had already broken to the rear. Alonzo Cushing's six cannon had been silenced. At the vortex of the Southern wave stood the 69th Pennsylvania. The enemy, wrote a captain in that regiment, "literally came right on top of our men."[12]

Within seconds, the combat inside the wall assumed a terrible fury. Someone in the 69th Pennsylvania ordered its right companies—I, A, and F—to refuse or to bend the regimental line up the slope. Companies I and A obeyed the instructions, but before Captain George Thompson could shout the command to his Company F, he was killed. The Southerners raced through the gap in the Pennsylvanians' line, engulfing Company F. The men of Company D, next in line, wheeled to the right. A new frenzy seized the combatants.[13]

Virginians and Pennsylvanians fired their weapons at point-blank range into each other. Union Private Joseph McKeever stated that "everybody was loading and firing as fast as they could." The Rebels seemed to have surrounded the Pennsylvanians, thought McKeever. "How they fired without killing all our men I do not know. We thought we were all gone." Colonel Dennis O'Kane, who had instructed his Keystone State volunteers not to fire until they saw the whites of the Southerners' eyes, now lay dying. Lieutenant Colonel Martin Tschudy was killed, and Major James Duffy severely wounded. Captain William Davis, a native of Ireland and a hatter in Philadelphia before the war, assumed command of the regiment.[14]

Men who had emptied their rifles wielded them as clubs. A Virginian crushed the skull of Private Hugh Bradley, who had himself been "a savage sort of a fellow" in the 69th Pennsylvania. The terribleness of the fighting, declared one Pennsylvanian, "struck horror to us all." Dozens of the Federals bolted to the rear. Some of the Virginians shouted, "Stop, you Yankee devils!"[15]

Farther up the slope, amid the shattered ranks of the Pennsylvanians, stood Alexander Webb, the brigade commander. "Webb was everywhere," claimed one of his men after the battle. Weeks later, he promised his wife that he would not expose himself again as he had on this day. But on July 3, as he explained to her, "the fate of a country depended upon individuals. No Genl. ever had more to depend upon his individual exertions than I had. . . . My men did not know me. It was necessary to establish myself. They were to be made to feel that I ordered no man to go where I would not go myself." Then, as a final assurance, he told her, "This is all past, there will not probably be another such an attack upon my lines."[16]

When the Virginians overwhelmed the 69th Pennsylvania and began to drive up the slope, Webb ran toward the right wing of the 71st Pennsylvania and the 72nd Pennsylvania at the crest. These brigade members and the four companies of the 106th Pennsylvania had been firing volleys into the Confederates. They had not budged from their position, although Webb had been waving at them to counterattack. Webb hurried directly to the flag of the 72nd Pennsylvania.[17]

The Confederates had raked these Pennsylvanians as they remained immobile along the ridge line. "Men dropped like ten-pins before the bowler," wrote a member of the 106th Pennsylvania. Dozens in the 72nd Pennsylvania were struck by the enemy fire. When Webb reached the latter unit, he grabbed the flagstaff, trying to jerk it from the hands of Sergeant William Finecy. The general and sergeant tugged at the staff, Finecy refusing to give it to Webb. The brigadier threatened to shoot the sergeant with his pistol if Finecy did not relinquish his grip.[18]

As the pair of men struggled for possession of the regimental colors, the Confederates swarmed up the slope. To the left of Webb, Lieutenant Frank Haskell of John Gibbon's staff tried to stem the rearward flow of men from the 69th Pennsylvania. "I met the tide of rabbits," Haskell claimed afterward with derision and exaggeration. "The damned red flags of the rebellion began to thicken and flaunt." Swinging his sword, Haskell struck some men on their backs but stopped few of them. The staff officer spurred his horse south for help from other units.[19]

A group of Confederates, primarily men from the 9th and 14th Virginia, charged toward Captain Andrew Cowan's five cannon of the 1st New York Independent Battery, posted south of the copse of trees. Earlier, Henry Hunt had cautioned Cowan to be careful when his gunners fired canister lest he hit men from the 69th Pennsylvania and 59th New York in front of the artillerists. With the retreat of the two regiments, Cowan's New Yorkers had a clear field of fire, and into it came the Virginians, led by a major, yelling, "Take the guns!" As one of the Pennsylvanians fled through the row of cannon, Corporal James Plunkett smashed a coffeepot over his head. The soldier kept running, with the pot over his face.[20]

The New Yorkers rammed double loads of canister into the cannon. When the Virginians closed to within less than twenty yards, the cannon leaped and roared, spewing a gale of iron slugs into the Rebels. The blasts had, in Cowan's words, "literally swept the enemy from my front." The Virginians lay in heaps, the wounded men giving the piles a seemingly moving life of their own. Later, Cowan walked to the fallen enemy, found the Confederate major's sword, and took it. Eventually, twenty-five years after the war, he returned it to some of Pickett's veterans.[21]

Farther south along the ridge, probably minutes before Armistead's troops pushed over the wall, nearly three hundred officers and men from Kemper's brigade broke through the Federal line and drove toward Battery B, 1st New York. Colonel Joseph Mayo of the 3rd Virginia wrote later that it was Kemper who gave the command to charge the battery, yelling, "There are the guns, boys, go for them." Mayo believed that "it was an injudicious order."[22]

The Southerners, mostly troops from the 11th Virginia, "marched up as tigers," said a Union gunner. When the attackers were almost to the guns, "we fed them canister," boasted another artillerist. A Virginia captain placed his hand on a muzzle, exclaiming, "This is ours!" Sergeant Louis D. Darveau replied, "You lie!" and killed the Confederate with a handspike. Some of the Virginians riddled the Union sergeant with bullets. The surviving Confederates turned and fled down the slope. "Few of them lived to get back," declared a New Yorker.[23]

In front of the copse of trees and among Cushing's abandoned cannon, meanwhile, the contingent of Virginians, led by Armistead, pressed toward the 72nd and 106th Pennsylvania. Since these Confederates had crossed the wall, their numbers had decreased with each step. Sergeant Thomas W. Shifflett, carrying the flag of the 14th Virginia, was hit in the face below an eye; the bullet exited through the back of his head. Amazingly, Shifflett survived the grievous wound and was paroled by the Federals. Twenty-four-year-old Colonel John Bowie Magruder, commander of the 57th Virginia, crumpled to the ground with a mortal wound. Struck in the chest by two minié balls, Magruder was in "most violent pain" but told his orderly to see that his horse was taken to the family home. He died two days later.[24]

Lieutenant Hutchings Carter grabbed the colors of the 53rd Virginia, which had fallen inside the wall when Private Robert Tyler Jones had been wounded a second time. The entire nine-member color guard of the regiment had been cut down, with eight of them killed. Carter took the colors and carried them up the slope. Later, after being taken a prisoner, unhurt, Carter would count seventeen bullet holes in his coat.[25]

"Never did men [do] more than these on that day," confided a captain of the 38th Virginia in his diary. In the forefront of them strode Armistead. When he reached Cushing's guns, another volley from the Pennsylvanians crashed into the Virginians. Armistead staggered and then sank to the ground. Near him, Lieutenant Colonel Rawley W. Martin of the 53rd Virginia fell with a wound in the leg. One of his men rushed to help Martin and collapsed from enemy gunfire, lifeless, upon the stricken officer.[26]

Valor alone could sustain flesh and blood only so long and so far before such lethal, scorching discharges. The Confederates on the slope near the clump of trees were like an island in gray and butternut, its mass diminishing with each new wave of musketry and cannon fire crashing against it. Then, from the south, came a river in blue, swamping the island of gray.

West of the ridge, in the Codori fields, the 13th and 16th Vermont advanced against the right flank of the Virginians in front of the stone wall. When the Vermonters came off the ridge and wheeled to the right at the outset of their attack, a number of men in the 13th Vermont paused and shook the hand of Private Benjamin Wright, who "bade us good by" as his life drained away from a wound. When the 16th Vermont came into line on the left of the 13th, the pair of New England regiments "charged together."[27]

THE CONFEDERATE COMMANDERS

GENERAL ROBERT E. LEE, C.S.A., commander of the Army of Northern Virginia, who brought his army into Pennsylvania seeking a showdown battle, and ordered the cannonade and infantry assault on the Union center on the afternoon of July 3, 1863.

(Left) LIEUTENANT GENERAL JAMES LONGSTREET, commander of the First Corps, Army of Northern Virginia, who despite his opposition to Lee's offensive tactics at Gettysburg was assigned to command the assault on Cemetery Ridge.

(Right) LIEUTENANT GENERAL AMBROSE POWELL HILL, commander of the Third Corps, Army of Northern Virginia, whose shadowy performance at Gettysburg on July 2 and 3 contributed to the Confederate defeat in the battle and has defied historical scrutiny.

(Bottom) LIEUTENANT GENERAL RICHARD S. EWELL, commander of the Second Corps, Army of Northern Virginia, who replaced Stonewall Jackson at the head of the famed "foot cavalry" and whose troops attempted to seize Culp's Hill on July 3.

Major General James Ewell Brown ("Jeb") Stuart, commander of the Cavalry Corps, Army of Northern Virginia. A flamboyant but excellent cavalry officer, Stuart joined the army at Gettysburg on July 2, after a controversial absence, and engaged Union cavalry on the afternoon of July 3, at the Rummel farm.

Major General George E. Pickett, division commander in the First Corps, who attained enduring fame when he led his three brigades of Virginians against the Union line at the "clump of trees" on July 3. After the repulse and decimation of his division, Pickett was in tears, muttering, "My brave men! My brave men!"

(*Left*) BRIGADIER GENERAL LEWIS A. ARMISTEAD, a brigade commander in Pickett's division, who led his men across the stone wall in front of the "clump of trees," where he fell with a mortal wound. He gave some of his personal effects to a staff officer to deliver to his old friend Union General Winfield S. Hancock.

(*Right*) BRIGADIER GENERAL JAMES L. KEMPER, a brigade commander in Pickett's division, who suffered a serious wound as he urged his Virginians up the slope of Cemetery Ridge and across the stone wall.

(*Bottom*) MAJOR GENERAL EDWARD JOHNSON, a division commander in the Second Corps, who directed the Confederate assaults against the Union line on Culp's Hill on July 2 and 3. Known as "Allegheny," Johnson was a general who "expects to do everything by fighting," in the words of a soldier.

(Left) BRIGADIER GENERAL J. JOHNSTON PETTIGREW, a brigade commander in Henry Heth's Third Corps division, who was given temporary command of the division on July 3, and led it beside Pickett's brigades in the afternoon assault. A brilliant and well-educated man, Pettigrew was mortally wounded on July 14 in a minor rear-guard action in Maryland.

(Right) MAJOR GENERAL ISAAC R. TRIMBLE, a redoubtable 61-year-old Marylander who had joined the army during its march into Pennsylvania. On July 3, Lee assigned Trimble the command of two brigades in the assault force. Trimble suffered a wound during the attack that resulted in the amputation of a leg. He was taken prisoner after the battle.

(Bottom) COLONEL E. PORTER ALEXANDER, commander of the First Corps artillery battalion, who was given tactical control of nearly half of the cannon used in the cannonade. Alexander's role in the day's operations was critical.

THE UNION GENERALS

MAJOR GENERAL GEORGE G. MEADE, U.S.A., commander of the Army of the Potomac, a Pennsylvanian who assumed command of the army three days before the battle. Although overshadowed by Lee, Meade performed masterfully at Gettysburg.

BRIGADIER GENERAL HENRY J. HUNT, commander of the artillery of the Army of the Potomac, whose brilliant leadership of the artillery units contributed significantly to the defeat of the Confederate infantry assault on Cemetery Ridge on July 3.

MAJOR GENERAL WINFIELD SCOTT HANCOCK, commander of the Second Corps, Army of the Potomac, another Pennsylvanian. His troops manned Cemetery Ridge on July 3 and repulsed the Confederate assault. A superb officer, Hancock suffered a wound during the attack but even while wounded urged a Union counterattack.

(*Left*) BRIGADIER GENERAL ALEXANDER HAYS, commander of the 3rd Division, Second Corps, whose "Blue Birds" held the line north of the "clump of trees." When his men defeated the Confederates, Hays grabbed a captured Confederate battle flag and dragged it on the ground as he rode along his ranks to the accompaniment of his men's cheers.

(*Right*) BRIGADIER GENERAL JOHN GIBBON, commander of the 2nd Division, Second Corps, whose veterans held the line in front of the "clump of trees." An excellent officer, Gibbon was wounded while urging his troops to stand fast as the Confederates crossed the stone wall.

(*Bottom*) BRIGADIER GENERAL ALEXANDER S. WEBB, commander of the Philadelphia Brigade in Gibbon's division. Webb's Pennsylvanians defended the stone wall at the outer angle or "The Angle" on July 3. He told his wife after the battle that he would try not to expose himself to danger again as he had during the assault.

(Left) MAJOR GENERAL HENRY W. SLOCUM, commander of the Twelfth Corps, Army of the Potomac, who told his fellow corps commanders at the council of war on July 2 that the army should "stay and fight it out" at Gettysburg. On July 3, his troops successfully defended Culp's Hill.

(Right) BRIGADIER GENERAL ALPHEUS S. WILLIAMS, division commander and temporary corps commander of the Twelfth Corps. When ordered to retake the works on Culp's Hill captured by the Confederates on the night of July 2, Williams remarked that it was "an order that I then thought was more easily made than executed."

(Bottom) BRIGADIER GENERAL GEORGE S. GREENE, brigade commander in John W. Geary's Twelfth Corps division, who at 62 was the oldest Union general at Gettysburg. Called affectionately "Old Pop" or "Old Man Greene" by his soldiers, Greene was the hero of the Union defense of Culp's Hill.

(Left) BRIGADIER GENERAL DAVID MCMURTRIE GREGG, commander of the 2nd Division, Cavalry Corps, Army of the Potomac, whose troopers fought Stuart's cavalrymen to a standstill on the afternoon of July 3 at Rummel's farm.

(Right) BRIGADIER GENERAL GEORGE ARMSTRONG CUSTER, commander of the Michigan Cavalry Brigade, who at 23 was the youngest general in the army. On July 3, during the cavalry engagement between Stuart and Gregg, Custer twice led a regiment in a counterattack, shouting to the men, "Come on, you Wolverines!"

(Below) A LITHOGRAPH of George Meade's council of war at his headquarters, the home of Lydia Leister, on the night of July 2. Meade stands in the forefront, listening to Winfield Scott Hancock. The generals decided to stand and fight the next day.

POSTWAR VIEW, LOOKING WEST from Cemetery Ridge, of the ground crossed by Confederate infantry on the afternoon of July 3. The outer angle, held by Alexander Webb's Philadelphia Brigade, lies in the left forefront. Emmitsburg Road is just beyond the angle, marked by the fence rails.

POSTWAR VIEW, LOOKING SOUTHWEST, of the ground from the position defended by the Union Second Corps to the Nicholas Codori farm, in the background. The present-day Codori barn is a postwar structure.

POSTWAR VIEW ALONG THE UNION POSITION on Cemetery Ridge, looking north toward the Bryan farm and Ziegler's Grove in the right background. Today's Hancock Avenue follows the length of the Union position.

POSTWAR VIEW, LOOKING SOUTHWEST, with the "clump of trees" to the left and rear of the horse. The fields in the distance were crossed by James Kemper's brigade of Virginians. The photographer stood near the modern Cyclorama Center.

POSTWAR VIEW, LOOKING NORTH, of the intersection of Emmitsburg Road and Baltimore Pike, at the south end of Gettysburg. Skirmishers from both armies fought each other throughout the morning of July 3 in this area. Modern-day buildings mark the intersection today.

POSTWAR VIEW, LOOKING NORTH, of the Lydia Leister house, George Meade's headquarters during the battle. The house suffered damage during the July 3 cannonade. Taneytown Road passes the house on the right.

POSTWAR VIEW, LOOKING SOUTH, of the Abraham Bryan barn and outbuilding, A free black man, Bryan and his family fled the area before the battle. On July 3, Confederate troops advanced up to and beyond the barn during their assault.

A DEAD SOLDIER ON THE BATTLEFIELD of Gettysburg. It is believed that he was killed by canister, fired from a cannon, because of the great damage done to his body. Note the severed hand in front of his rifle.

TAKEN WITHIN DAYS OF THE BATTLE, this photograph shows a section of the Union fieldworks on Culp's Hill. Behind these fortifications, the Federals resisted a series of Confederate attacks on July 2 and 3.

AN 1885 VIEW OF UNION BREASTWORKS on Culp's Hill. By then, the logs and stones used by the Federals had been removed.

VIEW OF TREES ON CULP'S HILL, showing the effects of cannon fire and musketry, which lasted for nearly seven hours on July 3. The modern line of works was rebuilt and is lower than the fortifications that were there on July 2–3, 1863.

A soldier in the 1st Minnesota who watched the Vermonters cross the fields wrote afterward that they marched "with as much apparent coolness, as much steadiness and with as perfect a line as I ever saw a regiment of veterans pass in review on a gala day." Captain Henry T. Owen of the 18th Virginia also saw them, and told a comrade later: "There off on our right was the grandest sight I have ever seen. A body of Yankees . . . coming at double quick 'right shoulder shift,' uniforms looking black in the distance muskets glittering in the sunlight and battle flags fluttering in the breeze created by their quickened motion."[28]

The Vermonters triggered a few volleys as they closed on the Rebels, who were "in great masses, without much order." The remnants of the 11th and 24th Virginia of Kemper's brigade and the 8th Virginia of Garnett's turned to face the Yankees. "Great sheets of flame" leaped from both lines, asserted Vermont Lieutenant Albert Clarke. The Federals pushed forward to within less than a dozen rods and delivered another "savage fire" into the Southerners. Clarke contended, "The lines were so near together that the blanched faces of men could be distinctly seen."[29]

A Virginian remembered that after the Vermonters opened fire "everything was a wild kaleidoscopic whirl." Captain Owen said that "in a few minutes all was confusion." He recalled, however, seeing two soldiers cross rifles, one firing up the slope, the other shooting at the Vermonters. A sergeant in the 13th Vermont had just finished shouting to a comrade, "Scott, aren't we giving them Hell?" when he was killed by a Confederate artillery round. Private William Wilson, in the same regiment, died in the fury. Three days earlier he had told a friend, "I shall never go home alive. We shall have a fight and I shall be killed." One Virginian, even as he kept firing rapidly, "seemed to be keeping tally of the dead" for his commanding officer.[30]

The combat, wrote Stannard in his diary, "beat everything that I ever saw or read of." The New Englanders' "withering fire" into the Virginians, declared the 13th Vermont's Colonel Wheelock G. Veazey, "completely destroyed their lines"; he added, "Those great masses of men seemed to disappear in a moment." Lieutenant Clarke described the "havoc" among the enemy as "dreadful." "Mortals could not stand such a fire longer. . . . Regiments had been annihilated," wrote Sergeant George Scott. "To retreat over that field of slaughter would be madness. They threw down their arms and surrendered."[31]

Squads of Vermonters rushed ahead into the crowd of Virginians, who had lifted their rifles above their heads. Lieutenant Stephen F. Brown, who had been under arrest for filling canteens from a spring against orders, had his sword taken away from him. When the flanking movement began, he picked up a camp hatchet. Now, wielding the hatchet as a weapon, Brown forced a fleeing Rebel officer to surrender. Private Piam O. Harris walked among the wounded and dead Confederates and found the flag of the 8th Virginia.[32]

The blue-clad captors ordered the prisoners to lie down as the fighting continued to rage around the clump of trees and along the wall. A number of Virginians had refused to surrender and were running toward Seminary Ridge. As one of them stated, "We made good time getting away." Stannard boasted in his report that the enemy gave up the struggle "not as conquerors, but as captives." He added that his nine-month troops "behaved like veterans." Corporal Francis Long of the 16th Vermont had a different assessment of the struggle. "I hope I never shall see another such a day as the 3rd of July," he confessed in a letter to his wife.[33]

о   о   о

BY THE TIME THE VERMONTERS had ripped apart the right flank of Pickett's division, additional Union regiments had reacted to the crisis in front of the copse of trees and had joined in the fighting. Like the Vermonters, these Federals had been blasting the Rebels with musketry before they rushed north along the ridge. The advent of these reinforcements heated the roiling combat to a white fury.[34]

Aligned on the left of Webb's Pennsylvanians, Colonel Norman Hall's veteran units led the Union counterattack. It was to Hall that Frank Haskell had ridden when Webb's line at the wall was shattered, telling the colonel that Webb needed help. Hall had had three regiments on the front line and two posted in reserve about one hundred yards to the rear. When the Virginians drove across the stone wall, however, the 59th New York and part of the 7th Michigan broke under the onslaught. With only the 20th Massachusetts left intact along the front, Hall ordered it to move "at once" and to strike the enemy flank.[35]

Lieutenant Colonel George N. Macy repeated Hall's orders to the Bay Staters, but the instructions could not be heard in the roar of gunfire. Consequently, the regiment "got into confusion," according to one member, and mistakenly began to withdraw. Officers ran to the front of the companies, waving their swords and pointing toward the trees. "Seeing the impossibility of executing any regular movement," Macy stated, he directed the companies to advance in a mass. He knew that "a hand to hand fight was coming."[36]

Behind the 20th Massachusetts, the 42nd New York and 19th Massachusetts were charging "side-by-side." Minutes earlier, Winfield Scott Hancock had stopped at the position of the 19th Massachusetts, pointed toward the clump of trees, and told Colonel Arthur F. Devereux "to get in God Damn quick." Devereux forwarded Hancock's order to Colonel James Mallon of the 42nd New York, instructing the latter officer to move at the double-quick. As Hancock rode to the Vermonters' position, where he was soon shot, the pair of regiments "made an impetuous dash" toward the Confederates. Colonel Hall appeared and "cheered us forward."[37]

The Virginians were, in Devereux's description, "just breaking through the little oak grove" when the Federal reserves arrived. The swarm of Yankees halted about fifteen paces from the Southerners, and both masses of men fired volleys. Major Edmund Rice of the 19th Massachusetts recalled, "I thought at the time I was the *bull's eye* for a good many of Pickets men." One bullet clipped off his cap, another knocked the sword from his hand, and a third struck the major in the abdomen. Color Sergeant Michael Cuddy carried the flag of the 42nd New York in the forefront of the regiment. Cut down with a mortal wound, Cuddy "rose by a convulsive effort" and waved the banner in the Rebels' faces. He had carried it since Fredericksburg in December 1862.[38]

In the 20th Massachusetts, Colonel Macy was flattened by a piece of an artillery shell, rose from the ground, and had his left hand shattered by a minié ball. He relinquished command to Captain Henry L. Abbott and headed for a field hospital, where a surgeon would amputate the hand. Both sides seemed immobilized as they lashed each other with gunfire. The Yankees were jammed together, "several files deep."[39]

Before long, more Federals joined the combat. Waved forward by staff officer Haskell came William Harrow's four regiments—the 19th Maine, 15th Massachusetts, 1st Minnesota, and 82nd New York. One member of the brigade wrote that the men had demanded that they charge the enemy before the command was given. "It was impossible to get there in order," wrote Colonel Francis Heath of the Maine unit. "Everyone wanted to be first and the men of the various commands were all mixed up. We went up more like a mob than a disciplined force."[40]

With the arrival of Harrow's troops, "the fight had become a perfect melee," stated a soldier in the 1st Minnesota, "and every man fought for him-self." Another Minnesotan declared, "We knew very well what we were there for and proceeded to business without ceremony." But a frenzy had gripped them that made the "business" a butchery at point-blank range. "If men ever became devils, that was one of the times," contended a Union lieutenant. "We were crazy with the excitement of the fight. We rushed in like wild beasts."[41]

Northerners and Southerners alike cursed, screamed, clubbed, stabbed, hurled rocks, fired rifles, tore cartridges and reloaded, looked after fallen comrades, yelled some more, and fired again. As it had been earlier in the day, now, in a spasm of time, a brief flickering in a life, ordinary and decent men slaughtered ordinary and decent men. Beneath a nondescript stand of trees on soil not fit for a good crop, they reaped a bloody harvest.[42]

Alexander Webb was struck in the groin by a bullet. Staff officer Frank Haskell suffered a severe bruise on his right leg from a spent minié ball that had hit his saddle first. The 19th Maine's Colonel Heath was knocked down by a piece of an artillery shell. While cheering on the troops, Captain John P. Blinn, a member of Harrow's staff, crumpled to the ground with a fatal wound. Sergeant Joseph H. Hervey of the 19th Massachusetts was "terribly mangled" by an artillery round. After Lieutenant Henry Ropes of the 20th Massachusetts died, his commander was moved to write in his report that the lieutenant's behavior was more exemplary "than I have ever witnessed in any other man." Privates and corporals lost their lives, with their passages un-noted.[43]

"The bullets seemed to come from front and both flanks," wrote a lieu-tenant in the 56th Virginia, "and I saw we could not hold the fence any longer." Some of the Virginians looked to the rear, searching for reinforce-ments, exclaiming, "Why dont they come!" At last, in an upheaval that spewed forth men, the Federals charged, breaking the stalemate on the slope. "Whether the command 'Charge!' was given by any general officer I do not know," remarked a Union lieutenant. "It seemed to me to come in a spon-taneous yell from the men, and instantly our line precipitated itself on the enemy."[44]

Officers and men from Webb's, Hall's, and Harrow's brigades and from ad-ditional units that had arrived poured down the ridge into the shreds of Pickett's division. In the forefront of the Union mass raced Corporal Henry D. O'Brien of the 1st Minnesota, holding the broken staff of the flag and wav-ing it before his comrades. A Southerner shot O'Brien in the hand, and he relinquished the banner to another bearer. For his bravery, O'Brien would be given a Medal of Honor.[45]

"The effect was electrical" upon the Virginians, bragged a Yankee. Massachusetts Sergeant William A. McGinnis yelled: "They're broke, boys! They're running! There they go! See 'em run!" Though many of the Rebels fled, knots of them resisted. Those who ran were cut down "like leaves," stated a Confederate. A private in the 14th Virginia recounted later: "It was almost as bad going back as it was coming forward. They continued to shoot at us." Hundreds of Virginians, however, gave up the struggle, either pleading with the Federals to cease fire, waving handkerchiefs, or shouting, "We surrender!"[46]

Still the bloodletting continued. The 19th Massachusetts's Major Edmund Rice, who some comrades claimed later got closer to the enemy than any Union officer, fell wounded. His leadership and bravery would earn him a Medal of Honor. A captain in the 71st Pennsylvania was killed "frightfully," and the regiment's color-bearer, William K. Bortman, led its counterattack, dying with the flag in his hands about ten feet from the stone wall. Lieutenant Sumner Paine of the 29th Massachusetts, only two months out of West Point, was yelling to a fellow officer, "Isn't this glorious," when he took a bullet in the chest near the wall and was gone.[47]

West of the wall, fortune finally deserted James Kemper. Mounted on horseback, an easy target, the brigadier had been spared until the end, or, as he said, "about the instant at which the general rout began." A bullet then struck him in the groin, and he toppled from the saddle. This was, in his words, "excruciatingly painful" and temporarily paralyzed his legs. Minutes later, some Federals found him and lifted him into a blanket. But a few of his Virginians saw him, and after either shooting or scattering the Yankees, they carried Kemper to the rear.[48]

Amid the carnage between the copse of trees and the stone wall, the victorious Northerners seized the trophies, the "damned red flags of rebellion." Captain Alexander McCuen of the 71st Pennsylvania beheaded the color-bearer of the 3rd Virginia with his sword and grabbed the banner. His fellow Pennsylvanian Captain Robert McBride captured Corporal L. P. Williams, who had been wounded, and the colors of the 56th Virginia. Two enlisted men in the Pennsylvania regiment, privates John Clapp and Isaac Tibbins, captured the flags of the 9th and 53rd Virginia, respectively.[49]

The 19th Massachusetts's Sergeant Benjamin Jellison flattened the color-bearer of the 57th Virginia with a fist and seized the banner; his comrade Private Benjamin Falls demanded the surrender of the wounded bearer of the 19th Virginia and gathered up the flag. Like Jellison, Corporal Joseph DeCastro knocked down the 14th Virginia's bearer and took the colors. Each of the three Massachusetts soldiers earned Medals of Honor for their actions.[50]

Other Union enlisted men brought in additional flags. Two members of the 82nd New York came away with the standards of the 1st and 7th Virginia. A soldier in the 16th Vermont captured the flag of the 8th Virginia, and a man in the 59th New York grasped the colors of the 18th Virginia. Private Marshall Sherman was awarded a Medal of Honor for his capture of the 28th Virginia's banner. The color-bearer of the 24th Virginia escaped and saved his standard.[51]

On the slope by the clump of trees, meanwhile, the Federals herded their prisoners rearward across the crest. Some of the Yankees still fired at the fleeing Confederates, and Union batteries chased them with shells and solid shots. The fight was not yet finished, but the Union soldiers knew that they had repulsed the enemy on this bloody patch of ground. To the north, in front of the stone wall defended by their comrades in Alexander Hays's division, they saw that the struggle had been decided.[52]

✿   ✿   ✿

ISAAC TRIMBLE'S TWO BRIGADES of North Carolinians, moving in direct support of Johnston Pettigrew's division, reached Emmitsburg Road as the Confederate assault rolled up the slope toward a climax. The advance of Trimble's units across the fields—"a wide, hot, and already crimson plain," according to Colonel William L. J. Lowrance—had been slowed by fences and fleeing men from Pettigrew's command. When John Brockenbrough's Virginians broke in a rout, James Lane's brigade, on the left of Trimble's line, began to outpace Lowrance's regiments and to oblique north. Trimble "checked" Lane's march. Nevertheless, the lines of the two brigades moved farther apart, creating a gap.[53]

Fortunately for the North Carolinians, the Union artillery had concentrated on Pettigrew's and Pickett's ranks, resulting in few casualties among Trimble's ten regiments. "The line moved forward handsomely and firmly," reported a staff officer. When the regiments approached Emmitsburg Road, however, a number of Federal batteries redirected their fire on them. Shell bursts and canister tore into the North Carolinians. "No one who was not in it," recalled a private, "can imagine the terrible fire of the batteries on the right and those Parrots on Round Top. And the batteries in front were *very busy*." [54]

The Confederates cheered for the "Old North State," and shoved down sections of the fence on the western side of the road. The enemy artillery discharges increased, ripping gaps in the Rebel ranks. "The air was sulphury as the infernal regions," thought a North Carolinian. Lieutenant Henry Moore of the 38th North Carolina stated, "Our men [were] falling in every direction." The Union fire, Moore added, was "terrible." Trimble wrote afterward, "The loss here was fearful, and I knew that no troops could long endure it." [55]

Scores, if not hundreds, of the North Carolinians turned and headed to the rear. "That fire was too much," confessed a private, "and we 'Turkeyed' in fine style." By now, the survivors of Pettigrew's decimated brigades were streaming down the slope, impelling the flight of Trimble's men. Trimble admitted later that he did not try to rally those who were retreating. He spurred his horse across the road, joining the officers and men who kept going toward the Union line. [56]

"The remaining few," as Lowrance described the troops left in his brigade, crossed the road and charged up the slope, following the path of Birkett Fry's Tennesseans and Alabamians. Union infantry and artillery hammered the North Carolinians. The colonel claimed that they reached or "touched" the enemy works, probably meaning the remains of the stone wall that extended north from the outer angle. The Federal musketry sliced into both flanks of the Confederates. With "no support in view," wrote Lowrance, his men began falling back without orders. [57]

Major Joseph H. Saunders of the 33rd North Carolina fell wounded in the attack. Struck in the mouth by a bullet that knocked out his teeth, Saunders was left for dead on the field. When his family in Chapel Hill received a report of his death, they held funeral services for him. But Saunders survived the wound, was captured by the Federals, and was subsequently imprisoned. Three months after the battle, the family learned that he was alive. But not until the spring of 1865 did Saunders return home. [58]

Lieutenant W. H. Winchester of the 13th North Carolina was struck down by artillery fire. The round mangled his right foot, with only the "heel-string" keeping it attached to his body. Winchester crawled toward the road, stopping near the ditch along the roadbed. Pulling out a knife, he asked a passing soldier to cut off the foot. When the man refused, Winchester did it himself. He would die later in a Union field hospital. [59]

On the left of Lowrance's regiments, the 7th North Carolina and the right wing of the 37th North Carolina of Lane's brigade veered to the right after they crossed the wall. These Rebels advanced only a short distance beyond the road before recoiling before the enemy fire. The entire color guard of the 7th North Carolina was either killed or wounded, and four company commanders went down with wounds. A minié ball hit the regiment's commander, Major J. McLeod Turner, striking his spinal cord and paralyzing him. The North Carolinians withdrew into the roadbed and lay down for a few minutes, sheltering themselves from the fury.[60]

Lane's other regiments—the 33rd, 18th, 28th, and the left wing of the 37th North Carolina—spilled across the second fence, moving over the ground bloodied by Joseph Davis's and James Marshall's North Carolinians and Mississippians. One of Lane's men believed that their ranks had been reduced to "only a skirmish line." They never had a chance. From their front on the crest behind the stone wall, on their left along the Bryan farm lane, and even in their rear west of Emmitsburg Road, Alexander Hays's Union veterans raked them in a scissors of musketry.[61]

The Yankees along Bryan's farm lane—the members of the 108th and 126th New York and 1st Massachusetts Sharpshooters—rested their rifles on the top rail of a fence and did "great execution." The Federals were, stated a New York captain, "quite close to the enemy's flank." Some of the Northerners shouted, "Come on, come on; come to death." At the head of the lane, the two-gun section of George Woodruff's Battery I, 1st United States Artillery, blasted Lane's troops with double loads of canister. Woodruff, however, lay dying beneath a tree in Ziegler's Grove, having been struck in the back by a bullet.[62]

Behind and to the left of the Confederates west of Emmitsburg Road, the 8th Ohio lashed the Rebels from a knoll along a fence. After the Ohioans had routed Brockenbrough's Virginians at Stevens Run, they had changed front on their left company and followed Pettigrew's troops toward Cemetery Ridge, firing at the enemy as they moved. "They seem to pay no attention to us," wrote an Ohioan, "who are a mere handful." Halting on the knoll, the 8th Ohio continued to pour point-blank musketry into the Confederates. A member of the regiment claimed that, when they triggered a volley at such a close range, "a moan went up from the field, distinctly to be heard."[63]

Lane stated in his report, "Both officers and men moved forward with a heroism unsurpassed." But no soldiers could withstand fire from three directions. It was a "great slaughter." The Confederate ranks simply melted away

before the gunfire and canister fire. "We got entirely broken up that afternoon," testified a private, "and noticed then that the 'Yanks' were harder to
push back than formerly." With Pettigrew's brigades in shreds and the troops
in flight, Lane's soldiers broke for the rear.[64]

Among the Confederate casualties were Pettigrew and Trimble. A canister
shot crushed the bones in Pettigrew's left hand, and his horse was killed
under him. Trimble, meanwhile, near the end of his brigades' advance beyond the road, suffered a bullet wound to the left leg that would result in the
amputation of the limb and his eventual capture by the Federals after the battle. When an aide asked the stricken Trimble if they should rally the troops,
the redoubtable fighter replied: "It's all over! Let the men go back."[65]

Hundreds of Tennesseans, Alabamians, Mississippians, and North Carolinians, however, were not so fortunate. The final repulse and flight of Pettigrew's and Trimble's troops occurred at about the same time Pickett's
Virginians were overwhelmed in front of the copse of trees. The "spirit of the
men was unrestrainable," noted an officer of Hays's troops; the Federals
leaped over the stone wall and scaled the fences, to race down the slope into
the shattered ranks of the Rebels. A North Carolina lieutenant confessed, "A
good many surrendered rather than risk getting out." The Southerners threw
down their weapons, waved handkerchiefs, and, in the words of a Yankee,
were "crying out mightily for quarter."[66]

Individual Federals gathered up Confederate battle flags. Officers and
men from the 1st Delaware, 12th New Jersey, 14th Connecticut, 39th New
York, 42nd New York, 126th New York, and 8th Ohio captured fourteen flags
from Pettigrew's and Trimble's twenty-two regiments and a battalion. Only
the flags of the 2nd Mississippi, 11th North Carolina, and 7th Tennessee were
saved by members of the regiments. The fate of six other banners remain unknown, although they were probably captured and reported as unidentified.
Sergeant Luke Byrn of the 2nd Mississippi had carried his flag almost to the
wall, then fell wounded on the ground, lay there concealing the colors all
night, and somehow returned to the Confederate lines. The other two standards were taken to the rear during the retreat.[67]

Several of the Northerners were awarded Medals of Honor for seizing the
enemy banners. Sergeant Major William B. Hincks, Corporal Christopher
Flynn, and Private E. W. Bacon of the 14th Connecticut earned medals for
the capture of flags from the 14th Tennessee, 52nd North Carolina, and 16th
North Carolina, respectively. The 126th New York's Captain Morris Brown,

Jr., found the flag of the 28th North Carolina, and Sergeant George H. Dore and Private Jerry Hall picked up unidentified colors. All three of the New Yorkers were given medals.[68]

Sergeant Daniel Miller and some comrades from the 8th Ohio rushed to Emmitsburg Road, forcing Confederates to surrender. Miller grabbed the color-bearer of the 38th Virginia of Lewis Armistead's brigade and took the flag. Private James Richmond captured an unidentified standard as a fellow Ohioan secured the colors of the 34th North Carolina. Miller and Richmond were also awarded Medals of Honor.[69]

What had been serried ranks of thousands of Confederate troops less than an hour before were now the bloodied shards of broken lines and broken men. Hundreds lay on the ground from near the edge of Seminary Ridge to within feet of the copse of trees; hundreds more stood in knots surrounded by Yankees; and hundreds of others were escaping from the awful carnage. Cannon fire from both Union and Confederate batteries still bellowed, adding more men to the slaughter heaps. The fury was unabated.

13

"It Is My Fault"

G EORGE PICKETT HAD WATCHED the decimation and repulse of his division from near the Nicholas Codori farm. His precise location during the Virginians' final thrust up the slope and across the stone wall has long been a source of historical dispute. Despite a few discreditable postwar allegations that Pickett remained in the rear during the charge, he probably crossed Emmitsburg Road and remained there until the retreat began. Once his three brigades closed on the Union line, Pickett could offer little direction to them. Instead, the general looked on as the whirlwind enveloped his men.[1]

Pickett's primary concern, once Richard Garnett's and James Kemper's brigades reached Emmitsburg Road, was the advance of the support troops to reinforce his division. As noted previously, he sent Captain Robert A. Bright to Longstreet with the message, "He would take the Hill, but could not hold it, without reinforcements." After spurring to the rear, Bright located Longstreet, who was sitting on a fence. The staff officer delivered Pickett's message and waited for a reply. Before Longstreet responded, the British army officer James Fremantle joined them.[2]

Bright recounted the conversation between Longstreet and Fremantle in a postwar letter. According to Bright, Fremantle spoke first: "General Longstreet, General Lee sent me here, and said you would put me in a position to see this charge. I would not have missed it for the world."

"I would," replied Longstreet; "the charge is over Colonel Fremantle; Captain Bright ride back and tell General Pickett what you heard me tell Colonel Fremantle."

Before Bright turned and rode away, however, Longstreet shouted to him, "Captain, you can tell Pickett that he can order [up] Wilcox's brigade."[3]

Bright hurried to the front and found Pickett on a hillside "which was the last descent before the ascent to the Stone Wall." Pickett reacted to Longstreet's words by sending Lieutenants Edward R. Baird and W. Stuart Symington and Bright to Cadmus Wilcox, hoping that one of them would survive the ride. All of the officers reached Wilcox and delivered the order. When Bright, the last of the trio, rejoined Pickett, a "heavy column of the enemy," as the staff officer described the situation on Cemetery Ridge, was turning "our left."[4]

At this point—probably thirty minutes or so after the main assault force had begun the advance—Pickett directed Bright to seek artillery support from Major James Dearing's batteries and his brother, Major Charles Pickett, to ask Longstreet for additional help. Neither staff officer succeeded in his mission. Captain William C. Marshall of Dearing's battalion told Bright that the gun crews had depleted nearly all of the ammunition and could not find the reserve ordnance train. Charles Pickett, who thought that when he left his brother "it was our final parting in this world," could not locate Longstreet and headed back toward the division.[5]

By then, it was too late for Pickett's, Pettigrew's, and Trimble's troops. The Virginians' cry referring to the support troops, "Why don't they come?," was a question that would embitter them and has haunted the history of the charge. The answer remains wrapped in uncertainty and is emblematic of Confederate command failures on this day.

At the center of the answer stood James Longstreet, who had direct authority over the nine brigades in the main assault force and Richard Anderson's five brigades in support. He had joined Porter Alexander along the artillery officer's line of cannon when the assault began. From there, he rode to a fence—most likely the one that ran from Spangler's Woods to Emmitsburg Road—dismounted to rest his horse, and continued to view the advance from a top rail. According to his chief of staff, Moxley Sorrel, "While Longstreet by no means approved the movement, his soldierly eye watched every feature of it. He neglected nothing that could help it and his anxiety for Pickett and the men was very apparent."[6]

Only ten minutes or so into the advance, when John Brockenbrough's brigade broke under artillery fire and volleys from the 8th Ohio, Longstreet reacted quickly. He sent Major Osmun Latrobe to direct Isaac Trimble to cover Johnston Pettigrew's left flank, and hurried Sorrel to Pickett to warn him about his right flank. Longstreet then ordered Anderson to move forward with the brigades of William Mahone, Carnot Posey, and Ambrose Wright in support of Pettigrew.[7]

When Longstreet's order to Anderson filtered down to the troops in the three brigades, the "men fell in promptly, and the line was dressed," wrote a Virginian with Mahone. He noticed, however, that "the men around me were solemn and silent." A fellow soldier in the brigade alleged later that a number of his comrades refused to obey the order. By the time the three brigades stepped out from Seminary Ridge, Pickett's and Pettigrew's units had become engulfed in the cauldron of hell on Cemetery Ridge.[8]

One of Posey's Mississippians confided in his diary that the three brigades "make a very feeble effort & accomplish nothing." When they reached the rise where the Confederate artillery was deployed, a courier rode up with instructions from Longstreet to halt. Anderson stated in his report that Longstreet said that a further advance "was useless, and would only involve unnecessary loss, the assault having failed." A Mississippi captain informed his mother in a letter that Longstreet's order "saved many lives, and while we were willing to go to the last man, we were thankful for it."[9]

Here Anderson's men waited as the survivors of Pickett's, Pettigrew's, and Trimble's commands streamed back from Cemetery Ridge. To the left, Edward Thomas's Georgians, lying in the Long Lane, moved forward to the ridge above Stevens Run, were hit by Union artillery fire, and retired. Who ordered Thomas to advance remains unknown. Beside the Georgians and Abner Perrin's South Carolinians in the roadbed, Robert Rodes prepared to go in. He had discretionary orders to attack if he saw an opportunity. For a handful of minutes, he thought that he could charge, but soon, he reported, it "was announced, and was apparent to me, that the attack had already failed."[10]

Richard Ewell, commander of Lee's Second Corps, meanwhile, had ridden to Seminary Ridge and watched the assault from there. As he looked on, Ewell scribbled a note to Jubal Early: "Longstreet & A. P. Hill are advancing in splendid style, if you see an opportunity, strike." A courier delivered it to Early in town, where his troops were posted in the streets and among the buildings. With Union artillery and infantry still firmly in place on Cemetery Hill, Early could do nothing except to sacrifice his own men.[11]

By this time, however, Cadmus Wilcox's Alabamians and David Lang's Floridians were crossing the fields toward Emmitsburg Road. When Pickett's three staff officers had delivered Longstreet's order to advance, Wilcox brought his troops to their feet. Although he had told Lang that morning that he would oppose such a movement, Wilcox obeyed the command. He did not, however, relay the order to Lang, who started his regiments only after he heard Alabama officers shout to their men, "Attention! Forward!" A Floridian confessed that when the command came to march it was "not obeyed with the same alacrity as was the case yesterday."[12]

The "crisis was over" on Cemetery Ridge, thought Porter Alexander when the two brigades started forward. The artillery officer watched them march, and "as they passed I could not help feeling a great pity for the useless loss of life they were incurring, for there was nothing for them to support." Because of the terrain, Wilcox, whom his men called "Old Billy Fixin," stated, "Not a man of the division that I was ordered to support could I see."[13]

When the twelve hundred Confederates topped the rise west of Emmitsburg Road, they came into view of Union artillerymen. The gun crews in Freeman McGilvery's line on southern Cemetery Ridge and from Little Round Top, fifty-nine cannon in all, hammered the oncoming Southerners. Wilcox described the punishment as a "terrific fire of artillery." Lieutenant James Wentworth of the 5th Florida wrote: "It was the hottest work I ever saw. My men were falling all around me with brains blown out, arms off and wounded in every description. I used every exertion in my power to cheer the men on." A shell burst above Wentworth's company, and the concussion knocked him unconscious.[14]

The Alabamians and Floridians struggled in crossing the fences along the road, exposing themselves more to the Federal gunners. Once over the rails, they yelled and pushed ahead into the low ground drained by Plum Run. "Our men fell fast and thick," wrote an officer in the 2nd Florida as they descended into the valley. Lang's Floridians kept going until they reached a fence along a skirt of woods. Here they scattered and sought shelter behind rocks and bushes.[15]

On their right, the Alabamians halted, scurrying for cover. Lieutenant Colonel Hilary A. Herbert of the 8th Alabama recalled that, as his soldiers went down the slope toward Plum Run, "I could hear their missiles, some of them grape shot, crashing through the bones of my men 'like hail-stones breaking through glass.' " Wilcox spurred his horse to the rear to ask for artillery support from Confederate batteries. He learned that they were out of ammunition.[16]

Caught in what Lang described as a "death trap," the Southerners opened a desultory fire. They held their position for only a few minutes. A Union infantryman stated later that the bushes were "twitching" from the bullets fired by the Yankees in front of the Confederates. Then, from the north, the 16th Vermont struck Lang's left flank.[17]

The Vermonters had been gathering prisoners from their counterattack on Pickett's troops when Colonel Wheelock Veazey saw the advance of Lang's and Wilcox's brigades. The colonel ordered his men to fall in, moved them by the left flank until they were opposite the enemy flank, and then faced the regiment to the front. Directing them not to fire, Veazey signaled the charge. The Vermonters cheered. On their left, four companies of the 14th Vermont scrambled off the ridge, moving against the enemy's front.[18]

"The movement was so sudden and rapid," wrote Veazey of his regiment's attack, "that the enemy could not change front to oppose us." Lang agreed, explaining in his report, "The men were by this time so badly scattered in the bushes and among the rocks that it was impossible to make any movement to meet or check the enemy's advance." To stay, Lang declared, meant "certain annihilation." He ordered a retreat.[19]

The Floridians bolted toward the rear, followed by the Alabamians. Wilcox wrote that he ordered the withdrawal of his brigade, but Herbert claimed that Wilcox was still with the artillery when the Federals struck. "It became evident that nothing could save us but a retreat," declared Herbert. He and the other regimental commanders conferred and agreed to get out. In fact, Wilcox had sent a courier with a command to withdraw, but the courier had been killed en route. Nevertheless, in the view of an Alabama soldier, the order "saved many lives."[20]

The Vermonters corralled dozens of prisoners, most of them from the 2nd and 8th Florida. Color Sergeant Charles C. Brink of the 16th Vermont captured the flag of the 2nd Florida. The colors had been made by a group of women in Tallahassee and had a "unique sunburst design" sewn on the standard battle flag. The Vermonters' brigade commander, George Stannard, asserted in his report that the Rebels "were scooped almost *en masse* into our lines."[21]

One of the Southern prisoners was Lieutenant Wentworth of the 5th Florida. Minutes after he had been flattened senseless by the explosion of an artillery round while urging his men forward, he awoke and stood up. Dazed and believing that the attack was still under way, he shouted for his troops to "give them hell." A Vermont private walked up to Wentworth and said that "they would give me hell if I did not surrender." The lieutenant complied.[22]

The Confederate captives went willingly and unguarded into the Union lines, wanting to escape the ongoing fighting. A number of Confederate cannon, with a few rounds left in the chests, opened fire, covering the flight of the Floridians and Alabamians and stopping the Vermonters' pursuit. Wilcox's and Lang's troops passed through the row of guns and halted at their original position. The Federals retired to Cemetery Ridge. For his decision to attack the Confederates and for his leadership in the action, Colonel Veazey of the 16th Vermont would be awarded a Medal of Honor.[23]

Wilcox and Lang together lost nearly five hundred in killed, wounded, and captured, more than 40 percent of their numbers. A Florida officer wrote his wife the next day that the brigade "was small before the fight, it is *very* much smaller now." Compounding the losses of friends and comrades was their belief that they had been needlessly sacrificed. The charge, in the estimation of an Alabamian, had been "a desperate undertaking almost a forlorn hope." Its only purpose to another Alabamian was "the loss of men." Porter Alexander described their advance as "at once both absurd and tragic." Lieutenant Colonel Herbert called it a "hopeless movement" that "I have never been able to understand. Gen. Wilcox never explained it—if he knew, as I suppose he did not." Many of the Confederate officers believed that it had been ordered to prevent a Union counterattack.[24]

Lang attributed some of the blame to Wilcox, who the Florida colonel thought had not obeyed the order to advance as promptly "as it should have been." During the morning, when the pair of officers had learned of their role as immediate support for Pickett's right flank, Wilcox had voiced to Lang his unwillingness to take his troops against the Union position. Perhaps the brigadier had acted reluctantly when Pickett's aides brought Longstreet's directive, but in the end it made little difference. Twelve hundred officers and men, exposed to the might of nearly sixty Union cannon in open fields, could not salvage a charge that had already been destroyed. Had the two brigades moved as soon as Pickett's line had passed their position, they probably would have prevented the flank attack of the 13th and 16th Vermont against James Kemper's men. Whether that would have altered the outcome at the copse of trees, with ample Union reserves at hand, seems unlikely. Far more additional Confederate troops, moving in immediate support, were needed if the attackers were to have had a chance of prevailing on the awful ridge.[25]

In the end, only the Floridians and Alabamians undertook a movement in support of the main assault force. By the time they went in, it was indeed "a forlorn hope." The evidence seems to indicate, however, that Lee expected a more active participation in the charge by other units than just Wilcox's and Lang's brigades. Lee apparently considered the fourteen brigades assigned to Longstreet's control as an integrated force that would be used in the assault. According to Brigadier General John Imboden, commander of a semi-independent cavalry force, Lee told him that night that if Pickett's, Pettigrew's, and Trimble's troops "had been supported as they were to have been—but, for some reason not yet fully explained to me, were not—we would have held the position and the day would have been ours."[26]

In his postwar writings, Porter Alexander supported Lee's statement to Imboden. "That Gen. Lee expected the attack to be at least better supported than it was is very certain," declared Alexander. The artillery officer wrote, further, that he "had heard a sort of camp rumor, that morning, that Gen. Lee said he intended to march every man he had upon the cemetery hill that day." Alexander attributed the failure of the support troops to march sooner to "a misunderstanding somewhere." Written orders, he thought, would have corrected any questions or uncertainties.[27]

Lee did not issue written orders. In his thinking, his discussions with Longstreet must have settled the question of the role of support troops. He had left the details to Longstreet, evidently expecting those units to advance in a timely fashion. Both men knew that the main assault force had to cross the fields as rapidly as possible, and that if the reinforcements were to bolster the attack they would have to advance soon after Pickett's, Pettigrew's, and Trimble's commands started forward. Alexander contended that, once the leading units had covered four hundred yards and the support troops had not moved, the "battle failed of being fought as Gen. Lee expected & wished."[28]

Longstreet must have either misunderstood Lee's plan for the reserve units or believed that his authority allowed him to act as his judgment dictated. He called for the brigades of Mahone, Posey, and Wright only after Brockenbrough's brigade had dissolved at Stevens Run, roughly ten minutes into the attack. He waited until Pickett's aide Bright came up—more than five minutes later—to send in Wilcox and Lang. Later, Longstreet had Moxley Sorrel ride to Lafayette McLaws with orders for that officer to cross Emmitsburg Road with his troops to cover the right flank of the attackers. In all cases, the response of the Confederates was too late.[29]

Longstreet halted the advance of Anderson's three brigades, believing that the assault had failed and not wanting to sacrifice more lives. But if Bright's account is accurate, Longstreet allowed Wilcox and Lang to go ahead after he had made that judgment about the attack. Did he send in the two brigades as cover for the retreat of the main force, or did he order them forward to comply, in part, with Lee's plans? Was Longstreet acting in opposition to the charge, refusing to expend more blood in a hopeless effort? None of these questions can be answered with assurance, but Longstreet's actions did spare lives, even if they did not fulfill Lee's wishes.[30]

Ultimately, Longstreet's decisions need to be judged against Lee's orders to him. The failure of the assault revealed that Lee needed more troops if the Confederates were to have a reasonable chance to succeed. But if Lee had planned to hurl Anderson's units and those in the Long Lane against the Union position, he would have stripped the entire center of his army of troops. If the outcome did not change with the advent of these additional thousands of men, Lee would risk the security of his army to a Union counterattack. There would have been a gap of nearly two miles in the heart of the Confederate position, with only the shattered remnants of defeated commands and cannon with little ammunition to stop the Federals. It would have been a gamble with enormous risks.[31]

The reports of Lee, Longstreet, A. P. Hill, Anderson, Rodes, and Wilcox indicate that the support troops were to advance either as necessary or after "any success" had been gained by the main assault units. Although their words do not offer unquestioned clarity, it appears that their understanding was different from Lee's as expressed in his statement to John Imboden that night: if the attackers "had been supported as they were to have been . . . we would have held the position and the day would have been ours." Perhaps Lee interpreted the lodgment on the slope of Cemetery Ridge as a success. But Longstreet viewed it otherwise, stopping the forward movement of the support troops, except for Wilcox and Lang. It cannot be doubted that Longstreet acted correctly when he ordered the halt, unwilling to add to the carnage in a failed operation. It cannot be doubted that Lee seemed to expect those troops to play a more active part.[32]

Behind the controversy lay the breakdown of the army's command system. Lee had brought his army into Pennsylvania in search of a decisive victory that could possibly result in Confederate independence. The July 3 afternoon assault against the Union center was his final attempt to attain that victory on this field. He understood the risks, but after hours of discussions and preparations, the use of reserves—a critical component of the operation—had not been clearly defined. Subordinates had interpreted their roles differently from what Lee expected. He and Longstreet seemed to act at cross-purposes. There should have been no questions or uncertainties left unsettled. It was a bad day for the Confederate high command, a worse one for the officers and men in the ranks. On Cemetery Ridge, meanwhile, a different story was transpiring.[33]

o   o   o

GEORGE G. MEADE RODE onto the crest of Cemetery Ridge minutes after the repulse of the Confederate charge. By his own admission later, "I did not myself see anything of the assaulting column." Accompanied by his son, George, and Lieutenant Ranald S. Mackenzie, an acting aide-de-camp, Meade saw only a group of Southern prisoners as he ascended the eastern slope of the ridge. Halting behind the position of Alexander Hays's division, Meade met Lieutenant John Egan of Battery I, 1st United States Artillery.[34]

Where was General Hays? Meade inquired of Egan. The young artillery officer pointed to the slope beyond the stone wall. Hays and Captain George P. Corts and Lieutenant David Shields of his staff were riding along the ridge, dragging captured Confederate battle flags on the ground. Hays's jubilant veterans were emitting "cheer after cheer" as the three riders passed through their ranks. They would encircle the division's entire line before halting. Shields, whom Hays had kissed on the cheek when the Rebels fled, called it "the grandest ride men ever took." [35]

Meade, however, had a more pressing concern and asked Egan "if they had turned," referring to the Confederates. Yes, replied Egan, because Hays had one of their flags. A "mighty cross" Meade barked back: "I don't care for their flags. Have they turned?" Again the lieutenant responded that they had, and Meade headed south along the crest toward the copse of trees.[36]

Soon a party of captured Southerners stopped Meade. One of them asked where they should go. Pointing to the rear, Meade told them "in a laughing way" to "go along that you will be well taken care of." At that moment, Confederate cannon reopened fire, the rounds howling across the ridge. "Why its hotter here than it was in front," exclaimed a Confederate as he and his comrades scattered toward the rear.[37]

Continuing on, Meade encountered Captain Frank Haskell of John Gibbon's staff, whom the general knew personally. "How is it going here?" asked Meade.

"I believe, General," said Haskell, "the enemy's attack is repulsed."

"What?" rebutted Meade. "Is the assault entirely repulsed?"

"It is, Sir," assured Haskell.[38]

Meade then turned to his son and remarked: "Well it seems to be all right here now, we ought to be hearing from Howard. Lets go over there." As they started toward Cemetery Hill, however, an artillery shell exploded nearby; a piece of it struck and killed the younger Meade's horse. The aide secured another mount and they rode off the ridge, moving rapidly through the fields east of the crest. Minutes later, Major William G. Mitchell of Winfield Scott Hancock's staff overtook the army commander.[39]

Reining up, Mitchell repeated an oral message that Hancock had dictated to him: "Tell General Meade that the troops under my command have repulsed the enemy's assault and that we have gained a great victory. The enemy is now flying in all directions in my front." When he finished, Mitchell added that Hancock had been "dangerously wounded." Meade removed his hat, leaned toward Mitchell, and said, "Say to General Hancock that I regret exceedingly that he is wounded, and that I thank him for the Country and for myself for the service he has rendered to day." As Meade resumed his ride to Cemetery Hill, Mitchell hurried south to rejoin his commander.[40]

Hancock had received ample attention by the time he sent Mitchell with the message to Meade. When the wounded general refused to leave the field until the enemy attack had been repulsed, his aides sent for an ambulance and Dr. Alexander N. Dougherty, medical director of the Second Corps. Hancock's staff officers and others moved him under the shade of a tree and waited for the surgeon. While there, Captain Henry Bingham of his staff joined the group. Bingham had not known of the general's wound until then, and Hancock sent him to inform John Caldwell that he now commanded the corps.[41]

Bingham returned shortly and gave Hancock a pair of spurs, a watch and chain, a seal, and a pocketbook that belonged to Hancock's old friend Confederate General Lewis Armistead. When the fighting at the copse of trees had reached a climax, Bingham rode onto the crest and met some privates who were carrying a wounded Southerner to the rear. Bingham ordered them back into line, but they replied that they had "an important prisoner," General Longstreet. The staff officer dismounted, saw that the man was suffering, and asked him his name. "General Armistead of the Confederate Army," came the reply.

"General," said the aide, "I am Captain Bingham of General Hancock's staff, and if you have anything valuable in your possession which you desire taken care of I will [take] care of it, for you."

Armistead inquired if it was General Winfield Scott Hancock. Yes, said Bingham. Hancock, responded the wounded officer, was "an old and valued friend of his," and he added that he wanted Bingham to give a message to his friend. "Tell General Hancock for me," as Bingham recounted his words, "that I have done him and done you all an injury which I shall *regret* or repent (I forget the exact word) the longest day I live." Then Bingham retrieved the items from Armistead and directed the soldiers to take him to the rear.[42]

The detail—probably Pennsylvanians from Alexander Webb's brigade—carried Armistead to the Eleventh Corps hospital, the home of George Spangler, located between Taneytown Road and Baltimore Pike. Dr. Daniel G. Brinton and another surgeon examined his injuries—bullet wounds to the "fleshy part" of his right arm and to the left leg, below the knee. Brinton described both as not "of a serious nature." Armistead told the surgeon, however, that "he had suffered much from over-exertion, want of sleep, and mental anxiety within the last few days." Nevertheless, Brinton wrote later that "his prospects of recovery seemed good."[43]

But Armistead lived less than two days, dying at the Spangler home on July 5. "I was astonished to learn of his death," wrote Brinton later. The doctor attributed it to "secondary fever & prostration." When the general's friends in Baltimore learned of his death, they traveled to Gettysburg, secured his body, and had it buried in St. Paul's Cemetery in Baltimore. For the old friends Hancock and Armistead, there would be a long passage, until Hancock's death in 1886, before they met again.[44]

Hancock, meanwhile, had been placed in an ambulance, attended to by Dr. Dougherty. The surgeon had removed a piece of a tenpenny nail from the general's wound. Occasional rounds from Confederate cannon still exploded over the ridge or whistled past. When the ambulance had proceeded to a relatively safe area, Hancock ordered it stopped. Although weakened by the loss of blood, he retained his combative nature and asked Dougherty to write a note to Meade as he dictated it. "I have never seen a more formidable attack," Hancock said, "and if the Sixth and Fifth Corps have pressed up, the enemy will be destroyed. The enemy must be short of ammunition, as I was shot with a tenpenny nail. I did not leave the field till the victory was entirely secured and the enemy was no longer in sight. . . . Not a rebel was in sight upright when I left." The note was given to a courier, and the ambulance rolled on toward a hospital.[45]

On Cemetery Ridge, the Federals, mostly Hancock's veterans, dealt with the aftermath of their victory. Celebration mixed with the grim reality of ground reddened by blood and gore. Death lingered, even when it seemed to have passed. Confederate artillery fire killed Lieutenant William Smith of the 1st Delaware, and a captain in the 69th Pennsylvania, as each of them carried a captured battle flag to headquarters in the rear. Another shell burst above the 13th Vermont as the regiment returned to its position, wounding two members and killing three. One of the slain was, wrote a comrade, "literally dismembered, one leg, bared of all but the shoe and stocking, being thrown several feet from the body."[46]

Their deaths added only a small amount to the sea of carnage that washed over the ridge and into Emmitsburg Road. The victors offered descriptions. The dead and wounded, stated one of them in a letter, "lay thicker than wheat sheaves. In some places they are winnows of human bodies." Lieutenant Gulian Weir told his father two days later, "July 3 was as exciting a fight I have yet been in. The enemy dead littered the field as far as I could see." In front of the copse of trees, according to the 20th Massachusetts's Captain Henry L. Abbott, "the rows of dead after the battle I found to be within 15 and 20 feet apart, as near hand to hand fighting as I ever care to see. The rebels behaved with as much pluck as any men in the world could; they stood there, against the fence, until they were nearly all shot down."[47]

Alexander Webb walked among the fallen near Alonzo Cushing's cannon and counted forty-two dead Virginians in the area where Armistead had been wounded. A captured Virginia lieutenant claimed that he had never seen so many corpses than between the stone wall and the clump of trees. In front of Hays's position, Lieutenant Lewis H. Crandell of the 125th New York tallied 156 slain Confederates in a two-acre section. Crandell went down to Emmitsburg Road and found the dead and wounded "thicker still behind the fence, they piled up." A member of the 12th New Jersey who also walked to the road noted that the dead seemed to be two to five feet deep. Captain Andrew H. Boyd of the 108th New York spoke for many men when he jotted in his diary under July 3, "It was an awful battle—the worst we have seen yet."[48]

Many of the Federals on the ridge had neither the inclination nor the time to count the enemy dead. Most of them sought shelter from the sporadic Confederate artillery fire, while details nudged prisoners to the rear, collected discarded arms, and attended to wounded comrades. In all, more than two thousand Southerners were herded to the rear, to be placed eventually on the farm of Daniel Sheaffer along Rock Creek. The eighty-two-man battalion of the 10th New York, a Zouave unit serving as the provost guard of Hays's division, escorted a majority of the captives to the rear. The rounds from their own batteries hurried the Rebels toward the Sheaffer farm.[49]

Later, wounded Confederates were gathered up and sent to field hospitals. Among these Southerners was Captain William Berkeley of the 8th Virginia. When Berkeley fell with a severe wound, he was taken to the Nicholas Codori house and carried into the cellar, where a dozen or more wounded men, both Northerners and Southerners, lay. As the gunfire roared and men cheered during the climax of the assault, they agreed that, whoever won, the others would be their prisoners. When Federals entered the cellar afterward, the Rebels became captives.[50]

Another of the prisoners was Private William B. Short of the 56th Virginia. A week earlier, Short had written to his wife, "I hope & trust to god that I dont wish to kile any of them & dont want to be kiled." Whether he managed not to kill a Federal is unknown, but he had been spared. Now, with his fellow Virginians, Short was headed for a Northern prison.[51]

Amid the carnage, however, there were still moments of humanity among foes. Private Kenneth Hickery of the 12th Massachusetts came upon a wounded Private Wesley Lewis Battle of the 37th North Carolina. Hickery, in his own words, "took care" of Battle, and the Southerner showed his gratitude by giving the Yankee his knife to keep. Nearby, Sergeant John Guiness of the 114th Pennsylvania gave a drink from his canteen to a dying Virginian. Guiness had kept the canteen strap across his shoulder as he did this, and as the dying man pulled on it, the two enemies' faces were inches apart. A paroxysm of pain coursed through the Rebel, and his grip tightened on the strap before he died. Unable to release the man's hold, Guiness cut the strap, leaving it with the Virginian.[52]

The 111th New York's commander, Colonel Clinton D. MacDougall, remembered that, as the enemy artillery fire subsided and as details attended to the fallen, he joined Hays at the general's headquarters at the Bryan farm. A stack of Confederate battle flags lay on the ground, and Hays asked the colonel to count them. Twenty-one, said MacDougall when he had finished. Moments later, one of Webb's aides appeared, requesting that Hays return the flags captured by Webb's Pennsylvanians. "How in hell did I get them if he captured them?" snarled Hays. Turning to David Shields, Hays said, "Oh,

'Dave!' pick out half a dozen flags and send them to General Webb as a present, with my compliments; we have so many here we don't know what to do with them and Webb needs them."[53]

Whether Shields delivered the banners went unreported. By this time, a sense of accomplishment infused the victors on Cemetery Ridge. A cheer echoed up and down the line when an erroneous rumor that James Longstreet had been captured raced through the ranks. At Meade's headquarters, a band played "Hail Columbia!" to the accompaniment of more cheers. One Maine soldier recalled that he thought of food and "then I was hungry." And Henry Abbott, who had viewed the dead closely, declared, "It was worth all our defeats."[54]

✿   ✿   ✿

A UNION ARTILLERY OFFICER, looking on from Cemetery Ridge, saw the receding eddies of what had barely an hour earlier been a tide of Confederate manpower. Its swells had reached nearly all the way to the crest of Cemetery Ridge before breaking against a wall of Federal cannon fire and musketry and ebbing away across the fields that stretched back to where the Rebels had come from. As the Northerner watched the survivors of the assault retreat, both the unscathed and the walking wounded, he observed that "no two men remained together." "Disorder" characterized the withdrawal, he claimed, as Union batteries continued to punish the shattered ranks.[55]

Although some Southerners asserted later that their regiments retired in order, the artillerist's description of the broken rivulets of men seems more accurate. The withdrawal turned into hundreds of individual efforts to escape capture and death or maiming. The Confederate soldiers had traveled into hell and only wanted to get out.[56]

Robert E. Lee had watched the assault from Seminary Ridge, sitting on a tree stump covered by an oilcloth, according to an eyewitness. He held Traveller's reins in his left hand, and rested his head in his right hand as if "he was in prayer." From where Lee sat, wrote a nearby officer, he "had a very good view of the battle." As the charge crested on Cemetery Ridge, Lee mounted Traveller and rode to the row of cannon, where he stopped beside Porter Alexander on a rise about four hundred yards west of the Peter Rogers house.[57]

Shortly, the British officer James Fremantle joined them. A cheer resounded suddenly from Cemetery Ridge, and Lee ordered Lieutenant Frederick M. Colston, a member of Alexander's staff who had been with the artillery commander when Lee arrived, to ride forward and determine whether the enemy "showed any signs of advancing." As Colston spurred his horse, the animal balked. The aide asked a passing soldier to hand him a stick and struck his mount with it. "Don't whip him, Captain," admonished Lee, "it does no good, I had a foolish horse once and kind treatment is the best." Embarrassed, Colston ceased, and the horse responded at last.[58]

Before Colston rode away, Lee turned to Alexander, remarking, "I can understand what they have to cheer for, but I thought that it might be our people." Minutes later, the survivors of the assault came walking toward Lee, Alexander, and Fremantle. The enemy were still firing at the retreating soldiers "as you would at a herd of game." Lee, thought Alexander, "then probably first appreciated the full extent of the disaster." The general nudged Traveller ahead, among the men, and said to them: "Fall back to the rear and reform your lines as well as you can. It was not your fault this time. It was all mine."[59]

Lee then stopped a litter party and asked whom they were carrying beneath the blanket. When told it was James Kemper, Lee said to the wounded officer, "General Kemper, I hope you are not badly hurt." The brigadier removed the blanket from his face and replied, "Yes, General, I think they have got me this time."

"Oh, I trust not! I trust not," responded Lee, adding, "It is my fault."[60]

Concerned about the possibility of an enemy counterattack, and visibly agitated about the plight of his troops, Lee spoke to a number of the officers and men. According to Fremantle, who stayed with Lee, the army commander said to them: "All this will come right in the end; we'll talk it over afterwards; but, in the meantime, all good men must rally. We want all good and true men just now." He repeated again and again, "My fault! My fault!"[61]

Cadmus Wilcox soon reined up his horse beside Lee. Wearing "a battered straw hat" and with tears in his eyes, the brigadier reported that he could not rally his Alabamians and that the cannon along Emmitsburg Road were in danger because most of the batteries had expended all of their ammunition. "Never mind, General, never mind," Lee said to Wilcox, "it is all my fault, and you young men must help me out the best you can."[62]

Lee had barely finished his reply when James Longstreet rode up. Lee met the corps commander with, "General, this is a bad business!" He then repeated what Wilcox had told him. Longstreet assured Lee that the batteries were not in danger: Lafayette McLaws's and John Hood's divisions remained in position and ready to react to a Union advance.[63]

Like Lee, Longstreet expected a Union counterattack. As he wrote later, "When the smoke cleared away, Pickett's Division was gone." If the Federals were to follow up their victory, the bloodied remnants of the Confederate assault force had to be re-formed. He directed his staff officers to rally the troops as he rode along the line of batteries, telling each artillery commander that the crews must hold at all costs. Either at his instructions or by Alexander's orders, every artillery crew with twenty rounds of ammunition was brought forward.[64]

During his ride along the line of cannon or after he spoke with Lee, Longstreet encountered Pickett. Various accounts indicate that the division commander was overwhelmed emotionally by the repulse and destruction of his command. When one officer asked Pickett, who was "crying," where he should rally the men, Pickett told him not to stop them but let them go to the previous night's campsite. Another officer claimed that Pickett asked chokingly, "Great God, where, oh! where is my division?" To a third officer he "almost sobbed out: 'My brave men! My brave men!' "[65]

When Longstreet and Pickett met, the latter said: "General, I am ruined. My division is gone; it is destroyed." Longstreet tried to console his old friend. Although accounts conflict, it appears that Lee did not speak personally with Pickett at this time, but sent a message via a staff officer that the Virginians had "made a name in history," and that "the blame rested on him, [Lee], for ordering them to do what was an impossibility."[66]

The efforts of Lee, Longstreet, their aides, and officers with the units managed to stem the rearward flow of some of the troops. The attackers evidently halted where they had begun the assault—Pickett's Virginians in the low ground behind the artillery, Pettigrew's and Trimble's men on the western slope of Seminary Ridge. Alexander, meanwhile, pushed a few batteries forward to check any Federal advance.[67]

Except for dots of skirmishers, the Yankees did not come in the aftermath of the repulse. Longstreet waited for more than an hour, until nearly five o'clock, before sending Moxley Sorrel with orders to have McLaws's and Hood's divisions withdraw to the positions they had occupied on July 2, before they attacked the Union left flank. When Sorrel delivered Longstreet's instructions to McLaws, the division commander objected, arguing that if Lee planned "to continue the contest" his troops held favorable ground for an attack. Longstreet's orders, replied Sorrel, allowed for "no discretion," and the two divisions had to retire. The contest on this field had ended.[68]

* * *

AFTER GEORGE MEADE had been assured that the Confederate assault had been repulsed, the army commander, accompanied by his son, rode to Cemetery Hill. On the crest, Meade had, in his word, a brief "interview" with Oliver Howard, commander of the Eleventh Corps. From there, the father and son returned to army headquarters at the Leister house. The wreckage of the overshots from the enemy cannonade lay everywhere—the row of dead horses, the damaged porch, the flattened fence, and the holes in the dwelling. During his stop at the house, Meade probably received Winfield Hancock's second message, in which the wounded corps commander urged a counterattack.[69]

When the Southern infantry had rolled forward in the charge, Union reserves from almost the entire length of the army's line had rushed to the support of the troops on Cemetery Ridge. One of the soldiers in the oncoming units told his wife later: "I have never seen anything so terribly grand as the valley in which we were moving. [It] appeared then If the whole of Pandemonium had been set loose." By the time the attackers had been beaten back, Meade had eighteen brigades from four corps either close at hand or available to assail the Confederates if they broke through on the ridge. This conglomerate of commands was still there if Meade chose to undertake a counterattack.[70]

Meade, however, never issued the order for a counterassault. He had few options—he could either use the Fifth and Sixth Corps in an attack against McLaws's and Hood's divisions on Lee's right flank, or he could use these units and/or the troops moved forward in support against the Confederate center. Neither choice offered certain success. McLaws's and Hood's brigades were posted, and the Federals would have to cross the same difficult ground west of Big and Little Round Top that had slowed the Confederates on July 2. In the center, the Yankees would have to advance over the open fields into the barrels of enemy cannon, as the Southerners had done. Meade could not have known how depleted the Confederate artillery chests were of long-range ammunition. He may have believed that the gray-jacketed gun crews possessed ample canister rounds.[71]

Instead—Meade did not address the matter in his report—the Union commander settled for what he and his army had achieved. The evidence lay before him in the number of Southern dead and wounded and the herds of prisoners. Lee had assailed Little Round Top and Cemetery Ridge on July 2 and failed; Culp's Hill had been secured, and now Lee's final effort, a magnificent charge, had been repulsed with staggering Southern casualties. The Army of the Potomac had won a decisive victory this day, and that was enough for George Meade. He chose the safe and wisest course.[72]

With his son by his side, Meade left headquarters and rode south along Cemetery Ridge to Little Round Top. On the eminence, he conferred with George Sykes, commander of the Fifth Corps. Meade ordered Sykes to conduct a reconnaissance in his front by clearing the woods east of the Wheatfield. Sykes forwarded it to Brigadier General Samuel W. Crawford, who assigned the duty to a brigade with a regiment from another brigade as support. There would be a brief spasm of fighting left in this long, terrible day.[73]

Before Meade had joined Sykes, however, Union cavalry in the fields and woods south of the Round Tops had been engaged in a struggle for parcels of ground. And to the east of the battlefield, a fierce encounter between Federal and Confederate horsemen had only recently ended. The day had belonged not only to infantrymen and artillerists, but also to those in the mounted units. There was an equality in hell.

14

"It Was Kill All You Can"

JOHN AND SARAH RUMMEL had purchased 168 acres of land about four miles east of Gettysburg, between York Pike and Hanover Road, in 1845. During the next eighteen years, they built a two-story log house with a balcony on the south end, a blacksmith shop, a springhouse, and a forty-by-seventy-foot barn. Sarah gave birth to a son, Isaac, and John worked the fields, providing for the family. They shared life with their neighbors—the Spanglers, Howards, Eckenrodes, and Lotts. Like that of all the families in Gettysburg and on the surrounding farms, the Rummels' rustic world changed forever on July 1, 1863.[1]

The battle at Gettysburg stayed distant from the Rummels during the first two days, except for the brief presence of Union cavalry in the area on the afternoon of July 2. By midmorning on July 3, however, the war had come to the Rummels and their neighbors: Union cavalrymen, outriders, and scouts for a mounted brigade appeared on the farm lanes and roads. The Federals were Michiganders from the brigade of Brigadier General George A. Custer. Unknown to the Rummels, the intersection of Low Dutch Road and Hanover Road had become an important crossroad. Low Dutch Road connected York Pike to Hanover Road and, beyond, to Baltimore Pike. The Rebels could use

Low Dutch Road as a route of advance to threaten the right flank of the Union army. The Rummel farm lay slightly more than a mile northwest of the intersection.[2]

By nightfall on July 2, Major General Alfred Pleasonton, commander of the Union Cavalry Corps, had only four of the command's eight brigades on the battlefield or in the area. Brigadier General David McM. Gregg and two brigades of his division were posted along Baltimore Pike south of the bridge over Rock Creek. Brigadier General Judson Kilpatrick's two-brigade division was on the march during the night, after its engagement with Confederate cavalry late in the day at Hunterstown, northeast of Gettysburg. Kilpatrick's troopers would arrive at Two Taverns, farther south of Gregg on Baltimore Pike, at daylight on July 3. Between them, Gregg and Kilpatrick counted roughly fifty-five hundred officers and men, with several batteries of horse artillery.[3]

The remaining four brigades—three in the division of Brigadier General John Buford and one from Gregg's division—guarded the army's southern flank and supply line in Maryland. On the morning of July 2, two of Buford's brigades, under colonels Thomas C. Devin and William Gamble, withdrew from Gettysburg to Taneytown, where they would remain until July 3, when they would march to Westminster. Brigadier General Wesley Merritt's Reserve Brigade, in Buford's command, occupied Emmitsburg, while Colonel Pennock Huey's regiments, from Gregg's division, had held Manchester since June 30. Only Merritt's brigade would be ordered to Gettysburg on July 3.[4]

Pleasonton had led the corps for just six weeks. A West Pointer, he had been given temporary command of it by Joseph Hooker on May 22. A short, slender man who dressed fastidiously and exuded confidence, Pleasonton was an ambitious self-promoter, with a reputation for untruthfulness and shameless ingratiation with superiors. His appointment caused grumbling throughout the army, typified by John Gibbon's assessment that it was "absurd when they have men as Buford & [Benjamin] Davis to put in the place." Another officer wrote that Pleasonton had owed his promotion to a simple fact, "he is always *in* at Head Quarters." A Massachusetts cavalry officer claimed, "It is the universal opinion that P's own reputation and P's late promotions are bolstered by systematic lying."[5]

Fortunately for Pleasonton, his appointment coincided with the emergence of the army's mounted arm. Throughout the campaign—at Brandy Station, Aldie, Middleburg, Upperville, and on July 1 at Gettysburg—the blue-jacketed horsemen held their own against their opponents, heralding a promising future. When George Meade assumed command of the army, he retained Pleasonton, who removed some brigade commanders and recommended for promotion Custer, Merritt, and Elon Farnsworth—young, aggressive officers. All three of them would have roles in the fighting on July 3.[6]

Before six o'clock on the morning of July 3, Pleasonton received orders from Meade to secure Baltimore Pike on the right of the Twelfth Corps and to guard the army's flanks. Pleasonton held Gregg's two brigades along the pike and sent instructions to Kilpatrick at Two Taverns to move with his two brigades to the army's left flank, in the area of the Round Tops, and to attack the enemy in that area. Merritt's brigade would be brought up from Emmitsburg to cooperate with Kilpatrick.[7]

The courier from Pleasonton delivered the order to Kilpatrick at eight o'clock. His men had reached Two Taverns four hours earlier, had slept for three hours, and were caring for their mounts or eating breakfast when the courier arrived. Before the troopers marched, however, Kilpatrick received a second message, which directed him to send Custer's brigade to the Low Dutch Road–Hanover Road intersection, where Gregg had been posted the previous day. Gregg had requested this change in orders, and Pleasonton agreed. In his report, Kilpatrick described the change as occurring "by some mistake."[8]

Custer's nineteen hundred Michiganders and Lieutenant Alexander C. M. Pennington's Battery M, 2nd United States Artillery, moved out before nine o'clock, following Low Dutch Road from Two Taverns. At twenty-three years of age, Autie Custer, as his family called him, was the youngest brigadier in the armies of the United States. He had been in command of the brigade only since June 29. Though he was last in his class at West Point—the second class to graduate in 1861—his rise from a staff officer to general had been nothing less than meteoric. Renowned for his personal bravery, ambition, and long curly blond hair, Custer was a striking figure who saw in warfare great opportunity for fame.[9]

When his Michigan volunteers first viewed their new commander, they were not sure what to make of him. He wore a uniform of black velvet trimmed with gold lace, a wide-collared blue navy shirt with silver stars sewn at the points of the collar, a wide-brimmed black felt hat, and boots with gilt spurs. A bright-red necktie completed the outfit. This resplendent uniform was unmistakable in combat or on a march, as Custer had intended it to be when he had it made. Almost at once, his troopers began calling him "the boy General of the Golden Lock."[10]

But Custer had quickly dispelled his men's doubts about his youth and his ability at Hanover on June 30, and at Hunterstown on July 2, where he personally led an attack down a narrow, fenced-in road and had a horse killed under him. The men saw that he would fight and do it in the forefront. On July 1, one of Meade's staff officers had written to his wife that Custer was "just fitted" for the cavalry, a "singular looking fellow." He added that the new brigadier "is a good officer & everyone likes him."[11]

The Michiganders covered the short distance from Two Taverns to the Low Dutch Road–Hanover Road crossroad in a half-hour or so, arriving soon after nine o'clock. Custer halted the regiments south of Hanover Road, in nearby fields, and drew two companies from each of the 5th and 6th Michigan Cavalry for scouting duties. The detachment from the 5th Michigan rode west on Hanover Road; the two companies of the 6th Michigan, under Major Peter Weber, continued north on Low Dutch Road. Weber's troopers had proceeded less than a mile when they turned into a crossroad that ran northwest along the edge of the Rummel farm. Weber halted on the brow of Cress Ridge in Rummel's Woods. Here, amid the stand of white oaks, the members of the 6th Michigan waited. About ten o'clock, they saw Confederate cavalrymen coming toward them from the north and west. The Michiganders turned and hurried back to report the information to Custer.[12]

*   *   *

THE SOUTHERN HORSEMEN seen by Weber's detachment were the leading elements of four Confederate brigades and batteries of horse artillery. They were coming from York Pike, following the narrow roads that crisscrossed the countryside from the pike to Hanover Road. Most important for Robert E. Lee's army, the bulk of the mounted units belonged to Major General Jeb Stuart's previously missing three brigades.[13]

Stuart had reported personally to Lee sometime between noon and 1:00 P.M. on July 2. Stuart probably arrived unaccompanied, riding ahead of his command, which was en route from Carlisle. One of Stuart's staff officers had located the army at Gettysburg on July 1, reported the cavalry's whereabouts to Lee, and returned with orders to join the army. Lee had not heard from his cavalry commander since June 24, hours before Stuart departed on a movement that virtually took him and his units out of the campaign. Consequently, the army had been deprived of Stuart's reconnaissance reports, crippling its movements until it stumbled into the collision at Gettysburg on July 1.

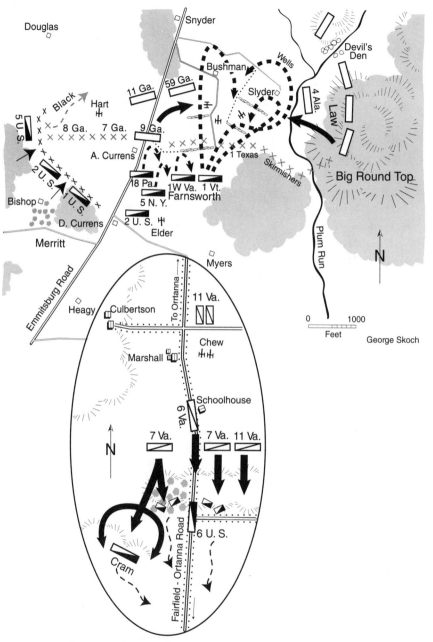

Douglas

Snyder

Devil's Den

Bushman

Wells

Slyder

4 Ala.

Law

11 Ga.   59 Ga.

Black

Hart

5 U.S.

8 Ga.   7 Ga.   9 Ga.

A. Currens

1 Texas

Skirmishers

Big Round Top

2 U.S.

1 U.S.

Bishop

18 Pa.

1 W Va. 1 Vt.

Farnsworth

5 N.Y.

D. Currens

2 U.S.

Elder

Merritt

Myers

Plum Run

N

Emmitsburg Road

Heagy   Culbertson

11 Va.

To Ortanna

0   1000

Feet

George Skoch

Chew

Marshall

Schoolhouse

6 Va.

N

7 Va.

7 Va. 11 Va.

Fairfield - Ortanna Road

6 U.S.

Cram

ACTIONS, SOUTH CAVALRY FIELD AND AT FAIRFIELD,
AFTERNOON OF JULY 3.

Stuart's misjudgment in his interpretation of Lee's orders has remained one of the campaign's most heated controversies.[14]

The meeting between Lee and Stuart resulted in an alleged sharp rebuke by Lee. But there are no eyewitness accounts, and neither man wrote about it. It had to be difficult for Stuart to receive Lee's disappointment, if not anger, over his absence. All Stuart had to offer in return was the capture of 125 wagons, Union prisoners, and an engagement with Federal cavalry at Hanover that delayed him further and forced him to detour around the enemy. This was not much for the price the army had paid.[15]

Toward evening, Stuart's units began arriving on the battlefield—the brigades of Colonel John R. Chambliss, Jr., and Brigadier General Fitzhugh Lee. Brigadier General Wade Hampton's troopers were delayed by the action at Hunterstown and halted south of that village. Chambliss's and Lee's men encamped north of York Pike, to the rear of Richard Ewell's Second Corps. When Ewell's infantrymen and artillerists saw the horsemen, "such joyful shouts as rent the air I never heard," recounted Major Norman R. Fitzhugh of Stuart's staff, "the cavalry for once was well received by the rest of the Army & we were glad to have the protection of our Infantry."[16]

Fitzhugh added in a letter to a sister, "We were tired & sore from so much & continuous marching, almost broken down from want of rest." Men and mounts were exhausted. They had suffered also from "the pangs of hunger," in the words of a North Carolina trooper, who declared in a letter, "I thought I knew some thing of the hardships of a soldier's life before but must confess that I did not." Stuart initially had the men remain in the saddles until his subordinates convinced him that they had to rest. A Virginia sergeant stated that dawn of July 3 "found our command in a poor condition to undergo the hardship of a battle with credit either to themselves or their country."[17]

During the night, Stuart received orders from Lee for the cavalry to operate beyond Ewell's left flank. What Lee intended for Stuart to accomplish is unclear, since Stuart stated in his report that he moved there "pursuant to instructions from" Lee. The army commander assigned Brigadier General Alfred G. Jenkins's Virginia brigade to Stuart. Jenkins had been knocked unconscious by a shell fragment while conducting a reconnaissance on July 2, and Colonel Milton J. Ferguson now led the brigade. Detachments for guard duty had reduced Ferguson's command to a battalion and eight companies from two regiments. In all, Stuart counted slightly more than five thousand officers and men, supported by thirteen cannon of horse artillery.[18]

When on the morning of July 3 the Confederate cavalry began the march is uncertain. Hampton's brigade backtracked through Hunterstown before turning south; the other three brigades moved across the fields north of York Pike. When they struck the road, east of Brinkerhoff's Ridge, the horsemen rode down narrow country roads toward Hanover Road. Ferguson's Virginians led the march, perhaps approaching Cress Ridge from the west, past the farms of Henry and George Trostle. Chambliss's regiments followed, halting in the low ground directly west of Rummel's Woods. Hampton, trailed by Fitz Lee, came up later, arriving between eleven and noon and stopping at the farms of the Miller and Stallworth families, north of the woods.[19]

Stuart and his staff accompanied the vanguard of the column. As Chambliss's and Ferguson's men dismounted in the fields west of Cress Ridge, Stuart rode to the crest and examined the ground and the location of Federal units. Stuart could see that the ridge dominated the terrain, with the fields of John Rummel and Jacob Lott, framed by stone walls and wooden fences, stretching toward Hanover Road. Little's Run, a shallow stream beginning at Rummel's springhouse, coursed south past Hanover Road. The ground was open—pastures and fields of grain—and offered opportunities for mounted attacks.[20]

Stuart brought up the 34th Virginia Battalion of Ferguson's brigade on foot. Armed with Enfield rifles with only ten rounds of ammunition for each man, the Virginians advanced to the Rummel farm buildings. Lieutenant Colonel Vincent A. Witcher deployed the five companies behind a stone wall that ran from the springhouse south through a meadow. Some of the Virginians scrambled into the barn. It was probably at this time that the Rebels took John Rummel as a prisoner, sending him on one of his horses to the rear. He remained with the Southerners throughout the day. Sarah Rummel was allowed to leave, and she fled to the home of Mrs. A. Eckenrode on Low Dutch Road.[21]

A handful of men from the 14th Virginia trailed Witcher's troopers and raided the Rummels' garden and springhouse, gathering up onions, milk, and molasses. They were enjoying their booty around the house when behind them two cannon from Cress Ridge opened fire. For reasons he never explained, Stuart had decided to test the Federals, bringing forward a section of the Louisiana Guard Artillery, a Second Corps unit temporarily attached to the cavalry. Captain Charles A. Green's gunners unlimbered their pair of ten-pound Parrotts and hurled shells toward the Low Dutch Road–Hanover Road intersection. It was not yet noon when the Louisianans pulled on the lanyards.[22]

The Confederate artillery discharges stirred up Custer and the Michiganders. When Weber sent the report of the approach of enemy cavalry, Custer kept the brigade south of Hanover Road, but deployed the 5th Michigan Cavalry as dismounted skirmishers north of the road and directed Pennington to unlimber his battery. The members of the 5th Michigan were armed with Spencer rifles, a .56-caliber weapon with a seven-shot magazine, or cylindrical tube, that fit into the stock. These Michiganders could deliver firepower beyond their numbers and were well chosen for this type of duty.[23]

Pennington's horse artillerists rolled their six three-inch Ordnance rifles onto a slight rise north of Hanover Road opposite the Joseph Spangler house. Setting the guns at a five-degree elevation, the Federals opened fire on the pair of Confederate cannon. A few rounds from Pennington's pieces caused Stuart to pull them back from the crest. The Union artillery fire also sent the foragers from the 14th Virginia Cavalry in a scurry to the rear.[24]

During the exchanges, the troopers of the 5th Michigan Cavalry pushed ahead, halting in the fields west and north of the Lott house. Less than four hundred yards to the northwest lay the Rummel buildings and Witcher's Virginians. By now the sun had heated the midday, and as a Michigan officer noted in his diary, "men and horses are suffering very much for water."[25]

The march of Hampton's and Fitz Lee's brigades, meanwhile, had been detected by the Federals on Cemetery Hill. In his report, Stuart wrote that he had "hoped to effect a surprise upon the enemy's rear," but the sighting of the two brigades had alerted the Northerners. As Stuart would discover, the disclosure of his movement brought additional Union cavalrymen to the Low Dutch Road–Hanover Road area.[26]

When the Federals on Cemetery Hill saw the enemy horsemen, Oliver Howard sent a dispatch to David Gregg noting that "large columns of the enemy's cavalry were moving toward the right of our line." At the same time, Gregg received an order from Pleasonton to relieve Custer and to send him to Kilpatrick, on the army's left flank. Gregg kept his cousin Colonel J. Irvin Gregg's brigade along Baltimore Pike as support for the Twelfth Corps and directed Colonel John B. McIntosh to take his brigade and to relieve Custer's Michiganders. McIntosh's men started minutes after noon, followed by the division commander.[27]

McIntosh's troopers probably proceeded south on Baltimore Pike to Two Taverns, turned left on Low Dutch Road, and arrived at the crossroad about one o'clock. McIntosh, whom one of his men described as "a very good officer but he is very unpopular in his command," met with Custer and learned about the situation. Custer had received the order to report to Kilpatrick and was waiting for McIntosh to appear. McIntosh had with him three regiments and a company—the 1st New Jersey Cavalry, 3rd Pennsylvania Cavalry, 1st Maryland Cavalry, and Company A, Purnell Legion Maryland Cavalry—and Captain Alanson M. Randol's Batteries E and G, 1st United States Artillery, numbering about nine hundred troopers and artillerymen.[28]

McIntosh posted the Pennsylvanians and Marylanders in a mounted column of squadrons in a clover field east of the Lott house and dismounted the New Jerseymen as skirmishers to replace the 5th Michigan Cavalry. As the Federals moved into position, the cannonade that preceded the infantry assault against Cemetery Ridge erupted, its thunder boiling and crashing from the west toward the cavalrymen. "The very ground shook and trembled," declared a Pennsylvanian, "and the smoke of the guns rolled out of the valley as tho there were thousands of acres of timber on fire." A North Carolinian with Stuart called it "the most incessant and terrific that I ever heard."[29]

Gregg arrived as McIntosh began his deployments. The division commander was thirty years old, a native Pennsylvanian and first cousin of the governor, Andrew Gregg Curtin, a West Pointer, and a horse soldier since his commission as a second lieutenant. He was a modest individual, an "accomplished gentleman" with a "retiring disposition." His quiet, unassuming demeanor fitted his calm temperament on a battlefield. He seemed to lack ambition, barring journalists from his command. "I do not propose," he remarked to a staff officer, "to have a picture reputation."[30]

The contrast, then, between the two men could have hardly been starker when Gregg reined up beside Custer. When they met, according to Gregg's subsequent account, Custer, dressed like the night in his velvet uniform glistening with braid, said: "General Gregg, you are going to have a big fight on your hands today. The woods beyond are full of the enemy."

"Well, in that case," replied Gregg, "I shall have to keep you to help me out."

"I will only be too glad to stay," said Custer, "if you will give the order."

Gregg issued the order, and as he stated in his report, Custer "was well pleased to remain with his brigade."[31]

From where they stood, it appeared indeed as if the Confederates were itching for a fight. On Cress Ridge, in front of Rummel's Woods, Stuart had aligned nine cannon—a pair of ten-pound Parrotts of the Louisiana Guard Artillery, two twelve-pound Napoleons, and one three-inch Ordnance rifle of Captain William M. McGregor's 2nd Stuart Horse Artillery, and four three-inch Ordnance rifles of Captain James Breathed's Virginia Battery. Unseen by the Federals, at the George Trostle farm west of the ridge, crews had unlimbered three guns, twelve-pound howitzers and three-inch Ordnance rifles, of Captain Thomas E. Jackson's Charlottesville Horse Battery. Except for the dismounted 34th Virginia Battalion at the Rummel farm, no other body of Confederate cavalry was visible.[32]

Gregg decided to test the Rebels' mettle. Randol's four cannon unlimbered in two sections—Lieutenant Earnest L. Kinney's guns about 250 yards to the right and in front of Pennington's battery, and Captain James Chester's pair of rifles farther to the front, near the orchard of the Anthony Howard farm. The 3rd Pennsylvania Cavalry of McIntosh's brigade was divided, two companies sent up Low Dutch Road to a woodlot northeast of the Lott house and six companies dismounted as support for the advanced skirmish line. The 5th Michigan Cavalry halted its withdrawal and joined the 1st New Jersey along the Union front. Custer bolstered the two regiments' position by ordering forward four companies of the 6th Michigan Cavalry to the west of Little's Run as protection for their left flank. A fight between the two opponents had been simmering for three or more hours. At two o'clock, as the Confederate infantry began the advance toward Cemetery Ridge to the west, it suddenly heated to a boil.[33]

The Confederate artillery crews reignited the combat, drawing an immediate response from the Union batteries. Pennington's and Randol's blue-jacketed gunners pounded Cress Ridge with solid shots and shells. It was an uneven struggle from the outset. "As a rule," Randol asserted later, "their Horse Art'y was so badly handled in battle we Art'y officers paid but little attention to it."[34]

Within minutes, the Federals' superiority in ammunition and cannon began to prevail. Captain Charles Green of the Louisiana Guard Artillery described the Northerners' response as "a severe fire." The Yankees disabled one cannon on the ridge and killed or wounded two dozen artillerymen and an equal number of horses. When the three pieces at the George Trostle farm joined in, firing "slowly" because of limited ammunition, the Federals rained percussion shells down on the crews. Within ten minutes, the bursts had killed half the horses and wounded four men. A Virginia cavalry officer declared, "The little artillery we used seemed of little service & I think most of it was soon silenced by the Federals."[35]

Five of the Confederate crews withdrew their guns—the Louisiana Guard Artillery on the ridge and the Charlottesville Horse Battery at the Trostle farm, the latter after depleting its artillery rounds. Pennington's Federals then targeted Rummel's barn, where Rebel sharpshooters were firing from holes and gaps between boards. One of the artillery officers admitted, however, that the fire "seemed to have little effect" upon the occupants.[36]

When the artillery duel began, McIntosh ordered the 1st New Jersey Cavalry on foot against the Rebels at the Rummel farm. The troopers went in, reached a rise above Little's Run, and halted at a rail fence. From behind the stone wall across the stream, the 34th Virginia Battalion opened fire—a "murderous" blast, in the estimation of a New Jerseyman. The Northerners answered in kind, and rifle fire flashed along both fences. Before long, the 5th Michigan Cavalry closed on the left of the New Jersey troopers, their Spencers adding to the mounting volume of gunfire. Across Little's Run, the four companies of the 6th Michigan Cavalry, also armed with Spencers, poured fire up the hollow into the flank of the Virginians.[37]

Stuart reacted to the enemy pressure by sending four companies each of the 14th and 16th Virginia down the slope against the Michiganders. Vincent Witcher of the 34th said later that the 16th counted fewer than fifty men and "was only a skeleton paper regiment," and that the 14th "was never famous for its gallantry." As these Virginians approached their comrades behind the stone wall, the 14th Virginia's Lieutenant William R. Gaines stopped to aid one of Witcher's men who had been wounded. When Gaines asked if he could help, the soldier growled, "Damn you go on into the fight, I will die in a few minutes."[38]

The members of the 14th and 16th Virginia Cavalry fought tenaciously. From behind a fence, they lashed the Northerners. Neither side could gain an advantage, although Witcher's men retreated from the stone wall after expending their ten rounds of ammunition. When a handful of the 5th Michigan Cavalry broke to the rear, Major Noah K. Ferry was shot in the head trying to rally them. "His death," wrote Colonel Russell A. Alger, "cast a deep gloom upon the whole brigade. He was a gallant soldier, an exemplary man." Behind the Michiganders and New Jerseymen, the six dismounted companies of the 3rd Pennsylvania Cavalry moved forward, adding their firepower to the struggle.[39]

On the Confederate left, beyond the Rummel farm, the 2nd Virginia Cavalry of Fitz Lee's brigade advanced along the road that ran from Low Dutch Road past the Rummel property to York Pike. Peter Weber's detachment of the 6th Michigan Cavalry had used it earlier in the morning. The narrow, fence-lined road skirted the northern edge of the woods where two companies of the 3rd Pennsylvania Cavalry had been posted by McIntosh. Some of the Pennsylvanians had been dismounted as skirmishers along the treeline, and it was toward them that Lee's Virginians came.[40]

Two companies of the Southerners pressed forward on foot down the undulating ground. They stopped to level sections of the post-and-rail fences, "which had been put there to stay, well rammed post morticed to receive the rail." Behind the skirmishers, the other companies of the regiment stayed in the saddles to charge through the gaps if necessary. When the opposing skirmishers came into range, they opened fire.[41]

Stuart wrote in his report, "I would have preferred a different method of attack." But "that entanglement," as he phrased it, had been "unavoidable," and he "determined to make the best fight possible." He had planned to hold the enemy in place around the Rummel and Lott farms with skirmishers and move a portion of his command behind Cress Ridge to strike Gregg's left flank. But the Federals' aggressiveness and the withdrawal of the 34th Virginia Battalion at the Rummel farm changed his plan. Stuart would clear out the Northerners with a mounted charge. He ordered forward his original command, the 1st Virginia Cavalry of Lee's brigade.[42]

As the Confederate regiment entered the fields east of Rummel's Woods, the 1st New Jersey Cavalry and 5th Michigan Cavalry were pulling back. Like Witcher's Virginians, they had used up their cartridges. Then, from the north, the thunder of a mounted attack rolled down the slope toward them. The Federals scattered, running for their horses and safety. Union artillerymen redirected their fire toward the 1st Virginia Cavalry, but the center of the battlefield had been swept of organized Yankees, and through it charged the Virginians. Their assault, thought Stuart, seemed "irresistible."[43]

Gregg reacted at once, directing Custer to counterattack with the 7th Michigan Cavalry, which had been kept in reserve south of Hanover Road near the Abraham Reever residence. Colonel William D. Mann waved them forward, shifting the formation from a column of fours into a close column of squadrons. At Hanover on June 30, the regiment had been briefly engaged, "not enough," wrote Lieutenant John A. Clark, "to satisfy my curiosity as the Rebs were disposed to keep at too great a distance. I had a curiosity to participate in a Battle and to know what it was to charge upon the enemy." Within minutes, Clark would know.[44]

Suddenly, George Custer appeared at the head of the regiment. He was one of the war's last knight-errants, a warrior imbued with a cause, following a road to glory. He reveled in fighting, for within its terrible confines he saw opportunity for fame. Fearless, he would not ask men to go where he would not lead them. Turning in his saddle, he shouted, "Come on, you Wolverines!"[45]

An officer in the 5th Michigan Cavalry admitted, "We stopped to see that charge." Custer had removed his hat, with his long blond hair flying above his shoulder. Captain William E. Miller of the 3rd Pennsylvania Cavalry, watching the Virginians, recalled, "A more determined and vigorous charge than that made by the 1st Virginia it was never my fortune to witness."[46]

The foes met at a post-and-rail fence that withstood the crash of the horses. The rear ranks of the Michigan regiment slammed into those in front, "breaking our columns into jelly and mixing us up like a mass of pulp." Major Luther S. Trowbridge of the 5th Michigan Cavalry described the collision with the fence as being "like the waves of the sea upon a rocky shore, until all were mixed in one confused and tangled mass."[47]

The Virginians and Michiganders were face to face at point-blank range. "Bullets were flying mightily thick," asserted a Northerner. Lieutenant Clark declared, "It was kill all you can do your best each for himself." The fury swirled along the fence as nearly seven hundred men used sabers, revolvers, and carbines. Custer's horse was struck, and he borrowed a bugler's mount. Numbers of Michiganders dismounted and knocked down sections of the fence. Through the gaps the Yankees "went pell-mell."[48]

The breakthrough scattered the Virginians, who bolted up the hillside. The Michiganders pursued, a surge of blue-jacketed horsemen roiling toward Rummel's Woods. Coming toward them, however, were more mounted Rebels—the 9th and 13th Virginia Cavalry of Chambliss's brigade, the 1st North Carolina and Jeff Davis Legion from Hampton's brigade, and squadrons of the 2nd Virginia Cavalry from Lee's brigade. Even Witcher's 34th Virginia Cavalry Battalion, with more ammunition, went back on foot to the Rummel farm and fired at the Michiganders.[49]

The Michiganders reached another fence along a lane that connected the Rummel house to Low Dutch Road. Stopped by the barrier, they halted their charge as the Confederates struck them in front and on both flanks. The Michiganders turned, racing toward the rear. A Pennsylvanian claimed that the Wolverines "ran back like sheep." As they passed near the Lott house in their flight, McIntosh rode into their midst, shouting, "For God's sake, men, if you are ever going to stand, stand now, for you are on your free soil!" But the broken ranks of the 7th Michigan Cavalry kept going. They had shattered an enemy attack only to be repulsed by an overwhelming counterthrust. "I had my curiosity fully gratified," Lieutenant Clark confessed in a letter, "& have not harkened for a fight since & do not think I should if I never participated in another."[50]

The Southerners pursued, receiving artillery fire from the Union batteries. Colonel Alger of the 5th Michigan Cavalry, meanwhile, had mounted a battalion of four companies and ordered Major Trowbridge to lead it against the oncoming Rebels. These Michiganders struck the right flank of Southerners, stopping the attack. Some of the dismounted Virginians who had followed "ran like lamplighters," according to Trowbridge, when the Federals counterattacked. The Confederates turned and retreated toward Cress Ridge. It seemed for a few minutes as if both opponents had had enough. Then, emerging from behind the ridge with drawn sabers, "glistening like silver in the bright sunlight," appeared more of Hampton's regiments.[51]

Hampton reported that the appearance of his remaining units—except for Cobb's Legion, which did not join in the attack—came as a "surprise" to him. He had been re-forming the 1st North Carolina and Jeff Davis Legion when one of his staff officers had mistakenly ordered in the rest of the brigade as support for Chambliss. "The disposition I had made of my command," he wrote, "contemplated an entirely different plan for the fight." Instead, Hampton, mounted on his horse, Captain, assumed command of the attack force. He had reputedly been the richest man in the South before the war, the owner of plantations in South Carolina. When the conflict began, he had outfitted and armed an entire unit, Hampton's Legion, and had arguably become Stuart's finest subordinate officer. It was now ten or fifteen minutes past three o'clock as the Southerners descended the ridge.[52]

The Confederates started out at a walk "in superb style." The pace quickened to a trot. "It was an inspiriting and imposing spectacle," declared one Michigan officer. A fellow member of the Union brigade added that the enemy's ranks "called forth a murmur of admiration" from the Yankees. When the Rebels spurred their mounts to a gallop, they began "yelling like demons," a tumultuous blend of men's voices in the air and horses' hooves against the ground. Hampton's officers shouted, "Keep to your sabers, men, keep to your sabers."[53]

Pennington's and Randol's Union gunners rammed charges of shells into their cannon and yanked the lanyards. A North Carolinian described the discharges as "a most galling fire." According to Lieutenant Chester, a staff officer from Gregg rode up with orders to withdraw his guns. "Tell the General to go to Hell," replied Chester, who admitted later that he was not "in a cheerful humor" at the time. The artillerists switched to canister as the Confederates closed the distance between them. The cavalrymen, claimed one Pennsylvanian, filled the gaps created by the canister "as if nothing had happened." Chester asserted that the enemy came "so near" his cannon "that I could hear their commands and see the buttons on their uniforms." [54]

From the rear of the batteries, however, the 1st Michigan Cavalry was advancing to the attack. When Gregg saw Hampton's men on the ridge, he ordered Colonel Charles H. Town to meet the Confederate charge. Town, whose life was draining away slowly from tuberculosis in his lungs, repeated the command and was making a speech when his troopers "cut him short." Details knocked down sections of fences along Hanover Road, opening a route for the Michiganders. They rode out of a hollow near the George Howard house, crossed the road, and shifted into a column of squadrons. By now, Custer had joined Town at the head of the regiment. [55]

Like their opponents, the Michiganders went forward at the trot. When they reached the plateau by the Union batteries, a bugler sounded the charge, and they spurred their horses into a gallop. They could see the enemy now, and, as one of them later stated, he thought his entire regiment "would be swallowed up." They waved their sabers and seemed to be "wild furious men." From the front, Custer shouted once more, "Come on, you Wolverines!" [56]

"They advanced to the charge of a vastly superior force with as much order and precision as if going upon parade," Custer boasted afterward of the regiment. Neither of the opponents slowed their pace. When they met, men and horses crashed into each other, the noise sounding "like the falling of timber." Horses somersaulted to the ground, hurling their riders into the air. Some men were crushed beneath the mounts. Sabers clanged against sabers; pistols were triggered into chests and faces. The Rebels yelled, "Yankee sons of bitches." It was a wild melee. A Wolverine struck Hampton on the head with his saber and was himself cut down by a blow from a Confederate. The field, wrote a South Carolinian, was "alive with moving squadrons." [57]

From the Confederate right, troopers from the 3rd Pennsylvania Cavalry, led by Captains Charles Treichel and William W. Rogers, and McIntosh's headquarters group charged toward the flag of the leading Southern regiment. Captain Walter S. Newhall of McIntosh's staff went directly at the colors. As Newhall reached for the staff, a Rebel shot him in the chin; the bullet exited at his cheek. These Federals numbered probably fewer than thirty officers and men and lost half in the combat. [58]

From the opposite flank of Hampton's ranks, Captain William E. Miller's battalion of the 3rd Pennsylvania Cavalry, posted in the woods north of the Lott house, entered the fighting. When the Confederate brigade advanced, Miller, who was ill with cramps and barely able to ride, had mounted his skirmishers and readied his troopers for an attack. His orders had been to hold the woods, but Miller saw an opportunity to strike the enemy column on the flank. He asked lieutenants William Brooke-Rawle and Miles G. Carter if they would support him if he were court-martialed for disobedience. When the lieutenants said that they should charge, Miller had his men fire a volley and form ranks. "The men were restive," wrote Miller, "and before I gave the order they started to charge."[59]

The Pennsylvanians—"We disobeyed our given orders and did what we thought best," declared one of them—drove ahead toward the mass of Confederates. Brooke-Rawle stated that as they attacked it appeared as if the head of the enemy force "seemed to fray at the edges and the current like an eddy seemed to be running back." Miller's nearly one hundred troopers struck the column at a point about two-thirds of its length from the front. Brooke-Rawle wrote that when his platoon hit the enemy it was "sucked" into the mass and surrounded. The Rebels called them "bad names" and shouted for the Federals to surrender. For a few minutes, said one Pennsylvanian, it "was awful."[60]

Miller's battalion cut through Hampton's ranks as if they were a lance of blue-clad horsemen. A group of Rebels wheeled to face the Pennsylvanians and then retired to the rear. In the mayhem, Miller suffered a wound to the arm. Private Elias G. Eyster captured a dismounted Confederate, but as he watched the action, his prisoner shot Eyster's horse and made him a captive. Sergeant Thomas Gregg rode up, slashing the Southerner with his saber. Before Gregg could react, however, another enemy trooper appeared and cleaved open the back of Gregg's head. The sergeant would survive the wound, but Eyster was hauled away as a prisoner.[61]

Still, the Confederate assault had been broken, "assailed in every direction." The Southerners began "sweeping back to the rear." Michiganders and Pennsylvanians chased them, but none of the pursuers went beyond the Rummel buildings. One of the Northerners remembered a Southern color-bearer, mounted on a gray horse, who stopped on the slope and defiantly waved his flag at the Federals as if he were daring them to try to take it. When Miller went to the rear, he met McIntosh, who congratulated the captain on his attack. Miller would receive a Medal of Honor for his initiative and personal bravery.[62]

This time, it was finished. Stuart decided to stop the fighting after the repulse of Hampton's charge. Officers gathered up stragglers and re-formed units. Comrades tended to wounded friends, and surgeons began the work of saving lives and repairing youthful bodies. In all, the Federals reported total casualties at 254, the Confederates 181. But wherever and in whatever numbers the wounded lay to be cared for, it was a "ghastly sight." Rummel's and his neighbors' barns served as field hospitals.[63]

Although the combined casualties amounted to less than 10 percent of those engaged, a cavalryman with Stuart claimed, "Mounted fights never lasted long, but there were more men killed and wounded in this fight than I ever saw on any field where the fighting was done mounted." In a span of roughly thirty to forty-five minutes, the opponents had fought each other in a series of vicious hand-to-hand encounters that toppled horses and killed and maimed men. For the Michigan troopers, who had never been in combat like this before, for instance, the engagement elicited such descriptions as "such fighting I never saw before," "cavalry never did such fighting before in America," and "the hardest Battle of the war." Their exaggerations resulted, in part, from their inexperience, and from the fact that, out of the 254 Union losses, 219 belonged to their brigade.[64]

In the end, however, their efforts and those of McIntosh's brigade thwarted Stuart's plans and secured the crucial Low Dutch Road–Hanover Road intersection. Had the Confederates been able to seize the crossroad and march to Two Taverns on Baltimore Pike, they would have been astride the Union army's main supply line and one of its two retreat routes. Stuart assessed the outcome in his report: "Had the enemy's main body been dislodged, as was confidently hoped and expected, I was in precisely the right position to discover it [a route to the Federals' rear] and improve the opportunity."[65]

Instead, David Gregg, Custer, McIntosh, and their officers and men prevailed. Union mounted units had been improving for months, as demonstrated during the initial weeks of the campaign and at Hanover three days earlier. On this field, however, the growing equality between the opponents was reaffirmed. The Yankee cavalry had come of age, and with new leaders such as Autie Custer, its promise seemed near at hand.[66]

Before nightfall, J. Irvin Gregg and his brigade joined his cousin's command on the field. Two infantry regiments from the Twelfth Corps arrived.

Stuart waited until after dark before pulling back to York Pike. When the Confederates retired, they released John Rummel but kept his horse. The farmer walked home. A trooper in the 7th Michigan wrote to his brother afterward: "I was verry anxious to have one big fight before the war should end & that fight I got at Gettysburg. I never want to se another one."[67]

◦   ◦   ◦

UNION BRIGADIER GENERAL JUDSON KILPATRICK would earn before long the nickname of "Kil-Cavalry" for his lavish expenditure of men and of horse-flesh. A small man, he had the temperament of a bantam rooster. Since his accession to command of the Third Cavalry Division on June 28, the twenty-seven-year-old 1861 graduate of West Point had sought fighting and had found it at Hanover and at Hunterstown. If given an opportunity or orders to assail the enemy, Kilpatrick would not hesitate to seize it.[68]

At eight o'clock on the morning of July 3, Kilpatrick received an order from Alfred Pleasonton to march to the left flank of the army near the Round Tops, to connect with Brigadier General Wesley Merritt's Reserve Brigade of John Buford's division, which would be moving north from Emmitsburg, and to attack the Confederate right flank. When Pleasonton's dispatch arrived, Kilpatrick's division was resting at Two Taverns on Baltimore Pike after an all-night ride to the village. Soon, another order came, directing George Custer's Michigan brigade to the Low Dutch Road–Hanover Road intersection, leaving Kilpatrick with only Brigadier General Elon Farnsworth's four regiments, which numbered about 1,925 officers and men. Later during the morning, Farnsworth started for the army's southern flank.[69]

The van of the Union column reached the area southwest of Big Round Top about 1:00 P.M., as the Confederate cannonade on Cemetery Ridge began. Farnsworth brought his regiments into line on the farm of George Bushman, posting most of the troopers in Bushman's Woods. His line consisted of, from left to right: the 18th Pennsylvania Cavalry, 1st West Virginia Cavalry, and 1st Vermont Cavalry. Behind the regiments, the crews of Lieutenant Samuel S. Elder's Battery E, 4th United States Artillery, unlimbered their four three-inch Ordnance rifles on a small, rocky knoll. As support for the battery, Farnsworth placed the 5th New York Cavalry in a ravine. Skirmishers dismounted and strung out along the northern edge of the woods. To the front, Southern pickets and a pair of batteries welcomed the Yankees with artillery fire and musketry. Elder's gunners replied with occasional rounds.[70]

The desultory exchange between the batteries and skirmishers lasted for more than two hours while the Confederate assault on Cemetery Ridge moved to a climax and repulse. Kilpatrick, who had joined Farnsworth, waited until the arrival of Merritt's brigade from Emmitsburg, Maryland. Merritt's men appeared on Emmitsburg Road from the south about three o'clock, having left the Maryland town at noon. While en route, Merritt had detached the 6th United States Cavalry to Fairfield, Pennsylvania, where a Confederate wagon train was reportedly foraging in the area. Merritt had with him slightly more than thirteen hundred officers and men in four regiments.[71]

Like Custer and Farnsworth, Merritt had been promoted from captain to brigadier general by Pleasonton on June 29. A native New Yorker and West Pointer, Merritt had not led his Regulars and volunteers in combat, but, as time would show, he was a highly capable horse soldier. When he arrived at the south end of the battlefield, he deployed his regiments in the fields on both sides of Emmitsburg Road north of the David Currens farm, dotting his front with dismounted skirmishers. His right-flank unit, companies of the 2nd United States Cavalry, stretched toward the left flank of Farnsworth's brigade. Captain William K. Graham's Battery K, 1st United States Artillery, unlimbered his six three-inch Ordnance rifles behind Merritt's cavalrymen.[72]

By the time Merritt's brigade arrived, the Confederates had fashioned a line of infantry, artillery, and cavalry to oppose the Federals. When the fighting ended on this portion of the battlefield on July 2, the division of John B. Hood had held a line from Rose's Woods, along Houck's Ridge, west of Little Round Top, south through Devil's Den, to the southwestern base of Big Round Top. Hood had been wounded early in his division's assault and had been succeeded by Brigadier General Evander Law. During the night, Law had rectified his line by shifting the Texas brigade into position on the left of Law's Alabama brigade, now under the command of Colonel James L. Sheffield of the 48th Alabama, covering the woods from the foot of Little Round Top to the base of Big Round Top. When the sun rose on July 3, Law's troops were in position.[73]

At daybreak, Law ordered three companies of the 47th Alabama to form a skirmish line south of Bushman's Woods and to cover the ground from the trees west to Emmitsburg Road, near the Currenses' house. Before long, one hundred troopers of the 1st South Carolina Cavalry, under Colonel John L. Black, and Captain James F. Hart's Washington Light Artillery of two Blakely rifles arrived in the area. Sent by James Longstreet and guided by his chief of

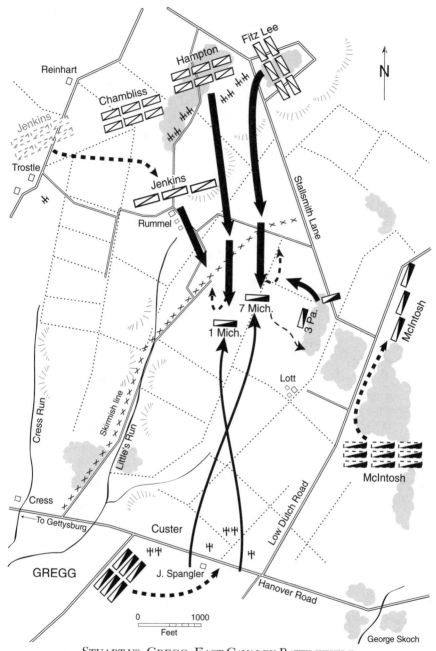

Reinhart

Jenkins

Trostle

Chambliss

Hampton

Fitz Lee

Jenkins

Rummel

Stallsmith Lane

N

7 Mich.

1 Mich.

3 Pa.

McIntosh

Lott

McIntosh

Cress Run

Skirmish line

Little's Run

Cress

To Gettysburg

Custer

GREGG

J. Spangler

Low Dutch Road

Hanover Road

George Skoch

0   1000
Feet

STUART VS. GREGG, EAST CAVALRY BATTLEFIELD,
AFTERNOON OF JULY 3.

staff, Moxley Sorrel, these units deployed in the fields west of Emmitsburg Road. Black sent vedettes farther south on the road, beyond the line of Alabamians. When Farnsworth's Union horsemen appeared, the Confederates withdrew, Black to a position north of the Currens farm and the Alabamians into the woods at the base of Big Round Top.[74]

In the meantime, the 1st Texas had been withdrawn from the line and sent to reinforce the South Carolinians and Alabamians. The Texans halted along the Bushman farm lane, behind a stone wall. They took rails from a nearby wooden fence and piled them on the wall. To their left, Sheffield extended a line of Alabamians at a right angle to his front, to face the Federals in Bushman's Woods. When Farnsworth's skirmishers cleared the trees, it was the Texans and Alabamians who met them with rifle fire.[75]

Earlier, Law had sent the 9th Georgia from Brigadier General George T. Anderson's brigade as support for Black's cavalrymen and Hart's pair of cannon. But when he learned of Farnsworth's arrival, Law followed with the rest of Anderson's regiments. The 7th and 8th Georgia led the march, filing into fields west of the road on the right of the 9th Georgia, whose members were aligned across the roadbed, near the stone farmhouse of the Alexander Currens family. The two regiments formed a line in front of Hart's gunners and on the left of Black's cavalrymen. Trailing behind and led personally by Law came the 11th and 59th Georgia. They extended the line farther south, on the right of the dismounted horsemen. As they shifted into position, Merritt's blue-clad troopers were advancing on foot in an attack.[76]

Kilpatrick's thin reserve of patience had drained away at last. He ordered both Farnsworth and Merritt to assail the enemy. The latter's troopers went in first, dismounted, as a heavy line of skirmishers. The Confederate line west of Emmitsburg Road resembled a crescent, and into it came the Federals. Hart's Rebel gunners opened fire, and when some of the Georgians rose from the ground in a wheatfield, blasting the Yankees, the attack stalled. The 11th and 59th Georgia raked the left flank of the Northerners. "Though every one fought like a tiger," noted Sergeant Samuel Crockett of the 1st United States in his diary, "we had to fall back." A Georgia major declared in a letter that the Southerners "soon gave them a good whipping. They ran after a hotly contested fight of about fifteen minutes." Merritt's feeble effort had ended almost as soon as it had begun.[77]

When Elon Farnsworth received Kilpatrick's order to undertake a mounted charge, he must have been stunned. He could see what one of his subordinates described later in a report: the Rebel position "is one that above all others is the worst for a cavalry charge—that is, behind stone fences so high as to preclude the possibility of gaining the opposite side without dismounting and throwing them down." The terrain was broken, undulating, with outcroppings of rocks, and dissected by fences. Although only the 1st Texas and three companies from the 47th Alabama lay in the front of the Federals, two batteries—Captain James Reilly's Rowan Artillery and Captain William K. Bachman's German Artillery, ten cannon in all—were posted on high ground about three hundred yards behind the Texans. Everything about the situation had the look of defeat.[78]

Farnsworth was a twenty-six-year-old Michigander who had entered the service in the fall of 1861 as an adjutant to his uncle, now Representative John Farnsworth, in the 8th Illinois Cavalry. At Brandy Station, he had commanded the regiment during the early phases of the engagement and was then appointed to Pleasonton's staff. The cavalry commander rewarded the able captain with promotion to brigadier general on June 29. Farnsworth had had enough experience to know that Kilpatrick's order portended heavy casualties.[79]

Farnsworth evidently sought the opinions of officers in his brigade, and when they questioned the wisdom of a mounted assault, he protested against it to Kilpatrick. The accounts of a number of subordinates who claimed to have heard either all or part of the exchange between the two generals described it as heated. According to one version of the conversation, Kilpatrick argued that he had been told the enemy was retreating. Farnsworth replied, "No successful charge can be made against the enemy in my front." Kilpatrick seemed "annoyed, not to say angered." He said: "Do you refuse to obey my orders? If you are afraid to lead this charge, I will lead it."

Rising in his stirrups, Farnsworth replied, "Take that back!"

"I did not mean it; forget it," Kilpatrick responded, and rose from his saddle "defiantly."

"General," said Farnsworth, "if you order the charge I will lead it, but you must take the awful responsibility."

With that, Farnsworth turned away and began issuing instructions to his regimental commanders.[80]

The 1st West Virginia Cavalry, led by Colonel Nathaniel P. Richmond, went in first, emerging from Bushman's Woods. The skirmishers of the 1st Texas fired at the Federals and then scattered as the cavalrymen charged. "The ground trembles as they came," said a Texan. When the West Virginians closed to within sixty yards, "our Boys rose," added the Rebel, "and pitched in to them." The volley from the Texans' Enfield rifles blew into the ranks of the troopers, knocking riders from their horses.[81]

The momentum of the attack carried the West Virginians over the wall and into the midst of the Texans. The horsemen slashed with their sabers as the infantrymen swung rifles, triggered blasts at close range, and even threw rocks. "The firing for a few minutes was front, rear and towards the flanks," stated one Confederate. Texas Private H. W. Berryman claimed that he personally gathered up five or six Union prisoners and "pointed to the rear and told them to git." Berryman watched as one of his comrades shot at a Yankee and "blew his brains out."[82]

The Federals rode about "in the greatest confusion." When they were "entirely surrounded," reported Major Charles E. Capehart of the regiment, Richmond shouted for them to cut their way out. The West Virginians either jumped their mounts over the wall or veered left or right to escape. They fled to the safety of Bushman's Woods. "Our regiment suffered terribly," wrote one of them, adding, "It cost us a fearful price." Nearly four hundred Federals participated in the attack, sustaining reported losses of twenty-one killed, thirty-four wounded, and forty-three captured, for a total of ninety-eight, or a 25-percent casualty rate.[83]

The Texans had no time to celebrate or to tend to their fallen men before more Union cavalrymen moved against them. These Southerners, who had numbered slightly fewer than two hundred when they manned the stone wall, were some of the finest combat soldiers in the army, and once again braced themselves as the 18th Pennsylvania Cavalry, supported by companies of the 5th New York Cavalry, charged. The Yankees advanced "with energy," wrote an officer, but Lieutenant Henry C. Potter of the 18th Pennsylvania avowed, "The Rebs in our front appeared by the thousands. They seemed to come out of the ground like bees."[84]

The Enfields flashed in a volley from the stone wall. "They gave us such a rattling fire," Potter wrote of the Texans, "we all gave way and retreated toward the woods." It was finished almost as soon as it had begun, with the Pennsylvanians and New Yorkers turning back toward the woods. Losses amounted to twenty officers and men in the two regiments.[85]

Farnsworth, meanwhile, had readied the 1st Vermont Cavalry, twelve companies in all, about four hundred officers and men. He divided the regiment into three battalions, four companies each under Lieutenant Colonel Addison W. Preston, Major William Wells, and Captain Henry C. Parsons. When they were forming ranks, Parsons noticed Captain Oliver T. Cushman, who was wearing "a white duck 'fighting jacket,' trimmed with yellow braid." Parsons objected to it, telling Cushman that it made him a conspicuous target. A "lady," replied the captain, had made it for him, and "no rebel bullet could pierce it." [86]

The Vermonters cleared the woods and spurred their mounts into "a full gallop" toward the Texans. The other regiments in the brigade had already retired, and, in the words of Bugler Joseph Allen, "The Texans had ceased firing, and we knew they were waiting to pick us off at closer range." The New Englanders raced ahead, "expecting the volley at short range." Seconds later, the Texans fired, but most of the bullets passed over the heads of the Vermonters. The cavalrymen reached the wall and went over it. The smoke was so thick that the Confederates "could not take accurate aim." [87]

Parsons's battalion led the charge. When they passed the Texans, they rode north—"The sun was blinding," according to Parsons—toward the John Slyder farm. At the stone farmhouse, Parsons's column turned east into a farm lane. Ahead of the Federals was the lower wooded slope of Big Round Top. [88]

Evander Law had watched the 1st Texas's valiant stand against the Union horsemen. When the 1st West Virginia Cavalry charged, the Confederate commander ordered the 9th, 11th, and 59th Georgia to move rapidly to the support of Reilly's and Bachman's batteries and sent an aide to his Alabama brigade at the foot of Big Round Top. Law told the staff officer that he should direct the first regimental commander he found in the woods to advance "in a run" to the rear. Riding east, the aide came upon the 4th Alabama, delivered Law's instructions, and then watched as the troops double-quicked through the trees to the edge of the woodline that overlooked the fields of the Slyder farm. Ahead of the Alabamians a column of enemy cavalry approached. [89]

An Alabama lieutenant yelled: "Cavalry, boys, cavalry! This is no fight, only a frolic, give it to them!" The Rebels stood and fired a volley. For a second time Parsons's men were fortunate, as the wave of bullets passed over their heads. Quickly, the Confederates reloaded and triggered another blast, a "random volley" in Parsons's description. This time they unhorsed some of the Vermonters. "Every time a man near was hit," recounted Bugler Allen, "I could hear the pat of the bullet." The Yankees could only see the enemy "by puffs of smoke." An Alabamian recalled, "Our boys really enjoyed that part of the battle." [90]

Parsons wheeled his column to the south, making the horses leap a stone wall. He halted his men in the shelter of a wooded hill and re-formed ranks. His rear squadron, however, had become separated and retreated across the meadow to Bushman's Woods. As they re-formed, Parsons saw William Wells's battalion, which "swept in a great circle to the right," crossing the tracks of Parsons's command.[91]

Wells's companies had cleared Bushman's Woods, to the right or east of Parsons's battalion, knifed through the skirmish line of Alabamians to the left of the Texans, and entered the meadow of the Slyder farm, then turned east and followed a low stone wall to the spur of Big Round Top. It was at this point in their attack that Parsons watched them pass. Farnsworth had accompanied Wells, and when the troopers reached the spur, the brigadier led them north through the woods behind the Alabama regiments deployed at the foot of the height. Many Confederates faced to the rear and shot at the passing column. "It was a swift, resistless charge," wrote Parsons, "over rocks, through timber, under close enfilading fire."[92]

Wells's battalion broke through the treeline into fields west of Devil's Den and Houck's Ridge. To their right on the ridge, Georgians of Brigadier General Henry L. Benning's brigade turned toward the Vermonters and lashed them with musketry. Gunners in a section of Bachman's battery near Emmitsburg Road wheeled to the left, unleashing their fire on the horsemen in the open ground. Farnsworth's horse was slain, and a corporal relinquished his mount to the general. Caught in a circle of closing death, the mounted column splintered into three groups.[93]

While one contingent raced south and then east and reached the safety of their lines, a second body of troopers angled toward the Bushman house and down its lane. This force passed through a gauntlet of fire as the 9th, 11th, and 59th Georgia, which had been rushed across the road by Law, triggered rounds at the riders. Most of them escaped the fusillades and even gobbled up some Texan skirmishers as prisoners before re-entering Bushman's Woods.[94]

The final group, led by Farnsworth and Wells, retraced their route toward the spur of Big Round Top. Gunfire from both sides sang through the column. As the Federals re-emerged into a field, the 15th Alabama came rushing into line across the cavalrymen's front. On the left of the 15th Alabama, the skirmishers of the 47th Alabama leveled their rifles. Preston's battalion, meanwhile, had joined Parsons, and squadrons from their commands were sent to support Wells's men. Time, however, had run its course for the Vermonters.[95]

A scissors of musketry cut into the ranks of the New Englanders. Farnsworth reeled in the saddle and toppled to the ground, struck in the chest, abdomen, and leg by five bullets. Subsequent accounts by Confederates alleging that he had committed suicide are bogus. In his report, Kilpatrick wrote of the fallen brigadier, "We can say of him, in the language of another, 'Good soldier, faithful friend, great heart, hail and farewell.' "[96]

The surviving Vermonters, slashing with their sabers, cut their way through. Wells, who would earn a Medal of Honor for this day, led one party to safety; other splinters of horsemen, including Parsons and his men, escaped in other directions. It had been, as Farnsworth and other officers stated, a senseless slaughter of good men, accomplishing nothing yet incurring a reported loss of thirteen killed, twenty-five wounded, and twenty-seven missing or captured.[97]

Kilpatrick's aggressiveness and misjudgment had led the Vermonters into a bloody trap. To one of the cavalrymen it seemed "as though all the powers of hell were waked to madness." A Texan, Sergeant D. H. Hamilton, summed up the combat tersely and accurately, "It was simply a picnic to fight cavalry under such conditions."[98]

·   ·   ·

THE MOOD OF THE MEMBERS of the 6th United States Cavalry could hardly have been better shortly after noon on July 3. Based upon the report of a farmer, their brigade commander, Wesley Merritt, had ordered the regiment to Fairfield, Pennsylvania, a village located eight miles southwest of Gettysburg, to intercept a Confederate wagon train that had been foraging in the area since the previous day. The civilian told Merritt that few guards protected the wagons. As the other regiments of the brigade marched from Emmitsburg, Maryland, to Gettysburg, the Regulars headed toward Fairfield.[99]

"All was excitement," recounted one of the Federals, "and you will not wonder when you imagine capturing a hundred wagons laden with spoils for confiscation, and the plundering and destruction of the same." En route, local folk welcomed them as they passed by, distributing bread, pies, and cakes to the grateful men. Young women smiled and wished them success. It must have appeared to the horse soldiers that it would indeed be a good day.[100]

The regiment's commander was Major Samuel Henry Starr, an old dragoon who had enlisted in 1832 as a private and had risen through the ranks. He was an unbending disciplinarian, as tough as dried rawhide, whom his men derisively called "Old Nose Bag" because of his method of punishing a trooper by placing the offender's head in a horse's nose bag. He wore a full grayish beard that gave him the appearance of a Biblical prophet possessed of hellfire and brimstone. Starr had commanded a volunteer regiment for a brief time during the war before returning to the Regular Army with a reduced rank. On this day, thought a cavalryman, he looked "as gloomy as usual."[101]

Starr had with him about four hundred officers and men—two companies were serving on duty at headquarters of the Cavalry Corps. When his column came to within two miles of Fairfield, he halted it and detached a squadron, under Captain George C. Cram, to scout along the valley's western rim, where they could see some enemy pickets on a nearby mountain. Cram, who was universally despised in the regiment and most often referred to as "Damn Cram," led his two companies along the bed of an unfinished railroad.[102]

The remaining companies proceeded into Fairfield, where Starr learned from residents that a number of enemy wagons had recently departed on Fairfield-Orrtanna Road toward Cashtown. Starr assigned Lieutenant Christian Balder and Companies F and L in pursuit. Riding north on the road, Balder's troopers spotted a few wagons less than a mile from town. A small detachment of Rebel pickets guarded the vehicles. Balder ordered a charge.[103]

As the Regulars attacked up the fence-lined road, the Confederates scattered, and the drivers lashed the wagon teams into a gallop. The Federals chased them for more than a mile until they saw a regiment of Confederate cavalry in the road. Balder ordered a retreat, and the two companies fled toward Fairfield. Starr, meanwhile, had brought up the other companies, halting them on the crest of a slight ridge. When Balder's men reached them, Starr dismounted four companies and deployed them on both sides of the road, half of them in an apple orchard, the other half behind a rail fence. He kept a battalion of four companies mounted in the road.[104]

Balder's detachment had encountered the 7th Virginia Cavalry of Brigadier General William E. ("Grumble") Jones. Ordered to protect the army's right flank and rear between Cashtown and Fairfield and to provide protection for the wagon train, Jones's three regiments and a battalion had arrived at Cashtown during the morning. One of the Virginians jotted in his diary that when the cannonade at Gettysburg began "the earth beneath seemed to tremble." The 7th Virginia Cavalry had led the march south toward Fairfield, and when its members saw the Union horsemen, they hurried in pursuit, reining up at the farmhouse of Benjamin Marshall. About three hundred yards ahead was the enemy in line on the ridge.[105]

"Grumble" Jones soon joined the regiment at the Marshall residence. A graduate of West Point, Jones was as good a cavalry officer as Jeb Stuart had in his corps. He had led his troopers with particular distinction at Brandy Station. A gruff, profane, disputatious man, he never cared much for Stuart personally or for the general's flamboyant style. But Jones possessed a combative fire and had instilled it in his command.[106]

When Jones arrived at the Marshall farm, he surveyed the ground and the enemy position. The country was open, with small fields framed by post-and-rail fences. To Jones, the best avenue of attack was on the road, although he noted in his report that the bordering fences were "too strong to be broken without the ax." Unable to ascertain the strength of the Federals, he nevertheless decided to charge them, explaining that "a vigorous assault must put even a small force on a perfect equality with a large one until a wide field could be prepared." He ordered in the 7th Virginia Cavalry.[107]

"With a wild yell," the Virginians surged down the narrow road in a long column. Starr's Regulars waited. When the van of the oncoming column closed within range, the Northerners unleashed a wall of fire from their .52-caliber single-shot breech-loading Sharps carbines. Horses and riders collapsed to the ground in the roadbed. Behind the fallen, their comrades turned and fled. Their commander, Lieutenant Colonel Thomas C. Marshall, admitted in his report that the regiment did not "close up as promptly as it should in this, no doubt, making our loss greater than it would otherwise have been." Jones was furious at his former command's performance, stating in his report that "a failure to rally promptly and renew the fight is a blemish in the bright history of this regiment."[108]

Jones called up support while cursing that one Yankee regiment might "whip my whole brigade." Captain R. Preston Chew's Ashby Horse Artillery rumbled down the road and into a field to the east. An artillerist recalled that the cannon were unlimbered "in a wheat field where the wheat was standing thick, and nearly as high as my head, and dead ripe. It looked like a shame to have war in such a field of wheat." At the Marshall house, the 6th Virginia Cavalry formed for another charge.[109]

When Starr saw the Confederate battery roll into position and more enemy horsemen appear, he decided to attack first with two of his mounted companies. He also ordered the squadron east of the road to join in the charge, but before they could mount up, their comrades swirled up the road toward the Rebels. Chew's gunners opened fire. Major Cabell E. Flournoy, commander of the 6th Virginia Cavalry, tried to inspire his veterans with a brief speech and then waved them forward. With sabers drawn, the Virginians went in. In the fields on either side of the road, men from the 7th Virginia, who had rallied, joined the attackers.[110]

The Confederates overwhelmed the charging Union squadron and splintered its ranks. For a few minutes, the opposing forces fought at close quarters with sabers and pistols. But Virginia numbers prevailed, routing the Federals. On came the Rebels toward Starr's position. They struck the Yankee line as the squadron east of the road was trying to mount its horses. The Regulars in the orchard fired a few rounds and were then overrun by the enemy horsemen. The Regulars were "caught in such a trap" and "had to cut our way out [and] run the gauntlet."[111]

In the melee, Lieutenant John Allan, adjutant of the 6th Virginia Cavalry, was killed. The previous night, he had written a note requesting that if he fell his body should be delivered to his wife's home in Baltimore. He listed the address and said that the person who did this would receive five hundred dollars. That night, his comrades gave his remains and note to some residents of Fairfield and requested that they fulfill Allan's wishes.[112]

Starr's decision to attack an enemy force of unknown strength, supported by artillery, cost him and his regiment dearly. The old dragoon was wounded, and Lieutenant Balder was killed amid the swirling action. More than two hundred of the Regulars surrendered or were ridden down by the Virginians and captured, including "Damn Cram," whose squadron arrived in time to be caught in the whirlwind. Among those who escaped was Sergeant George C. Platt. As a party of Confederates went after the regimental color-bearer, who lay on the ground trapped beneath his horse, Platt rode among the enemy, was cut by their sabers, but tore the flag from the staff and spurred away. His heroism earned him a Medal of Honor.[113]

The Virginians chased their opponents into and beyond Fairfield before abandoning the pursuit. On a day filled with the prospects of easy duty and easy pickings, the 6th United States Cavalry had been, in words of one of them, "cut to pieces." The casualties amounted to six killed, twenty-eight wounded, and 208 captured, or more than 60 percent of the command. Confederate losses totaled twelve killed, forty wounded, and six missing or captured. The Federals had made a stout fight of it before being overwhelmed. At the towns surrounding Gettysburg, as at Gettysburg itself, it was a day without mercy.[114]

✦   ✦   ✦

DEATH SEEMED UNWILLING TO LEAVE Gettysburg on July 3. It had worked fertile ground for three days, garnering a harvest unequaled in the annals of American history. It lingered into the early evening, returning to a plot of ground on the battlefield where it had been the previous day for one final, brief visit.

About six o'clock, Colonel William McCandless's brigade of Pennsylvania Reserve regiments from the Fifth Corps advanced from its position near the western base of Little Round Top with orders to clear Rose's Woods of enemy troops. George Sykes, the corps commander, had issued the order, complying with George Meade's request for a reconnaissance on his front. Supported by a Sixth Corps regiment on both their flanks, the Pennsylvanians moved into the Wheatfield and then wheeled to the left, or south, and entered the eastern end of Rose's Woods. A solitary Confederate battery had fired upon them, until the 139th Pennsylvania on their right forced it to withdraw.[115]

The Pennsylvanians moved diagonally through the trees, scattering a handful of enemy skirmishers, who disappeared to the west. Once the Federals had cleared the upper section of the woods, McCandless changed front to the rear, and the line pushed west along the length of the woods. Ahead of them, on a knoll, lay the 15th Georgia.[116]

The 15th Georgia, under Colonel Dudley M. DuBose, had been sent forward by its brigade commander, Henry L. Benning, at the direction of his division commander, Evander Law. Earlier, Benning had been informed by some of his pickets that Lafayette McLaws's division, on the brigade's left, had been ordered to withdraw. As noted previously, Longstreet had had Moxley Sorrel carry a message that required McLaws's and Law's troops to return to the positions they had held on July 2 before undertaking their assaults. When Law's staff officer reported to Benning with the instructions to occupy the hill, the Georgia brigadier had not been officially informed of the withdrawal. Consequently, the 15th Georgia entered Rose's Woods. Before long, however, another order came for Benning from Law, to pull back his brigade. As his other regiments began filing to the rear, the Pennsylvanians closed on the isolated 15th Georgia.[117]

DuBose's Georgians never had much of a chance. The Federal attack struck their left flank and front. From behind rocks and trees, the Georgians attempted a stand. But when the Pennsylvanians were within forty yards or less of the Confederates, DuBose ordered a retreat. The Georgians cleared the trees and rallied behind a stone wall, trying to slow down the enemy's pursuit. It was a mistake.[118]

The Pennsylvanians' line overlapped both flanks of the Georgians, and the Northerners raked the wall with frontal and enfilading fire. A half-dozen or more of the Georgians' color-bearers were shot down in succession. Unable to withstand such fearful musketry, DuBose ordered his men out. McCandless's veterans rushed the stone wall, capturing scores of Georgians. Sergeant James B. Thompson of the 1st Pennsylvania Rifles seized the flag of the Confederate regiment, for which act he would be awarded the Medal of Honor. Benning stated that DuBose "was fortunate to escape at all."[119]

The Pennsylvanians withdrew to the western edge of Rose's Woods and fashioned a line. Details escorted the prisoners to the rear as other groups collected piles of rifles that McCandless believed the Confederates had amassed to burn. The members of the 139th Pennsylvania hauled in a Union cannon that they had retaken during the advance. Samuel W. Crawford, McCandless's division commander, claimed later that his Pennsylvanians had fired the "last shots at Gettysburg." Whether they deserved the honor, such as it was, did not matter. For Gettysburg, the battle was finished.[120]

EPILOGUE

"This Place Called Gettysburg"

T HE SUN SET AT GETTYSBURG, PENNSYLVANIA, on July 3, 1863, at 7:32 P.M. Darkness settled in gradually, deepening across the fields and woodlots. Lamps tinted in amber the rooms of houses. Campfires created circles of light amid the blackness. To this place of death, night came as a long-awaited friend.[1]

"If ever I was glad to have night come I am tonight," one Union soldier confided in his diary. Although "there was great jubilation among us," wrote another Northerner, the prevailing mood among them, in the words of an officer, was "a great relief . . . a sense, as it were, that the worst was over." They were not sure if "Bobby" Lee would try it again the next day, but they had "a feeling that he had done his worst and failed." Rumors abounded, exaggerated or embellished with each retelling. "We had little idea" of how decisive a victory they had won, added the officer. The soldiers, recounted Frank Haskell, "talked only of the means of their own safety from destruction."[2]

Among those who had been spared, probably to a man in each army, there must have been a sense of gratitude and thankfulness. It could hardly have been otherwise. Darkness could not hide the grim reality of what they had been through. From Culp's Hill to beyond Big Round Top, they were awash in carnage. The smell and sounds of the bloodbath permeated the night.[3]

Private John Haley of the 17th Maine would recall, "So great was the stench from those who had fallen that none of us could eat, drink, or sleep." In the town, twelve-year-old Mary Elizabeth Montfort wrote, "The terrible smell all through the town is more than the time we found a dead rat behind the loose boards in the cellar." It hung in the air like a pall, enveloping all of those, civilian and soldier alike, who shared this terrible ground.[4]

Amid the putrefying corpses lay the wounded men, their bodies torn and broken by the combat. As it had the two previous nights, their agony rent the darkness. The night, wrote a Union captain, "was unearthly from the cries of the wounded who could not be cared for; the air was full of groans and prayers." Abner Doubleday remembered the "almost universal exclamation of those who felt their time had come, 'Oh, my God what will become of me!' "[5]

Ambulance details and comrades carried the suffering individuals to field hospitals in the rear. By nightfall, however, surgeons and assistants were overwhelmed by the unending stream of patients. A North Carolinian who had been assigned to hospital detail paused at eight o'clock to write to his father: "I have not been in the fight been looking after our wounded and a more sorrowful [sight] I never saw. Poor fellows lying wounded in every conceivable place and little or no attention paid them. The doctors dont examine unless amputation is necessary or it is extraordinarily dangerous. In fact they come in so fast that it is necessary."[6]

A Union doctor stated, "It soon became impossible to do much for [the wounded]. The few bandages in our medical knapsacks were already exhausted." One assistant at a Federal field hospital said that surgeons had eighteen amputating tables in use simultaneously. Although it might not have been a universal view, many soldiers agreed with a Virginian who declared that surgeons "are the instruments or agents of death instead of his victims."[7]

In fact, many of the unfortunate men would not survive the trauma and the unsanitary conditions. Their subsequent deaths only increased a staggering butcher's bill that had no precedent in American history. It was the sheer numbers of the dead who covered the battlefield that stunned even the veteran troops. Their graphic accounts offer the best description of the charnel house that Gettysburg had become after the fighting concluded on July 3.

Whether they wrote of what they had seen before the night came, or after they had time to view the field with another day's sun, their words testify to the magnitude of the slaughter. "O God, what a sight," a Pennsylvanian exclaimed in a letter to his wife. A Union chaplain asserted, "The stench was almost unendurable and the dead lay everywhere." A Floridian in David Lang's brigade declared, "I never saw the like of dead." A Regular Army artilleryman echoed the Confederate's assessment: "I have seen many a big battle, most of the big ones of the war, and I never saw the like."[8]

After a member of the Union Sixth Corps walked over a portion of the ground on July 4, he penned in his diary: "Such a horrible sight I never saw. On one part of the field the dead lay almost as thick as they could and in some places one on top of another. We have given the rebils a good whipping here." A New York officer who rode over it the next day told his brother, "I cannot accurately describe how dreadful it was," adding that "the scene would be sickening" if he did so.[9]

Private John H. Burrill of the 2nd New Hampshire admitted to his parents that he went across the battlefield "out of curiosity" on July 4. "Such a sight," he wrote afterward, "I never wish to see again. The men had turned black, their eyes had swollen out of their heads and they were twice their natural size. The stench of the field was awful." He confessed that he would rather go into another battle "than see the effects." A sixteen-year-old drummer boy, Jerry Collins of the 150th New York, recalled that "for the most part the dead were lying on their backs with wide-open expressionless eyes."[10]

The Union defenders of Culp's Hill and Cemetery Ridge, the scenes of the bloodiest combat on July 3, wrote of the aftermath, of the killing ground that they had occupied on this day. A soldier in the 111th Pennsylvania who had fought in Thomas Kane's brigade on Culp's Hill avowed, "It was one of the most awful sights I beheld for where the reble line was their dead were literaly piled in heaps." He noted that he also found a dead raccoon and two dead possums. A member of the same regiment remembered that he came upon a slain Confederate who had been killed by a ramrod that had pinned him to a tree.[11]

The Federals assigned to burial details received an issue of whiskey before they began their work. An Ohioan described the duty in his diary: "I have just returned from being one of the 'pall bearers' to the largest funeral I ever attended." He thought that they rolled nearly two hundred enemy dead into one trench. A Pennsylvanian recounted that, as they pushed the last Confederate, an orderly sergeant, into a mass grave, one of his comrades said, "There, damn you, call the roll and see if they are all there."[12]

The greatest concentration of dead, however, a blanket of bodies, was on the terrible slope between Emmitsburg Road and the position held by the Union Second Corps, marked by the clump of trees. Captain Benjamin W. Thompson of the 111th New York had been in the rear during the assault. Returning to the crest of Cemetery Ridge at sundown, he stopped and looked: "No words can depict the ghastly picture. The track of the great charge was marked by bodies of men in all possible positions, wounded, bleeding, dying and dead. Near the line where the final struggle occurred, the men lay in heaps, the wounded wiggling and groaning under the weight of the dead among whom they were entangled." Thompson's stomach sickened.[13]

Alexander Hays rode across the ground before sunrise on July 4. "I could scarcely find passage for my horse, for the dead and wounded," the general stated. "In one road it was impassable until I had them removed." A lieutenant from New York called the fields "the plains of slaughter." A private asserted that the slope in front of the stone wall held by Alexander Webb's Pennsylvanians "was literly covered with dead & wounded as far as we could see." Another private went farther out into fields toward the Confederate lines and said: "In many places it was inconvenient to walk without steping in clots of Human blood. It was Rebel blood so it did not seem so bad."[14]

A Massachusetts lieutenant gave a graphic picture to his mother of the effects of canister and other artillery rounds on human flesh at close range: "I thought I had seen the horror of war before, but the like of this battle is seldom seen. . . . Men with heads shot off, limbs shot off, men shot in two, and men shot in pieces, and little fragments so as hardly to be recognizable as any part of a man."[15]

The three-day battle exceeded anything in the previous experience of each army. The casualty totals present the stark truth that staggered the men in both armies. Although no figures can be precise for any engagement, the modern consensus places Union losses at 3,155 killed, 14,529 wounded or mortally wounded, and 5,365 missing, for a total of 23,049. The Confederates suffered losses of 3,903 killed, 18,735 wounded or mortally wounded, and 5,425 captured or missing, for a total of 28,063. When Lee's army retreated, it left behind at least five thousand of its wounded, bringing the total number of Southerners who were taken prisoner by the Federals to more than ten thousand. By nightfall on July 3, forty thousand officers and men from both armies, the dead and the wounded, lay either on the battlefield or in makeshift field hospitals. The enormity of the numbers awed the survivors and moved them to write of it.[16]

Of the fifty-one thousand casualties, approximately seventeen thousand were incurred on the final day, from the opening of the fighting at daybreak on Culp's Hill to the unequal struggle of the 15th Georgia in Rose's Woods an hour or so before sunset. Although no precise figures can be determined for all of the units, certain numbers can be derived from the records. At least 950 Northern soldiers lost their lives defending free soil at Gettysburg just on July 3.[17]

Like the Federals, the Confederates officially reported their casualty figures for the entire three days of battle. Except for George Pickett's division, which was engaged only on July 3, accurate figures on Southern losses on the final day are difficult, if not impossible, to calculate. It may be reasonably concluded, however, that the attacking forces on Culp's Hill and Cemetery Ridge suffered a casualty rate of one-third, if not higher. By that standard, the army lost nearly ten thousand in killed, wounded, and captured or missing on July 3.[18]

A modern study of Pickett's division on July 3 places its casualties at 499 killed or mortally wounded, 1,473 wounded, of whom 832 fell into Federal hands, and 681 nonwounded captured, for a total of 2,653. Although Union accounts report a larger number of prisoners taken immediately after the repulse, these claims might have included the walking wounded. In the end, the three brigades sustained losses of at least 42 percent of the command.[19]

To the survivors of the assault, Pickett's division seemed to have disappeared. A staff officer from another corps, who saw the division days later, thought that it "looked like two or three regiments." Lieutenant Colonel Powhatan B. Whittle of the 38th Virginia, in Lewis Armistead's brigade, observed in a letter soon after the battle, "My poor Regt is ruined." Whittle, who was wounded in the charge, claimed that on July 4 only seventy-three of 350 officers and men answered the roll call. A captain in the same regiment wrote in his diary, "I do not know who is living." Captain Charles Minor Blackford of Longstreet's staff, knowing how terrible the losses had been in the division, wrote on July 7: "Poor Virginia bleeds again at every pore. There will be few firesides in her midst where the voice of mourning will not be heard when the black-lettered list of losses is published."[20]

The summaries of casualties and the impressions of officers and men do not quite attest to the fearful destruction inflicted upon Pickett's division. Lewis Armistead and Richard Garnett, whose body was never recovered and was undoubtedly buried with his troops in a mass grave, had been killed or mortally wounded, James Kemper seriously wounded. Of the forty field officers present for duty—colonels, lieutenant colonels, and majors—twelve were either killed or mortally wounded, nine wounded, four wounded and captured, and one captured, for a total of twenty-six. Some regiments lost nearly all of their captains and lieutenants. Some companies suffered casualty rates of more than 80 percent. Company H, 56th Virginia, of Garnett's brigade, for instance, lost every officer and man except one private, out of thirty-seven in the attack. As Longstreet declared with justification immediately after the assault, "Pickett's Division was gone."[21]

Although the losses among the six brigades from A. P. Hill's Third Corps—the commands of Johnston Pettigrew and Isaac Trimble—are difficult to isolate for July 3, it would appear that they sustained a similar casualty rate to that of Pickett's division, if not slightly higher. Trimble suffered a crippling wound that necessitated amputation of a leg. When the army retreated, he was left behind as a prisoner. Colonel James K. Marshall was killed and Colonel Birkett D. Fry was wounded and captured while leading their brigades. The attrition among field officers amounted to 50 percent, with five killed or mortally wounded and eleven captured.[22]

Nearly nine out of every ten members of the 11th Mississippi, in Joseph Davis's brigade, fell in the assault or were taken prisoner. An officer in another unit, when he saw Davis's regiments reach Seminary Ridge, described them as "the frazzled remnant of the brigade." The 26th North Carolina, in Marshall's brigade, had lost more than five hundred on July 1, and added another 130 to the lists in the charge. A private alleged in a letter written on July 3 that the 11th North Carolina, in the same brigade, presented its flag to Henry Heth that night, "signifying that the Regt. could fight no longer." When it arrived at Gettysburg two days before, it had had about 650 officers and men; now it counted eighty. A soldier in the 2nd Mississippi claimed in his diary that of the sixty members in his regiment who advanced from Seminary Ridge only one was not a casualty. Like Pickett's Virginians, the Alabamians, Tennesseans, Mississippians, and North Carolinians had paid a terrible price.[23]

In the days and weeks immediately after the battle, the Confederates, particularly those who had survived or had witnessed the assault on Cemetery Ridge, tried to explain the sacrifice of lives and to derive meaning from the defeat. One artilleryman wrote with prescience when he told a family member, "The charge will be famous in history as one of the most gallant ever made." Many of them agreed that they had never been in or seen such a cannonade or attack. A North Carolinian put it tersely: "I have never heard such fighting before." Another man who crossed the fields asserted, "It was the hardest fite I ever was in." A private in the 22nd Virginia Battalion of John Brockenbrough's brigade informed his parents, "I have been through more since I left Virginia than ever did before in all my life and I am in hopes I will never see as hard a time again." [24]

They shared also a conviction of duty performed by men of valor. "There was not one of my men on the field," stated Major Joseph R. Cabell of the 38th Virginia in his report, "whom I was not proud to own as a member of the Regt. and as a Virginian." James Lane wrote that in his brigade "both officers and men moved forward with a heroism unsurpassed." Lieutenant Lemuel J. Hoyle of the 11th North Carolina observed less than two weeks later, "The fighting was perfectly fearful, and the slaughter tremendous. Our men fought with the accustomed valor and determination of Southern soldiers but in vain." A Mississippi private concluded, "There was nothing in it to brag about except the heroic gallantry of the men." [25]

Ironically, for the troops with Pettigrew and Trimble their bravery and sacrifice became lost, even discredited, over time. By the end of July, Richmond newspapers had framed the historical memory of the attack by crediting Pickett's Virginians with a near victory and blaming the men from the other states for the ultimate defeat. The press alleged that Pickett's soldiers went the farthest—the high tide of the Confederacy—and Pettigrew's and Trimble's officers and men did not support the Virginians and allowed the Federals to rake both flanks of the valiant Virginians. The controversy stretched into the decades, involving veterans of the charge, but the image of Virginians pouring over the stone wall toward the clump of trees in "Pickett's Charge" prevailed. Too many Alabamians, Tennesseans, Mississippians, and North Carolinians, however, lay dead and maimed on "the plains of slaughter" on the afternoon of July 3 for the Virginia interpretation to be creditable. [26]

Although this controversy arose soon after the campaign had ended and would fester into the next century, the participants in the assault agreed that, despite their bravery, what they had been asked to accomplish was beyond what flesh and blood could do. Their writings expressed a disquietude about the day's events. The Yankees, wrote one Southerner, "had such commanding positions it was almost impossible to dislodge them." A North Carolina officer believed that the enemy's "position was by far the most formidable we had ever encountered and was certainly impregnable." He continued, "The men came to the conclusion that an impossibility had been required of them." [27]

Other men offered their views—"we gained nothing but glory; and lost our bravest men"; "a second Fredericksburg affair, only the wrong way"; "I think we got *the* worst end of the bargain this time"; and "this day's work is *the mistake* of the campaign." One of Pettigrew's staff officers, writing several months later, noted, "It must remain always a sealed question, whether or not Cemetery Hill could have been taken with the forces engaged."[28]

Many of them thought that *"the mistake* of the campaign" rested with the army's commander. "Our wise Gen. Lee made a great mistake in making the attack," commented a South Carolinian. "I further think," stated an Alabamian in a letter to his mother, "that it was the worst piece of generalship I ever knew General Lee to exercise, in undertaking to storm the enemy's fortifications." The troops knew "that they were not responsible for the result." Colonel William H. A. Speer of the 28th North Carolina tried to explain Lee's decision: "The charge was almost the last hope as the heights had been stormed on both ends by a flank movement and could not be held, and then we had to storm it in front."[29]

For three days, the Army of Northern Virginia had fought and bled at Gettysburg, earning a victory on the first day and suffering defeat on the next two. Explanations for the defeat were offered almost as soon as the army marched away from the battlefield. One singular fact remains, however—the Union Army of the Potomac won the battle as it was fought. And it was fought or unfolded because of the decisions made by Robert E. Lee.

From the time Lee arrived on the battlefield in the early afternoon of July 1, he had taken the initiative or tactical control of the action. His troops' attacks on that day gave the initiative to him, and he chose not to relinquish it. In the aftermath of that first day's victory, he worked to overcome obstacles— Jeb Stuart's absence, Richard Ewell's hesitation to exploit the gains made on July 1, James Longstreet's opposition to an offensive on July 2, and the army's inability, as Lee described it, to achieve "a proper concert of action." As he also said, "A battle thus became, in a measure, unavoidable," and Lee decided to wage it where he had been drawn into it.[30]

Lee had an alternative at hand. He could have posted the army on Seminary Ridge in a defensive position and awaited attacks from the Federals. George Meade's council on July 2 indicates that he and his subordinates would have taken the offensive if circumstances required it. In his postwar writings, Porter Alexander argued that Lee should have acted on the defensive after July 1. Lee's decision otherwise, Alexander believed, was "a rather sad example of the forcing game."[31]

Lee had spent the past year, however, using "the forcing game." Against long odds, he had seen his army win battlefield victories and demoralize the enemy, most recently at Chancellorsville, by attacking. He had brought the army a long way from Fredericksburg into Pennsylvania. He had come into the Northern state for a showdown battle that might result in a political solution to the conflict. Although he had not wanted a battle on July 1, he had found the Federals on open ground and, in his view, vulnerable to defeat. It was an opportunity to be seized. Against the odds and against the closing window for Confederate independence, Lee chose the offensive. Limited success on July 2, as he interpreted it, induced him to resume the attacks the next day. Perhaps it was, as Colonel Speer concluded, "almost the last hope" for Lee and the army.[32]

For July 3, Lee wrote, "the general plan was unchanged"—assaults against both flanks of the Union army, augmented by Pickett's division. It had to be scrapped, however, when Pickett, who had not received orders to get to the field by dawn, failed to appear. The only aspect of Lee's original plan for the day that began on schedule was the effort to take Culp's Hill. Although the Federals initiated the combat there, Ewell's units were poised to strike and went forward soon afterward. The Confederate assaults on the naturally strong and well-fortified Union position never came close to a breakthrough. They were piecemeal, costly, and characteristic of the army's tactics on July 2 and 3. Ewell offered virtually no direction, and the burden fell on a division commander, Edward Johnson. Lee never seemed to appreciate the difficulties confronted by his troops at Culp's Hill.[33]

Faced with the need to cobble together another plan on the opposite end of the Confederate line, Lee settled upon the cannonade and infantry assault against Cemetery Ridge. In a July 4 letter to Jefferson Davis, Lee described it simply as "a more extensive attack." He seemed to have concluded that Meade must have weakened his center to bolster both flanks. With that conclusion, however, Lee "misjudged both the weakness of the enemy and the capabilities of his own army."[34]

The Army of Northern Virginia on the morning of July 3 at Gettysburg did not possess the capability to launch a successful assault, as envisioned and ordered by Lee. His artillery had neither the number and types of cannon nor enough long-range ammunition to wreak the havoc upon the enemy Lee thought would be necessary to shield the infantry. He also could not put enough troops in the assault force to break through the Union line and then hold it without depleting his center, a risk even Lee appeared hesitant to take. If he had used Pickett's division, Hill's entire corps, and Robert Rodes's brigades as the assault force—perhaps the requisite number to achieve a breakthrough—there would not have been an organized unit left in the army's center.[35]

For Lee and the army, consequently, everything had to fall in place. He would not have ordered the assault unless he believed that it could succeed. Despite hours of discussions and preparations, however, how could Lee and Longstreet not know of the limited supply of artillery ammunition? Why was the role of the reserve units not clearly understood, and why were precise orders not issued? And why did no one in the Confederate high command recognize the fences along Emmitsburg Road as a possibly disruptive—even deadly—barrier to the attacking infantry? These are questions whose definitive answers have defied historical inquiry.[36]

"We were not," wrote Porter Alexander, "the *machine* an army ought to be, either in organisation, or equipment." Alexander attributed some of the army's critical failings to inadequate staffs. Overlaid upon the army's organizational weaknesses, however, was Lee's method of command. Although it had worked so well in the past, his willingness to give his subordinates loose rein had become critically strained at Gettysburg, under Hill's and Ewell's inexperience and Longstreet's opposition. With so much at stake, with the decisive moment in the showdown battle that he had sought, Lee assumed, once again, his passive direction of details. If he expected or thought that he had ordered a more active and timely use of reserves, why did he not intervene? Once the plan had been fashioned, Lee evidently removed himself and his staff from the final preparations and the conduct of the cannonade and charge.[37]

The responsibility for the execution of the operation fell upon Longstreet and, to a lesser extent, A. P. Hill. The latter general, left with authority over two brigades in his corps, virtually disappeared during the assault. According to one artilleryman, Hill stood by a battery as the infantry charged and "looked at me as if he were dazed, if not confounded by the scene before him." When Union reinforcements rushed forward against the attack column, the gunners asked permission to open fire. Hill declined, saying that their ammunition was "too nearly exhausted to permit this." If true, it might have been the only order Hill issued.[38]

The direct burden for the assault's success or failure rested with "Old Pete" Longstreet. He had opposed the idea when Lee broached it and voiced his disagreement with it. As the morning lengthened, his mood darkened. Alexander believed that Longstreet "obeyed *reluctantly*," but "he owed it to Lee *to be reluctant* as failure was almost certain." Longstreet said afterward that it was suggested to him later that he should have stopped the infantry. He would have used such discretion if it were proper and Lee not present, but, as he wrote, "I never exercised discretion after discussing with General Lee the points of his orders, *and* when, after discussion, he had ordered the execution of his policy." [39]

Longstreet and his staff attended, then, to the details of the cannonade and the charge. When the artillery opened, he rode along the line, trying to allay the men's fears with a personal demonstration of courage. He tried briefly to shift responsibility to Alexander for the decision to start or not to start the infantry. Alexander's response reminded Longstreet that such a critical decision rested with *him*, and he exercised it. He ordered forward some of the reserves and canceled a further advance by three of Richard Anderson's brigades. He performed his duty against his better judgment. Whether he fulfilled Lee's designs as the commanding general thought them to be cannot be definitively answered. What seems certain about Longstreet was his admission to James Fremantle that he would have liked "very much" to miss or not see the charge.[40]

A void in the historical record was created by Lee's instruction to Pickett to destroy his report, which might have provided insight into the preparations and the charge. The report evidently was sharply critical of other generals and other units. Longstreet, who apparently read it, wrote, "Pickett's report was not so strong against the attack as mine before the attack was made but his was made in writing and of official record." Pickett was, according to an aide, "furious" when Lee returned it with instructions to delete sections of it. His brother, Charles, claimed that the general did not destroy it but sent a copy for safekeeping to his family in Richmond. When the Federals entered the city in April 1865, an uncle burned it.[41]

Pickett's and others' reports came after the Confederates had sustained a fearfully bloody defeat. But as the survivors streamed to the rear in its immediate aftermath, Lee met them and admitted a singular truth, "It is my fault." He gave an explanation to Davis about the day and the entire battle: "The conduct of the troops was all that I could desire or expect, and they deserve success so far as it can be deserved by heroic valor and fortitude. More may have been required of them than they were able to perform."[42]

Sergeant James B. Suddath of the 7th South Carolina offered his own assessment of the battle in a letter to his brother: "We like to have got our army destroyed just at the time we needed it the worst. It will learn Gen Lee a lesson he had too much confidence in his army he thought there was no place but he could take it but the mountains at Gettysburg was rather too much for him."[43]

Across the bloody fields from the Confederates, the outcome of the final day and of the battle brought different reactions and judgments. When the fury ended, the men of the Army of the Potomac knew that they had won not only a victory but redemption. Lee, thought a Union soldier, "supposed he could walk right over the Army of Potomac." Instead, wrote another Federal, he and his comrades "gave the rebels one of the damdest lickens that they have ever had." Captain David E. Beem of the 14th Indiana boasted in a letter to his wife on July 5, "The Army of the Potomac long resting under the disgrace of public opinion celebrated the glorious 4th of July with their guns still black with powder, and on the very field where they had vindicated their bravery."[44]

At Gettysburg, the Union army confronted its past and the possibility of a portentous defeat. By its performance, however, in the view of one historian, it "showed that there were limits to its capacity for self-inflicted damage." From privates in the ranks to the commanding general, the army had, indeed, earned vindication, exorcising some of its ghosts from the past.[45]

To be sure, the terrain, interior lines, numbers, and artillery ordnance favored the Federals. But at Gettysburg, unlike times in the past, leadership did not fail the rank and file. If the victory ultimately resulted from the prowess and bravery of the officers and men, George Meade and his senior subordinates reacted to the changing conditions on the battlefield with skill and alacrity. The outcome of the fighting on July 3 had been arguably decided during the morning.[46]

From the time Meade had arrived on the battlefield, before daylight on July 2, he acted cautiously, inspected his lines frequently, conferred often with subordinates, prepared plans systematically, and issued necessary instructions. It might have been, as Longstreet argued, that "we made the battle for him," and it might have been that Meade and his army could only have won a defensive battle. But that was the battle given him, and he exploited his army's advantages.[47]

At the council in the Leister house on the night of July 2, Meade set in motion the events and decisions that resulted in victory the next day. With the advice and support of his corps commanders, Meade's determination to stand and to give battle on the morrow was confirmed. Later that night, he issued the orders for the retaking of the lost works on Culp's Hill. And during the morning of July 3, he conferred with corps commanders, designating reserve units to respond to a crisis, worked closely with Henry Hunt on the disposition and use of artillery, and rode along the lines conducting further examinations. Meade was not present to witness the climax at Cemetery Ridge, but his preparations and orders had been executed by others. The arrival of Union reserve batteries and of nearly thirteen thousand troops in support of the front line testified to Meade's and others' masterful performances on the final day.[48]

When it had ended, he telegraphed Washington, first noting that "the army is in fine spirits," and then following with, "I do not think Lee will attack me again." Two days later, he wrote a brief summary to his wife: "The men behaved splendidly. I really think they are becoming soldiers." He followed with another letter on July 8: "I did and shall continue to do, my duty, to the best of my ability but knowing as I do that battles are often decided by accidents, and that no man of sense will say in advance what their result will be. I wish to be careful in bragging before the right time." His son, George, however, bragged in a letter to his mother: "I never saw such a time in my life. Papa formed his line of battle in the most admirable style, and handled his troops magnificently."[49]

From within the army and from Washington, Meade received credit for his performance. "He is already quite popular among the troops," claimed Lieutenant Cornelius Moore of the 57th New York on July 6, "as a natural consequence, having been successful in this his first fight." An artillery officer, Gulian V. Weir, informed his father two days after the battle, "I have also heard General McClellan will replace Meade in a short while. If this is true it will be a great loss. General Meade is the finest soldier we have yet in command."[50]

On July 7, at the order of President Abraham Lincoln, Meade was promoted to brigadier general in the Regular Army, to rank from July 3, "for skill, good conduct, and gallantry at the battle of Gettysburg." Congratulatory letters came from Generals John Pope, George McClellan, and Henry Halleck.[51]

In the end, Meade shared with others victory on the day a Union private said "will ever live in memory as a burning picture of bravery blood and death." His fellow victors included generals such as Winfield Scott Hancock, Henry Hunt, John Gibbon, Alpheus S. Williams, Alexander Hays, George Greene, Alexander Webb, George Stannard, and Thomas Kane; colonels such as Norman Hall, Thomas Smyth, and Charles Candy; soldiers such as the White Star Division on Culp's Hill, the Blue Birds of Alexander Hays, the

Philadelphia Brigade, the Vermonters of George Stannard, the Pennsylvanians of Thomas Kane, and the artillerists of Alonzo Cushing, William Arnold,
George Woodruff, James Rorty, Walter Perrin, and Freeman McGilvery. It
had been their day, and, with their comrades in other units, it had been their
battle.[52]

Images, burned into memory, last: Hancock on horseback riding along his
line during the cannonade; Hunt firing his revolver at the enemy as they came
over the wall; "Old Man" Greene walking behind the works on Culp's Hill;
Gibbon shouting encouragement amid the fury; Hays leading troops in a
manual of arms as the Confederates approached; Webb grabbing at a flag to
lead the counterattack; young Frank Haskell rushing in with reserves; Stannard hurrying his green Vermonters against the Rebel flank; and from the
east, an echo of "Come on, you Wolverines!"

A Southerner and a Northerner offered their assessments of the day. Tully
Simpson, a South Carolinian, stated a fortnight after the battle: "A few weeks
ago Genl Lee had the finest Army that ever was raised in ancient or modern
times—and commanded by as patriotic and heroic officers as ever drew a
sword in defence of liberty. But in an unfortunate hour and under disadvan-
tageous circumstances, he attacked the enemy." Charles Mattocks, a Mainer,
noted in his journal, "Friday, July 3d, 1863, was a sad day for Lee's army."[53]

٥　٥　٥

AFTER SUNDOWN ON JULY 3, Lee met with his senior officers and told them
that if Meade did not attack the next day the army would begin the return
march to Virginia. He followed the meeting with orders, and units began to
shift positions during the night. Early on July 4, he proposed a prisoner exchange to Meade, who rejected it because "it is not in my power to accede to
the proposed arrangement." Rain began falling in the afternoon—increasing
to a downpour, as if the skies were trying to wash away the blood. At last, after
nightfall, the Confederates marched south into the darkness.[54]

The retreat, slowed by the muddy roads and the fatigue of the men, continued through Maryland until the army reached the Potomac River. The
Federals pursued, paced by their cavalry, which overtook elements of the
Confederate wagon train and clashed with Jeb Stuart's troopers. The heavy
rains had swelled the river, forcing Lee's troops to build fieldworks in a defensive position until the waters subsided. Meade's army closed on the Rebel

lines. Meade conferred with his corps commanders, and they decided to test the works on July 14. By then the Potomac had fallen, and during the night of July 13–14, the Confederates crossed into Virginia. A rear-guard encounter at Falling Waters on the next morning ended the combat of the Gettysburg Campaign. Ironically, Johnston Pettigrew, who had survived the July 3 assault with only a slight wound, was mortally wounded in this minor action.[55]

One Georgia soldier, speaking for many of his comrades, was thankful to be in Virginia. Two days after his return, he wrote home: "I thought I knew it all, but this last campaign exceeds in hardships anything I ever experienced. I have been cold, hot, wet, dry, ragged, dirty, hungry, and thirsty, marched through clouds of dust, waded mud knee deep & suffered from fatigue & loss of sleep." He added, however, "Our army is far from being demoralised."[56]

In Gettysburg, meanwhile, the healing of broken men and of the community continued. Citizens from surrounding towns had brought wagon loads of provisions for the wounded soldiers. Most of the burial details had finished their gruesome duty. It was left to time and nature to cover the scars.[57]

When Lincoln came to Gettysburg in November to help dedicate the national cemetery, few of the scars had disappeared. The president and the thousands in the crowd knew that during the first week of July the nation had been at a crossroad. But as the Confederate tide receded from Cemetery Ridge on the afternoon of July 3, Major General Ulysses S. Grant was dictating terms for the surrender of the Southern garrison at Vicksburg, Mississippi. With what occurred at Gettysburg and Vicksburg, the nation passed the crossroad. Although nearly two more years of bloody and bitter warfare lay ahead, the struggle now followed a new road. When Lincoln's time came to speak on November 19, his few words gave the conflict definition, reminding the audience of the debt owed to those who had fallen and to those who continued the struggle for union and a "new birth of freedom."

Other voices, none so eloquent as Lincoln's, tried to explain what they witnessed and what it meant. They were ordinary men who had passed through three extraordinary days. One of them was Captain John Blinn of the 20th Massachusetts. He had suffered a mortal wound on July 3, and with the brief time left to him, he penned two letters home. One was to his wife, Cora: "I die in my countries cause. Don't mourn for me, but forget & be happy with some other man's love. My country called me out to die." The second one went to his mother, brother, and sister: "Your soldier boy is wounded but we whipped the enemy & the old flag is again glorious. My wound is a very serious one & I fear amputation may be necessary. I may die but Mother: God give you strength & grace to bear the affliction. My country called & I came to die upon her altar. God bless you & keep you. I can write no more."[58]

Georgian Sidney Richardson, who had been spared at Gettysburg, had seen the future and shared it with his parents: "But I am willing to fight them as long as General Lee says fight. But I think we are ruined now without going any further with it. One thing convinced me: that is when we went into Maryland and Pennsylvania. The [low] price of everything showed they did not feel the effects of this war, and I saw a great many men that are fit for service. . . . This war is hard to account for. It is no telling how it will end or when it will end."[59]

Like Richardson, Michigander Cyril Tyler was also uncertain about when the war would end. He was sure, however, as he told his father four days after the battle, that "we will have to fight them again soon. I dread it."[60]

The final voice belongs to a Union infantryman known only as Micah. He had helped in the repulse of the Confederate assault on Cemetery Ridge, grabbing a rifle from a comrade who had been shot in the head. Before the day ended, he wrote to his brother. "What men are these we slaughter like cattle," he asked, probably more to himself, "and still they come at us?" He doubted whether he would ever sleep again. But this Micah knew, "This place called Gettysburg shall surely be remembered in Hell for all of eternity."[61]

APPENDIX: ORDER OF BATTLE

MAJOR GENERAL GEORGE G. MEADE, USA, commanding
FIRST ARMY CORPS (Maj. Gen. John F. Reynolds)
    Maj. Gen. Abner Doubleday
    Maj. Gen. John Newton
  First Division (Brig. Gen. James S. Wadsworth)
    First Brigade (Brig. Gen. Solomon Meredith)
    —(Col. William W. Robinson)
      19th Indiana
      24th Michigan
      2nd Wisconsin
      6th Wisconsin
      7th Wisconsin
    Second Brigade (Brig. Gen. Lysander Cutler)
      7th Indiana
      76th New York
      84th New York (14th Militia)
      95th New York
      147th New York
      56th Pennsylvania (9 cos.)
  Second Division (Brig. Gen. John C. Robinson)
    First Brigade (Brig. Gen. Gabriel R. Paul)
    —(Col. Samuel H. Leonard)
    —(Col. Adrian R. Root)
    —(Col. Richard Coulter)
    —(Col. Peter Lyle)
    —(Col. Richard Coulter)

16th Maine
13th Massachusetts
94th New York
104th New York
107th Pennsylvania
Second Brigade (Brig. Gen. Henry Baxter)
12th Massachusetts
83rd New York (9th Militia)
97th New York
11th Pennsylvania
88th Pennsylvania
90th Pennsylvania
Third Division (Maj. Gen. Abner Doubleday)
—(Brig. Gen. Thomas A. Rowley)
First Brigade (Col. Chapman Biddle)
—(Brig. Gen. Thomas A. Rowley)
—(Col. Chapman Biddle)
80th New York (20th Militia)
121st Pennsylvania
142nd Pennsylvania
151st Pennsylvania
Second Brigade (Col. Roy Stone)
—(Col. Langhorne Wister)
—(Col. Edmund L. Dana)
143rd Pennsylvania
149th Pennsylvania
150th Pennsylvania
Third Brigade (Brig. Gen. George J. Stannard)
—(Col. Francis V. Randall)
13th Vermont
14th Vermont
16th Vermont
Artillery Brigade (Col. Charles S. Wainwright)
Maine Light, 2nd Battery (B) (Capt. James A. Hall)
Maine Light, 5th Battery (E) (Capt. Greenleaf T. Stevens)
1st New York Light, Batteries L & E (Capt. Gilbert H. Reynolds)
—(Lieut. George Breck)
1st Pennsylvania Light, Battery (B) (Capt. James H. Cooper)
4th United States, Battery (B) (Lieut. James Stewart)

SECOND ARMY CORPS (Maj. Gen. Winfield S. Hancock)
—(Brig. Gen. John Gibbon)
—(Maj. Gen. Winfield S. Hancock)
  First Division (Brig. Gen. John C. Caldwell)
    First Brigade (Col. Edward E. Cross)
    —(Col. H. Boyd McKeen)
    5th New Hampshire
    61st New York
    81st Pennsylvania
    148th Pennsylvania
    Second Brigade (Col. Patrick Kelly)
    28th Massachusetts
    63rd New York (2 cos.)
    69th New York (2 cos.)
    88th New York (2 cos.)
    116th Pennsylvania (4 cos.)
    Third Brigade (Brigadier General Samuel K. Zook)
    —(Lieut. Col. John Fraser)
    52nd New York
    57th New York
    66th New York
    140th Pennsylvania
    Fourth Brigade (Col. John R. Brooke)
    27th Connecticut (2 cos.)
    2nd Delaware
    64th New York
    53rd Pennsylvania
    145th Pennsylvania (7 cos.)
  Second Division (Brig. Gen. John Gibbon)
  —(Brig. Gen. William Harrow)
  —(Brig. Gen. John Gibbon)
    First Brigade (Brig. Gen. William Harrow)
    —(Col. Francis E. Heath)
    19th Maine
    15th Massachusetts
    1st Minnesota and 2nd Co. Minnesota Sharpshooters
    82nd New York (2nd Militia)
    Second Brigade (Brig. Gen. Alexander S. Webb)
    69th Pennsylvania
    71st Pennsylvania

72nd Pennsylvania
106th Pennsylvania
Third Brigade (Col. Norman J. Hall)
59th New York
19th Massachusetts
20th Massachusetts
7th Michigan
42nd New York
59th New York (4 cos.)
Unattached
Massachusetts Sharpshooters 1st Co.
Third Division (Brig. Gen. Alexander Hays)
First Brigade (Col. Samuel S. Carroll)
14th Indiana
4th Ohio
8th Ohio
7th West Virginia
Second Brigade (Col. Thomas A. Smyth)
—(Lieut. Col. Francis E. Pierce)
14th Connecticut
1st Delaware
12th New Jersey
10th New York Battalion
108th New York
Third Brigade (Col. George L. Willard)
—(Col. Eliakim Sherrill)
—(Lieut. Col. James L. Bull)
39th New York (4 cos.)
111th New York
125th New York
126th New York
Artillery Brigade (Capt. John G. Hazard)
1st New York Light, Battery (G) and 14th New York Battery
(Lieut. Albert S. Sheldon)
—(Capt. James M. Rorty)
—(Lieut. Robert E. Rogers)
1st Rhode Island, Battery (A) (Capt. William A. Arnold)
1st Rhode Island, Battery (B) (Lieut. T. Fred Brown)
1st United States, Battery (I)
(Lieut. George A. Woodruff)
—(Lieut. Tully McCrea)

4th United States, Battery (A) (Lieut. Alonzo H. Cushing)

—(Sgt. Frederick Fuger)

THIRD ARMY CORPS (Maj. Gen. Daniel E. Sickles)

—(Maj. Gen. David B. Birney)

First Division (Maj. Gen. David B. Birney)

—(Brig. Gen. J. H. Hobart Ward)

First Brigade (Brig. Gen. Charles K. Graham)

—(Col. Andrew H. Tippin)

57th Pennsylvania (8 cos.)

63rd Pennsylvania

68th Pennsylvania

105th Pennsylvania

114th Pennsylvania

141st Pennsylvania

Second Brigade (Brig. Gen. J. H. Hobart Ward)

—(Col. Hiram Berdan)

20th Indiana

3rd Maine

4th Maine

86th New York

124th New York

99th Pennsylvania

1st United States Sharpshooters

2nd United States Sharpshooters (8 cos.)

Third Brigade (Col. P. Regis De Trobriand)

17th Maine

3rd Michigan

5th Michigan

40th New York

110th Pennsylvania (6 cos.)

Second Division (Brig. Gen. Andrew A. Humphreys)

First Brigade (Brig. Gen. Joseph B. Carr)

1st Massachusetts

11th Massachusetts

16th Massachusetts

12th New Hampshire

11th New Jersey

26th Pennsylvania

Second Brigade (Col. William R. Brewster)

70th New York

71st New York

72nd New York
73rd New York
74th New York
120th New York
Third Brigade (Col. George C. Burling)
2nd New Hampshire
5th New Jersey
6th New Jersey
7th New Jersey
8th New Jersey
115th Pennsylvania
Artillery Brigade (Capt. George E. Randolph)
—(Capt. A. Judson Clark)
1st New Jersey Light, 2nd Battery (B) (Capt. A. Judson Clark)
—(Lieut. Robert Sims)
1st New York, Battery (D) (Capt. George B. Winslow)
New York Light, 4th Battery (Capt. James E. Smith)
1st Rhode Island Light, Battery (E) (Lieut. John K. Bucklyn)
—(Lieut. Benjamin Freeborn)
4th United States, Battery (K) (Lieut. Francis W. Seeley)
—(Lieut. Robert James)
FIFTH ARMY CORPS (Maj. Gen. George Sykes)
First Division (Brig. Gen. James Barnes)
First Brigade (Col. William S. Tilton)
18th Massachusetts
22nd Massachusetts
1st Michigan
118th Pennsylvania
Second Brigade (Col. Jacob B. Sweitzer)
9th Massachusetts
32nd Massachusetts
4th Michigan
62nd Pennsylvania
Third Brigade (Col. Strong Vincent)
—(Col. James C. Rice)
20th Maine
16th Michigan
44th New York
83rd Pennsylvania
Second Division (Brig. Gen. Romeyn B. Ayres)

First Brigade (Col. Hannibal Day)
3rd United States (6 cos.)
4th United States (4 cos.)
6th United States (5 cos.)
12th United States (8 cos.)
14th United States (8 cos.)
Second Brigade (Col. Sidney Burbank)
2nd United States (6 cos.)
7th United States (4 cos.)
10th United States (3 cos.)
11th United States (6 cos.)
17th United States (7 cos.)
Third Brigade (Brig. Gen. Stephen H. Weed)
—(Col. Kenner Garrard)
140th New York
146th New York
91st Pennsylvania
155th Pennsylvania
Third Division
First Brigade (Col. William McCandless)
1st Pennsylvania Reserves (9 cos.)
2nd Pennsylvania Reserves
6th Pennsylvania Reserves
13th Pennsylvania Reserves
Third Brigade (Col. Joseph W. Fisher)
5th Pennsylvania Reserves
9th Pennsylvania Reserves
10th Pennsylvania Reserves
11th Pennsylvania Reserves
12th Pennsylvania Reserves (9 cos.)
Artillery Brigade (Capt. Augustus P. Martin)
Massachusetts Light, 3rd Battery (C) (Lieut. Aaron F. Walcott)
1st New York Light, Battery (C) (Capt. Almont Barnes)
1st Ohio Light, Battery (L) (Capt. Frank C. Gibbs)
5th United States, Battery (D) (Lieut. Charles E. Hazlett)
—(Lieut. Benjamin F. Rittenhouse)
5th United States, Battery (I) (Lieut. Malbone F. Watson)
—(Lieut. Charles C. MacConnell)
SIXTH ARMY CORPS (Maj. Gen. John Sedgwick)
First Division (Brig. Gen. Horatio G. Wright)

First Brigade (Brig. Gen. Alfred T. A. Torbert)
1st New Jersey
2nd New Jersey
3rd New Jersey
15th New Jersey
Second Brigade (Brig. Gen. Joseph J. Bartlett)
5th Maine
121st New York
95th Pennsylvania
96th Pennsylvania
Third Brigade (Brig. Gen. David A. Russell)
6th Maine
49th Pennsylvania (4 cos.)
119th Pennsylvania
5th Wisconsin
Second Division (Brig. Gen. Albion P. Howe)
Second Brigade (Col. Lewis A. Grant)
2nd Vermont
3rd Vermont
4th Vermont
5th Vermont
6th Vermont
Third Brigade (Brig. Gen. Thomas H. Neill)
7th Maine (6 cos.)
33rd New York (detach.)
43rd New York
49th New York
77th New York
61st Pennsylvania
Third Division (Maj. Gen. John Newton)
—(Brig. Gen. Frank Wheaton)
First Brigade (Brig. Gen. Alexander Shaler)
65th New York
67th New York
122nd New York
23rd Pennsylvania
82nd Pennsylvania
Second Brigade (Col. Henry L. Eustis)
7th Massachusetts
10th Massachusetts

37th Massachusetts

2nd Rhode Island

Third Brigade (Brig. Gen. Frank Wheaton)

—(Col. David J. Nevin)

62nd New York

93rd Pennsylvania

98th Pennsylvania

139th Pennsylvania

Artillery Brigade (Col. Charles H. Tompkins)

Massachusetts Light, 1st Battery (A)

New York Light, 1st Battery

New York Light, 3rd Battery

1st Rhode Island Light, Battery (C)

1st Rhode Island Light, Battery (G)

2nd United States, Battery (D)

2nd United States, Battery (G)

5th United States, Battery (F)

ELEVENTH ARMY CORPS (Maj. Gen. Oliver O. Howard)

—(Maj. Gen. Carl Schurz)

—(Maj. Gen. Oliver O. Howard)

First Division (Brig. Gen. Francis C. Barlow)

—(Brig. Gen. Adelbert Ames)

First Brigade (Col. Leopold von Gilsa)

41st New York (9 cos.)

54th New York

68th New York

153rd Pennsylvania

Second Brigade (Brig. Gen. Adelbert Ames)

—(Col. Andrew L. Harris)

17th Connecticut

25th Ohio

75th Ohio

107th Ohio

Second Division

(Brig. Gen. Adolph von Steinwehr)

First Brigade (Col. Charles R. Coster)

134th New York

154th New York

27th Pennsylvania

73rd Pennsylvania

Second Brigade (Col. Orlando Smith)
33rd Massachusetts
136th New York
55th Ohio
73rd Ohio
Third Division (Maj. Gen. Carl Schurz)
—(Brig. Gen. Alexander Schimmelfennig)
—(Maj. Gen. Carl Schurz)
First Brigade (Brig. Gen. Alexander Schimmelfennig)
—(Col. George Von Amsberg)
82nd Illinois
45th New York
157th New York
61st Ohio
74th Pennsylvania
Second Brigade (Col. Wladimir Krzyzanowski)
58th New York
119th New York
82nd Ohio
75th Pennsylvania
26th Wisconsin
Artillery Brigade (Maj. Thomas W. Osborn)
1st New York Light, Battery (I) (Capt. Michael Weidrich)
New York Light, 13th Battery (Lieut. William Wheeler)
1st Ohio Light, Battery (I) (Capt. Hubert Dilger)
1st Ohio Light, Battery (K) (Capt. Lewis Heckman)
United States, Battery (G) (Lieut. Bayard Wilkeson)
—(Lieut. Eugene A. Bancroft)
TWELFTH ARMY CORPS (Maj. Gen. Henry W. Slocum)
—(Brig. Gen. Alpheus S. Williams)
First Division (Brig. Gen. Alpheus S. Williams)
—(Brig. Gen. Thomas H. Ruger)
First Brigade (Col. Archibald L. McDougall)
5th Connecticut
20th Connecticut
3rd Maryland
123rd New York
145th New York
46th Pennsylvania

Second Brigade (Brig. Gen. Henry H. Lockwood)
1st Maryland Potomac Home Brigade
1st Maryland Eastern Shore
150th New York
Third Brigade (Brig. Gen. Thomas H. Ruger)
—(Col. Silas Colgrove)
27th Indiana
2nd Massachusetts
13th New Jersey
107th New York
3rd Wisconsin
Second Division (Brig. Gen. John W. Geary)
First Brigade (Col. Charles Candy)
5th Ohio
7th Ohio
29th Ohio
66th Ohio
28th Pennsylvania
147th Pennsylvania (8 cos.)
Second Brigade (Col. George A. Cobham, Jr.)
—(Brig. Gen. Thomas L. Kane)
—(Col. George A. Cobham, Jr.)
29th Pennsylvania
109th Pennsylvania
111th Pennsylvania
Third Brigade (Brig. Gen. George S. Greene)
60th New York
78th New York
102nd New York
137th New York
149th New York
Artillery Brigade (Lieut. Edward D. Muhlenberg)
1st New York Light, Battery (M) (Lieut. Charles E. Winegar)
Pennsylvania Light, Battery (E) (Lieut. Charles A. Atwell)
4th United States, Battery (F) (Lieut. Sylvanus T. Rugg)
5th United States, Battery (K) (Lieut. David H. Kinzie)
CAVALRY CORPS (Maj. Gen. Alfred Pleasonton)
First Division (Brig. Gen. John Buford)
First Brigade (Col. William Gamble)
8th Illinois
12th Illinois (6 cos.)

3rd Indiana (6 cos.)

8th New York

Second Brigade (Col. Thomas C. Devin)

6th New York

9th New York

17th Pennsylvania

3rd West Virginia (2 cos.)

Reserve Brigade (Brig. Gen. Wesley Merritt)

6th Pennsylvania

1st United States

2nd United States

5th United States

6th United States

Second Division (Brig. Gen. David McM. Gregg)

First Brigade (Col. John B. McIntosh)

1st Maryland (11 cos.)

Purnell (Maryland) Legion Co. (A)

1st Massachusetts

1st New Jersey

1st Pennsylvania

3rd Pennsylvania

3rd Pennsylvania Artillery Section Battery (H)

Third Brigade (Col. J. Irvin Gregg)

1st Maine (10 cos.)

10th New York

4th Pennsylvania

16th Pennsylvania

Third Division (Brig. Gen. Judson Kilpatrick)

—(Col. Nathaniel P. Richmond)

First Brigade (Brig. Gen. Elon J. Farnsworth)

5th New York

18th Pennsylvania

1st Vermont

1st West Virginia (10 cos.)

Second Brigade (Brig. Gen. George A. Custer)

1st Michigan

5th Michigan

6th Michigan

7th Michigan (10 cos.)

Horse Artillery

  1st Brigade (Capt. James M. Robertson)

    9th Michigan Battery

    6th New York Battery

    2nd United States, Batteries (B & L)

    2nd United States, Battery (M)

    4th United States, Battery (E)

  2nd Brigade (Capt. John C. Tidball)

    1st United States, Batteries (E & G)

    1st United States, Battery (K)

    2nd United States, Battery (A)

ARTILLERY RESERVE (Brig. Gen. Robert O. Tyler)

  —(Capt. James M. Robertson)

  1st Brigade (Regular) (Capt. Dunbar R. Ransom)

    1st United States, Battery (H) (Lieut. Chandler P. Eakin)

    3rd United States, Batteries (F & K) (Lieut. John G. Turnbull)

    4th United States, Battery (C) (Lieut. Evan Thomas)

    5th United States, Battery (C) (Lieut. Gulian V. Weir)

  1st Volunteer Brigade (Lieut. Col. Freeman McGilvery)

    Massachusetts Light, 5th Battery (E) (Capt. Charles A. Phillips)

    Massachusetts Light, 9th Battery (Capt. John Bigelow)

    New York Light, 15th Battery (Capt. Patrick Hart)

    Pennsylvania Light, Batteries (C & F) (Capt. James Thompson)

  2nd Volunteer Brigade (Capt. Elijah D. Taft)

    Connecticut Light, 2nd Battery (Capt. John W. Sterling)

    New York Light, 5th Battery (Capt. Elijah D. Taft)

  3rd Volunteer Brigade (Capt. James F. Huntington)

    New Hampshire Light, 1st Battery (Capt. Frederick M. Edgell)

    1st Ohio Light, Battery (H) (Lieut. George W. Norton)

    1st Pennsylvania Light, Batteries (F & G)

      (Capt. R. Bruce Ricketts)

    West Virginia Light, Battery (C) (Capt. Wallace Hill)

  4th Volunteer Brigade (Capt. Robert H. Fitzhugh)

    Maine Light, 6th Battery (F) (Lieut. Edwin B. Dow)

    Maryland Light, Battery (A) (Capt. James H. Rigby)

    1st New Jersey Light, Battery (A) (Lieut. Agustin N. Parsons)

    1st New York Light, Battery (G) (Capt. Nelson Ames)

    1st New York Light, Battery (K) (Capt. Robert H. Fitzhugh)

    11th New York Battery (Capt. Robert H. Fitzhugh)

TRAIN GUARD 4th New Jersey (4 cos.) (Maj. Charles Ewing)

THE ARMY OF NORTHERN VIRGINIA
GENERAL ROBERT E. LEE, CSA, commanding
FIRST ARMY CORPS (Lieut. Gen. James Longstreet)
McLaws' Division (Maj. Gen. Lafayette McLaws)
Kershaw's Brigade (Brig. Gen. Joseph B. Kershaw)
2nd South Carolina
3rd South Carolina
7th South Carolina
8th South Carolina
15th South Carolina
3rd South Carolina Battalion
Semmes' Brigade (Brig. Gen. Paul J. Semmes)
—(Col. Goode Bryan)
10th Georgia
50th Georgia
51st Georgia
53rd Georgia
Barksdale's Brigade (Brig. Gen. William Barksdale)
—(Col. Benjamin G. Humphreys)
13th Mississippi
17th Mississippi
18th Mississippi
21st Mississippi
Wofford's Brigade (Brig. Gen. William T. Wofford)
16th Georgia
18th Georgia
24th Georgia
Cobb's (Georgia) Legion
Phillips' (Georgia) Legion
Artillery (Col. Henry Coalter Cabell)
1st North Carolina Artillery Battery (A) (Capt. Basil C. Manly)
Pulaski (Georgia) Artillery (Capt. John C. Fraser)
—(Lieut. W. J. Furlong)
1st Richmond Howitzers (Capt. Edward S. McCarthy)
Troup (Georgia) Artillery (Capt. Henry H. Carlton)
—(Lieut. C. W. Motes)
Pickett's Division (Brig. Gen. George E. Pickett)
Garnett's Brigade (Brig. Gen. Richard B. Garnett)
—(Maj. C. S. Peyton)
8th Virginia
18th Virginia

19th Virginia
28th Virginia
56th Virginia
Kemper's Brigade (Brig. Gen. James L. Kemper)
—(Col. Joseph Mayo, Jr.)
1st Virginia
3rd Virginia
7th Virginia
11th Virginia
24th Virginia
Armistead's Brigade (Brig. Gen. Lewis A. Armistead)
—(Col. William R. Aylett)
9th Virginia
14th Virginia
38th Virginia
53rd Virginia
57th Virginia
Artillery (Maj. James Dearing)
Fauquier (Virginia) Artillery (Capt. Robert M. Stribling)
Hampden (Virginia) Artillery (Capt. William H. Caskie)
Richmond Fayette Artillery (Capt. Miles C. Macon)
Lynchburg (Virginia) Artillery (Capt. Joseph G. Blount)
Hood's Division (Maj. Gen. John B. Hood)
—(Brig. Gen. Evander M. Law)
Law's Brigade (Brig. Gen. Evander M. Law)
—(Col. James L. Sheffield)
4th Alabama
15th Alabama
44th Alabama
47th Alabama
48th Alabama
Robertson's Brigade (Brig. Gen. Jerome B. Robertson)
3rd Arkansas
1st Texas
4th Texas
5th Texas
Anderson's Brigade (Brig. Gen. George T. Anderson)
—(Lieut. Col. William Luffman)
7th Georgia
8th Georgia
9th Georgia

11th Georgia
59th Georgia
Benning's Brigade (Brig. Gen. Henry L. Benning)
2nd Georgia
15th Georgia
17th Georgia
20th Georgia
Artillery (Maj. Mathis W. Henry)
Branch (North Carolina) Artillery (Capt. Alexander C. Latham)
German (South Carolina) Artillery (Capt. William K. Bachman)
Palmetto (South Carolina) Light Artillery (Capt. Hugh R. Garden)
Rowan (North Carolina) Artillery (Capt. James Reilly)
Artillery Reserve (Col. James B. Walton)
Alexander's Battalion (Col. Edward P. Alexander)
Ashland (Virginia) Artillery (Capt. Pichegru Woolfolk, Jr.)
—(Lieut. James Woolfolk)
Bedford (Virginia) Artillery (Capt. Tyler C. Jordan)
Brooks (South Carolina) Artillery (Lieut. S. C. Gilbert)
Madison (Louisiana) Artillery (Capt. George V. Moody)
Virginia (Richmond) Battery (Capt. William W. Parker)
Virginia (Bath) Battery (Capt. Osmond B. Taylor)
Washington (Louisiana) Artillery
    (Maj. Benjamin F. Eshleman)
1st Company (Capt. Charles W. Squires)
2nd Company (Capt. John B. Richardson)
3rd Company (Capt. Merritt B. Miller)
4th Company (Capt. Joe Norcom)
—(Lieut. H. A. Battles)
SECOND ARMY CORPS (Lieut. Gen. Richard S. Ewell)
Early's Division (Maj. Gen. Jubal A. Early)
Hays' Brigade (Brig. Gen. Harry T. Hays)
5th Louisiana
6th Louisiana
7th Louisiana
8th Louisiana
9th Louisiana
Smith's Brigade (Brig. Gen. William Smith)
31st Virginia
49th Virginia
52nd Virginia

Hoke's Brigade (Col. Isaac E. Avery)
—(Col. A. C. Godwin)
6th North Carolina
21st North Carolina
57th North Carolina
Gordon's Brigade (Brig. Gen. John B. Gordon)
13th Georgia
26th Georgia
31st Georgia
38th Georgia
60th Georgia
61st Georgia
Artillery (Lieut. Col. Hilary P. Jones)
Charlottesville (Virginia) Artillery
(Capt. James McD. Carrington)
Courtney (Virginia) Artillery (Capt. William A. Tanner)
Louisiana Guard Artillery (Capt. Charles A. Green)
Staunton (Virginia) Artillery (Capt. Asher W. Garber)
Rodes' Division (Maj. Gen. Robert E. Rodes)
Daniel's Brigade (Brig. Gen. Junius Daniel)
32nd North Carolina
43rd North Carolina
45th North Carolina
53rd North Carolina
2nd North Carolina Battalion
Iverson's Brigade (Brig. Gen. Alfred Iverson)
5th North Carolina
12th North Carolina
20th North Carolina
23rd North Carolina
Doles' Brigade (Brig. Gen. George Doles)
4th Georgia
12th Georgia
21st Georgia
44th Georgia
Ramseur's Brigade (Brig. Gen. Stephen D. Ramseur)
2nd North Carolina
4th North Carolina
14th North Carolina
30th North Carolina

O'Neal's Brigade (Col. Edward A. O'Neal)

3rd Alabama

5th Alabama

6th Alabama

12th Alabama

26th Alabama

Artillery (Lieut. Col. Thomas H. Carter)

Jeff Davis (Alabama) Artillery (Capt. William J. Reese)

King William (Virginia) Artillery (Capt. William P. Carter)

Morris (Virginia) Artillery (Capt. Richard C. M. Page)

Orange (Virginia) Artillery (Capt. Charles W. Fry)

Johnson's Division (Maj. Gen. Edward Johnson)

Steuart's Brigade (Brig. Gen. George H. Steuart)

1st Maryland Battalion Infantry

1st North Carolina

3rd North Carolina

10th Virginia

23rd Virginia

37th Virginia

Nicholls' Brigade (Col. Jesse M. Williams)

1st Louisiana

2nd Louisiana

10th Louisiana

14th Louisiana

15th Louisiana

Stonewall Brigade (Brig. Gen. James Walker)

2nd Virginia

4th Virginia

5th Virginia

27th Virginia

33rd Virginia

Jones's Brigade (Brig. Gen. John M. Jones)

—(Lieut. Col. Robert H. Dungan)

21st Virginia

25th Virginia

42nd Virginia

44th Virginia

48th Virginia

50th Virginia

Artillery (Maj. James W. Latimer)
   1st Maryland Battery (Capt. William F. Dement)
   Alleghany (Virginia) Artillery (Capt. John C. Carpenter)
   Chesapeake (Maryland) Artillery (Capt. William D. Brown)
   Lee (Virginia) Battery (Capt. Charles I. Raine)
   —(Lieut. William M. Hardwicke)
Artillery Reserve (Col. J. Thompson Brown)
First Virginia Artillery (Capt. Willis J. Dance)
   2nd Richmond (Virginia) Howitzers (Capt. David Watson)
   3rd Richmond (Virginia) Howitzers (Capt. Benjamin H. Smith, Jr.)
   Powhatan (Virginia) Artillery (Lieut. John M. Cunningham)
   Rockbridge (Virginia) Artillery (Capt. Archibald Graham)
   Salem (Virginia) Artillery (Lieut. Charles B. Griffin)
Nelson's Battalion (Lieut. Col. William Nelson)
   Amherst (Virginia) Artillery (Capt. Thomas J. Kirkpatrick)
   Fluvanna (Virginia) Artillery (Capt. John L. Massie)
   Georgia Battery (Capt. John Milledge, Jr.)
THIRD ARMY CORPS (Lieut. Gen. Ambrose P. Hill)
 Anderson's Division (Maj. Gen. Richard H. Anderson)
  Wilcox's Brigade (Brig. Gen. Cadmus M. Wilcox)
    8th Alabama
    9th Alabama
    10th Alabama
    11th Alabama
    14th Alabama
  Wright's Brigade (Brig. Gen. Ambrose R. Wright)
    —(Col. William Gibson)
    3rd Georgia
    22nd Georgia
    48th Georgia
    2nd Georgia Battalion
  Mahone's Brigade (Brig. Gen. William Mahone)
    6th Virginia
    12th Virginia
    16th Virginia
    41st Virginia
    61st Virginia
  Perry's Brigade (Col. David Lang)
    2nd Florida
    5th Florida
    8th Florida

Posey's Brigade (Brig. Gen. Carnot Posey)
12th Mississippi
16th Mississippi
19th Mississippi
48th Mississippi
Artillery (Sumter Battalion) (Maj. John Lane)
Company A (Capt. Hugh M. Ross)
Company B (Capt. George M. Patterson)
Company C (Capt. John T. Wingfield)
Heth's Division (Maj. Gen. Henry Heth)
—(Brig. Gen. James J. Pettigrew)
1st Brigade (Brig. Gen. James J. Pettigrew)
11th North Carolina
26th North Carolina
47th North Carolina
52nd North Carolina
2nd Brigade (Col. John M. Brockenborough)
40th Virginia
47th Virginia
55th Virginia
22nd Virginia Battalion
3rd Brigade (Brig. Gen. James J. Archer)
—(Col. Birkett D. Fry)
—(Lieut. Col. Samuel G. Shepherd)
5th Alabama Battalion
13th Alabama
1st Tennessee (Provisional Army)
7th Tennessee
14th Tennessee
4th Brigade (Brig. Gen. Joseph R. Davis)
2nd Mississippi
11th Mississippi
42nd Mississippi
55th North Carolina
Artillery (Lieut. Col. John Garnett)
Donaldsville (Louisiana) Artillery (Capt. Victor Maurin)
Huger (Virginia) Artillery (Capt. Joseph D. Moore)
Lewis (Virginia) Artillery (Capt. John W. Lewis)
Norfolk Light Artillery Blues (Capt. Charles R. Grandy)

Pender's Division (Maj. Gen. William D. Pender)
—(Brig. Gen. James H. Lane)
—(Maj. Gen. Isaac R. Trimble)
—(Brig. Gen. James H. Lane)
1st Brigade (Col. Abner Perrin)
1st South Carolina (Provisional Army)
1st South Carolina Rifles
12th South Carolina
13th South Carolina
14th South Carolina
2nd Brigade (Brig. Gen. James H. Lane)
—(Col. Clark M. Avery)
—(Brig. Gen. James H. Lane)
—(Col. Clark M. Avery)
7th North Carolina
18th North Carolina
28th North Carolina
33rd North Carolina
37th North Carolina
3rd Brigade (Brig. Gen. Edward L. Thomas)
14th Georgia
35th Georgia
45th Georgia
49th Georgia
4th Brigade (Brig. Gen. Alfred M. Scales)
—(Lieut. Col. G. T. Gordon)
—(Col. W. Lee. J. Lowrance)
13th North Carolina
16th North Carolina
22nd North Carolina
34th North Carolina
38th North Carolina
Artillery (Maj. William T. Poague)
Albemarle (Virginia) Artillery (Capt. James W. Wyatt)
Charlotte (North Carolina) Artillery (Capt. Joseph Graham)
Madison (Mississippi) Light Artillery (Capt. George Ward)
Warrenton (Virginia) Battery (Capt. James V. Brooke)
Artillery Reserve (Col. R. Lindsay Walker)
McIntosh's Battalion (Maj. D. G. McIntosh)
Danville (Virginia) Artillery (Capt. R. Sidney Rice)
Hardaway (Alabama) Artillery (Capt. William B. Hurt)

2nd Rockbridge (Virginia) Artillery (Lieut. Samuel Wallace)

Richmond (Virginia) Battery (Capt. Marmaduke Johnson)

Pegram's Battalion (Maj. William J. Pegram)

—(Capt. E. B. Brunson)

Crenshaw (Virginia) Battery (Capt. William G. Crenshaw)

Fredericksburg (Virginia) Artillery (Capt. Edward A. Marye)

Letcher (Virginia) Artillery (Capt. Thomas A. Brander)

Pee Dee (South Carolina) Artillery (Lieut. William E. Zimmerman)

Purcell (Virginia) Artillery (Capt. Joseph McGraw)

CAVALRY

Stuart's Division (Maj. Gen. James E. B. Stuart)

Hampton's Brigade (Brig. Gen. Wade Hampton)

—(Col. Laurence S. Baker)

1st North Carolina

1st South Carolina

2nd South Carolina

Cobb's (Georgia) Legion

Jeff Davis (Mississippi) Legion

Phillips' (Georgia) Legion

Fitz Lee's Brigade (Brig. Gen. Fitzhugh Lee)

1st Maryland Battalion

1st Virginia

2nd Virginia

3rd Virginia

4th Virginia

5th Virginia

Robertson's Brigade (Brig. Gen. Beverly H. Robertson)

4th North Carolina

5th North Carolina

Jenkins' Brigade (Brig. Gen. Albert G. Jenkins)

—(Col. Milton J. Ferguson)

14th Virginia

16th Virginia

17th Virginia

34th Virginia Battalion

36th Virginia Battalion

Jackson's (Virginia) Battery

Jones's Brigade (Brig. Gen. William E. Jones)

6th Virginia

7th Virginia

11th Virginia

W.H.F. Lee's Brigade (Col. John R. Chambliss, Jr.)
  2nd North Carolina
  9th Virginia
  10th Virginia
  13th Virginia
Stuart Horse Artillery (Maj. Robert F. Beckham)
  Breathed's (Virginia) Battery (Capt. James Breathed)
  Chew's (Virginia) Battery (Capt. R. Preston Chew)
  Griffin's (Maryland) Battery (Capt. William H. Griffin)
  Hart's (South Carolina) Battery (Capt. James F. Hart)
  McGregor's (Virginia) Battery (Capt. William M. McGregor)
  Moorman's (Virginia) Battery (Capt. Marcellus M. Moorman)
Imboden's Command (Brig. Gen. John D. Imboden)
  18th Virginia
  62nd Virginia Infantry, Mounted
  Virginia Partisan Rangers
  Virginia (Staunton) Battery

NOTES

ᵴᵴ
ᵴ

Abbreviations

AAS	American Antiquarian Society
ADAH	Alabama Department of Archives and History
ANB	Antietam National Battlefield
B&L	Johnson and Buel, eds., *Battles and Leaders of the Civil War*
BP	*Bachelder Papers*
BPL	Bancroft Public Library
BU	Brown University
CHS	Chicago Historical Society
CMU	Central Michigan University
CSL	Connecticut State Library
CTHS	Connecticut Historical Society
CV	*Confederate Veteran*
DCHS	Dutchess County Historical Society
DHSTC	DeWitt Historical Society of Tompkins County
DPA	Delaware Public Archives
DU	Duke University
ECU	East Carolina University
ECHS	Erie County Historical Society
EU	Emory University
FSA	Florida State Archives
GC	Gettysburg College
GHS	Georgia Historical Society
GNMP	Gettysburg National Military Park
HSP	Historical Society of Pennsylvania

HU	Harvard University
IHS	Indiana Historical Society
IU	Indiana University
LC	Library of Congress
LSU	Louisiana State University
LVA	Library of Virginia
MC	Museum of the Confederacy
MDAH	Mississippi Department of Archives and History
MDHS	Maryland Historical Society
MGA	Middle Georgia Archives
MHS	Massachusetts Historical Society
MNBP	Manassas National Battlefield Park
MNHS	Minnesota Historical Society
MSA	Mississippi State Archives
MCHM	Monroe County Historical Museum
NA	National Archives
NCDAH	North Carolina Department of Archives and History
NHHS	New Hampshire Historical Society
NYHS	New-York Historical Society
NYSL	New York State Library
OHS	Ohio Historical Society
OR	U.S. War Department, *The War of the Rebellion: Official Records of the Union and Confederate Armies*
PHMC	Pennsylvania Historical and Museum Commission
PML	Pierpont Morgan Library
PU	Princeton University
QU	Queen's University
SAHS	St. Augustine Historical Society
SHSP	*Southern Historical Society Papers*
SHSW	State Historical Society of Wisconsin
SOR	*Supplement to the Official Records of the Union and Confederate Armies*
TSLA	Tennessee State Library and Archives
TU	Tulane University
UC	University of Chicago
UGA	University of Georgia
UM	University of Michigan
UNC	University of North Carolina
UR	University of Rochester
USAMHI	United States Army Military History Institute
USC	University of South Carolina

UT	University of Texas
UVA	University of Virginia
UVT	University of Vermont
VHS	Virginia Historical Society
VTHS	Vermont Historical Society
WL	Washington and Lee University
WLM	War Library and Museum
WM	The College of William and Mary
WMU	Western Michigan University
WRHS	Western Reserve Historical Society
YU	Yale University

Prologue

1. Byrne and Weaver, *Haskell*, p. 110.
2. Quaife, ed., *From the Cannon's Mouth*, p. 221.
3. Sickles et al., "Further Recollections," p. 276; *OR*, 27, 1, p. 127; *CV*, 21, p. 387.
4. Rollins, "George Gordon Meade," p. 77; McLean and McLean, eds., *Gettysburg Sources*, 2, p. 83; Coddington, *Gettysburg Campaign*, p. 442; Gallagher, ed., *Three Days*, p. 231; Fishel, *Secret War*, p. 527.
5. *OR*, 27, 1, p. 72; George G. Meade–Margaret, July 5, 1863, Meade Collection, HSP.
6. McLean and McLean, eds., *Gettysburg Sources*, 2, p. 80; "Sketches from the Battle-Fields of the War: Gettysburg—The Second Day," p. 2, Gibbon Papers, HSP; Cleaves, *Meade*, p. 155; Coddington, *Gettysburg Campaign*, p. 449.
7. Byrne and Weaver, *Haskell*, p. 134; George G. Meade–Margaret, July 8, 1863, Meade Collection, HSP; Cleaves, *Meade*, pp. 142, 143; Tagg, *Generals*, pp. 1, 13, 33, 45, 65, 81, 103, 121, 143, 147.
8. "Sketches from the Battle-Fields," p. 3, Gibbon Papers, HSP; Gallagher, ed., *Three Days*, p. 234; Coddington, *Gettysburg Campaign*, pp. 442, 450; Quaife, ed., *From the Cannon's Mouth*, p. 229; *OR*, 27, 1, p. 74.
9. "Sketches from the Battle-Fields," pp. 10, 12, Gibbon Papers, HSP; *OR*, 27, 1, p. 73.
10. *OR*, 27, 1, pp. 73, 74; Gibbon, *Personal Recollections*, pp. 140–44; Tucker, *High Tide*, p. 310; McLean and McLean, eds., *Gettysburg Sources*, 2, p. 87; Gibbon, "Another View," p. 708.
11. Gibbon, *Personal Recollections*, p. 145.
12. John Gibbon–Henry J. Hunt, May 31, 1879, Hunt Papers, LC.
13. Nye, *Here Come the Rebels!*, p. 43.
14. Wert, *General James Longstreet*, p. 247.
15. Ibid., p. 247.

16. Ibid., pp. 242–43, 247, 248.
17. Ibid., p. 248.
18. *OR,* 25, 2, p. 810.
19. Wert, *General James Longstreet,* pp. 248–50; Nye, *Here Come the Rebels!,* chap. 1.
20. Nye, *Here Come the Rebels!,* pp. 43–45; *SHSP,* 4, p. 98.
21. W. H. Taylor, *Four Years,* p. 101; Sword, *Southern Invincibility,* p. 170; Henry M. Talley–My Dear Mother, June 11, 1863, Brown Papers, NCDAH.
22. William H. Sanders–Matthew, July 16, 1863, Sanders Papers, ADAH.
23. Wert, *Brotherhood,* p. 241.
24. Coddington, *Gettysburg Campaign,* chap. 3.
25. Wert, *General James Longstreet,* p. 251.
26. Ibid., p. 251.
27. Coddington, *Gettysburg Campaign,* chap. 4.
28. Ibid.
29. Bud–My Dear Sister, July 18, 1863, Bud Letter, PML; Everson and Simpson, eds., *"Far, Far from Home,"* p. 250; Iowa M. Royster–Ma, June 29, 1863, Royster Papers, UNC.
30. Robert Stafford–Aunt, August 27, 1863, Stafford Correspondence, PML; Jeremiah M. Tate–sister Mary, July 19, 1863, Tate Letters, PML; Charles J. Batchelor–My dear Father, October 18, 1863, Batchelor Papers, LSU.
31. Benjamin L. Farinholt–Lelia, July 1, 1863, Farinholt Papers, VHS; William A. Miller–Sister, July 1, 1863, 18th Virginia Infantry File, GNMP; I. V. Reynolds–Wife, July 20, 1863, Reynolds Papers, DU.
32. T. W. Holley–Eliza, July 10, 1863, Holley Papers, DU; Bud–My Dear Sister, July 18, 1863, Bud Letter, PML; Dobbins, ed., *Grandfather's Journal,* p. 148; William H. Sanders–Matthew, July 16, 1863, Sanders Papers, ADAH; J. W. Stevens, *Reminiscences,* p. 107; Everson and Simpson, eds., *"Far, Far from Home,"* p. 251; William A. Miller–Sister, July 1, 1863, 18th Virginia Infantry File, GNMP.
33. Charles J. Batchelor–My dear Father, October 18, 1863, Batchelor Papers, LSU; Benjamin L. Farinholt–Lelia, July 1, 1863, Farinholt Papers, VHS; Ferdinand J. Dunlap–Sister, July 22, 1863, Dunlap Letters, USAMHI.
34. Loehr, *War History,* p. 35; Wert, *General James Longstreet,* pp. 252–53; Nye, *Here Come the Rebels!,* chaps. 15–17.
35. *OR,* 27, 3, pp. 913, 915, 923; Nye, *Here Come the Rebels!,* chap. 19; Longstreet, *From Manassas To Appomattox,* pp. 341–43.
36. *Annals,* p. 307; *OR,* 27, 2, pp. 307, 321; Wert, *General James Longstreet,* p. 254.
37. Longstreet, *From Manassas to Appomattox,* pp. 346, 347; Sorrel, *Recollections,* p. 155; Wert, *General James Longstreet,* pp. 254–55.
38. Wert, *General James Longstreet,* p. 255.
39. Ibid.

40. *OR*, 27, 3, pp. 369, 373; Coddington, *Gettysburg Campaign*, pp. 130–33; Henry Clare–My dear Wm, June 30, 1863, Clare Letters, GC.
41. *OR*, 27, 3, p. 373; *Annals*, p. 207; Coddington, *Gettysburg Campaign*, pp. 37, 209.
42. Coddington, *Gettysburg Campaign*, pp. 214, 215.
43. Ibid., pp. 224–25.
44. Ibid., pp. 229–35; Schildt, *Roads*, chaps. 12, 13; Busey and Martin, *Regimental Strengths*, pp. 16, 129.
45. Wert, *General James Longstreet*, pp. 256–57; Martin, *Gettysburg*, chaps. 3, 4.
46. Martin, *Gettysburg*, chap. 5; Busey and Martin, *Regimental Strengths*, pp. 16, 150, 172.
47. Martin, *Gettysburg*, chap. 8, casualties on pp. 465–66.
48. Ibid., chap. 9; Wert, *General James Longstreet*, pp. 258, 259.
49. Wert, *General James Longstreet*, pp. 258, 259; Lord, ed., *Fremantle Diary*, p. 205.
50. *OR*, 27, 2, p. 308.
51. Ibid., 27, 3, pp. 458, 459, 461.
52. Coddington, *Gettysburg Campaign*, pp. 297–98, 357, 358; Schildt, *Roads*, pp. 522, 523, 524, 532, 533.
53. Coddington, *Gettysburg Campaign*, p. 323; Paine Diary, NYHS.
54. Coddington, *Gettysburg Campaign*, pp. 330–32; Ladd and Ladd, eds., *BP*, 1, p. 223.
55. Coddington, *Gettysburg Campaign*, pp. 331, 332.
56. Ibid., pp. 330–32.
57. Wert, *General James Longstreet*, chap. 13; *Annals*, p. 424.
58. H. W. Pfanz, *Gettysburg: The Second Day*, chaps. 8–13; Wert, *General James Longstreet*, pp. 274–78; Williams, "From Sumter," p. 98.
59. H. W. Pfanz, *Gettysburg: The Second Day*, chaps. 8–13; Wert, *General James Longstreet*, p. 274.
60. H. W. Pfanz, *Gettysburg: The Second Day*, chap. 14.
61. Ibid., chaps. 15–17; Coddington, *Gettysburg Campaign*, p. 442.
62. W. H. Taylor, *Four Years*, p. 99.
63. *OR*, 27, 2, p. 320.
64. David E. Maxwell–Father, July 8, 1863, Maxwell Papers, VHS.

1. Night on the Battlefield

1. Benedict, *Army Life*, p. 169.
2. Penny and Laine, *Struggle*, p. 107; Meinhard, "First Minnesota," p. 85; Wheelock G. Veazey–G. G. Benedict, July 11, 1864, Veazey Papers, VTHS.
3. Elmore, "Torrid Heat," p. 13; Mahood, *"Written In Blood,"* p. 137; McDonald,

"Diary," UT; Private Felix Brannigan, 73rd New York, excerpt of letter, n.d., Brake Collection, USAMHI; Philo H. Conklin–Friend Mary, July 31, 1863, Johnson Family Papers, USAMHI; Wheelock G. Veazey–G. G. Benedict, July 11, 1864, Veazey Papers, VTHS; Byrne and Weaver, *Haskell*, p. 128.

4. Muffly, ed., *Story*, p. 173; Jacob Slagle–Brother, September 13, 1863, Slagle Letters, PML.
5. Muffly, *Story*, pp. 172, 173; Jacob Slagle–Brother, September 13, 1863, Slagle Letters, PML.
6. *OR*, 27, 1, p. 597; Nathan Hayward–Father, July 8, 1863, Hayward Papers, MHS.
7. George H. Patch Journal, June 16–July 4, 1863, Patch Papers, VHS; Council A. Bryon–Nell, November 17, 1863, Bryan Papers, FSA; Private Felix Brannigan, 73rd New York, excerpt of letter, n.d., Brake Collection, USAMHI; Diary of James Beverly Clifton, Clifton Collection, NCDAH; Hagerty, *Collis' Zouaves*, p. 245; McDonald, "Diary," UT.
8. Benedict, *Army Life*, p. 171.
9. Thompson, " 'This Hell,' " p. 20.
10. Henry Clare–My dear William, July 5, 1863, Clare Letters, GC; Page, *History*, p. 142; Tully McCrae, "Reminiscences About Gettysburg," 1st U.S. Artillery, Battery I File, GNMP.
11. Henry Clare–My dear William, July 5, 1863, Clare Letters, GC; Page, *History*, p. 142; Hadden, "Granite Glory," p. 57.
12. H. S. Stevens, *Souvenir*, pp. 15, 16; Wheelock G. Veazey–G. G. Benedict, July 11, 1864, Veazey Papers, VTHS; Henry Clare–My dear William, July 5, 1863, Clare Letters, GC; Ladd and Ladd, eds., *BP*, 2, p. 871; Elmore, "Torrid Heat," p. 13.
13. Penny and Laine, *Struggle*, p. 104; Raus, *Generation*, pp. 25–26.
14. Penny and Laine, *Struggle*, pp. 104–6.
15. McCarty Collection, UT; H. W. Pfanz, *Gettysburg: The Second Day*, pp. 127, 195; Pledger, "Major Martin," p. 3, UT.
16. McCarty Collection, UT.
17. Vest, Diary, MC; "The Gettysburg Campaign," pp. 4, 5, Alexander Papers, UNC; R. K. Krick, *Parker's Virginia Battery*, p. 180.
18. Warner, *Generals in Gray*, p. 3; *OR*, 27, 2, pp. 429–30.
19. "The Gettysburg Campaign," p. 5, Alexander Papers, UNC.
20. Ibid.
21. *OR*, 27, 2, p. 434; R. K. Krick, *Parker's Virginia Battery*, p. 180; Squires, "Last of Lee's Battle Line," LC.
22. "The Gettysburg Campaign," p. 5, Alexander Papers, UNC.
23. The best description of the July 2 fighting on Culp's Hill is in H. W. Pfanz, *Gettysburg: Culp's Hill*, chap. 13; *OR*, 27, 2, p. 446.
24. H. W. Pfanz, *Gettysburg: Culp's Hill*, pp. 190–95, 207; *OR*, 27, 1, 766, 826;

"History Twelfth Corps," p. 36, Love Papers, LC; Charles F. Morse–Mother, July 17, 1863, Morse Papers, MHS; Busey and Martin, *Regimental Strengths,* p. 116.

25. H. W. Pfanz, *Gettysburg: Culp's Hill,* pp. 207, 211–13.

26. Busey and Martin, *Regimental Strengths,* p. 151; H. W. Pfanz, *Gettysburg: Culp's Hill,* chap. 13; *OR,* 27, 1, p. 827; Charles Anderson Raine Memoir, 23rd Virginia Infantry File, GNMP.

27. Ladd and Ladd, eds., *BP,* 2, p. 842.

28. *OR,* 27, 1, pp. 766, 826; H. W. Pfanz, *Gettysburg: Culp's Hill,* pp. 204, 223; O'Brien, " 'Perfect Roar,' " p. 87; "History Twelfth Corps," p. 36, Love Papers, LC.

29. *Philadelphia Public Ledger,* July 10, 1863; James S. Hyde, "The Gettysburg Campaign of the 137th New York," 137th New York Infantry File, GNMP; *Pennsylvania at Gettysburg,* 1, p. 219; *OR,* 27, 1, p. 851; H. W. Pfanz, *Gettysburg: Culp's Hill,* p. 227.

30. *OR,* 27, 1, pp. 851, 853; *Philadelphia Public Ledger,* July 10, 1863; H. W. Pfanz, *Gettysburg: Culp's Hill,* p. 227.

31. *Pennsylvania at Gettysburg,* 1, p. 219; Veale, *109th Regiment,* p. 13; Boyle, *Soldiers True,* p. 125; H. W. Pfanz, *Gettysburg: Culp's Hill,* p. 227.

32. Boyle, *Soldiers True,* p. 125; H. W. Pfanz, *Gettysburg: Culp's Hill,* p. 227.

33. *Philadelphia Public Ledger,* July 10, 1863; *Pennsylvania at Gettysburg,* 1, p. 220; Veale, *109th Regiment,* p. 14; Account of Thomas Leiper Kane, n.d., Rothermel Papers, PHMC; H. W. Pfanz, *Gettysburg: Culp's Hill,* pp. 227–28.

34. O'Brien, " 'Perfect Roar,' " p. 87; H. W. Pfanz, *Gettysburg: Culp's Hill,* pp. 228–29; *Philadelphia North American,* June 29, 1913; M. Shroyer Diary, Boardman Collection, USAMHI; Coco, *Strange and Blighted Land,* p. 25.

35. *OR,* 27, 1, pp. 780, 783; E. R. Brown, *Twenty-Seventh Indiana,* pp. 373, 374; H. W. Pfanz, *Gettysburg: Culp's Hill,* p. 230.

36. *OR,* 27, 1, pp. 780, 783, 784; Morhous, *Reminiscences,* p. 50; Chapman Diary, pp. 35, 36, CSL; Rugg Diary and Memorandum, CSL; L. R. Coy–Sarah, July 6, 1863, 123rd New York Infantry File, GNMP; Packer, Diary, CSL.

37. Charles F. Morse–Mother, July 17, 1863, Morse Papers, MHS; *OR,* 27, 1, p. 813.

38. Charles F. Morse–Mother, July 17, 1863; John A. Fox–Charles F. Morse, April 22, 1878, both in Morse Papers, MHS; *OR,* 27, 1, p. 813; John Hill–Friends, July 5, 1863, Hill Letters, USAMHI; H. W. Pfanz, *Gettysburg: Culp's Hill,* pp. 232–33.

39. Charles F. Morse–Mother, July 17, 1863; John A. Fox–Charles F. Morse, April 22, 1878, both in Morse Papers, MHS; John Hill–Friends, July 5, 1863, Hill Letters, USAMHI; Milano, "Call of Leadership," p. 73; *OR,* 27, 1, p. 813.

40. Quaife, ed., *From the Cannon's Mouth,* p. 229; E. R. Brown, *Twenty-seventh Indiana,* pp. 373, 374.

41. H. W. Pfanz, *Gettysburg: Culp's Hill*, pp. 288–89; Walter Clark, ed., *Histories*, 3, p. 6.

42. David Hunter–Mother, July 2, 1863, 2nd Virginia Infantry File, GNMP.

43. Hadden, "Granite Glory," p. 57.

2. Lee and Meade

1. Freeman, *R. E. Lee*, 3, p. 107; Frassanito, *Early Photography*, pp. 65, 66; Magner, *Traveller*, p. 4.

2. Warner, *Generals in Gray*, pp. 179–82.

3. Gallagher, *Confederate War*, pp. 8, 10, 63, 85, 284.

4. E. P. Alexander, *Memoirs*, p. 111; Freeman, *R. E. Lee*, 4, pp. 178, 179; Wert, *General James Longstreet*, pp. 127–28.

5. E. P. Alexander–Frederick Colston, February 9, 1904, Campbell-Colston Papers, UNC; Gallagher, ed., *Fighting For*, p. 91.

6. Polley, *Hood's Texas Brigade*, p. 153; Tucker, *Lee and Longstreet*, p. 234; Gallagher, ed., *Fighting For*, p. 265.

7. Roland, "Lee's Invasion Strategy," p. 36; Harsh, *Confederate Tide Rising*, pp. 57, 58.

8. Harsh, *Confederate Tide Rising*, pp. 57, 65, 66.

9. Ibid., pp. 57, 59, 62, 66; Roland, "Lee's Invasion Strategy," p. 36; Harsh, *Taken at the Flood*, p. 492.

10. Harsh, *Confederate Tide Rising*, pp. 59–62, 68–70; Harsh, *Taken at the Flood*, pp. 20, 490, 492.

11. *OR*, 27, 3, pp. 868–69.

12. Ibid., pp. 880–81.

13. Ibid., p. 881; E. M. Thomas, *Robert E. Lee*, p. 302; Roland, "Lee's Invasion Strategy," p. 38; Woodworth, *Davis and Lee*, pp. 241, 243.

14. Wert, *General James Longstreet*, pp. 246–47, 266; W. H. Taylor, *Four Years*, p. 91.

15. *OR*, 27, 2, pp. 308, 321; Ladd and Ladd, eds., *BP*, 2, pp. 925–26; Gallagher, ed., *Lee*, p. 437.

16. *OR*, 27, 2, p. 308.

17. Wert, *General James Longstreet*, pp. 257–58; *Annals*, p. 421.

18. Gallagher, ed., *Second Day*, p. 32; Harsh, *Confederate Tide Rising*, p. 70; Griffith, *Battle Tactics*, p. 35; *SHSP*, 4, p. 79.

19. Tucker, *Lee and Longstreet*, p. 96.

20. Gallagher, ed., *Third Day*, p. 43; Gallagher, ed., *Fighting For*, p. 110; Coddington, *Gettysburg Campaign*, pp. 444, 445; Luvaas, "Lee," p. 7; *SHSP*, 5, pp. 91, 92; Diary, Porter Papers, DU.

21. Coddington, *Gettysburg Campaign*, pp. 425–29.

22. *OR*, 27, 2, p. 308; Gallagher, ed., *Lee*, p. 14; Coddington, *Gettysburg Cam-*

paign, p. 446; Bandy and Freeland, eds., *Gettysburg Papers,* 1, pp. 70, 71; *CV,* 21, p. 62.

23. Gallagher, ed., *Lee,* p. 17; Sorrel, *Recollections,* p. 162.

24. Harsh, *Confederate Tide Rising,* pp. 59, 62, 66, 70; Gallagher, *Confederate War,* pp. 116, 127; Griffith, *Battle Tactics,* pp. 198–99; *CV,* 21, p. 62.

25. Lord, ed., *Fremantle Diary,* pp. 197–98; McLean and McLean, eds., *Gettysburg Sources,* 1, pp. 34–36; Ratchford, *Some Reminiscences,* p. 37; Moses, Autobiography, p. 58, UNC.

26. E. M. Thomas, *Robert E. Lee,* pp. 277, 278, 301; "A Reunion of Confederate Officers and Their Ladies," McIntosh Papers, USAMHI.

27. James C. Biddle–My own darling Wife, July 6, 1863, Biddle Civil War Letters, HSP; *OR,* 27, 1, p. 72.

28. Warner, *Generals in Blue,* pp. 315–16; Tagg, *Generals,* pp. 1–2.

29. Warner, *Generals in Blue,* p. 316; Tagg, *Generals,* pp. 2–3; Cleaves, *Meade,* chaps. 6–7.

30. James C. Biddle–My own darling little Wife, July 1, 1863, Biddle Civil War Letters, HSP; Quaife, ed., *From the Cannon's Mouth,* p. 223; George Meade–Mama, July 1, 1863, Meade Collection, HSP.

31. Quaife, ed., *From the Cannon's Mouth,* p. 221; Clement Hoffman–Mother, July 5, 1863, Hoffman Papers, USAMHI; Acker, *Inside,* p. 293; Nevins, ed., *Diary,* p. 242.

32. Acker, *Inside,* pp. 289, 293; Agassiz, ed., *Meade's Headquarters,* p. 25; John Gibbon–My darling Mama, June 29, 30, 1863, Gibbon Papers, HSP.

33. Nevins, ed., *Diary,* p. 227; R. G. Scott, ed., *Fallen Leaves,* p. 189; Tagg, *Generals,* pp. 2, 3; Agassiz, ed., *Meade's Headquarters,* pp. 25, 39, 57, 272.

34. Agassiz, ed., *Meade's Headquarters,* pp. 73, 167; J. D. Smith, *History,* p. 77; Tagg, *Generals,* p. 3.

35. Byrne and Weaver, *Haskell,* p. 132; J. D. Scott, *Fallen Leaves,* p. 189.

36. Agassiz, ed., *Meade's Headquarters,* p. 8; Byrne and Weaver, *Haskell,* p. 132; Acker, *Inside,* p. 289; Benedict Diary, CHS.

37. Nevins, ed., *Diary,* pp. 227, 228; George Meade–Mama, July 1, 1863, Meade Collection, HSP; Rollins, "George Gordon Meade," p. 65.

38. Rollins, "George Gordon Meade," pp. 62–65.

39. Ibid., pp. 63, 66–73.

40. Ibid., pp. 73–77.

41. Ibid., p. 77.

3. "The Whole Hillside"

1. Tagg, *Generals,* p. 162; Motts, "To Gain a Second Star," pp. 65, 67, 68.

2. Tagg, *Generals,* p. 162; Collins, *Memoirs,* p. 137.

3. Collins, *Memoirs*, p. 137; Ladd and Ladd, eds., *BP,* 1, p. 293.

4. Collins, *Memoirs*, p. 137; Bird, "Summary," p. 2, USAMHI; Trowbridge, "Field of Gettysburg," p. 619; Philo B. Buckingham–My Dear Wife, July 17, 1863, Buckingham Letter, AAS.

5. *OR*, 27, 1, p. 856; *Washington Post,* July 9, 1899; Ladd and Ladd, eds., *BP,* 1, p. 293; *New York at Gettysburg,* 1, p. 264.

6. *OR*, 27, 1, p. 856; Bandy and Freeland, eds., *Gettysburg Papers*, 2, p. 821; Green Diary, UNC.

7. Sauers, ed., *Fighting Them Over,* pp. 357–58; Ladd and Ladd, eds., *BP,* 1, pp. 293, 295; *New York at Gettysburg,* 1, p. 63; *B&L,* 3, p. 316; Motts, "To Gain a Second Star," pp. 71, 73; Powell Memoirs, OHS.

8. Collins, *Memoirs*, p. 139; see chap. 1 above.

9. Ladd and Ladd, eds., *BP,* 1, p. 218; *OR*, 27, 1, pp. 768, 775; Tucker, *High Tide,* pp. 310, 322; Quaife, ed., *From the Cannon's Mouth*, pp. 3–8; Hamblen, *Connecticut Yankees*, p. 68; Tagg, *Generals*, pp. 146–47.

10. *OR*, 27, 1, p. 775; Byrne and Weaver, *Haskell*, p. 133; Tagg, *Generals*, pp. 143–45.

11. *OR*, 27, 1, p. 775; H. W. Pfanz, *Gettysburg: Culp's Hill*, p. 200; Coddington, *Gettysburg Campaign*, p. 453; Ladd and Ladd, eds., *BP,* 1, p. 219.

12. Busey and Martin, *Regimental Strengths*, p. 88; Quaife, ed., *From the Cannon's Mouth*, p. 230; H. W. Pfanz, *Gettysburg: Culp's Hill*, pp. 228, 229, 232, 286.

13. Quaife, ed., *From the Cannon's Mouth*, p. 230; *OR*, 27, 1, p. 775; O'Brien, " 'Perfect Roar,' " p. 81.

14. *OR*, 27, 1, pp. 827, 828; H. W. Pfanz, *Gettysburg: Culp's Hill*, pp. 228, 229, 286; Busey and Martin, *Regimental Strengths*, p. 88.

15. Coddington, *Gettysburg Campaign*, p. 467; H. W. Pfanz, *Gettysburg: Culp's Hill*, pp. 232, 286; Quaife, ed., *From the Cannon's Mouth*, pp. 227, 228; Topps, "Dutchess County Regiment," pp. 51, 52; Busey and Martin, *Regimental Strengths*, p. 88.

16. *OR*, 27, 1, pp. 761, 801, 870; Coco, *Concise Guide*, pp. 25, 73; *New York at Gettysburg,* 3, p. 1265.

17. *OR*, 27, 1, pp. 870, 873, 899; Coco, *Concise Guide,* pp. 25, 73; H. W. Pfanz, *Gettysburg: Culp's Hill*, pp. 285–87.

18. *OR*, 27, 1, p. 775; Ladd and Ladd, eds., *BP,* 1, p. 219; Quaife, ed., *From the Cannon's Mouth*, p. 230.

19. *OR*, 27, 1, p. 775; Ladd and Ladd, eds., *BP,* 1, p. 219; Quaife, ed., *From the Cannon's Mouth*, p. 230.

20. *SOR*, 5, p. 400; H. W. Pfanz, *Gettysburg: Culp's Hill*, pp. 207, 288; Charles J. Batchelor–My dear Father, October 18, 1863, Batchelor Papers, LSU; Zable, "Paper Read," p. 3, TU.

21. H. W. Pfanz, *Gettysburg: Culp's Hill*, pp. 286, 288; Hands Memoir, p. 98, UVA; *OR*, 27, 2, p. 510.

22. Tagg, *Generals*, pp. 269–70; Stiles, *Four Years*, p. 218.
23. Stiles, *Four Years*, p. 218; Tagg, *Generals*, p. 270; Brown Memoirs, TSLA.
24. *OR*, 27, 2, pp. 447, 504; Coddington, *Gettysburg Campaign*, pp. 454, 468.
25. *OR*, 27, 2, p. 447; D. C. Pfanz, *Richard S. Ewell*, pp. 313, 318, 319.
26. *OR*, 27, 2, p. 447; D. C. Pfanz, *Richard S. Ewell*, pp. 318–19.
27. *OR*, 27, 2, pp. 447, 568, 605; H. W. Pfanz, *Gettysburg: Culp's Hill*, p. 288.
28. *OR*, 27, 2, p. 568; H. W. Pfanz, *Gettysburg: Culp's Hill*, pp. 286, 288, 289; "North Carolina Troops at Gettysburg," North Carolina Troops File, GNMP; Busey and Martin, *Regimental Strengths*, pp. 150, 161, 164, 166.
29. The best description and analysis to date of Ewell's performance at Gettysburg is in D. C. Pfanz, *Richard S. Ewell*, chap. 21; see also Gallagher, ed., *Lee*, p. 11, for Lee's assessment of Ewell's generalship; Brown Memoirs, TSLA.
30. McCollough Diary, LC; "North Carolina Troops at Gettysburg," North Carolina Troops File, GNMP; Clemens, " 'Diary' of John H. Stone," p. 132.
31. *OR*, 27, 1, pp. 775, 870, 873, 899; Brady, ed., *Hurrah*, p. 252; *New York at Gettysburg*, 3, p. 1265.
32. *OR*, 27, 1, pp. 870, 899; "History Twelfth Corps," p. 38, Love Papers, LC.
33. *OR*, 27, 1, pp. 775, 828; "History Twelfth Corps," p. 38, Love Papers, LC; Hands Memoir, p. 98, UVA; Boyle, *Soldiers True*, p. 126.
34. David Ballenger–My dear Nancy, July 8, 1863, Ballenger Papers, USC; *Mobile Evening News*, July 24, 1863; *OR*, 27, 1, pp. 863, 865, 868; 2, pp. 513, 532, 537, 538.
35. *OR*, 27, 2, pp. 513, 593; *Mobile Evening News*, July 24, 1863.
36. Zable, "Paper Read," pp. 3, 4, TU.
37. *OR*, 27, 2, pp. 537, 538; S. Newton Bosworth–My dear friend, July 16, 1863, Bosworth Family Papers, USAMHI; Jones Memoirs, VHS.
38. *OR*, 27, 2, pp. 532, 537, 538, 539.
39. Ibid., 1, pp. 828, 844; Eugene Powell–J. B. Bachelder, March 23, 1886, Bachelder Papers, GNMP; Powell Memoirs, OHS.
40. Eugene Powell–J. B. Bachelder, March 23, 1886, Bachelder Papers, GNMP; Ladd and Ladd, eds., *BP*, 3, p. 1508; *OR*, 27, 1, p. 844; *Ohio Memorials*, p. 36; Powell Memoirs, OHS.
41. Eugene Powell–J. B. Bachelder, March 23, 1886, Bachelder Papers, GNMP; Powell Memoirs, OHS; William Sayre–Father and Mother Brothers and Sisters, July 5, 1863, Sayre Letters, USAMHI.
42. *OR*, 27, 1, p. 844; 2, p. 532; Ladd and Ladd, eds., *BP*, 2, pp. 1226, 1248.
43. *OR*, 27, 1, p. 829; Tagg, *Generals*, pp. 155–56; Tucker, *High Tide*, p. 322.
44. Winey, *Union Army Uniforms*, p. 19.
45. *OR*, 27, 1, pp. 829, 841, 842; Secheverell, *Journal History*, pp. 70, 71; O'Brien, " 'Perfect Roar,' " p. 90.

46. *OR*, 27, 1, pp. 857, 865; Rudy Diary, DHSTC; Sword and Shotwell, "Two New York Swords," p. 38; Collins, *Memoirs*, pp. 143, 144.

47. Perry Norton–Father, July 9, 1863, Norton Brothers Letters, USAMHI.

48. *OR*, 27, 1, pp. 841, 842, 843, 857; Wilder, *History*, p. 37; O'Brien, " 'Perfect Roar,' " pp. 89, 90; Parmeter Diary, OHS; James S. Hyde, "Gettysburg Campaign," 137th New York Infantry File, GNMP.

49. *OR*, 27, 1, pp. 287, 829, 841, 843, 845, 857; James S. Hyde, "Gettysburg Campaign," 137th New York Infantry File, GNMP; Ladd and Ladd, eds., *BP*, 1, pp. 331, 332; Parmeter Diary, OHS; Secheverell, *Journal History*, p. 71; O'Brien, " 'Perfect Roar,' " pp. 90, 92; H. E. Brown, *28th Regiment P.V.V.I.*, p. 6; *Pennsylvania at Gettysburg*, 1, p. 204.

50. O'Brien, " 'Perfect Roar,' " p. 90; Parmeter Diary, OHS.

51. *OR*, 27, 1, pp. 865, 868; O'Brien, " 'Perfect Roar,' " p. 92; James William Thomas Diary, Dielman Collection, MDHS.

52. *OR*, 27, 1, p. 853; Ladd and Ladd, eds., *BP*, 3, p. 1510; Hands Memoir, p. 98, UVA.

53. *OR*, 27, 1, pp. 846, 849, 853, 855; Ladd and Ladd, eds., *BP*, 3, p. 1510; Busey and Martin, *Regimental Strengths*, p. 95; Boyle, *Soldiers True*, p. 126.

54. *OR*, 27, 1, pp. 849, 853, 855; *Pennsylvania at Gettysburg*, 1, pp. 220, 570, 571; Ladd and Ladd, eds., *BP*, 3, pp. 1511, 1512; Boyle, *Soldiers True*, p. 127.

55. Tagg, *Generals*, pp. 159–60.

56. "Notes of a Conversation with General Kane," Thomas L. Kane File, GNMP; Ladd and Ladd, eds., *BP*, 1, pp. 160, 161.

57. *Philadelphia North American*, June 29, 1913; Tagg, *Generals*, p. 159.

58. James T. Miller–Sister, August 2, 1863, Miller Papers, UM; Firebaugh Diary, USAMHI; Hands Memoir, p. 98, UVA; Clemens, " 'Diary' of John H. Stone," p. 132.

59. *SOR*, 5, p. 395; Goldsborough, *Maryland Line*, p. 106; B. H. Coffman–Wife, July 12, 1863, Coffman Letters, USAMHI.

60. Clemens, " 'Diary' of John H. Stone," p. 133; Hands Memoir, p. 100, UVA; Dayton, ed., *Diary*, p. 83.

61. *OR*, 27, 1, p. 849; Rollins and Shultz, *Guide*, pp. 126–28; *Pennsylvania at Gettysburg*, 1, p. 220; James T. Miller–Sister, August 2, 1863, Miller Papers, UM; Boyle, *Soldiers True*, p. 127; Diary of James William Thomas, Dielman Collection, MDHS.

62. *OR*, 27, 1, pp. 828, 846; *Pennsylvania at Gettysburg*, 2, p. 717; Kross, "July 3rd Action," p. 10; O'Brien, " 'Perfect Roar,' " p. 89.

63. *OR*, 27, 1, pp. 806, 828, 846; Kross, "July 3rd Action," p. 10; Elmore, "Courage Against the Trenches," p. 92; Busey and Martin, *Regimental Strengths*, p. 94; *Pennsylvania at Gettysburg*, 1, p. 571; *Snyder County Tribune*, June 22, 1882.

64. Busey and Martin, *Regimental Strengths*, p. 94; *OR*, 27, 1, pp. 836, 837, 839, 846; *Pennsylvania at Gettysburg*, 2, p. 718; Boyle, *Soldiers True*, p. 126.

65. *Philadelphia North American*, June 29, 1913.

66. *OR*, 27, 1, p. 806; Busey and Martin, *Regimental Strengths*, p. 92; Gallagher, ed., *Three Days*, pp. 181, 182; Tagg, *Generals*, p. 151.

67. Topps, "Dutchess County Regiment," pp. 49, 50; Tagg, *Generals*, p. 152; *OR*, 27, 1, p. 806.

68. *OR*, 27, 1, p. 766; Tagg, *Generals*, p. 151.

69. *OR*, 27, 1, pp. 804, 806; Ladd and Ladd, eds., *BP*, 1, p. 636; Topps, "Dutchess County Regiment," pp. 47, 52.

70. *OR*, 27, 1, pp. 784, 793; Croffut and Morris, *Military and Civil History*, p. 385; Hamblen, *Connecticut Yankees*, p. 80; Abner C. Smith–Wife & Children, July 4, 1863, Smith Letters, USAMHI; Tagg, *Generals*, p. 149.

71. *OR*, 27, 1, p. 793; Ladd and Ladd, eds., *BP*, 3, pp. 1457, 1458; Chapman Diary, CSL; "20th Connecticut Volunteers," Love Papers, LC.

72. *OR*, 27, 1, p. 793; Ladd and Ladd, eds., *BP*, 3, pp. 1457, 1458; Croffut and Morris, *Military and Civil History*, p. 386; Storrs, *"Twentieth Connecticut,"* pp. 92, 93; Chapman Diary, CSL; Abner C. Smith–Wife & Children, July 4, 1863, Smith Letters, USAMHI.

73. *OR*, 27, 1, pp. 784, 795; Rugg Diary, CSL; John C. Gourlie–Father, July 3, 1863, Gourlie Letters, USAMHI; Hamblen, *Connecticut Yankees*, pp. 66–67; Morhous, *Reminiscences*, p. 50; Marvin, *Fifth Regiment*, p. 275.

74. *OR*, 27, 1, pp. 784, 801; Cruikshank Memoir, p. 126, BPL; Morhous, *Reminiscences*, p. 50; Hamblen, *Connecticut Yankees*, p. 81.

75. *OR*, 27, 1, pp. 784, 794, 801; Ladd and Ladd, eds., *BP*, p. 1458; Morhous, *Reminiscences*, p. 50; Cruikshank Memoir, p. 126, BPL.

76. *OR*, 27, 1, pp. 784, 794, 801.

77. Ladd and Ladd, eds., *BP*, 1, p. 157; Thomas H. Ruger–George F. Morse, July 29, 1903, 27th Indiana Infantry File, GNMP.

78. *OR*, 27, 1, p. 781; Ladd and Ladd, eds., *BP*, 1, p. 364; William M. Snow–George W. Morse, March [?], 1902; Thomas H. Ruger–George W. Morse, July 29, 1903, both in 27th Indiana Infantry File, GNMP.

79. *OR*, 27, 1, pp. 781, 818; Everett W. Pattison–Charles F. Morse, May 22, 1917, Morse Papers, MHS; Toombs, *New Jersey Troops*, p. 274; William M. Snow–George W. Morse, March [?], 1902, 27th Indiana Infantry File, GNMP.

80. *OR*, 27, 1, p. 813.

81. Jones, *Giants*, pp. 48, 49.

82. *OR*, 27, 1, p. 813; 2, p. 521; Ammen, ed., "Maryland Troops," 1, p. 132, USAMHI; Raus, *Generation*, p. 20; Busey and Martin, *Regimental Strengths*, p. 93; Ladd and Ladd, eds., *BP*, 1, p. 158.

83. Milano, "Call of Leadership," pp. 69, 71, 75; *SOR*, 5, p. 223; E. R. Brown, *Twenty-Seventh Indiana*, pp. 380, 381.

84. *OR*, 27, 1, p. 814; Charles F. Morse–Mother, July 17, 1863, Morse Papers, MHS; William Cogswell–William Schorder, Adjutant General, December 11, 1863, 2nd Massachusetts Infantry File, GNMP; *SOR*, 5, p. 223.

85. *OR*, 27, 1, p. 817; *SOR*, 5, p. 223; Morse, *History*, p. 16; Charles F. Morse–Mother, July 17, 1863; Diary, 9:30 A.M., July 3, 1863, Morse Papers, MHS; William Cogswell–William Schorder, Adjutant General, December 11, 1863, 2nd Massachusetts Infantry File, GNMP.

86. William Cogswell–William Schorder, Adjutant General, December 11, 1863, 2nd Massachusetts Infantry File, GNMP; Charles F. Morse–Mother, July 17, 1863, Morse Papers, MHS; *OR*, 27, 1, p. 817; Morse, *History*, p. 17.

87. E. R. Brown, *Twenty-Seventh Indiana*, pp. 382–84; Ladd and Ladd, eds., *BP*, 3, p. 1773; Report of J.Q.A. Nadenbousch, Nadenbousch Papers, DU; Diary of Thomas B. Boone, Brake Collection, USAMHI.

88. Douglas, *I Rode with Stonewall*, p. 249; *OR*, 27, 2, pp. 489, 521.

89. Douglas, *I Rode with Stonewall*, pp. 250, 252, 260; R. Long, "Confederate Prisoners," p. 98; *OR*, 27, 2, p. 489.

90. E. R. Brown, *Twenty-Seventh Indiana*, p. 383; William Cogswell–William Schorder, Adjutant General, December 11, 1863, 2nd Massachusetts Infantry File, GNMP; Charles F. Morse–Mother, July 17, 1863, Morse Papers, MHS; Morse, *Letters*, pp. 142, 146; Charles L. Warner–Mother, July 9, 1863, Warner Papers, USAMHI.

91. Charles F. Morse–Mother, July 17, 1863, Morse Papers, MHS; William Cogswell–William Schorder, Adjutant General, December 11, 1863, 2nd Massachusetts Infantry File, GNMP; *OR*, 27, 1, pp. 814, 816, 817; *SOR*, 5, p. 223; War Department, "Record," 1, p. 38, LC; Ladd and Ladd, eds., *BP*, 1, p. 158; "List of Killed, Wounded & Missing . . . July 3, 1863," 2nd Massachusetts, Volunteer Infantry Papers, USAMHI.

92. "33rd Regiment New York Volunteers," Love Papers, LC; Ladd and Ladd, eds., *BP*, 1, pp. 146, 365; *OR*, 27, 1, p. 781.

93. William M. Snow–George W. Morse, March [?], 1902, 27th Indiana Infantry File, GNMP.

94. John A. Fox–Charles F. Morse, April 30, 1878, Morse Papers, MHS.

95. *OR*, 27, 1, pp. 812, 813; evidence in support of Colgrove can be found in E. R. Brown, *Twenty-Seventh Indiana*, pp. 379, 380; George W. Morse–Silas Colgrove and Theodore F. Colgrove, June 25, 1904, 27th Indiana Infantry File, GNMP.

4. "None but Demons"

1. *New York at Gettysburg*, 2, p. 623.
2. Unidentified 137th New York Soldier–Father & Mother, July 7, 1863, 137th New York Infantry File, GNMP; H. E. Brown, *28th Regt. P.V.V.I.*, p. 6.
3. *OR*, 27, 1, p. 829; 2, pp. 513, 526, 593; Coddington, *Gettysburg Campaign*, pp. 465, 470; Boyle, *Soldiers True*, p. 127; Kross, "July 3rd Action," p. 10.
4. Collins, *Memoirs*, p. 141; *OR*, 27, 1, pp. 846, 855; Kross, "July 3rd Action," p. 12; *Pennsylvania at Gettysburg*, 1, p. 220.
5. *OR*, 27, 1, p. 846; 2, p. 526; Kross, "July 3 Action," pp. 10, 12.
6. *OR*, 27, 2, p. 530; J. L. Johnson, *University Memorial*, p. 476; Moore, *Story*, pp. 139, 200.
7. *OR*, 27, 2, pp. 513, 528; Zable, "Paper," p. 4, TU.
8. *OR*, 27, 2, p. 593; *SOR*, 5, p. 403; David Ballenger–My dear Nancy, July 8, 1863, Ballenger Papers, USC; Jeremiah M. Tate–sister Mary, July 19, 1863, Tate Letters, PML.
9. James T. Miller–Parents, July 6, 1863, Miller Papers, UM.
10. Hyde Diary, USAMHI.
11. Parmeter Diary, OHS; Rudy Diary, DHSTC; James T. Miller–Sister, August 2, 1863, Miller Papers, UM; Eddy, *History*, p. 263; Marquis and Tevis, *History*, pp. 96–97; *OR*, 27, 1, p. 858.
12. Cook and Benton, eds., "Dutchess County Regiment," p. 35; Rudy Diary, DHSTC; Marquis and Tevis, *History*, p. 98; Parmeter Diary, OHS; James T. Miller–Sister, August 2, 1863, Miller Papers, UM.
13. Collins, *Memoirs*, p. 143; Unidentified 137th New York Soldier–Father & Mother, July 7, 1863, 137th New York Infantry File, GNMP.
14. *OR*, 27, 1, pp. 805, 810; Sauers, ed., *Fighting Them Over*, p. 393; "150th New York Infantry," Love Papers, LC.
15. Benton, *As Seen from the Ranks*, p. 3; "150th New York Infantry," Love Papers, LC; *New York at Gettysburg*, 2, p. 635; Richard Titus–Father, July 9, 1863, Titus Letters, DCHS.
16. *OR*, 27, 1, p. 810; Cook and Benton, eds., "Dutchess County Regiment," p. 35; Topps, "Dutchess County Regiment," p. 52; Richard Titus–Father, July 28, 1863, Titus Letters, DCHS; Kaminsky, ed., *War*, p. 106.
17. *OR*, 27, 1, pp. 868, 869; Collins, *Memoirs*, p. 140; Raus, *Generation*, p. 84.
18. *OR*, 27, 1, p. 868.
19. H. E. Brown, *28th Regt. P.V.V.I.*, p. 6.
20. *OR*, 27, 1, pp. 810, 833; James T. Miller–Sister, August 2, 1863, Miller Papers, UM; Hyde Diary, USAMHI.
21. Walter Clark, ed., *Histories*, 1, p. 148; McCullough Diary, LC.

22. *Mobile Evening News,* July 24, 1863; McKim, *Soldier's Recollections,* pp. 184, 185, 201.

23. John Futch–Kind Wife, July 12, 1863, Futch Letters, NCDAH; Ammen, ed., "Maryland Troops," 1, p. 135, USAMHI.

24. *New York at Gettysburg,* 1, p. 260; Coddington, *Gettysburg Campaign,* p. 466.

25. *OR,* 27, 1, pp. 681, 682; H. W. Pfanz, *Gettysburg: Culp's Hill,* p. 324; Hug Diary, USAMHI; Busey and Martin, *Regimental Strengths,* p. 75.

26. *OR,* 27, 1, p. 682; *New York at Gettysburg,* 2, pp. 845, 846; Sanford N. Truesdell–[Ozias E. Truesdell], July 9, 1863, Truesdell Family Papers, CSL.

27. Sanford N. Truesdell–[Ozias E. Truesdell], July 9, 1863, Truesdell Family Papers, CSL; *New York at Gettysburg,* 2, pp. 845, 849; Willard Norton–Sister, July 11, 1863, Norton Brothers Papers, USAMHI.

28. *New York at Gettysburg,* 1, p. 71; 3, pp. 1265, 1266; *OR,* 27, 1, p. 824; 2, pp. 511, 512; Ladd and Ladd, eds., *BP,* 1, pp. 133, 134; Toombs, *Reminiscences,* p. 80; E. R. Brown, *Twenty-Seventh Indiana,* pp. 386, 388; Kross, "July 3rd Action," p. 8.

29. *OR,* 27, 1, pp. 489, 521; *New York at Gettysburg,* 1, pp. 71, 389; Kross, "July 3rd Action," p. 8; H. W. Pfanz, *Gettysburg: Culp's Hill,* p. 112.

30. *OR,* 27, 2, pp. 511, 519, 568; 3, p. 499; Ammen, ed., "Maryland Troops," 1, p. 132, USAMHI; "North Carolina Troops at Gettysburg," North Carolina Troops File, GNMP.

31. D. C. Pfanz, *Richard S. Ewell,* p. 319; McKim, *Soldier's Recollections,* p. 203; Brown Memoirs, TSLA; *OR,* 27, 2, p. 568.

32. Tagg, *Generals,* pp. 272–73; Clemens, " 'Diary' of John H. Stone," p. 131.

33. *OR,* 27, 2, p. 511; Kross, "July 3rd Action," pp. 12–13; H. W. Pfanz, *Gettysburg: Culp's Hill,* p. 311.

34. *OR,* 27, 2, p. 511; Goldsborough, *Maryland Line,* p. 106; Taylor, "War Story," TSL; undated articles from the *Telegram,* 2nd Maryland Battalion of Infantry File, GNMP.

35. *OR,* 27, 1, p. 849; 2, p. 511; Boyle, *Soldiers True,* p. 128; *Pennsylvania at Gettysburg,* 2, p. 718; David Nichol–Father, July 9, 1863, Nichol Papers, USAMHI; Brady, ed., *Hurrah,* p. 258; undated articles from the *Telegram,* 2nd Maryland Battalion of Infantry File, GNMP; Secheverell, *Journal History,* p. 71.

36. *OR,* 27, 2, p. 511; *SOR,* 5, p. 400; McKim, *Soldier's Recollections,* p. 188; undated articles from the *Telegram,* 2nd Maryland Battalion of Infantry File, GNMP; David Nichol–Father, July 9, 1863, Nichol Papers, USAMHI; Diary of James William Thomas, Dielman Collection, MDHS.

37. Hands Memoir, p. 101; Diary of James William Thomas, Dielman Collection, MDHS; Goldsborough, *Maryland Line,* pp. 109, 110; undated articles from the *Telegram,* 2nd Maryland Battalion of Infantry File, GNMP; Walter Clark, ed., *Histories,* 1, p. 196.

38. *OR*, 27, 1, p. 808; Ladd and Ladd, eds., *BP*, 1, p. 636; Toomey, *Marylanders*, p. 27.
39. *OR*, 27, 1, p. 808; McKim, *Soldier's Recollections*, pp. 183, 185, 186.
40. *OR*, 27, 2, p. 511; McKim, *Soldier's Recollections*, pp. 183, 204; Diary of James William Thomas, Dielman Collection, MDHS; Goldsborough, *Maryland Line*, p. 109; Taylor, "War Story," TSLA; Walter Clark, ed., *Histories*, 1, p. 196.
41. Ladd and Ladd, eds., *BP*, 2, p. 1131; *Pennsylvania at Gettysburg*, 2, p. 718; *Snyder County Tribune*, June 22, 1882.
42. Ladd and Ladd, eds., *BP*, 1, p. 636; Account of Thomas Leiper Kane, Rothermel Papers, PHMC.
43. *OR*, 27, 2, pp. 568, 569, 572, 573, 574, 575, 577; Kross, "July 3rd Action," p. 13; "North Carolina Troops at Gettysburg," North Carolina Troops File, GNMP; Walter Clark, ed., *Histories*, 3, p. 6.
44. *OR*, 27, 2, pp. 568, 569, 575, 577.
45. Ibid., pp. 519, 526; Kross, "July 3rd Action," p. 13.
46. *OR*, 27, 1, p. 844; 2, pp. 519, 526; Ladd and Ladd, eds., *BP*, 2, p. 1248; Kross, "July 3rd Action," p. 13.
47. *OR*, 27, 2, p. 519; B. H. Coffman–Wife, July 12, 1863, Coffman Letters, USAMHI; Givens B. Strickler, Biographical Sketch, McDowell Correspondence, WL.
48. Ladd and Ladd, eds., *BP*, 1, p. 297; *Washington Post*, July 9, 1899; O'Brien, " 'Perfect Roar,' " p. 94; Joseph A. Moore–John P. Nicholson, September 25, 1899, 147th Pennsylvania Infantry File, GNMP; Parmeter Diary, OHS.
49. *OR*, 27, 2, p. 519.
50. Ibid., 1, pp. 830, 831, 841; 2, p. 523; *Washington Post*, July 9, 1899; Ladd and Ladd, eds., *BP*, 1, p. 297; O'Brien, " 'Perfect Roar,' " p. 94; H. W. Pfanz, *Gettysburg: Culp's Hill*, pp. 325, 326; Sanford N. Truesdell–[Ozias E. Truesdell], July 9, 1863, Truesdell Family Papers, CSL; Boyle, *Soldiers True*, p. 128.
51. Rudy Diary, DHSTC; Diary of J.T.H., Boardman Collection, USAMHI.
52. William Sayre–Father and Mother Brothers and Sisters, July 5, 1863, Sayre Letters, USAMHI; Sanford N. Truesdell–[Ozias E. Truesdell], July 9, 1863, Truesdell Family Papers, CSL.
53. Hyde Diary, USAMHI; Coco, *Strange and Blighted Land*, p. 17; James S. Hyde, "The Gettysburg Campaign of the 137th New York," 137th New York Infantry File, GNMP.
54. John L. Harding–Sister, July 18, 1863, Harding Papers, IU; Walton, ed., *Civil War Courtship*, p. 50; L. R. Coy–Sarah, July 6, 1863, 123rd New York Infantry File, GNMP.
55. H. W. Pfanz, *Gettysburg: Culp's Hill*, p. 369.
56. *B&L*, 3, p. 317; Ladd and Ladd, eds., *BP*, 2, p. 978; William T. Shimp–Dearest Annie, July 18, 1863, Shimp Papers, USAMHI; Caleb Hadley Beal–Parents, July

5, 1863, Beal Papers, MHS; Jacobs, "Later Rambles," p. 167; Kaminsky, ed., *War,* p. 106.

57. Coco, *Strange and Blighted Land,* p. 19; Coco, *Wasted Valor,* p. 25.

58. *OR,* 27, 2, pp. 340–42; O'Brien, " 'Perfect Roar,' " p. 95.

59. *OR,* 27, 2, p. 341; Frassanito, *Early Photography,* pp. 124–28; Frye, *2nd Virginia,* p. 55.

60. *OR,* 27, 1, pp. 173–87; Busey, *These Honored Dead,* passim.

61. H. E. Brown, *28th Regt. P.V.V.I.,* p. 7; William T. Shimp–Dearest Annie, July 18, 1863, Shimp Papers, USAMHI; Ladd and Ladd, eds., *BP,* 1, p. 221.

62. W. H. Proffit–R. L. Proffit, July 9, 1863, Proffit Family Papers, UNC; Casper Henkel–Cousin, July 12, 1863, 37th Virginia Infantry File, GNMP; Green Diary, p. 20 1/2, UNC; B. H. Coffman–Wife, July 12, 1863, Coffman Letters, USAMHI; Firebaugh Diary, UNC; Thomas F. Boatwright–My Darling Wife, July 9, 1863, Boatwright Papers, UNC.

63. McKim, *Soldier's Recollections,* p. 182.

64. C. W. Turner, ed., *Ted Barclay,* p. 90.

65. *OR,* 27, 2, p. 504; D. C. Pfanz, *Richard S. Ewell,* p. 319.

66. *OR,* 27, 2, pp. 448, 490, 505.

67. Ibid., 1, pp. 794, 795, 798; 3, p. 500; L. R. Coy–Sister, July 6, 1863, 123rd New York Infantry File, GNMP; Marvin, *Fifth Regiment,* p. 280; Packer Diary, CSL; William Williams–My dear Wife, July 29, 1863, Williams Letters, USAMHI; *New York at Gettysburg,* 2, pp. 541, 859.

68. *OR,* 27, 1, pp. 762, 764, 832.

69. Ibid., pp. 759, 775, 832; Ira S. Jeffers–Parents, July 6, 1863, Jeffers Papers, US-AMHI.

70. *OR,* 27, 1, p. 833.

71. Ladd and Ladd, eds., *BP,* 1, pp. 218–19.

72. Chapman Diary, pp. 40, 41, CSL; Chapman, *Civil War Diary,* p. 24.

5. "No Fifteen Thousand Men"

1. Longstreet, *From Manassas to Appomattox,* p. 387; *Annals,* p. 429; Gallagher, ed., *Second Day,* p. 10.

2. Wert, *General James Longstreet,* chaps. 1–9, quotes pp. 198, 200.

3. Ibid., chap. 12, quote on p. 252; Lord, ed., *Fremantle Diary,* pp. 46, 189, 190; Williams, "From Sumter," p. 98.

4. Lord, ed., *Fremantle Diary,* p. 198; *Annals,* p. 433; Wert, *General James Longstreet,* p. 252.

5. *B&L,* 3, p. 246; Wert, *General James Longstreet,* pp. 244–47.

6. *B&L,* 3, p. 246; Wert, *General James Longstreet,* p. 247.

7. Wert, *General James Longstreet*, pp. 246–47.

8. *B&L*, 3, p. 339; *Annals*, p. 421; Wert, *General James Longstreet*, pp. 256–57; *Washington Post*, June 11, 1893.

9. Longstreet wrote different versions of this conversation, so the precise words are impossible to reconstruct. See *B&L*, 3, p. 339; *Annals*, p. 421; Longstreet, *From Manassas to Appomattox*, pp. 358–59; Wert, *General James Longstreet*, p. 257.

10. Longstreet, *From Manassas to Appomattox*, p. 358; Lord, ed., *Fremantle Diary*, p. 205; Moses, *Autobiography*, pp. 60, 61, UNC; Wert, *General James Longstreet*, p. 259.

11. Wert, *General James Longstreet*, pp. 260–61.

12. Sorrel, *Recollections*, p. 157; Wert, *General James Longstreet*, chaps. 13, 14; Ross, *Cities*, p. 55.

13. Ross, *Cities*, p. 56; Sorrel, *Recollections*, p. 170; *Annals*, p. 429; Longstreet, *From Manassas to Appomattox*, pp. 385, 386; Coddington, *Gettysburg Campaign*, pp. 455, 456, 457.

14. Gallagher, ed., *Third Day*, p. 46; Coddington, *Gettysburg Campaign*, p. 457.

15. Gallagher, ed., *Fighting For*, pp. 120, 242; Gallagher, ed., *Second Day*, p. 10; Wert, *General James Longstreet*, p. 283.

16. Longstreet, *From Manassas to Appomattox*, pp. 385, 386; *Annals*, p. 429; Coddington, *Gettysburg Campaign*, p. 457; Gallagher, ed., *Third Day*, p. 45.

17. Charles Marshall–H. T. Owen, January 28, 1878; Charles Pickett–H. T. Owen, March 30, 1878, both in Owen Papers, VHS; E. P. Reeve–Wife, June 28, 1863, Reeve Papers, UNC; Stone, ed., "Diary of William Heyser," n. p.; Georg and Busey, *Nothing but Glory*, p. 8.

18. James Kemper–E. P. Alexander, September 20, 1869, Dearborn Collection, HU; W. Harrison, *Pickett's Men*, p. 88; Edward R. Baird–H. T. Owen, Owen Papers, VHS; Georg and Busey, *Nothing but Glory*, pp. 18, 19.

19. Gallagher, ed., *Third Day*, pp. 45, 46; Wert, *General James Longstreet*, p. 282; Charles Marshall–H. T. Owen, January 28, 1878; James Longstreet–H. T. Owen, April 21, 1878, both in Owen Papers, VHS.

20. Powell and Clement, eds., *War Recollections*, p. 51; *Annals*, p. 442; Georg and Busey, *Nothing but Glory*, pp. 23–25.

21. Coddington, *Gettysburg Campaign*, p. 458; *Annals*, p. 429; Longstreet, *From Manassas to Appomattox*, p. 387.

22. *OR*, 27, 2, p. 320; Coddington, *Gettysburg Campaign*, p. 459; *Annals*, p. 312; Thomas J. Goree–James Longstreet, May 17, 1875, Longstreet Papers, UNC.

23. Longstreet, *From Manassas to Appomattox*, p. 386; *Annals*, p. 432; Penny and Laine, *Struggle*, pp. 109, 112; Laney, "Wasted Gallantry," p. 44; Coddington, *Gettysburg Campaign*, p. 458; *OR*, 27, 2, p. 359.

24. *OR*, 27, 2, p. 320.

25. Longstreet, *From Manassas to Appomattox*, p. 386; Gallagher, ed., *Third Day*, p. 46; Coddington, *Gettysburg Campaign*, p. 459.
26. Coddington, *Gettysburg Campaign*, pp. 459, 460, 463, 464.
27. Ibid., pp. 421–22, 459; Gottfried, "Wright's Charge," pp. 73, 77, 78, 81; H. W. Pfanz, *Gettysburg: The Second Day*, pp. 387–89; E. P. Alexander, *Military Memoirs*, pp. 421–22.
28. Coddington, *Gettysburg Campaign*, pp. 463–64.
29. Ibid., pp. 463–64.
30. Ibid., p. 459; Georg and Busey, *Nothing but Glory*, p. 206; *Annals*, p. 441; Boggs, ed., *Alexander Letters*, p. 249.
31. Rollins, "Second Wave," pp. 102, 102n; Griffith, *Battle Tactics*, pp. 143–45.
32. Coddington, *Gettysburg Campaign*, p. 463; Longstreet, *From Manassas to Appomattox*, p. 386; *B&L*, 3, pp. 342, 343.
33. *Annals*, p. 429; *B&L*, 3, pp. 342–43.
34. *Annals*, p. 429; Longstreet, *From Manassas to Appomattox*, p. 387.
35. Coddington, *Gettysburg Campaign*, pp. 460–62; Rollins, "Second Wave," p. 102; *OR*, 27, 2, pp. 308, 320, 359.
36. Coddington, *Gettysburg Campaign*, pp. 461, 462; Tagg, *Generals*, pp. 334, 342.
37. *OR*, 27, 2, p. 320; Coddington, *Gettysburg Campaign*, pp. 460, 461; *Annals*, p. 312; Rollins, "Second Wave," pp. 108, 110; E. P. Alexander–Frederick Colston, November 24, 1894, April 7, 1898, both in Campbell-Colston Family Papers, UNC.
38. *OR*, 27, 2, pp. 360, 614, 615; H. W. Pfanz, *Gettysburg: The Second Day*, p. 385.
39. *OR*, 27, 2, p. 556; Frassanito, *Early Photography*, p. 183; H. W. Pfanz, *Gettysburg: The Second Day*, p. 385.
40. *OR*, 27, 2, pp. 320, 359, 360; Rollins, "Second Wave," pp. 102–7.
41. Coddington, *Gettysburg Campaign*, pp. 463, 464.
42. Ibid., p. 463; Gallagher, ed., *Three Days*, pp. 272, 278; Rollins, "Lee's Artillery," p. 46.
43. Rollins, "Lee's Artillery," pp. 46, 51; Gallagher, ed., *Three Days*, p. 274.
44. Rollins, "Lee's Artillery," pp. 47, 52; "The Gettysburg Campaign," p. 6, Alexander Papers, UNC.
45. Rollins, "Lee's Artillery," pp. 47, 50–53; Gallagher, ed., *Three Days*, p. 274; "The Gettysburg Campaign," p. 7, Alexander Papers, UNC.
46. "The Gettysburg Campaign," pp. 6–8, Alexander Papers, UNC.
47. Warner, *Generals in Gray*, pp. 234–35; Gallagher, ed., *Three Days*, pp. 272, 274, 275, 283.
48. Rollins, "Lee's Artillery," p. 48.
49. Georg and Busey, *Nothing but Glory*, p. 228; Busey and Martin, *Regimental Strengths*, pp. 144–46; Ladd and Ladd, eds., *BP*, 3, p. 1776; Young, "Pettigrew's Brigade at Gettysburg," p. 555.

50. *OR,* 27, 2, pp. 329–46; Motts, "Brave and Resolute Force," p. 30.
51. *OR,* 27, 2, pp. 343–45; Busey and Martin, *Regimental Strengths,* pp. 173–77, 181, 185–88; Clark, ed., *Histories,* 1, p. 698; 5, pp. 134, 158; undated newspaper clipping, Robbins Papers, UNC; J. J. Young–Zebulon Vance, July 4, 1863, 26th North Carolina Infantry File, GNMP; Louis G. Young–William J. Baker, February 10, 1864, Winston Papers, NCDAH; M. W. Taylor, "North Carolina," pp. 78, 80, 86, 89; Brooks, "22nd Battalion Virginia Infantry," p. 11, MC; Motts, "Brave and Resolute Force," p. 29; Coddington, *Gettysburg Campaign,* p. 462.
52. Louis G. Young–William J. Baker, February 10, 1864, Winston Papers, NCDAH; Young, "Pettigrew's Brigade at Gettysburg," p. 555; George M. Whiting–Editor, March 18, 1867, Paris Papers, UNC; Ladd and Ladd, eds., *BP,* 3, p. 1776; Coddington, *Gettysburg Campaign,* p. 462; *Annals,* p. 441.
53. Woodworth, *Davis and Lee,* p. 245; Gallagher, ed., *Lee,* p. 261; Thomas, *Robert E. Lee,* p. 302.
54. *OR,* 27, 2, p. 359; Gallagher, ed., *Lee,* p. 437; Boggs, ed., *Alexander Letters,* p. 249; *Annals,* p. 620; Longstreet, *From Manassas to Appomattox,* p. 387.

6. "We Were on the Eve"

1. Georg and Busey, *Nothing but Glory,* pp. 19, 23; James Kemper–E. P. Alexander, September 20, 1869, Dearborn Collection, HU; Levin C. Gayle Diary, 9th Virginia Infantry File, GNMP; Rollins, ed., *Pickett's Charge,* pp. 49, 50, 52, 54; Lewis, *Recollections,* p. 77.
2. D. B. Dameron, "Recollections of Some of the Incidents of the Battle of Gettysburg, Pa., July 3, 1863," Daniel Papers, UVA; Georg and Busey, *Nothing but Glory,* pp. 23–27; Diary, Lippitt Papers, UNC; *New York Times,* May 1, 1893; Harrison, *Pickett's Men,* pp. 90, 91; Johnston, *Story,* p. 203; Loving Diary, LVA; John or William Cocke–Parents and Sister, July 11, 1863, Cocke Family Papers, VHS.
3. Diary, Lippitt Papers, UNC; Johnston, *Story,* p. 203; Georg and Busey, *Nothing but Glory,* p. 25; Coddington, *Gettysburg Campaign,* pp. 68, 115.
4. Georg and Busey, *Nothing but Glory,* p. 9; Loehr, *War History,* p. 1; Wallace, *1st Virginia Infantry,* pp. 1, 8; Wallace, *3rd Virginia Infantry,* p. 1; Riggs, *7th Virginia Infantry,* p. 1; Divine, *8th Virginia Infantry,* p. 1; Trask, *9th Virginia Infantry,* p. 1; Crews and Parrish, *14th Virginia Infantry,* p. 2; J. I. Robertson, Jr., *18th Virginia Infantry,* pp. 2–3; Jordan and Thomas, *19th Virginia Infantry,* p. 2; Gunn, *24th Virginia Infantry,* p. 4; Fields, *28th Virginia Infantry,* p. 3; Gregory, *38th Virginia Infantry,* p. 3; Powell and Clement, eds., *War Recollections,* p. 5.
5. Sorrel, *Recollections,* p. 48; Moses, Autobiography, p. 58, UNC; Lord, ed., *Fremantle Diary,* p. 197; Gordon, *General George E. Pickett,* pp. 77, 107.

6. Gordon, *General George E. Pickett*, pp. 6, 12, 15, 28, 35, 51; Warner, *Generals in Gray*, p. 239.

7. Gordon, *General George E. Pickett*, pp. 2, 3, 75–77.

8. Wert, *General James Longstreet*, pp. 45, 210; Sorrel, *Recollections*, p. 48.

9. *B&L*, 3, p. 343; Motts, "Brave and Resolute Force," p. 31; *OR*, 27, 2, p. 359.

10. Georg and Busey, *Nothing but Glory*, p. 25; W. W. Scott, *History of Orange County*, p. 187; Warner, *Generals in Gray*, p. 169; R. M. Powell, *Recollections*, p. 34; *B&L*, 3, p. 345.

11. Georg and Busey, *Nothing but Glory*, p. 5; Richard B. Garnett–My dear Mrs. Dandridge, June 25, 1863, Bedinger-Dandridge Family Correspondence, DU; Davis, "Death," p. 110; Hunton, *Autobiography*, p. 89.

12. George E. Pickett–LaSalle Corbell, October 11, 1862, Inman Papers, BU; Wert, *Brotherhood*, pp. 70–71, 85–89; Warner, *Generals in Gray*, p. 99.

13. Wert, *Brotherhood*, pp. 70–71, 88–90.

14. Ibid., pp. 89–90; Warner, *Generals in Gray*, p. 99; Elliott Johnston–My dear Madam, July 18, 1863, Chisolm Papers, VHS.

15. Elliott Johnston–My dear Madam, July 18, 1863, Chisolm Papers, VHS; W. Harrison, *Pickett's Men*, pp. 20, 21; George E. Pickett–LaSalle Corbell, October 11, 1862, Inman Papers, BU; Georg and Busey, *Nothing but Glory*, p. 119.

16. Gallagher, ed., *Third Day*, p. 94; Warner, *Generals in Gray*, p. 11.

17. Gallagher, ed., *Third Day*, pp. 99, 101–5.

18. Ibid., pp. 111–12; Tagg, *Generals*, p. 243.

19. Gallagher, ed., *Third Day*, pp. 115–17; Tagg, *Generals*, pp. 243–44; W. Harrison, *Pickett's Men*, p. 35.

20. D. B. Dameron, "Recollections of Some of the Incidents of the Battle of Gettysburg, Pa., July 3, 1863," Daniel Papers, UVA; Ladd and Ladd, eds., *BP*, 2, p. 1191; Georg and Busey, *Nothing but Glory*, pp. 25–26; Durkin, ed., *John Dooley*, p. 102; Reardon, *Pickett's Charge*, pp. 6, 7; Report of Colonel Joseph Mayo, July 26, 1863, Pickett Papers, DU; Harrison, *Pickett's Men*, pp. 90–91; Johnston, *Story*, p. 204.

21. Ladd and Ladd, eds., *BP*, 2, p. 1191; W. Harrison, *Pickett's Men*, p. 91; Georg and Busey, *Nothing but Glory*, p. 38; Clayton G. Coleman–John W. Daniel, July 1, 1904, Daniel Papers, UVA.

22. Lewis, *Recollections*, pp. 77–78; Compton, "Reminiscences," p. 9, USAMHI; Diary of Levin C. Gayle, 9th Virginia Infantry File, GNMP; Powell and Clement, eds., *War Recollections*, p. 39.

23. W. Harrison, *Pickett's Men*, p. 91; J.S.D. Cullen–My Dear Lottie, July 8, 1863, Carrington Family Papers, VHS; J. C. Granberry–John W. Daniel, March 25, 1905, Daniel Papers, UVA; J. I. Robertson, Jr., *18th Virginia Infantry*, p. 21.

24. Powell and Clement, eds., *War Recollections*, p. 39; Rollins, *"Damned Red*

Flags," p. 149; Account of John Holmes Smith, July 4, 5, 1904, Daniel Papers, UVA; Rollins, ed., *Pickett's Charge*, p. 54.

25. Louis G. Young–William J. Baker, February 10, 1864, Winston Papers, NCDAH; Haskell, *Haskell Memoirs*, p. 41; C. N. Wilson, *Most Promising Young Man*, pp. 23, 24, 26, 27, 32; Tucker, *High Tide*, p. 95.

26. C. N. Wilson, *Most Promising Young Man*, p. 36; Tucker, *High Tide*, p. 95; Tagg, *Generals*, pp. 343–44; Haskell, *Haskell Memoirs*, p. 41.

27. *OR*, 27, 2, pp. 650–51; Louis G. Young–William J. Baker, February 10, 1864, Winston Papers, NCDAH; Young, "Pettigrew's Brigade," pp. 553, 554.

28. *OR*, 27, 2, pp. 607, 608, 650; War Department, "Record," 1, p. 19, LC; *SHSP*, 7, p. 92.

29. Undated newspaper clipping, Robbins Papers, UNC; *OR*, 27, 2, p. 650; Fortesque Diary, pp. 151, 153, WLM; Peel Diary, p. 24, MDAH; *SHSP*, 7, p. 92.

30. *OR*, 27, 2, p. 650; C. N. Wilson, *Most Promising Young Man*, p. 65; Tucker, *High Tide*, p. 103; Long, "Confederate Prisoners," p. 100.

31. *OR*, 27, 2, p. 650; M. W. Taylor, "Col. James Keith Marshall," pp. 78–80; Haskell, *Haskell Memoirs*, p. 41.

32. *OR*, 27, 2, p. 650; Tagg, *Generals*, pp. 352–53; Warner, *Generals in Gray*, p. 68.

33. *OR*, 27, 2, p. 650; Brooks, "22nd Battalion Virginia Infantry," p. 11, MC; W. S. Christian–John W. Daniel, October 24, 1903, Daniel Papers, UVA; Tagg, *Generals*, pp. 346–47.

34. Peel Diary, p. 24, MDAH; G. H. Faribault, "Extracts from an Article Entitled 'Pettigrew's Old Brigade,' " Paris Papers, UNC; W. B. Taylor–Mother, July 25, 1863, 11th North Carolina Infantry File, GNMP.

35. Collett Leventhorpe–Charles C. Jones, April 13, 1887, C. C. Jones Papers, DU; R. M. Tuttle–Mr. Bright, June 3, 1903, Daniel Papers, UVA; M. W. Taylor, "North Carolina," p. 86; C. N. Wilson, *Most Promising Young Man*, pp. 61, 62; Freeman, *Lee's Lieutenants*, 3, p. 181; James Longstreet–Henry Heth, February 14, 1897, Longstreet Papers, MC.

36. *OR*, 27, 2, pp. 359, 666; Lane, "Lane's N. Carolina Brigade," pp. 5, 6, USAMHI.

37. *OR*, 27, 2, p. 666; Clark, ed., *Histories*, 1, p. 698; M. W. Taylor, "North Carolina," pp. 80, 81, 88, 89; *SOR*, 5, p. 67; Freeman, *Lee's Lieutenants*, 3, p. 150; Ladd and Ladd, eds., *BP*, 3, p. 1776; R. K. Krick, *Lee's Colonels*, p. 244.

38. *OR*, 27, 2, p. 666; Harris, "Historical Sketches," p. 35, SHSW; Rollins, ed., *Pickett's Charge*, p. 250; I. R. Trimble, "North Carolinians at Gettysburg," p. 57.

39. Tagg, *Generals*, pp. 333–34; Isaac Trimble–John B. Bachelder, n.d., Bachelder Papers, NHHS; Freeman, *Lee's Lieutenants*, 3, p. 182.

40. Tagg, *Generals*, pp. 328–29; Warner, *Generals in Gray*, p. 310.

41. Tagg, *Generals*, pp. 328–29.

42. Freeman, *Lee's Lieutenants*, 3, pp. 34, 94–95.

43. I. R. Trimble, "North Carolinians at Gettysburg," p. 57; Tagg, *Generals*, p. 328; Ladd and Ladd, eds., *BP*, 2, p. 932.

44. Clark M. Avery–My Dear Sir, July 28, 1863, Caldwell Papers, UNC; Ladd and Ladd, eds., *BP*, 3, p. 1776.

45. *OR*, 27, 2, pp. 608, 614, 619; Gottfried, "Mahone's Brigade," p. 75.

46. *OR*, 27, 2, pp. 608, 614, 619; David Lang–John B. Bachelder, October 16, 1893, Lang Letterbooks, FSA.

47. David Lang–John B. Bachelder, October 16, 1893, Lang Letterbooks, FSA.

48. Ibid.

49. *SHSP*, 7, p. 92; Gallagher, ed., *Fighting For*, p. 258; Coddington, *Gettysburg Campaign*, pp. 491–92.

50. Ladd and Ladd, eds., *BP*, 1, p. 517.

51. *OR*, 27, 2, p. 320.

52. "The Gettysburg Campaign," p. 5, Alexander Papers, UNC; *OR*, 27, 2, p. 434; R. K. Krick, *Parker's Virginia Battery*, p. 180; Memoir of Washington Artillery, p. 27, MC.

53. "The Gettysburg Campaign," pp. 6, 7, Alexander Papers, UNC; Gallagher, ed., *Fighting For*, p. 247; *OR*, 27, 2, p. 351.

54. "The Gettysburg Campaign," p. 7, Alexander Papers, UNC; R. K. Krick, *Parker's Virginia Battery*, pp. 180, 181; Rollins, "Failure . . . Pickett's Charge," p. 34.

55. *B&L*, 3, p. 361; Gallagher, ed., *Fighting For*, p. 253; E. P. Alexander, *Military Memoirs*, p. 418; "The Gettysburg Campaign," p. 6, Alexander Papers, UNC.

56. Gallagher, ed., *Fighting For*, p. 332; Wert, *General James Longstreet*, p. 212; *SHSP*, 5, pp. 50, 52–53, 201, 202.

57. Gallagher, ed., *Fighting For*, pp. 245, 246.

58. "The Gettysburg Campaign," p. 6, Alexander Papers, UNC.

59. E. P. Alexander–My dear Colston, April 7, 1898, Campbell-Colston Family Papers, UNC; Gallagher, ed., *Fighting For*, p. 252; E. P. Alexander, *Military Memoirs*, p. 416.

60. E. P. Alexander–My dear Colston, April 7, 1898, Campbell-Colston Family Papers, UNC; Gallagher, ed., *Fighting For*, p. 252; E. P. Alexander, *Military Memoirs*, pp. 388, 417; "The Gettysburg Campaign," p. 10, Alexander Papers, UNC.

61. Gallagher, ed., *Fighting For*, p. 248; "The Gettysburg Campaign," pp. 8, 11, Alexander Papers, UNC.

62. Ladd and Ladd, eds., *BP*, 1, p. 484; Coco, *Concise Guide*, p. 43; Rollins, "Failure . . . at Gettysburg," p. 49; Rollins, "Failure . . . Pickett's Charge," pp. 32–33; Busey and Martin, *Regimental Strengths*, p. 130.

63. Rollins, "Failure . . . Pickett's Charge," p. 32; Haskell, *Haskell Memoirs*, pp. 46, 47; *SOR*, 5, pp. 348, 349.

64. *OR*, 27, 2, p. 375; Coco, *Concise Guide*, p. 60; Rollins, "Failure . . . Pickett's

Charge," p. 32; "North Carolina Troops at Gettysburg," North Carolina Troops File, GNMP.

65. Coco, *Concise Guide*, p. 60; Graves, *History*, p. 32; Rollins, "Failure . . . Pickett's Charge," p. 33.

66. *OR*, 27, 2, pp. 375, 434; Memoir of Washington Artillery, MC; Coco, *Concise Guide*, p. 60; Rollins, "Failure . . . Pickett's Charge," p. 32.

67. *OR*, 27, 2, pp. 375, 434; Rollins, "Failure . . . Pickett's Charge," p. 32.

68. *OR*, 27, 2, p. 388; Gallagher, ed., *Fighting For*, p. 253; *CV*, 9, p. 215; Warner, *Generals in Gray*, pp. 69–70; James Dearing–My darling Mother, July 26, 1863, Dearing Family Papers, UVA; War Department, "Record," 1, p. 15, LC; Georg and Busey, *Nothing but Glory*, p. 19.

69. "The Gettysburg Campaign," p. 10, Alexander Papers, UNC.

70. *OR*, 27, 2, p. 388; Virginia Troops File, GNMP; War Department, "Record," 1, p. 15, LC; Coco, *Concise Guide*, p. 61; Rollins, "Failure . . . Pickett's Charge," p. 32.

71. Coco, *Concise Guide*, p. 60; *B&L*, 3, p. 362; *Sumter Herald*, April 29, 1902; Ladd and Ladd, eds., *BP*, 1, p. 484; Boggs, ed., *Alexander Letters*, p. 249; "The Gettysburg Campaign," p. 8, Alexander Papers, UNC; Rollins, "Failure . . . Pickett's Charge," pp. 32–33.

72. Magner, *Traveller*, p. 46; E. P. Alexander, *Military Memoirs*, p. 420; "The Gettysburg Campaign," p. 6, Alexander Papers, UNC; *B&L*, 3, p. 358; Rollins, "Lee's Artillery," pp. 48, 50.

73. *OR*, 27, 2, p. 610; Virginia Troops File, GNMP; "The Gettysburg Campaign," p. 9, Alexander Papers, UNC; Busey and Martin, *Regimental Strengths*, p. 172; Rollins, "Failure . . . Pickett's Charge," pp. 32–33.

74. *OR*, 27, 2, p. 610; M. F. Cockrell, ed., *Gunner*, p. 73; Virginia Troops File, GNMP; "North Carolina Troops at Gettysburg," North Carolina Troops File, GNMP; Rollins, "Failure . . . Pickett's Charge," p. 32.

75. *OR*, 27, 2, pp. 610, 635; Virginia Troops File, GNMP; Rollins, "Failure . . . Pickett's Charge," pp. 32, 33.

76. *OR*, 27, 2, p. 675; Virginia Troops File, GNMP; War Department, "Record," 1, p. 22; Rollins, "Failure . . . Pickett's Charge," p. 32.

77. *OR*, 27, 2, p. 604; Virginia Troops File, GNMP; Rollins, "Failure . . . Pickett's Charge," p. 33; George L. Christian–John Daniel, April 4, July 4, 1898, Daniel Papers, UVA.

78. *OR*, 27, 2, p. 603; Virginia Troops File, GNMP; Rollins, "Failure . . . Pickett's Charge," p. 32.

79. *OR*, 27, 2, p. 456; Virginia Troops File, GNMP; Moore, *Story*, p. 198; H. W. Pfanz, *Gettysburg: Culp's Hill*, pp. 169–70; Rollins, "Failure . . . Pickett's Charge," pp. 32–33.

80. Rollins, "Failure . . . Pickett's Charge," pp. 30–35; James Dearing–My darling

Mother, July 26, 1863, Dearing Family Papers, UVA; Coddington, *Gettysburg Campaign*, pp. 250, 251.

81. Gallagher, ed., *Three Days*, pp. 271, 272, 273, 278; Rollins, "Failure . . . Pickett's Charge," p. 39.

82. Gallagher, ed., *Fighting For*, p. 336; David G. McIntosh–Jennings C. Wise, June 8, 1916, McIntosh Papers, USAMHI; Thomas J. Goree–James Longstreet, May 17, 1875, Longstreet Papers, DU.

83. *OR*, 27, 2, p. 352; "The Gettysburg Campaign," p. 9, Alexander Papers, UNC; M. F. Cockrell, ed., *Gunner*, p. 74.

84. Gallagher, ed., *Three Days*, pp. 271–75, 283; Rollins, "Failure . . . Pickett's Charge," p. 39; Chamberlaine, *Memoirs*, p. 71.

85. Account of Captain Benjamin F. Little, 52nd North Carolina Infantry File, GNMP; Ladd and Ladd, eds., *BP*, 1, p. 518; Thomas J. Goree–James Longstreet, July 30, 1894, Longstreet Papers, UNC; Lindsley, ed., *Military Annals of Tennessee*, pp. 248, 249; *Annals*, pp. 431–32.

86. Coddington, *Gettysburg Campaign*, p. 464; Wert, *General James Longstreet*, p. 129; *SHSP*, 5, p. 91.

87. Freeman, *Lee's Lieutenants*, 3, p. 148; Coddington, *Gettysburg Campaign*, pp. 464, 490, 491; E. P. Alexander–Frederick Colston, January 14, 1895, Campbell-Colston Family Papers, UNC; Krolick, "Lee and Longstreet," p. 40.

88. Rollins, ed., *Pickett's Charge*, p. 65.

89. E. P. Alexander–Frederick Colston, October 20, November 24, 1903, both in Campbell-Colston Family Papers, UNC; Kross, "July 3rd Action," p. 18.

90. Coddington, *Gettysburg Campaign*, pp. 425, 426.

91. Wert, *General James Longstreet*, pp. 153–55.

92. E. P. Alexander–My dear Colston, April 7, 1898, Campbell-Colston Family Papers, UNC.

93. Longstreet, *From Manassas to Appomattox*, p. 388; *Washington Post*, June 11, 1893.

94. *OR*, 27, 2, pp. 321, 359; Longstreet, *From Manassas to Appomattox*, pp. 389, 390; Freeman, *Lee's Lieutenants*, 3, p. 149; Coddington, *Gettysburg Campaign*, p. 501; Gallagher, ed., *Three Days*, pp. 281, 282; Wert, *General James Longstreet*, p. 287.

95. Walter Harrison, *Pickett's Men*, pp. 90–91; *Annals*, p. 430.

96. Ladd and Ladd, eds., *BP*, p. 484; Gallagher, ed., *Lee*, p. 440; Lord, ed., *Fremantle Diary*, p. 211.

7. "They Are Determined"

1. Byrne and Weaver, *Haskell*, p. 139.

2. Agassiz, ed., *Meade's Headquarters*, pp. 12, 29, 30.

3. Scott, ed., *Fallen Leaves,* p. 189; Israel Thickstun–Brother Comp, July 6, 1863, Thickstun Family Papers, USAMHI.

4. Rollins, "George Gordon Meade," p. 78.

5. Ibid., p. 78; James C. Biddle–My own darling little Wife, July 1, 1863, Biddle Civil War Letters, HSP.

6. Rollins, "George Gordon Meade," p. 78; Magner, *Traveller,* p. 6; George G. Meade–Margaret, July 8, 1863, Meade Collection, HSP.

7. Coddington, *Gettysburg Campaign,* pp. 476–77, 480; Rollins, "George Gordon Meade," p. 78.

8. Coddington, *Gettysburg Campaign,* pp. 269, 275; *OR,* 27, 1, p. 261; John Newton–Henry J. Hunt, May 13, 1879, Hunt Papers, LC; Jacob Slagle–Brother, September 13, 1863, Slagle Letters, PML.

9. Agassiz, ed., *Meade's Headquarters,* p. 9; Nevins, ed., *Diary,* p. 256; Byrne and Weaver, *Haskell,* p. 133; Tagg, *Generals,* p. 13.

10. *OR,* 27, 1, p. 261; John Newton–Henry J. Hunt, May 13, 1879, Hunt Papers, LC; Coddington, *Gettysburg Campaign,* pp. 476–77, 480.

11. *OR,* 27, 1, pp. 175, 261, 380, 663, 669; John Newton–Henry J. Hunt, May 13, 1879, Hunt Papers, LC; Coddington, *Gettysburg Campaign,* p. 477.

12. *OR,* 27, 1, p. 262; Christiancy Diary, UVA; Coddington, *Gettysburg Campaign,* chap. 15, p. 477.

13. Agassiz, ed., *Meade's Headquarters,* pp. 146, 266; Tagg, *Generals,* p. 65; Nevins, ed., *Diary,* p. 228.

14. *OR,* 27, 1, pp. 177–78, 262, 485, 536, 544; Agassiz, ed., *Meade's Headquarters,* p. 266; Cavada Diary, HSP; John Newton–Henry J. Hunt, May 13, 1879, Hunt Papers, LC; Busey and Martin, *Regimental Strengths,* p. 46.

15. Coddington, *Gettysburg Campaign,* p. 477; *OR,* 27, 1, pp. 593, 602, 654.

16. Tagg, *Generals,* p. 81; Byrne and Weaver, *Haskell,* p. 133; Acker, ed., *Inside,* p. 343; Gibbon, *Personal Recollections,* p. 131; Agassiz, ed., *Meade's Headquarters,* pp. 9, 26, 80.

17. Agassiz, ed., *Meade's Headquarters,* pp. 37, 108; Byrne and Weaver, *Haskell,* p. 132; H. Blanchard–Dearest Mother, July 11, 1863, Blanchard Letter, USAMHI.

18. Byrne and Weaver, *Haskell,* p. 132; Tagg, *Generals,* pp. 103–5; Busey and Martin, *Regimental Strengths,* p. 16.

19. *OR,* 27, 1, pp. 663, 665, 674, 678; Ladd and Ladd, eds., *BP,* 1, p. 375; Coddington, *Gettysburg Campaign,* pp. 477, 481.

20. *OR,* 27, 1, pp. 175–82, 261; Busey and Martin, *Regimental Strengths,* pp. 20, 32, 46, 56, 71, 72, 75, 76; Coddington, *Gettysburg Campaign,* p. 481; John Newton–Henry J. Hunt, May 13, 1879, Hunt Papers, LC.

21. *OR,* 27, 3, p. 499.

22. Cleaves, *Meade,* p. 127; George G. Meade–Dearest Love, July 3, 1863, Meade Collection, HSP.

23. Warner, *Generals in Blue*, p. 242; Tagg, *Generals*, p. 187.

24. Rollins and Shultz, "Combined and Concentrated Fire," p. 40; Coco, *Concise Guide*, pp. 89–91.

25. Warner, *Generals in Blue*, p. 242; Tagg, *Generals*, p. 188.

26. Sears, *Chancellorsville*, p. 68.

27. Ibid., pp. 320, 331, 373; Gallagher, ed., *Three Days*, p. 287.

28. Gallagher, ed., *Three Days*, p. 287; Rollins and Shultz, "Combined and Concentrated Fire," p. 49; Philo B. Buckingham–My Dear Wife, July 17, 1863, Buckingham Letter, AAS; Coco, *Concise Guide*, p. 16.

29. Rollins and Shultz, "Combined and Concentrated Fire," pp. 40, 49; Tagg, *Generals*, p. 188; *OR*, 27, 1, p. 232; Ladd and Ladd, eds., *BP*, 1, pp. 426–27.

30. *OR*, 27, 1, p. 237; Ladd and Ladd, eds., *BP*, 1, p. 675; Shultz, "Double Canister," pp. 15, 16.

31. *OR*, 27, 1, pp. 237, 238, 878; Ladd and Ladd, eds., *BP*, 1, p. 228; Tagg, *Generals*, p. 190.

32. *OR*, 27, 1, pp. 747, 748, 749; Nevins, ed., *Diary*, pp. 238, 246, 247; Rollins and Shultz, "Combined and Concentrated Fire," pp. 54, 55; Henney Diary, US-AMHI; Crumb, ed., *Eleventh Corps Artillery*, pp. 26, 70; Shultz, "Double Canister," p. 8.

33. *OR*, 27, 1, pp. 748, 749; Crumb, ed., *Eleventh Corps Artillery*, p. 70; Rollins and Shultz, "Combined and Concentrated Fire," pp. 54, 59, 60.

34. *OR*, 27, 1, pp. 238, 477, 478; "The Gettysburg Campaign," p. 4, Alexander Papers, UNC; Gallagher, ed., *Three Days*, p. 287.

35. *OR*, 27, 1, p. 238; Ladd and Ladd, eds., *BP*, 3, p. 1977; Shultz, "Double Canister," p. 9; Tully McCrae, "Reminiscences About Gettysburg, 3 March 1904," p. 2, Brake Collection, USAMHI.

36. Bryan Farm Files, GNMP; Frassanito, *Early Photography*, p. 233; Coco, *Strange and Blighted Land*, p. 52; Shultz and Rollins, "Measuring Pickett's Charge," p. 116; Hartwig, "It Struck Horror," p. 90; Georg, " 'Common Pride,' " p. 438, GNMP.

37. *OR*, 27, 1, pp. 238, 478; Ladd and Ladd, eds., *BP*, 1, p. 341; Shultz, "Double Canister," p. 10.

38. *OR*, 27, 1, p. 478; Shultz, "Double Canister," p. 11.

39. *New York at Gettysburg*, 3, p. 1325; *OR*, 27, 1, pp. 480, 481; Shultz, "Double Canister," pp. 11–12.

40. *OR*, 27, 1, p. 690; *New York Herald*, July 2, 1911; Coco, *Concise Guide*, p. 72.

41. *OR*, 27, 1, pp. 881, 883, 890, 901; Patrick Hart–Henry J. Hunt, July 7, 1879, Hunt Papers, LC; Coco, *Concise Guard*, p. 36; Rollins and Shultz, "Combined and Concentrated Fire," p. 47.

42. *OR*, 27, 1, pp. 883, 890, 901; Appleton et al., *History*, p. 654; *Maine at Gettysburg*, pp. 326, 329; Croffut and Morris, *Military and Civil History*, p. 388; Ladd

and Ladd, eds., *BP*, 1, p. 170; Coco, *Concise Guide*, pp. 36, 70–75; Rollins and Shultz, "Combined and Concentrated Fire," p. 47.

43. *OR*, 27, 1, pp. 238, 883; Appleton et al., *History*, p. 666; Ladd and Ladd, eds., *BP*, 1, p. 170; John Bigelow–Henry J. Hunt, November 4, 1875, Hunt Papers, LC; Shultz, *"Double Canister,"* p. 13; Rollins and Shultz, "Combined and Concentrated Fire," p. 47.

44. *OR*, 27, 1, p. 659; Shultz, *"Double Canister,"* p. 14.

45. *OR*, 27, 1, p. 238; Ladd and Ladd, eds., *BP*, 1, pp. 228, 428; *B&L*, 3, p. 371.

46. *OR*, 27, 1, p. 238; Ladd and Ladd, eds., *BP*, 1, pp. 228, 229, 428–30; Nevins, ed., *Diary*, pp. 248–49; Magner, *Traveller*, p. 46; Griffith, *Battle Tactics*, p. 168.

47. Rollins and Shultz, "Combined and Concentrated Fire," pp. 54–56; Gallagher, ed., *Three Days*, p. 292; Rollins, "George Gordon Meade," p. 80; Griffith, *Battle Tactics*, p. 167.

48. Bee, *Boys*, p. 143.

49. Thomas W. Gardner–Sister, June 23, 1863, Gardner Letter, USAMHI.

50. Coddington, *Gettysburg Campaign*, pp. 333, 416–28; Garcelon Diary, USAMHI.

51. Campbell, " 'Remember Harper's Ferry!,' " p. 102; Nevins, ed., *Diary*, p. 248; David M. Smith–[Family], July 10, 1863, Smith Letters, PML; Silliker, ed., *Rebel Yell*, p. 103.

52. Byrne and Weaver, *Haskell*, p. 92; Walker, *History*, pp. 108, 164, 167, 170; Gallagher, ed., *Third Day*, p. 138.

53. Tagg, *Generals*, p. 33; Bandy and Freeland, eds., *Gettysburg Papers*, 2, pp. 1021, 1025; Byrne and Weaver, *Haskell*, p. 133.

54. Warner, *Generals in Blue*, pp. 202–3; J. D. Smith, *History*, p. 77; Byrne and Weaver, *Haskell*, p. 133; Agassiz, ed., *Meade's Headquarters*, pp. 82, 134; Bandy and Freeland, eds., *Gettysburg Papers*, 2, p. 1021; Walker, *General Hancock*, p. 137.

55. Bandy and Freeland, eds., *Gettysburg Papers*, 2, p. 1021; Agassiz, ed., *Meade's Headquarters*, pp. 134, 189; John W. Geary–Henry J. Hunt, July 17, 1879, Hunt Papers, LC; Hancock, *Reminiscences*, p. 97.

56. Walker, *General Hancock*, p. 138; *OR*, 27, 1, pp. 176–77, 372; Busey and Martin, *Regimental Strengths*, p. 33; Coddington, *Gettysburg Campaign*, p. 476; Map of Pickett's Charge, July 3rd: Longstreet's Assault File, #1, GNMP.

57. Tagg, *Generals*, p. 53; Coddington, *Gettysburg Campaign*, p. 98; G. T. Fleming, ed., *Life of Hays*, p. 404.

58. Walker, *History*, pp. 288, 289; Agassiz, ed., *Meade's Headquarters*, p. 92; Bandy and Freeland, eds., *Gettysburg Papers*, 2, p. 903; *New York at Gettysburg*, 2, p. 799; Alexander S. Webb–Wife, August 8, 1863, Webb Papers, YU; Tagg, *Generals*, p. 53.

59. *OR*, 27, 1, p. 457; Samuel S. Carroll–Winfield S. Hancock, July 23, 1876, Bates Collection, PHMC; Sawyer, *Military History*, p. 126.

60. *Report of Joint Committee*, p. 12; Statement of Chaplain Henry S. Stevens, June 10, 1905, Stevens Papers, NCDAH; Ladd and Ladd, eds., *BP*, 2, p. 1070; Campbell, " 'Remember Harper's Ferry!,' " p. 99; Map of Pickett's Charge, July 3rd: Longstreet's Assault File, #1, GNMP.

61. Ladd and Ladd, eds., *BP*, 1, pp. 339, 340; Daniel Woodall–Sister, July 31, 1863, Woodall Papers, DPA; Campbell, " 'Remember Harper's Ferry!,' " pp. 98, 99; Murray, *Redemption*, pp. 29, 34, 102, 103, 109.

62. Mahood, *"Written in Blood"*, pp. 130, 131, 135; Willson, *Disaster*, pp. 170–71; Lewis H. Crandell–Ernie, July 6, 1863, Crandell Account, USAMHI; C. D. Mac-Dougall–C. A. Richardson, June 30, 1886, 111th New York Infantry File, GNMP.

63. Map of Pickett's Charge, July 3rd: Longstreet's Assault File, #1, GNMP; Statement of Chaplain Henry S. Stevens, June 10, 1905, Stevens Papers, NCDAH; Busey and Martin, *Regimental Strengths*, pp. 33, 42; Ladd and Ladd, eds., *BP*, 3, pp. 1737, 1739, 1742, 1743, 1745, 1747, 1761; Trinque, "Confederate Battle Flags," pp. 112, 113; G. T. Fleming, ed., *Life of Hays*, pp. 404, 409, 418.

64. Wert, *Brotherhood*, pp. 74, 98, 99; Tagg, *Generals*, pp. 44–45.

65. Wert, *Brotherhood*, chaps. 6–10, quotes on pp. 98, 196.

66. John Gibbon–My dear dear Mama, June 22, 1863, Gibbon Papers, HSP.

67. Ibid.; Agassiz, ed., *Meade's Headquarters*, pp. 103, 107; Byrne and Weaver, *Haskell*, p. 134.

68. Trinque, "Confederate Battle Flags," p. 121; Map of Pickett's Charge, July 3rd: Longstreet's Assault File, #1, GNMP; Tagg, *Generals*, p. 49; John Gibbon–My darling Mama, June 30, 1863, Gibbon Papers, HSP.

69. Banes, *History*, pp. 8, 10, 11, 16; Lash, "Philadelphia Brigade," pp. 97–98, 99; Hartwig, "It Struck Horror," p. 89; Agassiz, ed., *Meade's Headquarters*, p. 307.

70. Lash, "Philadelphia Brigade," pp. 99, 101; Ladd and Ladd, eds., *BP*, 1, pp. 294, 295; Ward, *History*, pp. 161, 163, 165.

71. Alexander S. Webb–Wife, August 8, 1863, Webb Papers, YU; Winey, *Union Army Uniforms*, p. 33; Lash, "Philadelphia Brigade," p. 102; *Pennsylvania at Gettysburg*, 1, p. 552; Rollins, ed., *Pickett's Charge*, pp. 292, 293; J. B. Bachelder, "The 72nd Penn'a Monument Cast," newspaper clipping, n.d., McPherson Papers, LC; W. Penn Smith–P. F. Rothermel, November 25, 1867, Rothermel Papers, PHMC.

72. Hartwig, "It Struck Horror," pp. 90, 91, 92; R. Penn Smith–P. F. Rothermel, November 25, 1867, Rothermel Papers, PHMC; Banes, *History*, p. 187.

73. Map of Pickett's Charge, July 3rd: Longstreet's Assault File, #1, GNMP; Tagg, *Generals*, pp. 51–52.

74. *OR*, 27, 1, p. 445; Bruce, *Twentieth Regiment*, pp. 10–11, 283, 445; *New York at Gettysburg*, 1, pp. 59, 312; Miller and Mooney, *Civil War*, p. 50; R. G. Scott, ed., *Fallen Leaves*, pp. 3, 186; Waitt, ed., *History*, p. 234.

75. Tagg, *Generals*, p. 47; Warner, *Generals in Blue*, pp. 210–11; R. G. Scott, ed.,

Fallen Leaves, p. 191; Letter of E. H. Cleavins, September 27, 1882, Silbey Collection, NA.

76. *OR,* 27, 1, pp. 420, 422, 423; Trinque, "Confederate Battle Flags," p. 121; *New York at Gettysburg,* 2, p. 664; Meinhard, "First Minnesota," pp. 81–84; Moe, *Last Full Measure,* pp. 271, 272, 275, 281.

77. Hage, "Battle of Gettysburg," p. 254; Holcombe, *History,* pp. 347, 365.

78. *OR,* 27, 1, pp. 423, 425; Hadden, "Granite Glory," p. 63; William Peacock–Sarah, August 20, 1863, Peacock Letters, USAMHI.

79. *OR,* 27, 1, pp. 321, 325; Theodore B. Gates–P. F. Rothermel, April 28, 1868, Rothermel Papers, PHMC; Ladd and Ladd, eds., *BP,* 1, pp. 268, 269.

80. Coffin, *Nine Months,* pp. 147, 177, 191, 214; Winey, *Union Army Uniforms,* p. 46; Ladd and Ladd, eds., *BP,* 1, pp. 52, 53.

81. Coffin, *Nine Months,* p. 147; Tagg, *Generals,* p. 30; Ladd and Ladd, eds., *BP,* 1, pp. 53, 54.

82. *OR,* 27, 1, p. 349; Francis Long–Wife, July 2, 1863, Picerno Collection.

83. *OR,* 27, 1, pp. 174, 349; Ladd and Ladd, eds., *BP,* 1, pp. 95, 96; *Pennsylvania at Gettysburg,* 2, p. 741; Busey and Martin, *Regimental Strengths,* pp. 27–29.

84. Gibbon, *Personal Recollections,* p. 146.

85. Ibid., p. 146; Byrne and Weaver, *Haskell,* pp. 145–46; Ladd and Ladd, eds., *BP,* 3, p. 1360.

86. Byrne and Weaver, *Haskell,* p. 146; *OR,* 27, 1, pp. 203, 290; Rollins, "George Gordon Meade," p. 80; Bandy and Freeland, eds., *Gettysburg Papers,* 2, p. 750; Coddington, *Gettysburg Campaign,* p. 476; *New York at Gettysburg,* 2, pp. 715, 716.

87. George Meade–Mama, July 1, 1863, Meade Collection, HSP.

8. "Bloodthirsty Business"

1. J. D. Smith, *History,* p. 70; Ward, *History,* p. 165; Bandy and Freeland, eds., *Gettysburg Papers,* 2, p. 947; Archer, "Remembering," p. 71; H. S. Stevens, *Souvenir,* p. 16.

2. Ladd and Ladd, eds., *BP,* 2, pp. 872, 1001; *New York at Gettysburg,* 2, p. 890; D. S. Thomas, *Ready . . . Aim . . . Fire!,* p. 11; Griffith, *Battle Tactics,* p. 85.

3. Campbell, " 'Remember Harper's Ferry!,' " p. 100; Bandy and Freeland, eds., *Gettysburg Papers,* 2, p. 947.

4. Ladd and Ladd, eds., *BP,* pp. 768, 962; Ward, *History,* p. 165; Wheelock G. Veazey–G. G. Benedict, July 11, 1864, Veazey Papers, VTHS; Chamberlin, *History,* p. 150; J. D. Smith, *History,* p. 79; *Maine at Gettysburg,* p. 295; Thomas M. Littlejohn, "Recollections of a Confederate Soldier," 1st South Carolina Infantry File, GNMP; Rollins, "Second Wave," p. 105; Kirkpatrick Diary, UT; Bee, *Boys,* p. 149.

5. Wright, "Story," p. 607, GNMP; Archer, "Remembering," p. 71; Mahood, "Written In Blood," p. 141; Ward, *History*, p. 165.

6. *OR*, 27, 2, p. 663; Ladd and Ladd, eds., *BP*, 2, p. 1001.

7. Hamblen, *Connecticut Yankees*, p. 91; H. S. Stevens, *Souvenir*, p. 16; Page, *History*, p. 142; Campbell, " 'Remember Harper's Ferry!,' " p. 100; Murray, *Redemption*, pp. 119, 120; C. A. Richardson–John B. Bachelder, August 18, 1889, Wheeler Papers, GNMP; *Philadelphia North American*, June 29, 1913.

8. Beyer and Keydel, eds., *Deeds*, pp. 249–50.

9. Bee, *Boys*, p. 149; Gallagher, ed., *Third Day*, p. 140.

10. Ladd and Ladd, eds., *BP*, 3, p. 1752.

11. John L. Street–Father and Mother, July 6, 1863, Street Papers, GNMP.

12. *OR*, 27, 1, pp. 478, 519; 2, pp. 379, 380; K. M. Brown, *Cushing*, p. 225; James E. Decker–Sister, July 6, 1863, Decker Letters, USAMHI; Washburn, *Complete Military History*, p. 50; Hartwig, "It Struck Horror," p. 94; Coffin, *Nine Months*, p. 213.

13. R. K. Krick, *Parker's Virginia Battery*, p. 182.

14. *OR*, 27, 2, p. 598; Kitzmiller, "Accounts," USAMHI; H. W. Pfanz, *Gettysburg: Culp's Hill*, pp. 134–38; Ladd and Ladd, eds., *BP*, 2, p. 747.

15. *OR*, 27, 1, pp. 457, 459, 714–16, 719, 720; 2, p. 598; Blackford Diary, USAMHI; Samuel Pickens Diary, 5th Alabama Infantry File, GNMP.

16. *OR*, 27, 2, p. 598; Blackford Diary, USAMHI.

17. Kitzmiller, "Accounts," USAMHI; Lieutenant Augustus Horstmann Diary, 45th New York Infantry File, GNMP; Ladd and Ladd, eds., *BP*, 2, p. 1097; *New York at Gettysburg*, 1, p. 381; Buell, *Cannoneer*, pp. 91, 92.

18. H. W. Pfanz, *Gettysburg: Culp's Hill*, pp. 150–51.

19. Ibid., pp. 134–38; William W. Ker–John P. Nicholson, May 1, 1894, 73rd Pennsylvania Infantry File, GNMP; Blackford Diary, USAMHI.

20. H. W. Pfanz, *Gettysburg: Culp's Hill*, pp. 141–42; Frassanito, *Early Photography*, pp. 119, 121; Coco, *Strange and Blighted Land*, p. 309; *Philadelphia North American*, July 4, 1909.

21. Eskridge, "War Reminiscences," p. 2, USAMHI; Coles and Waters, "Forgotten Sacrifice," p. 42; Crumb, ed., *Eleventh Corps Artillery*, p. 29.

22. Bliss Farm Buildings File, GNMP; Christ, *"Over,"* p. 5; H. S. Stevens, *Souvenir*, p. 16.

23. Christ, *"Over,"* pp. 5, 6, 14, 18, 19; Bowen Diary, p. 8, USAMHI; *Final Report*, p. 109; Archer, "Remembering," p. 73.

24. Bowen Diary, pp. 8, 9, USAMHI; Christ, *"Over,"* pp. 3, 21, 23, 35, 40; Ladd and Ladd, eds., *BP*, 3, p. 1390; Winschel, "Posey's Brigade," pp. 96, 98, 99.

25. Poriss and Poriss, *While My Country*, pp. 71, 77; *OR*, 27, 1, p. 470; Winschel, "Posey's Brigade," p. 99; *Final Report*, p. 113; Haines, *History*, p. 39.

26. Haines, *History*, p. 39; Christ, *"Over,"* pp. 4, 5; H. S. Stevens, *Souvenir,* p. 18.
27. Haines, *History*, pp. 39, 40; *Final Report*, pp. 111, 113; *OR*, 27, 1, p. 470; Poriss and Poriss, *While My Country*, p. 77; Richard Thompson–My dear Sister Em & Bill, July 4, 1863, 12th New Jersey Infantry File, GNMP.
28. *Final Report*, pp. 113, 114, 116; *OR*, 27, 1, p. 470; Bandy and Freeland, eds., *Gettysburg Papers*, 2, pp. 957, 958; Richard Thompson–My dear Sister Em & Bill, July 4, 1863, 12th New Jersey Infantry File, GNMP; Christ, *"Over,"* pp. 58–62; Winschel, "Posey's Brigade," p. 99.
29. *OR*, 27, 1, p. 467; H. S. Stevens, *Souvenir,* pp. 17, 18; Ladd and Ladd, eds., *BP*, 3, pp. 397, 399; Loren H. Goodrich–Friends, July 17, 1863, Goodrich Papers, CTHS.
30. Winschel, "Posey's Brigade," p. 99; Loren H. Goodrich–Friends, July 17, 1863, Goodrich Papers, CTHS; H. S. Stevens, *Souvenir,* pp. 18, 19; Christ, *"Over,"* pp. 69–72.
31. *OR*, 27, 1, p. 467; Testament of Lieutenant Wilbur D. Fiske, October 7, 1870, Silbey Collection, NA; Ladd and Ladd, eds., *BP*, 3, p. 2007.
32. *OR*, 27, 1, p. 467; Ladd and Ladd, eds., *BP*, 3, p. 2007; Christ, *"Over,"* pp. 72–73.
33. *OR*, 27, 1, p. 467; Carmichael, *Lee's Young Artillerist*, p. 103; "The Gettysburg Campaign," p. 9, Alexander Papers, UNC.
34. *OR*, 27, 1, p. 467; Ladd and Ladd, eds., *BP*, 1, p. 399; H. S. Stevens, *Souvenir,* pp. 19–20; Christ, *"Over,"* pp. 74–75.
35. Ladd and Ladd, eds., *BP*, 2, pp. 1179, 1180, 1188; G. T. Fleming, ed., *Life of Hays*, p. 431; Christ, *"Over,"* pp. 74, 75.
36. H. S. Stevens, *Souvenir,* p. 20; Ladd and Ladd, eds., *BP*, 2, p. 1180; 3, pp. 2007, 2008; Christ, *"Over,"* pp. 75–76.
37. Ladd and Ladd, eds., *BP*, 3, p. 2008; H. S. Stevens, *Souvenir,* p. 21; G. T. Fleming, ed., *Life of Hays*, p. 432; Testament of Wilbur D. Fiske, October 7, 1870, Silbey Collection, NA.
38. Testament of Wilbur D. Fiske, October 7, 1870, Silbey Collection, NA; Bliss Farm Buildings File, GNMP; Christ, *"Over,"* pp. 76, 118–21.
39. "Weather Conditions During the Battle of Gettysburg," Kauffman Collection, USAMHI; Bandy and Freeland, eds., *Gettysburg Papers*, 2, p. 947; Elmore, "Torrid Heat," pp. 14, 19, 20; Elliott Diary, USAMHI; William Clark, *History*, p. 142; Baird, "Reminiscences," p. 33, UM; Appleton et al., *History*, p. 660; Diary, Fry Papers, USAMHI.
40. Byrne and Weaver, *Haskell*, p. 144; Buell, *Cannoneer,* p. 92; Carmichael, *Lee's Young Artillerist*, p. 103.
41. Galwey, *Valiant Hours*, pp. 112, 113; undated newspaper clipping, 1st New York Artillery, Battery B File, GNMP; Coffin, *Nine Months*, p. 215; Sturtevant, *Pictorial History*, p. 289.

42. Ladd and Ladd, eds., *BP*, 2, p. 963; Diary of Lieutenant William H. Crennell, 140th New York Infantry File, GNMP.

43. Hagerty, *Collis' Zouaves*, pp. 245, 246; *Philadelphia Press*, July 4, 1888; Cavada Diary, HSP; William B. Baker–Parents, July 5, 1863, W. B. Baker Papers, UNC.

44. Shultz, *"Double Canister,"* pp. 7, 18, 19, 20.

45. Schaff, "The Gettysburg Week," p. 21; Logbook of Gouverneur Warren, Warren Papers, NYSL; "Civil War Union Soldier's 1863 Diary," USAMHI; J. W. Sebritz–My Dear Aunt, July 3, 1863, Lindsay Papers, UNC.

46. "E. P. Alexander," p. 23.

47. Ibid., p. 23; Gallagher, ed., *Fighting For,* p. 254; Ladd and Ladd, eds., *BP*, 1, p. 485; Gallagher, ed., *Lee,* pp. 440–42.

48. Wert, *General James Longstreet,* pp. 288–89; "E. P. Alexander," p. 24.

49. Gallagher, ed., *Lee,* pp. 441, 442; Wert, *General James Longstreet,* p. 288; Ladd and Ladd, eds., *BP*, 1, p. 486.

50. Gallagher, ed., *Lee,* p. 442; Ladd and Ladd, eds., *BP*, 1, p. 486; Gallagher, ed., *Fighting For,* p. 255.

51. *OR*, 27, 2, p. 733; Longstreet, *From Manassas to Appomattox,* pp. 390, 391.

52. Kross, "July 3rd Action," p. 57; Owen, *In Camp,* pp. 248, 249, 250; Jacobs, *Notes,* p. 35; *Philadelphia North American,* June 29, 1913; Fortesque Diary, WLM; Memoir Washington Artillery, MC; Blackford, ed., *Letters,* p. 187.

9. "The Air Seethed"

1. Wise, *Long Arm,* p. 677; *Sumter Herald,* April 29, 1902; Rollins, ed., *Pickett's Charge,* p. xxi; Elmore, "Grand Cannonade," pp. 110–11; Wert, *General James Longstreet,* p. 289.

2. *OR*, 27, 2, pp. 388, 610; Rollins, *"Damned Red Flags,"* pp. 150, 151.

3. Rozier, ed., *Granite Farm Letters,* p. 125; William Calder–My Dearest Mother, July 8, 1863, Calder Papers, UNC; Fleming Thompson–Sister & Mother, July 17, 1863, Thompson Papers, UT; B. R. Kinney–W. H. Badgett, July 18, 1863, 14th North Carolina Infantry File, GNMP.

4. Bee, *Boys,* p. 149; Wright, "Story," pp. 608, 609, GNMP.

5. O'Connell Memoir, p. 57, USAMHI; Hartwig, "It Struck Horror," p. 95; Albert Stokes Emmell, " 'Now Is the Time for Buck & Ball': The Life & Civil War Experience of Albert Stokes Emmell," 12th New Jersey Infantry File, GNMP; William P. Oberlin–Annie, July 10, 1863, Oberlin Civil War Letters, USAMHI.

6. Silliker, ed., *Rebel Yell,* p. 103; McLean and McLean, eds., *Gettysburg Sources,* 1, p. 76; William Danforth–My dear Wife, July 4, 1863, Danforth Papers, MNHS; Josiah C. Fuller–My own dear wife, July 4, 1863, Fuller Letters, PML; Alfred P. Carpenter–[?], July 30, 1863, Carpenter Papers, MNHS; Francis Heath–John B.

Bachelder, October 12, 1889, 19th Maine Infantry File, GNMP; Alexander S. Webb–Father, July 17, 1863, Webb Papers, YU.

7. G. T. Fleming, ed., *Life of Hays,* p. 442; Washburn, *Complete Military History,* pp. 50, 52; Archer, "Remembering," p. 74; Ladd and Ladd, eds., *BP,* 2, pp. 1069, 1070.

8. G. T. Fleming, ed., *Life of Hays,* p. 442; Washburn, *Complete Military History,* p. 50; *OR,* 27, 1, p. 465.

9. Campbell, " 'Remember Harper's Ferry!,' " pp. 103, 104.

10. Washburn, *Complete Military History,* p. 52; Ladd and Ladd, eds., *BP,* 2, p. 1068.

11. *OR,* 27, 1, p. 476; *New York at Gettysburg,* 2, p. 801; Ladd and Ladd, eds., *BP,* 3, pp. 1743, 1754, 1759; S. B. McIntyre–C. D. MacDougall, June 27, 1890, 111th New York Infantry File, GNMP.

12. Alexander Hays–A. G. Curtin, April 15, 1864, Records Group 79, NA.

13. Ladd and Ladd, eds., *BP,* 2, pp. 1068–69.

14. G. T. Fleming, ed., *Life of Hays,* pp. 451, 452.

15. R. Penn Smith–Isaac J. Wistar, July 29, 1863, Wistar Papers, GNMP; Byrne and Weaver, *Haskell,* pp. 151, 152; Ladd and Ladd, eds., *BP,* 1, p. 18.

16. F. E. Heath, "Account of the 19th Maine at Gettysburg," Records of the Adjutant General, MSA; Waitt, ed., *History,* p. 237; *Minneapolis State Atlas,* August 26, 1863; Moe, *Last Full Measure,* p. 285.

17. "Sketches from . . . Gettysburg—The Third Day," pp. 1–3, Gibbon Papers, HSP.

18. Byrne and Weaver, *Haskell,* p. 155.

19. Gibbon, *Personal Recollections,* pp. 147–50; McLean and McLean, eds., *Gettysburg Sources,* 2, p. 136; Moe, *Last Full Measure,* p. 284.

20. *OR,* 27, 1, p. 352; Blinn Civil War Diary, UVT; Ladd and Ladd, eds., *BP,* 1, pp. 59, 60; Coffin, *Nine Months,* pp. 218, 219.

21. Hubler, "Narrative," p. 13, USAMHI; Chamberlin, *History,* p. 151; Jacob Slagle–Brother, September 13, 1863, Slagle Letters, PML.

22. *OR,* 27, 2, pp. 456, 603; *New York at Gettysburg,* 3, p. 1247; Crumb, ed., *Eleventh Corps Artillery,* pp. 32, 34.

23. *OR,* 27, 1, p. 706; Crumb, ed., *Eleventh Corps Artillery,* pp. 31, 32, 34, 72; G. A. Turner, ed., *Civil War Letters,* p. 126; Carl Schurz–Frank Moore, June 6, 1865, Schurz Letter, PU; Diary of Lieutenant Augustus Horstmann, 45th New York Infantry File, GNMP; James S. Jones–Sister Cad, September 15, 1863, Jones Letter, USAMHI.

24. Crumb, ed., *Eleventh Corps Artillery,* p. 31; Diary of Lieutenant Augustus Horstmann, 45th New York Infantry File, GNMP; *OR,* 27, 1, pp. 305, 308; Nevins, ed., *Diary,* p. 249.

25. Nevins, ed., *Diary,* p. 249; Crumb, ed., *Eleventh Corps Artillery,* p. 36; Benedict, *Vermont in the Civil War,* 2, p. 466; Galwey, *Valiant Hours,* p. 113; Stevens and Knowlton, *Address,* p. 21.

26. Walker, *History,* p. 292; Patrick Diary, LC; Whitehouse and Whitehouse, "Daily Register," UM.

27. *OR,* 27, 1, p. 597; Hage, "Battle of Gettysburg," p. 256; Tallman Memoirs, p. 59, USAMHI; Marvin Diary, MNHS; Bandy and Freeland, eds., *Gettysburg Papers,* 1, pp. 282, 283.

28. Rhodes, ed., *All for the Union,* p. 116; Whitmore Diary, MHS; John Brislin–My Dear Friend, September 2, 1863, Brislin Letters, USAMHI; Diary, Furst Papers, USAMHI.

29. Paine Diary, NYHS; James C. Biddle–My own darling Wife, July 8, 1863, Biddle Civil War Letters, HSP; Gallagher, ed., *Three Days,* p. 238.

30. George G. Meade–John B. Bachelder, December 4, 1869, Rothermel Papers, PHMC; Agassiz, ed., *Meade's Headquarters,* p. 13.

31. George G. Meade–John B. Bachelder, December 4, 1869, Rothermel Papers, PHMC; James C. Biddle–My own darling Wife, July 8, 1863, Biddle Civil War Letters, HSP; Ladd and Ladd, eds., *BP,* 2, pp. 852, 857; Paul A. Oliver–Sam Oliver, July 8, 1863, Oliver Collection, PU.

32. George G. Meade–John B. Bachelder, December 4, 1869, Rothermel Papers, PHMC; Crumb, ed., *Eleventh Corps Artillery,* p. 37.

33. *OR,* 27, 1, p. 480; Ladd and Ladd, eds., *BP,* 1, pp. 229, 430; 3, p. 1360; Wafer Diary, QU.

34. *OR,* 27, 1, pp. 272, 480; Ladd and Ladd, eds., *BP,* 1, p. 229.

35. *OR,* 27, 1, pp. 372, 373; Ladd and Ladd, eds., *BP,* 1, p. 229.

36. Ladd and Ladd, eds., *BP,* 1, p. 229; *OR,* 27, 1, p. 480.

37. *Marietta Sunday Observer,* August 11, 1918; Eldridge B. Platt–Father and Mother Brothers and Sisters, July 17, 1863, Platt Papers, UNC; Byrne and Weaver, *Haskell,* p. 150; Walker, *History,* p. 293.

38. Crumb, ed., *Eleventh Corps Artillery,* p. 34; *OR,* 27, 1, pp. 894, 895; Goldsborough, *Maryland Line,* p. 324; C. B. Brockway–D. McConaughy, March 5, 1864, Rothermel Papers, PHMC; "The Gettysburg Campaign," p. 9, Alexander Papers, UNC; E. P. Alexander–H. J. Hunt, June 27, 1879, Hunt Papers, LC.

39. Daniel Memoir, p. 16, VHS; O'Farrell Diary, MC; Carmichael, "Never Heard Before," p. 110.

40. Bingham, "Memoirs of Hancock," WRHS; *OR,* 27, 1, p. 888; Ladd and Ladd, eds., *BP,* 3, p. 1798; Patrick Hart–Henry J. Hunt, July 7, 15, 1879, Hunt Papers, LC.

41. *OR,* 27, 1, pp. 885, 888, 898; Ladd and Ladd, eds., *BP,* 1, p. 170; 3, p. 1798; Appleton et al., *History,* p. 652; Patrick Hart–Henry J. Hunt, July 7, 15, 1879; J. E. Spear–Henry J. Hunt, July 18, 1879; John Bigelow–H. J. Hunt, November 4, 1875, all in Hunt Papers, LC.

42. Ladd and Ladd, eds., *BP,* 1, pp. 229, 230, 428, 429, 430, 444; Nevins, ed., *Diary,* p. 252; John Gibbon–Henry J. Hunt, May 31, 1879, Hunt Papers, LC.

43. Ladd and Ladd, eds., *BP,* 1, pp. 229, 230, 428, 429, 430; John Gibbon–Henry J.

Hunt, May 31, 1879, Hunt Papers, LC; Coddington, *Gettysburg Campaign*, p. 481.

44. O'Connell, Memoir, p. 57, USAMHI; Vest Diary, MC; R. K. Krick, *Parker's Virginia Battery*, p. 182; Henry Clare–My dear William, July 5, 1863, Clare Letters, GC.

45. J. H. Rhodes, *History*, pp. 202, 203, 204, 207, 209; *OR*, 27, 1, p. 443; Adams, *Reminiscences*, p. 70.

46. *OR*, 27, 1, pp. 432, 480; *Gettysburg Compiler*, June 7, 1887; *Buffalo Evening News*, May 29, 1894.

47. *OR*, 27, 1, p. 480; *New York at Gettysburg*, 3, p. 1180; Nevins, ed., *Diary*, p. 252.

48. R. G. Scott, ed., *Fallen Leaves*, p. 184n.

49. *OR*, 27, 2, pp. 435, 678; *Sumter Herald*, April 29, 1902; Account of Joseph L. Thompson, n.d.; Account of John Holmes Smith, July 4, 5, 1904; W.H.H. Winston–John W. Daniel, June 10, 1905, all in Daniel Papers, UVA.

50. Carmichael, *Lee's Young Artillerist*, pp. 103, 104; *OR*, 27, 2, pp. 352, 379, 381, 382, 384, 604; Robert W. Stribling–My dear Major, March 7, 1904, Daniel Papers, UVA; Henry C. Cabell, "A Visit to the Battle-field of Gettysburg, 1887," p. 7, Cabell Family Papers, VHS; Walter Clark, ed., *Histories*, 1, p. 544.

51. John H. Lewis, "Recollections from 1860 to 1865," 9th Virginia Infantry File, GNMP.

52. Colston, "Campaign of Gettysburg," UNC; Durkin, ed., *John Dooley*, p. 103.

53. Rollins, ed., *Pickett's Charge*, pp. 91, 92; Wallace, *3rd Virginia Infantry*, pp. 37, 98; Report of Colonel Joseph Mayo, July 26, 1863, Pickett Papers, DU; W. H. Stewart, *Pair of Blankets*, p. 100.

54. Walthall, "Reminiscences," USAMHI; Account of J. Risque Hutter, n.d.; Account of John Holmes Smith, July 4, 5, 1904; W.H.H. Winston–John W. Daniel, June 10, 1905, all in Daniel Papers, UVA; Johnston, *Story*, p. 207.

55. Edmund Berkeley–John W. Daniel, September 26, [?], Daniel Papers, UVA; Shotwell, "Virginia and North Carolina," p. 89; Divine, *8th Virginia Infantry*, p. 22; *OR*, 27, 2, p. 385; Coco, *Wasted Valor*, p. 116; *SOR*, 5, p. 308.

56. James Hodges Walker, "The Charge of Picketts Division by a Participant," 9th Virginia Infantry File, GNMP; Lewis, *Recollections*, p. 78; B. L. Farinholt–John W. Daniel, April 15, 1905; Erasmus Williams, "14th Virginia Infantry at Gettysburg," both in Daniel Papers, UVA; Armistead Ledger, MC; Powell and Clement, eds., *War Recollections*, p. 43; W. H. Stewart, *Pair of Blankets*, p. 101.

57. L. J. Wilson, *Confederate Soldier*, p. 120; George W. Whiting–Editor, March 18, 1867, Paris Papers, UNC; Ladd and Ladd, eds., *BP*, 1, p. 518; William H. Winn–My dear Sister, July 8, 1863, Winn Papers, DU; Peel Diary, MDAH.

58. Rollins, *"Damned Red Flags,"* pp. 145, 146.

59. Ibid., p. 146; Priest, *Into the Fight*, p. 72.

60. Mosely Diary, USAMHI; Diary of John Shipp, Shipp Family Papers, VHS; Cock-

rell and Ballard, eds., *Mississippi Rebel,* pp. 196, 197; Diary of George Washington Hall, 14th Georgia Infantry File, GNMP; Todd, Reminiscences, p. 131, UNC; Houghton and Houghton, *Two Boys,* p. 34; Lightsey, *Veteran's Story,* p. 36; Memoir, Bernard Papers, UNC; Raymond J. Reid–Hal, September 4, 1863, Reid Papers, SAHS; David Ballenger–My dear Nancy, July 8, 1863, Ballenger Papers, USC; John B. Crawford–Wife, July 8, 1863, Crawford Civil War Letters, MDAH.

61. Account of John Holmes Smith, n.d., Daniel Papers, UVA; *Buffalo Evening News,* May 29, 1894; Dawson, *Reminiscences,* p. 95; James Kemper–E. P. Alexander, September 20, 1869, Dearborn Collection, HU.

62. James Kemper–E. P. Alexander, September 20, 1869, Dearborn Collection, HU.

63. Ladd and Ladd, eds., BP, 1, p. 484; 3, pp. 1360–61; Priest, *Into the Fight,* has a list of seventy-nine officers and men who wrote about the cannonade's length of time. Priest concludes that it lasted about an hour (pp. 194–98). See also James Dearing–My darling Mother, July 26, 1863, Dearing Family Papers, UVA; *OR,* 27, 2, pp. 388, 389, 610; 3, p. 500.

64. Appleton et al., *History,* p. 652; *B&L,* 3, pp. 373–74; *OR,* 27, 1, p. 480; Byrne and Weaver, *Haskell,* p. 156; Rollins, "Failure . . . Pickett's Charge," p. 40.

65. *OR,* 27, 1, pp. 239, 480; Byrne and Weaver, *Haskell,* p. 156; Rollins, "Failure . . . Pickett's Charge," p. 40; Shultz, *"Double Canister,"* pp. 32, 33.

66. Rollins, "Failure . . . Pickett's Charge," p. 40; Shultz, *"Double Canister,"* p. 25.

67. Rollins, "Failure . . . Pickett's Charge," p. 40; Shultz, *"Double Canister,"* p. 25.

68. Rollins, "Failure . . . Pickett's Charge," pp. 26, 29, 30, 35; Frederick Fuger, "Personal Recollections Battle of Gettysburg," p. 19, Webb Papers, YU; "The Gettysburg Campaign," p. 9, Alexander Papers, UNC; Wise, *Long Arm,* pp. 665–68; Louis G. Young–William J. Baker, February 10, 1864, Winston Papers, NCDAH.

69. Coddington, *Gettysburg Campaign,* pp. 498, 499; Rollins, "Failure . . . Pickett's Charge," p. 26.

70. *OR,* 27, 1, p. 239; Ladd and Ladd, eds., *BP,* 1, p. 430.

71. Crumb, ed., *Eleventh Corps Artillery,* pp. 36, 37, 39, 40; Ladd and Ladd, eds., *BP,* 1, p. 430; *OR,* 27, 1, p. 239; Rollins, "George Gordon Meade," pp. 79–80.

72. *OR,* 27, 1, p. 239; Ladd and Ladd, eds., *BP,* 1, p. 430; Shultz, *"Double Canister,"* pp. 32–35.

73. *OR,* 27, 1, p. 239; Ladd and Ladd, eds., *BP,* 1, pp. 431, 445; Shultz, *"Double Canister,"* pp. 44, 46, 53.

74. *OR,* 27, 1, pp. 239, 893; Ladd and Ladd, eds., *BP,* 1, p. 622; Shultz, *"Double Canister,"* pp. 30–31.

75. *OR,* 27, 1, p. 239; Ladd and Ladd, eds., *BP,* 1, p. 441; Griffith, *Battle Tactics,* p. 168.

76. Boggs, ed., *Alexander Letters,* p. 250; Ladd and Ladd, eds., *BP,* 1, p. 489.

77. Ladd and Ladd, eds., *BP,* 1, pp. 486–88.

78. Ibid., p. 489; "E. P. Alexander," p. 24; Boggs, ed., *Alexander Letters,* p. 250.

79. Ladd and Ladd, eds., *BP*, 1, p. 489; Boggs, ed., *Alexander Letters*, p. 250; Gallagher, ed., *Fighting For*, pp. 258–59; Alexander, *Military Memoirs*, p. 423; "E. P. Alexander," p. 24.

80. Thomas R. Friend–Charles Pickett, December 10, 1904, Pickett Papers, VHS.

10. "Like Feathers"

1. *B&L*, 3, p. 345; *Annals*, p. 431; George E. Pickett–[Sallie Corbell], July 9, 1863, Brake Collection, USAMHI; *New York Times*, May 1, 1893; Sorrel, *Recollections*, p. 162; Gallagher, ed., *Fighting For*, p. 260.

2. Longstreet, *From Manassas to Appomattox*, p. 392; Magner, *Traveller*, p. 46; *OR*, 27, 2, p. 360; Haskell, *Haskell Memoirs*, p. 50; conversation based on account of Alexander in Gallagher, ed., *Fighting For*, p. 261; Ladd and Ladd, eds., *BP*, 1, pp. 489, 490.

3. Rawley W. Martin–Sylvester Chamberlin, August 11, 1897; B. L. Farinholt–John W. Daniel, April 15, 1905, both in Daniel Papers, UVA; Shultz and Rollins, "Measuring Pickett's Charge," p. 117; Coddington, *Gettysburg Campaign*, p. 252; D. S. Thomas, *Ready . . . Aim . . . Fire!*, p. 36.

4. Edmund Berkeley–John W. Daniel, September 26, [?], Daniel Papers, UVA; *Baltimore Sun*, December 28, 1903; V. A. Topscott–Robert A. Bright, January 7, 1904, Southall Papers, WM.

5. Rollins, ed., *Pickett's Charge*, pp. 53, 54; Rawley W. Martin–Sylvester Chamberlin, August 11, 1897, Daniel Papers, UVA.

6. Report of Colonel Joseph Mayo, July 26, 1863, Pickett Papers, DU; Georg and Busey, *Nothing but Glory*, p. 27; James L. Kemper–A. D. Pollock, January 12, 1865, Janney-Pollock Family Papers, UVA; James L. Kemper–W. H. Swallow, February 4, 1886, Bachelder Papers, NHHS.

7. Account of J. Risque Hutter, n.d., Daniel Papers, UVA; Durkin, ed., *John Dooley*, p. 105.

8. *OR*, 27, 2, p. 386; Georg and Busey, *Nothing but Glory*, pp. 31–33; *CV*, 38, p. 175; Berkeley, "War Reminiscences," p. 40, MNBP; Edmund Berkeley–John W. Daniel, September 26, [?], Daniel Papers, UVA; William H. Taylor, "Some Experiences," p. 119.

9. Rollins, *"Damned Red Flags,"* p. 154; J.S.D. Cullen–My Dear Lottie, July 8, 1863, Carrington Family Papers, VHS.

10. Powell and Clement, eds., *War Recollections*, p. 49; *Philadelphia Press*, July 4, 1887; Lewis, *Recollections*, p. 79; *CV*, 2, p. 271; Dawson, *Reminiscences*, p. 96; Georg and Busey, *Nothing but Glory*, pp. 35, 85.

11. Rawley W. Martin–Sylvester Chamberlain, August 11, 1904; Account of F. M. Bailey, n.d., both in Daniel Papers, UVA; Rawley W. Martin–Robert A. Bright,

January 25, 1904, Southall Papers, WM; Lewis, *Recollections,* p. 79; Dawson, *Reminiscences,* p. 96.

12. Peel Diary, p. 28, MDAH; Lane, "Lane's N. Carolina Brigade," p. 9, USAMHI; Longstreet, *From Manassas to Appomattox,* pp. 392, 393.

13. Trinque, "Confederate Battle Flags," p. 110; Winschel, "Heavy Was Their Loss," p. 79; Rollins, *"Damned Red Flags,"* p. 179; Ladd and Ladd, eds., *BP,* 1, p. 518; Map of Pickett's Charge, July 3rd: Longstreet's Assault File, #1, GNMP.

14. Rollins, *"Damned Red Flags,"* pp. 182, 184; M. M. Brown, *University Greys,* p. 44; Map of Pickett's Charge, July 3rd: Longstreet's Assault File, #1, GNMP; Peel Diary, p. 28, MDAH.

15. Rollins, *"Damned Red Flags,"* p. 184; W. S. Christian–John W. Daniel, n.d., Daniel Papers, UVA; Brooks, "22nd Battalion Virginia Infantry," p. 11, MC.

16. W. S. Christian–John W. Daniel, n.d., Daniel Papers, UVA; Report of R. M. Mayo, August 13, 1863, Heth Collection, MC; R.E.L. Krick, *40th Virginia Infantry,* p. 30; Brooks, "22nd Battalion Virginia Infantry," p. 11, MC.

17. Rollins, *"Damned Red Flags,"* p. 185; William G. Morris–W. Saunders, October 1, 1877, Morris Papers, UNC; Map of Pickett's Charge, July 3rd: Longstreet's Assault File, #1, GNMP.

18. *OR,* 27, 2, p. 386; Georg and Busey, *Nothing but Glory,* p. 207; Loehr, *War History,* p. 36; Shotwell, "Virginia and North Carolina," p. 91; O. W. Barrow, "Sketch of Henry Guards," Maury Papers, DU; Account of F. M. Bailey, n.d.; Rawley W. Martin–Sylvester Chamberlain, August 11, 1897, both in Daniel Papers, UVA; "Weather Conditions During the Battle of Gettysburg," Kauffman Collection, USAMHI; Elmore, "Torrid Heat," p. 20; *Atlanta Journal,* December 7, 1901; Powell and Clement, eds., *War Recollections,* p. 40; Lewis, *Recollections,* p. 79.

19. *OR,* 27, 2, p. 386; Elmore, "Torrid Heat," pp. 14, 15; James Hodges Walker, "The Charge of Pickett's Division by a Participant," 9th Virginia Infantry File, GNMP; Walter Clark, ed., *Histories,* 3, p. 91; Georg and Busey, *Nothing but Glory,* p. 206; Rollins, ed., *Pickett's Charge,* p. 85; Riggs, *7th Virginia Infantry,* p. 25.

20. Byrne and Weaver, *Haskell,* pp. 114, 115; Agassiz, ed., *Meade's Headquarters,* p. 100.

21. *Augusta Daily Constitutionalist,* July 23, 1863; M. W. Taylor, "Ramseur's Brigade," p. 37; David Champion, "Reminiscences," 14th Georgia Infantry File, GNMP; William Calder–My Dearest Mother, July 8, 1863, Calder Papers, UNC.

22. Report of Colonel Joseph Mayo, July 26, 1863, Pickett Papers, DU; Compton, "Reminiscences," p. 15, USAMHI; Thomas R. Friend–Charles Pickett, December 10, 1894, Pickett Papers, VHS; Report of Captain W. W. Bentley, July 9, 1863, 24th Virginia Infantry File, GNMP; Ladd and Ladd, eds., *BP,* 2, p. 1191; James L. Kemper–A. D. Pollock, January 12, 1865, Janney-Pollock Family Papers, UVA.

23. Henry C. Cabell, "A Visit to the Battle-field of Gettysburg," p. 8, Cabell Family Papers, VHS; W. S. Christian–John W. Daniel, October 24, 1903, Daniel Papers,

UVA; Ladd and Ladd, eds., *BP*, 2, p. 933; Christ, *"Over,"* p. 79; Imhof, *Gettysburg*, p. 163.

24. Shultz and Rollins, "Measuring Pickett's Charge," pp. 114, 116, 117; Georg and Busey, *Nothing but Glory*, p. 206; Imhof, *Gettysburg*, p. 5; Winschel, "Posey's Brigade," p. 96.

25. Coffin, *Nine Months*, p. 221; Wright, "Story," p. 610, GNMP; Ladd and Ladd, eds., *BP*, 3, p. 1409; Ford, *Story*, p. 276.

26. Loren H. Goodrich–Friends, July 17, 1863, Goodrich Papers, CTHS; Winschel, "Heavy Was Their Loss," p. 81; Mahood, *"Written In Blood,"* p. 145; Haines, *History*, p. 42.

27. Bee, *Boys*, p. 149; *OR*, 27, 1, p. 431.

28. Tully McCrae, "Reminiscences About Gettysburg," 1st U.S. Artillery, Battery I File, GNMP; *Reunions*, p. 12; R. G. Scott, ed., *Fallen Leaves*, p. 188; Nathan Hayward–Father, July 8, 1863, Hayward Papers, MHS; Osborn, "Reminiscence," p. 4, GC.

29. Osborn, "Reminiscence," p. 4, GC; H. S. Stevens, *Souvenir*, pp. 27, 29; Archer, "Remembering," p. 75; Bandy and Freeland, eds., *Gettysburg Papers*, 2, p. 963; Seville, *History*, pp. 81, 82; J. B. Hardenburgh–T. B. Gates, October 9, 1878, Gates Papers, NYHS; Byrne and Weaver, *Haskell*, p. 159.

30. *OR*, 27, 1, p. 473; Belknap Diary, USAMHI; G. R. Stewart, *Pickett's Charge*, p. 166; Map of Pickett's Charge, July 3rd: Longstreet's Assault File, #1, GNMP; Mahood, *"Written In Blood,"* pp. 144, 153; G. T. Fleming, ed., *Life of Hays*, p. 439.

31. Stevens and Knowlton, *Address*, p. 22; Haines, *History*, p. 41; Bandy and Freeland, eds., *Gettysburg Papers*, 2, p. 906; G. T. Fleming, ed., *Life of Hays*, p. 439; *OR*, 27, 1, p. 466.

32. "Sketches from . . . : Gettysburg—The Third Day," pp. 4–5, Gibbon Papers, HSP; Magner, *Traveller*, p. 46; John Gibbon–My Dear Hunt, September 6, 1884, Gibbon Letters, PML; *OR*, 27, 1, p. 417; Gibbon, *Personal Recollections*, pp. 150, 151; Byrne and Weaver, *Haskell*, p. 160.

33. Byrne and Weaver, *Haskell*, p. 159; Stevens and Knowlton, *Address*, p. 22; Gibbon, *Personal Recollections*, p. 151.

34. *OR*, 27, 1, p. 428; *Gettysburg Compiler*, June 7, 1887; Frederick Fuger, "Personal Recollections Battle of Gettysburg," pp. 17, 18, Webb Papers, YU; *Buffalo Evening News*, May 29, 1894; Lash, "Philadelphia Brigade," p. 104; Rollins, ed., *Pickett's Charge*, p. 311.

35. Hartwig, "It Struck Horror," pp. 96, 97.

36. *OR*, 27, 1, pp. 428, 690; Ladd and Ladd, eds., *BP*, 1, p. 281; *Webb*, p. 65; *New York Herald*, July 2, 1911; Andrew Cowan–Alexander S. Webb, November 6, 1885, Webb Papers, YU; War Department, "Record," 6, p. 22, LC.

37. *OR*, 27, 1, p. 690; Ladd and Ladd, eds., *BP*, 1, pp. 281, 282; 2, pp. 1146, 1148;

Webb, p. 65; *New York Herald,* July 2, 1911; Andrew Cowan–Alexander S. Webb, November 6, 1885, Webb Papers, YU; War Department, "Record," 6, p. 22, LC.

38. *OR,* 27, 1, pp. 239, 753, 879, 880; Gallagher, ed., *Fighting For,* p. 262; Ladd and Ladd, eds., *BP,* 2, p. 1126; Gallagher, ed., *Three Days,* pp. 298, 303; Shultz, "Double Canister," pp. 35, 36, 44–47, 50, 51, 53; Rollins, "Failure . . . Pickett's Charge," p. 40.

39. *OR,* 27, 1, pp. 885, 893, 898, 900, 901; Peel Diary, p. 29, MDAH; Crumb, ed., *Eleventh Corps Artillery,* p. 40.

40. *Southern Bivouac,* 4, p. 567; Crumb, ed., *Eleventh Corps Artillery,* p. 40; *Pennsylvania at Gettysburg,* 2, p. 911.

41. Crumb, ed., *Eleventh Corps Artillery,* p. 42; Gallagher, ed., *Three Days,* p. 298; Peel Diary, p. 29, MDAH.

42. *OR,* 27, 1, pp. 884, 885, 893, 898, 901; J. E. Spear–Henry J. Hunt, July 18, 1879, Hunt Papers, LC; M. W. Taylor, "Ramseur's Brigade," p. 37; Crews and Parrish, *14th Virginia Infantry,* p. 40; Shultz, "Double Canister," p. 42; Coco, *Concise Guide,* p. 71.

43. Compton, "Reminiscences," p. 13, USAMHI; Durkin, ed., *John Dooley,* p. 105; Benjamin B. Humphreys–Lafayette McLaws, January 6, 1878, McLaws Papers, UNC.

44. V. F. Jordan, ed., *Captain Remembers,* p. 85; W.H.H. Winston–John W. Daniel, June 10, 1905; Account of John Holmes Smith, July 4, 5, 1904, both in Daniel Papers, UVA; Rollins, "Damned Red Flags," pp. 152, 155, 160.

45. R. A. Bright–Charles Pickett, October 15, 1892, Pickett Papers, VHS; Durkin, ed., *John Dooley,* p. 109; Coco, *Wasted Valor,* pp. 127, 128.

46. Gallagher, ed., *Fighting For,* p. 262.

47. Account of John Holmes Smith, July 4, 5, 1904, Daniel Papers, UVA; Report of Colonel Joseph Mayo, July 26, 1863, Pickett Papers, DU; Rollins, ed., *Pickett's Charge,* pp. 163, 164; Ladd and Ladd, eds., *BP,* 2, p. 984; James L. Kemper–E. P. Alexander, September 20, 1869, Dearborn Collection, HU.

48. *OR,* 27, 2, p. 386; *Buffalo Evening News,* May 29, 1894; Young and Young, *56th Virginia Infantry,* p. 179; H. C. Michie–John W. Daniel, January 27, 1904, Daniel Papers, UVA.

49. Rollins, "Damned Red Flags," p. 155.

50. Powell and Clement, eds., *War Recollections,* p. 43; W. B. Robertson–Mattie, July 28, 1863; F. M. Bailey–John W. Daniel, December 22, 1904, both in Daniel Papers, UVA.

51. John C. Timberlake–Editors, *Richmond Dispatch,* Draft #1 [1887], Timberlake Letter, VHS; George E. Pickett–Samuel Cooper, August 11, 1863, 53rd Virginia Infantry File, GNMP; *Philadelphia Press,* July 4, 1887; Rawley W. Martin–Sylvester Chamberlain, August 11, 1907, Daniel Papers, UVA; Rollins, "Damned Red Flags," pp. 174, 175.

52. Crews and Parrish, *14th Virginia Infantry*, p. 39.

53. Report of Major Joseph R. Cabell, July 11, 1863, Armistead Ledger, MC; James J. Phillips–F. H. Smith, July 18, 1863, 9th Virginia Infantry File, GNMP.

54. *OR*, 27, 2, p. 651; McLean and McLean, eds., *Gettysburg Sources*, 1, p. 141; *SOR*, 5, p. 409; George M. Whiting–Editor, March 18, 1867, Paris Papers, UNC.

55. *SOR*, 5, p. 168; *OR*, 27, 2, pp. 360, 647; Brooks, "22nd Battalion Virginia Infantry," p. 13, MC; Rollins, *"Damned Red Flags,"* p. 184; Shultz and Rollins, "Measuring Pickett's Charge," pp. 114, 116.

56. Busey and Martin, *Regimental Strengths*, p. 42; Ladd and Ladd, eds., *BP*, 1, pp. 625, 663; Galwey, *Valiant Hours*, pp. 115, 116; Sawyer, *Military History*, pp. 126, 129; Christ, *"Over,"* p. 79.

57. W. S. Christian–John W. Daniel, October 24, 1903, Daniel Papers, UVA; *SOR*, 5, p. 415; Diary of Thomas J. Luttrell, 40th Virginia Infantry File, GNMP; James H. Lane–Messrs. Editors, September 7, 1877, Grimes Papers, UNC; Brooks, "22nd Battalion Virginia Infantry," pp. 11, 13, MC; *Raleigh Observer*, November 29, 1877; Ladd and Ladd, eds., *BP*, 3, p. 1800; M. W. Taylor, "Ramseur's Brigade," p. 38.

58. Report of R. M. Mayo, August 13, 1863, Heth Collection, MC; *SOR*, 5, p. 415; W. S. Christian–John W. Daniel, October 24, 1903, Daniel Papers, UVA; Diary of Thomas J. Luttrell, 40th Virginia Infantry File, GNMP.

59. Armistead Ledger, MC; Rawley W. Martin–Sylvester Chamberlain, August 11, 1897, Daniel Papers, UVA; *OR*, 27, 1, pp. 706, 750; 2, pp. 647, 651; Walter Clark, ed., *Histories*, 5, p. 127; Crumb, ed., *Eleventh Corps Artillery*, p. 42.

60. Acker, *Inside*, pp. 309–10; Longacre, *To Gettysburg and Beyond*, p. 133; James E. Decker–Sister, July 6, 1863, Decker Letters, USAMHI; Gibbon, *Personal Recollections*, p. 179.

61. Account of John Holmes Smith, July 4, 5, 1904, Daniel Papers, UVA; Christopher Mead–Wife, July 6, 1863, Brake Collection, USAMHI; Hadden, "Granite Glory," p. 59; Wheelock G. Veazey–G. G. Benedict, July 11, 1864, Veazey Papers, VTHS; *Gettysburg Compiler*, June 7, 1887; Page, *History*, pp. 142, 150, 151.

62. Gallagher, ed., *Third Day*, p. 141.

11. Into the "Vortex of Death"

1. *OR*, 27, 1, pp. 417, 454, 465; *B&L*, 3, p. 388; Byrne and Weaver, *Haskell*, pp. 160, 161; Bee, *Boys*, p. 150.

2. *OR*, 27, 2, p. 647; Statement of Chaplain Henry S. Stevens, June 10, 1905, Stevens Papers, NCDAH; Page, *History*, p. 152; Metts, *Longstreet's Charge*, p. 4; Gregory, *38th Virginia Infantry*, p. 40; *SOR*, 5, p. 168.

3. Archer, "Remembering," p. 77; undated newspaper clipping, Robbins Papers, UNC; Lindsley, ed., *Military Annals of Tennessee*, p. 250.

4. W. P. Jesse–John W. Daniel, March 31, 1905, Daniel Papers, UVA; *Buffalo Evening News,* May 29, 1904; *OR,* 27, 1, p. 417; undated newspaper clipping, Robbins Papers, UNC; Long, "Confederate Prisoners," p. 107.
5. Ladd and Ladd, eds., *BP,* 2, p. 914; Lindsley, *Military Annals of Tennessee,* p. 250; Statement of Chaplain Henry S. Stevens, June 10, 1905, Stevens Papers, NCDAH.
6. *OR,* 27, 1, pp. 417, 454, 465; Griffith, *Battle Tactics,* p. 149; Christopher Mead–Wife, July 6, 1863, 12th New Jersey Infantry File, GNMP; David M. Smith–[Family], July 10, 1863, Smith Letters, PML.
7. Trinque, "Confederate Battle Flags," p. 116; Tully McCrae, "Reminiscences About Gettysburg, 3 March 1904," Brake Collection, USAMHI; Map of Pickett's Charge, July 3rd: Longstreet's Assault File, #1, GNMP; T. H. Smith, ed., "Story," p. 122.
8. Kross, "July 3rd Action," p. 57; Shultz and Rollins, "Measuring Pickett's Charge," p. 117; Map of Pickett's Charge, July 3rd: Longstreet's Assault File, #1, GNMP.
9. Benedict, *Short History,* p. 11; Ladd and Ladd, eds., *BP,* 1, pp. 49, 55, 56, 60; Francis Long–Wife, July 5, 1863, Picerno Collection; R. W. Douthat–John W. Daniel, January 14, 1905, Daniel Papers, UVA; *OR,* 27, 1, p. 1042; Coffin, *Nine Months,* pp. 227, 228.
10. *OR,* 27, 1, p. 884; Coffin, *Nine Months,* p. 228; *St. Paul Pioneer,* August 9, 1863; Shultz, *"Double Canister,"* p. 42; Menges Memoirs, p. 7, USAMHI; Sauers, ed., *Fighting Them Over,* p. 440; Map of Pickett's Charge, July 3rd: Longstreet's Assault File, #1, GNMP.
11. Report of Colonel Joseph Mayo, July 26, 1863, Pickett Papers, DU; R. A. Bright–Charles Pickett, October 15, 1892; W. Stuart Symington–Charles Pickett, October 17, 1892; Thomas R. Friend–Charles Pickett, December 10, [?], all in Pickett Papers, VHS; Account of F. M. Bailey, n.d.; James E. Poindexter–John W. Daniel, September 14, 1903, both in Daniel Papers, UVA; E. P. Alexander–Frederick Colston, November 24, 1894, Campbell-Colston Family Papers, UNC.
12. *OR,* 27, 2, p. 435; *SOR,* 5, pp. 341, 349; Gallagher, ed., *Fighting For,* p. 262; J. Merrick Reid–E. P. Alexander, March 15, 1901, Alexander Papers, UNC; *Sumter Herald,* April 29, 1902.
13. J. Merrick Reid–E. P. Alexander, March 15, 1901, Alexander Papers, UNC; *OR,* 27, 1, p. 888; 2, p. 435; *SOR,* 5, p. 349; Haskell, *Haskell Memoirs,* pp. 50–51; Memoirs, p. 34, Haskell Papers, DU; *Sumter Herald,* April 29, 1902; C.H.C. Brown–J. B. Walton, n.d., Walton Papers, TU.
14. "Sketches from . . . : Gettysburg—The Third Day," p. 6, Gibbon Papers, HSP; Todd Diary, USAMHI.
15. Ladd and Ladd, eds., *BP,* 2, p. 777; Bruce, *Twentieth Regiment,* p. 294; Wright, "Story," p. 611, GNMP; Moe, *Last Full Measure,* p. 288; R. G. Scott, ed., *Fallen Leaves,* p. 188.

16. Moe, *Last Full Measure*, p. 288; Ladd and Ladd, eds., *BP*, 3, p. 1403; *Gettysburg Compiler*, June 7, 1887; Bruce, *Twentieth Regiment*, p. 294; Cyril Tyler–Father, July 7, 1863, 7th Michigan Infantry File, GNMP.

17. Todd Diary, USAMHI; Henry Clare–My dear William, July 5, 1863, Clare Letters, GC; Frank Whittemore–Parents, July 5, 1863, Whittemore Letter, USAMHI; Hartwig, "It Struck Horror," p. 97.

18. Map of Pickett's Charge, July 3rd: Longstreet's Assault File, #1, GNMP; Bell, *11th Virginia Infantry*, p. 40; Trinque, "Confederate Battle Flags," pp. 121, 123.

19. Tucker, *Lee and Longstreet*, p. 119; Account of J. Risque Hutter, n.d., Daniel Papers, UVA; Bell, *11th Virginia Infantry*, pp. 79–80.

20. James J. Hunt–John Daniel, October 28, 1904, Daniel Papers, UVA; Riggs, *7th Virginia Infantry*, pp. 24, 88; Rollins, *"Damned Red Flags,"* p. 159.

21. James L. Kemper–A. D. Pollock, January 12, 1865, Janney-Pollock Family Papers, UVA.

22. Report of Captain Alphonso N. Jones, n.d., Brake Collection, USAMHI; Report of Colonel Joseph Mayo, July 23, 1863, Pickett Papers, DU; Statement of J. W. Wray, n.d., Daniel Papers, UVA.

23. Map of Pickett's Charge, July 3rd: Longstreet's Assault File, #1, GNMP; Trinque, "Confederate Battle Flags," pp. 120, 122; Wood, *Reminiscences*, p. 46; *OR*, 27, 2, p. 386.

24. Divine, *8th Virginia Infantry*, p. 22; *SOR*, 5, p. 309; Hunton, *Autobiography*, pp. 90–91; Edmund Berkeley–Eppa Hunton, III, February 9, [?], Berkeley Letter, VHS; Eppa Hunton–John W. Daniel, July 25, 1904, Daniel Papers, UVA.

25. Divine, *8th Virginia Infantry*, pp. iv, 22, 56; Edmund Berkeley–Eppa Hunton, III, February 9, [?], Berkeley Letter, VHS; Edmund Berkeley–John W. Daniel, September 26, [?], Daniel Papers, UVA.

26. Divine, *8th Virginia Infantry*, pp. 21, 77; Coco, *Wasted Valor*, pp. 116, 117.

27. Rollins, *"Damned Red Flags,"* pp. 164, 165; Account of Henry A. Carrington, n.d., Daniel Papers, UVA; J.S.D. Cullen–My Dear Lottie, July 8, 1863, Carrington Family Papers, VHS.

28. *OR*, 27, 2, p. 387; Fields, *28th Virginia Infantry*, pp. 26, 81.

29. W. P. Jesse–John W. Daniel, March 30, 1908, Daniel Papers, UVA; Rollins, *"Damned Red Flags,"* p. 170; Fields, *28th Virginia Infantry*, p. 27.

30. Map of Pickett's Charge, July 3rd: Longstreet's Assault File, #1, GNMP; K. M. Brown, *Cushing*, pp. 242, 248; *Buffalo Evening News*, May 29, 1894.

31. *Buffalo Evening News*, May 29, 1894; *OR*, 27, 2, p. 386; Hartwig, "It Struck Horror," p. 97; Thomas Moon Reminiscences, 4th U.S. Artillery, Battery A File, GNMP.

32. *OR*, 27, 1, p. 452; A. F. Devereux–M. S. O'Donnell, May 24, 1889, Devereux Papers, WRHS; Ladd and Ladd, eds., *BP*, 3, pp. 1627, 1628, 1706; *SOR*, 5, p. 213;

Gettysburg Compiler, June 7, 1878; Rollins, ed., *Pickett's Charge,* p. 293; Hartwig, "It Struck Horror," p. 97; Lash, "Philadelphia Brigade," pp. 105, 106.

33. K. M. Brown, *Cushing,* pp. 7, 248–51, 259; Frederick Fuger, "Personal Recollections Battle of Gettysburg," p. 18, Webb Papers, YU; W. B. Cushing–John B. Bachelder, December 16, 1866, Silbey Collection, NA; *Burlington Free Press and Times,* June 2, 1911; Thomas Moon Reminiscences, 4th U.S. Artillery, Battery A File, GNMP; *OR,* 27, 1, p. 480.

34. *OR,* 27, 1, p. 417; Sauers, *"Advance The Colors!,"* p. 189; Trinque, "Confederate Battle Flags," p. 121; Hartwig, "It Struck Horror," p. 98; Ladd and Ladd, eds., *BP,* 3, p. 1403; John Buckley–John Bachelder, n.d., Buckley Papers, GNMP.

35. Frank Whittemore–Parents, July 5, 1863, Whittemore Letter, USAMHI; *OR,* 27, 2, p. 386; Lash, "Philadelphia Brigade," p. 108; Hartwig, "It Struck Horror," p. 98.

36. *CV,* 14, p. 81; Ladd and Ladd, eds., *BP,* 3, p. 1901; Reardon, *Pickett's Charge,* p. 24; Magner, *Traveller,* p. 31; Georg and Busey, *Nothing but Glory,* p. 119; Davis, "Death," p. 113; Elliott Johnston–My dear Madam, July 18, 1863, Chisolm Papers, VHS.

37. Robert B. Dameron–John W. Daniel, n.d.; J. P. Jones–John W. Daniel, July 24, 1904, both in Daniel Papers, UVA; *Buffalo Evening News,* May 29, 1894.

38. Ladd and Ladd, eds., *BP,* 1, p. 519.

39. Trinque, "Confederate Battle Flags," pp. 110–12; Map of Pickett's Charge, July 3rd: Longstreet's Assault File, #1, GNMP; G. T. Fleming, ed., *Life of Hays,* p. 406.

40. *New York at Gettysburg,* 2, p. 802; Lindsley, *Military Annals of Tennessee,* p. 250; Ladd and Ladd, eds., *BP,* 1, p. 519.

41. Ladd and Ladd, eds., *BP,* 1, p. 519; James M. Simpson–My own dear Mother, July 8, 1863, Allen and Simpson Family Papers, UNC.

42. Ladd and Ladd, eds., *BP,* 1, p. 519; Reardon, *Pickett's Charge,* p. 13; Trinque, "Confederate Battle Flags," p. 115; Metts, *Longstreet's Charge,* p. 4.

43. Page, *History,* p. 153; Hamblen, *Connecticut Yankees,* p. 105; Archer, "Remembering," p. 77; *OR,* 27, 1, p. 467; Map of Pickett's Charge, July 3rd: Longstreet's Assault File, #1, GNMP.

44. Rollins, ed., *Pickett's Charge,* pp. 301–2; Shultz, *"Double Canister,"* pp. 55–57; Map of Pickett's Charge, July 3rd: Longstreet's Assault File, #1, GNMP; Account of G. V. Weir; Homer Baldwin–My dear Father, July 7, 1863, both in 5th U.S. Artillery, Battery C File, GNMP.

45. *OR,* 27, 2, p. 647; Rollins, *"Damned Red Flags,"* pp. 180, 181; Page, *History,* p. 152.

46. *OR,* 27, 1, p. 467; Ladd and Ladd, eds., *BP,* 1, p. 408; Bee, *Boys,* p. 145.

47. *OR,* 27, 2, p. 647; A. S. Van de Graaff–My dear Wife, July 8, 1863, 5th Alabama Battalion File, GNMP; Rollins, *"Damned Red Flags,"* pp. 180–82; Trinque,

"Confederate Battle Flags," p. 117; Bee, *Boys,* p. 150; *Lebanon Democrat,* August 10, 1890.

48. Bee, *Boys,* p. 144; Archer, "Remembering," p. 77.
49. James M. Simpson–My own dear Mother, July 8, 1863, Allen and Simpson Family Papers, UNC.
50. *OR,* 27, 1, pp. 454, 465; Louis G. Young–William J. Baker, February 10, 1864, Winston Papers, NCDAH; Bandy and Freeland, eds., *Gettysburg Papers,* 2, p. 909; Ladd and Ladd, eds., *BP,* 3, p. 1977; Tully McCrae, "Reminiscences About Gettysburg, 3 March 1904," p. 6, Brake Collection, USAMHI; Map of Pickett's Charge, July 3rd: Longstreet's Assault File, #1, GNMP.
51. Poriss and Poriss, *While My Country,* p. 78; Longacre, *To Gettysburg and Beyond,* pp. 132, 135; *Final Report,* p. 82; Rollins, ed., *Pickett's Charge,* p. 269; Ladd and Ladd, eds., *BP,* 3, p. 1362.
52. Bee, *Boys,* p. 150.
53. Lemuel J. Hoyle–My Dear Mother, July 12, 1863, Hoyle Papers, UNC.
54. M. W. Taylor, "Col. James Keith Marshall," p. 87; Louis G. Young–William J. Baker, February 10, 1864, Winston Papers, NCDAH; Walter Clark, ed., *Histories,* 5, p. 153; M. W. Taylor, "North Carolina," p. 83; R. K. Krick, *Lee's Colonels,* pp. 273, 296; Benjamin F. Little–My Dear Wife, July 20, 1863, Little Papers, UNC.
55. *SOR,* 5, p. 411; *OR,* 27, 2, pp. 644, 645; Bowen Diary, p. 9, USAMHI; George M. Whiting–Editor, March 18, 1867, Paris Papers, UNC; Walter Clark, ed., *Histories,* 1, p. 590; Louis G. Young–William J. Baker, February 10, 1864, Winston Papers, NCDAH; Ashe, "Charge at Gettysburg," p. 20; Rollins, *"Damned Red Flags,"* pp. 182, 183.
56. Chapman, *More Terrible Than Victory,* p. 113; *SOR,* 5, pp. 409, 411; Walter Clark, ed., *Histories,* 2, p. 374; 5, p. 152; J. Jones–H. K. Burgwyn, July 30, 1863, Grimes Papers, UNC; Metts, *Longstreet's Charge,* pp. 6, 8; Henry W. Newton–M.C.S. Noble, August 8, 1913, Noble Papers, UNC; *OR,* 27, 2, p. 645.
57. Haines, *History,* p. 42; *OR,* 27, 2, p. 644; *SOR,* 5, p. 411.
58. *OR,* 27, 2, p. 651; M. W. Taylor, "North Carolina," p. 82; Map of Pickett's Charge, July 3rd: Longstreet's Assault File, #1, GNMP.
59. *OR,* 27, 2, p. 650; R. K. Krick, *Lee's Colonels,* pp. 45, 49, 86, 122, 150, 184, 250, 259, 293, 327, 335; Coco, *Wasted Valor,* pp. 119, 120; Winschel, "Heavy Was Their Loss," p. 82.
60. Peel Diary, p. 30, MDAH; Rollins, *"Damned Red Flags,"* p. 184; Winschel, "Heavy Was Their Loss," pp. 82, 83.
61. Rollins, *"Damned Red Flags,"* p. 184; Winschel, "Heavy Was Their Loss," p. 83; *CV,* 19, p. 66; McLean and McLean, eds., *Gettysburg Sources,* 1, pp. 144, 145; Peel Diary, pp. 30, 31, MDAH.
62. *Galveston Daily News,* June 21, 1896; War Department, "Records," 1, p. 21, LC;

Walter Clark, ed., *Histories,* 3, pp. 299, 301; Rollins, *"Damned Red Flags,"* p. 185; Winschel, "Heavy Was Their Loss," p. 83; *CV,* 8, p. 166.

63. Rollins, *"Damned Red Flags,"* pp. 184–85.

64. *OR,* 27, 2, pp. 644, 651; M. W. Taylor, "North Carolina," p. 82.

65. *OR,* 27, 1, pp. 374, 417; Winfield S. Hancock–P. F. Rothermel, December 31, 1868, January 21, 1869, Rothermel Papers, PHMC; Benedict, *Vermont in the Civil War,* 2, p. 483; Wright, " 'Don't Let Me Bleed to Death,' " p. 89.

66. Benedict, *Army Life,* p. 180; Winfield S. Hancock–P. F. Rothermel, December 31, 1868, Rothermel Papers, PHMC; Benedict, *Vermont in the Civil War,* 2, p. 483.

67. Winfield S. Hancock–P. F. Rothermel, December 31, 1868, Rothermel Papers, PHMC; Benedict, *Army Life,* p. 183; *OR,* 27, 1, p. 366; Ladd and Ladd, eds., *BP,* 1, p. 56; 3, pp. 1363, 1364, 1949; Wright, " 'Don't Let Me Bleed to Death,' " pp. 87, 91.

68. Winfield S. Hancock–P. F. Rothermel, December 31, 1868, Rothermel Papers, PHMC; Wright, " 'Don't Let Me Bleed to Death,' " p. 91.

69. Winfield S. Hancock–P. F. Rothermel, December 31, 1868, Rothermel Papers, PHMC; Wright, " 'Don't Let Me Bleed to Death,' " pp. 87, 91.

70. Ladd and Ladd, eds., *BP,* 3, p. 1759; G. T. Fleming, ed., *Life of Hays,* p. 442.

71. G. T. Fleming, ed., *Life of Hays,* pp. 404, 406; Ladd and Ladd, eds., *BP,* 3, pp. 1759, 1762; Murray, *Redemption,* p. 135; *OR,* 27, 1, p. 454.

72. *OR,* 27, 2, p. 454; Washburn, *Complete Military History,* p. 50; Shultz, *"Double Canister,"* p. 54; Ladd and Ladd, eds., *BP,* 3, pp. 1759, 1977; S. B. McIntyre–C. D. MacDougall, June 27, 1890, 111th New York Infantry File, GNMP.

12. "Come On"

1. Lewis, *Recollections,* p. 81; Gregory, *38th Virginia Infantry,* p. 43; Erasmus Williams, "14th Virginia Infantry at Gettysburg," Daniel Papers, UVA.

2. Rawley W. Martin–Sylvester Chamberlain, August 11, 1907, Daniel Papers, UVA; Gregory, *38th Virginia Infantry,* p. 40; *Philadelphia Press,* July 4, 1887.

3. *Philadelphia Press,* July 4, 1887.

4. Gregory, *38th Virginia Infantry,* p. 43; M. A. Cogbill–E. Scott Gibbs, September 28, 1894, Pickett Papers, VHS; Map of Pickett's Charge, July 3rd: Longstreet's Assault File, #1, GNMP; Powell and Clement, eds., *War Recollections,* p. 44.

5. Powell and Clement, eds., *War Recollections,* pp. 46, 48; Rollins, ed., *Pickett's Charge,* pp. 178, 179; Georg and Busey, *Nothing but Glory,* p. 437.

6. *SOR,* 5, p. 333; Report of Major Joseph R. Cabell, July 11, 1863, Armistead Ledger, MC; W. H. Stewart, *Pair of Blankets,* p. 111; Rawley Martin–Robert A. Bright, January 25, 1904, Southall Papers, WM; M. A. Cogbill–E. Scott Gibbs, September 28, 1894, Pickett Papers, VHS.

7. Rawley Martin–Robert A. Bright, January 25, 1904, Southall Papers, WM; Report of Major Joseph R. Cabell, July 11, 1863, Armistead Ledger, MC; D. B. Easley–Howard Townsend, July 24, 1913, Easley Papers, USAMHI; *SOR,* 5, p. 333; Powhatan B. Whittle–Brother, July 8, 1863, Whittle Papers, UNC; Gregory, *38th Virginia Infantry,* pp. 42, 92, 131.

8. R. K. Krick, *Lee's Colonels,* pp. 271, 280, 296; James J. Phillips–F. H. Smith, July 18, 1863, 9th Virginia Infantry File, GNMP.

9. McLean and McLean, eds., *Gettysburg Sources,* 2, p. 118; R. K. Krick, *Lee's Colonels,* pp. 283, 367; Neathery, *Neathery Siblings,* pp. 47–48.

10. Powell and Clement, eds., *War Recollections,* pp. 44, 48; Rollins, ed., *Pickett's Charge,* p. 179.

11. *Philadelphia Press,* July 4, 1887; Rawley Martin–Robert A. Bright, January 25, 1904, Southall Papers, WM; W. A. Cogbill–E. Scott Gibbs, September 28, 1894, Pickett Papers, VHS; Hartwig, "It Struck Horror," p. 97; Alexander S. Webb–Father, July 17, 1863, Webb Papers, YU; Account of F. M. Bailey, n.d.; Rawley W. Martin–Sylvester Chamberlain, August 11, 1897, both in Daniel Papers, UVA.

12. Rawley W. Martin–Sylvester Chamberlain, August 11, 1907, Daniel Papers, UVA; Alexander S. Webb–Father, July 17, 1863, Webb Papers, YU; Hartwig, "It Struck Horror," p. 97; *OR,* 27, 1, pp. 428, 431, 448.

13. Alexander S. Webb–Father, July 17, 1863, Webb Papers, YU; Hartwig, "It Struck Horror," pp. 91, 97, 98; *Gettysburg Compiler,* June 7, 1887; McDermott, *Brief History,* p. 32; Ladd and Ladd, eds., *BP,* 3, pp. 1410, 1411.

14. *OR,* 27, 1, p. 431; McDermott, *Brief History,* pp. 32, 33; Ladd and Ladd, eds., *BP,* 3, pp. 1412, 1414; Hartwig, "It Struck Horror," p. 98; Raus, *Generation,* p. 120.

15. Ladd and Ladd, eds., *BP,* 3, p. 1412; *OR,* 27, 1, p. 417; Rollins, ed., *Pickett's Charge,* p. 313; Hartwig, "It Struck Horror," p. 100; *Buffalo Evening News,* May 29, 1894.

16. *OR,* 27, 1, p. 428; Gibbon, *Personal Recollections,* p. 180; Alexander S. Webb–Dearest Annie, July 27, 1863; Andrew Cowan–Alexander S. Webb, December 6, 1885, both in Webb Papers, YU; Lash, "Philadelphia Brigade," p. 108.

17. *OR,* 27, 1, p. 434; Ladd and Ladd, eds., *BP,* 1, p. 19; Rollins, ed., *Pickett's Charge,* pp. 293, 316; *Pennsylvania at Gettysburg,* 1, p. 554; R. Penn Smith–Isaac J. Wistar, July 29, 1863, Wistar Papers, GNMP; Ward, *History,* pp. 165, 166.

18. *Pennsylvania at Gettysburg,* 1, p. 554; J. B. Bachelder, "The 72nd Penn'a Monument Case," newspaper clipping, n.d., McPherson Papers, LC; Alexander S. Webb–P. F. Rothermel, January [?], Rothermel Papers, PHMC; Ladd and Ladd, eds., *BP,* 2, p. 966; Sword, "Alexander Webb," p. 94; Sauers, *"Advance The Colors!,"* 1, pp. 195, 196; Banes, *History,* p. 194.

19. Byrne and Weaver, *Haskell,* pp. 159, 160, 164, 165; *OR,* 27, 1, p. 431; *SOR,* 5, p. 215.

20. Map of Pickett's Charge, July 3rd: Longstreet's Assault File, #1, GNMP; *OR*, 27, 1, p. 690; *SOR*, 5, pp. 213, 214; Ladd and Ladd, eds., *BP*, 2, p. 1156; *New York Herald*, July 2, 1911; *New York at Gettysburg*, 3, p. 1277; Account of Andrew Cowan, n.d., Webb Papers, YU.
21. *OR*, 27, 1, p. 690; *SOR*, 5, p. 215; *New York at Gettysburg*, 3, p. 1277; Ladd and Ladd, eds., *BP*, 2, pp. 1156, 1157; *New York Herald*, July 2, 1911.
22. Map of Pickett's Charge, July 3rd: Longstreet's Assault File, #1, GNMP; Letter of James E. Decker, July 6, 1863, Pettit's Battery Letters, GNMP; Rollins, ed., *Pickett's Charge*, p. 147.
23. Letter of E. Corbin, July 4, 1863; Letter of James E. Decker, July 6, 1863, both in Pettit's Battery Letters, GNMP; Rollins, *"Damned Red Flags,"* p. 162; *New York at Gettysburg*, 3, p. 1184; undated newspaper clipping, 1st New York Artillery, Battery B File, GNMP.
24. Muller, History, p. 18, MNHS; Crews and Parrish, *14th Virginia Infantry*, pp. 40, 41; E. M. Magruder–Sister, [August 1863], Magruder Papers, DU; J. L. Johnson, *University Memorial*, p. 753; Coco, *Wasted Valor*, p. 129; W. H. Stewart, *Pair of Blankets*, p. 108.
25. Powell and Clement, eds., *War Recollections*, pp. 44, 46, 48; Rollins, ed., *Pickett's Charge*, pp. 178, 179.
26. Gregory, *38th Virginia Infantry*, p. 43; Ladd and Ladd, eds., *BP*, 3, p. 1705; D. B. Easley–Howard Townsend, July 24, 1913, Easley Papers, USAMHI; R. Penn Smith–Isaac J. Wistar, July 29, 1863, Wistar Papers, GNMP; Alexander S. Webb–Father, July 17, 1863; Frederick Fuger, "Personal Recollections Battle of Gettysburg," p. 18, both in Webb Papers, YU; C. L. Farinholt–John W. Daniel, April 15, 1905; Rawley W. Martin–Sylvester Chamberlain, August 11, 1907, both in Daniel Papers, UVA; John C. Timberlake–Editors, *Richmond Dispatch*, Draft #1, [1887], Timberlake Letter, VHS; Powell and Clement, eds., *War Recollections*, pp. 1, 48.
27. *OR*, 27, 1, p. 1042; Ladd and Ladd, eds., *BP*, 1, pp. 60, 61; Benedict, *Vermont in the Civil War*, 2, pp. 468, 469; Wheelock G. Veazey–G. G. Benedict, July 11, 1864, Veazey Papers, VTHS; Coffin, *Nine Months*, p. 230.
28. Alfred P. Carpenter–[?], July 30, 1863, Carpenter Papers, MNHS; H. T. Owen–H. A. Carrington, January 27, 1878, Daniel Papers, UVA.
29. *OR*, 27, 1, pp. 350, 353, 1042; Ladd and Ladd, eds., *BP*, 1, pp. 56, 60, 61; Coffin, *Nine Months*, p. 233; Benedict, *Vermont in the Civil War*, 2, p. 469; Wheelock G. Veazey–G. G. Benedict, July 11, 1864, Veazey Papers, VTHS; Map of Pickett's Charge, July 3rd: Longstreet's Assault File, #1, GNMP.
30. Rollins, ed., *Pickett's Charge*, p. 147; H. T. Owen–H. A. Carrington, January 27, 1878, Daniel Papers, UVA; McLean and McLean, eds., *Gettysburg Sources*, 1, p. 78; Coffin, *Nine Months*, pp. 185, 234.

31. Ladd and Ladd, eds., *BP*, 1, p. 56; *OR*, 27, 1, pp. 350, 1042; Coffin, *Nine Months,* pp. 233, 235; Wheelock G. Veazey–G. G. Benedict, July 11, 1864, Veazey Papers, VTHS.

32. *OR*, 27, 1, p. 350; Benedict, *Vermont in the Civil War*, 2, pp. 469, 470; Sturtevant, *Pictorial History*, p. 229; Rollins, "*Damned Red Flags*," pp. 178–79.

33. *OR*, 27, 1, p. 350; Coffin, *Nine Months*, p. 236; Jacob Slagle–Brother, September 13, 1863, Slagle Letters, PML; Account of John Holmes Smith, July 4, 5, 1904, Daniel Papers, UVA; Francis Long–Wife, July 5, 1863, Picerno Collection.

34. Coddington, *Gettysburg Campaign*, p. 518; *OR*, 27, 1, pp. 439, 445, 451; *SOR*, 5, p. 165; A. C. Plaisted–J. B. Bachelder, June 11, 1870, Bachelder Papers, NHHS; Map of Pickett's Charge, July 3rd: Longstreet's Assault File, #1, GNMP.

35. *OR*, 27, 1, pp. 439, 445, 451; Ladd and Ladd, eds., *BP*, 1, p. 252; Henry L. Abbott–My Dear Sir, July 28, 1863, Paine Papers, MHS; Byrne and Weaver, *Haskell*, pp. 165–66.

36. *OR*, 27, 1, pp. 439, 445; Ladd and Ladd, eds., *BP*, 1, pp. 252, 253; Mason Diary, UC; W. Raymond Lee–Alexander S. Webb, April 22, 1864, Webb Papers, YU.

37. *OR*, 27, 1, pp. 451, 452; Edmund Rice–Alexander S. Webb, August 1, 1871, Webb Papers, YU; A. F. Devereux–E. D. Townsend, May 1, 1878, Records Group 94, NA; John Reynolds, "The Nineteenth Massachusetts at Gettysburg, July 2–3–4," p. 8, 19th Massachusetts Infantry File, GNMP; Ladd and Ladd, eds., *BP*, 3, p. 1609.

38. *SOR*, 5, p. 165; *OR*, 27, 1, pp. 451, 452; A. F. Devereux–E. D. Townsend, May 1, 1878, Records Group 94, NA; Edmund Rice–John B. Bachelder, July 27, 1886, Silbey Collection, NA; Beyer and Keydel, eds., *Deeds*, p. 235.

39. *OR*, 27, 1, p. 439; George N. Macy–C. C. Paine, July 23, 1863, Paine Papers, MHS; Ladd and Ladd, eds., *BP*, 1, p. 253; W. Raymond Lee–Alexander S. Webb, April 22, 1864, Webb Papers, YU; Miller and Mooney, *Civil War*, p. 52.

40. A. C. Plaisted–J. B. Bachelder, June 11, 1870, Bachelder Papers, NHHS; Bond, Reminiscences, MNHS; Earle, *History*, p. 22; Francis Heath–John B. Bachelder, October 12, 1889, 19th Maine Infantry File, GNMP; Albert Davis–Mother, July 17, 1863, Davis Letters, UM; Byrne and Weaver, *Haskell*, pp. 166, 167.

41. *St. Paul Pioneer,* August 9, 1863; Wright, "Story," p. 612, GNMP; *Minneapolis Journal,* June 30, 1897.

42. Wright, "Story," p. 612, GNMP; *Minneapolis Journal*, June 30, 1897; *St. Paul Pioneer,* August 9, 1863; Meinhard, "First Minnesota," p. 87; Ladd and Ladd, eds., *BP*, 3, pp. 1709, 1710; *B&L*, 3, p. 389; Samuel Roberts–H. N. Newton, February 3, 1890, Roberts Papers, UNC; Henry L. Abbott–My Dear Sir, July 28, 1863, Paine Papers, MHS.

43. *Webb*, p. 17; Byrne and Weaver, *Haskell*, p. 88; Winfield S. Hancock–P. F. Rothermel, December 31, 1868, Rothermel Papers, PHMC; Waitt, ed., *History*, p. 250; *OR*, 27, 1, pp. 421, 446; *Maine at Gettysburg*, p. 297.

44. *Buffalo Evening News,* May 29, 1894; Bandy and Freeland, eds., *Gettysburg Papers,* 2, p. 613; *Minneapolis State Atlas,* August 26, 1863; Rollins, ed., *Pickett's Charge,* p. 222.

45. *OR,* 27, 1, pp. 319, 322, 374, 444; *St. Paul Daily Press,* July 25, 1863; Waitt, ed., *History,* p. 250; Beyer and Keydel, eds., *Deeds,* p. 250.

46. *OR,* 27, 1, pp. 319, 322, 374, 444; *Minneapolis State Atlas,* August 26, 1863; Ladd and Ladd, eds., *BP,* 1, p. 393; Wright, "1st Minnesota at Gettysburg," p. 612, MNHS; Theodore B. Gates–P. F. Rothermel, April 28, 1868, Rothermel Papers, PHMC; Chamberlin, *History,* p. 151; V. A. Tapscott–John W. Daniel, February 29, 1904, Daniel Papers, UVA; *Buffalo Evening News,* May 29, 1894; Neathery, *Neathery Siblings,* p. 53; Moe, *Last Full Measure,* p. 289; Loren H. Goodrich–Friends, July 17, 1863, Goodrich Papers, CTHS; Burns Diary, p. 60, USAMHI; Waitt, ed., *History,* p. 250.

47. Poirer, "Norwich at Gettysburg," pp. 121, 122; Rollins, ed., *Pickett's Charge,* p. 298; R. Penn Smith–Isaac J. Wistar, July 29, 1863, Wistar Papers, GNMP; Henry L. Abbott–C. C. Paine, July 13, 28, 1863, Paine Papers, MHS.

48. Ladd and Ladd, eds., *BP,* 2, p. 1192; Colin Mackingil–Madam, July 24, 1863, Kemper Papers, UVA; James L. Kemper–E. P. Alexander, September 20, 1869, Dearborn Collection, HU.

49. *Gettysburg Compiler,* June 7, 1887; Rollins, "*Damned Red Flags,*" pp. 173, 174; Trinque, "Confederate Battle Flags," p. 127.

50. Ladd and Ladd, eds., *BP,* 3, p. 1991; Beyer and Keydel, eds., *Deeds,* p. 235; Rollins, "*Damned Red Flags,*" pp. 168, 174, 176; Trinque, "Confederate Battle Flags," p. 127; George H. Patch–Father and Mother, July 6, 1863, Patch Letters, USAMHI.

51. Trinque, "Confederate Battle Flags," p. 127; Riggs, *7th Virginia Infantry,* p. 26; Rollins, "*Damned Red Flags,*" p. 173; Alfred P. Carpenter–[?], July 30, 1863, Carpenter Papers, MNHS; *St. Paul Pioneer,* August 9, 1863; Charles Merrick–Mim, July 6, 1863, Merrick Papers, WRHS; Nathan Hayward–Father, July 8, 1863, Hayward Papers, MHS.

52. *OR,* 27, 1, pp. 375, 690; Ladd and Ladd, eds., *BP,* 1, pp. 282, 283; Moe, *Last Full Measure,* p. 289; Ralph Rea–Cousin, July 8, 1863, 7th Michigan Infantry File, GNMP.

53. *OR,* 27, 2, pp. 659, 671; *Raleigh Observer,* November 29, 1877.

54. *OR,* 27, 2, pp. 659, 666, 671; *Raleigh Observer,* November 29, 1877; Ladd and Ladd, eds., *BP,* 3, p. 1776.

55. Walter Clark, ed., *Histories,* 2, p. 693; *Raleigh Observer,* November 29, 1877; Ladd and Ladd, eds., *BP,* 3, p. 1776; Harris, "Historical Sketches," pp. 36, 37, SHSW; Rollins, ed., *Pickett's Charge,* p. 252; I. R. Trimble, "North Carolinians at Gettysburg," p. 58.

56. *OR,* 27, 2, pp. 666, 671; Ladd and Ladd, eds., *BP,* 3, p. 1776; Rollins, ed.,

Pickett's Charge, p. 252; I. R. Trimble, "North Carolinians at Gettysburg," p. 58.

57. *OR,* 27, 2, pp. 671–72; M. W. Taylor, "North Carolina," p. 78; Trinque, "Confederate Battle Flags," p. 120; Clark M. Avery–My Dear Sir, July 18, 1863, Caldwell Papers, UNC.

58. Walter Clark, ed., *Histories,* 3, p. 155; Long, "Maj. Joseph H. Saunders," pp. 102, 104, 106; M. W. Taylor, "North Carolina," p. 76n.

59. Walter Clark, ed., *Histories,* 1, p. 672.

60. Harris, "Historical Sketches," p. 37, SHSW; William G. Morris–W. Saunders, October 1, 1877, Morris Papers, UNC; M. W. Taylor, "North Carolina," pp. 79, 80; *Raleigh Observer,* November 29, 1877.

61. *OR,* 27, 2, pp. 659, 666; Rollins, ed., *Pickett's Charge,* pp. 251, 252; Walter Clark, ed., *Histories,* 2, p. 693; Map of Pickett's Charge, July 3rd: Longstreet's Assault File, #1, GNMP.

62. Ladd and Ladd, eds., *BP,* 2, pp. 986, 1001; 3, pp. 1977, 1979; Campbell, "Remember Harper's Ferry!," p. 106; Mahood, *"Written In Blood,"* p. 150; G. T. Fleming, ed., *Life of Hays,* pp. 438, 439; *New York at Gettysburg,* 2, p. 890; Simons, *Regimental History,* p. 137; James Moore–My Dear Friend, July 5, 1863, Moore Papers, UR; Washburn, *Complete Military History,* pp. 50, 51; Shultz, *"Double Canister,"* p. 54.

63. *OR,* 27, 1, p. 462; Ladd and Ladd, eds., *BP,* 2, pp. 1132, 1133; Galwey, *Valiant Hours,* p. 117; Sawyer, *Military History,* p. 131.

64. *OR,* 27, 2, p. 667; Alexander Diary, UNC; Ladd and Ladd, eds., *BP,* 3, p. 1777; Floyd Memoir, p. 8, VHS; Thomas L. Norwood–My Dear Father, July 16, 1863, Norwood Papers, UNC; Bee, *Boys,* p. 145; Willoughby F. Avery–Cousin Mary, July 28, 1863, Caldwell Papers, UNC; Rollins, ed., *Pickett's Charge,* p. 252.

65. M. W. Taylor, "North Carolina," p. 83; Ladd and Ladd, eds., *BP,* 2, pp. 933, 934, 1199; Patrick Diary, LC; Rollins, ed., *Pickett's Charge,* p. 233.

66. H. S. Stevens, *Souvenir,* pp. 31, 32; Young, "Pettigrew's Brigade at Gettysburg," p. 556; Joseph H. Saunders–Editors of the *Observer,* September 22, 1877; Joseph A. Engehard–Editors of the *Observer,* September 27, 1877, both in Grimes Papers, UNC; Reardon, *Pickett's Charge,* p. 15; G. M. Whiting–John Paris, April 27, 1869, Paris Papers, UNC; Belknap Diary, USAMHI.

67. Trinque, "Confederate Battle Flags," pp. 109, 127; Rollins, *"Damned Red Flags,"* pp. 184, 185, 227, 228.

68. *OR,* 27, 1, pp. 467, 468, 473; Page, *History,* pp. 155, 156, 166; H. S. Stevens, *Souvenir,* p. 32; Ladd and Ladd, eds., *BP,* 1, pp. 316, 317; *New York at Gettysburg,* 2, pp. 907, 908.

69. *OR,* 27, 1, p. 462; Galwey, *Valiant Hours,* pp. 118, 119; Ladd and Ladd, eds., *BP,* 1, pp. 625, 663; Sawyer, *Military History,* p. 132; Rollins, *"Damned Red Flags,"* p. 188.

13. "It Is My Fault"

1. R. A. Bright–Charles Pickett, October 15, 1892; W. Stuart Symington–Charles Pickett, October 17, 1892; Charles Pickett–Joseph Bryan, November 11, 1894; Thomas R. Friend–Charles Pickett, December 10, 1894, all in Pickett Papers, VHS; Cockrell, "Where Was Pickett," Cockrell Collection, UVA; discussion of the postwar controversy about Pickett's location in the attack is in Georg and Busey, *Nothing but Glory,* pp. 194–205; Kross, "July 3rd Action," p. 57.
2. R. A. Bright–Charles Pickett, October 15, 1892, Pickett Papers, VHS; Lord, ed., *Fremantle Diary,* p. 212.
3. R. A. Bright–Charles Pickett, October 15, 1892, Pickett Papers, VHS; for Fremantle's abbreviated and slightly different version of the conversation, see Lord, ed., *Fremantle Diary,* p. 212.
4. R. A. Bright–Charles Pickett, October 15, 1892; W. Stuart Symington–Charles Pickett, October 17, 1892; Charles Pickett–Joseph Bryan, November 11, 1894, all in Pickett Papers, VHS; *OR,* 27, 2, p. 620.
5. R. A. Bright–Charles Pickett, October 15, 1892; Charles Pickett–Joseph Bryan, November 11, 1894, both in Pickett Papers, VHS.
6. *B&L,* 3, p. 346; Lord, ed., *Fremantle Diary,* pp. 211, 212; Sorrel, *Recollections,* p. 163.
7. *OR,* 27, 2, pp. 360, 615; Longstreet, *From Manassas to Appomattox,* p. 393; Sorrel, *Recollections,* p. 164; Moses, Autobiography, p. 51, UNC; Ross, *Cities,* p. 58.
8. *OR,* 27, 2, pp. 615, 625; Todd, Reminiscences, p. 132, UNC; Gottfried, "Mahone's Brigade," p. 73; Memoir, p. 18, Bernard Papers, UNC.
9. Kirkpatrick Diary, p. 55, UT; Todd, Reminiscences, p. 132, UNC; Memoir, pp. 18–19, Bernard Papers, UNC; *OR,* 27, 2, pp. 360, 615, 625; John S. Lewis–My very dear Mother, July 21, 1863, Harry Lewis Papers, UNC; Dobbins, ed., *Grandfather's Journal,* p. 149.
10. *OR,* 27, 2, pp. 557, 625; James W. Carter–Mrs. Bell A. Montfort, July 8, 1863, Montfort-Pope-Spain Families Collection, MGA; Henderson, *12th Virginia Infantry,* p. 57.
11. Daniel Memoir, p. 16, VHS; D. C. Pfanz, *Richard S. Ewell,* p. 320; "North Carolina at Gettysburg," North Carolina Troops File, GNMP; Seymour Journal, UM.
12. *OR,* 27, 2, p. 620; Wilcox, "Postwar Notations on Gettysburg Report," Wilcox Papers, LC; Gallagher, ed., *Fighting For,* p. 256; David Lang–John B. Bachelder, October 16, 1893, Lang Letterbooks, FSA; Pigman Diary, GHS.
13. Gallagher, ed., *Fighting For,* pp. 256, 264, 265; *OR,* 27, 2, p. 620; Rollins, ed., *Pickett's Charge,* p. 183.
14. *OR,* 27, 2, p. 620; Shultz, *"Double Canister,"* p. 59; John B. Bachelder–John W. Daniel, December 15, 1875, Bachelder Letters, USAMHI; Coles and Waters,

"Forgotten Sacrifice," p. 45; Groene, ed., "Civil War Letters," p. 355; Ladd and Ladd, eds., *BP*, 1, p. 171; Alloway Diary, HSP; James A. Gardner–John P. Nicholson, October 22, 1902, 1st Pennsylvania Artillery, Cooper's Battery B File, GNMP.

15. *OR*, 27, 2, p. 632; David Lang–John B. Bachelder, October 16, 1893, Lang Letterbooks, FSA; War Department, "Record," 1, pp. 19, 20, LC; Elmore, "Florida Brigade," p. 54; Raymond J. Reid–Hal, September 4, 1863, Reid Papers, SAHS.

16. *OR*, 27, 2, p. 620; H. A. Herbert–E. P. Alexander, August 18, 1903, Alexander Papers, UNC; Hilary A. Herbert, "A Short History of the 8th Alabama Regiment," McLaws Papers, DU; Cadmus Wilcox–Thomas S. Mills, July 17, 1863, Wilcox Papers, LC.

17. Cadmus Wilcox–Thomas S. Mills, July 17, 1863, Wilcox Papers, LC; Coffin, *Nine Months*, pp. 238, 239; *OR*, 27, 1, p. 1042.

18. *OR*, 27, 1, p. 1042; Benedict, *Short History*, pp. 12, 13; Benedict, *Vermont in the Civil War*, 2, p. 474.

19. Benedict, *Vermont in the Civil War*, 2, p. 474; *OR*, 27, 2, p. 632.

20. *OR*, 27, 2, p. 620; H. A. Herbert–E. P. Alexander, August 18, 1903, Alexander Papers, UNC; Hilary A. Herbert, "A Short History of the 8th Alabama Regiment," McLaws Papers, DU; letter of an Alabama soldier to his mother, July 21, 1863, Alabama Troops File, GNMP.

21. *OR*, 27, 1, pp. 350, 382, 1042; Benedict, *Vermont in the Civil War*, 2, p. 475; Coles and Waters, "Forgotten Sacrifice," p. 44; War Department, "Record," 1, p. 19, LC; *Florida Soldiers*, pp. 42–206.

22. Coles and Waters, "Forgotten Sacrifice," p. 45.

23. *OR*, 27, 1, p. 1042; 2, p. 633; Wheelock G. Veazey–G. G. Benedict, July 11, 1864, Veazey Papers, VTHS.

24. *OR*, 27, 2, p. 620, 632; *Florida Soldiers*, pp. 42–206; E. H. Shore–Wife, August 16, 1863, Shore Papers, EU; Groene, ed., "Civil War Letters," p. 355; Isaac Sidney Barineau–My Dear Sister, July 15, 1863, Barineau Collection, USAMHI; Thomas C. Elder–My Dear Wife, July 4, 1863, Elder Papers, VHS; letter of an Alabama soldier to mother, July 21, 1863, Alabama Troops File, GNMP; Fleming Thompson–Sister & Mother, July 17, 1863, Thompson Papers, UT; E. P. Alexander, *Military Memoirs*, p. 425; Council A. Bryan–My dear Wife, July 25, 1863, Bryan Papers, FSA; H. A. Herbert–E. P. Alexander, August 18, 1903, Alexander Papers, UNC.

25. David Lang–John B. Bachelder, October 16, 1893, Lang Letterbooks, FSA; Ladd and Ladd, eds., *BP*, 1, p. 230; Coddington, *Gettysburg Campaign*, p. 463.

26. Gallagher, ed., *Fighting For*, pp. 255, 278, 282; *OR*, 27, 2, p. 360; Coddington, *Gettysburg Campaign*, p. 529; Boggs, ed., *Alexander Letters*, pp. 249, 250; Rollins, "Second Wave," p. 101.

27. Gallagher, ed., *Fighting For,* pp. 255, 256, 278, 280; Boggs, ed., *Alexander Letters,* pp. 249, 250.

28. Gallagher, ed., *Fighting For,* pp. 278, 280; E. P. Alexander–My dear Colston, April 7, 1898, Campbell-Colston Family Papers, UNC.

29. Gallagher, ed., *Fighting For,* p. 256; *OR,* 27, 2, p. 360; Longstreet, *From Manassas to Appomattox,* p. 393; Sorrel, *Recollections,* pp. 163, 164; *OR,* 27, 2, p. 359; Lafayette McLaws–Braxton Bragg, April 22, 1864, McLaws Papers, WRHS.

30. R. A. Bright–Charles Pickett, October 15, 1892, Pickett Papers, VHS; Lord, ed., *Fremantle Diary,* pp. 212–13; Coddington, *Gettysburg Campaign,* p. 529.

31. Rollins, "Second Wave," p. 101; Coddington, *Gettysburg Campaign,* p. 463.

32. *OR,* 27, 2, pp. 320–21, 360, 608, 614–15, 620; Rollins, "Second Wave," pp. 101, 102–13.

33. Gallagher, ed., *Fighting For,* pp. 255, 278, 280–83; Coddington, *Gettysburg Campaign,* p. 463; Rollins, "Second Wave," pp. 102–13.

34. George G. Meade–John B. Bachelder, December 4, 1869; John Egan–George Meade, February 8, 1870, both in Rothermel Papers, PHMC; George Meade–Alexander S. Webb, November 11, 1883, Webb Papers, YU; Ladd and Ladd, eds., *BP,* 1, p. 389.

35. John Egan–George Meade, February 8, 1870, Rothermel Papers, PHMC; Ladd and Ladd, eds., *BP,* 1, pp. 317, 341, 389; 2, p. 854; Belknap Diary, USAMHI; Rollins, *"Damned Red Flags,"* pp. 191, 193–94; Receipt, July 17, 1863, Les Jensen–Lewis Leigh, Jr., December 9, 1977, both in Bull Receipt, USAMHI; Washburn, *Complete Military History,* p. 53; G. T. Fleming, ed., *Life of Hays,* pp. 424, 464.

36. George G. Meade–John B. Bachelder, December 4, 1869; John Egan–George Meade, February 8, 1870, both in Rothermel Papers, PHMC; Ladd and Ladd, eds., *BP,* 1, p. 389.

37. Ladd and Ladd, eds., *BP,* 2, pp. 854–55.

38. George G. Meade–John B. Bachelder, December 4, 1869, Rothermel Papers, PHMC; George Meade–Alexander S. Webb, November 11, 1883, Webb Papers, YU; Byrne and Weaver, *Haskell,* pp. 173, 174.

39. George Meade–Alexander S. Webb, November 11, 1883, Webb Papers, YU; W. G. Mitchell–W. S. Hancock, January 10, 1866; W. S. Hancock–P. F. Rothermel, December 13, 1870; William G. Mitchell–P. F. Rothermel, December 19, 1870, all in Rothermel Papers, PHMC.

40. W. G. Mitchell–W. S. Hancock, January 10, 1866; W. S. Hancock–P. F. Rothermel, December 19, 1870, both in Rothermel Papers, PHMC; Ladd and Ladd, eds., *BP,* 1, pp. 320, 321.

41. A. N. Dougherty–William G. Mitchell, extract of letter, January 2, 1869; Henry Bingham–W. S. Hancock, January 5, 1869, both in Rothermel Papers, PHMC.

42. The description of the Armistead-Bingham incident is taken from Henry Bingham–W. S. Hancock, January 5, 1869, Rothermel Papers, PHMC.

43. D. G. Brinton–Henry H. Bingham, March 22, 1869, Bachelder Papers, NHHS; Coco, *Vast Sea*, p. 105; Ladd and Ladd, eds., *BP*, 1, p. 358.

44. Warner, *Generals in Gray*, p. 12; D. G. Brinton–Henry H. Bingham, March 22, 1869, Bachelder Papers, NHHS; Ladd and Ladd, eds., *BP*, 1, pp. 358–59; Clipping from *Gettysburg Times*, January 14, 1939, Brake Collection, USAMHI.

45. Winfield S. Hancock–P. F. Rothermel, December 31, 1868; A. N. Dougherty–William G. Mitchell, extract of letter, January 2, 1869, both in Rothermel Papers, PHMC; *OR*, 27, 1, p. 366.

46. Seville, *History*, p. 82; Ladd and Ladd, eds., *BP*, 3, pp. 1365, 1399; Benedict, *Army Life*, pp. 185, 186.

47. Albert Stokes Emmell, "Now Is the Time for Buck & Ball: The Life & Civil War Experience of Albert Stokes Emmell," 12th New Jersey Infantry File, GNMP; Gulian V. Weir–Dearest Father, July 5, 1863, 5th United States Artillery, Battery C File, GNMP; R. G. Scott, ed., *Fallen Leaves*, p. 188.

48. Ladd and Ladd, eds., *BP*, 1, pp. 19, 85; *Philadelphia Press*, July 4, 1887; Lewis H. Crandell–Ennie, July 6, 1863, Crandell Account, USAMHI; Bowen Diary, p. 9, USAMHI; Washburn, *Complete Military History*, p. 124.

49. *OR*, 27, 1, pp. 465, 471, 476; Ladd and Ladd, eds., *BP*, 1, pp. 356, 384, 385; 3, pp. 1362, 1911, 1912; R. Penn Smith–Isaac J. Wistar, July 29, 1863, Wistar Papers, GNMP; Sheaffer Farm Claims, GNMP; William P. Oberlin–Annie, July 10, 1863, Oberlin Civil War Letters, USAMHI; *Cleveland Plain Dealer*, July 13, 1863; Sword, "Captain George F. Tait," pp. 83–85.

50. Edmund Berkeley–John W. Daniel, September 26, [?], Daniel Papers, UVA.

51. William B. Short–Babie, June 26, August 18, 1863, Short Letters, MC.

52. Kenneth Hickery–Friend Battle, April 16, [?], 37th North Carolina Infantry File, GNMP; Hagerty, *Collis' Zouaves*, p. 248.

53. Rollins, *"Damned Red Flags,"* pp. 194–95.

54. Ladd and Ladd, eds., *BP*, 3, p. 1365; *New York at Gettysburg*, 3, p. 1308; *Reunions*, p. 13; Miller and Mooney, *Civil War*, p. 52.

55. Crumb, ed., *Eleventh Corps Artillery*, p. 43.

56. Walter Clark, ed., *Histories*, 2, pp. 43, 478.

57. J. Thompson Brown–Frederick M. Colston, March 25, 1903, Alexander Papers, UNC; Tucker, *Lee and Longstreet*, p. 120; Kennedy Diary, UNC; Gallagher, ed., *Fighting For*, p. 265; Ladd and Ladd, eds., *BP*, 1, p. 490; Colston, "Campaign of Gettysburg," UNC; War Department, "Record," 1, p. 13, LC.

58. Colston, "Campaign of Gettysburg," UNC; Ladd and Ladd, eds., *BP*, 1, p. 490; Gallagher, ed., *Fighting For*, pp. 265–66.

59. Colston, "Campaign of Gettysburg," UNC; *B&L*, 3, p. 366. For Porter Alexander's two versions of Lee's words to the men, see Gallagher, ed., *Fighting For*,

p. 266, and interview in *New York Times*, May 1, 1893. I have relied on the latter one, because Alexander declared in the article that he was "certain" of the words.

60. Gallagher, ed., *Fighting For*, p. 266; Charles Marshall–H. T. Owen, January 28, 1878, Owen Papers, VHS.

61. Sorrel, *Recollections*, p. 164; Lord, ed., *Fremantle Diary*, p. 214; *Lebanon Democrat*, August 10, 1899; Thomas J. Goree–James Longstreet, May 17, 1875, Longstreet Papers, UNC; G. R. Stewart, *Pickett's Charge*, p. 257.

62. Wilcox, postwar notations on Gettysburg Report, Wilcox Papers, LC; Lord, ed., *Fremantle Diary*, p. 215; Rollins, ed., *Pickett's Charge*, p. 165; *London Times*, August 18, 1863.

63. Wilcox, postwar notations on Gettysburg Report, Wilcox Papers, LC; M. W. Taylor, "Unmerited Censure," pp. 76, 80; Thomas J. Goree–James Longstreet, May 17, 1875, Longstreet Papers, UNC.

64. *Annals*, p. 431; *B&L*, 3, p. 347; White, "Gettysburg," pp. 326–27.

65. *CV*, 19, p. 287; H. T. Owen–H. A. Carrington, January 27, 1878, Daniel Papers, UVA; Dawson, *Reminiscences*, p. 97; Loehr, *War History*, p. 38; Wood, *Reminiscences*, p. 47.

66. *CV*, 19, p. 287; Loehr, *War History*, p. 38; Blackford, ed., *Letters*, p. 188.

67. *OR*, 27, 2, pp. 376, 379, 389; H. T. Owen–H. A. Carrington, January 27, 1878, Daniel Papers, UVA; *B&L*, 3, p. 347; R. K. Krick, *Parker's Virginia Battery*, p. 185.

68. *B&L*, 3, p. 348; McLaws, "Gettysburg," McLaws Papers, DU; *Philadelphia Weekly Press*, April 21, 1886.

69. George G. Meade–John B. Bachelder, December 4, 1869, Rothermel Papers, PHMC; *OR*, 27, 1, p. 366.

70. *OR*, 27, 1, pp. 262, 521, 524, 785; William Williams–My dear Wife, July 29, 1863, Williams Letters, USAMHI; Cavada Diary, HSP; Ladd and Ladd, eds., *BP*, 2, pp. 998, 1150; 3, p. 1801; Byrnes Diary, DU; *Maine at Gettysburg*, p. 214; *New York at Gettysburg*, 3, p. 1033; Cook and Benton, eds., *"Dutchess County Regiment,"* p. 38; Rollins, "George Gordon Meade," pp. 80, 82; Coddington, *Gettysburg Campaign*, p. 533.

71. Coddington, *Gettysburg Campaign*, pp. 533–34.

72. Ibid., p. 534.

73. George G. Meade–John B. Bachelder, December 4, 1869, Rothermel Papers, PHMC; *OR*, 27, 1, p. 654; Rollins, *"Damned Red Flags,"* p. 196.

14. "It Was Kill All You Can"

1. Hoffman, "Bit of History"; Hoffman, interview with author, August 11, 2000.

2. Hoffman, interview with author, August 11, 2000; Macomber Diary, CMU; Ladd and Ladd, eds., *BP*, 2, pp. 1206, 1287.

3. *OR*, 27, 1, pp. 914, 916, 956, 977; Gregg, "Army of the Potomac," p. 11, LC; Busey and Martin, *Regimental Strengths*, pp. 104, 106, 107, 108, 110.

4. *OR*, 27, 1, pp. 914, 916, 928, 970.

5. Wert, *Custer*, pp. 74–75; John Gibbon–My dearest Mama, June 2, 1863, Gibbon Papers, HSP; Byrne and Weaver, *Haskell*, pp. 133–34.

6. Wert, *Custer*, pp. 75–91.

7. *OR*, 27, 1, pp. 914, 916, 992; 3, p. 502; Gregg, "Army of the Potomac," p. 11, LC.

8. *OR*, 27, 1, pp. 956, 992; Gregg, "Army of the Potomac," p. 11, LC; Ladd and Ladd, eds., *BP*, 2, pp. 1219, 1287; Krolick, "Forgotten Field," p. 80.

9. Ladd and Ladd, eds., *BP*, 2, pp. 1219, 1287; Krolick, "Forgotten Field," p. 80; Busey and Martin, *Regimental Strengths*, p. 108; Wert, *Custer*, chaps. 1–5.

10. Wert, *Custer*, pp. 82–85; Agassiz, ed., *Meade's Headquarters*, p. 17; Sauers, ed., *Fighting Them Over*, p. 473; Meyer, *Civil War*, pp. 48–49.

11. Wert, *Custer*, pp. 85–89; James C. Biddle–My own darling little Wife, July 1, 1863, Biddle Civil War Letters, HSP.

12. *SOR*, 5, p. 271; Ladd and Ladd, eds., *BP*, 2, p. 1206; 3, p. 1532; George G. Briggs–J. B. Bachelder, March 26, 1886, 7th Michigan Cavalry File, GNMP; *Michigan at Gettysburg*, p. 146; Hoffman, interview with author, August 11, 2000; Hoffman, Map of East Cavalry Battlefield.

13. *OR*, 27, 2, p. 697; Hoffman, interview with author, August 11, 2000; Hoffman, Map of East Cavalry Battlefield.

14. Shevchuk, "Lost Hours," p. 70; Gallagher, ed., *Fighting For*, pp. 228, 277; Thomas, *Bold Dragoon*, chap. 12; Nesbitt, *Saber and Scapegoat*, passim.

15. Shevchuk, "Lost Hours," p. 70; Thomas, *Bold Dragoon*, pp. 247, 248.

16. *OR*, 27, 1, pp. 697, 724; Shevchuk, "Lost Hours," pp. 73, 74; Ladd and Ladd, eds., *BP*, 2, p. 1343; Norman R. Fitzhugh–Sister, July 16, 1863, Corse Papers, UNC.

17. Norman R. Fitzhugh–Sister, July 16, 1863, Corse Papers, UNC; James W. Biddle–My dear Pa, July 16, 1863, Biddle Letters, DU; Thomas, *Bold Dragoon*, p. 247; Ladd and Ladd, eds., *BP*, 2, p. 1340.

18. *OR*, 27, 2, pp. 497, 697; Shevchuk, "Wounding," pp. 61, 63; Brown Memoirs, TSLA; Ladd and Ladd, eds., *BP*, 2, pp. 1170, 1246, 1290; 3, pp. 1331, 1420; Diary, Bailey Letters and Diary, USAMHI; Virginia Troops File, GNMP; V. A. Witcher–John W. Daniel, March 15, 1900, Daniel Papers, UVA; Busey and Martin, *Regimental Strengths*, pp. 195–97, 199, 201.

19. *OR*, 27, 2, pp. 697, 698, 724; Ladd and Ladd, eds., *BP*, 3, p. 1377; Hoffman, Map of East Cavalry Battlefield.

20. *OR*, 27, 2, p. 698; Ladd and Ladd, eds., *BP*, 1, p. 209; 2, p. 1290; Hoffman, interview with author, August 11, 2000; Hoffman, Map of East Cavalry Battlefield.

21. *OR*, 27, 2, p. 697; V. A. Witcher–John W. Daniel, March 15, 1900, Daniel Pa-

pers, UVA; Ladd and Ladd, eds., *BP,* 2, p. 1229; Hoffman, interview with author, August 11, 2000.

22. "Ferguson Brigade Line," 14th Virginia Cavalry File, GNMP; *OR,* 27, 2, pp. 497, 697; Ladd and Ladd, eds., *BP,* 2, pp. 1170, 1170n; 3, pp. 1380, 1381, 1384.

23. *SOR,* 5, p. 271; Ladd and Ladd, eds., *BP,* 2, pp. 1176, 1287; 3, p. 1532; William Brooke Rawle–Henry J. Hunt, November 8, 1894, Hunt Papers, LC; Wayne C. Mann–Author, March 9, 1994, Mann Letter; J. Robertson, *Michigan,* p. 404; Wert, *Custer,* p. 87.

24. Ladd and Ladd, eds., *BP,* 3, p. 1427; Map, July 3rd: East Cavalry Field (Gregg vs. Stuart) File, GNMP; *OR,* 27, 2, p. 697; "Ferguson Brigade Line," 14th Virginia Cavalry File, GNMP.

25. Ladd and Ladd, eds., *BP,* 2, pp. 1082, 1084, 1176, 1206, 1259, 1287; George G. Briggs–J. B. Bachelder, March 26, 1886, 7th Michigan Cavalry File, GNMP; Wert, *Custer,* p. 90.

26. *OR,* 27, 1, p. 956; 2, p. 697.

27. *OR,* 27, 1, pp. 956, 977, 1059; Ladd and Ladd, eds., *BP,* 2, pp. 898, 1075; Gregg, "Army of the Potomac," p. 11, LC.

28. *OR,* 27, 1, pp. 956, 1050; Rawle et al., *History,* pp. 270, 271, 554; Kidd, *Personal Recollections,* pp. 139, 140; J. Robertson, *Michigan,* p. 409; Allan L. Bevan–Sister, August 11, 1863, Bevan Papers, USAMHI; Raus, *Generation,* pp. 30, 143; Busey and Martin, *Regimental Strengths,* p. 104.

29. *OR,* 27, 1, p. 1050; Ladd and Ladd, eds., *BP,* 2, pp. 1263, 1264; Longacre, *Cavalry,* p. 225; James W. Biddle–My dear Pa, July 16, 1863, Biddle Letters, DU.

30. Warner, *Generals in Blue,* pp. 187–88; *Annals,* p. 468; Longacre, *Cavalry,* p. 50.

31. Gregg, *Second Cavalry Division,* p. 11; *Philadelphia North American,* June 29, 1913; *OR,* 27, 1, p. 956.

32. *OR,* 27, 2, p. 497; Ladd and Ladd, eds., *BP,* 2, pp. 1170, 1225, 1246; 3, pp. 1331, 1420; Virginia Troops File, GNMP; H. B. McClellan–Henry J. Hunt, January 1, 1887, Hunt Papers, LC; Micajah Woods–My Dear Father, July 10, 1863, Woods Papers, UVA; Pennington's Battery, U.S. Regulars: Artillery File, GNMP.

33. *OR,* 27, 1, p. 956; Ladd and Ladd, eds., *BP,* 1, p. 652; 2, pp. 1079, 1084, 1122, 1123, 1259, 1265; 3, p. 1431; Rawle et al., *History,* pp. 273, 274, 554; *Michigan at Gettysburg,* p. 148; *SOR,* 5, p. 264; *Annals,* p. 475; William Brooke Rawle–Henry J. Hunt, November 8, 1884, Hunt Papers, LC; William Brooke-Rawle–William E. Miller, June 12, 1878, Rawle Papers, HSP; Hoffman, interview with author, August 11, 2000.

34. *OR,* 27, 1, p. 497; Ladd and Ladd, eds., *BP,* 2, pp. 1077, 1078, 1079, 1252; 3, p. 1427; Virginia Troops File, GNMP.

35. *OR,* 27, 2, p. 497; Ladd and Ladd, eds., *BP,* 2, pp. 1078, 1079, 1085, 1225; 3, pp. 1417, 1427, 1428; Virginia Troops File, GNMP; Micajah Woods–My Dear Fa-

ther, July 10, 1863, Woods Papers, UVA; E. E. Bouldin, "Some of the Cavalry at Gettysburg," Daniel Papers, UVA.

36. *OR*, 27, 2, p. 497; Micajah Woods–My Dear Father, July 10, 1863, Woods Papers, UVA; Virginia Troops File, GNMP; Ladd and Ladd, eds., *BP*, 2, pp. 1078, 1085.

37. *SOR*, 5, pp. 264, 271; V. A. Witcher–John W. Daniel, March 15, 1900, Daniel Papers, UVA; Ladd and Ladd, eds., *BP*, 1, p. 652; 2, pp. 1123, 1176, 1207, 1229, 1237, 1264, 1265; 3, p. 1431; *Final Report*, p. 91; *Michigan at Gettysburg*, p. 149; Rawle et al., *History*, pp. 273, 276.

38. V. A. Witcher–John W. Daniel, March 15, 1900, Daniel Papers, UVA; Ladd and Ladd, eds., *BP*, 2, p. 1290; 3, pp. 1440, 1441, 1444, 1446, 1481; Hoffman, interview with author, August 11, 2000; Hoffman, Map of East Cavalry Battlefield.

39. Ladd and Ladd, eds., *BP*, 2, pp. 652, 1271, 1294; *SOR*, 5, p. 271; Rawle et al., *History*, pp. 275, 276; William Brooke-Rawle–William E. Miller, June 12, 1878, Rawle Papers, HSP; Husby and Wittenberg, eds., *Under Custer's Command*, p. 37; *Final Report*, p. 92; Hoffman, Map of East Cavalry Battlefield.

40. Ladd and Ladd, eds., *BP*, 2, pp. 1112, 1114, 1117, 1264, 1265, 1385; Rawle et al., *History*, p. 274; Hoffman, Map of East Cavalry Battlefield.

41. Ladd and Ladd, eds., *BP*, 2, pp. 1113, 1117, 1378, 1385; Edward C. Brugh–T. T. Munford, April 27, 1886, Munford-Ellis Family Papers, DU.

42. *OR*, 27, 2, pp. 697, 698.

43. Ibid., p. 698; *SOR*, 5, p. 271; Harris, *Michigan Brigade*, p. 13; Ladd and Ladd, eds., *BP*, 2, pp. 1176, 1207, 1265; 3, p. 1448; Rawle et al., *History*, pp. 274, 275; William B. Baker–Parents, July 5, 1863, W. B. Baker Papers, UNC.

44. Ladd and Ladd, eds., *BP*, 2, pp. 1265, 1266; 3, p. 1532; Wert, *Custer*, pp. 92, 93; William Brooke-Rawle–William E. Miller, June 12, 1878, Rawle Papers, HSP; J. A. Clark–My Dear Friend, July 30, 1863, Clark Papers, UM.

45. Wert, *Custer*, pp. 93, 173, 229–30.

46. L. S. Trowbridge–Wife, July [?], 1863; L. S. Trowbridge–R. A. Alger, February 19, 1886, both in 5th Michigan Cavalry File, GNMP; Meyer, *Civil War*, p. 50; *B&L*, 3, p. 404.

47. Sources conflict over whether the fence was a post-and-rail structure or a stone wall topped by rails, but the contemporary accounts favor a post-and-rail fence. See W. O. Lee, comp., *Personal*, p. 155; Urwin, *Custer Victorious*, p. 77; *Michigan at Gettysburg*, p. 151; Gregg, "Army of the Potomac," p. 11, LC; Ladd and Ladd, eds., *BP*, 2, pp. 1207, 1257; Wert, *Custer*, p. 93.

48. Ladd and Ladd, eds., *BP*, 2, pp. 1257, 1266; J. A. Clark–My Dear Friend, July 30, 1863, Clark Papers, UM; Wert, *Custer*, p. 93; Rawle et al., *History*, p. 276; W. O. Lee, comp., *Personal*, p. 155; *Michigan at Gettysburg*, p. 152.

49. Ladd and Ladd, eds., *BP*, 1, pp. 209, 210; 2, pp. 1117, 1201, 1230, 1237, 1266;

OR, 27, 2, pp. 698, 724; *B&L,* 3, p. 404; Urwin, *Custer Victorious,* p. 78; *Michigan at Gettysburg,* p. 152.

50. *Michigan at Gettysburg,* p. 152; *OR,* 27, 2, pp. 698, 724; Ladd and Ladd, eds., *BP,* 2, pp. 1117, 1257; 3, p. 1341; *B&L,* 3, p. 404; William Brooke-Rawle–William E. Miller, June 12, 1878, Rawle Papers, HSP; Longacre, *Cavalry,* p. 231; J. A. Clark–My Dear Friend, July 30, 1863, Clark Papers, UM.

51. Ladd and Ladd, eds., *BP,* 1, p. 209; 2, pp. 1190, 1207, 1266; 3, pp. 1448, 1449; R. A. Alger–John B. Bachelder, January 4, 1886, 5th Michigan Cavalry File, GNMP; Kidd, *Personal Recollections,* pp. 149, 150, 152.

52. *OR,* 27, 2, pp. 724–25; Magner, *Traveller,* p. 46; William Brooke-Rawle–David McM. Gregg, May 29, 1879, Rawle Papers, HSP; Rawle et al., *History,* p. 554.

53. William Brooke-Rawle–William E. Miller, June 12, 1878, Rawle Papers, HSP; Kidd, *Personal Recollections,* p. 153; Rawle et al., *History,* p. 276; James Kidd–Father & Mother, July 9, 1863, Kidd Papers, UM; *Annals,* p. 481.

54. Ladd and Ladd, eds., *BP,* 1, pp. 654, 655; 2, pp. 1079, 1080, 1087–90, 1266, 1267; *Philadelphia North American,* June 29, 1913; James W. Biddle–My dear Pa, July 16, 1863, Biddle Letters, DU; James Kidd–Father & Mother, July 9, 1863, Kidd Papers, UM; David McM. Gregg–[J. Edward Carpenter], December 27, 1877, Gregg Papers, HSP.

55. Ladd and Ladd, eds., *BP,* 3, pp. 1434, 1490; Meyer, *Civil War,* p. 52; Wert, *Custer,* p. 94; Harris, *Michigan Brigade,* pp. 12, 13.

56. Ladd and Ladd, eds., *BP,* 3, pp. 1434, 1435, 1490; Rawle et al., *History,* p. 279; C. M. Norton–A. E. Mathews, July 3, 1886; A. E. Mathews–John B. Bachelder, June 11, 1887, both in 1st Michigan Cavalry File, GNMP; Rawle et al., *History,* p. 279.

57. J. Robertson, *Michigan,* p. 410; *B&L,* 3, p. 404; Rawle et al., *History,* p. 300; Ladd and Ladd, eds., *BP,* 3, pp. 1435, 1436, 1492; Cauthen, ed., *Family Letters,* p. 94; "Personal Reminiscences of Gettysburg, by a Confederate Cavalryman," Smith Papers, DU; Kidd, *Personal Recollections,* pp. 154, 155.

58. Ladd and Ladd, eds., *BP,* 2, pp. 1080, 1222, 1223, 1253, 1254, 1267; Newhall, *Memoir,* pp. 111, 112; Frederick C. Newhall–Father, July 4, 1863, Newhall Letters, HSP.

59. William Brooke-Rawle–William E. Miller, June 12, 1878, Rawle Papers, HSP; Ladd and Ladd, eds., *BP,* 1, pp. 652, 653, 658; *Philadelphia North American,* June 29, 1913; Speese, *Story,* p. 7.

60. John [?]–Folks, July 4, 1863, John Letter, USAMHI; Ladd and Ladd, eds., *BP,* 1, pp. 653, 658; *Philadelphia Weekly Times,* September 14, 1878; *Philadelphia North American,* June 29, 1913; Rawle et al., *History,* p. 279; Speese, *Story,* p. 7; William Brooke-Rawle–William E. Miller, June 12, 1878, Rawle Papers, HSP.

61. Ladd and Ladd, eds., *BP*, 1, pp. 653, 658, 659; *Gettysburg Times*, February 15, 1947; *Philadelphia Weekly Times*, September 14, 1878; William Brooke-Rawle–William E. Miller, June 12, 1878, Rawle Papers, HSP; *Philadelphia North American*, June 29, 1913; Speese, *Story*, p. 9.

62. Ladd and Ladd, eds., *BP*, 1, pp. 653, 654, 658; *Philadelphia Weekly Times*, September 14, 1878; Gregg, "Army of the Potomac," p. 16, LC; William Brooke-Rawle–William E. Miller, June 12, 1878, Rawle Papers, HSP; Speese, *Story*, p. 9.

63. *OR*, 27, 1, p. 957; Wert, *Custer*, p. 95; Ladd and Ladd, eds., *BP*, 2, pp. 1114, 1230, 1231; 3, p. 1493.

64. Haden, *J.E.B. Stuart's Cavalry*, p. 25; Macomber Diary, CMU; Edward Corselius–Mother, July 4, 1863, Corselius Papers, UM; Andrew Newton Buck–Brothers & Sisters, July 9, 1863, Buck Family Papers, UM; Barbour Diary, UM; Wert, *Custer*, p. 95.

65. *OR*, 27, 2, p. 699.

66. J. Robertson, *Michigan*, p. 410.

67. *OR*, 27, 1, pp. 781, 791; 2, p. 699; James Kidd–Father & Mother, July 9, 1863, Kidd Papers, UM; Hoffman, interview with author, August 11, 2000; William H. O'Brien–Brother, October 21, 1863, O'Brien Family Papers, UM.

68. Warner, *Generals in Blue*, p. 266; *OR*, 27, 3, p. 356; Sauers, ed., *Fighting Them Over*, p. 473.

69. *OR*, 27, 1, pp. 914, 916, 992, 993; Busey and Martin, *Regimental Strengths*, p. 107.

70. *OR*, 27, 1, p. 993; Penny and Laine, *Struggle*, pp. 116, 142; Shevchuk, "1st Texas," p. 84; Map, July 3rd: South Cavalry Field File, GNMP.

71. *OR*, 27, 1, pp. 943, 993; Ladd and Ladd, eds., *BP*, 2, p. 916; Account of Private Samuel James Crockett, July 3rd: South Cavalry Field File, GNMP; Shevchuk, "Cavalry Fight at Fairfield," p. 106; Busey and Martin, *Regimental Strengths*, p. 102.

72. Warner, *Generals in Blue*, p. 321; Ladd and Ladd, eds., *BP*, 2, p. 916; Penny and Laine, *Struggle*, pp. 134, 142; Frassanito, *Early Photography*, p. 180.

73. Penny and Laine, *Struggle*, pp. 100–108, 134, 142, 182; Thomas L. McCarty, "1st Texas," July 3rd: Farnsworth File, GNMP; Shevchuk, "1st Texas," p. 82.

74. Penny and Laine, *Struggle*, p. 112; Black, *Crumbling Defenses*, pp. 39–41; Ladd and Ladd, eds., *BP*, 2, pp. 1215, 1216, 1241; 3, p. 1344; Coco, *Concise Guide*, p. 83.

75. Shevchuk, "1st Texas," pp. 84, 85; Penny and Laine, *Struggle*, pp. 120–24, 132; McCarty Collection, UT; Thomas L. McCarty, "1st Texas," July 3rd: Farnsworth File, GNMP.

76. *OR*, 27, 2, pp. 397, 400, 402; Ladd and Ladd, eds., *BP*, 3, pp. 1370, 1872; Penny and Laine, *Struggle*, pp. 117, 134; Wittenberg, "Merritt's Regulars," pp. 117, 119.

77. *OR*, 27, 2, pp. 400, 403; Ladd and Ladd, eds., *BP*, 2, pp. 916, 917, 1216, 1217, 1242, 1370; 3, pp. 1872, 1873; Black, *Crumbling Defenses*, pp. 41, 42; Penny and Laine, *Struggle*, pp. 133–35; Samuel Crockett Diary, 1st U.S. Cavalry File, GNMP; *CV*, 21, p. 336.

78. *OR*, 27, 1, pp. 993, 1012, 1018; H. C. Parsons, "Farnsworth's Charge and Death," 1st Vermont Cavalry File, GNMP; Wittenberg, *Gettysburg's Forgotten Cavalry Actions*, pp. 25, 31; John H. Bennett, "1st Vermont Cavalry," July 3rd: Farnsworth File, GNMP; "North Carolina Troops at Gettysburg," North Carolina Troops File, GNMP; Coco, *Concise Guide*, p. 77.

79. Tagg, *Generals*, pp. 182–83; Penny and Laine, *Struggle*, pp. 139–40.

80. John W. Bennett, "1st Vermont Cavalry"; Henry Clay Potter, "Personal Experiences of Henry Clay Potter (Capt. 18th Penna. Cavalry) in Battle of Gettysburg," both in July 3rd: Farnsworth File, GNMP; H. C. Parsons, "Farnsworth's Charge and Death," 1st Vermont Cavalry File, GNMP; Wittenberg, *Gettysburg's Forgotten Cavalry Actions*, pp. 25–26.

81. *OR*, 27, 1, pp. 1018, 1019; *New York Times*, July 3, 1913; Shevchuk, "1st Texas," p. 85; Thomas L. McCarty, "1st Texas," July 3rd: Farnsworth File, GNMP; *CV*, 8, p. 240.

82. *OR*, 27, 1, p. 1019; Thomas L. McCarty, "1st Texas"; Letter of H. W. Berryman, July 9, 1863, both in July 3rd: Farnsworth File, GNMP; *New York Times*, July 3, 1913; James H. Hendrick–Mother, July 8, 1863, Brake Collection, USAMHI.

83. *OR*, 27, 1, pp. 186, 1019; Shevchuk, "1st Texas," pp. 85–86; Letter of H. W. Berryman, July 9, 1863, July 3rd: Farnsworth File, GNMP; *Athens Messenger*, August 13, 1863; Busey and Martin, *Regimental Strengths*, p. 107.

84. *OR*, 27, 1, pp. 1009, 1012; Sauers, ed., *Fighting Them Over*, p. 485; Shevchuk, "1st Texas," pp. 85, 86; J. Andrew Witt–John B. Bachelder, May 17, 1888, July 3rd: Farnsworth File, GNMP; Klingensmith, "Cavalry Regiment's First Campaign," p. 65.

85. *OR*, 27, 1, pp. 186, 1009, 1012; J. Andrew Witt–John B. Bachelder, May 17, 1898; Account of John W. Philips, n.d., both in July 3rd: Farnsworth File, GNMP; Klingensmith, "Cavalry Regiment's First Campaign," p. 65.

86. *OR*, 27, 1, p. 1013; *B&L*, 3, p. 394; Wittenberg, *Gettysburg's Forgotten Cavalry Actions*, p. 27; H. C. Parsons, "Farnsworth's Charge and Death," 1st Vermont Cavalry File, GNMP; Busey and Martin, *Regimental Strengths*, p. 107; Winey, *Union Army Uniforms*, pp. 27–28.

87. *OR*, 27, 1, p. 1013; *B&L*, 3, p. 395; "1st Vermont Cavalry," July 3rd: Farnsworth File, GNMP; George T. Balch, Statement, October 14, 1863, Balch Statement, USAMHI.

88. *B&L*, 3, p. 395; Sauers, ed., *Fighting Them Over*, p. 478; Wittenberg, *Gettysburg's Forgotten Cavalry Actions*, pp. 29–31; Penny and Laine, *Struggle*, p. 142.

89. Ladd and Ladd, eds., *BP*, 2, p. 496; Henry L. Figures–Sister, July 8, 1863, Fig-

ures Letters, PML; Wittenberg, *Gettysburg's Forgotten Cavalry Actions,* pp. 29, 32; Penny and Laine, *Struggle,* p. 142.

90. Wittenberg, *Gettysburg's Forgotten Cavalry Actions,* p. 32; *B&L,* 3, p. 395; Sauers, ed., *Fighting Them Over,* pp. 478–79; "1st Vermont Cavalry," July 3rd: Farnsworth File, GNMP; "Diary of Turner Vaughan," p. 589.

91. Sauers, ed., *Fighting Them Over,* p. 479; *B&L,* 3, p. 395; Wittenberg, *Gettysburg's Forgotten Cavalry Actions,* p. 32; Penny and Laine, *Struggle,* p. 142.

92. *B&L,* 3, p. 395; Ladd and Ladd, eds., *BP,* 3, p. 1547; Wittenberg, *Gettysburg's Forgotten Cavalry Actions,* p. 32; George T. Balch, Statement, October 14, 1863, Balch Statement, USAMHI; Ide, "First Vermont Cavalry," p. 17; Penny and Laine, *Struggle,* p. 142.

93. Wittenberg, *Gettysburg's Forgotten Cavalry Actions,* pp. 32–34; *B&L,* 3, p. 395; Ladd and Ladd, eds., *BP,* 1, p. 497; Ide, "First Vermont Cavalry," p. 17.

94. Ladd and Ladd, eds., *BP,* 1, p. 497; Account of George Hillyer, July 3rd: South Cavalry Field File, GNMP; *B&L,* 3, p. 395; Wittenberg, *Gettysburg's Forgotten Cavalry Actions,* p. 34.

95. *B&L,* 3, p. 395; Ladd and Ladd, eds., *BP,* 3, p. 1557; Henry L. Figures–Sister, July 8, 1863, Figures Letters, PML; Wittenberg, *Gettysburg's Forgotten Cavalry Actions,* p. 35.

96. "1st Texas"; "Farnsworth—Did He Or Didn't He?," both in July 3rd: Farnsworth File, GNMP; Black, *Crumbling Defenses,* p. 43; Ladd and Ladd, eds., *BP,* 3, pp. 1557, 1559, 1560; *Philadelphia Press,* July 4, 1888; Wesson Diary, USAMHI; Wittenberg, *Gettysburg's Forgotten Cavalry Actions,* pp. 45–52; *OR,* 27, 1, p. 993.

97. *OR,* 27, 1, pp. 186, 1013; 2, p. 396; Ladd and Ladd, eds., *BP,* 3, pp. 1557, 1558; *B&L,* 3, pp. 395–96; Sauers, ed., *Fighting Them Over,* p. 479; Blinn Civil War Diary, UVT; Beyer and Keydel, eds., *Deeds,* p. 239.

98. *Wheeling Daily Intelligencer,* July 15, 1863; Shevchuk, "1st Texas," p. 90.

99. *OR,* 27, 1, p. 948; *Proceedings,* p. 3, Starr Papers, UT; Shevchuk, "Cavalry Fight at Fairfield," p. 106; Wittenberg, *Gettysburg's Forgotten Cavalry Actions,* p. 70.

100. Carter, *From Yorktown to Santiago,* p. 97; Wittenberg, *Gettysburg's Forgotten Cavalry Actions,* p. 71.

101. Shevchuk, "Cavalry Fight at Fairfield," p. 107; Wittenberg, *Gettysburg's Forgotten Cavalry Actions,* pp. 68, 69, 71.

102. *OR,* 27, 1, p. 948; Busey and Martin, *Regimental Strengths,* p. 98; *Proceedings,* p. 3, Starr Papers, UT; Shevchuk, "Cavalry Fight at Fairfield," p. 106; Wittenberg, *Gettysburg's Forgotten Cavalry Actions,* p. 71.

103. Shevchuk, "Cavalry Fight at Fairfield," p. 107; Carter, *From Yorktown to Santiago,* p. 95; *Proceedings,* p. 3, Starr Papers, UT.

104. *Proceedings,* p. 3, Starr Papers, UT; *National Tribune,* June 6, 1891; Shevchuk,

"Cavalry Fight at Fairfield," pp. 108, 110; Statement of James McDowell, April 4, 1895, Platt Letters, USAMHI.

105. *OR,* 27, 2, pp. 752, 756; Nunnelee, "Diary"/Memoir, MC; Hawse Diary, UVA; T. Alexander, "Gettysburg Cavalry Operations," p. 40.

106. *OR,* 27, 2, p. 752; Warner, *Generals in Gray,* pp. 166–67; Longacre, *Cavalry,* p. 30.

107. *OR,* 27, 2, p. 752.

108. Ibid., pp. 752, 756, 760; W. N. McDonald, *History,* pp. 154, 155.

109. *OR,* 27, 2, pp. 752, 756; W. N. McDonald, *History,* p. 155; Neese, *Three Years,* pp. 188, 189.

110. *OR,* 27, 2, p. 752; Statement of James McDowell, April 6, 1895, Platt Letters, USAMHI; W. N. McDonald, *History,* p. 155; Carter, *From Yorktown to Santiago,* p. 96; Shevchuk, "Cavalry Fight at Fairfield," p. 113; Wittenberg, *Gettysburg's Forgotten Cavalry Actions,* p. 78; Opie, *Rebel Cavalryman,* p. 172.

111. *OR,* 27, 2, pp. 752, 756, 760; W. N. McDonald, *History,* pp. 155, 156; *Proceedings,* pp. 4, 5, Starr Papers, UT; Carter, *From Yorktown to Santiago,* pp. 96, 97; *National Tribune,* August 6, 1891; Knapp Diary, WMU.

112. Shevchuk, "Cavalry Fight at Fairfield," p. 113; Coco, *Wasted Valor,* pp. 110–11.

113. *Proceedings,* pp. 4, 5, Starr Papers, UT; Carter, *From Yorktown to Santiago,* pp. 97, 98; *National Tribune,* August 6, 1891; Shevchuk, "Cavalry Fight at Fairfield," pp. 113, 115, 116; Statement of James McDowell, April 6, 1895; O. W. Bennett–Lewis H. Carpenter, April 24, [?], both in Platt Letters, USAMHI.

114. *OR,* 27, 1, p. 948; 2, pp. 752, 756, 760; Carter, *From Yorktown to Santiago,* p. 98; Shevchuk, "Cavalry Fight at Fairfield," p. 115.

115. *OR,* 27, 1, pp. 654, 657, 685; Thomson and Rauch, *History,* pp. 273, 274; *Pennsylvania at Gettysburg,* 1, p. 283.

116. *OR,* 27, 1, pp. 654, 657; 2, pp. 416, 423; *Pennsylvania at Gettysburg,* 1, p. 283.

117. *OR,* 27, 2, pp. 416, 417, 423.

118. *OR,* 1, p. 654; 2, pp. 417, 423; Thomson and Rauch, *History,* p. 274.

119. *OR,* 27, 1, pp. 654, 655; 2, pp. 417, 423, 424; *SOR,* 5, p. 205; *CV,* 13, p. 250; Rollins, *"Damned Red Flags,"* p. 196. McCandless reported that his men captured two hundred Georgians; Benning placed the figure at eighty or ninety.

120. *OR,* 27, 1, pp. 657, 658, 685; Thomson and Rauch, *History,* p. 274; Samuel W. Crawford–My dear Mr. Smith, July 12, 1886, Crawford Letters, GC.

Epilogue: "This Place Called Gettysburg"

1. Elmore, "Torrid Heat," p. 19.

2. Whitmore Diary, MHS; Palmer, *Second Brigade,* p. 199; Longhenry, "Yankee Piper," pp. 3–25, ANB; Nevins, ed., *Diary,* pp. 249–50; Byrne and Weaver, *Haskell,* p. 185.

3. Ladd and Ladd, eds., *BP*, 2, p. 998.

4. Ibid., p. 998; Bloom, " 'We Never Expected a Battle,' " p. 181.

5. Ladd and Ladd, eds., *BP*, 2, p. 1002; Abner Doubleday–Samuel P. Bates, April 10, 1874, Bates Papers, LC.

6. George P. Erwin–Father, July 3, 1863, Erwin Papers, UNC.

7. Maust, "Union Second Corps Hospital," pp. 54–55; extract of a letter of E. Corbin, July 5, 1863, Pettit's Battery Letters, GNMP; William B. Clement–Wife, May 31, 1863, Clement Papers, NCDAH; Kennedy Diary, UNC; Diary of a 57th Virginia Surgeon, Lippitt Papers, UNC.

8. George Cramer–Wife, July 11, 1863, 11th Pennsylvania Infantry File, GNMP; Joseph Hopkins Twichell–My darling Sis, July 6, 1863, Twichell Civil War Letters, YU; Isaac Sidney Barineau–My Dear Sister, July 15, 1863, Barineau Collection, USAMHI; Homer Baldwin–My dear Father, July 7, 1863, 5th United States Artillery, Battery C File, GNMP.

9. Whitmore Diary, MHS; Henry P. Clare–William Clare, July 5, 1863, Clare Papers, DU.

10. John H. Burrill–Parents, July 13, 1863, Burrill Letters, USAMHI; Jerry Collins–S. G. Jack, February 21, 1903, Collins Papers, DCHS.

11. James T. Miller–Sister, August 8, 1863, Miller Papers, UM; Blanchard Memoir, p. 8, ECHS.

12. Blanchard Memoir, pp. 8–9, ECHS; Rudy Diary, DHSTC; *National Tribune,* June 9, 1887.

13. Thompson, " 'This Hell,' " pp. 22–23.

14. G. T. Fleming, ed., *Life of Hays,* p. 421; Nevins, ed., *Diary,* p. 252; Henry Clare–My dear William, July 5, 1863, Clare Letters, GC; David M. Smith–[Family], July 10, 1863, Smith Letters, PML; Coco, *Strange and Blighted Land,* p. 58.

15. Blight, ed., *When This Cruel War Is Over,* p. 239.

16. The figures used are a composite of those in R. K. Krick, comp., *Gettysburg Death Roster,* p. 17; Coco, *Strange and Blighted Land,* p. 2; Busey, *These Honored Dead,* p. 6. The officially reported casualties are listed in *OR,* 27, 1, pp. 173–87; 2, pp. 338–346.

17. Busey, *These Honored Dead,* passim; Aldrich, *History,* p. 219; Cowtam, *Services,* p. 210; Hamblen, *Connecticut Yankees,* pp. 123–24; James E. Decker–Sister, July 6, 1863, Decker Letters, USAMHI; Muster Report, 4th United States Artillery, Battery A File, GNMP.

18. See above chap. 4 for Confederate numbers and losses on Culp's Hill; Georg and Busey, *Nothing but Glory,* p. 226; G. R. Stewart, *Pickett's Charge,* p. 263; *OR,* 27, 2, pp. 338–46.

19. Georg and Busey, *Nothing but Glory,* p. 226; G. R. Stewart, *Pickett's Charge,* p. 263; *OR,* 27, 2, p. 339; See above chap. 13 for Union numbers on captives.

20. Howard, *Recollections*, p. 214; Powhatan B. Whittle–Brother, July 8, 1863, Whittle Papers, UNC; Granville W. Belcher–My Dear Caroline, July 16, 1863, Belcher Papers, DU; Blackford, *Letters*, p. 190, Griggs Book, MC.

21. R. K. Krick, *Lee's Colonels*, pp. 28, 35, 46, 68, 70, 73, 114, 117, 128, 135, 151, 157, 177, 212, 240, 244, 247, 248, 267, 270, 275, 280, 283, 286, 296, 322, 337, 348, 356, 362, 367, 369, 371, 374; Harrison, *Pickett's Men*, p. 103; Wallace, *3rd Virginia Infantry*, p. 38; Divine, *8th Virginia Infantry*, p. 25; Trask, *9th Virginia Infantry*, p. 26; James J. Phillips–F. H. Smith, July 18, 1863, 9th Virginia Infantry File, GNMP; Crews and Parrish, *14th Virginia Infantry*, pp. 42, 43; Gregory, *38th Virginia Infantry*, pp. 42, 43; Loving Diary, LVA; R. E. Dunn–Brother, July 19, 1863, Dunn Family Papers, VHS; H. C. Michie–Robert W. Douthat, April 23, 1906, Douthat Papers, NA; E. M. Magruder–Sister, c. August 1863, Magruder Papers, DU; J. C. Carrington–Eppa Hunton, September 29, 1903; H. C. Michie–John Daniel, January 27, 1904, both in Daniel Papers, UVA; Davis, "Death," pp. 113–14.

22. R. K. Krick, *Lee's Colonels*, pp. 27, 33, 39, 45, 47, 49, 62, 63, 64, 80, 81, 86, 90, 94, 99, 121, 122, 125, 138, 146, 149, 150, 178, 184, 187, 197, 210, 213, 222, 224, 226, 233, 243, 245, 248, 250, 252, 258, 273, 293, 294, 296, 300, 305, 308, 316, 327, 329, 335, 336, 351, 354, 373, 377; G. R. Stewart, *Pickett's Charge*, p. 263; Patrick Diary, LC.

23. Winschel, "Heavy Was Their Loss," p. 83; Cockrell and Ballard, eds., *Mississippi Rebel*, p. 198; George P. Erwin–Father, July 3, 1863, Erwin Papers, UNC; *OR*, 27, 2, p. 667; Taylor, "Col. James Keith Marshall," p. 88; Sherrill Diary, MC; *North Carolina Standard*, July 17, 28, 1863; Harris, "Historical Sketches," p. 37, SHSW; Walter Clark, ed., *Histories*, 1, pp. 380, 590; Rowland, *Military History*, pp. 50, 56, 124; Speer, ed., *Voices*, pp. 107, 109; Vairin Diary, p. 75, MDAH.

24. Charles R. "Dick" Phelps–Aunt, July 9, 1863, Phelps Papers, UVA; H. W. Barrow–Christian Pfohl, July 19, 1863, Pfohl Papers, UNC; John B. Gordon–My *own precious wife*, July 7, 10, 1863, Gordon Family Papers, UGA; W. J. Kincheloe–Sister, July 10, 1863, Daniel Papers, UVA; Marcus Hefner–Wife, July 10, 1863, Hefner Papers, NCDAH; William J. Hatchett–My Dear Parents, July 7, 1863, Hatchett Family Papers, USAMHI.

25. Report of Major Joseph R. Cabell, July 11, 1863, Armistead Ledger, MC; *OR*, 27, 2, p. 667; Noah Deaton–Sister, August 12, 1863, Deaton Papers, DU; Lemuel J. Hoyle–My Dear Mother, July 12, 1863, Hoyle Papers, UNC; Cockrell and Ballard, eds., *Mississippi Rebel*, p. 199.

26. The best examination of the controversy is in Reardon, *Pickett's Charge*, passim; Motts, " 'Brave and Resolute Force,' " p. 29.

27. George Bowles–Absent Friend, August 4, 1863, Bowles-Jordan Letters, UVA; Rozier, ed., *Granite Farm Letters*, p. 115; Speer, ed., *Voices*, p. 107; John C.

Granbery–Ella F. Granbery, July 8, 1863, Granbery Papers, UVA; R. K. Krick, *Parker's Virginia Battery,* p. 191; William H. Sanders–Matthew, July 16, 1863, Sanders Papers, ADAH.

28. G. R. Stewart, *Pickett's Charge,* p. 235; J. J. Young–Zebulon B. Vance, July 4, 1863, Vance Correspondence, NCDAH; J.S.D. Cullen–My dear Lottie, July 8, 1863, Daniel Papers, UVA; Walter H. Taylor–Sister, July 7, 1863, Taylor Papers, LVA; Jacob B. Click–Old Friend Lucius, July 17, 1863, Click Papers, DU; Gaston Saunders–My Dear Mother, July 15, 1863, Saunders Papers, UNC; Kennedy Diary, UNC; Louis G. Young–William J. Baker, February 10, 1864, Winston Papers, NCDAH.

29. Alexander McNeill–Tine, July 8, 1863, 2nd South Carolina Infantry File, GNMP; David Ballenger–My dear Mother, July 18, 1863, Ballenger Papers, USC; William H. Sanders–Matthew, July 16, 1863, Sanders Papers, ADAH; Speer, ed., *Voices,* p. 107.

30. *OR,* 27, 2, pp. 308, 320; Lee, *Recollections,* p. 102; Maurice, ed., *Aide-De-Camp,* p. 222.

31. *OR,* 27, 2, p. 308; Gallagher, ed., *Fighting For,* pp. 110, 120, 233, 234.

32. *OR,* 27, 2, p. 308; Griffith, *Battle Tactics,* p. 38; Harsh, *Confederate Tide Rising,* p. 70.

33. *OR,* 27, 2, p. 320; "The Gettysburg Campaign," p. 1, Alexander Papers, UNC; see chaps. 3, 4 above.

34. *OR,* 27, 2, p. 298; Bandy and Freeland, eds., *Gettysburg Papers,* 1, p. 72; *Annals,* p. 433; Harsh, *Confederate Tide Rising,* p. 70.

35. Kross, "July 3rd Action," p. 18.

36. See chap. 6 above; *OR,* 27, 2, p. 321.

37. E. P. Alexander–Frederick Colston, February 9, 1904, Campbell-Colston Family Papers, UNC; E. M. Thomas, *Robert E. Lee,* pp. 302, 303.

38. George L. Christian–John Daniel, July 4, 1898, Daniel Papers, UVA.

39. James Longstreet–D. E. Sickles, September 19, 1902, Longstreet Papers, HSP; *Annals,* p. 414; Hamilton, ed., *Papers,* 2, p. 27; E. P. Alexander–Mr. Bancroft, October 30, 1904, Longstreet Papers, DU; *B&L,* 3, p. 345.

40. See chaps. 10–13 above; Lord, ed., *Fremantle Diary,* p. 212; Longstreet, *From Manassas to Appomattox,* pp. 393–95.

41. *OR,* 27, 3, p. 1075; Walter Taylor–Charles Venable, October 8, 1892; James Longstreet–J. Van Holt Nash, October 30, 1892, both in Taylor Papers, LVA; W. Stuart Symington–Frederick M. Colston, December 21, 1903, Alexander Papers, UNC; Charles Pickett–Lida Perry, March 24, 1896, Pickett Papers, DU; Charles Pickett–James Longstreet, October 17, 1892, Longstreet Papers, EU.

42. *OR,* 27, 2, p. 309.

43. Williams, ed., "From Sumter," p. 100.

44. William A. Allison–Stock, July 18, 1863, Allison Letters, PML; Samuel B.

Carter–Vincent B. Brewer, July 9, 1863, Carter Letter, USAMHI; Hager, Civil War Memoirs, UVA; David E. Beem–My dear Wife, July 5, 1863, Beem Papers, IHS.

45. Griffith, *Battle Tactics*, p. 38.
46. Ibid.
47. Ibid.; Tucker, *Lee and Longstreet*, p. 227.
48. See chaps. 7, 10–13 above.
49. *OR*, 27, 1, p. 75; 3, p. 499; George G. Meade–Margaret, July 5, 8, 1863; George Meade–My Dear Mama, July 6, 1863, all in Meade Collection, HSP.
50. Moore, "Cornie," p. 120, USAMHI; Gulian V. Weir–Dearest Father, July 5, 1863, 5th U.S. Artillery, Battery C File, GNMP.
51. Edwin M. Stanton–George G. Meade, July 7, 1863; John Pope–My dear Meade, July 10, 1863; George B. McClellan–My dear General, July 11, 1863; Henry W. Halleck–Major Genl Meade, July 28, 1863, all in Meade Collection, HSP.
52. Ladd and Ladd, eds., *BP*, 2, p. 920.
53. Everson and Simpson, eds., *"Far, Far From Home,"* p. 257; Racine, *"Unspoiled Heart,"* p. 52.
54. *OR*, 27, 2, pp. 311, 326; 3, p. 514; D. C. Pfanz, *Richard S. Ewell*, pp. 320, 321; McDonald, ed., *Make Me a Map*, p. 158; John D. Imboden–M. S. O'Donnell, August 4, 1891, Imboden Letter, USAMHI; Diary, Alexander Papers, UNC.
55. J. S. Bartlett, Recollections, p. 4, Bartlett Papers, UNC; Cadwallader Jones–Sister, August 28, 1863, Jones Papers, UNC; Diary, Alexander Papers, UNC; Latrobe Diary, VHS; Coddington, *Gettysburg Campaign*, chap. 20.
56. Theodore Fogel–My Dear Sister, July 16, 1863, Fogel Papers, EU.
57. William M. Clark–My Dear Sister, July 5, 1863, 147th Pennsylvania Infantry File, GNMP; Hartwig, "It Struck Horror," p. 99; *OR*, 27, 1, pp. 25, 378; *CV*, 21, p. 537.
58. John P. Blinn–My Darling Cora, July 4, 1863, 20th Massachusetts Infantry File, GNMP; John P. Blinn–Mother, Brother & Sister, July 4, 1863, Adams Papers, GNMP.
59. Lane, ed., *"Dear Mother,"* p. 259.
60. Cyril Tyler–Father, July 7, 1863, 7th Michigan Infantry File, GNMP.
61. Sword, *Southern Invincibility*, p. 181.

BIBLIOGRAPHY

Unpublished Sources

Alabama Department of Archives and History, Montgomery, Ala.:
 Sanders, William Henry. Papers
American Antiquarian Society, Worcester, Mass.:
 Buckingham, Philo B. Letter, July 17, 1863
Antietam National Battlefield, Library, Sharpsburg, Md.:
 Longhenry, Ludolph. "A Yankee Piper in Dixie." Seventh Wisconsin Infantry
  File
Bancroft Public Library, Salem, N.Y.:
 Cruikshank, Robert. Memoir
Brown University, John Hay Library, Providence, R.I.:
 Inman, Arthur Crew. Papers
Central Michigan University, Clark Historical Library, Mount Pleasant, Mich.:
 Macomber, Dexter M. Diary. Typescript
Chicago Historical Society, Chicago, Ill.:
 Benedict, Edwin D. Diary
The College of William and Mary, The Earl Gregg Swem Library, Manuscripts
  Department, Williamsburg, Va.:
 Southall, George Washington. Papers
Connecticut Historical Society, Hartford, Conn.:
 Goodrich, Loren H. Papers
Connecticut State Library, Hartford, Conn.:
 Chapman, Horatio Dana. Diary
 Clark, Charles H. Letter, July 4, 1863
 Packer, Warren W. Diary

Rugg, Harlan P. Diary and Memorandum
Truesdell Family. Papers
Delaware Public Archives, Dover, Del.:
Woodall, Daniel. Papers
DeWitt Historical Society of Tompkins County, Ithaca, N.Y.:
Rudy, Henry. Diary
Duke University, William R. Perkins Library, Special Collections, Durham, N.C.:
Bedinger-Dandridge Family. Correspondence
Belcher, Granville W. Papers
Biddle, Samuel Simpson. Letters
Byrnes, William. Diary
Cain, Patrick H. Letters
Clare, William Keating. Papers
Click, Jacob B. Papers
Deaton, Noah. Papers
Dula, A. J. Papers
Harden Family. Papers
Haskell, John C. Papers
Holley, Turner W. Papers
Jones, Charles Colcock. Papers
Jones, George W. Papers
Longstreet, James. Papers
Magruder, John Bowie. Papers
Maury, Richard L. Papers
McLaws, Lafayette. Papers
Munford-Ellis Family. Papers
Nadenbousch, J.Q.A. Papers
Pickett, George Edward. Papers
Porter, John Richardson. Papers
Reynolds, Isaac V. Papers
Smith, Stephens Calhoun. Papers
Winn, John and Philip James. Papers
Dutchess County Historical Society, Poughkeepsie, N.Y.:
Collins, Jerry. Papers
Funk, Peter. Diary
Titus, Richard. Letters
Emory University, Robert W. Woodruff Library, Special Collections, Atlanta, Ga.:
Fogel, Theodore. Papers
Gourdin, Robert N. Papers
Longstreet, James. Papers
Shore, Augustine. Papers

Erie County Historical Society, Erie, Pa.:
    Blanchard, C. H. Memoir
Florida State Archives, Tallahassee, Fla.:
    Bryan, Council A. Papers
    Lang, David. Letterbooks
Georgia Historical Society, Savannah, Ga.:
    Pigman, William Penn. Diary
Gettysburg College, Library, Special Collections, Gettysburg, Pa.:
    Clare, Henry Pentland. Letters
    Crawford, Samuel W. Letters
    Jacobs, Michael. Letters. Photocopies
    Osborn, Stephen Allen. "Reminiscence of the Civil War."
Gettysburg National Military Park, Library, Gettysburg, Pa.:
    1st Michigan Cavalry File
    1st New York Artillery, Battery B File
    1st New York Independent Battery, Cowan's Battery File
    1st Pennsylvania Artillery, Cooper's Battery B File
    1st Pennsylvania Light Artillery, Hampton's Battery File
    1st South Carolina Infantry File
    1st U.S. Artillery, Battery I File
    1st U.S. Cavalry File
    1st Vermont Cavalry File
    2nd Maryland Battalion of Infantry File
    2nd Massachusetts Infantry File
    2nd South Carolina Infantry File
    2nd Virginia Infantry File
    4th U.S. Artillery, Battery A, Cushing's Battery File
    5th Alabama Battalion of Infantry File
    5th Alabama Infantry File
    5th Michigan Cavalry File
    5th U.S. Artillery, Battery C File
    6th Michigan Cavalry File
    6th Virginia Infantry File
    7th Michigan Cavalry File
    7th Michigan Infantry File
    9th Virginia Infantry File
    11th North Carolina Infantry File
    11th Pennsylvania Infantry File
    12th New Jersey Infantry File
    14th Georgia Infantry File
    14th North Carolina Infantry File

14th Tennessee Infantry File
14th Virginia Cavalry File
18th Virginia Infantry File
19th Maine Infantry File
19th Massachusetts Infantry File
20th Massachusetts Infantry File
23rd Virginia Infantry File
24th Virginia Infantry File
26th North Carolina Infantry File
27th Indiana Infantry File
37th North Carolina Infantry File
37th Virginia Infantry File
40th Virginia Infantry File
45th New York Infantry File
52nd North Carolina Infantry File
53rd Virginia Infantry File
66th Ohio Infantry File
69th Pennsylvania Infantry File
73rd Pennsylvania Infantry File
111th New York Infantry File
123rd New York Infantry File
137th New York Infantry File
140th New York Infantry File
147th Pennsylvania Infantry File
Alabama Troops: General Information File
Bachelder, John B. Papers
Bliss Farm Buildings File
Bryan Farm Files
Buckley, John. Papers
Georg, Kathleen R. " 'A Common Pride And Fame': The Attack and Repulse of
    Pickett's Division at Gettysburg July 3, 1863," n.d.
Gregory A. Coco Collection:
    Adams, John E. Papers
    Parmater, N. L. Diary. Typescript
    Pettit's Battery. Letters
    Sheaffer, Daniel. Farm Claims
    Sherman, George W. Papers
    Street, John L. Papers
    Wheeler, Charles M. Papers
    Wright, James A. "The Story of Co. F, 1st Minn. Inf." Typescript copy
Gettysburg Newspaper Clippings

July 3rd: Farnsworth's Charge and Death File
July 3rd: Longstreet's Assault File, #1
July 3rd: South Cavalry Field File
Kane, Thomas L. File
"The Left Flank During Pickett's Charge: Pender's Division in Longstreet's
    Assault by Gen. Lane" File
North Carolina Troops: General Information File
Tennessee Troops: General Information File
U. S. Regulars: Artillery File
Virginia Troops: General Information File
Wistar, Isaac Jones. Papers
Harvard University, The Houghton Library, Cambridge, Mass.:
    Dearborn, Frederick M. Collection
Historical Society of Pennsylvania, Philadelphia, Pa.:
    Alloway, John W. Diary
    Biddle, James Cornell. Civil War Letters
    Cavada, Adolphus F. Diary
    Gibbon, John. Papers
    Gregg, David McMurtrie. Papers
    Longstreet, James. Papers
    Lynch, John Wheat. Letters
    Meade, George G. Collection
    Newhall, Walter Symonds. Letters, 1862–1863
    Rawle, William Brooke. Papers
Hoffman, Daniel:
    "A Bit of History Through the Eyes of John Rummel." Private
    Interview with author, August 11, 2000
    Map of East Cavalry Battlefield. Private
Indiana Historical Society, Indianapolis, Ind.:
    Beem, David E. Collection
Indiana University, Lilly Library, Manuscripts Department, Bloomington, Ind.:
    Harding, John L. Papers
Library of Congress, Washington, D. C.:
    Bates, Samuel P. Papers
    Gregg, David McM. "Army of the Potomac in the Gettysburg Campaign." David
        McM. Gregg Papers
    Hotchkiss, Jedediah. Papers
    Hunt, Henry J. Papers
    Love, John J. H. Papers
    McCullough, S. Thomas. Diary
    McPherson, Edward. Papers

Miscellaneous Manuscripts Collection:
    Shriver, William. Collection
    Squires, W.H.T. "The Last of Lee's Battle Line." Washington Artillery of New
        Orleans Papers
    Patrick, Marsena R. Diary
    War Department Battlefield Commission. "A Record of the Positions of Troops on
        the Battlefield"
    Wilcox, Cadmus. Papers
Library of Virginia, Richmond, Va.:
    Denoon, Charles E. Papers
    Loving, Edwin Baker. Diary
    Taylor, Walter H. Papers
    Welsh, John P. Letters
Louisiana State University, Hill Memorial Library, Special Collections, Baton
        Rouge, La.:
    Batchelor, Albert A. Papers
Maine State Archives, Augusta, Me.:
    Records of the Adjutant General of Maine
Manassas National Battlefield Park, Library, Manassas, Va.:
    Berkeley, Edmund. "War Reminiscences and Others of a Son of the Old
        Dominion." 8th Virginia Infantry File
Mann, Wayne C. Letter to author, March 9, 1994
Maryland Historical Society, Baltimore, Md.:
    Dielman, Louis H. Collection. #2163
Massachusetts Historical Society, Boston, Mass.:
    Beal, Caleb Hadley. Papers
    Failing, Elliot P. Diary. Failing-Knight Papers
    Hayward, Nathan. Papers
    Morse, Charles F. Papers
    Paine, Sumner. Papers
    Whitmore, George A. Diary
Middle Georgia Archives, Washington Library, Macon, Ga.:
    Montfort-Pope-Spain Families. Collection
Minnesota Historical Society, St. Paul, Minn.:
    Bond, Daniel. Reminiscences
    Carpenter, Alfred P. Papers
    Danforth, William. Papers
    Folwell, William W. Papers
    Marvin, Matthew. Diary
    Muller, Charles. History
    Wright, James A. "First Minnesota at Gettysburg"

Mississippi Department of Archives and History, Jackson, Miss.:
    Crawford, John Berryman. Civil War Letters
    Hill, William H. Diary
    Peel, William. Diary
    Vairin, A.L.P. Diary
    Wilson, J. J. Papers
Monroe County Historical Museum, Archives, Monroe, Mich.:
    Custer, George A. Collection
Museum of the Confederacy, Eleanor S. Brockenbrough Library,
    Richmond, Va.:
    Andrews, John Oliver. "War Record of John Oliver Andrews."
        Typescript
    Armistead, Lewis A. Ledger
    Bond, Frank A. "Personal Reminiscences of the Great War Between the States."
        Typescript
    Brooks, Thomas. "The Twenty-Second Battalion Virginia Infantry."
        Typescript
    C.S.A. Core Collection:
        Covington, Joseph G. Letters
    Godsey, William Archer. Memoir. Typescript
    Griggs, George K. Book
    Heth, Henry. Collection
    Longstreet, James. Papers
    Memoir of Member of Washington Artillery. Typescript
    Myers, Robert P. Papers
    Nunnelee, Lewis T. "Diary"/Memoir
    O'Farrell, John. Diary
    Sherrill, A. M. Diary
    Short, William B. Letters
    Vest, John Henry. Diary
National Archives, Washington, D.C.:
    Compiled Service Records. Records Group 94
    Douthat, Robert W. Papers
    Federal Land Claims
    Records Group 79
    Silbey, Franklin R. Collection. John B. Bachelder Papers
New Hampshire Historical Society, Concord, N.H.:
    Bachelder, John B. Papers
New-York Historical Society, New York, N.Y.:
    Gates, Theodore Burr. Papers
    Paine, William H. Diary

New York State Library, Special Collections, Albany, N.Y.:
    Warren, Gouverneur K. Papers
North Carolina Department of Archives and History, Raleigh, N.C.:
    Brown, Henry C. Papers
    Clifton, James Beverly. Collection
    Futch, John. Letters
    Hefner, Marcus. Papers
    Stevens, Henry S. Papers. Private Collections, P.C. 962
    Vance, Zebulon B. Correspondence, June 1–July 20, 1863
    Winston, Francis D. Papers
Ohio Historical Society, Columbus, Ohio:
    Parmeter, Nathaniel Z. Diary
    Powell, Eugene. Memoirs
    Tanner, Augustus B. Papers
Pennsylvania Historical and Museum Commission, Harrisburg, Pa.:
    Bates, Samuel P. Collection
    Rothermel, Peter F. Papers
Picerno, Nicholas P. Private Collection. Claremont, N.H.
Pierpont Morgan Library, Gilder Lehrman Collection,
        New York, N.Y.:
    Allison, William A. Letters
    Bud. Letter, July 18, 1863
    Figures, Henry L. Letters
    Fuller, Josiah C. Letters
    Gibbon, John. Letters
    Slagle, Jacob. Letters
    Smith, David M. Letters
    Stafford, Robert. Correspondence
    Tate, Jeremiah M. Letters
Princeton University, Princeton, N.J.:
    Andre de Coppet Collection:
        Schurz, Carl. Letter, June 6, 1865
    Oliver, Paul Ambrose. Collection
Queen's University, Kingston, Ontario, Canada:
    Wafer, Francis Moses. Diary. Typescript
St. Augustine Historical Society, St. Augustine, Fla.:
    Reid, Raymond J. Papers
State Historical Society of Wisconsin, Madison, Wisc.:
    Haskell, Frank. Letters, Wisconsin History Commission
    Harris, J. S. "Historical Sketches of the Seventh Regiment North Carolina
        Troops"

Tennessee State Library and Archives, Manuscript Division, Nashville, Tenn.:
    Brown, Campbell. Memoirs, Brown-Ewell Papers
    Taylor, Oliver. "The War Story of a Confederate Soldier Boy"
Tulane University, Howard-Tilton Memorial Library, New Orleans, La.:
    Louisiana Historical Association, Civil War Collections:
        Walton, J. B. Papers
        Zable, David. "Paper Read by Co'l David Zable at Meeting of Army of
            Northern Virginia Louisiana Division, December 12th, 1903"
United States Army Military History Institute, Archives, Carlisle Barracks, Pa.:
    Boardman, Susan. Collection
    Brake, Robert L. Collection
    Civil War Miscellaneous Collection:
        149th Pennsylvania Infantry Regiment Papers. Typescript
        Auld, Isaac McQueen. Letters. Typescript
        Barineau, Ann. Collection
        Belknap, Charles Wesley. Diary
        Bevan, Allan L. Papers
        Blackford, Eugene. Diary
        Bowen, George A. Diary. Typescript
        "Civil War Union Soldier's 1863 Diary." Typescript
        Compton, Edward Howard. "Reminiscences of Edward Howard Compton: A
            Survivor of Second Battle of Manassas and the Battle of Gettysburg"
        Crandell, Lewis H. Account of Gettysburg
        Decker, James Edson. Letters. Typescript
        Elliott, Joseph P. Diary
        Firebaugh, Samuel Argus. Diary. Typescript
        Garcelon, Charles A. Diary
        Goggin, James M. Letter
        Gourlie, John C. Letters
        Hill, John D. Letters. Typescript
        Hubler, Simon. "Narrative of Simon Hubler, First Sergeant, late of Co. 'I' 143
            Reg. Pa. Vol. Inf." Typescript
        Hug, Andrew. Diary. Typescript
        Imboden, John D. Letter, August 4, 1891
        Kenney, James W. Letters and Diary
        Linn, John B. "Journal of My Trip to the Battlefield at Gettysburg July 1863."
            Typescript
        Lynch, Christopher Goodhand. Papers
        McIntosh, David G. Papers
        "The Ninth Massachusetts Volunteer Infantry, in the War Against the U.S. of
            America: Outline of a Diary." Typescript

Oberlin, William Penn. Civil War Letters. Typescript

O'Connell, John. Memoir

Peacock, William H. Letters

Platt, George C. Letters

Sayre, William Moore. Letters. Typescript

Shimp, William T. Papers

Slagle, Jacob F. Letter, September 13, 1863

Todd, Joseph. Diary

Walthall, Howard Malcolm. "Reminiscences." Typescript

Whittemore, Franklin. Letter, July 5, 1863

Williams, William R. Letters

Civil War Times Illustrated Collection:

Atticks, J. C. Diary

Baker, I. Norval. Diary and Memoir

Bird, Edward Archer. "Summary of His Visit to the Battlefield of Gettysburg"

Burrill, John H. Letters. Typescript

Coon, Steuben H. Papers

Eskridge, William Harrison. "War Reminiscences." Typescript

Fry, Jesse. Papers

Hatchett Family. Papers

Hawk, George W. W. Letters. Typescript

Henney, Henry. Diary. Typescript

Jones, Benjamin A. Memoir. Typescript

Kitzmiller, Anna Garlach. "Accounts of Experiences in Gettysburg During Military Operations There"

Menges, Jacob R. Memoirs. Typescript

Squires, Charles W. "The Last of Lee's Battle Line." Edited by W.H.T. Squires

Wesson, Silas D. Diary. Typescript

Thomas Clemens Collection:

Ammen, S. Z., Ed. "Maryland Troops in the Confederate Army from Original Sources." Vol. I, 1879

Moore, Gilbert C., Jr., Ed. "Cornie: The Civil War Letters of Lt. Cornelius L. Moore Co. I, 57th Regiment, New York State Volunteers"

Gregory A. Coco Collection/Harrisburg Civil War Round Table Collection:

Bailey, William Britton, Jr. Letters and Diary

Coffman, B. H. Letters

Dunlap, Ferdinand J. Letters

Easley, D. B. Papers

Hancock, Winfield Scott. Papers

Harrisburg Civil War Round Table Collection:
  Brislin, John. Letters
  Furst, Luther C. Papers
  Hoffman, Clement. Papers
  Kauffman, George. Collection
  Nichol, David. Papers
Jeffers, Ira S. Papers
Johnson Family. Papers
Lewis Leigh Collection:
  2nd Massachusetts Volunteer Infantry. Papers
  Balch, George T. Statement, October 14, 1863
  Blackford, Eugene. Letters
  Bosworth Family. Papers
  Bull, James M. Receipt for Captured Flag, July 17, 1863
  Carter, Samuel B. Letter, July 9, 1863
  Gardner, Thomas W. Letter, June 23, 1863
  Gookin, Daniel. Journal
  Hoitt, William B. Letters
  Jones, James S. Letter, September 15, 1863
  Patch, George H. Letters
M.O.L.L.U.S. Collection:
  Hancock, Winfield Scott. Papers
Northwest Corner Civil War Round Table Collection:
  Dawes, Rufus R. Letters
  Lane, James H. "Lane's N. Carolina Brigade in the Battle of
    Gettysburg"
  Smith, Abner C. Letters. Typescript
  Treichler, James M. Memoirs. Typescript
Norwich Civil War Round Table Collection:
  Hyde, James S. Diary. Typescript
Pennsylvania "Save the Flag" Collection:
  Burns, William J. Diary. Typescript
Peters Collection/Lewis Leigh Collection:
  Bachelder, John B. Letters
Ralph G. Poriss Collection:
  Blanchard, H. Letter, July 11, 1863
  Figures, Henry S. Letters
  John. Letter, July 4, 1863
  Mosely, Josiah W. Diary
  Norton Brothers. Letters

Charles Rhodes III Collection:
  Tallman, William H. Memoirs
  Thickstun Family. Papers
  Warner, Charles L. Papers
University of Chicago, Regenstein Library, Chicago, Ill.:
  Mason, Herbert C. Diary, Lincoln Collection, Civil War Diaries—1863
  Truesdell, Sanford. Letters
University of Georgia, Hargrett Rare Books and Manuscript Library, Athens, Ga.:
  Gordon Family. Papers
  Laroque Collection
University of Michigan, Ann Arbor, Mich.:
  Bentley Historical Library:
    Baird, William. "Reminiscences." Baird Family Papers
    Barbour, George W. Diary
    Buck Family. Papers
    Corselius, George. Papers
    Davis, Albert. Letters
    Kidd, James Harvey. Papers
    Lockley, George. Diary
    O'Brien Family. Papers
  William L. Clements Library:
    Alger, Russell A. Papers
    Schoff Civil War Collection:
      Clark, John A. Papers
      Miller, James T. Papers
      Seymour, Isaac. Journal
      Wilcoxson, William B. Papers
University of North Carolina, Wilson Library, Chapel Hill, N.C.:
  Southern Historical Collection:
    Alexander, Edward Porter. Papers
    Alexander, William D. Diary
    Allen and Simpson Family. Papers
    Baker, Blanche. Papers
    Baker, William B. Papers
    Bartlett, J. S. Papers
    Bernard, George S. Papers
    Boatwright, Thomas F. Papers
    Calder, William. Papers
    Caldwell, Tod Robinson. Papers
    Campbell-Colston Family. Papers

Corse, Montgomery D. Papers

Eaton, Samuel W. Papers

Erwin, George Phifer. Papers

Firebaugh, Samuel Angus. Diary, 1862–1864

Green, James E. Diary

Grimes, Bryan. Papers

Hoyle, Lemuel J. Papers

Humphreys, Benjamin G. "A History of the Sunflower Guards."

    J.F.H. Claiborne Papers

Jones, Cadwallader J. Papers

Jones, Edmund W. Papers

Kennedy, Francis M. Diary

Lane, John R. Papers

Lewis, Harry. Papers

Lewis, William Gaston. Papers

Lindsay, Robert Goodloe. Papers

Lippitt, Charles. Papers

Little, Benjamin F. Papers

Long, Armistead L. Papers

Longstreet, James. Papers

McLaws, Lafayette. Papers

Morris, William Groves. Papers

Moses, Raphael J. Autobiography

Noble, Marcus C. S. Papers

Norwood, Joseph Caldwell. Papers

Paris, John. Papers

Pettit, William B. Papers

Pfohl, Christian Thomas. Papers

Platt, Eldridge B. Papers

Polk, Leonidas Lafayette. Papers

Proffit Family. Papers

Reeve, Edward Payson. Papers

Robbins, William M. Papers

Roberts, Samuel. Papers

Royster, Iowa M. Papers

Saunders, Joseph. Papers

Todd, Westwood A. Reminiscences

Venable, Charles S. Papers

Waldrop, Richard Woolfolk. Papers

Whittle, Lewis N. Papers

Willis, Charles Ashley. Diary

University of Rochester, Library, Rochester, N.Y.:
Moore, James. Papers
University of South Carolina, South Caroliniana Library, Columbia, S.C.:
Ballenger, David. Papers
University of Texas, Center for American History, Manuscript Collections, Austin, Texas:
Kirkpatrick, James J. Diary
McCarty, Thomas L. Collection
McDonald, Wilfred. "Diary of a Federal Soldier in the Civil War"
Pledger, Anne Granbery. "Major W. H. 'Howdy' Martin, Fourth Texas Infantry, 1823–1898." Mrs. E. M. Schiwetz Papers
Pomeroy, Nicholas. "Reminiscences of the American Civil War 1861–1865"
Proceedings at the Fifth Annual Reunion of the Survivors of the Sixth U.S. Cavalry, Fairfield, Pa., Tuesday, July 3rd, 1888. Samuel Henry Starr Papers
Thompson, Fleming. Papers, 1861–1865
University of Vermont, Burlington, Vt.:
Blinn, Charles H. Civil War Diary
University of Virginia, Alderman Library, Special Collections, Charlottesville, Va.:
Bowles-Jordan. Letters. #6450
Christiancy, Henry C. Diary. #10,070
Cockrell, Monroe F. "Where Was Pickett at Gettysburg?" October 1, 1949. Monroe F. Cockrell Collection. #3393
Daniel, John W. Papers
Dearing Family. Papers. #3117
Granbery, John Cowper. Papers. #4942
Hager, Jonathan Benjamin. Civil War Memoirs, 1862–1863. #9044
Hands, Washington. Memoir
Hawse, Jasper. Diary. #5188a
Heth-Selden. Papers. #5071
Holladay Family. Papers. #9703-f
Janney-Pollock Family. Papers. #5209
Johnston, Clement Dixon. Papers. #6693
Kemper, James Lawson. Papers. #4098
Phelps, Charles R. Papers. #2920
Williams, Henry Kinchen. "My Travels and Scenes During the War Between the North and South Commencing May 1861, Ending April 1865." #1752
Woods, Micajah. Papers. #10,279
Vermont Historical Society, Montpelier, Vt.:
Veazy, Wheelock Graves

Virginia Historical Society, Richmond, Va.:
   Berkeley, Edmund. Letter, February 9, [?]
   Cabell Family. Papers
   Carrington Family. Papers
   Chisolm, William Garnett. Papers
   Cocke Family. Papers
   Daniel, John Warwick. Memoir
   Duffey, Edward Samuel. Diary
   Dunn Family. Papers
   Elder, Thomas Claybrook. Papers
   Farinholt, Benjamin Lyons. Papers
   Floyd, Augustus Evander. Memoir. Typescript
   Hawes, Katherine Heath. Papers
   Jones, Benjamin Anderson. Memoirs
   Latrobe, Osmun. Diary, 1862–1865. Typescript
   Maxwell, David Elwell. Papers
   McClellan, Henry Brainerd. Papers
   Owen, Henry Thweatt. Papers
   Patch, George H. Papers
   Pickett, Charles. Papers
   Shipp Family. Papers
   Talley, Henry M. Papers
   Timberlake, John Corbett. Letter
   Venable, Charles Scott. Papers
Virginia Military Institute, Preston Library, Lexington, Va.:
   Bentley, William. Alumni File
   Stuart, William Dabney. Papers
War Library and Museum, Philadelphia, Pa.:
   Fortesque, Louis R. Diary
Washington and Lee University, Leyburn Library, Special Collections, Lexington,
      Va.:
   McDowell, William George. Correspondence and Short Biographies
   Welsh Family. Papers, 1817–1886
Western Michigan University, Kalamazoo, Mich.:
   Ball, William. Letters. Ed Ridgeway Collection. Regional History Collections
   Knapp, Ran R. Diary. DeYoung Henry Collection
Western Reserve Historical Society, Cleveland, Ohio:
   Bingham, Henry H. "Memoirs of Hancock," 1872
   Devereaux, Arthur F. Papers
   McLaws, Lafayette. Papers. William P. Palmer Collection
   Merrick, Charles. Papers

Yale University, Beinecke Rare Book and Manuscript Library, New Haven, Conn.:
    Twichell, Joseph Hopkins. Civil War Letters
    Webb, Alexander S. Papers

Newspapers

Athens [Ohio] *Messenger*
Atlanta Journal
Augusta Daily Constitutionalist
Baltimore Sun
Buffalo Evening News
Burlington Free Press and Times
Cleveland Plain Dealer
Doylestown [Pa.] *Daily Intelligencer*
Galveston Daily News
Gettysburg Compiler
Gettysburg Times
Harrisburg Patriot Union
Lebanon [Tenn.] *Democrat*
London Times
Marietta [Ohio] *Sunday Observer*
Minneapolis Journal
Minneapolis State Atlas
Mobile Evening News
National Tribune
New York Herald
New York Times
North Carolina Standard
Philadelphia North American
Philadelphia Press
Philadelphia Public Ledger
Philadelphia Weekly Press
Philadelphia Weekly Times
Raleigh Observer
St. Paul Daily Press
St. Paul Pioneer
Snyder County [Pa.] *Tribune*
Sumter [S.C.] *Herald*
Toledo Blade
Washington Post
Wheeling Daily Intelligencer

Published Books and Articles

Acker, J. Gregory, ed. *Inside the Army of the Potomac: The Civil War Experience of Captain Francis Adams Donaldson.* Mechanicsburg, Pa.: Stackpole Books, 1998.

Adams, John G. B. *Reminiscences of the Nineteenth Massachusetts Regiment.* Boston: Wright & Potter, 1899.

Agassiz, George R., ed. *Meade's Headquarters 1863–1865: Letters of Colonel Theodore Lyman from the Wilderness to Appomattox.* Boston: Atlantic Monthly Press, 1922.

Aldrich, Thomas M. *The History of Battery A First Regiment Rhode Island Light Artillery in the War to Preserve the Union 1861–1865.* Providence: Snow & Farnham, 1904.

Alexander, E. P. *Military Memoirs of a Confederate.* Reprint. Bloomington: Indiana University Press, 1962.

Alexander, Ted. "Gettysburg Cavalry Operations, June 27–July 3, 1863." *Blue & Gray Magazine,* vol. 6, no. 1 (October 1988).

The Annals of the War Written by Leading Participants North and South. Reprint. Dayton, Ohio: Morningside House, 1988.

Appleton, Nathan, et al. *History of the Fifth Massachusetts Battery.* Boston: Luther E. Cowles, 1902.

Archer, John M. "Remembering the 14th Connecticut Volunteers." *Gettysburg Magazine,* no. 9, July 1993.

Ashe, S. A. "The Charge at Gettysburg." *North Carolina Booklet,* vol. 1, no. 11 (March 10, 1902).

Bandy, Ken, and Florence Freeland, eds. *The Gettysburg Papers.* Two vols. Dayton, Ohio: Press of Morningside Bookshop, 1978.

Banes, Charles H. *History of the Philadelphia Brigade.* Philadelphia: J. B. Lippincott, 1876.

Bean, W. G. "A House Divided: The Civil War Letters of a Virginia Family." *Virginia Magazine of History and Biography,* vol. 54, no. 4 (October 1951).

Bee, Robert L. *The Boys from Rockville: Civil War Narratives of Sgt. Benjamin Hirst, Company D, 14th Connecticut Volunteers.* Knoxville: University of Tennessee Press, 1998.

Bell, Robert T. *11th Virginia Infantry.* Lynchburg, Va.: H. E. Howard, 1985.

Benedict, George G. *Army Life in Virginia.* Burlington, Vt.: Free Press Association, 1895.

———. *A Short History of the 14th Vermont Regt.* Bennington, Vt.: Press of C. A. Pierce, 1887.

———. *Vermont in the Civil War: A History of the Part Taken by the Vermont Sol-*

diers and Sailors in the War for the Union, 1861–65. Two vols. Burlington, Vt.: Free Press Association, 1886–88.

Benton, Charles E. *As Seen from the Ranks: A Boy in the Civil War.* New York and London: G. P. Putnam's Sons, 1902.

Beyer, W. F., and O. F. Keydel, eds. *Deeds of Valor: How America's Civil War Heroes Won the Congressional Medal of Honor.* Reprint. Stamford, Conn.: Longmeadow Press, 1994.

Black, John Logan. *Crumbling Defenses, or Memoirs and Reminiscences of John Logan Black.* Ed. E. D. McSwain. Macon, Ga.: n.p., 1960.

Blackford, Susan Leigh, ed. *Letters from Lee's Army, or Memoirs of Life In and Out of the Army in Virginia During the War Between the States.* New York: Charles Scribner's Sons, 1947.

Blight, David W., ed. *When This Cruel War Is Over: The Civil War Letters of Charles Harvey Brewster.* Amherst: University of Massachusetts Press, 1992.

Bloom, Robert L. " 'We Never Expected a Battle': The Civilians at Gettysburg, 1863." *Pennsylvania History,* vol. 55, no. 4 (October 1988).

Boggs, Marion Alexander, ed. *The Alexander Letters 1787–1900.* Athens: University of Georgia Press, 1980.

Boyle, John Richards. *Soldiers True: The Story of the One Hundred and Eleventh Regiment Pennsylvania Veteran Volunteers, and of Its Campaigns in the War for the Union, 1861–1865.* New York: Eaton & Mains, 1903.

Brady, James P., ed. *Hurrah for the Artillery!: Knap's Independent Battery "E," Pennsylvania Light Artillery.* Gettysburg, Pa.: Thomas Publications, 1992.

Brown, Edmund Randolph. *The Twenty-Seventh Indiana Volunteer Infantry in the War of the Rebellion 1861 to 1865: First Division 12th and 20th Corps.* n.p.: E. R. Brown, 1899.

Brown, H. E. *The 28th Regt. P.V.V.I., the 147th Regt. P.V.V.I., and Knap's Ind. Battery "E." at Gettysburg, July 1, 2, 3, 1863.* N.p.: n.p., n.d.

Brown, Kent Masterson. *Cushing of Gettysburg: The Story of a Union Artillery Commander.* Lexington: University Press of Kentucky, 1993.

Brown, Maud Morrow. *The University Greys: Company A Eleventh Mississippi Regiment Army of Northern Virginia 1861–1865.* Richmond, Va.: Garrett and Massie, 1940.

Bruce, George A. *The Twentieth Regiment of Massachusetts Volunteer Infantry 1861–1865.* Boston and New York: Houghton, Mifflin and Company, 1906.

Bryant, Edwin E. *History of the Third Regiment of Wisconsin Veteran Volunteer Infantry 1861–1865.* Madison, Wisc.: Veteran Association of the Regiment, 1891.

Buell, Augustus. *The Cannoneer: Recollections of Service in the Army of the Potomac.* Washington, D.C.: National Tribune, 1897.

Busey, John W. *These Honored Dead: The Union Casualties at Gettysburg.* Hightstown, N.J.: Longstreet House, 1988.

Busey, John W., and David G. Martin. *Regimental Strengths at Gettysburg.* Baltimore: Gateway Press, 1982.

Byrne, Frank L., and Andrew T. Weaver. *Haskell Of Gettysburg: His Life and Civil War Papers.* Madison: State Historical Society of Wisconsin, 1970.

Campbell, Eric A. "The Aftermath and Recovery of Gettysburg, Part 1." *Gettysburg Magazine,* no. 11, July 1994.

———. " 'Remember Harper's Ferry!': The Degradation, Humiliation, and Redemption of Col. George L. Willard's Brigade, Part 2." *Gettysburg Magazine,* no. 8, January 1993.

Carmichael, Peter S. *Lee's Young Artillerist: William R. J. Pegram.* Charlottesville and London: University Press of Virginia, 1995.

———. "Never Heard Before on the American Continent." *Gettysburg Magazine,* no. 10, January 1994.

Carter, W. H. *From Yorktown to Santiago with the Sixth U.S. Cavalry.* Baltimore: Lord Baltimore Press, 1900.

Cauthen, Charles Edward, ed. *Family Letters of Three Wade Hamptons, 1782–1901.* Columbia, S.C.: n.p., 1953.

Chamberlaine, William W. *Memoirs of the Civil War Between the Northern and Southern Sections of the United States of America 1861 to 1865.* Washington, D.C.: Press of Byron S. Adams, 1912.

Chamberlin, Thomas. *History of the One Hundred and Fiftieth Regiment Pennsylvania Volunteers, Second Regiment, Bucktail Brigade.* Reprint. Baltimore: Butternut and Blue, 1986.

Chapman, Horatio Dana. *Civil War Diary of a Forty-Niner.* Hartford, Conn.: Allis, 1929.

Chapman, Craig S. *More Terrible Than Victory: North Carolina's Bloody Bethel Regiment 1861–1865.* Washington, D.C., and London: Brassey's, 1998.

Christ, Elwood W. *"Over a Wide, Hot, . . . Crimson Plain": The Struggle for the Bliss Farm at Gettysburg July 2nd and 3rd, 1863.* Baltimore: Butternut and Blue, 1993.

Clark, Walter, ed. *Histories of the Several Regiments and Battalions from North Carolina in the Great War 1861–'65.* Five vols. Reprint. Wendell, N.C.: Broadfoot's Bookmart, 1982.

Clark, William. *History of Hampton Battery F Independent Pennsylvania Light Artillery.* Pittsburgh and Akron: Werner, 1909.

Cleaves, Freeman. *Meade of Gettysburg.* Norman: University of Oklahoma Press, 1960.

Clemens, Thomas G. "The 'Diary' of John H. Stone, First Lieutenant, Company B,

2nd Maryland Infantry, C.S.A." *Maryland Historical Magazine,* vol. 85 (Summer 1990).

Cockrell, Monroe F., ed. *Gunner with Stonewall: Reminiscences of William Thomas Poague.* Reprint. Jackson, Tenn.: McCowat-Mercer Press, 1957.

Cockrell, Thomas D., and Michael B. Ballard, eds. *A Mississippi Rebel in the Army of Northern Virginia: The Civil War Memoirs of Private David Holt.* Baton Rouge and London: Louisiana State University Press, 1995.

Coco, Gregory A. *A Concise Guide to the Artillery At Gettysburg.* Gettysburg, Pa.: Thomas Publications, 1998.

———. *A Strange and Blighted Land—Gettysburg: The Aftermath of a Battle.* Gettysburg, Pa.: Thomas Publications, 1995.

———. *A Vast Sea Of Misery: A History and Guide to the Union and Confederate Field Hospitals at Gettysburg July 1–November 20, 1863.* Gettysburg, Pa.: Thomas Publications, 1988.

———. *Wasted Valor: The Confederate Dead at Gettysburg.* Gettysburg, Pa.: Thomas Publications, 1990.

———, ed. *From Ball's Bluff to Gettysburg . . . and Beyond: The Civil War Letters of Private Roland E. Bowen, 15th Massachusetts Infantry 1861–1864.* Gettysburg, Pa.: Thomas Publications, 1994.

Coddington, Edwin B. *The Gettysburg Campaign: A Study in Command.* New York: Charles Scribner's Sons, 1968.

Coffin, Howard. *Nine Months to Gettysburg: Stannard's Vermonters and the Repulse of Pickett's Charge.* Woodstock, Vt.: Countryman Press, 1997.

Coles, David J., and Zack C. Waters. "Forgotten Sacrifice: The Florida Brigade at the Battle of Gettysburg." *Apalachee,* vol. 11 (1996).

Collins, George K. *Memoirs of the 149th Regt. N.Y. Vol. Inft. 3d Brig., 2d Div., 12th and 20th A.C.* Syracuse, N.Y.: George K. Collins, 1891.

Confederate Veteran. Forty vols. Reprint. Wilmington, N.C.: Broadfoot Publishing Company, 1987–88.

Cook, S. G., and Charles E. Benton, eds. *The "Dutchess County Regiment" in the Civil War: Its Story as Told by Its Members.* Danbury, Conn.: Danbury Medical Printing Co., 1907.

Cooksey, Paul Clark. "The Plan for Pickett's Charge." *Gettysburg Magazine,* no. 22, January 2000.

Cowtam, Charles W. *Services of the Tenth New York Volunteers (National Zouaves) in the War of the Rebellion.* New York: Charles H. Ludwig, 1882.

Crews, Edward R., and Timothy A. Parrish. *14th Virginia Infantry.* Lynchburg, Va.: H. E. Howard, 1995.

Croffut, W. A., and John M. Morris. *The Military and Civil History of Connecticut During the War of 1861–1865.* New York: Ledyard Bell, 1869.

Crumb, Herb S., ed. *The Eleventh Corps Artillery at Gettysburg: The Papers of Major Thomas Ward Osborn, Chief of Artillery.* Hamilton, N.Y.: Edmonston Publishing, 1991.

Cutrer, Thomas W., ed. *Longstreet's Aide: The Civil War Letters of Major Thomas J. Goree.* Charlottesville and London: University Press of Virginia, 1995.

Davis, Stephen. "The Death and Burials of General Richard Brooke Garnett." *Gettysburg Magazine,* no. 5, July 1991.

Dawson, Francis W. *Reminiscences of Confederate Service 1861–1865.* Ed. Bell I. Wiley. Baton Rouge and London: Louisiana State University Press, 1980.

Dayton, Ruth Woods, ed. *The Diary of a Confederate Soldier: James E. Hall.* Berryville, Va.: Virginia Book Co., 1961.

"Diary of Turner Vaughan, Co. 'C,' 4th Alabama Regiment, C.S.A., Commenced March 4th, 1863, and Ending February 12th, 1864." *Alabama Historical Quarterly,* vol. 18 (1956).

Divine, John E. *8th Virginia Infantry.* Lynchburg, Va.: H. E. Howard, 1983.

Dobbins, Austin C., ed. *Grandfather's Journal: Company B Sixteenth Mississippi Infantry Volunteers Harris' Brigade Mahone's Division Hill's Corps, A.N.V. May 27, 1861–July 15, 1865.* Dayton, Ohio: Morningside House, 1988.

Douglas, Henry Kyd. *I Rode with Stonewall.* Chapel Hill: University of North Carolina Press, 1940.

Downey, Fairfax. *The Guns at Gettysburg.* New York: David McKay, 1958.

Dunaway, Wayland Fuller. *Reminiscences of a Rebel.* New York: Neale Publishing Company, 1913.

Durkin, Joseph T., ed. *John Dooley Confederate Soldier: His War Journal.* Georgetown, D.C.: Georgetown University Press, 1945.

Earle, David M. *History of the Excursion of the Fifteenth Massachusetts Regiment and Its Friends to the Battle-Fields of Gettysburg, Pa., Antietam, Md., Ball's Bluff, Virginia, and Washington, D.C., May 31–June 12, 1886.* Worcester, Mass.: Press of Charles Hamilton, 1886.

Eddy, Richard. *History of the Sixtieth Regiment New York State Volunteers.* Philadelphia, Pa.: Crissy & Markley, 1864.

Elmore, Thomas L. "Courage Against the Trenches: The Attack and Repulse of Steuart's Brigade on Culp's Hill." *Gettysburg Magazine,* no. 7, July 1992.

———. "The Florida Brigade at Gettysburg." *Gettysburg Magazine,* no. 15, July 1996.

———. "The Grand Cannonade: A Confederate Perspective." *Gettysburg Magazine,* no. 19, July 1998.

———. "Torrid Heat and Blinding Rain: A Meteorological and Astronomical Chronology of the Gettysburg Campaign." *Gettysburg Magazine,* no. 13, July 1995.

"E. P. Alexander and Pickett's Charge." *Civil War Times Illustrated,* vol. 17, no. 1 (April 1978).

Everson, Guy R., and Edward H. Simpson, Jr., eds. *"Far, Far from Home": The Wartime Letters of Dick and Tally Simpson, Third South Carolina Volunteers.* New York and Oxford: Oxford University Press, 1994.

Fields, Frank E., Jr. *28th Virginia Infantry.* Lynchburg, Va.: H. E. Howard, 1985.

Final Report of the Gettysburg Battle-Field Commission of New Jersey. Reprint. Hightstown, N.J.: Longstreet House, 1997.

Fishel, Edwin C. *The Secret War for the Union: The Untold Story of Military Intelligence in the Civil War.* Boston and New York: Houghton Mifflin, 1996.

Fleming, Francis P. *Memoir of Capt. C. Seton Fleming of the Second Florida Infantry, C.S.A.* Reprint. Alexandria, Va.: Stonewall House, 1985.

Fleming, George Thornton, ed. *Life and Letters of Alexander Hays.* Pittsburgh, Pa.: Gilbert Adams Hays, 1919.

Florida Soldiers: CSA 2nd, 5th, 8th Florida Infantry. Special Archives Publication Number 92. St. Augustine: Florida Department of Military Affairs, 1989.

Ford, Andrew E. *The Story of the Fifteenth Regiment Massachusetts Volunteer Infantry in the Civil War 1861–1864.* Clinton, Mass.: Press of W. J. Coulter, 1898.

Frassanito, William A. *Early Photography at Gettysburg.* Gettysburg, Pa.: Thomas Publications, 1995.

Freeman, Douglas Southall. *Lee's Lieutenants: A Study in Command.* Three vols. New York: Charles Scribner's Sons, 1942–44.

————. *R. E. Lee: A Biography.* Four vols. New York and London: Charles Scribner's Sons, 1932–34.

Frye, Dennis E. *2nd Virginia Infantry.* Lynchburg, Va.: H. E. Howard, 1984.

Gallagher, Gary W. *The Confederate War.* Cambridge, Mass., and London: Harvard University Press, 1997.

————, ed. *Fighting for the Confederacy: The Personal Recollections of General Edward Porter Alexander.* Chapel Hill and London: University of North Carolina Press, 1989.

————, ed. *Lee: The Soldier.* Lincoln and London: University of Nebraska Press, 1996.

————, ed. *The Second Day at Gettysburg: Essays on Confederate and Union Leadership.* Kent, Ohio, and London: Kent State University Press, 1993.

————, ed. *The Third Day at Gettysburg & Beyond.* Chapel Hill and London: University of North Carolina Press, 1994.

————, ed. *Three Days at Gettysburg: Essays On Confederate and Union Leadership.* Kent, Ohio, and London: Kent State University Press, 1999.

Galwey, Thomas Francis. *The Valiant Hours.* Ed. W. S. Nye. Harrisburg, Pa.: Stackpole Company, 1961.

Gambone, A. M. *Hancock at Gettysburg . . . and Beyond.* Baltimore: Butternut and Blue, 1997.

Georg, Kathleen R., and John W. Busey. *Nothing but Glory: Pickett's Division at Gettysburg.* Hightstown, N.J.: Longstreet House, 1987.

Gibbon, John. "Another View of Gettysburg." *North American Review,* vol. 152, no. 415 (June 1891).

———. *Personal Recollections of the Civil War.* Reprint. Dayton, Ohio: Morningside Bookshop, 1978.

Goldsborough, W. W. *The Maryland Line in the Confederate Army, 1861–1865.* Reprint. Gaithersburg, Md.: Butternut Press, 1983.

Gordon, Lesley J. *General George E. Pickett in Life & Legend.* Chapel Hill and London: University of North Carolina Press, 1998.

Gottfried, Bradley M. "Mahone's Brigade: Insubordination or Miscommunication?" *Gettysburg Magazine,* no. 18, January 1998.

———. "Wright's Charge on July 2, 1863: Piercing the Union Line or Inflated Glory." *Gettysburg Magazine,* no. 17, July 1997.

Graves, Joseph A. *The History of the Bedford Light Artillery.* Reprint. Gaithersburg, Md.: Butternut Press, 1980.

Gregg, David McM. *The Second Cavalry Division of the Army of the Potomac in the Gettysburg Campaign.* Philadelphia: Military Order of the Loyal Legion of the United States, 1907.

Gregory, G. Howard. *38th Virginia Infantry.* Lynchburg, Va.: H. E. Howard, 1988.

Griffith, Paddy. *Battle Tactics of the Civil War.* New Haven and London: Yale University Press, 1989.

Groene, Bertram H., ed. "Civil War Letters of Colonel David Lang." *Florida Historical Quarterly,* vol. 54, no. 3 (1976).

Gunn, Ralph White. *24th Virginia Infantry.* Lynchburg, Va.: H. E. Howard, 1987.

Hadden, R. Lee. "The Granite Glory: The 19th Maine at Gettysburg." *Gettysburg Magazine,* no. 13, July 1995.

Haden, B. J. *J.E.B. Stuart's Cavalry.* Charlottesville, Va.: Progress Publishing Co., n.d.

Hage, Anne A. "The Battle of Gettysburg as Seen by Minnesota Soldiers." *Minnesota History,* vol. 38, no. 6 (June 1963).

Hagerty, Edward J. *Collis' Zouaves: The 114th Pennsylvania Volunteers in the Civil War.* Baton Rouge and London: Louisiana State University Press, 1997.

Haines, William P. *History of the Men of Co. F, with Description of the Marches and Battles of the 12th New Jersey Vols.* Camden, N.J.: C. S. Magrath, 1897.

Hamblen, Charles P. *Connecticut Yankees at Gettysburg.* Ed. Walter L. Powell. Kent, Ohio, and London: Kent State University Press, 1993.

Hamilton, J. G. deRoulhac, ed. *The Papers of Randolph Abbott Shotwell.* Two vols. Raleigh: North Carolina Historical Commission, 1929–31.

Hancock, Almira Russell. *Reminiscences of Winfield Scott Hancock.* New York: Charles L. Webster & Company, 1887.

Harris, Samuel. *The Michigan Brigade of Cavalry at the Battle of Gettysburg and Why I Was Not Hung.* Reprint. Rochester, Mich.: Rochester Historical Commission, 1992.

Harrison, Kathleen Georg. "Gettysburg—The Third Day, July 3, 1863." *Blue & Gray Magazine,* vol. 5, no. 6 (July 1988).

Harrison, Walter. *Pickett's Men: A Fragment of War History.* Reprint. Gaithersburg, Md.: Olde Soldier Books, 1987.

Harsh, Joseph L. *Confederate Tide Rising: Robert E. Lee and the Making of Southern Strategy, 1861–1862.* Kent, Ohio, and London: Kent State University Press, 1998.

————. *Taken at the Flood: Robert E. Lee and Confederate Strategy in the Maryland Campaign of 1862.* Kent, Ohio, and London: Kent State University Press, 1999.

Hartwig, Scott D. "It Struck Horror to Us All." *Gettysburg Magazine,* no. 4, January 1991.

Haskell, John Cheves. *The Haskell Memoirs.* Ed. Gilbert E. Govan and James W. Livingood. New York: G. P. Putnam's Sons, 1960.

Henderson, William D. *12th Virginia Infantry.* Lynchburg, Va.: H. E. Howard, 1984.

Historical Sketch of Co. "D." 13th Regiment, N.J. Vols. New York: D. H. Gildersleeve & Co., 1875.

Holcombe, R. I. *History of the First Regiment Minnesota Volunteer Infantry 1861–1864.* Reprint. Gaithersburg, Md.: Ron R. Van Sickle Military Books, 1987.

Houghton, W. R., and M. B. Houghton. *Two Boys in the Civil War and After.* Montgomery, Ala.: Paragon Press, 1912.

Howard, McHenry. *Recollections of a Maryland Confederate Soldier and Staff Officer Under Johnston, Jackson and Lee.* Reprint. Dayton, Ohio: Morningside Bookshop, 1975.

Hunton, Eppa. *Autobiography of Eppa Hunton, 1822–1908.* Richmond, Va.: William Byrd Press, 1933.

Husby, Karla Jean, and Eric J. Wittenberg, eds. *Under Custer's Command: The Civil War Journal of James Henry Avery.* Washington, D.C.: Brassey's, 2000.

Ide, Horace K. "The First Vermont Cavalry in the Gettysburg Campaign." Ed. Elliott W. Hoffman. *Gettysburg Magazine,* no. 14, January 1996.

Imhof, John D. *Gettysburg, Day Two: A Study In Maps.* Baltimore: Butternut and Blue, 1999.

Jacobs, Michael. "Later Rambles over the Field of Gettysburg." *United States Service Magazine,* January 1864.

————. *Notes on the Rebel Invasion of Maryland and Pennsylvania and the Battle of*

Gettysburg July 1st, 2nd and 3rd, 1863. Gettysburg, Pa.: Times Printing House, 1909.

Johnson, John Lipscomb. *The University Memorial: Biographical Sketches of Alumni of the University of Virginia Who Fell in the Confederate War.* Baltimore: Turnbull Brothers, 1871.

Johnson, Robert Underwood, and Clarence Clough Buel, eds. *Battles and Leaders of the Civil War.* Four vols. Reprint. New York and London: Thomas Yoseloff, 1956.

Johnston, David E. *The Story of a Confederate Boy in the Civil War.* Portland, Ore.: Glass & Prudhomme, 1914.

Jones, Wilbur D., Jr. *Giants in the Cornfield: The 27th Indiana Infantry.* Shippensburg, Pa.: White Mane Publishing Co., 1997.

Jordan, Erwin L., Jr., and Herbert A. Thomas, Jr. *19th Virginia Infantry.* Lynchburg, Va.: H. E. Howard, 1987.

Jordan, Virginia Fitzgerald, ed. *The Captain Remembers: The Papers of Captain Richard Irby.* Blackstone, Va.: Nottoway County Historical Association, 1975.

Kaminsky, Virginia Hughes, ed. *A War to Petrify the Heart: The Civil War Letters of a Dutchess County, N.Y., Volunteer, Richard T. Van Wyck.* Hensonville, N.Y.: Black Dome Press, 1997.

Kidd, James H. *Personal Recollections of a Cavalryman with Custer's Michigan Cavalry Brigade in the Civil War.* Reprint. Alexandria, Va.: Time-Life Books, 1983.

Klingensmith, Harold A. "A Cavalry Regiment's First Campaign: The 18th Pennsylvania at Gettysburg." *Gettysburg Magazine,* no. 20, January 1999.

Krick, Robert E. L. *40th Virginia Infantry.* Lynchburg, Va.: H. E. Howard, 1985.

Krick, Robert K. *Lee's Colonels: A Biographical Register of the Field Officers of the Army of Northern Virginia.* Dayton, Ohio: Morningside Bookshop, 1979.

———. *Parker's Virginia Battery, C.S.A.* Wilmington, N.C.: Broadfoot Publishing Company, 1989.

———, comp. *The Gettysburg Death Roster: The Confederate Dead at Gettysburg.* Dayton, Ohio: Morningside Bookshop, 1985.

Krolick, Marshall D. "Forgotten Field: The Cavalry Battle East of Gettysburg On July 3, 1863." *Gettysburg Magazine,* no. 4, January 1991.

———. "Lee and Longstreet at Gettysburg." *Virginia Country's Civil War,* vol. 5.

Kross, Gary. "July 3rd Action at Culp's Hill." *Blue & Gray Magazine,* vol. 16, no. 5 (June 1999).

Ladd, David L., and Audrey J. Ladd, eds. *The Bachelder Papers: Gettysburg in Their Own Words.* Three vols. Dayton, Ohio: Morningside House, 1994–95.

Lane, Mills, ed. *"Dear Mother: Don't grieve about me. If I get killed, I'll only be dead":
Letters from Georgia Soldiers in the Civil War.* Savannah, Ga.: Beehive Press, 1977.

Laney, Daniel M. "Wasted Gallantry: Hood's Texas Brigade at Gettysburg." *Gettysburg Magazine,* no. 16, January 1997.

Lash, Gary G. "The Philadelphia Brigade at Gettysburg." *Gettysburg Magazine,* no. 7, July 1992.

Lee, Robert E. *Recollections and Letters of General Robert E. Lee.* Garden City, N.Y.: Garden City Publishing Co., 1924.

Lee, William O., comp. *Personal and Historical Sketches and Facial History of and by Members of the Seventh Regiment Michigan Volunteer Cavalry 1862–1865.* Detroit: 7th Michigan Cavalry Association, [1902].

Lewis, John H. *Recollections from 1860 to 1865.* Washington, D.C.: Peake and Company, 1895.

Lightsey, Ada Christine. *The Veteran's Story.* Meridian, Miss.: Meridian News, n.d.

Lindsley, John Berrien, ed. *The Military Annals of Tennessee.* First Series. Nashville: J. M. Lindsley & Co., 1886.

Livermore, Thomas L. *Days and Events 1860–1866.* Boston and New York: Houghton Mifflin, 1920.

Loehr, Charles T. *War History of the Old First Virginia Infantry Regiment, Army of Northern Virginia.* Reprint. Dayton, Ohio: Morningside Bookshop, 1970.

Long, A. L. *Memoirs of Robert E. Lee: His Military and Personal History.* New York: J. M. Stoddart & Company, 1886.

Long, Roger. "The Confederate Prisoners of Gettysburg." *Gettysburg Magazine,* no. 2, July 1990.

————. "Maj. Joseph H. Saunders, 33rd North Carolina, C.S.A." *Gettysburg Magazine,* no. 10, January 1994.

Longacre, Edward G. *The Cavalry at Gettysburg: A Tactical Study of Mounted Operations during the Civil War's Pivotal Campaign 9 June–14 July 1863.* Rutherford, Madison, and Teaneck, N.J.: Fairleigh Dickinson University Press, 1986.

————. *Custer and His Wolverines: The Michigan Cavalry Brigade, 1861–1865.* Conshohocken, Pa.: Combined Books, 1997.

————. *To Gettysburg and Beyond: The Twelfth New Jersey Volunteer Infantry, II Corps, Army of the Potomac, 1862–1865.* Hightstown, N.J.: Longstreet House, 1988.

Longstreet, James. *From Manassas to Appomattox: Memoirs of the Civil War in America.* Philadelphia: J. B. Lippincott, 1896.

Lord, Walter, ed. *The Fremantle Diary: Being the Journal of Lieutenant Colonel James Arthur Lyon Fremantle, Coldstream Guards, on His Three Months in the Southern States.* Boston: Little, Brown, 1954.

Luvaas, Jay. "Lee and the Operational Art: The Right Place, The Right Time." *Parameters: US Army War College Quarterly,* vol. 22, no. 3 (Autumn 1992).

Magner, Blake A. *Traveller & Company: The Horses of Gettysburg.* Gettysburg, Pa.: Farnsworth House Military Impressions, 1995.

Mahood, Wayne. *"Written in Blood": A History of the 126th New York Infantry in the Civil War.* Hightstown, N.J.: Longstreet House, 1997.

Maine at Gettysburg: Report of Maine Commissioners Prepared by the Executive Committee. Reprint. Gettysburg, Pa.: Stan Clark Military Books, 1994.

Marquis, D. R., and D. R. Tevis. *The History of the Fighting Fourteenth.* Brooklyn: Brooklyn Eagle Press, 1911[?].

Martin, David G. *Gettysburg: July 1.* Conshohocken, Pa.: Combined Books, 1995.

Marvin, Edwin E. *The Fifth Regiment Connecticut Volunteers: A History Compiled from Diaries and Official Reports.* Hartford, Conn.: Wiley, Waterman & Eaton, 1889.

Maurice, Frederick, ed. *An Aide-de-Camp of Lee: Being the Papers of Colonel Charles Marshall, Sometime Aide-de-Camp, Military Secretary, and Assistant Adjutant General on the Staff of Robert E. Lee 1862–1865.* Boston: Little, Brown, 1927.

Maust, Roland R. "The Union Second Corps Hospital at Gettysburg, July 2 to August 8, 1863." *Gettysburg Magazine,* no. 10, January 1994.

McDermott, Anthony W. *A Brief History of the 69th Regiment Pennsylvania Veteran Volunteers, from Its Formation Until Final Muster Out of the United States Service.* Philadelphia: D. J. Gallagher & Co., 1889.

McDonald, Archie P., ed. *Make Me a Map of the Valley: The Civil War Journal of Stonewall Jackson's Topographer.* Dallas: Southern Methodist University Press, 1973.

McDonald, William N. *A History of the Laurel Brigade, Originally the Ashby Cavalry of the Army of Northern Virginia and Chew's Battery.* Reprint. Arlington, Va.: R. W. Beatty, 1969.

McKim, Randolph H. *A Soldier's Recollections: Leaves from the Diary of a Young Confederate.* Reprint. Alexandria, Va.: Time-Life Books, 1984.

McLean, James L., Jr., and Judy W. McLean, eds. *Gettysburg Sources.* Three vols. Baltimore: Butternut and Blue, 1986–90.

Meinhard, Robert W. "The First Minnesota at Gettysburg." *Gettysburg Magazine,* no. 5, July 1991.

Metts, James I. *Longstreet's Charge at Gettysburg, Pa.: Historical Essay.* N.p.: n.p., n.d.

Meyer, Henry C. *Civil War Experiences Under Bayard, Gregg, Kilpatrick, Custer, Raulston, and Newberry 1862, 1863, 1864.* New York: Knickerbocker Press, 1917.

Michigan at Gettysburg: July 1st, 2nd and 3rd, 1863. June 12th, 1889. Reprint. Hightstown, N.J.: Longstreet House, 1998.

Milano, Anthony J. "A Call of Leadership: Lt. Col. Charles Redington Mudge, U.S.V., and the Second Massachusetts Infantry at Gettysburg." *Gettysburg Magazine,* no. 6, January 1992.

Miller, Richard F., and Robert F. Mooney. *The Civil War: The Nantucket Experience, Including the Memoirs of Joshia Fitch Murphey.* Nantucket, Mass.: Wesco Publishing, 1994.

Moe, Richard. *The Last Full Measure: The Life and Death of the First Minnesota Volunteers.* New York: Henry Holt, 1993.

Moore, Edward A. *The Story of a Cannoneer Under Stonewall Jackson.* Reprint. Freeport, N.Y.: Books for Libraries Press, 1971.

Morhous, Henry C. *Reminiscences of the 123rd Regiment, N.Y.S.V., Giving a Complete History of Its Three Years Service in the War.* Reprint. Fort Edward, N.Y.: Washington County Historical Society, 1995.

Morse, Charles F. *History of the Second Massachusetts Regiment of Infantry, Gettysburg.* Boston: George H. Ellis, 1882.

———. *Letters Written During the Civil War 1861–1865.* Boston: n.p., 1889.

Motts, Wayne E. " 'A Brave and Resolute Force.' " *North & South,* vol. 2, no. 5 (1999).

———. "To Gain a Second Star: The Forgotten George S. Greene." *Gettysburg Magazine,* no. 3, July 1990.

Muffly, J. W., ed. *The Story of Our Regiment: A History of the 148th Pennsylvania Vols.* Des Moines, Iowa: Kenyon, 1904.

Murray, R. L. *The Redemption of the "Harper's Ferry Cowards": The Story of the 111th and 126th New York State Volunteer Regiments at Gettysburg.* Wolcott, N.Y.: R. L. Murray, n.d.

Neathery, J. Marshall. *Neathery Siblings Had Eight Ancestors in the Civil War: Five of Them at Gettysburg.* Rolesville, N.C.: J. Marshall Neathery, 1996.

Neese, George M. *Three Years in the Confederate Horse Artillery.* Reprint. Dayton, Ohio: Morningside Bookshop, 1983.

Nesbitt, Mark. *Saber and Scapegoat: J.E.B. Stuart and the Gettysburg Controversy.* Mechanicsburg, Pa.: Stackpole Books, 1994.

Nevins, Allan, ed. *A Diary of Battle: The Personal Journals of Colonel Charles S. Wainwright 1861–1865.* Reprint. Gettysburg, Pa.: Stan Clark Military Books, n.d.

Newhall, Walter S. *A Memoir.* Philadelphia: Caxton Press of C. Sherman, Son & Co., 1864.

New York at Gettysburg: Final Report on the Battlefield of Gettysburg. Three vols. Albany: J. B. Lyon, 1900.

Nye, Wilbur Sturtevant. *Here Come the Rebels!* Reprint. Dayton, Ohio: Morningside Bookshop, 1988.

O'Brien, Kevin E. " 'A Perfect Roar of Musketry': Candy's Brigade in the Fight for Culp's Hill." *Gettysburg Magazine,* no. 9, July 1993.

Ohio Memorials at Gettysburg: Report of the Gettysburg Memorial Commission. Reprint. Baltimore: Butternut and Blue, 1998.

Opie, John N. *A Rebel Cavalryman with Lee, Stuart And Jackson.* Reprint. Dayton, Ohio: Morningside Bookshop, 1972.

Owen, William Miller. *In Camp and Battle with the Washington Artillery of New Orleans.* Reprint. Gaithersburg, Md.: Butternut Press, n.d.

Page, Charles D. *History of the Fourteenth Regiment, Connecticut Vol. Infantry.* Meriden, Conn.: Horton, 1906.

Palmer, E. F. *The Second Brigade: or Camp Life.* Montpelier, Vt.: E. I. Walton, 1864.

Pennsylvania at Gettysburg: Ceremonies at the Dedication of the Monuments. Two vols. Harrisburg, Pa.: William Stanley Ray, 1904.

Penny, Morris M., and J. Gary Laine. *Struggle for the Round Tops: Law's Alabama Brigade at the Battle of Gettysburg, July 2–3, 1863.* Shippensburg, Pa.: Burd Street Press, 1999.

Pfanz, Donald C. *Richard S. Ewell: A Soldier's Life.* Chapel Hill and London: University of North Carolina Press, 1998.

Pfanz, Harry W. *Gettysburg: Culp's Hill and Cemetery Hill.* Chapel Hill and London: University of North Carolina Press, 1993.

———. *Gettysburg: The Second Day.* Chapel Hill and London: University of North Carolina Press, 1987.

Poirer, Robert G. "Norwich at Gettysburg: The Citizen-Soldier Academy's Contribution to Victory." *Gettysburg Magazine,* no. 14, January 1996.

Polley, J. B. *Hood's Texas Brigade: Its Marches, Its Battles, Its Achievements.* Reprint. Dayton, Ohio: Morningside Bookshop, 1988.

Poriss, Gerry Harden, and Ralph G. Poriss. *While My Country Is in Danger: The Life and Letters of Lieutenant Colonel Richard S. Thompson.* Hamilton, N.Y.: Edmonston Publishing, 1994.

Powell, Kathryne Hobson, and Maud Carter Clement, eds. *War Recollections of Confederate Veterans of Pittsylvania County, Virginia, 1861–1865.* n.p.: Randall O. Reynolds, n.d.

Powell, Robert M. *Recollections of a Texas Colonel at Gettysburg.* Ed. Gregory A. Coco. Gettysburg, Pa.: Thomas Publications, 1990.

Priest, John Michael. *Into the Fight: Pickett's Charge at Gettysburg.* Shippensburg, Pa.: White Mane Books, 1998.

Quaife, Milo M., ed. *From the Cannon's Mouth: The Civil War Letters of General Alpheus S. Williams.* Detroit: Wayne State University Press and the Detroit Historical Society, 1959.

Racine, Philip N. *"Unspoiled Heart": The Journal of Charles Mattocks of the 17th Maine.* Knoxville: University of Tennessee Press, 1994.

Ratchford, J. W. *Some Reminiscences of Persons and Incidents of the Civil War.* Reprint. Austin, Texas: Shoal Creek Publishers, 1971.

Raus, Edmund J., Jr. *A Generation on the March: The Union Army at Gettysburg.* Lynchburg, Va.: H. E. Howard, 1987.

Rawle, William Brooke, et al. *History of the Third Pennsylvania Cavalry Sixtieth Regiment Pennsylvania Volunteers in the American Civil War 1861–1865.* Philadelphia: Franklin, 1905.

Reardon, Carol. *Pickett's Charge in History and Memory.* Chapel Hill and London: University of North Carolina Press, 1997.

Reidenbaugh, Lowell. *27th Virginia Infantry.* Lynchburg, Va.: H. E. Howard, 1993.

———. *33rd Virginia Infantry.* Lynchburg, Va.: H. E. Howard, 1987.

Report of Joint Committee, to Mark the Positions Occupied by the 1st and 2d Delaware Regiments at the Battle of Gettysburg, July 2d and 3d, 1863. Reprint. Hightstown, N.J.: Longstreet House, 1998.

Reunions of the Nineteenth Maine Regiment Association. Augusta, Me.: Sprague, Owen & Nash, 1878.

Rhodes, John H. *The History of Battery B First Regiment Rhode Island Light Artillery in the War to Preserve the Union 1861–1865.* Reprint. Baltimore: Butternut and Blue, 1997.

Rhodes, Robert Hunt, ed. *All for the Union: The Civil War Diary and Letters of Elisha Hunt Rhodes.* New York: Orion Books, 1991.

Riggs, David F. *7th Virginia Infantry.* Lynchburg, Va.: H. E. Howard, 1982.

Robertson, James I., Jr. *4th Virginia Infantry.* Lynchburg, Va.: H. E. Howard, 1982.

———. *18th Virginia Infantry.* Lynchburg, Va.: H. E. Howard, 1984.

Robertson, John. *Michigan in the War.* Lansing: W. S. George & Co., 1880.

Roland, Charles P. "Lee's Invasion Strategy." *North & South,* vol. 1, no. 6 (1998).

Rollins, Richard. *"The Damned Red Flags of the Rebellion": The Confederate Battle Flag at Gettysburg.* Redondo Beach, Calif.: Rank and File Publications, 1997.

———. "The Failure of Confederate Artillery at Gettysburg: Ordnance and Logistics." *North & South,* vol. 3, no. 2 (2000).

———. "The Failure of the Confederate Artillery in Pickett's Charge." *North & South,* vol. 3, no. 4 (2000).

———. "George Gordon Meade and the Defense of Cemetery Ridge." *Gettysburg Magazine,* no. 19, July 1998.

———. "Lee's Artillery Prepares for Pickett's Charge." *North & South,* vol. 2, no. 7 (1999).

———. "The Second Wave of Pickett's Charge." *Gettysburg Magazine,* no. 18, January 1998.

———, ed. *Pickett's Charge: Eyewitness Accounts.* Redondo Beach, Calif.: Rank and File Publications, 1994.

Rollins, Richard, and David L. Shultz. "A Combined and Concentrated Fire: The Federal Artillery at Gettysburg, July 3, 1863." *North & South,* vol. 2, no. 3 (1999).

————. *Guide to Pennsylvania Troops at Gettysburg.* Redondo Beach, Calif.: Rank and File Publications, 1996.

Rosenblatt, Emil, and Ruth Rosenblatt, eds. *Hard Marching Every Day: The Civil War Letters of Private Wilbur Fisk, 1861–1865.* Lawrence: University Press of Kansas, 1992.

Ross, Fitzgerald. *Cities and Camps of the Confederate States.* Ed. Richard Barksdale Harwell. Urbana: University of Illinois Press, 1958.

Rowland, Dunbar. *Military History of Mississippi 1803–1898.* Reprint. Spartanburg, S.C.: Reprint Company, 1978.

Rozier, John, ed. *The Granite Farm Letters: The Civil War Correspondence of Edgeworth & Sallie Bird.* Athens and London: University of Georgia Press, 1988.

Sauers, Richard A. *"Advance The Colors!": Pennsylvania Civil War Battle Flags.* Two vols. Harrisburg, Pa.: Capitol Preservation Committee, 1987, 1991.

————, ed. *Fighting Them Over: How the Veterans Remembered Gettysburg in the Pages of the National Tribune.* Baltimore: Butternut and Blue, 1998.

Sawyer, Franklin. *A Military History of the 8th Regiment Ohio Vol. Inf'y: Its Battles, Marches and Army Movements.* Cleveland: Fairbanks & Co., 1881.

Schaff, Philip. "The Gettysburg Week." *Scribner's Magazine,* vol. 16 (July–December 1894).

Schildt, John W. *Roads to Gettysburg.* Parsons, W.Va.: McClain, 1982.

Schurz, Carl. "The Battle of Gettysburg." *McClure's Magazine,* vol. 29 (May–October 1907).

Scott, Robert Garth, ed. *Fallen Leaves: The Civil War Letters of Major Henry Livermore Abbott.* Kent, Ohio, and London: Kent State University Press, 1991.

Scott, W. W. *A History of Orange County, Virginia.* Reprint. Berryville, Va.: Chesapeake Book Company, 1962.

Sears, Stephen W. *Chancellorsville.* Boston and New York: Houghton Mifflin, 1996.

Secheverell, John H. *Journal History of the Twenty-Ninth Ohio Veteran Volunteers, 1861–1865.* Cleveland: n.p., 1883.

Seville, William P. *History of the First Regiment, Delaware Volunteers, from the Commencement of the "Three Months'" Service to the Final Muster-Out at the Close of the Rebellion.* Reprint. Baltimore: Gateway Press, 1986.

Shevchuk, Paul M. "The Cavalry Fight at Fairfield, Pennsylvania, July 3, 1863." *Gettysburg Magazine,* no. 1, July 1989.

————. "The 1st Texas Infantry and the Repulse of Farnsworth's Charge." *Gettysburg Magazine,* no. 2, July 1990.

————. "The Lost Hours of 'Jeb' Stuart." *Gettysburg Magazine,* no. 4, January 1991.

————. "The Wounding of Albert Jenkins, July 2, 1863." *Gettysburg Magazine*, no. 3, July 1990.

Shotwell, Randolph. "Virginia and North Carolina in the Battle of Gettysburg." *Our Living and Our Dead*, vol. 4 (March–August, 1876).

Shultz, David. *"Double Canister at Ten Yards": The Federal Artillery and the Repulse of Pickett's Charge*. Redondo Beach, Calif.: Rank and File Publications, 1995.

Shultz, David, and Richard Rollins. *The Baltimore Pike Artillery Line and Kinzie's Knoll*. Redondo Beach, Calif.: Rank and File Publications, 1997.

————. "Measuring Pickett's Charge." *Gettysburg Magazine*, no. 17, July 1997.

Sickles, Daniel E., D. McM. Gregg, John Newton, and Daniel Butterfield. "Further Recollections of Gettysburg." *North American Review*, vol. 152, no. 412 (March 1891).

Silliker, Ruth L., ed. *The Rebel Yell & the Yankee Hurrah: The Civil War Journal of a Maine Volunteer*. Camden, Me.: Down East Books, 1985.

Simons, Ezra D. *A Regimental History: The One Hundred and Twenty-Fifth New York State Volunteers*. New York: Judson, 1888.

Smith, John Day. *The History of the Nineteenth Regiment of Maine Volunteer Infantry 1862–1865*. Minneapolis: Great Western Printing Company, 1909.

Smith, Timothy H., ed. "The Story of Albertus McCreary: A Boy's Experience of the Battle." *Gettysburg Magazine*, no. 17, July 1997.

Sorrel, G. Moxley. *Recollections of a Confederate Staff Officer*. Ed. Bell Irvin Wiley. Reprint. Jackson, Tenn.: McCowat-Mercer Press, 1958.

Southern Bivouac. Six vols. Reprint. Wilmington, N.C.: Broadfoot Publishing Company, 1993.

Southern Historical Society Papers. Fifty-two vols. Reprint. Millwood, N.Y.: Kraus Reprint Co., 1977.

Speer, Allen Paul, ed. *Voices from Cemetery Hill: The Civil War Diary, Reports, and Letters of Colonel William Henry Asbury Speer (1861–1864)*. Johnson City, Tenn.: Overmountain Press, 1997.

Speese, Andrew Jackson. *Story of Companies H, A and C, Third Pennsylvania Cavalry at Gettysburg, July 3, 1863*. n.p.: n.p., 1906.

Stevens, H. S. *Souvenir of Excursion to Battlefields by the Society of the Fourteenth Connecticut Regiment and Reunion at Antietam September 1891*. Washington, D.C.: Gibson Bros., 1893.

Stevens, H. S., and J. W. Knowlton. *Address Delivered at the Dedication of Monument of the 14th Connecticut Volunteers at Gettysburg, Pa., July 3rd, 1884*. Middletown, Conn.: n.p., 1884.

Stevens, John W. *Reminiscences of the Civil War*. Reprint. Powhatan, Va.: Derwent Books, 1982.

Stewart, George R. *Pickett's Charge: A Microhistory of the Final Attack at Gettysburg, July 3, 1863*. Boston: Houghton Mifflin, 1959.

Stewart, William H. *A Pair of Blankets: War-Time History in Letters to the Young People of the South*. Ed. Benjamin H. Trask. Wilmington, N.C.: Broadfoot Publishing Company, 1990.

Stiles, Robert. *Four Years Under Marse Robert*. Reprint. Dayton, Ohio: Morningside Bookshop, 1977.

Stone, Jane Dice, ed. "Diary of William Heyser." *The Kittichtinny Historical Society Papers*, Number 16, Mercersburg, Pa.: Kittichtinny Historical Society, 1978.

Storrs, John W. *The "Twentieth Connecticut": A Regimental History*. Ansonia, Conn.: Press of the "Naugatuck Valley Sentinel," 1886.

Sturtevant, Ralph Orson. *Pictorial History Thirteenth Regiment Vermont Volunteers War Of 1861–1865*. Reprint. Newport, Vt.: Tony O'Connor Civil War Enterprises, 1999.

Supplement to the Official Records of the Union And Confederate Armies. Ninety-five vols. Wilmington, N.C.: Broadfoot Publishing Company, 1994–1999.

Sword, Wiley. "Alexander Webb and His Colt Navy Revolver: In the 'Pinch of the Fight' During 'Pickett's Charge' at Gettysburg." *Gettysburg Magazine*, no. 15, July 1996.

———. "Capt. George F. Tait and the 10th New York Zouaves Encounter 'Pickett's Charge.' " *Gettysburg Magazine*, no. 16, January 1997.

———. *Southern Invincibility: A History of the Confederate Heart*. New York: St. Martin's Press, 1999.

Sword, Wiley, and Mike Shotwell. "Two New York Swords in the Fight for Culp's Hill: Colonel James C. Lane's and Captain Nicholas Grumbach's." *Gettysburg Magazine*, no. 10, January 1994.

Tagg, Larry. *The Generals of Gettysburg: The Leaders of America's Greatest Battle*. Campbell, Calif.: Savas Publishing Company, 1998.

Taylor, Michael W. "Col. James Keith Marshall: One of Three Brigade Commanders Killed in the Pickett-Pettigrew-Trimble Charge." *Gettysburg Magazine*, no. 15, July 1996.

———. "North Carolina in the Pickett-Pettigrew-Trimble Charge at Gettysburg." *Gettysburg Magazine*, no. 8, January 1993.

———. "Ramseur's Brigade in the Gettysburg Campaign: A Newly Discovered Account by Capt. James I. Harris, Co. I, 30th Regt. N.C.T." *Gettysburg Magazine*, no. 17, July 1997.

———. "The Unmerited Censure of Two Maryland Staff Officers, Maj. Osmun Latrobe and First Lt. W. Stuart Symington." *Gettysburg Magazine*, no. 13, July 1995.

Taylor, Walter H. *Four Years with General Lee*. Reprint. Bloomington: Indiana University Press, 1962.

Taylor, William H. "Some Experiences of a Confederate Assistant Surgeon." *Transactions of the College of Physicians of Philadelphia*, vol. 28 [1906].

Thomas, Dean S. *Ready . . . Aim . . . Fire!: Small Arms Ammunition in the Battle of Gettysburg*. Gettysburg, Pa.: Thomas Publications, 1993.

Thomas, Emory M. *Bold Dragoon: The Life Of J.E.B. Stuart*. New York: Harper & Row, 1986.

———. *Robert E. Lee: A Biography*. New York and London: W. W. Norton, 1995.

Thompson, Benjamin W. " 'This Hell of Destruction': The Benjamin W. Thompson Memoir, Part II." *Civil War Times Illustrated*, vol. 12, no. 6 (October 1973).

Thomson, O. R. Howard, and William H. Rauch. *History of the "Bucktails": Kane Rifle Regiment of the Pennsylvania Reserve Corps*. Reprint. Dayton, Ohio: Morningside House, 1988.

Toombs, Samuel. *New Jersey Troops in the Gettysburg Campaign from June 5 to July 31, 1863*. Orange, N.J.: Evening Mail Publishing House, 1888.

———. *Reminiscences of the War, Comprising a Detailed Account of the Experiences of the Thirteenth Regiment New Jersey Volunteers in Camp, on the March, and in Battle*. Reprint. Hightstown, N.J.: Longstreet House, 1994.

Toomey, Daniel Carroll. *Marylanders at Gettysburg*. Baltimore: Toomey Press, 1994.

Topps, David. "The Dutchess County Regiment." *Gettysburg Magazine*, no. 12, January 1995.

Trask, Benjamin H. *9th Virginia Infantry*. Lynchburg, Va.: H. E. Howard, 1984.

Trimble, Isaac R. "North Carolinians at Gettysburg." *Our Living and Our Dead*, vol. 4 (March–August, 1876).

Trimble, Tony L. "Paper Collars: Stannard's Brigade at Gettysburg." *Gettysburg Magazine*, no. 2, July 1990.

Trinque, Bruce A. "Arnold's Battery and the 26th North Carolina." *Gettysburg Magazine*, no. 12, January 1995.

———. "Confederate Battle Flags in the July 3rd Charge." *Gettysburg Magazine*, no. 21, July 1999.

Trowbridge, J. T. "The Field of Gettysburg." *Atlantic Monthly*, vol. 16 (1865).

Tucker, Glenn. *High Tide at Gettysburg: The Campaign in Pennsylvania*. Indianapolis and New York: Bobbs-Merrill, 1958.

———. *Lee and Longstreet at Gettysburg*. Indianapolis: Bobbs-Merrill, 1968.

Turner, Charles W., ed. *Ted Barclay, Liberty Hall Volunteers: Letters from the Stonewall Brigade (1861–1864)*. Natural Bridge Station, Va.: Rockbridge, 1992.

Turner, George A., ed. *Civil War Letters from Soldiers and Citizens of Columbia County, Pennsylvania*. New York: American Heritage Custom Publishing, 1996.

Urwin, Gregory J. W. *Custer Victorious: The Civil War Battles of General George Armstrong Custer*. Rutherford, N.J.: Associated University Presses, 1983.

U.S. War Department. *The War of the Rebellion: A Compilation of the Official Records of the Union And Confederate Armies.* One hundred and twenty-eight vols. Washington, D.C.: Government Printing Office, 1880–1901.

Veale, Moses. *The 109th Regiment Penna. Veteran Volunteers: An Address Delivered at the Unveiling of Their Monument on Culps Hill, Gettysburg, Pa., September 11, 1889.* Philadelphia: James Beale, 1890.

Waitt, Ernest Linden, ed. *History of the Nineteenth Regiment Massachusetts Volunteer Infantry.* Salem, Mass.: Salem Press Co., 1906.

Walker, Francis A. *General Hancock.* New York: D. Appleton and Company, 1894.

———. *History of the Second Army Corps in the Army of the Potomac.* Reprint. Gaithersburg, Md.: Olde Soldier Books, 1990.

Wallace, Lee A., Jr. *1st Virginia Infantry.* Lynchburg, Va.: H. E. Howard, 1985.

———. *3rd Virginia Infantry.* Lynchburg, Va.: H. E. Howard, 1986.

Walton, William, ed. *A Civil War Courtship: The Letters of Edwin Weller from Antietam to Atlanta.* Garden City, N.Y.: Doubleday, 1980.

Ward, Joseph R. C. *History of the One Hundred and Sixth Regiment Pennsylvania Volunteers, 2d Brigade, 2d Division, 2d Corps, 1861–1865.* Philadelphia: Grant, Faires, & Rodgers, 1883.

Warner, Ezra J. *Generals in Blue: Lives of the Union Commanders.* Baton Rouge and London: Louisiana State University Press, 1981.

———. *Generals in Gray: Lives of the Confederate Commanders.* Baton Rouge: Louisiana State University Press, 1970.

Washburn, George H. *A Complete Military History and Record of the 108th Regiment N.Y. Vols. from 1862 to 1864.* Rochester, N.Y.: E. R. Andrews, 1894.

Webb and His Brigade at the Angle Gettysburg. Albany: J. B. Lyon Company, 1916.

Wert, Jeffry D. *A Brotherhood of Valor: The Common Soldiers of the Stonewall Brigade, C.S.A., and the Iron Brigade, U.S.A.* New York: Simon & Schuster, 1999.

———. *Custer: The Controversial Life of George Armstrong Custer.* New York: Simon & Schuster, 1996.

———. *General James Longstreet: The Confederacy's Most Controversial Soldier.* New York: Simon & Schuster, 1993.

White, H. "Gettysburg Thirty Years After." *Nation,* vol. 56, no. 1453 (May 4, 1893).

Wilder, Theodore. *The History of Company C, Seventh Regiment, O.V.I.* Oberlin, Ohio: J.B.T. Marsh, 1866.

Williams, Frank B., Jr., ed. "From Sumter to the Wilderness: Letters of Sergeant James Butler Suddath, Co. E, 7th Regiment, S.C.V." *South Carolina Historical Magazine,* vol. 63, no. 2 (April 1962).

Willson, Arabella M. *Disaster, Struggle, Triumph: The Adventures of 1000 "Boys in Blue," From August, 1862, to June, 1865.* Albany: Argus Company, 1870.

Wilson, Clyde N. *The Most Promising Young Man of the South: James Johnston Petti-*

grew and His Men at Gettysburg. Abilene, Texas: McWhiney Foundation Press, 1998.

Wilson, LeGrand James. *The Confederate Soldier.* Edited by James W. Silver. Memphis, Tenn.: Memphis State University Press, 1973.

Winey, Michael J. *Union Army Uniforms at Gettysburg.* Gettysburg, Pa.: Thomas Publications, 1998.

Winschel, Terrence J. "Heavy Was Their Loss: Joe Davis' Brigade at Gettysburg, Part II." *Gettysburg Magazine,* no. 3, July 1990.

———. "The Jeff Davis Legion at Gettysburg." *Gettysburg Magazine,* no. 12, January 1995.

———. "Posey's Brigade at Gettysburg, Part II." *Gettysburg Magazine,* no. 5, July 1991.

Wise, Jennings Cropper. *The Long Arm of Lee: The History of the Artillery of the Army of Northern Virginia.* Reprint. New York: Oxford University Press, 1959.

Wittenberg, Eric J. *Gettysburg's Forgotten Cavalry Actions.* Gettysburg, Pa.: Thomas Publications, 1998.

———. "Merritt's Regulars on South Cavalry Field: Oh, What Could Have Been." *Gettysburg Magazine,* no. 16, January 1997.

Wood, William Nathaniel. *Reminiscences of Big I.* Ed. Bell Irvin Wiley. Reprint. Wilmington, N.C.: Broadfoot Publishing Company, 1987.

Woodworth, Steven E. *Davis and Lee at War.* Lawrence: University Press of Kansas, 1995.

Wright, Steven J. " 'Don't Let Me Bleed To Death': The Wounding of Maj. Gen. Winfield Scott Hancock." *Gettysburg Magazine,* no. 6, January 1992.

Young, Louis G. "Pettigrew's Brigade at Gettysburg." *Our Living and Our Dead,* vol. 1, no. 6 (February 1875).

Young, William, Jr., and Patricia C. Young. *56th Virginia Infantry.* Lynchburg, Va.: H. E. Howard, 1990.

INDEX

☙☙
☙

Page numbers in *italics* refer to maps.